The Principles
of Psychology

The Principles of Psychology

William James

Volume III

Notes, Appendixes, Apparatus, General Index

HARVARD UNIVERSITY PRESS
Cambridge, Massachusetts
and London, England
1981

CENTER FOR
SCHOLARLY EDITIONS
AN APPROVED EDITION
MODERN LANGUAGE
ASSOCIATION OF AMERICA

Library of Congress Cataloging in Publication Data
James, William, 1842–1910.
The principles of psychology.
(The works of William James)
Vol. 3: Notes, appendixes, apparatus, general index.
1. Psychology. I. Title. II. Series: James,
William, 1842–1910. Works. 1975. [DNLM: 1. Psychology.
BF 121 J29p]
BF121.J2   1981   150   81–4194
ISBN 0–674–70559–9 (v. 1)   AACR2
ISBN 0–674–70555–6

Contents

Notes

Notes

The William James Collection is housed in the Houghton Library of Harvard University. It can be identified by the call number 'MS Am 1092', with, sometimes, either 'b' or 'f' as a prefix and a decimal following the numeral '2'. Many books from James's library are also preserved there; many of these are sufficiently identified by their call numbers, which begin either with 'WJ' or 'AC'. Other books from his library are in Harvard's Widener Library and elsewhere, and in such cases their location is stated. Still others were sold and have not been located. However, Ralph Barton Perry made a list, noting markings and annotations; this unpublished list can be consulted at Houghton.

Since work on this edition began, the Houghton Library has reclassified the manuscripts and many letters in the James Collection. A new and detailed guide was prepared in the spring of 1977. The new call numbers are used in the present notes. Apparently, in time, the 'WJ' class will be eliminated, but thus far only a few books have been affected. Some books have been transferred recently from Widener into Houghton, while others, reported by Perry as sold or not listed at all, have turned up in the Widener stacks. The concluding volumes of this edition will contain a complete account of James's library and will give the then current call numbers and locations. Since the same volumes will contain James's annotations, extensively indexed, only those annotations are noted in the present volume which appear to have a direct bearing upon the text at hand.

James was a very active reader who filled his books with annotations and markings. The term 'markings' refers to underlining, vertical lines in margins, exclamation points, question marks, the notation 'N.B.', and 'Qu' for 'quote'. James's style of marking is distinctive: the N.B.'s are such that the same vertical stroke serves for both the 'N' and the 'B', while his underlining often has a peculiar waver. Furthermore, James habitually filled the flyleaves of his books with indexes, in some cases simply jotting down a page number or two, in others, noting numerous subjects and marking passages for attention or quotation. Pages singled out in this fashion usually have markings. Thus, for books protected in Houghton, the risk of error in attributing a given marking to James is slight. The risk is greater for materials in open stacks such as those in Widener, where the only claim made is that the book was owned or used by James and that there are markings. Where the books have been sold, we are totally dependent upon Perry's reports.

In the *Principles*, as in all of his writings, James did not seek out available English translations of texts he wished to quote. He did not avoid published translations, but most of the time, he either did the work himself or had passages translated especially for him. Such private translations were compared with the originals. Usually they are fairly free, but without distortions. James was especially free with italics, adding or deleting them as suited his purpose. This looseness remains in the present edition and, except for a few cases, is not commented upon in the notes. Because of the sheer bulk of text involved, it is not possible to provide originals of translated passages, as is done in some earlier volumes of this edition. Neither is it possible in the notes to supply passages deleted by James.

In the *Principles* there are some two thousand references and, in most cases, the works mentioned were actually consulted by James. This is obvious from his reading notes and marginal entries. But at other times, his patience seems to have run out and he borrowed both the fact and the reference. Thus, some of the references towards the end of the chapter on "Discrimination and Comparison" (pp. 512–518), giving the latest results, appear to have been borrowed from Wundt. Where James cites no source but provides only a name, the original source is indicated in the present notes even when it is likely that James used some intermediary.

The chapter on hypnotism is something of an oddity; while James mentions many names, he provides practically no definite references. This suggests that the chapter was written while James was away from his library. Clearly, James had read much more in the field than is indicated by his scanty references.

It seems that just about every German physiologist at one time or another published his own physiological *Archiv*. This leads to much confusion especially when French and English titles are added and words abbreviated. To avoid confusion, complete titles are given, except for the short titles listed below. Several frequently cited books are also cited by short title.

It is to be understood that whenever a book or pamphlet is listed as preserved in a library, James's personal copy of a work by the author being treated in the note is being referred to. With very rare exceptions, books in Houghton from James's library are annotated.

Works by James already published in the present edition are cited in this edition, identified as WORKS, while others are cited in the original editions.

SHORT TITLES

Archives de Physiologie for *Archives de Physiologie Normale et Pathologique*
Archiv für Anatomie und Physiologie for *Archiv für Physiologie*, the *physiologische Abtheilung*, edited by Emil Du Bois-Reymond, of the *Archiv für Anatomie und Physiologie*
Archiv für Physiologie for *Archiv für die gesammte Physiologie des Menschen und der Thiere*, edited by Eduard Friedrich Wilhelm Pflüger
Archiv für Psychiatrie for *Archiv für Psychiatrie und Nervenkrankheiten*
Grundzüge for Wilhelm Wundt, *Grundzüge der physiologischen Psychologie*
Handbuch for Hermann Helmholtz, *Handbuch der physiologischen Optik*
Hermann's *Handbuch* for *Handbuch der Physiologie*, edited by Ludimar Hermann, 6 vols. (Leipzig: Vogel, 1879–1881)
Jahresbericht for *Jahresberichte über die Fortschritte der Anatomie und Physiologie*, edited by Fr. Hofmann and G. Schwalbe, and *Jahresbericht über die Fortschritte der Anatomie und Physiologie*, edited by Ludimar

Hermann and G. Schwalbe; in both cases, for the *zweite Abtheilung:*
Physiologie
Philosophical Transactions for *Philosophical Transactions of the Royal*
Society of London, series B in 1887 and after
Proceedings of the SPR for *Proceedings of the Society for Psychical Research*
(English)
Revue Philosophique for *Revue Philosophique de la France et de l'Étranger*
Sitzungsberichte (Berlin) for *Sitzungsberichte der königlich preussischen*
Akademie der Wissenschaften zu Berlin
Sitzungsberichte (Vienna) for *Sitzungsberichte der kaiserlichen Akademie der*
Wissenschaften, mathematisch-naturwissenschaftliche Classe (Vienna)
Vierteljahrsschrift for *Vierteljahrsschrift für wissenschaftliche Philosophie*

5.2 instruction] For an account of James's teaching of psychology, including excerpts from letters, see Ralph Barton Perry, *The Thought and Character*
of William James, 2 vols. (Boston: Little, Brown, 1935), II, 10–24. Few, if
any, teaching notes have survived; however, the Harvard University Archives
preserves student notes for Philosophy 5 for 1880–1881, a course in psychology. These notes (HUC 8880.370.5) taken by George Albert Burdett are
nearly illegible and of poor quality, but reveal a strong emphasis on physiology in the course. Also in the Archives are student notes for Philosophy 2,
logic and psychology: in the 1887–1888 notes (HUC 8887.370.2), Bain's
Senses and the Intellect is the main psychological text; in the 1889–1890
notes (HUC 8889.370.4), Ladd's *Elements of Physiological Psychology*. Preserved in Houghton are numerous printed examination papers for James's
courses, including the early psychology ones (bMS Am 1092.9 [4521–4522]).
As an assistant professor of physiology in 1875–1876, James announced a
graduate course on the relations between physiology and psychology and this
seems to have been his first psychology course. In 1876–1877, James's
Natural History 2 was a course in physiological psychology with Spencer's
Principles of Psychology as a text. The following year, he used Taine's *On*
Intelligence in Philosophy 4. Each of James's courses, except for the early
graduate ones, is listed in the appropriate *Annual Report of the President of*
Harvard College, with information about the texts used and the number of
students.

5.11 *wer*] Goethe, *Faust*, ed. Erich Trunz (Hamburg: Christian Vegner,
1963), p. 11 (line 97).

5.23 abridgment] "The Spatial Quale," *Journal of Speculative Philosophy*,
13 (January 1879), 64–87; reprinted in *Essays in Psychology*, WORKS.

7.14 Volkmann] Wilhelm Fridolin Volkmann, Ritter von Volkmar (1822–
1877), Czechoslovakian philosopher and psychologist, *Lehrbuch der Psy-*
chologie vom Standpunkte des Realismus und nach genetischer Methode,
2nd ed., 2 vols. (Cöthen: Schulze, 1875–1876). A third edition, revised, was
published in 1884–1885.

7.17 Sully's] James Sully (1842–1923), British philosopher and psychologist, *Outlines of Psychology with Special Reference to the Theory of Edu-*
cation (New York: D. Appleton, 1884) (WJ 584.51.2). Houghton preserves
copies of four letters from James to Sully (bMS Am 1092.1) and sixteen
originals from Sully to James (bMS Am 1092, letters 1118–1133). Also at

Houghton is *The Human Mind: A Text-Book of Psychology* (London: Longmans, Green, 1892) (WJ 584.51). Perry reports that two works by Sully, both mentioned in the present notes, were sold.

7.17 Dewey's] John Dewey (1859–1952), *Psychology* (New York: Harper & Brothers, 1887). Perry reports, without identifying editions, that a copy of this work was sold. For the relations between James and Dewey see Perry, II, 514–533. Their correspondence is at Houghton (bMS Am 1092.9 [128–144, 885–889]).

7.17–18 Baldwin's] James Mark Baldwin (1861–1934), American philosopher and psychologist, *Handbook of Psychology: Senses and Intellect* (New York: Henry Holt, 1889) (WJ 406.49.2). Later Baldwin published a companion volume, *Handbook of Psychology: Feeling and Will* (New York: Henry Holt, 1891) (WJ 406.49). Also at Houghton is *Mental Development in the Child and the Race: Methods and Processes* (New York: Macmillan, 1895) (WJ 406.49.4) as well as a collection of clippings of articles by Baldwin (WJ 406.49.5). Perry reports that marked copies of *Social and Ethical Interpretations in Mental Development* (1897) and *Thought and Things, or Genetic Logic*, vol. I (1906) were sold. Some letters from James to Baldwin appear in Baldwin's autobiography, *Between Two Wars: 1861–1921*, 2 vols. (Boston: Stratford Co., 1926). Copies of these and other letters are at Houghton (bMS Am 1092.1). Letters from Baldwin to James are also at Houghton (bMS Am 1092, letters 28–30).

7.22 Mill] John Stuart Mill (1806–1873). In addition to works mentioned in the present notes, James's library contained a marked copy of the *Autobiography* (1873), reported as sold. For a note on references in James's manuscripts to Mill see *A Pluralistic Universe*, WORKS, note to 7.21.

7.22 Lotze] Rudolph Hermann Lotze (1817–1881), German philosopher. In addition to works mentioned in the present notes, Houghton preserves the *Geschichte der Aesthetic in Deutschland* (Munich: Cotta, 1868) (WJ 751.88.2), *Outlines of Metaphysic*, trans. George T. Ladd (Boston: Ginn, 1886) (WJ 751.88.16), and six German pamphlets bound as one volume (WJ 751.88). Perry reports that the *Grundzüge der Psychologie* (1881) was sold. For Lotze and James's psychology see Otto F. Kraushaar, "Lotze's Influence on the Psychology of William James," *Psychological Review*, 43 (1936), 235–257.

7.22–23 Renouvier] Charles Renouvier (1815–1903), French philosopher. For the correspondence between James and Renouvier, Renouvier's writings on James, and works by Renouvier from James's library, in addition to those mentioned in the present notes, see *Essays in Philosophy*, WORKS, note to 23.1.

7.23 Hodgson] Shadworth Hollway Hodgson (1832–1912), British philosopher. In addition to works mentioned in the present notes, Houghton preserves *The Metaphysic of Experience*, 4 vols. (London: Longmans, Green, 1898) (WJ 539.18.2), and pamphlets (WJ 539.18) (WJ 539.18.8). The correspondence between James and Hodgson is also at Houghton (bMS Am 1092.9 [188–225, 969–998]). For the relations between them see Perry, I, 611–653.

7.23 Wundt] Wilhelm Wundt (1832–1920), German psychologist and philosopher. In addition to works mentioned in the present notes, Houghton preserves the *System der Philosophie* (Leipzig: W. Engelmann, 1889) (WJ 796. 59.6). For James's view of Wundt see his letter to Carl Stumpf, February 6, 1887 (*The Letters of William James*, ed. Henry James, 2 vols. [Boston: Atlantic Monthly Press, 1920], I, 262–267).

7.24 Wright] Chauncey Wright (1830–1875), American philosopher. For the relations between Wright and James see Perry, I, 520–532.

7.25 Peirce] Charles Sanders Peirce (1839–1914). The correspondence between James and Peirce is at Houghton (bMS Am 1092, letters 657–759; bMS Am 1092.9 [3370–3427]). Numerous excerpts can be found in Perry.

7.25 Hall] Granville Stanley Hall (1844–1924), American psychologist, a graduate student at Harvard from 1876 to 1878. For the relations between James and Hall see Dorothy Ross, *G. Stanley Hall: The Psychologist as Prophet* (Chicago: University of Chicago Press, 1972). James's letters to Hall are in the Clark University Archives, Worcester, Mass., with copies at Houghton; Hall's letters to James are at Houghton (bMS Am 1092.9 [165–180]).

7.25–26 Putnam] James Jackson Putnam (1846–1918), Boston physician, a student with James in the Harvard Medical School. Sixteen letters from James to Putnam are in the Countway Library of Medicine, Boston (H MS C 4.2); Houghton has copies of five letters from James to Putnam (bMS Am 1092.1) and one original from Putnam to James (bMS Am 1092, letter 778). Some of this correspondence appears in Nathan G. Hale, ed., *James Jackson Putnam and Psychoanalysis: Letters between Putnam and Sigmund Freud, Ernest Jones, William James, Sandor Ferenczi, and Morton Prince, 1877–1917* (Cambridge, Mass.: Harvard University Press, 1971).

7.26 Royce] Josiah Royce (1855–1916), American philosopher, one of James's closer personal friends. For a note on some of the books by Royce from James's library see *Pragmatism*, WORKS, note to 16.5. Their correspondence is at Houghton (bMS Am 1092.9 [529–560, 3594–3641]). For the relations between them see Perry, I, 778–824.

15.18 Herbart] Johann Friedrich Herbart (1776–1841), German philosopher. Perry notes that a marked copy of Herbart's *Metaphysik*, ed. Hartenstein (1851), was sold, probably meaning thereby *Schriften zur Metaphysik* from the *Sämmtliche Werke*, ed. G. Hartenstein.

16.17 death's] From Shakespeare's *Sonnets*, XXX.

18.38 Ladd] George Trumbull Ladd (1842–1921), American philosopher and psychologist, *Elements of Physiological Psychology: A Treatise of the Activities and Nature of the Mind* (New York: Charles Scribner's Sons, 1887) (WJ 448.17). Pt. III, ch. 3 (pp. 633–667) is titled "Real Connection of Brain and Mind." A letter from Ladd asking for a thorough review is pasted in in James's copy. James's review is in the *Nation*, 44 (June 2, 1887), 473, with emphasis on Ladd's view of the soul. James comments upon this interpretation of Ladd on the soul in "The Knowing of Things Together," *Psychological Review*, 2 (March 1895), 120n, reprinted in *Essays in Philosophy*, WORKS, p. 84n. Ladd reviewed the *Principles*, "Psychology as So-called 'Natural Science'," *Philosophical Review*, 1 (January 1892), 24–53, to which James replied in "A Plea for Psychology as a 'Natural Science'," *Philosophical Review*, 1 (March 1892), 146–153, reprinted in *Collected Essays and Reviews*

(New York: Longmans, Green, 1920) and *Essays in Psychology*, WORKS. Also preserved are Ladd's *Psychology: Descriptive and Explanatory* (New York: Charles Scribner's Sons, 1894) (WJ 448.17.4) and *Philosophy of Mind* (New York: Charles Scribner's Sons, 1895) (WJ 448.17.2); while the *Philosophy of Knowledge* (1897) was sold.

19.24 Spencerian] The importance of Herbert Spencer (1820–1903) for James's thought is made clear by the extensive annotations, often sharply critical, in his copies of Spencer's works. Furthermore, the James Collection contains some 60 sheets of notes on Spencer (bMS Am 1092.9 [4484–4494]), to be published in the volume of manuscript remains. Perry (I, 474–493) includes excerpts on Spencer from James's courses and James's letter to Spencer, April 21, 1879, asking whether an enclosed summary of Spencer on knowledge correctly represents Spencer's position. Spencer's reply, endorsing James's interpretation, is at Houghton (Autograph File). In the drastically altered second edition of *The Principles of Psychology*, 2 vols. (New York: D. Appleton, 1871–1873) (WJ 582.24.6), I, 387 (sec. 173), Spencer holds that "from the lowest to the highest forms of life, the increasing adjustment of inner to outer relations is one indivisible progression." James criticizes this view in "Remarks on Spencer's Definition of Mind as Correspondence," *Journal of Speculative Philosophy*, 12 (January 1878), 1–18, reprinted in *Essays in Philosophy*, WORKS. For a similar criticism see p. 381, below.

22.14 Pflüger] Eduard Friedrich Wilhelm Pflüger (1829–1910), German physiologist, holds that consciousness is present throughout the whole nervous system in *Die sensorischen Functionen des Rückenmarks der Wirbelthiere nebst einer neuen Lehre über die Leitungsgesetze der Reflexionen* (Berlin: A. Hirschwald, 1853). James's unannotated copy is in Houghton (Phil 6103.8*), in a volume of pamphlets from James's library titled *Reflexe und Hemmungen*, which also includes Pflüger's *Über das Hemmungs-Nervensystem für die peristaltischen Bewegungen* (Berlin: A. Hirschwald, 1857). Pflüger, who sometimes speaks of the "spinal soul," was involved in a controversy with Lotze over this point. For a discussion of this controversy and additional references see Franklin Fearing, *Reflex Action: A Study in the History of Physiological Psychology* (Baltimore: Williams & Wilkins, 1930), pp. 161–186.

22.14 Lewes] George Henry Lewes (1817–1878), English philosopher and writer. Perry reports that four volumes of the five making up the three series of *Problems of Life and Mind* were sold. Lewes discusses the presence of consciousness in the spinal cord in *Problems*, second series, *The Physical Basis of Mind* (London: Trübner, 1877), pp. 413–493, problem IV on "The Reflex Theory," and in *The Physiology of Common Life* (see p. 85n). James's review of *The Physical Basis of Mind* is sharply critical, *Nation*, 25 (November 8, 1877), 290. For additional references to Lewes on the spinal cord see Fearing.

22.32 Goltz] Friedrich Leopold Goltz (1834–1902), German physiologist, *Beiträge zur Lehre von den Functionen der Nervencentren des Frosches* (Berlin: A. Hirschwald, 1869), p. 70. James's copy was given to Harvard but has not been located. A letter from Goltz to James is pasted in in James's copy of *Über die Verrichtungen des Grosshirns: Gesammelte Abhandlungen* (Bonn: Emil Strauss, 1881) (Phil 6116.5), in Widener. Reprinted in this work are accounts of experiments on dogs from the *Archiv für Physiologie*, beginning in 1876. Goltz with various collaborators continued to use the title "Über die Verrichtungen des Grosshirns" in the *Archiv* after 1881: 5th report, 34 (1884), 450–505; 6th report, 42 (1888), 419–467; 7th report, 51 (1892), 570–614. While in Europe in the summer of 1880, James indicates a desire to meet Goltz (Perry, I, 382).

23.12 Liebmann] Otto Liebmann (1840–1912), German philosopher, *Zur Analysis der Wirklichkeit* (Strassburg: Karl J. Trübner, 1876), p. 489. Works by this author from James's library will be listed in the volume of manuscript remains.

24.3 Martin's] Henry Newell Martin (1848–1896), Irish-born biologist, active in the United States, *The Human Body: An Account of Its Structure and Activities and the Conditions of Its Healthy Working* (New York: Henry Holt, 1881), in the American Science Series. James relied heavily upon Martin for the physiological portions of *Psychology: Briefer Course* (New York: Henry Holt, 1892).

24.12 Holden's] Luther Holden (1815–1905), British physician and anatomist, *A Manual of the Dissection of the Human Body* (1851). In some editions this work also bears on the spine the title *A Manual of Anatomy*.

24.13 Foster] Michael Foster (1836–1907), British physiologist, *A Course of Elementary Practical Physiology* (London: Macmillan, 1876). In the first edition, Foster is "assisted by" John Newport Langley (1852–1925), British physiologist; in the fifth, they are named as co-authors, while in later ones, Langley is additionally named as an editor.

24.14 Morrell's] George Herbert Morrell, *The Student's Manual of Comparative Anatomy, and Guide to Dissection*, pt. I (London: Longman & Co., 1872).

27.7 generation] For a history of the study of the functions of the brain, with biographical sketches of leading figures and excerpts from their writings, see Edwin Clarke and C. D. O'Malley, *The Human Brain and Spinal Cord* (Berkeley: University of California Press, 1968). English translations are indicated in the bibliography.

27.8 Meynert] Theodor Meynert (1833–1892), psychiatrist, active in Austria. In Widener are James's annotated copies of *Zur Mechanik des Gehirnbaues* (Vienna: W. Braumüller, 1874) (Phil 6122.44) and *Psychiatrie. Klinik der Erkrankungen des Vorderhirns*, pt. I (Vienna: W. Braumüller, 1884) (Phil 6962.5), and an unannotated copy of *Klinische Vorlesungen über Psychiatrie auf wissenschaftlichen Grundlagen*, 2 vols. (Vienna: W. Braumüller, 1889–1890) (Phil 6962.5.5). Houghton preserves *Psychiatry: A Clinical Treatise on Diseases of the Fore-Brain* (New York: G. P. Putnam's Sons, 1885) (*AC 85.J2376.Zz885m).

27.15 vivisectional] This account of experiments on frogs appears in part to be based on Goltz, *Nervencentren des Frosches*, but James himself is known to have dissected frogs. For his view of vivisection see the *Nation*, 20 (February 25, 1875), 128–129, and 22 (June 29, 1876), 415. In his review of "Experimental and Critical Contribution to the Physiology of the Semicircular Canals," *American Journal of Otology*, 2 (1880), 341–343, James notes that in an unfinished experiment he removed semicircular canals from some frogs to test theories of vertigo.

Notes

29.9 Robin] Charles Philippe Robin (1821–1885), French anatomist, "Observations anatomiques et physiologiques faites sur des suppliciés par décollation," *Journal de l'Anatomie et de la Physiologie Normales et Pathologiques de l'Homme et des Animaux*, 6 (1869), 69–102, especially p. 90.

34.32 Darwin's] Charles Darwin, *The Descent of Man, and Selection in Relation to Sex*, 2 vols. (London: John Murray, 1871). A copy of this work (1871) was sold.

37.10 FIG. 3] Figures 3 and 4, while not copies, seem based on Meynert's figure 60, *Psychiatry*, p. 158. The child and flame example is found in *Psychiatry*, pp. 160–161, and *Zur Mechanik des Gehirnbaues*, p. 18. James's index to *Psychiatry* contains "Sensations of innervation, 159–163-4."

39.9 Gall] Franz Josef Gall (1758–1828), German-born physiologist, founder of phrenology, often credited with the general conception of localization of functions in the brain.

39.27 Spurzheim] Johann Kaspar Spurzheim (1776–1832), German-born physiologist, collaborated with Gall. Spurzheim died in Boston while giving a course of lectures there and at Harvard.

40.37 Lange] Friedrich Albert Lange (1828–1875), German philosopher, *Geschichte des Materialismus und Kritik seiner Bedeutung in der Gegenwart*, 2nd ed., 2 vols. (Iserlohn: J. Baedeker, 1873–1875), II, 344–345. Perry reports that both volumes, with annotations, were sold. James is not using an available English translation. 'Wunderbares Pferd' is translated as 'queer horse'.

41.15 Jackson] John Hughlings Jackson (1835–1911), British neurologist, "On Epilepsies and on the After Effects of Epileptic Discharges," *West Riding Lunatic Asylum Medical Reports*, 6 (1876), 266–309, quotation from pp. 267–268. For James, Jackson shines "with the genius of interpretation. . . . The man who will do most service to brain physiology to-day will be not he who scoops most cerebral material from dogs and monkeys, but he who makes most guesses, simple guesses, . . . as to what *may possibly* be the elementary forms of functioning of this mysterious organ" (Review of H. C. Bastian, *The Brain as an Organ of Mind*, in the *Nation*, 31 [September 23, 1880], 224). Several unmarked offprints are in Widener (Phil 6103.2).

41.19 Meynert] *Psychiatry*, p. 39; *Zur Mechanik des Gehirnbaues*, pp. 18, 19.

42.5 Munk] Hermann Munk (1839–1912), German physiologist. Munk's earlier investigations are collected in his *Über die Functionen der Grosshirnrinde. Gesammelte Mittheilungen aus den Jahren 1877–80 mit Einleitung und Anmerkungen* (Berlin: A. Hirschwald, 1881). The second edition (1890) contains additional papers cited by James from the *Sitzungsberichte* (Berlin). Munk's "Of the Visual Area of the Cerebral Cortex, and Its Relation to Eye Movements," *Brain*, 13 (1890), 45–70, surveys the localization controversy. For James's meeting with Munk see *Letters*, I, 213–214.

42.10 Flourens] Jean Pierre Marie Flourens (1794–1867), French physiologist, *Recherches expérimentales sur les propriétés et les fonctions du système nerveux, dans les animaux vertébrés* (1824).

42.13 Hitzig] Eduard Hitzig (1838–1907), German psychiatrist, and Gustav Theodor Fritsch (1838–1927), German physiologist, "Über die elektrische Erregbarkeit des Grosshirns," *Archiv für Anatomie, Physiologie und wissen-*

schaftliche Medicin, 1870, pp. 300–332. In Widener is an annotated copy of *Untersuchungen über das Gehirn* (Berlin: A. Hirschwald, 1874) (Phil 6117.35), containing the above paper, and an unannotated copy of *Über den Quärulant-enwahnsinn* (Leipzig: Vogel, 1895) (Phil 6457.11). For James's evaluation of Hitzig see the *Nation*, 20 (June 3, 1875), 377–378.

42.15 Ferrier] David Ferrier (1843–1928), British physician and neurologist, *The Functions of the Brain* (1876). James's annotated copy in Widener is of the second edition (London: Smith, Elder, 1886) (Phil 6115.3.6) and is dated December 1886. According to James, Ferrier's work leaves the impression of "masterly sobriety and judiciousness" (*Nation*, 24 [June 14, 1877], 355–356).

42.18 Munk's] Munk concludes his first report (March 23, 1877), *Über die Functionen*, 1st ed., pp. 10–20, with criticisms of Ferrier.

42.26 Rolando] Luigi Rolando (1773–1831), Italian physiologist, described a structure of the brain which bears his name; see figure 6 (p. 45).

43.34 François-Franck's] Charles Albert François-Franck (1849–1921), French physiologist, *Leçons sur les fonctions motrices du cerveau (réactions volontaires et organiques) et sur l'épilepsie cérébrale* (Paris: Doin, 1887), pp. 311–336, titled "Excitabilité corticale."

43.36 Paneth] Josef Paneth (1857–1890), Austrian physiologist, "Über Lage, Ausdehnung und Bedeutung der absoluten motorischen Felder auf der Hirn-oberfläche des Hundes," *Archiv für Physiologie*, 37 (1885), 523–561.

44.1 Fig. 5] Ferrier, 2nd ed., p. 247, for both figure and legend.

44.1 Sylvius] Franciscus Sylvius (de le Boë) (1614–1672), German chemist and physiologist.

44.23 Loeb] Jacques Loeb (1859–1924), German-born physiologist, later active in the United States, "Beiträge zur Physiologie des Grosshirns," *Archiv für Physiologie*, 39 (1886), 265–346. In Widener are James's unmarked copies, inscribed to him by Loeb, of *Der Heliotropismus der Thiere und seine Über-einstimmung mit dem Heliotropismus der Pflanzen* (Würzburg: Georg Hertz, 1890) (S 7808.51.5), *Einleitung in die vergleichende Gehirnphysiologie und vergleichende Psychologie* (Leipzig: J. A. Barth, 1899) (Phil 5821.4), *Unter-suchungen zur physiologischen Morphologie der Thiere*, 2 vols. (Würzburg: Georg Hertz, 1891–1892) (S 7810.51). A collection of pamphlets given to Harvard was not found. A marked copy of *Comparative Physiology of the Brain and Comparative Psychology* (1900) was sold. Three letters from Loeb to James are at Houghton (bMS Am 1092, letters 509–511).

45.21 Schäfer] Victor Alexander Haden Horsley (1857–1916), British physi-cian and physiologist, and Edward Albert Schafer (Schäfer, Sharpey-Schafer) (1850–1935), British physiologist, "A Record of Experiments upon the Functions of the Cerebral Cortex," *Philosophical Transactions* (B), 179 (1888), 1–45; figure 6 is from p. 6, figure 7, from p. 10, the discussion, from p. 13. Horsley's *Structure and Functions of the Brain and Spinal Cord* (1892) was given to Harvard but has not been seen.

45.23 Goltz] See note to 22.32.

46.13 Exner] Sigmund Exner (1846–1926), Austrian physiologist, *Unter-suchungen über die Localisation der Functionen in der Grosshirnrinde des*

Menschen (Vienna: W. Braumüller, 1881), pp. 88–125, describes one by one 167 cases of brain tumor and gives the location of each in a series of figures. James's figures 8 and 9 are Exner's figures A and C of Plate II. In James's copy in Widener (Phil 6114.12.5), in James's hand, there are instructions to copy the two figures for use in the book and a partially erased remark on figure A, "never injured without symp to." In Widener is James's marked copy of an abstract of this work, *Biologisches Centralblatt*, 1 (January 10, 1882), 627–635, together with other pamphlets (Phil 6103.2). Also in Widener is an annotated copy of *Entwurf zu einer physiologischen Erklärung der psychischen Erscheinungen*, vol. I (Leipzig: Deuticke, 1894) (Phil 6114.12[1]).

46.23 Beevor] Charles Edward Beevor (1854–1908), British physician and physiologist, and Victor Horsley, "A Further Minute Analysis by Electric Stimulation of the So-called Motor Region of the Cortex Cerebri in the Monkey (Macacus sinicus)," *Philosophical Transactions* (B), 179 (1888), 205–256.

48.2-3 Flechsig's] Paul Emil Flechsig (1847–1929), German physiologist and psychiatrist, *Die Leitungsbahnen im Gehirn und Rückenmark des Menschen auf Grund entwickelungsgeschichtlicher Untersuchungen* (Leipzig: W. Engelmann, 1876), pp. 263–264. In Widener is an annotated copy of *Gehirn und Seele*, 2nd ed. (Leipzig: Veit, 1896) (Phil 6115.6.7), while *Plan des menschlichen Gehirns* (Leipzig: Veit, 1883) was given to Widener, but rejected in 1967.

48.10 Edinger] Ludwig Edinger (1855–1918), German neurologist, *Zwölf Vorlesungen über den Bau der nervösen Centralorgane. Für Ärzte und Studirende*, 2nd ed. (Leipzig: Vogel, 1889), p. 155.

49.25 'Wernicke'] Carl Wernicke (1848–1905), German psychiatrist, *Der aphasische Symptomencomplex: Eine psychologische Studie auf anatomischer Basis* (Breslau: Max Cohn & Weigert, 1874). James's annotated copy is in Widener (Phil 6400.6). Also in Widener is an unannotated copy of *Über den wissenschaftlichen Standpunkt in der Psychiatrie* (Cassel: Fischer, 1880) (Phil 6972.2.15) and an annotated copy of *Grundriss der Psychiatrie in klinischen Vorlesungen*, 2 vols. (Leipzig: Thieme, 1894–1896) (Phil 6972.2.10). James reviewed the last mentioned work in the *Psychological Review*, 4 (1897), 225–227.

50.1 Broca] Pierre Paul Broca (1824–1880), French physician and anthropologist, *Mémoires d'anthropologie*, V (Paris: C. Reinwald, 1888), 1–161, reprints numerous papers under the common title "Siège de la faculté du langage articulé," including the paper James appears to have in mind, "Perte de la parole, ramollissement chronique et destruction partielle du lobe antérieur gauche du cerveau," *Bulletins de la Société d'Anthropologie*, 1st series, vol. 2 (April 18, 1861), pp. 235–238.

50.39 Nothnagel] Carl Wilhelm Hermann Nothnagel (1841–1905), Austrian physician, and Bernard Naunyn (1839–1925), German physician, *Über die Localisation der Gehirnkrankheiten* (Wiesbaden: J. F. Bergmann, 1887), p. 34. James's unannotated copy is in Widener (Phil 6963.5).

51.28 Ferrier] James seems to have in mind Ferrier's results as reported in the first edition of *The Functions of the Brain* (New York: G. P. Putnam's

Sons, 1876), pp. 144, 164. In the second edition, the same subject is treated in ch. 9, pt. 1 (pp. 270–305), on "The Visual Centre."

51.34 Munk] Each of the seven reports in *Über die Functionen*, 1st ed., deals with vision centers and Ferrier's investigations. On pp. 28–57, in his third report (March 15, 1878), Munk discusses his experiments on monkeys at greater length. The distinction between sensorial and psychic blindness, 'Rindenblindheit' and 'Seelenblindheit', appears in most of the reports, as does the notion of restitution in cases of psychic blindness. The hemiopic character of certain disturbances is treated in the third report.

51.39 Hammond's] William Alexander Hammond (1828–1900), American physician, *A Treatise on the Diseases of the Nervous System* (1871). In the sixth edition, rewritten and enlarged (New York: D. Appleton, 1876), ch. 7 (pp. 166–205) is titled "Aphasia." In Widener are James's copies of *On Certain Conditions of Nervous Derangement* (New York: G. P. Putnam's Sons, 1881) (Phil 6317.1B) and *Sleep and Its Derangements* (Philadelphia: J. B. Lippincott, 1869) (Phil 7050.5.2).

52.21 Goltz] Goltz is known as a leading opponent of localizationism.

52.30 Munk's] Munk describes his experiments on doves in section 4 of his twelfth report, *Über die Functionen der Grosshirnrinde: Gesammelte Mittheilungen*, 2nd ed. (Berlin: A. Hirschwald, 1890), pp. 191–211, the first of four reports with the common title "Über die centralen Organe für das Sehen und das Hören bei den Wirbelthieren," which originally appeared in five installments in the *Sitzungsberichte* (Berlin), 1883, no. 34, pp. 793–827; 1884, no. 24, pp. 549–568; 1886, no. 7, pp. 111–136, no. 8, pp. 179–188; 1889, no. 31, pp. 615–632.

52.36 Schrader] Max E. G. Schrader (d. 1903), German physician, "Zur Physiologie des Vogelgehirns," *Archiv für Physiologie*, 44 (November 1888), 175–238.

52.39 Christiani] Arthur Christiani (1843–1887), German physiologist, *Zur Physiologie des Gehirnes* (Berlin: Enslin, 1885). James's annotated copy is in Widener (Phil 6112.22). Chs. 5–7 (pp. 83–165), titled "Die Frage von der Localisation der Sehfunction," give a history of the discussion. An unsigned review of this book in *Science*, 6 (October 30, 1885), 379–380, appears to be by James. James's copy contains a letter from Christiani to an unidentified reviewer of the book.

53.23 Brown-Séquard] Charles Édouard Brown-Séquard (1817–1894), Mauritian physiologist, gives a survey of his views on inhibition (see p. 77, note 73) in "De quelques règles générales relatives à l'inhibition," *Archives de Physiologie*, 5th series, vol. 1 (October 1889), pp. 751–761. James's unmarked copy of "On Localization of Functions in the Brain," *Boston Medical and Surgical Journal*, 93 (July 29, 1875), 119–125, is in Widener (Phil 6103.2).

53.26 Goltz] For the term 'Ausfallserscheinungen' see *Über die Verrichtungen*, p. 40; for Goltz's view of inhibition, pp. 39–41.

53.38 Munk] Munk attacks Schrader in his fifteenth report (*Sitzungsberichte* [Berlin], 1889, no. 31, pp. 619–621), but the sentence in quotation marks was not found.

54.2 Munk] See notes to 42.5 and 51.34.

54.9 Hitzig] Christiani, pp. 138–165, discusses the work of these five authors and others. Hitzig and Luciani in particular are presented as writing against Munk. Hitzig's own account of his involvement in these controversies is given in his "Alte und neue Untersuchungen über das Gehirn," *Archiv für Psychiatrie*, 34 (1901), 1–38; 35 (1902), 275–392, 585–611; 36 (1902), 1–96; 37 (1903), 299–467, 849–1013.

54.14 Loeb] While pp. 272–278 of Loeb's "Beiträge zur Physiologie des Grosshirns" deal specifically with hemiamblyopia, the subject is discussed throughout the paper.

54.37 Lannegrace] See note to 57.33–34.

54.39 Christiani] In ch. 2 (pp. 19–30) Christiani describes his experiments with rabbits, while in chs. 3 and 4 (pp. 31–82), he discusses Munk's work.

54.40 Munk] See note to 52.30.

55.1 FIG. 12] Figures 12 and 13 are figures 1 and 2 in Munk's *Über die Functionen*, 1st ed.; they also appear in *Sitzungsberichte* (Berlin), 1886, no. 7, opposite p. 136.

55.26 Luciani] Luigi Luciani (1840–1919), Italian physiologist, and Giuseppe Seppilli, *Die Functions-Localisation auf der Grosshirnrinde an thierexperimenten und klinischen Fällen nachgewiesen*, trans. M. O. Fraenkel (Leipzig: Denicke, 1886), pp. 81–88, 103–114. Houghton preserves James's annotated copies of *Il cervelletto; nuovi studi di fisiologia normale e patologica* (Florence: Coi tipi dei successori Le Monnier, 1891) (WJ 841.52) and *I preludi della vita; discorso inaugurale* (Florence: Fiorentino, 1892) (WJ 841.52.2).

55.27 Goltz] See note to 22.32.

55.29 Loeb] See note to 44. 23.

55.30 Berlin] See note to 52.30.

56.7 FIG. 14] Luciani and Seppilli, p. 147.

56.12 Ferrier] *The Functions of the Brain*, 2nd ed., p. 273.

57.17 Ferrier] David Ferrier, *The Localisation of Cerebral Disease: Being the Gulstonian Lectures of the Royal College of Physicians for 1878* (London: Smith, Elder, 1878), pp. 116–119, claims that in experiments on monkeys a lesion of the occipital lobes was never followed by motor or sensory disturbance. He also cites reports of mental patients with such lesions and no defects in vision.

57.32 Ferrier] See note to 51.28.

57.32 Brown] Sanger Monroe Brown (1852–1928), Canadian-born neurologist, and Edward Albert Schafer, "An Investigation into the Functions of the Occipital and Temporal Lobes of the Monkey's Brain," *Philosophical Transactions* (B), 179 (1888), 303–327.

57.33–34 Lannegrace] Paul Jean Justinien Lannegrace (1852–1892), French physiologist, "Influence des lesions corticales sur la vue," *Archives de Médecine Expérimentale et d'Anatomie Pathologique*, 1 (1889), 87–114, 289–324. The report is by Albert Eulenburg (1840–1917), German physician, *Neuro-*

logisches Centralblatt, 8 (February 15, 1889), 108–110; (July 15, 1889), 420–422.

58.3 Seguin] Edward Constant Seguin (1843–1898), American neurologist, "A Contribution to the Pathology of Hemianopsia of Central Origin (Cortex-Hemianopsia)" *Journal of Nervous and Mental Disease*, 13 (January 1886), 1–38. Figure 15 is from p. 35. The legend is James's.

59.1 Henschen] Salomon Eberhard Henschen (1847–1930), Swedish physician, "On the Visual Path and Centre," *Brain*, 16 (1893), 170–180.

59.2 Vitzou] Alexandre N. Vitzou, Rumanian physiologist, "Effets de l'ablation totale des lobes occipitaux sur la vision, chez le chien," *Archives de Physiologie*, series 5, vol. 5 (October 1893), pp. 688–698.

59.19 Nothnagel] Nothnagel and Naunyn, p. 13.

59.30 Wilbrand] Hermann Wilbrand (b. 1851), German physician, *Die Seelenblindheit als Herderscheinung und ihre Beziehungen zur homonymen Hemianopsie zur Alexie und Agraphie* (Wiesbaden: J. F. Bergmann, 1887) (WJ 794.48), pp. 51–66.

59.32 Lissauer] Heinrich Lissauer (1861–1891), German neurologist, "Ein Fall von Seelenblindheit nebst einem Beitrage zur Theorie derselben," *Archiv für Psychiatrie*, 21 (1889), 222–270.

60.32 Freund] Carl Samuel Freund (b. 1862), German neurologist, "Über optische Aphasie und Seelenblindheit," *Archiv für Psychiatrie*, 20 (1889), 276–297, 371–416.

60.38 Charcot] Jean Martin Charcot (1825–1893), French neurologist. Preserved in Widener is James's annotated copy of *Leçons sur les localisations dans les maladies du cerveau*, 1st fascicle (Paris: Aux bureaux du *Progrès Médical*, 1876) (Phil 6952.23), and an unannotated copy of Charcot and A. Pitres (see note to 203.24), *Étude critique et clinique de la doctrine des localisations motrices dans l'écorce des hémisphères cérébraux de l'homme* (Paris: Alcan, 1883) (Phil 6952.23.10). For the case, see below pp. 705–706.

60.41 Bruns] Ludwig Bruns (1858–1916), German neurologist, and B. Stölting, German physician, "Ein Fall von Alexie mit rechtsseitiger homonymer Hemianopsie ('subcorticale Alexie' WERNICKE)," *Neurologisches Centralblatt*, 7 (September 1, 1888), 481–490; (September 15, 1888), 509–520.

61.33 Mauthner] Ludwig Mauthner (1840–1894), Austrian physician, *Gehirn und Auge* (Wiesbaden: J. F. Bergmann, 1881), pp. 487–507, section on "Seelenblindheit."

61.36 Bernard] Désiré Antoine François Bernard (b. 1853), French physician, *De l'aphasie et de ses diverses formes* (Paris: Aux Bureaux du *Progrès Médical*, 1885), ch. 5 (pp. 71–144), "De la cécité verbale."

61.37 Ballet] Gilbert Ballet (1853–1916), French physician, *Le Langage intérieur et les diverses formes de l'aphasie* (Paris: Alcan, 1886), ch. 8 (pp. 100–115), "De l'effacement partiel ou total des images visuelles des mots. —La cécité verbale."

61.37 Ross's] James Ross (1837–1892), British physician, *On Aphasia:*

Being a Contribution to the Subject of the Dissolution of Speech from Cerebral Disease (London: J. & A. Churchill, 1887), pp. 74–77, describes several degrees of "psychical blindness."

61.38 Binet] Alfred Binet (1857–1911), French psychologist, "Sur les rapports entre l'hémianopsie et la mémoire visuelle," *Revue Philosophique*, 26 (November 1888), 481–488. Works by Binet from James's library will be listed in the volume of manuscript remains. For a letter from Binet to James see note to 717.35.

61.39 Wernicke's] Carl Wernicke, *Lehrbuch der Gehirnkrankheiten für Aerzte und Studirende*, III (Berlin: Fischer, 1883), 554–559.

61.41 Monakow] Constantin von Monakow (1853–1930), Russian-born, Swiss neuropsychiatrist, "Experimentelle und pathologisch-anatomische Untersuchungen über die optischen Centren und Bahnen," *Archiv für Psychiatrie*, 20 (1889), 714–787.

62.8 FIG. 16] Luciani and Seppilli, p. 159.

62.9 Ferrier] David Ferrier and Gerald Francis Yeo (1845–1909), Irish-born physiologist, "A Record of Experiments on the Effects of Lesion of Different Regions of the Cerebral Hemispheres," *Philosophical Transactions* (B), 175 (1884), 479–564. Ferrier reports the same result in *The Functions of the Brain*, 2nd ed., pp. 307–308.

62.11 Brown] See note to 57.32.

62.19 Ferrier] David Ferrier, "Schäfer on the Temporal and Occipital Lobes," *Brain*, 11 (April 1888), 7–30.

62.20 Schäfer] Edward Albert Schafer, "On the Functions of the Temporal and Occipital Lobes: A Reply to Dr. Ferrier," *Brain*, 11 (July 1888), 145–165. On p. 151, Schafer presents evidence to show that Ferrier's monkey was not deaf.

62.27 Dog X] Luciani and Seppilli, pp. 120–124.

63.11 Starr] Moses Allen Starr (1854–1932), American neurologist, "The Pathology of Sensory Aphasia, with an Analysis of Fifty Cases in which Broca's Centre was not Diseased," *Brain*, 12 (July 1889), 82–99.

64.1–2 Charcot's] James perhaps has in mind Charcot's "Des différentes formes de l'aphasie," *Progrès Médical*, 11 (June 9, 1883), 441–444; continued as "Des variétés de l'aphasie" (June 16), 469–471; (June 23), 487–488; (July 7), 521–523; and concluded with the original title (November 3), 859–861. See also p. 65n.

65.1 FIG. 17] This figure is not a facsimile copy from Nothnagel and Naunyn. Their tables 3 and 4 represent a single brain with three shaded regions. Two of these correspond to the Broca and Wernicke regions of James's figure 11, the third, to the angular convolution of figure 17.

65.15 Ferrier] *The Functions of the Brain*, 2nd ed., ch. 9, pt. 3 (pp. 312–323), on "The Olfactory and Gustatory Centres."

65.16 Munk] Munk discusses the sense of smell in his seventh report (July 2, 1880), *Über die Functionen*, 1st ed., pp. 121–133.

65.22 Bastian's] Henry Charlton Bastian (1837–1915), British physician and biologist, *The Brain as an Organ of Mind* (New York: D. Appleton, 1880), chs. 28–30 (pp. 601–690). James's copy is in Widener (Phil 6111.10.2). James reviewed the work in the *Nation*, 31 (September 23, 1880), 224–225. Also in Widener is *On Paralysis from Brain Disease in Its Common Forms* (New York: D. Appleton, 1875) (Phil 6951.18) and pamphlets.

66.1 FIG. 18] Ross, p. 124.

66.4 FIG. 19] Luciani and Seppilli, p. 165.

66.8 Mills] Charles Karsner Mills (1845–1931), American neurologist, "Cerebral Localization in Its Practical Relations," *Transactions of the Congress of American Physicians and Surgeons*, 1 (1889), 184–284.

67.3 Hitzig] For Hitzig's view of the muscle sense see *Untersuchungen über das Gehirn*, pp. 59–60.

67.11 Schiff] Moritz Schiff (1823–1896), Swiss physiologist, *Lezioni di fisiologia sperimentale sul sistema nervoso encefalico*, compiled by Pietro Marchi, 2nd ed. (Florence: Cammelli, 1873), pp. 527–531. James's annotated copy in Widener (Phil 6128.37) is dated Florence, January 1873. His index contains the entry "Sensibility of centres, 247, 282, 285, 267, 294, 439, 527."

67.11 Herzen] Alexandre Herzen (1839–1906), French physiologist. Houghton preserves James's unmarked copy of *Expériences sur les centres modérateurs de l'action réflexe* (Turin: H. Lœscher, 1864) (Phil 6103.8*), while a marked copy of *Le Cerveau et l'activité cérébrale* (1887) was sold from James's library.

67.34 *Functions*] 2nd ed., pp. 374–377. On p. 375 of his copy, James notes: "Corroborated for monkeys by Horsley and Schafer. Phil. Trans. vol. 179, p. 15" (see note to 45.21).

67.37 *Brain*] Moritz Schiff, "On the Excitable Area of the Cortex, and Its Relations to the Columns of the Spinal Cord. *A Reply to* Professor Horsley," *Brain*, 9 (October 1886), 289–310.

67.38 Bechterew] Wladimir Bechterew (Vladimir Mikhailovich Bekhterev) (1857–1927), Russian physician, "Wie sind die Erscheinungen zu verstehen, die nach Zerstörung des motorischen Rindenfeldes an Thieren auftreten?", *Archiv für Physiologie*, 35 (1885), 137–145.

67.41 Goltz] See note to 22.32.

68.2 Ferrier] On p. 23 of their paper (see note to 45.21), Horsley and Schafer note that Ferrier assisted in some of their experiments and cite Ferrier's *Functions*, 2nd ed., pp. 341ff, as evidence that Ferrier now accepts their position.

68.24 FIG. 20] Luciani and Seppilli, p. 296, depicting the *"senso-motorischen Sphäre"* (p. 295).

68.28 *Functions*] 2nd ed.

68.32 *Transactions*] See note to 66.8.

69.19 Putnam] James assisted Putnam in at least one localization experi-

Notes

ment, on the problem of restricting electrical stimulation to definite portions of the brain; see Putnam's "Contribution to the Physiology of the Cortex Cerebri," *Boston Medical and Surgical Journal*, 91 (July 16, 1874), 49-52.

69.36 Exner's] Exner explains what his plate 25 represents on p. 180.

69.37 Ferrier's] 2nd ed., pp. 108-148, 360-364.

69.39 Mills] Nothing in Starr's "Pathology of Sensory Aphasia" or his other writings was found fitting James's original reference to "Starr, *loc. cit.* p. 272." The reference does fit Charles Karsner Mills (see note to 66.8), where on p. 272 Mills writes: "I can see no reason for requiring a muscular sense entirely distinct from other acknowledged forms of sensibility." While Mills does not refer to Nothnagel by name, he does remark that some facts which have been brought forward concerning the muscular sense and the parietal lobe are not convincing.

69.40 Leyden] Ernst Viktor von Leyden (1832-1910), German physician, and M. Jastrowitz, *Beiträge zur Lehre von der Localisation im Gehirn und über deren praktische Verwerthung* (Leipzig: Thieme, 1888), p. 72.

71.36 *Philosophical*] See note to 45.21.

71.37 *Transactions*] From Victor Horsley's remarks in a "Discussion on Cerebral Localization," *Transactions of the Congress of American Physicians and Surgeons*, 1 (1889), 329-354.

71.38 Beevor] See note to 46.23.

72.7 FIG. 21] For the essay by Paneth see note to 43.36. Figure 21 is half of figure 1 in table 6 in Paneth. The legend is James's.

72.23 Luys] Jules Luys (1828-1897), French anatomist and physician, *The Brain and Its Functions* (New York: D. Appleton, 1882), p. 66. In Widener is James's annotated copy of the French edition, dated January 1877, *Le Cerveau et ses fonctions* (Paris: Baillière, 1876) (Phil 6121.7.3). Also in Widener are unannotated copies of *Recherches sur le système nerveux cérébro-spinal: Sa structure, ses fonctions et ses maladies* (Paris: Baillière, 1865) (Phil 6121.7.5), dated Paris, November 1868; *Leçons sur la structure et les maladies du système nerveux* (Paris: Baillière, 1875) (Phil 6121.7.21); and *Leçons cliniques sur les principaux phénomènes de l'hypnotisme dans leurs rapparts avec la pathologie mentale* (Paris: Carré, 1890) (Phil 6681.12). In Houghton is James's annotated copy of *Études de physiologie et de pathologie cérébrales* (Paris: Baillière, 1874) (Phil 6121.7.9B).

72.23 Horsley] Horsley and Schafer, "A Record of Experiments," p. 17 (see note to 45.21).

72.24 Mercier] Charles Arthur Mercier (1852-1919), British psychiatrist, *The Nervous System and the Mind: A Treatise on the Dynamics of the Human Organism* (London: Macmillan, 1888), p. 124. James's annotated copy is in Widener (Phil 6122.31). Perry reports that an annotated copy of *Sanity and Insanity* (1892) was sold. The date given could well be an error.

73.16 Marique] Joseph M. Louis Marique (b. 1856), Belgian physician, *Recherches expérimentales sur le mécanisme de fonctionnement des centres psycho-moteurs du cerveau* (Brussels: Gustave Mayolez, 1885).

Notes

73.16   Exner] Sigmund Exner and Josef Paneth, "Versuche über die Folgen der Durchschneidung von Associationsfasern am Hundehirn," *Archiv für Physiologie*, 44 (1889), 544-555.

73.29   Wundt] In the present edition of *The Principles of Psychology*, four editions of Wundt's *Grundzüge der physiologischen Psychologie* are cited. Houghton preserves James's annotated copies of the first edition (Leipzig: W. Engelmann, 1874) (WJ 796.59.2) and of the second, 2 vols. (Leipzig: W. Engelmann, 1880) (WJ 796.59.4). Perry reports that both volumes of the fourth edition (Leipzig: W. Engelmann, 1893), with some annotations, were sold. Neither volume of the third edition (Leipzig: W. Engelmann, 1887) has been located. James's index to the first edition of the *Grundzüge* has no entry for apperception, but the index in vol. II of the second, contains the entry "Apperception I, 492, II, 304." James's extensive comments on I, 492 indicate considerable perplexity. "Is this merely a statement of the conditions of feeling or is it an explanation of it as the pleasure of the Ap^{tgt} [Apperceptionsthätigkeit] rather than that of the man. Is the A. *that in* the man that feels the pleasure?" "This account seems to me to embody every defect. It is neither psychological nor physiological. One doesn't know whether the reaction d. Ap. thatgkt *is* the pleasure or is *followed* by the pleasure. One doesnt know whether the reaction which is unpleasant is a reaction towards the unpleasant thing or towards the other things whose Apperception is gehemmt." "He seems to mean that sensations wh. *bind* apperception so that it turns with difficulty *to others* are unpleasant on account of this difficulty." James expressed similar criticisms of apperception in "The Knowing of Things Together," *Essays in Philosophy*, WORKS, p. 80n. James reviewed the first edition of the *Grundzüge* in the *North American Review*, 121 (July 1875), 195-201.

74.37   Clifford's] William Kingdon Clifford (1845-1879), British mathematician and philosopher, *Lectures and Essays*, ed. Leslie Stephen and Frederick Pollock, 2 vols. (London: Macmillan, 1879), II, 72: "But the inferred existence of your feelings, of objective groupings among them similar to those among my feelings, and of a subjective order in many respects analogous to my own,—these inferred existences are in the very act of inference *thrown out* of my consciousness." Thus, such inferred existences are to be called ejects. Perry reports that both volumes of this edition were sold.

75.32   Freusberg] Adolf Freusberg (b. 1849), German physiologist, "Über die Erregung und Hemmung der Thätigkeit der nervösen Centralorgane," *Archiv für Physiologie*, 10 (1875), 174-208.

75.34   Ferrier's] 2nd ed.

75.34   Vulpian] Edme Félix Alfred Vulpian (1826-1887), French physiologist and physician, *Leçons sur la physiologie générale et comparée du système nerveux*, recorded by Ernest Brémond (Paris: Baillière, 1866), p. 548.

75.36   Maudsley] Henry Maudsley (1835-1918), British physiologist and psychologist, *The Physiology of Mind: Being the First Part of a Third Edition, Revised, Enlarged, and in Great Part Rewritten, of "The Physiology and Pathology of Mind"* (London: Macmillan, 1876), pp. 138ff, 197ff, 241ff. James's annotated copy is in Widener (Phil 6122.1.15). Also in Widener are annotated copies of *The Pathology of Mind: Being the Third Edition of the*

Notes

Second Part of the "Physiology and Pathology of Mind," Recast, Enlarged, and Rewritten (New York: D. Appleton, 1880) (Phil 6962.2.9B), and *Natural Causes and Supernatural Seemings* (London: Kegan Paul, Trench, 1886) (Phil 7068.86.50). James's copy of *Body and Mind: An Inquiry into Their Connection and Mutual Influence, Specially in Reference to Mental Disorders* (London: Macmillan, 1870) was given to Widener, but rejected in 1967. James reviewed *The Physiology of Mind* in the *Nation*, 24 (June 14, 1877), 355–356. For other reviews see note to 1149.39.

75.37 Lewes's] See note to 22.14.

76.35 Goltz] Friedrich Leopold Goltz and Adolf Freusberg, "Über die Functionen des Lendenmarks des Hundes," *Archiv für Physiologie*, 8 (1874), 460–498.

76.37 Loeb] See note to 44.23.

76.39 Schrader] See note to 52.36.

76.40 *Nervous*] Mercier, ch. 3 (pp. 59–80), "Muscular Actions, Their Co-Ordination and Inhibition"; ch. 6 (pp. 116–145), "The Nervous Mechanism of Co-Ordination and Inhibition." Mercier's article is titled "Inhibition," *Brain*, 11 (October 1888), 361–386.

77.16 Carville] C. Carville and Henri Duret (1849–1921), French physician, "Les Fonctions des hemisphères cérébraux," *Archives de Physiologie*, 2nd series, vol. 2 (1875), pp. 352–491.

77.33 Brown-Séquard] See note to 53.23.

77.37 Brunton's] Thomas Lauder Brunton (1844–1916), British physician and pharmacologist, *A Text-Book of Pharmacology, Therapeutics and Materia Medica*, adapted to the United States Pharmacopœia by Francis H. Williams (Philadelphia: Lea Brothers, 1885), pp. 154–158. James's copy has not been identified and his reference fits other editions. Brunton's "On the Nature of Inhibition, and the Action of Drugs upon It" appeared in *Nature*, 27 (March 1, 1883), 419–422; (March 8, 1883), 436–439; (March 15, 1883), 467–468; (March 22, 1883), 485–487.

77.39 Herzen] An abstract of Alexandre Herzen and N. Löwenthal, "Un Cas d'exstirpation bilatérale du gyrus sigmoïde chez un jeune chien," *Recueil Zoologique Suisse*, 4 (1886), 71–87, appeared in *Jahresbericht*, vol. 15, pt. 2 (1888) (covering the literature of 1886), p. 38.

78.34 Pflüger's] See note to 22.32.

78.35 *Neurologisches*] Friedrich Leopold Goltz, "Der Hund ohne Gross-hirn," *Neurologisches Centralblatt*, 8 (June 15, 1889), 372–373.

80.17 Steiner's] Isidor Steiner (1849–1914), German physiologist, *Untersuchungen über die Physiologie des Froschhirns* (Braunschweig: Vieweg, 1885).

80.35 Pflüger's] Max E. G. Schrader, "Zur Physiologie des Froschgehirns," *Archiv für Physiologie*, 41 (July 1887), 75–90.

80.36 *Ibid.*] See note to 52.36.

80.40 Berlin] Isidor Steiner, "Über das Grosshirn der Knochenfische,"

Sitzungsberichte (Berlin) 1886, vol. 1, pp. 5–9. Vulpian's work led Steiner to continue his investigations, "Über das Gehirn der Knochenfische," *Sitzungsberichte*, 1886, vol. 2, pp. 1133–1135.

80.41 *Comptes*] Edme Félix Alfred Vulpian, "De l'hémi-anesthésie alterne comme symptôme de certaines lésions du bulbe rachidien," *Comptes Rendus Hebdomadaires des Séances de l'Académie des Sciences*, 102 (January 11, 1886), 90–96.

81.40 *Comptes*] Vulpian, "Sur la persistance des mouvements volontaires chez les poissons osseux à la suite de l'ablation des lobes cérébraux," *Comptes Rendus Hebdomadaires des Séances de l'Académie des Sciences*, 102 (June 28, 1886), 1526–1530. The text quoted is from pp. 1529–1530. Vulpian is commenting on Steiner's first paper.

82.37 Seguin] Case 3 in Seguin, pp. 6, 20 (see note to 58.3).

82.40 *Loc.*] See note to 52.36.

83.2 'Ausfallserscheinung'] See p. 53.

83.32 Goltz] See note to 22.32.

83.32 Schrader] See note to 52.36.

83.35 Soltmann's] Hermann Julius Otto Soltmann (1844–1912), German physician. Paneth and Bechterew identify two articles by Soltmann in the *Jahrbuch für Kinderheilkunde und physische Erziehung*: "Experimentelle Studien über die Functionen des Grosshirns der Neugeborenen," n.s. 9 (1876), 106–148; "Über das Hemmungsnervensystem der Neugebornen," n.s. 11 (1877), 101–114.

83.38 Paneth's] Josef Paneth, "Über die Erregbarkeit der Hirnrinde neugeborener Hunde," *Archiv für Physiologie*, 37 (October 1885), 202–208.

83.41 Bechterew] Wladimir Bechterew, "Über die Erregbarkeit verschiedener Hirnbezirke bei neugeborenen Thieren," *Neurologisches Centralblatt*, 8 (September 15, 1889), 513–521.

84.32 Münsterberg] Hugo Münsterberg (1863–1916), German-born psychologist, James's colleague at Harvard. For relations between James and Münsterberg, including excerpts from letters, see Perry, II, 138–154. The correspondence between them is at Houghton (bMS Am 1092.9 [357–392, 3263–3305]). Houghton preserves the following annotated works, a few inscribed to James from Münsterberg: *Die Willenshandlung. Ein Beitrag zur physiologischen Psychologie* (Freiburg i. B.: J. C. B. Mohr, 1888) (WJ 757.62.6); *Beiträge zur experimentellen Psychologie*, 4 pts. (Freiburg i. B.: J. C. B. Mohr, 1889–1892) (WJ 757.62); *Grundzüge der Psychologie*, vol. I (Leipzig: J. A. Barth, 1900) (WJ 757.62.2); *Science and Idealism* (Boston: Houghton, Mifflin, 1906) (WJ 757.62.8); *Philosophie der Werte* (Leipzig: J. A. Barth, 1908) (*AC 85.J2376.Zz908m); and pamphlets (WJ 757.62.4) (WJ 757.62.10) (WJ 757.62.12). Perry reports that annotated copies of *Psychology and Life* (1899) and *Psychotherapy* (1909) were sold. On p. 134 of James's copy of *Die Willenshandlung*, there is the following: "Bechterew Jbr. XV, 38. bestätigte Soltmann Neurol Cbl 1889." The article by Soltmann has not been identified.

84.42 Pflüger's] See note to 52.36.

85.28 Schiff] Moritz Schiff, *Lehrbuch der Muskel- und Nervenphysiologie* (Lahr: M. Schauenburg, 1858-1859). James could be referring to the whole section, "Psychische Thätigkeit des Rückenmarks," pp. 213-222.

85.32 Lewes] George Henry Lewes, *The Physiology of Common Life*, 2 vols. (Edinburgh: William Blackwood and Sons, 1859-1860), II, 81-272, on "The Mind and the Brain."

85.35-36 Rosenthal] Isidor Rosenthal (1836-1915), German physiologist, "Über Reflexe," *Biologisches Centralblatt*, 4 (June 15, 1884), 247-256.

85.36 Mendelssohn] Moritz Mendelssohn, "Untersuchungen über Reflexe," third report, *Sitzungsberichte* (Berlin), 1885, vol. I, pp. 107-111.

86.41 Schrader's] See note to 52.36.

88.6 Locke's] James's copy of the 31st edition of *An Essay Concerning Human Understanding* (London: William Tegg, 1853) (WJ 551.13) is dated September 1876. James is referring to p. 276 (bk. II, ch. 32, sec. 6). In his copy the passage is marked with cross-references to pp. 294, 301-302, 412, 450, 445, 490, 276.

89.31 Valentin] Gabriel Gustav Valentin (1810-1883), German-born physiologist, "Die Interferenzen elektrischer Erregungen," *Archiv für Physiologie*, 7 (1873), 458-496.

89.31 Stirling] William Stirling (1851-1932), British physiologist, "On the Summation of Electrical Stimuli Applied to the Skin," *Journal of Anatomy and Physiology*, 10 (October 1875), 324-376; previously published in German as "Über die Summation elektrischer Hautreize," *Berichte über die Verhandlungen der königlich sächsischen Gesellschaft der Wissenschaften zu Leipzig* (mathematisch-physische Classe), 26 (1874), 372-440.

89.32 Ward] James Ward (1843-1925), British philosopher and psychologist, "Über die Auslösung von Reflexbewegungen durch eine Summe schwacher Reize," *Archiv für Anatomie und Physiologie*, 1880, pp. 72-91. For the relations between James and Ward see Perry, II, 644-657. Their correspondence is at Houghton (bMS Am 1092.9 [649-661, 3829-3854]). Also at Houghton is James's copy of *Naturalism and Agnosticism*, 2 vols. (London: Adam and Charles Black, 1899) (WJ 592.75).

89.33 Sewall] Henry Sewall (1855-1936), American physician and physiologist, "On the Effect of Two Succeeding Stimuli upon Muscular Contraction," *Studies from the Biological Laboratory* (Johns Hopkins University, session 1878-1879), vol. 1, no. 2 (1880), pp. 29-56.

89.34 Kronecker] Karl Hugo Kronecker (1839-1914), German physiologist. The *Archiv für Anatomie und Physiologie*, 1880, pp. 437-438 contains an abstract of Kronecker's "Über die Erregung der Gefässnervencentren durch Summation elektrischer Reize," describing work done with R. Nicolaides, of the Physiological Institute of Berlin. The complete paper, with Kronecker and Nicolaides as authors, appears in the same *Archiv*, 1883, pp. 27-42.

89.35 Exner] Sigmund Exner, "Zur Kenntniss von der Wechselwirkung der Erregungen im Centralnervensystem," *Archiv für Physiologie*, 28 (1882), 487-506.

89.35 Eckhard] Conrad Eckhard (1822–1905), German physiologist, "Physiologie des Rückenmarks und des Gehirns mit Ausschluss der Grosshirnrinde," in Hermann's *Handbuch*, vol. II, pt. 2 (1879), pp. 3–188. In Houghton is James's copy of *Experimentalphysiologie des Nervensystems* (Giessen: Emil Roth, 1867) (WJ 721.45), dated September 1867.

89.38 Hermann] Ludimar Hermann (1834–1914), German physiologist, "Allgemeine Nervenphysiologie," in Hermann's *Handbuch*, vol. II, pt. 1 (1879), pp. 3–196; "Allgemeine Muskelphysik," in Hermann's *Handbuch*, vol. I, pt. 1 (1879), pp. 3–260.

89.39 Wundt] 2nd ed., I, 243–251.

89.39 Richet] Charles Robert Richet (1850–1935), French physiologist. Letters from Richet to James are at Houghton (bMS Am 1092, letters 796–806). In Widener is James's annotated copy of *L'Homme et l'intelligence: Fragments de physiologie et de psychologie* (Paris: Alcan, 1884) (Phil 5257.6). James's index contains "Summation of stimuli 24–9, 468." Richet's paper in the *Revue Philosophique* is titled "Les Origines et les modalités de la mémoire: Essai de psychologie générale," 21 (June 1886), 561–590; and in the *Physiologie expérimentale. Travaux du laboratoire de M. Marey*, "De l'addition latente des excitations électriques dans les nerfs et dans les muscles," 3 (1877), 97–105.

90.35 Kronecker] Karl Hugo Kronecker and Granville Stanley Hall, "Die willkürliche Muskelaction," *Archiv für Anatomie und Physiologie*, 1879, pp. 11–47 of the supplement.

90.36 Schoenlein] Karl Ernest Schoenlein (1859–1899), German biologist, "Zu Frage nach der Natur der Anfangszuckung," *Archiv für Anatomie und Physiologie*, 1882, pp. 357–368.

90.36 Sertoli] Enrico Sertoli (1842–1910), Italian physiologist. *Jahresbericht*, vol. 11, pt. 2 (1883) (literature of 1882), p. 25, contains an abstract of Sertoli's "Contribuzioni alla fisiologia generale dei muscoli lisci."

90.37 De Watteville] Armand de Watteville (1846–1925), Swiss-born physiologist, editor of *Brain*, "Über die Summirung von Reizen in den sensiblen Nerven des Menschen," *Neurologisches Centralblatt*, 2 (April 1, 1883), 144–147.

90.38 Gruenhagen] Alfred Wilhelm Gruenhagen (1842–1912), German physiologist, "Über ächte Interferenz- und Summationsvorgänge nervöser Thätigkeitszustände," *Archiv für Physiologie*, 34 (1884), 301–309.

90.39 Bubnoff] N. Bubnoff and Rudolf Peter Heinrich Heidenhain (1834–1897), German physiologist, "Über Erregungs- und Hemmungsvorgänge innerhalb der motorischen Hirncentren," *Archiv für Physiologie*, 26 (1881), 137–200; quotation from pp. 156–157.

91.34 Exner] See note to 89.35.

91.38 Lewes] Lewes, *The Physical Basis of Mind*, pp. 478–479, cites Ernst Wilhelm, Ritter von Brücke (1819–1892), German physiologist, from his *Vorlesungen über Physiologie*.

91.40 Romanes] George John Romanes (1848–1894), Canadian-born naturalist, *Mental Evolution in Animals* (London: Kegan Paul, Trench, 1883)

(WJ 577.53), p. 163. Romanes cites a letter from Allen Thomson (1809–1884), Scottish biologist.

91.41 Mach] Ernst Mach (1838–1916), Austrian physicist and philosopher. In 1882 James heard Mach lecturing in Prague. Mach's letters to James are at Houghton (bMS Am 1092, letters 538–543). Also at Houghton are five books by Mach from James's library, among them *Die Analyse der Empfindungen*, 4th ed. (Jena: Gustav Fischer, 1903) (WJ 753.13). James appears to be using the first edition of this work, *Beiträge zur Analyse der Empfindungen* (Jena: Gustav Fischer, 1886). Mach discusses a sparrow's behavior on pp. 35n–36n. For James's meeting with Mach see *Letters*, I, 212. Works by Mach from James's library will be listed in the volume of manuscript remains.

92.16 Helmholtz] Hermann Ludwig Ferdinand von Helmholtz (1821–1894), German physiologist and physicist, is usually credited with being the first to measure the speed of an impulse as it travels in the nervous system. His first experiments on frogs are reported in "Vorläufiger Bericht über die Fortpflanzungsgeschwindigkeit der Nervenreizung," *Archiv für Anatomie und Physiologie* (anatomische Abtheilung), 1850, pp. 71–73 of supplement. James studied with Helmholtz in 1868 (Perry, I, 151), while in 1893, Helmholtz visited James at Chocorua (*Letters*, I, 347).

92.24 Franklin] James is alluding to the inscription on Jean Antoine Houdon's bust of Benjamin Franklin, "He snatched the thunderbolt from heaven, then the sceptre from tyrants," usually traced to the Roman poet Manilius.

92.38 Fowler] Richard Fowler (1765–1863), British physician, *Some Observations on the Mental State of the Blind, and Deaf, and Dumb, Suggested by the Case of Jane Sullivan, Both Blind, Deaf, Dumb, and Uneducated* (Salisbury: W. B. Brodie, 1843), p. 14.

93.25 Ludwig's] Carl Friedrich Wilhelm Ludwig (1816–1895), German physiologist, in 1847 first described the kymograph, an instrument for recording variations in blood pressure.

93.28 Hipp's] An electric chronoscope, an instrument for measuring very short intervals of time, was invented by Charles Wheatstone (1802–1875), British physicist and inventor, and modified by Matthäus Hipp (1813–1893), German-born inventor.

94.2 'psychodometer'] Sigmund Exner calls his instrument a neuramoebimeter in "Experimentelle Untersuchung der einfachsten psychischen Processe," *Archiv für Physiologie*, 7 (1873), 601–660; 8 (1874), 526–537; 11 (1875), 403–432, 581–602; see especially the appendix to the first part. Heinrich Obersteiner (1847–1922), German physiologist, worked with Exner in some of the experiments. His account of a very similar instrument can be found in "Über eine neue einfache Methode zur Bestimmung der psychischen Leistungsfähigkeit des Gehirnes Geisteskranker," *Archiv für pathologische Anatomie und Physiologie und für klinische Medicin*, 59 (1874), 427–458.

94.5 FIG. 22] This reaction timer is described and pictured on pp. 312–313 of Joseph Weatherhead Warren (1849–1916), "The Effect of Pure Alcohol on the Reaction Time, with a Description of a New Chronoscope," *Journal of Physiology*, 8 (December 1887), 311–348. Warren was a physician who from 1881 to 1891 taught at the Harvard Medical School. He called this the Bowditch neuramoebimeter after Henry Pickering Bowditch (1840–1911),

American physiologist, professor at the Harvard Medical School. James's correspondence with Bowditch is at Houghton (bMS Am 1092.9 [77–84, 772–818]).

94.28 Marey] Étienne Jules Marey (1830–1904), French physiologist, *La Méthode graphique dans les sciences expérimentales et principalement en physiologie et en médecine* (Paris: G. Masson, [1878]), pp. 133–166, titled "Chronographie."

94.32 Holmes] Oliver Wendell Holmes (1809–1894), American author and physician, professor at the Harvard Medical School. Two letters from Holmes to James are at Houghton (bMS Am 1092, letters 385–386).

94.33 Jastrow] Joseph Jastrow (1863–1944), American psychologist, "An Easy Method of Measuring the Time of Mental Processes," *Science*, 8 (September 10, 1886), pp. 237–241 of supplement. Perry reports that James's copy of *Fact and Fable in Psychology* (1900) was given to the Harvard libraries, but it has not been located.

95.40 Cattell] James McKeen Cattell (1860–1944), American psychologist, "The Time Taken up by Cerebral Operations," *Mind*, 11 (1886), 220–242, 377–392, 524–538. James's numerous letters to Cattell are in the Library of Congress.

96.28 *Physiologische*] 2nd ed. See also note to 73.29.

96.33 Staude's] Otto Staude (1857–1928), "Der Begriff der Apperception in der neueren Psychologie," *Philosophische Studien*, vol. 1, no. 2 (1882), pp. 149–212. This periodical was edited by Wundt. In James's set of the *Philosophische Studien* (WJ 140.70), there are several critical comments about Staude's article.

96.35 Marty] Anton Marty (1847–1914), Swiss philosopher of language, "Über Sprachreflex, Nativismus und absichtliche Sprachbildung," *Vierteljahrsschrift*, 8 (1884), 456–478; 10 (1886), 69–105, 346–364; 13 (1889), 195–220, 304–344; 14 (1890), 55–84, 443–484; 15 (1891), 251–284, 445–467; 16 (1892), 104–122. In Houghton is James's copy of the sixth installment as well as Marty's review of *The Principles of Psychology*, in the *Zeitschrift für Psychologie und Physiologie der Sinnesorgane*, 3 (May 1892), 297–333 (WJ 700.5). The review is inscribed to James. It is extensively annotated.

96.37 Exner] See note to 94.2.

96.38 Richet] Charles Richet, "De la durée des actes psychiques élémentaires," *Revue Philosophique*, 6 (October 1878), 393–396, a discussion of the paper by Kries and Auerbach cited by James on p. 497n.

97.38 Exner] See note to 94.2. On p. 618 Exner gives an actual date for the experiments referred to by James simply as "some experiments."

97.39 Wundt] 2nd ed.

98.10 Delbœuf] Joseph Remi Léopold Delbœuf (1831–1896), Belgian philosopher and psychologist, *Théorie générale de la sensibilité* (Brussels: F. Hayez, 1876), p. 57: "L'organe adventice est donc ce qui rend la sensation possible: *il est la condition du .sens adventice*, c'est-à-dire *de la faculté de recevoir d'une manière différenciée les changements extérieurs différenciés.*"

Thirteen letters from Delbœuf to James are at Houghton (bMS Am 1092, letters 152-164). Also at Houghton is James's copy of *La Psychologie comme science naturelle* (Paris: Baillière, 1876) (WJ 617.48). For works by Delbœuf sold from James's library see *Some Problems of Philosophy*, WORKS, note to 76.19.

98.13 Exner's] See note to 94.2.

98.23 "Everyone"] Vol. 7, p. 615.

98.32 *Physiologische*] 2nd ed.

98.33 Cattell's] See note to 95.40.

98.45 Lipps] Theodor Lipps (1851-1914), German psychologist and philosopher, *Grundtatsachen des Seelenlebens* (Bonn: Max Cohen & Sohn, 1883) (WJ 750.71), pp. 179-188. In addition to works cited in the present notes, Houghton has *Vom Fühlen, Wollen, und Denken. Eine psychologische Skizze* (Leipzig: J. A. Barth, 1902) (WJ 750.71.4). Given to Widener but not now catalogued is James's copy of *Zur Psychologie der Suggestion* (1897).

99.1 Lange] Ludwig Lange (1863-1936), German psychologist, "Neue Experimente über den Vorgang der einfachen Reaction auf Sinneseindrücke," *Philosophische Studien*, vol. 4, no. 4 (1888), pp. 479-510.

99.10 Wundt] *Grundzüge*, 3rd ed., II, 265-267.

100.2 Lange's] "Neue Experimente," p. 493.

100.9 Wundt's] *Grundzüge*, 2nd ed., II, 219-291, ch. 16 on "Apperception und Verlauf der Vorstellungen."

100.24 Buccola] Gabriele Buccola (1854-1885), Italian psychiatrist, *La legge del tempo nei fenomeni del pensiero: Saggio di psicologia sperimentale* (Milan: Fratelli Dumolard, 1883), p. 147.

100.26 Exner] See note to 94.2.

100.27 Herzen] Alexandre Herzen, "Il tempo fisiologico in rapporto all'età," *Archivio per l'Antropologia e la Etnologia*, 9 (1879), 351-352.

100.39 Exner] Sigmund Exner, "Physiologie der Grosshirnrinde," in Hermann's *Handbuch*, vol. II, pt. 2 (1879), pp. 189-350; pp. 252-280, for section on "Das zeitliche Verhalten psychischer Impulse."

100.39 Ribot's] Théodule Armand Ribot (1839-1916), French psychologist, *La Psychologie allemande contemporaine: (École expérimentale)* (Paris: Baillière, 1879), pp. 299-338. Ch. 8 is titled "De la durée des actes psychiques." The title as originally given by James comes closer to the French original than to the English translation, *German Psychology of To-day, the Empirical School*, trans. James Mark Baldwin (New York: Charles Scribner's Sons, 1886). Widener preserves James's unannotated copy of Ribot's *Essai sur les passions* (Paris: Alcan, 1907) (Phil 5400.18.15). Also in Widener, with annotations, bound as a single volume with a letter to James from Ribot, are *Les Maladies de la mémoire* (Paris: Baillière, 1881) and *Les Maladies de la volonté* (Paris: Baillière, 1883) (Phil 5545.22.2). Other letters from Ribot are at Houghton (bMS Am 1092, letters 788-795), as well as copies of letters from James to Ribot (bMS Am 1092.1).

100.41 Gilman] Benjamin Ives Gilman (1852-1933), American psychologist and author, was a graduate student in psychology at Harvard in 1883-1885.

101.12 Hirsch] Wundt, 2nd ed., II, 223n, cites Adolph Hirsch (1830-1901), Swiss geodesist, "Chronoskopische Versuche über die Geschwindigkeit der verschiedenen Sinneseindrücke und der Nerven-Leitung," *Untersuchungen zur Naturlehre des Menschen und der Thiere*, ed. Jacob Moleschott, 9 (1865), 183-199; Wilhelm Gottlieb Hankel (1814-1899), German physicist, "Über einen Apparat zur Messung sehr kleiner Zeiträume," *Annalen der Physik und Chemie*, 132 (1867), 134-165; and pp. 645, 648, 649 of Exner (see note to 94.2).

101.16 Goldscheider] Alfred Goldscheider (1858-1935), German physiologist, has several papers on reaction time. James could be referring to the report "Über die Reactionszeit der Temperaturempfindungen," *Archiv für Anatomie und Physiologie*, 1887, pp. 469-473.

101.17 Vintschgau] Maximilian von Vintschgau (1832-1913), Austrian physiologist, and E. Steinach, "Über die Reactionszeit von Temperatursempfindungen," *Archiv für Physiologie*, 41 (1887), 367-370.

101.21 Vintschgau] M. von Vintschgau and J. Hönigschmied, "Versuche über die Reactionszeit einer Geschmacksempfindung," pt. 3, *Archiv für Physiologie*, 14 (1876), 529-592. James is rounding off Vintschgau's (p. 575) 0. 1598 and 0.2196.

101.26 Vintschgau] M. von Vintschgau, "Physiologie des Geschmackssinns und des Geruchssinns," in Hermann's *Handbuch*, vol. III, pt. 2 (1880), pp. 145-286 (pp. 272-286, on smell).

101.27 Beaunis] Henri Étienne Beaunis (1830-1921), French psychologist, *Recherches expérimentales sur les conditions de l'activité cérébrale et sur la physiologie des nerfs*, 2 vols. (Paris: Baillière, 1884-1886), I, 49-80, section on "Recherches sur le temps de réaction des sensations olfactives."

101.36-37 Orschansky] Isaak G. Orschansky (Orshanskii) (b. 1851), Russian physiologist, "Zur Lehre von der Willensthätigkeit. Über willkürliche Impulse und Hemmungen," *Archiv für Anatomie und Physiologie*, 1889, pp. 173-198.

101.42 *Physiologische*] 2nd ed.

102.3 Vintschgau] Buccola, p. 103, cites Vintschgau, Hermann's *Handbuch*, vol. III, pt. 2, p. 204.

102.4 Buccola] Buccola, p. 106, lists a minimum, maximum, and median reaction time for every individual tested and type of odor. James gives medians.

102.8 Herzen] Alexandre Herzen, *Grundlinien einer allgemeinen Psychophysiologie* (Leipzig: Ernst Günthers Verlag, 1889), p. 101. The copy in Widener (Phil 6117.1), acquired December 24, 1889, has on the back flyleaf "101" in what appears to be James's hand.

102.19 Hall] Granville Stanley Hall and Johannes von Kries (1853-1928), German physiologist, "Über die Abhängigkeit der Reactionszeiten vom des

Reizes," *Archiv für Anatomie und Physiologie*, 1879, pp. 1–10 of supplement.

102.31 Vintschgau] Sigmund Exner, Hermann's *Handbuch*, vol. II, pt. 2, p. 270 (see note to 100.39), cites Michael Joseph Dietl (1847–1887), German physiologist, and M. von Vintschgau, "Das Verhalten der physiologischen Reactionszeit unter dem Einfluss von Morphium, Caffée und Wein," *Archiv für Physiologie*, 16 (January 1878), 316–372.

102.39 *Journal*] See note to 94.5.

103.2 Buccola] Pp. 189–195, "Alimenti nervosi e sostanze farmacologiche."

103.5 Hall] Granville Stanley Hall, "Reaction-time and Attention in the Hypnotic State," *Mind*, 8 (April 1883), 170–182.

103.5 James] William James, "Reaction-Time in the Hypnotic Trance," *Proceedings of the American Society for Psychical Research*, 1 (December 1887), 246–248. The experiments on Harvard College seniors were performed in 1885.

103.8 Gad] Johannes Gad (1842–1926), German physiologist, "Über die Reactionszeit für Erregung und für Hemmung," *Archiv für Anatomie und Physiologie*, 1887, pp. 363–370.

103.9 Orschansky] See note to 101.36–37.

103.25 Mosso] Angelo Mosso (1846–1910), Italian physiologist, describes his plethysmograph, a device for recording variations in the amount of blood in an organ, in *La Paura* (Milan: Fratelli Treves, 1884), p. 116 and in *Über den Kreislauf des Blutes im menschlichen Gehirn* (Leipzig: Veit, 1881), p. 45. In Widener is a copy of *Fear*, trans. E. Lough and F. Kiesaw (London: Longmans, Green, 1896) (*Cg Phil 5401.1.10).

103.30 FIG. 23] *Über den Kreislauf*, p. 51.

103.32 François-Franck] Lesson 22, pp. 203–210, "Recherche des effets circulatoires d'origine corticale, indépendants de l'état épileptique."

104.1 Ludwig] Mosso worked in Ludwig's laboratory in Leipzig.

104.4 Mosso's] The tilting table is pictured in *La Paura*, p. 119.

104.21 female] *Über den Kreislauf*, p. 74.

104.37 *Über*] Pp. 39–45.

104.39 Gley] Eugène Gley (1857–1930), French physiologist, "Essai critique sur les conditions physiologiques de la pensée. État du pouls carotidien pendant le travail intellectuel," *Archives de Physiologie*, 13 (1881), 742–759. Gley summarizes his results on p. 757 and on p. 756 expresses his agreement with Mosso.

105.2 Martin] Henry Newell Martin, "The Physiology of Secretion," *Transactions of the Medical and Chirurgical Faculty of the State of Maryland* (81st session, April 1879) (Baltimore, 1879), pp. 48–74. Quotation is from p. 73.

105.15 Lombard] Josiah Stickney Lombard, American physician, *Experimental Researches on the Regional Temperature of the Head under Conditions of Rest, Intellectual Activity, and Emotion* (London: H. K. Lewis, 1879). It is difficult to say whether James's "60,000 observations" is correct, since

Lombard himself does not seem to give a single total.

106.12 Amidon] Royal Wells Amidon (b. 1853), American neurologist, *A New Study of Cerebral Cortical Localization. The Effect of Willed Muscular Movements on the Temperature of the Head* (New York: G. P. Putnam's Sons, 1880), pp. 48–53; reprinted from the *Archives of Medicine*, 3 (April 1880), 117–173.

106.31 *'Ohne*] A widely quoted saying from Jacob Moleschott (1822–1893), Dutch physiologist and philosopher.

106.37 Herzen] Alexandre Herzen, "De l'échauffement des centres nerveux par le fait de leur activité," *Revue Philosophique*, 3 (January 1877), 36–50, a discussion of Moritz Schiff, "Recherches sur l'échauffement des nerfs et des centres nerveux à la suite des irritations sensorielles et sensitives," *Archives de Physiologie*, 2 (1869), 157–178, 330–351; 3 (1870), 5–25, 198–214, 323–333, 451–462.

107.5 Agassiz] Louis Agassiz (1807–1873), Swiss-born naturalist, one of James's teachers at Harvard. In his "Answers to Correspondents," Mark Twain advises an aspiring author to eat two "middling-sized whales," because according to Agassiz, "the phosphorus in it makes brain" (*Sketches New and Old* [New York: Gabriel Wells, 1922], p. 70).

107.14 Edes] Robert Thaxter Edes (b. 1838), American physician, "The Excretion of Phosphoric Acid by the Kidneys as Affected by Mental Labor," *Archives of Medicine*, 10 (August 1883), 40–46. James is referring to p. 44.

107.32 "The] A widely quoted remark by Pierre Jean Georges Cabanis (1757–1808), French materialist, *Rapports du physique et du moral de l'homme*, 2nd ed., 2 vols. (Paris: Crapelet, 1805), I, 152–153. Perry reports that a copy of the edition of 1844 of this work was sold with "thought is a brain secretion 137–138" on the flyleaf. For the text see *Essays in Religion and Morality*, WORKS, pp. 84n–85n. Karl Vogt (1817–1895), German naturalist, expressed a similar view.

107.38 Mendel] Emanuel Mendel (1839–1907), German physician, "Die Phosphorsäure im Urin von Gehirnkranken," *Archiv für Psychiatrie*, 3 (1872), 636–672. James's copy of *Genie und Entartung* (1894) is listed as given to Widener, but it has not been identified.

107.39 Mairet] Albert Mairet (1852–1935), French psychiatrist, "De la nutrition du système nerveux à l'état physiologique et pathologique," *Archives de Neurologie*, 9 (1885), 232–251, 360–391; 10 (1885), 76–83.

107.39 Beaunis] "Recherches sur l'influence de l'activité cérébrale sur la sécrétion urinaire et specialement sur l'élimination de l'acide phosphorique," *Recherches expérimentales*, I, 3–47.

107.40 Richet] Charles Richet, "Le Travail psychique et la force chimique," *Revue Scientifique*, 38 (December 18, 1886), 788–789.

110.29 Dumont] Léon Dumont (1837–1877), French author, "De l'habitude," *Revue Philosophique*, 1 (April 1876), 321–366, text from pp. 323–324.

114.22 Carpenter] William Benjamin Carpenter (1813–1885), British physiologist, *Principles of Mental Physiology, with Their Applications to the Training and Discipline of the Mind, and the Study of Its Morbid Conditions* (New York: D. Appleton, 1874) (WJ 511.77), pp. 339–345. In James's copy these and other pages are cut out in conformity with James's instructions on the title page.

114.34 Fiske's] John Fiske (1842–1901), American historian and philosopher, *Outlines of Cosmic Philosophy, Based on the Doctrine of Evolution, with Criticisms of the Positive Philosophy*, 2 vols. (London: Macmillan, 1874), II, 142–146. One letter to James is at Houghton (bMS Am 1092, letter 195). Books by Fiske from James's library will be listed in the volume of manuscript remains.

114.35 Spencer's] Herbert Spencer, *The Principles of Biology*, 2 vols. (London: Williams and Norgate, 1864–1867), II, 346–361. Marked copies of both volumes were sold, with vol. I dated 1864. "Physical Synthesis" is part V of *The Principles of Psychology*, I, 507–628.

115.12 Brown-Séquard's] No source is given in Carpenter.

115.42 Masius] Jean Baptiste Nicolas Voltaire Masius (1836–1912), Belgian physiologist, "De le régénération de la moelle épinière," *Archives de Biologie*, 1 (1880), 696–717. The *Archives* were edited by Édouard van Beneden and Charles van Bambeke, but were not published at Liège. Masius and Beneden were professors at Liège.

118.38 Schneider] Georg Heinrich Schneider (1846–1904), German educator, *Der menschliche Wille vom Standpunkte der neueren Entwickelungstheorien (Des "Darwinismus")*, (Berlin: Dümmler, 1882) (WJ 779.39), pp. 417–419.

118.39 Spencer's] *The Principles of Psychology*, I, 585–603, especially pp. 585–586 (sec. 254).

118.40 *Physiology*] Maudsley, pp. 154–155. James's index contains the entry "utility of cord educat^n, 154."

121.40 Houdin] Jean Eugène Robert-Houdin (1805–1871), French conjurer. Carpenter is quoting from an unidentified edition of *Confidences d'un prestidigiteur* as translated by R. Shelton Mackenzie. The quoted text is on p. 49 of the edition examined, *Life of Robert Houdin, the King of the Conjurers* (Philadelphia: Porter & Coates, c1859).

122.40 Hartmann] Eduard von Hartmann (1842–1906), German philosopher, *Philosophy of the Unconscious*, trans. William Chatterton Coupland, 3 vols. (London: Trübner, 1884), ch. 2 of pt. A (pp. 72–78), "Unconscious Ideation in the Execution of Voluntary Movement." Works by von Hartmann from James's library will be listed in the volume of manuscript remains.

123.39 *Mental*] Pp. 19–20.

125.39 Huxley's] Thomas Henry Huxley (1825–1895), English biologist and essayist, repeats the anecdote in several works, among them *Lessons in Elementary Physiology* (London: Macmillan, 1866), p. 286 (in lesson 11). Preserved is *A Manual of the Anatomy of Vertebrated Animals* (London: J. & A. Churchill, 1871) (WJ 540.97). James reviewed Huxley's *Lectures on the Elements of Comparative Anatomy* (1864) in the *North American Review*,

100 (January 1865), 290–298.

127.3 Bain's] Alexander Bain (1818–1903), Scottish philosopher and psychologist, *The Emotions and the Will*, 3rd ed. (London: Longmans, Green, 1875) (WJ 506.41), ch. 9 (pp. 440–459), "The Moral Habits." Not all of the annotations are by James. Bain also has a chapter on moral habits in *Mental and Moral Science* (London: Longmans, Green, 1868) (WJ 506.41.2), but this work shows few signs of use by James.

127.22 Bain] *The Emotions and the Will*, 3rd ed., pp. 440–441.

127.39 Baumann] Julius Baumann (1837–1916), German philosopher, *Handbuch der Moral nebst Abriss der Rechtsphilosophie* (Leipzig: S. Hirzel, 1879). The Goethe anecdote is on p. 39. A marked copy of this work was sold. Other works from James's library will be listed in the volume of manuscript remains.

128.39 Bahnsen] Julius August Bahnsen (1830–1881), German philosopher, *Beiträge zur Charakterologie. Mit besonderer Berücksichtigung pädagogischer Fragen*, 2 vols. (Leipzig: F. A. Brockhaus, 1867), I, 209. The second quotation is from I, 208.

129.6 Mill] John Stuart Mill, *A System of Logic: Ratiocinative and Inductive*, 2 vols., 8th ed. (London: Longmans, Green, Reader, and Dyer, 1872) (WJ 555.51), II, 429. Mill is quoting Novalis.

130.39 Scudder] Vida Dutton Scudder (1861–1954), American author and educator, "The Moral Dangers of Musical Devotees," *Andover Review*, 7 (January 1887), 46–53.

131.3 Jefferson's] Joseph Jefferson (1829–1905), American actor. In *Rip Van Winkle as Played by Joseph Jefferson* (Toronto: George N. Morang, 1899), p. 130, Rip says: "Well, I swore off drinkin'; but as this is the first time I see you, I won't count this one."

133.5 'No] See p. 185.

133.32 Hodgson] Shadworth Hodgson, *Time and Space: A Metaphysical Essay* (London: Longman, Green, Longman, Roberts, and Green, 1865) (WJ 539.18.6), p. 280. James's copy is dated December 1875.

134.6 Descartes] For works by Descartes from James's library, in addition to those mentioned in the present notes, see *Some Problems of Philosophy*, WORKS, note to 13.24. In James's copy of *Les Passions de l'âme* (Paris, 1650) (*FC 6.D4537.649pc), p. 22 (pt. I, article 13) is marked and 'reflex' written in the margin. In his index to *Les Méditations métaphysiques*, 3rd ed. (Paris, 1673) (*AC 85.J2376.Zz673d), James has "Reflex action 269, 270," a reference to the conclusion of the first part of Descartes' responses to the fourth set of objections.

134.21 Hodgson] In *The Theory of Practice: An Ethical Enquiry*, 2 vols. (London: Longmans, Green, Reader, and Dyer, 1870), I, 417–418, Hodgson retracts ch. 5, sec. 30 of *Time and Space* and denies that states of consciousness are ever the "causæ existendi" of other states of consciousness and of changes in nerve movements. James's annotated set was sold.

134.27 Spalding] Douglas Alexander Spalding (c. 1840–1877), British naturalist. The author of Spalding's obituary in *Mind*, 3 (1878), 153–154, accuses

Notes

Spalding of believing himself to be the first to propose, in scattered contributions to *Nature*, that "animals and men are conscious automata."

134.32 Huxley] Thomas Henry Huxley, "On the Hypothesis that Animals are Automata, and Its History," *Fortnightly Review*, n.s. 16 (November 1, 1874), 555–580, reprinted in *Method and Results: Essays* (London: Macmillan, 1893).

134.34 writer] Parts of what may be this essay have survived (bMS Am 1092.9 [4409]). On fol. 11a, James refers to three unidentified articles on volition (1862–1863) by Jacob Augustus Lockhart Clarke (1817–1880), British anatomist.

135.22 Clifford] *Lectures and Essays*, II, 53–57, 163–165.

137.36 Pflüger] For both Pflüger and Lewes see notes to 22.14.

139.39 Mercier] Pp. 8–9.

139.40 *Op.*] Pp. 10–11.

140.9 Hume's] David Hume, *An Enquiry Concerning Human Understanding* (sec. VII, pt. 2), in *Essays Moral, Political, and Literary*, ed. T. H. Green and T. H. Grose, 2 vols. (London: Longmans, Green, 1875) (WJ 540.54), II, 61.

140.35 all] John Bartlett, *Familiar Quotations*, 10th ed. (Boston: Little, Brown, 1921), p. 11, traces this saying to the collection of proverbs by John Heywood (1546), and on p. 976, to ch. 33 of *Don Quixote* in the translation by Peter Anthony Motteux. Hegel speaks of the night in which "all cows are black" in the Preface to *The Phenomenology of Mind*, trans. J. B. Baillie, 4th impression (London: George Allen & Unwin, 1955), p. 79.

140.40 Lotze] James could be referring to Lotze's discussion of causality in *Metaphysic*, trans. Bernard Bosanquet (Oxford: Claredon, 1884) (WJ 751. 88.12), pp. 101–107 (secs. 55–58). For similar comments by James see *Some Problems of Philosophy*, WORKS, note to 49.7.

146.19 Spencer] *The Principles of Psychology*, I, 280–281 (sec. 125).

146.36 Fick] Probably Adolf Fick (1829–1901), German physiologist.

147.1 Allen] Charles Grant Blairfindie Allen (1848–1899), Canadian-born naturalist and writer. James's index to *Physiological Æsthetics* (London: Henry S. King, 1877) (WJ 503.49) contains the entries "Rebuts objection from noxious pleasures 27" and "*Pain* a sign of destruction; *displeasure* of merely excessive waste, 40." For James's review and the correspondence between them see *The Will to Believe*, WORKS, note to 174.36.

148.23 theory] For James's later views concerning mental compounds see "The Knowing of Things Together," *Essays in Philosophy*, WORKS, and "The Compounding of Consciousness," *A Pluralistic Universe*, WORKS.

149.39 *Psychology*] I, 158.

150.7 Tyndall] John Tyndall (1820–1893), British physicist, *Fragments of Science for Unscientific People*, 5th ed. (London: Longmans, Green, 1868), p. 420, from the address "Scope and Limit of Scientific Materialism" (1868).

150.30 *Ibid.*] I, 625.

150.32 Belfast] John Tyndall, "Inaugural Address" (on becoming president of the British Association for the Advancement of Science), *Nature*, 10 (August 20, 1874), 309–319.

150.35 Helmholtz] Hermann Helmholtz, *Handbuch der physiologischen Optik* (Leipzig: Voss, 1867), p. 445. For the text see below, pp. 590–591.

150.40 *Psychology*] I, 293–294. In James's copy on I, 294, 'without break' is underlined and marked "! N B." The exclamation point was added at a later reading.

151.29 *Psychology*] I, 434–435. For a similar criticism see "The Sentiment of Rationality," *Essays in Philosophy*, WORKS, p. 37.

152.5 girl] Frederick Marryat (1792–1848), British novelist, *Mr Midshipman Easy* (1836; rpt. London: J. M. Dent, 1896), p. 9.

152.33 *Ibid.*] I, 403.

152.35 Spencer] Herbert Spencer, "Replies to Criticisms," *Fortnightly Review*, 20 (n.s. vol. 14) (November 1, 1873), 581–595; (December 1, 1873), 715–739. In James's set of the *Review* in Widener (P 188.2), there are annotations in the second installment, including on p. 737, "what an ass! Did he never hear of hypothesis." In Spencer's *Principles of Psychology*, James is referring to I, 103–107, 248–249, 559–562.

153.10 Fick] Adolf Fick, *Lehrbuch der Anatomie und Physiologie der Sinnesorgane* (Lahr: M. Schauenburg, 1864), p. 31.

153.41 *Lehrbuch*] Pp. 29–30.

154.10 Taine] See note to 162.31.

156.39 *Principles*] I, 148–152. In James's copy, on I, 149, there is the note, "Brown, vol. I, p. 139 gives the true interpretation," which has not been traced, while on p. 150, "Blow fire—blow harder it goes out."

157.20 Spencer] Herbert Spencer, *First Principles of a New System of Philosophy* (New York: D. Appleton, 1877) (WJ 582.24.4), pp. 211–218.

159.22 Helmholtz] *Handbuch*, p. 279 (sec. 20).

160.30 Mill's] II, 439–444.

161.38 Montgomery] Edmund Duncan Montgomery (1835–1911), Scottish-born philosopher, active in the United States, "The Dependence of Quality on Specific Energies," *Mind*, 5 (January 1880), 1–29. For James's comments on a later paper by Montgomery see *Letters*, I, 254–255. An annotated copy of *Philosophical Problems in the Light of Vital Organization* (1907) was sold.

161.39 Royce] Josiah Royce, " 'Mind-Stuff' and Reality," *Mind*, 6 (July 1881), 365–377.

161.39 Lotze] Hermann Lotze, *Microcosmus: An Essay Concerning Man and His Relation to the World*, trans. Elizabeth Hamilton and E. E. Constance Jones, 2 vols. Vol. I of James's set (WJ 751.88.14) is (New York: Scribner and Welford, 1885), while vol. II is (Edinburgh: T. T. Clark, 1885). James is referring to I, 158–163. On I, 160–161 of James's copy, there are several marginal comments apparently made with teaching in mind. Also preserved is James's copy of the German original, *Mikrokosmus*, 2nd ed., 3 vols. (Leipzig: S. Hirzel, 1869–1872) (WJ 751.88.6). The first volume is dated June 1876; the second, shows no signs of reading. In Houghton is Lotze's *Metaphysik* (Leipzig: S. Hirzel, 1879) (WJ 751.88.8). Sec. 242 is on pp. 478–480, sec. 260, pp. 514–517. On p. 478, James has: "Verschiedene Vorstellungen können sich nicht *von selbst* zusam̃en setzen. Um eine Resultante zu haben muss ein Einheitliches Wesen dazukom̃en das die verschiedene Wirkungen combianirt." While Lotze does have an *Outlines of Metaphysic*, the work actually mentioned by James, James's reference does not fit that work, but rather Lotze's *Grundzüge der Psychologie* (Leipzig: S. Hirzel, 1881), pp. 56–59. The form of reference shows that he is not referring to the English translation by George T. Ladd, *Outlines of Psychology* (Boston: Ginn, 1886), where the same sections are numbered 62–64.

162.25 Reid's] Thomas Reid (1710–1796), Scottish philosopher, *Essays on the Intellectual Powers of Man*, in *The Works of Thomas Reid, D. D.*, ed. William Hamilton, 5th ed. (Edinburgh: Maclachlan and Stewart, 1858), pp. 396–398. Perry reports that this edition was sold. While Perry also lists Reid's *Essays on the Powers of the Human Mind* among books sold, a three-volume set (Edinburgh: Bell & Bradfute, 1812), with annotations in vol. I like those described by Perry, remained in the James house until the summer of 1978 when it was sold to the Pangloss Bookshop, Cambridge, Mass., and is now in my possession. In Houghton is James's unannotated copy of *An Inquiry into the Human Mind on the Principles of Common Sense* (Edinburgh: 1764) (Phil 2240.30[B]*) and an annotated copy of the *Essays on the Intellectual Powers of Man*, abridged by James Walker, 10th ed. (Philadelphia: E. H. Butler, 1861) (WJ 575.41).

162.26 Bowne's] Borden Parker Bowne (1847–1910), American philosopher, *Metaphysics: A Study in First Principles* (New York: Harper & Brothers, 1882), pp. 361–376. Perry reports that an annotated copy of this work was sold. For a note on the relations between James and Bowne see *Some Problems of Philosophy*, WORKS, note to 66.38.

162.26 Mivart] St. George Jackson Mivart (1827–1900), British naturalist, *Nature and Thought: An Introduction to a Natural Philosophy* (London: Kegan Paul, Trench, 1882), pp. 98–101.

162.27 Gurney] Edmund Gurney (1847–1888), British aesthetician and psychical researcher, "Monism," *Mind*, 6 (April 1881), 153–173. James discusses Gurney's work in "What Psychical Research Has Accomplished," in *The Will to Believe*. For their relations see *The Will to Believe*, WORKS, notes to 225.38 and 228.11.

162.29 Clifford] William Kingdon Clifford, "On the Nature of Things-in-Themselves," *Mind*, 3 (1878), 57–67 (*Lectures and Essays*, II, 71–88).

162.30 Fechner] Gustav Theodor Fechner (1801–1887), German philosopher, physicist, and psychologist, *Elemente der Psychophysik*, 2 vols. (Leipzig: Breitkopf und Härtel, 1860) (WJ 727.13), II, 526–543. James's copy is dated Berlin, December 1867. Chapter 4 of *A Pluralistic Universe* is devoted to a general assessment of Fechner's thought; for James's varying evaluations of Fechner see *A Pluralistic Universe*, WORKS, notes to 68.28–80.19.

162.31 Taine] Hippolyte Adolphe Taine (1828–1893), French philosopher and psychologist, *On Intelligence*, trans. T. D. Haye, 2 vols. (New York: Henry Holt, 1875), I, 100–152. Houghton preserves James's copy of the French, *De l'intelligence*, 2 vols. (Paris: Hachette, 1870) (WJ 684.41). For additional works from James's library see *Some Problems of Philosophy*, WORKS, note to 37.36. James reviewed *On Intelligence* in the *Nation*, 15 (August 29, 1872), 139–141, the translation by Haye in an earlier one-volume edition.

162.31 Haeckel] Ernst Heinrich Haeckel (1834–1919), German biologist and philosopher, *Gesammelte populäre Vorträge aus dem Gebiete der Entwickelungslehre*, 2 vols. (Bonn: Emil Strauss, 1878–1879), I, 143–181.

162.32 Duncan] William Stewart Duncan (b. 1839), *Conscious Matter or the Physical and the Psychical Universally in Causal Connection* (London: David Bogue, 1881). In back of the Widener copy (Phil 478.1), in James's hand, there is a series of numbers "52, 33, 35, 63, 93, 118, 122," page references to discussions of combinations of mental elements.

162.33 Zöllner] Johann Carl Friedrich Zöllner (1834–1882), German physicist, *Über die Natur der Cometen. Beiträge zur Geschichte und Theorie der Erkenntniss*, 2nd ed. (Leipzig: W. Engelmann, 1872), pp. 320ff. For works from James's library see *The Will to Believe*, WORKS, note to 22.34.

162.33 Barratt] Alfred Barratt (1844–1881), British philosopher and lawyer, *Physical Ethics or the Science of Action: An Essay* (London: Williams and Norgate, 1869); *Physical Metempiric* (London: Williams and Norgate, 1883) (WJ 506.77). In James's copy, no marginalia related to mind-stuff were found. In his diary for August 23, 1905, James notes that he is reading *Physical Metempiric* (MS Am 1092.9 [4553]).

162.34 Soury] Jules Auguste Soury (1842–1915), French writer, "Über die hylozoistischen Ansichten der neuern Philosophen," *Kosmos: Zeitschrift für Entwickelungslehre und einheitliche Weltanschauung*, 10 (1881–1882), 241–256, 321–334, 401–412.

162.35 Main] Alexander Main, miscellaneous writer. The following appeared in *Mind*: "Mr. Hodgson on Mr. Lewes's View of Philosophy," 1 (April 1876), 292–294; "The Automatic Theory of Animal Activity," 1 (July 1876), 431–434; "The Uniformity of Nature," 1 (October 1876), 566–567; "Mr. Hodgson on 'Cogito ergo sum'," 2 (January 1877), 126–128; "Some Questionable Propositions in Ferrier's 'Institutes'," 2 (July 1877), 402–409; and the following in the *Revue Philosophique*: "Caractères contradictoires de la théorie automatique de l'activité animale," 2 (July 1876), 86–88; "L'Uniformité de la nature," 2 (July 1876), 88–91; discussion of Alexander Bain, *L'Ame et le corps*, 2 (October 1876), 419–422; "Une Idole moderne," 3 (January 1877), 51–53; "Cause et effet," 3 (May 1877), 502–504; "Cause et volonté," 4 (October 1877), 402–404.

162.36 Frankland] Frederick William Frankland (1854–1916), British-born mathematician and philosophical writer, "The Doctrine of Mind-Stuff," *Mind*, 6 (January 1881), 116–120.

162.36–37 Whittaker] Thomas Whittaker (1856–1935), British philosopher and author, "'Mind-stuff' from the Historical Point of View," *Mind*, 6 (October 1881), 498–513.

162.37 Prince] Morton Prince (1854–1929), American physician and psychiatrist, *The Nature of Mind and Human Automatism* (Philadelphia: J. B. Lippincott, 1885) (WJ 471.41.2). Also at Houghton is James's copy of *The Dissociation of a Personality* (New York: Longmans, Green, 1906) (WJ 471. 41).

162.38 Riehl] Alois Riehl (1844–1924), Austrian philosopher, *Der philosophische Kriticismus und seine Bedeutung für die positive Wissenschaft*, 2 vols. (Leipzig: W. Engelmann, 1876–1887) (WJ 776.23), vol. II, pt. 2, pp. 176–216 (sec. 2, ch. 2), "Über das Verhältniss der psychischen Erscheinungen zu den materiellen Vorgängen." In his copy, on p. 180, James comments "hylozoism," while on p. 181, "This is a terribly pretentious way of setting to work to expound his thesis, which is simply that the 'physical' cause of consciousness is 'in itself' unknown to us, and *if known* would seem 'der Sache nach' homogeneous ['one' above 'homogeneous'] with the consciousness itself—hence no paradox in the causal relation. All most weitschweifig in the exposition!" On the back flyleaf, James writes: "The 'Grund' of reality presents itself in two aspects physical and mental, neither of which it *is*, for both are its Erscheinungen. As 'quantitative' we find these phenomena 'begreiflich' when we bring them into the mechanical system of which the principle relating one phenomenon to another is that of Identity, as embodied in the conservation of 'force.' The wirksamkeit, however, in itself, is something qualitative, and although *will* is nearer to it than anything non-mental can be, yet it is not will."

163.32 'mental] In his index to vol. I of Mill's *Logic*, James has the entry "Mental chemistry 514," a reference to bk. III, ch. 10, sec. 4. For Mill's text see *A Pluralistic Universe*, WORKS, note to 85.11.

163.32 'psychic] See p. 907.

163.38–39 Brentano] Franz Brentano (1838–1917), German philosopher, *Psychologie vom empirischen Standpunkte*, I (Leipzig: Duncker & Humblot, 1874) (WJ 709.24), p. 209. James's index contains the entry "209 Siamese twins."

164.26 Ward] In Houghton is James's cutting of Ward's "Psychology" from the 9th ed. (1886) of the *Encyclopædia Britannica* (WJ 592.75.2), an article which according to James "marks the transition of English psychology from one epoch to another" (Perry, II, 59). Ward writes: "Are we, then, (1) quoting J. S. Mill's words, 'to accept the paradox that something which *ex hypothesi* is but a series of feelings, can be aware of itself as a series?'" Ward cites the conclusion of ch. 12 of *An Examination of Sir William Hamilton's Philosophy*, but does not identify the edition. Also at Houghton (WJ 592. 75.2) is James's cutting of Ward's "Psychology" from the 10th ed.

164.29 Bain] Alexander Bain, "Mr. James Ward's 'Psychology'," *Mind*, 11 (October 1886), 457–477.

166.14 Leibnitz] Houghton preserves James's annotated set of the *Œuvres philosophiques de Leibniz*, ed. Paul Janet, 2 vols. (Paris: Ladrange, 1866) (WJ 749.41). James is translating from the *Nouveaux essais sur l'entendement humain* (*Œuvres*, I, 15).

166.32 Colsenet] Edmond Eugène Colsenet (1847–1925), French philosopher, *La Vie inconsciente de l'esprit* (Paris: Baillière, 1880).

166.33 Laycock] Thomas Laycock (1812–1876), British physician, *Mind and Brain: Or, the Correlations of Consciousness and Organisation; With Their Applications to Philosophy, Zoology, Physiology, Mental Pathology, and the Practice of Medicine*, 2 vols. (Edinburgh: Sutherland and Knox, 1860), pt. 2, ch. 5 (I, 159–173), on "Unconscious Existence." James's copy was given to Harvard, but it has not been located.

166.34 Carpenter] *Principles of Mental Physiology*, pp. 515–543, "Of Unconscious Cerebration."

166.34 Cobbe] Frances Power Cobbe (1822–1904), British author and philanthropist, *Darwinism in Morals, and Other Essays* (London: Williams and Norgate, 1872), pp. 305–334.

166.35 Bowen] Francis Bowen (1811–1890), American philosopher, professor at Harvard, *Modern Philosophy, from Descartes to Schopenhauer and Hartmann*, 4th ed. (New York: Charles Scribner's Sons, 1877), pp. 429–480, on Hartmann's philosophy of the unconscious. James's copy of this edition was sold.

166.36 Hutton] Richard Holt Hutton (1826–1897), British journalist and essayist, "Latent Thought," *Contemporary Review*, 24 (July 1874), 201–211.

166.37 Mill] Perry reports that two editions of *An Examination of Sir William Hamilton's Philosophy* were sold from James's library, a copy of the 4th edition dated 1872 and an edition in two volumes dated 1865. Widener has a copy of vol. I from James's library (Boston: William V. Spencer, 1865) (Phil 2138.30[1]). Some of the many markings appear to be by James, while the annotations are not. Vol. II of this edition, not annotated and signed by Henry James, has been sold and is now in my possession. Unless James specifies another edition, the 4th (London: Longmans, Green, Reader, and Dyer, 1872) will be used in the present notes. Ch. 15, pp. 341–358, is titled "Sir William Hamilton's Doctrine of Unconscious Mental Modifications."

166.38 Lewes] George Henry Lewes, *Problems of Life and Mind*, 3rd series, 2 vols. (London: Trübner, 1879), II, 143–204, 240–249, "The Nature of Consciousness and Unconsciousness" (prob. II, ch. 10), "The Triple Process" (prob. III, ch. 2). In the latter section Lewes does not directly deal with the unconscious. Rather, he divides the sensory process into the stages of excitation, co-ordination and discharge. James's reference could be an error for, for example, *The Physical Basis of Mind*, pp. 353–366, on "Consciousness and Unconsciousness" (prob. III, ch. 4).

166.39 Thompson] Daniel Greenleaf Thompson (1850–1897), American author, *A System of Psychology*, 2 vols. (London: Longmans, Green, 1884), I, 428–438, "Unconscious Activities."

166.39 Baldwin] James Mark Baldwin, *Handbook of Psychology: Senses and Intellect*, pp. 43–68, "Consciousness."

167.39 Mill] 4th ed., p. 346.

167.40 Stewart] Dugald Stewart (1753–1828), Scottish philosopher. Perry reports that an annotated copy of vol. I of Stewart's *Elements of the Philosophy of the Human Mind* (1818) was sold. James's edition has not been identified, since several editions appeared that year. Vol. I of the New York (James Eastburn, 1818) edition will be used in the present notes. Ch. 2 (I, 79–100) is titled "Of Attention." For Stewart's text see pp. 383–384.

169.37   Maude] John Edward Maude (1855–1885), English-born clergyman, studied philosophy at Harvard where he became acquainted with James. Maude's posthumous *Foundations of Ethics* (New York: Henry Holt, 1887) was edited by James. "The Unconscious in Education," *Education*, 2 (March 1882), 394–409; (May 1882), 459–476, was written while a student at the Harvard Divinity School.

170.9   Wundt] James could be referring to Wundt's discussion of "geistige Anlagen," *Grundzüge*, 2nd ed., II, 318–327.

170.37   Hering] Ewald Hering (1834–1918), German physiologist, *Zur Lehre vom Lichtsinne* (Vienna: Carl Gerold's Sohn, 1878). For Hering's text see p. 668n. In addition to works mentioned in the present notes, in Houghton is *Über das Gedächtniss als eine allgemeine Function der organisirten Materie* (Vienna, 1870) (WJ 737.76.2). For James's visit to Hering see *Letters*, I, 212.

171.37   Wundt] Wilhelm Wundt, *Über den Einfluss der Philosophie auf die Erfahrungswissenschaften. Akademische Antrittsrede gehalten zu Leipzig* (Leipzig: W. Engelmann, 1876), pp. 10–11.

171.38   Helmholtz] Hermann Helmholtz, *Die Thatsachen in der Wahrnehmung* (Berlin: A. Hirschwald, 1879) (WJ 737.51), p. 27.

171.39   *Über*] Arthur Schopenhauer (1788–1860), *Über die vierfache Wurzel des Satzes vom zureichenden Grunde*, ed. Julius Frauenstädt, 3rd ed. (Leipzig: F. A. Brockhaus, 1864), pp. 59–65. James's edition has not been identified and his reference fits several editions. For James's attitude towards Schopenhauer see *Some Problems of Philosophy*, WORKS, note to 19.20.

171.40   Zöllner's] Pp. 342–425, contains two sections, "Zur Geschichte und Theorie der unbewussten Schlüsse" and "Die Theorie der unbewussten Schlüsse in ihrer Anwendung auf die Gesichtswahrnehmungen."

172.39   Helmholtz] See pp. 477, 487–493.

176.17   Lipps's] In his index to *Grundtatsachen des Seelenlebens*, James has the entry "Clear idea vs. clear object 37–8." Lipps' 'Wahrnehmung' and 'Gesichtsbild' are both translated as 'perception'.

179.34   'ejected'] See note to 74.37.

180.31   Leibnitzian] James's index to vol. II of Leibniz's *Œuvres* contains the entry "mind stuff 586, 369, 519."

180.38–39   Herbart] In *A Text-Book in Psychology*, trans. Margaret K. Smith (New York: D. Appleton, 1891), p. 119 (sec. 150; sec. 109 in 1st German edition [1816]), Herbart states: "The soul is a simple essence, not merely without parts, but also without any kind of diversity or multiplicity in its quality; hence it has no space relations."

180.39   Lotze] In his copy of *Microcosmus*, on pp. 162 and 163, in reference to bk. II, ch. 1, sec. 5, James has "polyzoism" and "How does he bring in the 'ruling monad'?" This chapter deals with "The Existence of the Soul." Lotze writes: "If the ruling monad is that soul which forms our ego, and whose internal motions we are seeking to understand, the interior of the other monads at least to us inquirers remains absolutely closed" (I, 163).

184.37–38 Robertson] George Croom Robertson (1842–1892), British philosopher, "Psychology and Philosophy," *Mind*, 8 (January 1883), 1–21. In James's file of *Mind* at Houghton (Phil 22.4.6*), this essay is heavily marked. James's correspondence with Robertson is at Houghton (bMS Am 1092.9 [504–528, 3536–3552]).

184.38 Ward] James Ward, "Psychological Principles," *Mind*, 8 (April 1883), 153–169; (October 1883), 465–486.

184.38 Dewey] John Dewey, "The Psychological Standpoint," *Mind*, 11 (January 1886), 1–19. In James's copy (Phil 22.4.6*), this essay is heavily annotated.

185.37 Huxley] "This conception of the relations of states of consciousness with molecular changes in the brain—of *psychoses* with *neuroses* . . . " ("On the Hypothesis," p. 575 [see note to 134.32]).

186.7 Locke] *Essay*, p. 4 (pt. I, ch. 1, sec. 8).

186.18 Hume's] David Hume, *A Treatise of Human Nature*, ed. T. H. Green and T. H. Grose, 2 vols. (London: Longmans, Green, 1874) (WJ 540.42.2), I, 311 (bk. I, pt. 1, sec. 1).

186.18 Hamilton's] William Hamilton (1788–1856), Scottish philosopher. An annotated copy of vol. I of Hamilton's *Lectures*, in an unidentified edition of 1859, was sold. Where in the *Principles* James gives page references, they fit the *Lectures on Metaphysics and Logic*, ed. H. L. Mansel and John Veitch, 4 vols. (Edinburgh: William Blackwood and Sons, 1859–1860), and this will be used in the present notes. James seems to be referring to lecture XX of the *Lectures on Metaphysics*, II, 10–13.

186.24 FEELING] James discusses the term 'feeling' in "On Some Omissions of Introspective Psychology," *Mind*, 9 (January 1884), 19n.

186.39 Mill's] I, 51–57. On p. 55, attached by a guideline to 'Feeling', James has "What is his generic name for state of mind?" Opposite Mill's remark that "Feeling . . . is a genus, of which Sensation, Emotion, and Thought, are subordinate species," James has "Is this definition or doctrine? see 58."

187.5 Ueberweg] Friedrich Ueberweg (1826–1871), German philosopher, *System of Logic and History of Logical Doctrines*, trans. Thomas M. Lindsay (London: Longmans, Green, 1871), p. 86.

187.12 Brentano] I, 24–25, 11–12. James's index to the *Psychologie* contains "Ueberweg 183–4, Vorstellungen substantial 215–6, 226, 11–2, 24–5, 119, 158, 184."

187.29 Comte] Auguste Comte (1798–1857), French philosopher, *Cours de philosophie positive*, 6 vols. (Paris: Bachelier, 1830–1842), I, 34–37. James's edition has not been identified.

188.33 Mill] John Stuart Mill, *Auguste Comte and Positivism*, 3rd ed. (London: Trübner, 1882), p. 64.

189.34 Wundt] Wilhelm Wundt, *Logik: Eine Untersuchung der Principien der Erkenntniss und der Methoden wissenschaftlicher Forschung*, 2 vols. (Stuttgart: Enke, 1880-1883), II, 482-483. A marked copy was sold.

190.11 Mohr] Jakob Mohr, *Grundlage der empirischen Psychologie* (Leipzig: Mutze, 1882) (WJ 756.40), p. 47. The quoted text is marked in James's copy.

191.9 Sully] James Sully, *Illusions: A Psychological Study* (New York: D. Appleton, 1881), ch. 8 (pp. 189-211), "Illusions of Introspection." An annotated copy was sold.

191.30 Hartley] David Hartley (1705-1757), British philosopher. Nothing by Hartley from James's library is known.

191.30 Brown] Thomas Brown (1778-1820), Scottish philosopher. An annotated copy of *Lectures on the Philosophy of the Human Mind*, 10th ed., was sold, probably a reference to the one-volume edition (Edinburgh: William Tait, 1837), the edition used in the present notes.

191.34-35 Lavoisier] Antoine Laurent Lavoisier (1743-1794), French chemist.

192.4 Weber] Ernst Heinrich Weber (1795-1878), German physiologist, who sometimes worked with his brothers, Wilhelm Eduard (1804-1891), physicist, and Eduard Friedrich Wilhelm (1806-1871), anatomist.

192.4 Vierordt] Karl von Vierordt (1818-1884), German physician. Preserved is *Der Zeitsinn nach Versuchen* (Tübingen: Laupp, 1868) (WJ 790.24), dated by James, July 1876.

193.18 Darwin] Darwin's earliest questionnaires date from 1839-1840. In 1867 he distributed a widely circulated questionnaire on the expression of the emotions.

193.18 Galton] Francis Galton (1822-1911), British scientist. Preserved is *Inquiries into Human Faculty and Its Development* (New York: Macmillan, 1883) (WJ 531.52), with a letter from Galton to James pasted in. Another letter to James is also at Houghton (bMS Am 1092, letter 156). A copy of *Natural Inheritance* was sold. Much of Galton's work on the heredity of genius is based on questionnaires.

195.40 Bowne's] *Metaphysics*, p. 408: "When we figure the mind as a tablet with pictures on it, we also conceive of ourselves as looking at the picture, and then we mistake our imagined perception of the picture for its perception by the impressed mind."

198.28 Locke] *Essay*, p. 58 (bk. II, ch. 1, sec. 13).

198.36 Spence] Payton Spence, physician, in the *Journal of Speculative Philosophy*: "Time and Space Considered as Negations," 13 (October 1879), 337-346; "Atomic Collision and Non-Collision; or, the Conscious and Unconscious States of Matter. A New Theory of Consciousness," 14 (July 1880), 286-298.

198.37 Garver] Madison Monroe Garver (1847-1941), American physicist and librarian, "Periodic Character of Voluntary Nervous Action," *American Journal of Science*, 3rd series, vol. 20 (September 1880), pp. 189-193.

199.34 Malebranche] Nicolas de Malebranche (1638–1715), French philosopher, *De la recherche de la vérité*, in *Œuvres de Malebranche*, III (Paris: Charpentier, 1871), 339–348. Preserved is vol. I of this edition (WJ 653.49).

199.35 Wolff] Christian Wolff (1679–1754), German philosopher, *Psychologia Rationalis* (Verona, 1737) (Phil 3910.40.5), p. 22. This is one of sixteen volumes from James's library in Widener, in the Phil 3910 class, from several 18th century editions, with few markings or annotations. These volumes are additionally identified as from the library of Henry James, Sr.

199.36 Hamilton] *Lectures on Metaphysics and Logic*, I, 310–337.

199.37 Bascom] John Bascom (1827–1911), American educator, *The Science of Mind* (New York: G. P. Putnam's Sons, 1881), pp. 72–78.

199.37 Jouffroy] Théodore Simon Jouffroy (1796–1842), French philosopher, *Mélanges philosophiques*, 2nd ed. (Paris: Ladrange, 1838), pp. 290–312.

199.38 Holland] Henry Holland (1788–1873), British physician, *Chapters on Mental Physiology* (London: Longman, Brown, Green, and Longmans, 1852), p. 80.

199.39 Brodie] Benjamin Collins Brodie (1783–1862), British physician, *Psychological Inquiries: In a Series of Essays, Intended to Illustrate the Mutual Relations of the Physical Organization and the Mental Faculties* (London: Longman, Brown, Green, and Longmans, 1854), p. 147.

199.39 Chesley] E. M. Chesley, "Does the Mind Ever Sleep?" *Journal of Speculative Philosophy*, 11 (1887), 72–78.

199.40 Ribot] Théodule Ribot, *Les Maladies de la personnalité* (Paris: Alcan, 1885), pp. 8–10.

199.41 Lotze] *Metaphysic*, p. 533 (sec. 307).

201.6 Janet] Pierre Janet (1859–1947), French psychologist, *L'Automatisme psychologique: Essai de psychologie expérimentale sur les formes inférieures de l'activité humaine* (Paris: Alcan, 1889) (WJ 642.59). James's index contains the entries "La distraction des hysteriques, 188," "Catalepsie par distraction, 237," "Suggestions par distraction 239." All of the works by Janet from James's library will be listed in the volume of manuscript remains.

201.6 Binet] Articles by Binet in the *Open Court* are "Proof of Double Consciousness in Hysterical Individuals," 3 (July 25, 1889), 1739–1741; "The Relations between the Two Consciousnesses of Hysterical Individuals," 3 (August 1, 1889), 1751–1754; "The Graphic Method and the Doubling of Consciousness," 3 (November 7, 1889), 1919–1922; in the *Revue Philosophique*: "Recherches sur les altérations de la conscience chez les hystériques," 27 (February 1889), 135–170; "La Vision mentale," 27 (April 1889), 337–373; "Recherche sur les mouvements volontaires dans l'anesthésie hystérique," 28 (November 1889), 470–500; "La Concurrence des états psychologiques," 29 (February 1890), 138–155.

201.16 Janet] James is translating freely from *L'Automatisme*, pp. 188–189.

201.25 Janet] *L'Automatisme*, p. 238.

202.11 "I] The eyeglass episode has not been found.

202.16–17 Salpêtrière] A hospital in Paris in which in 1880 Jean Martin Charcot established a clinic for the treatment of nervous diseases. Both Binet and Janet made there many of their observations. It is possible that in 1882 James visited it (Perry, II, 723).

202.25 'colored] Binet, "Recherches sur les altérations," p. 163.

202.31 Her] Binet, p. 158.

203.16 Pierre Janet] In his index to *L'Automatisme*, James refers to many cases of this type, among them "Subconscient calculation, 325, 363," "The conscious self ignores all that this subc. s. does, and replaces it by an hallucination 326."

203.16 Jules Janet] Jules Janet (1861–1945), French psychologist, "L'Hystérie et l'hypnotisme, d'après la théorie de la double personnalité," *Revue Scientifique*, 3rd series, vol. 18 (May 19, 1888), pp. 616–623.

203.24 Bernheim] Hippolyte Bernheim (1840–1919), French hypnotist, *Suggestive Therapeutics: A Treatise on the Nature and Uses of Hypnotism*, trans. Christian A. Herter (New York: G. P. Putnam's Sons, 1889), p. 49. In Widener is an annotated copy of *Hypnotisme, suggestion, psychothérapie: Études nouvelles* (Paris: Doin, 1891) (Phil 6671.5).

203.24 Pitres] Albert Pitres (1848–1928), French psychiatrist, *Des anesthésies hystériques* (Bordeaux: Gounouilhou, 1887). In Widener is an unmarked copy of *Recherches sur les lésions du centre ovale des hémisphères cérébraux étudiées au point de vue des localisations cérébrales* (Paris: Aux bureaux du *Progrès Médical*, 1877) (Phil 6125.16). See also note to 60.38.

204.15 Janet] *L'Automatisme*, pp. 281–282.

205.2 Janet] Jules Janet, p. 622.

205.17 Lucie] *L'Automatisme*, p. 239.

205.24 Janet] *L'Automatisme*, pp. 240–241.

206.12 Gurney] Edmund Gurney, "Peculiarities of Certain Post-Hypnotic States," *Proceedings of the SPR*, 4 (May 1887), 268–323.

206.28 Beaunis] "Études physiologiques et psychologiques sur le somnambulisme provoqué," pp. 1–106 of *Recherches expérimentales*, vol. II.

206.31 Janet's] *L'Automatisme*, pp. 255–256.

206.39 *Proceedings*] William James, "Notes on Automatic Writing," *Proceedings of the American Society for Psychical Research*, vol. I, no. 4 (March 1889), pp. 548–564.

207.6 Léonie 3] In his index to *L'Automatisme*, James has "L's 3 states & children 132-3, 160." See also pp. 365–367.

207.17 Janet] *L'Automatisme*, p. 314.

207.31 Janet] *L'Automatisme*, pp. 267–268. The Algiers story is on pp. 328–329.

208.5 Léonie's] James's index to *L'Automatisme* contains the entry "Pieds de nez after a year 316."

210.38 Descartes] *Les Passions*, pp. 46-51 (pt. I, articles 32-34).

211.10 Bowen] Francis Bowen, *Lowell Lectures, on the Application of Metaphysical and Ethical Science to the Evidences of Religion* (Boston: Charles C. Little and James Brown, 1849), p. 55.

211.12 Walter] Johnston Estep Walter (1843-1924), American clergyman and educator, *The Perception of Space and Matter* (Boston: Estes and Lauriat, 1879), pp. 241-253 (pt. II, section I, ch. 3), "The Soul is Extended." In "The Perception of Space," *Mind*, 12 (April 1887), p. 206n, while discussing the idea of the soul as an extended substance, James praises Walter's book as a "work of unusual critical ability." James also refers to Noah Porter (1811-1892), American philosopher, *Human Intellect*, p. 130. This reference fits *The Human Intellect with an Introduction upon Psychology and the Soul*, 2nd ed. (New York: Charles Scribner, 1869).

211.13 Fichte] Immanuel Hermann Fichte (1796-1879), German philosopher, *Psychologie. Die Lehre vom bewussten Geiste des Menschen, oder Entwickelungsgeschichte des Bewusstseins, begründet auf Anthropologie und innerer Erfahrung*, I (Leipzig: F. A. Brockhaus, 1864) (WJ 728.12), pp. 35-53, "Die Raumverhältnisse der Seelen- und Geistwesens." Perry reports that an annotated copy, dated Dresden, July 1867, of Fichte's *Anthropologie* (1860), was sold.

211.13 Ulrici] Hermann Ulrici (1806-1884), German philosopher, *Leib und Seele. Grundzüge einer Psychologie des Menschen*, 2nd ed., 2 vols. (Leipzig: Weigel, 1874), I, 204. James's edition of this work has not been identified; however, his reference on p. 402n fits the second edition.

211.18 Plato] Preserved at Houghton is James's set of *The Dialogues of Plato*, trans. B. Jowett, 4 vols. (Oxford: Clarendon, 1871) (WJ 835.70). Plato discusses the location of these powers in *Timaeus*, 69-70 (II, 563 in the Jowett translation).

211.20 Aristotle] *On the Parts of Animals*, 647ª-647ᵇ.

211.35 Hamilton's] *Lectures on Metaphysics and Logic*, II, 127-128 (lecture 25 of the *Lectures on Metaphysics*).

211.37 Volkmann] *Lehrbuch der Psychologie*, I, 81-89. In sec. 16, Volkmann develops his own view and concludes with a bibliographical note. James's remark about the blood and other organs is based on Volkmann, I, 83.

212.34 Lotze] Hermann Lotze, *Medicinische Psychologie oder Physiologie der Seele* (Leipzig: Weidmann, 1852) (WJ 751.88.4). James's copy is dated Berlin, January 1867 and Dresden, July 1868. James is referring to pp. 115-122, "Von dem Sitze der Seele." Inserted between pp. 114-115, in James's early handwriting, there are the following notes: "§ 10. On the seat of the Soul. [¶] He attributes to the Soul locality without extension, and makes this conceivable by placing it a given point in an *amorphous* mass of matter which receives the different impulses of the other nerve elements and transmits ['a part of' *del.*] them ['at least' *del.*] with their different qualities with more or less diminished force to the soul. We shall afterwards see that the only direct physical receptiveness of the soul is of qualities, and we need not doubt that so simple a channel can transmit the infinite number of qualities of wh. we take cognizance any more than we doubt that the simple air can transmit as many qualities of sound &c as it does—The exact determination of this seat he does not attempt, although he thinks it may be on the passage of N. fibres. [¶] In *105* & *106* He admits the possibility of the soul flying from point to point according as the point becomes stimulated. But to be attracted to the particular point which is stimulated, again supposes a *dynamic* connection if not a local between each point and the soul, so that after all the movability does not appear neccessary. [¶] [This speculation seems all perfectly vain. The assumption of an amorphous target for the physical shocks to impinge on, in *one point* of wh. the soul is, is really nothing else than the assumption of an extended soul. And on the other hand the assumption in the end of a dynamic connection of soul and organ being possible without a local connextion seems to do away entirely with the need even of a locality for the soul.—The perpetual see-sawing of the author between sensuous conceptions of the thing, & merely negative conceptions (justified by saying that the sensuous conceptions are equally incomprehensible when closely looked at) shows how empty the whole course of the thought is." James is also referring to *Microcosmus*, I, 290–315, "Of the Seat of the Soul"; *Metaphysic*, pp. 509–534 (secs. 291–307), "The Physical Basis of Mental Activity"; *Grundzüge der Psychologie*, pp. 63–67, "Vom Sitze der Seele."

212.37 Fechner] *Elemente der Psychophysik*, II, 381–428, "Über den Sitz der Seele."

216.37–38 *acquaintance*] For other treatments of this distinction see *The Meaning of Truth*, WORKS, pp. 18–20, 30–31, 87–88, and elsewhere.

216.40 Lotze] Hermann Lotze, *Logik* (Leipzig: S. Hirzel, 1874) (WJ 751. 88.8), pp. 484–486, 519–522. On p. 519 (at sec. 326), James writes: "Der Subject nimmt Theil am Inhalt seiner Vostellungen," while on p. 521 (sec. 327), "Alles Wissen bedarf der Thätigkeit des Subjects, auch wenn es ein wahres Wissen ist." Also in Houghton is *Logic*, trans. B. Bosanquet (Oxford: Clarendon, 1884) (WJ 751.88.10).

217.39 Grote] John Grote (1813–1866), British philosopher, *Exploratio Philosophica: Rough Notes on Modern Intellectual Science*, Part I (Cambridge: Deighton, Bell, and Co., 1865) (WJ 535.67). On p. 60, Grote develops the distinction between acquaintance and knowledge about. On p. 60, James comments: "First & second intention" and refers to p. 122. James's index has "Relativity of Knowledge 60 sq."

217.39 Helmholtz] Hermann Helmholtz, *Popular Lectures on Scientific Subjects*, trans. E. Atkinson (London: Longmans, Green, 1873), pp. 308–309.

219.1 We] In *The Re-Organisation of Philosophy. An Address Delivered Before the Aristotelian Society* (London: Williams and Norgate, 1886) (WJ 539.18), p. 9, Shadworth Hodgson, as one of the two meanings of the term, states that 'experience' indicates the "stream or content of actual consciousness as it occurs in consciousness." See also the quotation from Bain, pp. 237n–238n.

223.37 Constans] Augustin Constans (b. 1811), French government official, *Relation sur une épidémie d'hystéro-démonopathie en 1861*, 2nd ed. (Paris: Delahaye, 1863). James's copy was given to Widener, but it has not been located.

223.38 Chiap] Fernando Franzolini (1840–1905), Italian physician, *L'Epi-*

demia di istero-demonopatie in Verzegnis studiata dai dottori Giuseppe Chiap e Fernando Franzolini (Reggio Emilia: Stefano Calderini e Figlio, 1879).

223.39 Kerner's] Andreas Justinus Kerner (1786–1862), German poet and physician, *Nachricht von dem Vorkommen des Besessenseyns eines dämonisch-magnetischen Leidens und seiner schon im Alterthum bekannten Heilung durch magisch-magnetisches Einwirken* (Stuttgart: J. G. Cotta, 1836). James's unmarked copy is in Widener (24244.21 [B]). Other works by Kerner from James's library will be listed in the volume of manuscript remains.

224.39 *Philosophy*] Shadworth Hodgson, *The Philosophy of Reflection*, 2 vols. (London: Longmans, Green, 1878) (WJ 539.18.4), I, 248–249, 290.

226.39 *Populäre*] Hermann Helmholtz, *Populäre wissenschaftliche Vorträge*, III (Braunschweig: Vieweg, 1876), 72.

226.40 Fick] Adolf Fick, "Dioptrik. Nebenapparate des Auges," in Hermann's *Handbuch*, vol. III, pt. 1 (1879), pp. 3–234.

234.24–25 Brentano's] *Psychologie*, bk. II, ch. 4, "Von der Einheit des Bewusstseins," I, 204–232.

234.28 Wills] James Wills, "An Essay on Accidental Association," *Transactions of the Royal Irish Academy*, vol. 21, pt. 2 (1848), pp. 87–104 (read in 1845–1846).

237.16 Zeno's] James treats Zeno's paradoxes at length in *A Pluralistic Universe* and *Some Problems of Philosophy*.

238.38 Bain] 3rd ed. The passage is marked with an exclamation point in James's copy.

239.33 Green] Thomas Hill Green (1836–1882), English philosopher, "Can There be a Natural Science of Man?" *Mind*, 7 (1882), 1–29, 161–185, 321–348.

239.37 Destutt] Antoine Louis Claude, comte Destutt de Tracy (1754–1836), French philosopher, *Élémens d'idéologie*, 3rd ed., I (Paris: Courcier, 1817), p. 48.

240.7 Laromiguière] Pierre Laromiguière (1756–1837), French philosopher, *Leçons de philosophie sur les principes de l'intelligence, ou sur les causes et sur les origines des idées*, 5th ed., 2 vols. (Paris: Brunot-Labbe, 1833), II, 69–70. In the Widener copy of vol. II (Phil 5251.30.5), on the flyleaf in James's hand, pp. 65, 69–70, and 184 are listed, with the remark "Resumé p. 101–3." Only one due date is stamped in the volume—October 10, 1885.

240.18 Cardaillac] Jean Jacques Séverin de Cardaillac (1766–1845), French philosopher, *Études élémentaires de philosophie*, I (Paris: Firmin Didot Frères, 1830), pp. 80–89.

240.43 Brown] *Lectures on the Philosophy of the Human Mind*, pp. 288–289.

241.30 *Principles*] I, 163–165.

242.36 Paulhan] Frédéric Paulhan (1856–1931), French psychologist, "Les Phénomènes affectifs au point de vue de la psychologie générale," *Revue Philosophique*, 20 (1885), 449–484, 583–600. One letter from Paulhan to

James is at Houghton (bMS Am 1092, letter 650).

245.7 'twig'] *The Century Dictionary and Cyclopedia* (ᶜ1900), VIII, 6551, after explaining that 'twig' means to comprehend, understand, perceive, discover, quotes James's sentence as an illustration of such usage.

246.16 Galton] See pp. 696–702.

247.33 Mozart] From a letter by Mozart quoted by Otto Jahn, *W. A. Mozart*, 4 vols. (Leipzig: Breitkopf und Härtel, 1856–1859), III, 424. The authenticity of the letter has been questioned.

249.27 *Mental*] P. 280.

249.29 Stricker] Salomon Stricker (1834–1898), Hungarian pathologist, *Vorlesungen über allgemeine und experimentelle Pathologie* (Vienna: W. Braumüller, 1877–). This work was published in installments, and 1879 may well be the date of publication of the third installment, the installment cited by James. However, this could not be verified because in the copies examined the title pages of the later installments were lost during binding. Perry reports that this work, with an 1879 date, bound in a single volume with Stricker's *Studien über die Sprachvorstellungen* (1880), *Studien über die Bewegungsvorstellungen* (1882), and *Studien über die Association der Vorstellungen* (1883), was sold. The *Pathologie* contained the notes "association 55" and "'fringe', 547, 501, 462-3."

249.30 Romanes] George John Romanes, *Mental Evolution in Man: Origin of Human Faculty* (New York: D. Appleton, 1889) (WJ 577.53.2). James's index contains the entry "fringe 82." In James's copy, there is a clipping of a review of this work by James in an unidentified periodical.

249.32 Maguire] Thomas Maguire, Irish philosopher, *Lectures on Philosophy*, first series (London: Kegan Paul, Trench, 1885), p. 211. Maguire is criticizing James's "On Some Omissions of Introspective Psychology," *Mind*, 9 (January 1884), 1–26, parts of which are incorporated into the present chapter; reprinted in full in *Essays in Psychology*, WORKS.

251.11–12 *"Qu'importe*] From the poem "La Coupe et les lèvres," by Alfred de Musset (1810–1857), French poet, *Premières poésies* (Paris: Charpentier, 1878), p. 230.

251.37 Campbell] George Campbell (1719–1796), Scottish theologian and rhetorician, *The Philosophy of Rhetoric* (1776). It has not been established which printing of the about 60 available to him was used by James. Textual evidence indicates the New York, 1873 edition (Harper & Brothers), used in the present notes, or an edition much like it. James is quoting from p. 278 (the title of ch. 7) and pp. 280-282.

254.30 Story'] Jean Story (pseudonym), *Substantialism: or, Philosophy of Knowledge* (Boston: Franklin Press, 1879), p. 141. The work is copyrighted by a J. S. Thompson Frohock.

254.31 Tarde] Joseph Remi Léopold Delbœuf, *Le Sommeil et les rêves considérés principalement dans leurs rapports avec les théories de la certitude et de la mémoire* (Paris: Alcan, 1885), pp. 226n–227n, quoting a personal communication by Jean Gabriel Tarde (1843-1904), French sociologist.

256.1 Hegel's] For works by Hegel from James's library see *The Will to Believe*, WORKS, note to 196.12. James's main discussions of Hegel are "On Some Hegelisms," *The Will to Believe*, WORKS, and "Hegel and His Method," *A Pluralistic Universe*, WORKS.

256.10 Galton] See pp. 696–702.

256.33 writer] See p. 1088.

256.40 Ballard] Melville Ballard, instructor at the Columbia Institution for the Instruction of the Deaf and Dumb and Blind (now Gallaudet College). For a discussion of Ballard's reliability, and another narrative by a deaf-mute, see James's "Thought before Language: A Deaf-Mute's Recollections," *Philosophical Review*, 1 (November 1892), 613–624.

259.35 Porter] Samuel Porter (1810–1901), American educator, instructor at the National Deaf-Mute College, Washington, D.C., "Is Thought Possible without Language?" *Princeton Review*, 57th year (January 1881), pp. 104–128.

259.36 Ireland] William Wotherspoon Ireland (1832–1909), Scottish physician, *The Blot upon the Brain: Studies in History and Psychology* (New York: G. P. Putnam's Sons, 1886), pp. 270–288, "The Relation of Words to Thought." James's copy was given to Widener, but it has not been located.

259.37 Romanes] In *Mental Evolution in Man*, p. 83n, Romanes refers to a series of letters on the subject in *Nature* in 1887 and 1888, by himself, Max Müller, Galton, Mivart, and others.

259.38 Müller] Friedrich Max Müller (1823–1900), German-born philologist, *The Science of Thought* (New York: C. Scribner's Sons, 1887), pp. 30–64.

260.20 Berkeley] George Berkeley, *A Treatise Concerning the Principles of Human Knowledge*, ed. Charles P. Krauth (Philadelphia: J. B. Lippincott, 1874) (WJ 507.76), p. 187 (Introduction, sec. 19). Perry reports that annotated copies of vols. I and II of *The Works of George Berkeley*, ed. Alexander Campbell Fraser (1871), were sold.

261.40 *Problems*] II, 470–478.

261.41 Egger] Victor Émile Egger (1848–1909), French psychologist, *La Parole intérieure: Essai de psychologie descriptive* (Paris: Baillière, 1881) (WJ 622.32), pp. 241–321.

263.24 Herzen] Alexandre Herzen, "Les Trois phases successives du retour à la conscience après une syncope," *Revue Philosophique*, 21 (1886), 671–672.

263.30 Shoemaker] George Erety Shoemaker (b. 1857), American physician, "Recollections after Ether-Inhalation—Psychical and Physiological," *Therapeutic Gazette*, 10 (August 16, 1886), 521–526. The quotation is from p. 522. The *New York Evening Post* version was not seen.

264.3 Spencer] Herbert Spencer, "Consciousness under Chloroform," *Mind*, 3 (October 1878), 555–564. Spencer does not identify his informant.

264.30 Kant] See p. 341.

264.30 Ferrier] James Frederick Ferrier (1808–1864), Scottish philosopher, *Institutes of Metaphysic: The Theory of Knowing and Being* (Edinburgh: Wm. Blackwood, 1854), p. 79. Houghton preserves a copy of this edition (WJ 527.78), identified as from James's library, with annotations by Henry James, Sr., and no indications of use by James. The *Institutes* became vol. I of the three-volume *Philosophical Works of the Late James Frederick Ferrier.*

264.33 Hamilton] William Hamilton, *Discussions on Philosophy and Literature, Education and University Reform*, 2nd ed. (London: Longman, Brown, Green and Longmans, 1853), p. 47. Widener preserves a copy of this work from the library of Henry James, Sr., given together with James's books (Phil 2035.30.1).

264.36 Mansel] Henry Longueville Mansel (1820–1871), English philosopher, *Metaphysics or the Philosophy of Consciousness Phenomenal and Real* (Edinburgh: Adam and Charles Black, 1860), p. 58. For works by Mansel from James's library see *Some Problems of Philosophy*, WORKS, note to 33.25.

264.40 Green] Thomas Hill Green, "Introduction" to David Hume, *A Treatise of Human Nature*, I, 12. Perry reports that Green's *Works* (1885), perhaps only vol. I containing the "Introduction," were sold.

266.39 *Lectures*] Pp. 289–290.

267.30 Kant] See p. 341.

267.39 Mill's] James Mill (1773–1836), British philosopher and historian, *Analysis of the Phenomena of the Human Mind*, ed. John Stuart Mill, with notes by Alexander Bain, Andrew Findlater, George Grote, and J. S. Mill, 2 vols. (London: Longmans, Green, Reader, and Dyer, 1869) (WJ 550.50), I, 264.

270.12 Joubert] The remark by Joseph Joubert (1754–1824), French writer, seems quoted from Egger, p. 221. In his index to *La Parole intérieure*, James has "Joubert 221."

270.14 Egger] P. 227.

270.32 work] Both chs. 5 and 6, pp. 213–321, deal with "La Parole intérieure et la pensée."

270.34 Egger] P. 215.

273.36 Lange] Friedrich Albert Lange, *Geschichte des Materialismus*, II, 421–422.

274.21 Helmholtz] See pp. 487–488, 666.

277.1 Schopenhauer] In *Die Welt als Wille und Vorstellung*, 2 vols. (Leipzig: F. A. Brockhaus, 1859) (*AC 85.J2376.Zz859s), II, 362–363, Schopenhauer summarizes his claim that human actions flow from character and motive and states that the full argument is in his *Preisschrift über die Freiheit des Willens*.

278.14 Lotze] *Microcosmus*, I, 250.

282.40 "Who] Shakespeare, *Othello* (act 3, scene 3).

283.42 Locke's] *Essay*, pp. 253–254.

286.25 *active*] George Frederick Stout (1860–1944), English philosopher and psychologist, *Analytic Psychology*, 2 vols. (London: Swan Sonnenschein, 1896) (WJ 583.67), I, 143–179, in the chapter on "The Concept of Mental Activity," criticizes James's discussion. James responds in "The Experience of Activity," *Essays in Radical Empiricism*, WORKS, p. 86n. In James's copy of Stout, there are a number of marginal comments. On I, 143, in part in reference to Stout's remark that according to F. H. Bradley, the current use of 'activity' is a scandal (see *Essays in Radical Empiricism*, WORKS, note to 80.13), James writes: "good example of english method of asking 'What do you mean' by a word. Bradley only omits to say what follows on the the term as thus defined? What difference accrues?—One may say it is a question of *who* are the dramates personae in the game of life? Or is there a *game* of life, or only happenings with comments of feeling on results." On p. 161, where Stout quotes 286.34–287.4, James writes: "I say this in a somewhat different connexion, (the inner self) no incompatible with a feeling of activity being subjectively *involved* in these cephalic experiences." James seems to have treated Stout's criticism in a lecture because on p. 161 he also has "How does he criticise W.J." On p. 162, where Stout quotes 287.6–287.12, James writes: "But why are these b. p. [bodily processes] not *active*? The question I was discussing was not as to the *existence* of an activity, but as to *who* was the actor, soul or muscle." While on p. 163: "Yes, but what is the *process*? spiritual or muscular? In either case it is active" and "We have 3 ideas to distinguish here: 1) the activity as such of a supposed spiritual agent; 2) activity as part of the 'content'; 3) the process as such feeling its own current. I was concerned only in denying 1. Cf. 201-2 [WORKS, pp. 199–200]." On p. 164: "These criticisms seem to carry weight, & make it appear as if the activity feeling were not limited to so restricted a portion of the 'content' as these muscular experiences. W.J." On p. 179, "But grant that our mental life is active:—what follows? What does active mean farther than being like our mental life?" For a note on the relations between James and Stout see *Some Problems of Philosophy*, WORKS, note to 110.20.

290.13 Ferrier] James seems not to be quoting, but rather paraphrasing such statements as that "the only object which any intelligence ever has, or ever can have any cognisance of is, itself-in-union-with-whatever-it-apprehends" (*Institutes of Metaphysic*, p. 98).

291.38 Souriau] Paul Souriau (1852–1926), French philosopher of art, "La Conscience de soi," *Revue Philosophique*, 22 (November 1886), 449–472.

293.5 "Is] Quoted by Bain, *The Emotions and the Will*, 3rd ed., p. 206.

293.38 Bain] Pp. 192–200, ch. 10 of the section on "The Emotions."

294.25 Thackeray] William Makepeace Thackeray, *The Book of Snobs*, ch. 3, *The Works of William Makepeace Thackeray*, XXII (New York: Charles Scribner's Sons, 1904), 21.

294.33 Guiteau] Charles Guiteau (d. June 30, 1882) assassinated James Garfield in 1881. The *New York Times*, July 1, 1882, p. 1, quotes Guiteau's speech on the gallows: "The American press has a large bill to settle with the righteous Father for their vindictiveness in this matter," that is, for demanding Guiteau's execution. However, the *Nation*, 35 (July 6, 1882), 1, emphasizes the desire for notoriety as part of Guiteau's motivation.

296.36 Carlyle] Thomas Carlyle (1795–1881), Scottish historian and essayist, *Sartor Resartus: The Life and Opinions of Herr Teufelsdröckh*, 3rd ed. (London: Chapman and Hall, 1849) (*AC 85.J2376.Zz849c), pp. 207–208.

297.17 Carlyle] P. 207.

297.32 Epictetus] *The Works of Epictetus*, trans. Thomas Wentworth Higginson (Boston: Little, Brown, 1866), pp. 6, 10, 105 (from the *Discourses*).

299.3 Aurelius] *The Thoughts of the Emperor M. Aurelius Antoninus*, trans. George Long (Boston: Ticknor and Fields, 1864) (*AC 85.J2376.Zz864a), p. 130 (bk. IV, sec. 23). In James's copy, dated February 1865, the passage is marked and with cross-references to pp. 259, 144.

299.34 Horwicz] Adolf Horwicz (1831–1894), German philosopher, *Analyse der qualitativen Gefühle* (Magdeburg: A. & R. Faber, 1878), p. 262; vol. II, pt. 2 of *Psychologische Analysen auf physiologischer Grundlage* (1872–) (WJ 739.78).

302.3 Job's] Job, xiii, 15.

302.4 Aurelius's] *Thoughts*, p. 193 (bk. VII, sec. 41).

308.37 "For] Ralph Waldo Emerson, "Threnody," *Poems* (Boston: Houghton, Mifflin, 1885), p. 135; vol. IX of the Riverside Edition of *Emerson's Complete Works*.

309.39 Lotze] *Microcosmus*, I, 248–254.

311.39 *Psychologische*] Pp. 267–270.

312.21 Bain] *The Emotions and the Will*, 3rd ed., pp. 201–214, ch. 11 of "The Emotions." The quotation is from pp. 203–204, 206, 205. James ignores paragraph divisions and section numbering. In James's copy pp. 203–204 are marked and with 'Reflective' in the margin.

313.45 *Microcosmus*] I, 696–706.

315.32 Kant] *Critique of Pure Reason*, B133. Heavily annotated is James's copy of the German edition by Erich Adickes (Berlin: Mayer & Müller, 1889) (*AC 85.J2376.Zz889k); for other works by Kant see *Some Problems of Philosophy*, WORKS, note to 14.6.

319.29 Hume] See pp. 332–334.

319.29 Herbart] See p. 335n.

323.22 Hodgson] Shadworth Hodgson, *Time and Space*, p. 177. In James's copy, the passage is marked with a cross-reference to pp. 191–192 and to J. J. Baumann, *Philosophie als Orientierung über die Welt* (Leipzig: S. Hirzel, 1873) (WJ 706.89), pp. 114–115. James's index to Baumann contains "Ich 114."

329.8 Hodgson] Shadworth Hodgson, *The Method of Philosophy: An Address* (privately printed, 1882) (WJ 539.18), p. 27.

329.17 Wayland] Francis Wayland (1796–1865), American clergyman and educator, *The Elements of Intellectual Philosophy* (Boston: Phillips, Sampson, 1854), p. 15.

330.36 *Metaphysik*] P. 487. James is not using the English translation. In his copy of the *Medicinische Psychologie*, between pp. 66–67 and 80–81,

James inserted the following: "§6. Of the connexion of body & soul generally. He tries to establish the possibility of an action of material & spiritual substances upon each other. ['against' *del.*] In the first place he says (53,-4, -5) that the idea of spiritual substance, whatever a wide-spread prejudice may say to the contrary, is just as clear as that of matter. Neither can be thought of but in some determined state. The reason why we are so often dissatisfied with all knowledge which does not lead to sensible intuition is that the 'formal concept' of matter, i. e. the *conditions* of its determinations & their relations to each other are better known to us that those of spirit. As objects of 'intellectual intuition,' as qualities of being, they *(i.e. M. & Sp.) [inserted with a caret] stand to us on a par,—The primitive way of thinking seems to be ['for all objects' *del.*] that of conceiving of all objects as ideal qualitative essences, and in later German philosophy this method has had great play. But it is fruitless to try to descend from these into the infinite detail which characterizes the relations of objects to each other. [There seems no *logical* weakness in this method. It fails rather because, ['letting' *del.*] it is mindful in its distinctions almost exclusively of the relations of things to one very narrow standard, viz. *our feelings.* Were our feelings a less specialized form of existence it would be more successful. By considering things in their relation to motion, which appears merely to be the most general form of existence, we immediately master an immense network of their relations to each other.]—As soon as we have worked out our aim of determining the conditions of the *states* of the soul, it will seem as familiar to us as matter is. [It seems at all events strange that a substance *in* which we are, as we are supposed to be in the soul, shd. appear more foreign to us than external matter]

In 56–60 he replies to the objection that interaction between incorporeal & corporeal is inconceivable by pointing out that so is interaction between corporeals equally inconceivable. It is false even in physics that cause & effect obtain only between things homogeneous. *The [inserted with caret] Homogeneity is always a relative term, and Body & soul are also homogeneous in so far as they are both modifications of *Substance.* [!]

60.   Innefficiency [*stet*] of bodiless 'Ideas' to act on matter. They can only do so when conceived as affections of a substantial soul. [Better they can only be conceived of as affections &. Let 'em exist alone and by his previous argument they can act on matter as well as it on itself] . . . .

(In 63 he propounds his private spiritualistic conception to be that the essence of matter is itself spiritual and material phenomena are only its shadow, so that the interaction is between things homogeneous after all)."

In connection with secs. 243–245 (pp. 480–487) of the *Metaphysik*, James comments on p. 480, "Was mit dem Ausdruck Seelen *Substanz* gemeint wird," on p. 482, "Einheit einer Substanz. Kañ nicht mehr als Einheit des Selbstbewusstseins," on p. 483, "Eine Gleichniss von Kant." His index to the *Metaphysik* includes the following: " 'Substance' 481, 496-7, 84," "Kant & soul-substance #244," "immortality 487."

331.2 Locke] *Essay*, pp. 226–227 (bk. II, ch. 27, secs. 16–19). On p. 226, where Locke writes that "self is that conscious thinking thing (whatever substance made up of, . . . it matters not)," attached by a guideline to 'it matters not' James comments "practicalism." The same passage is marked "N.B. 229-30." On p. 227, James has: "What is the *practically* important principle of identity? soul body or self?"

331.38 *Metaphysic*] Pp. 427–430.

332.25 *Treatise*] I, 533–535 (bk. I, pt. IV, sec. 6).

334.38 Appendix] I, 559–560.

335.38 Herbart] James could be thinking of the following: "The simple nature of the soul is totally unknown and will forever remain so. It is as little an object of speculative as of empirical psychology" (*A Text-Book in Psychology*, p. 120 [sec. 153]). Herbart discusses the "I" in *Psychologie als Wissenschaft, neu gegründet auf Erfahrung, Metaphysik, und Mathematik*, 2 vols. (Königsberg: Unzer, 1824–1825), I, 85–93 (secs. 24–26).

336.22 Taine] *On Intelligence*, I, 209–210; II, 108 (French edition, I, 206; II, 187). In his index inserted between I, 242–243 of *De l'intelligence*, James has "plank image 206." On I, 387, James comments: "In vol. II, 187, 219 (pp. 366, 386 of 8ᵛᵒ engl. ed.) he speaks of a character existing the same in all our representations, the character of inwardness, and this abstracted he calls the ego. But this is anything but a total, a sum, a compound, it is a constant element." The octavo is the one-volume edition of 1871.

338.40 *Analysis*] II, 174–175.

338.41 *Examination*] Pp. 262–263. Italics are James's.

339.3 chapter] Ch. 12 (4th ed., pp. 240–249), "The Psychological Theory of the Belief in Matter, how Far Applicable to Mind." James quotes from pp. 247–248.

341.33 "The] B135.

341.37 *Kritik*] B137.

342.23 'not] Kant, B157.

342.25 "the] Kant, A346=B404.

342.39 "the] Kant, B131.

345.37 Morris] George Sylvester Morris (1840–1889), American philosopher, *Kant's Critique of Pure Reason: A Critical Exposition* (Chicago: Griggs, 1882), p. 224n.

345.39 Cohen] Hermann Cohen (1842–1918), German philosopher, *Kants Theorie der Erfahrung* (Berlin: Dümmler, 1871), p. 138, in reference to the *Prolegomena zu einer jeden künftigen Metaphysik*, in *Sämmtliche Werke*, ed. Karl Rosenkranz and F. W. Schubert, III (Leipzig: Voss, 1838) (*AC 85. J2376.Zz838k), p. 65 (sec. 22 [21a in other editions]). An annotated copy of Cohen's work was sold.

346.10-11 Rosenkranz] Johann Karl Friedrich Rosenkranz (1805–1879), German philosopher. In his *Index Rerum* (bMS Am 1092.9 [4520]), under Rosenkranz, James lists the *Psychologie*, 3rd ed. (1863) and the autobiographical *Von Magdeburg bis Königsberg* (1873). Except for writings in connection with editions of Kant and Hegel, nothing by Rosenkranz from James's library is known.

346.11 Erdmann] Johann Eduard Erdmann (1805–1892), German philosopher.

347.13 Green] Thomas Hill Green, *Prolegomena to Ethics*, ed. A. C. Bradley (Oxford: Clarendon, 1883) (WJ 535.22), p. 61 (sec. 57). From 347.14 to 347.15 has not been located.

347.22 "we] Pp. 65 (sec. 61), 70 (sec. 64).

348.39 *Loc.*] Pp. 69-70.

349.18 "ghastly] From Tennyson's "In Memoriam A. H. H.," *The Works of Alfred Lord Tennyson* (London: Macmillan, 1905), p. 249.

349.24 Hume's] See p. 333.

349.31 Caird] Edward Caird (1835-1908), Scottish philosopher, *Hegel* (Philadelphia: J. B. Lippincott, 1883), p. 149. Perry reports that a copy of this work (1883) was sold. One letter from Caird to James is at Houghton (bMS Am 1092, letter 62).

351.46 Brown] Pp. 75-76.

352.39 Brown] P. 72. From Alexander Pope and others, *Memoirs of Martinus Scriblerus*, in *The Works of Alexander Pope*, ed. William Roscoe, VII (London, 1824), 85 (ch. 12).

353.19-20 Carpenter] *Principles of Mental Physiology*, p. 457, from Frances Power Cobbe, *Hours of Work and Play* (Philadelphia: J. B. Lippincott, 1867), p. 100.

353.36 Gurney] Edmund Gurney, Frederic William Henry Myers, Frank Podmore, *Phantasms of the Living*, 2 vols. (London: Society for Psychical Research, 1886), I, 126-158. James's copy is in Houghton (Phil 7068.86. 20*B).

353.38 Hodgson] Richard Hodgson (1855-1905), Australian-born psychical researcher, and S. J. Davey, "The Possibilities of Mal-Observation and Lapse of Memory from a Practical Point of View," *Proceedings of the SPR*, 4 (May 1887), 381-495. For a note on James and Hodgson see *The Will to Believe*, WORKS, note to 227.31. Davey is an unidentified psychical researcher, see *The Will to Believe*, WORKS, note to 232.1, for date of death.

354.37 Royce] Josiah Royce, "Hallucination of Memory and 'Telepathy'," *Mind*, 13 (April 1888), 244-248; "Report of the Committee on Phantasms and Presentiments," *Proceedings of the American Society for Psychical Research*, vol. I, no. 4 (March 1889), pp. 350-428.

355.27 *Maladies*] Pp. 84-85.

355.29 Strümpell] Adolf von Strümpell (1853-1925), German physician, "Beobachtungen über ausgebreitete Anästhesien und deren Folgen für die willkürliche Bewegung und das Bewusstsein," *Deutsches Archiv für klinische Medicin*, 22 (1878), 321-361.

355.43 Taine] *De l'intelligence*, 3rd ed., 2 vols. (Paris: Hachette, 1878), II, 462.

356.37 Griesinger] Wilhelm Griesinger (1817-1868), German psychiatrist, *Die Pathologie und Therapie der psychischen Krankheiten*, 2nd ed. (Stuttgart: Krabbe, 1867) (WJ 734.41), pp. 49-50. James's copy is signed, Paris, 1868. On p. 50, James has a cross-reference to p. 170. He did not use the available English translation.

356.38 *Proceedings*] See note to 206.39.

357.37 *l'intelligence*] 3rd ed., II, 465–468. On II, 461n, Taine states that the cases are those discussed by Krishaber in his book, but that he had direct access to Krishaber's journal of observations.

357.37 Krishaber's] Maurice Krishaber (1836–1883), French physician, *De la névropathie cérébro-cardiaque* (Paris: G. Masson, 1873). James's copy is in Widener (Phil 6320.5), with the following in back: "153, 163, 165, 171" and "Memory 142, 153."

358.1 Fisher] From a letter to James, December 26, 1887 (bMS Am 1092.9 [4410]), by Chester Irving Fisher (d. 1905), American physician, at the time superintendent of the State Almshouse, Tewksbury, Mass.

358.31 Azam] Eugène Azam (1822–1899), French physician, "Amnésie périodique, ou doublement de la vie," *Revue Scientifique*, 2nd series, vol. 10 (May 20, 1876), pp. 481–489; *Hypnotisme, double conscience et altérations de la personnalité* (Paris: Baillière, 1887).

359.17 Rieger] Conrad Rieger (1855–1939), German psychiatrist, *Der Hypnotismus* (Jena: Gustav Fischer, 1884) (WJ 776.22), pp. 109–115. James is quoting from p. 113.

359.36 Mitchell] Silas Weir Mitchell (1829–1914), American neurologist and author, "Mary Reynolds: A Case of Double Consciousness," *Transactions of the College of Physicians of Philadelphia*, 10 (1888), 366–389. Widener preserves two unannotated copies of the reprint (Philadelphia: Wm. J. Dornan, 1889) (Phil 7039.6A and .6B), with the former inscribed to James by the author. Also in Widener is James's annotated copy of Mitchell's *Lectures on Diseases of the Nervous System Especially in Women* (Philadelphia: Henry C. Lea's Son, 1881) (Phil 6322.11). In Houghton are six letters from Mitchell to James (bMS Am 1092, letters 553–558). James is quoting from the *Transactions*, pp. 369–370, 373–374, 375–376, 383–384. The article "Mary Reynolds: A Case of Double Consciousness," *Harper's New Monthly Magazine*, 20 (May 1860), 807–812, is by William Swan Plumer (1802–1880), American clergyman and author.

363.39 Winslow's] Forbes Winslow (1844–1913), British psychiatrist, *On Obscure Diseases of the Brain, and Disorders of the Mind: Their Incipient Symptoms, Pathology, Diagnosis, Treatment, and Prophylaxis* (Philadelphia: Blanchard & Lea, 1860). Chs. 13–17 (pp. 291–376), all deal with memory. In his annotated copy in Widener (Phil 6972.5.2B), James has "homicide with delusion 68–9."

364.3 Janet] Pierre Janet, *L'Automatisme*, pp. 87–88, 105. Janet himself (p. 105) describes the change as one from a visual to a motor type. For the terms 'motor' and 'visual' see *Œuvres complètes de J. M. Charcot*, III (Paris: Aux bureaux du *Progrès Médical*, 1890), 190–191.

364.29 Janet] *L'Automatisme*, pp. 107, 108, 97.

364.38 Janet] *L'Automatisme*, p. 97.

364.39 Janet] See note to 203.16.

365.18 Janet] *L'Automatisme*, pp. 108–109.

365.24 *phase*] *L'Automatisme*, p. 50: "période des attitudes passionnelles."

365.30 Lucie's] *L'Automatisme*, p. 106.

366.3 "This] *L'Automatisme*, pp. 128–129, 132–133.

367.20 "This] *L'Automatisme*, p. 89.

367.25 Bourru] Henri Bourru and Prosper Ferdinand Burot, French physicians, *Variations de la personnalité* (Paris: Baillière, 1888). A marked copy of this work was sold. The viper incident and change of personality is found on pp. 20–22; paralysis of the right side, p. 27; a picture of Louis V. in "État de Bicêtre," opposite p. 37. Bicêtre is the location of an asylum near Paris in which Louis V. was for a time hospitalized.

368.26 Janet's] James's index to *L'Automatisme* contains "Proof that anaesthesia entails amnesia 97, 99."

368.27 Locke's] *Essay*, pp. 224–225 (bk. II, ch. 27, sec. 14).

369.7 Wigan]' Arthur Ladbroke Wigan, British physician, *The Duality of the Mind: Proved by the Structure, Functions, and Diseases of the Brain, and by the Phenomena of Mental Derangement, and Shewn to Be Essential to Moral Responsibility* (London: Longman, Brown, Green, and Longmans, 1844), pp. 394–395.

369.13 Bourne] In Widener is a pamphlet about the conversion of Ansel Bourne, *A Narrative of the Wonderful Facts in the Case of Ansel Bourne* (Fall River, Mass., 1877) (Phil 6990.26.5).

369.33 *Loc.*] Jules Janet, "L'Hystérie et l'hypnotisme," p. 619.

369.37 Dufay] Jean François Charles Dufay (1815–1898), French physician and political figure, "La Notion de la personnalité," *Revue Scientifique*, 18 (July 15, 1876), 69–71.

369.42 Hodgson] In the *Proceedings of the SPR*, 7 (April 1891), 1, it is reported that a paper on Bourne by James and Richard Hodgson was read for them on March 6, 1891. Presumably it is this paper which appears under Hodgson's name as "A Case of Double Consciousness," *Proceedings of the SPR*, 7 (July 1891), 221–257. On pp. 232–233, 241–249, Hodgson describes how James became involved and how together they questioned Bourne after James had hypnotised him. On pp. 254–255 there is a note by James dated May 30, 1890.

371.37 Newbold] The testimony of William Romaine Newbold (1865–1926), American educator, is given by Hodgson, pp. 250–253.

371.40 Bourne] The testimony of Louis H. Read and Guy Hinsdale (1858–1948), American physician, is given by Hodgson, pp. 232, 253–254.

373.7 Dean] Sidney Dean (1818–1901), American clergyman and author. In "Notes on Automatic Writing," in giving Dean's account, James notes that he himself has seen the hieroglyphs, and that these and similar marks were not recognized by language experts.

374.39 medium] Leonore Piper (1859–1950), American trance medium, whose control at times identified himself as Dr. Phinuit. Many of James's writings about Mrs. Piper appear in Gardner Murphy and Robert O. Ballou, *William James on Psychical Research* (New York: Viking Press, 1960).

375.38 Stevens] E. Winchester Stevens (1822?-1885), *The Watseka Wonder;* . . . *A Narrative of the Leading Phenomena Occurring in the Case of Mary Lurancy Vennum* (Chicago: Religio-Philosophical Publishing House, [1879]). James's copy is in Widener (Phil 7039.8). James is using a reprint (Chicago: Religio-Philosophical Publishing House, 1887), published together with Plumer's "Mary Reynolds" (Phil 7039.8.1). James is quoting from pp. 14-15.

376.20 "She] (1887), pp. 28-29.

376.29 "perfectly] (1887), p. 31.

377.9 hands] In "Notes on Automatic Writing," pp. 549-550, James describes in more detail three tests for anesthesia.

378.13 Myers] Frederic William Henry Myers (1843-1901), British essayist and psychical researcher, in the *Proceedings of the SPR*: "On a Telepathic Explanation of Some So-called Spiritualistic Phenomena," 2 (December 1884), 217-237, part I of the series continued as "Automatic Writing," 3 (May 1885), 1-63; 4 (May 1887), 209-261; part IV appeared with the additional title "The Dæmon of Socrates," 5 (June 1889), 522-547.

378.16 Jackson's] Spencer's student and friend, Jackson discusses the evolution of the brain, but the view attributed to him has not been found. Jackson holds that the left side of the brain is the "leading [motor] side," and the right, "the automatic [motor] side" (*Selected Writings of John Hughlings Jackson*, ed. James Taylor, 2 vols. [London: Hodder and Stoughton, 1931], I, 39). See also note to 769.15.

378.38 Maudsley's] Henry Maudsley, "The Double Brain," *Mind*, 14 (April 1889), 161-187.

378.38 Luys's] Jules Luys, "Étude sur le dédoublement des opérations cérébrales et sur le rôle isolé de chaque hémisphère dans les phénomènes de la pathologie mentale," *L'Encéphale: Journal des Maladies Mentales et Nerveuses*, 8 (September–October 1888), 516-537.

378.39 Brown-Séquard] Charles Édouard Brown-Séquard, "Have We Two Brains or One?" *Forum*, 9 (August 1890), 627-643.

380.21 Bain] Alexander Bain, *The Senses and the Intellect*, 3rd ed. (London: Longmans, Green, 1868) (WJ 506.41.4). James's index contains "Selective attention 559, 580." On p. 370 of *The Emotions and the Will* James asks, "What can the will do towards commanding the sequence of its thoughts?" and attaches this with a guideline to Bain's "What the will can do is to fix the Attention."

383.38 Waitz] Theodor Waitz (1821-1864), German philosopher, *Lehrbuch der Psychologie als Naturwissenschaft* (Braunschweig: Vieweg, 1849), pp. 631-632. An annotated copy, dated May 3, 1870, was sold. Waitz is referring to Adrien Léonard, *Essai sur l'éducation des animaux, le chien pris pour type* (Lillie: Leleux, 1842).

384.27 Jevons] William Stanley Jevons (1835-1882), English logician and economist, "The Power of Numerical Discrimination," *Nature*, 3 (February 9,

1871), 281-282.

384.34 *Elements*] P. 78.

384.35 *Lectures*] I, 254. In a note Hamilton refers to works by Charles Bonnet (1720-1793), Swiss naturalist and philosophical writer, Abraham Tucker (1705-1774), English philosopher, Destutt de Tracy, and others.

385.22 Cattell] James McKeen Cattell, "Über die Trägheit der Netzhaut und des Sehcentrums," *Philosophische Studien*, 3 (1885), 94-127; quotation from p. 127.

385.37 Dietze] Georg Dietze (b. 1857), German psychologist, "Untersuchungen über den Umfang des Bewusstseins bei regelmässig auf einander folgenden Schalleindrücken," *Philosophische Studien*, 2 (1884), 362-393.

385.40 Bechterew] Wladimir Bechterew, "Das Bewusstsein und seine Grenzen," *Neurologisches Centralblatt*, 8 (May 1, 1889), 272-273, an abstract of a paper originally published in Russian.

385.45 *Revue*] Frédéric Paulhan, "La Simultanéité des actes psychiques," *Revue Scientifique*, 39 (May 28, 1887), 684-689. James quotes from p. 687 in an inverted order.

386.35 Wolff] Christian Wolff, *Psychologia Empirica Methodo Scientifica per Tractata* (Verona, 1736), pp. 108-109. James's copy is in Widener (Phil 3910.35.5 [F]).

388.38 Pflüger's] See note to 94.2.

389.39 *Ibid.*] II, 262-263.

391.6 Tschisch] Woldemar von Tschisch (Tchisch; Vladimir Fedorovich Chizh) (1855-1923), Russian physician, "Über die Zeitverhältnisse der Apperception einfacher und zusammengesetzter Vorstellungen, untersucht mit Hülfe der Complicationsmethode," *Philosophische Studien*, 2 (1885), 603-634.

391.13 Bessel] Friedrich Wilhelm Bessel (1784-1846), German astronomer.

391.19 FIG. 35] Figure 35 is from Wundt's *Grundzüge*, 2nd ed., II, 270; the quotation is from II, 269-270.

393.41 Wundt] Wilhelm Wundt, *Vorlesungen über die Menschen- und Thierseele*, 2 vols. (Leipzig: Voss, 1863), I, 37-42, 365-371. Only vol. II is preserved (WJ 796.59.8). Also preserved is the English translation by J. E. Creighton and E. B. Titchener of the 2nd ed. (1892) (London: Swan Sonnenschein, 1894) (WJ 796.59.10), with annotations primarily for teaching purposes.

395.40 Herbart] II, 225-226.

396.34 Wesley] John Wesley (1703-1791), English clergyman, founder of Methodism. Widener preserves volume I of L. Tyerman, *The Life and Times of the Rev. John Wesley, M.A., Founder of the Methodists* (London: Hodder and Stoughton, 1870) (Br 2123.25.45B).

396.34 Hall] Robert Hall (1764-1831), English clergyman.

396.39 Hamilton] *Lectures on Metaphysics and Logic*, I, 259-260. Hamilton is referring to Joseph Justus Scaliger (1540-1609), Protestant scholar; Girolamo Cardano (1501-1576), Italian scientist and philosopher; François Vieta (1540-1603), French mathematician; Guillaume Budé (1468-1540), French scholar.

397.35   *Mental*] *Principles of Mental Physiology*, pp. 138-139.

397.37   Cattell] See note to 95.40.

398.31   logic] From 1884-1885 to 1889-1890, James's Philosophy 2 covered both logic and psychology. In view of his frequently stated dislike of logic (see Perry, II, 680-681), it is possible that this remark is autobiographical.

399.1   FIG. 36] This figure seems based on Helmholtz, *Atlas von elf Tafeln* (figures to accompany the *Handbuch*) (Leipzig: Voss, 1867), table 11, figure X. James omits a pair of black diamonds, one just above the other, in each of the two halves. The Houghton copy (Phil 5643.8*), while not from James's library, has annotations in James's hand.

399.3-4   Helmholtz] *Handbuch*, p. 770 (sec. 32).

399.22   Helmholtz] *Handbuch*, p. 772 (sec. 32).

400.37   Hamilton] *Lectures on Metaphysics and Logic*, I, 258. In notes Hamilton provides references to the works of Claude Adrien Helvétius (1715-1771), French philosopher; Georg Louis Leclerc de Buffon (1707-1788), French naturalist; Georges Cuvier (1769-1832), French naturalist; Philip Dormer Stanhope, fourth Earl of Chesterfield (1694-1773), English statesman and author.

402.37   Lotze] Pp. 478-479.

402.37   Fechner] Gustav Theodor Fechner, *Revision der Hauptpuncte der Psychophysik* (Leipzig: Breitkopf und Härtel, 1882), pp. 269-284. Ch. 19 is titled "Aufmerksamkeitsverhältnisse."

402.38   Müller] Georg Elias Müller (1850-1934), German psychologist, *Zur Theorie der sinnlichen Aufmerksamkeit* (Leipzig: A. Edelmann, [1873]), pp. 2-16.

402.39   Stumpf] Carl Stumpf (1848-1936), German psychologist, *Tonpsychologie*, 2 vols. (Leipzig: S. Hirzel, 1883-1890) (WJ 783.89), I, 71. In addition to works mentioned in the present notes, Houghton preserves *Erscheinungen und psychische Funktionen* (Berlin: 1891-1907) (WJ 783.89. 4F) and a collection of pamphlets (WJ 783.89.4). The correspondence between them is at Houghton (bMS Am 1092.9 [620-642, 3778-3811]). For the relations between them see Perry, II, 173-204. Stumpf has published "William James nach seinen Briefen. Leben. Charakter. Lehre," *Kant-Studien*, 32 (1927), 205-241, reprinted as a pamphlet (Berlin: Rolf Heise, 1928).

403.33   *Tonpsychologie*] I, 71-72.

404.38   *Elements*] I, 81-82.

404.39   *Physiologische*] II, 226-227.

405.41   *Op.*] II, 238-239.

406.38   Cattell] On p. 233 of "The Time Taken up by Cerebral Operations" (see note to 95.40), Cattell reports that he cannot recall a single case of premature reaction.

409.27 *Op.*] *Grundzüge*, 2nd ed.

409.28 Cattell] See note to 95.40.

409.34 Obersteiner] Heinrich Obersteiner, "Experimental Researches on Attention," *Brain*, 1 (January 1879), 439-453.

409.36 Bertels] Arved Bertels, Latvian physician, *Versuche über die Ablenkung der Aufmerksamkeit* (Dorpat: H. Laakmann, 1889).

413.32 Mach] Ernst Mach, "Zur Theorie des Gehörorgans," *Sitzungsberichte* (Vienna), vol. 48, no. 3 (October 1863), pp. 283-300.

414.29 Hering] Ewald Hering, "Der Raumsinn und die Bewegungen des Auges," in Hermann's *Handbuch*, vol. III, pt. 1 (1879), pp. 343-601.

415.33 Exner's] See pp. 387-388.

416.4 'Spannung'] See p. 405. The word was not found in Exner.

416.9 Lewes's] *Problems of Life and Mind*, 3rd series, II, 107-108.

416.38 Helmholtz] Hermann Helmholtz, *Die Lehre von den Tonempfindungen, als physiologische Grundlage für die Theorie der Musik*, 3rd ed. (Braunschweig: Vieweg, 1870), pp. 85-88. Perry reports that an annotated copy of this edition was sold. James is not quoting the translation by Alexander J. Ellis, *On the Sensations of Tone as a Physiological Basis for the Theory of Music*, 2nd ed. (London: Longmans, Green, 1885).

417.39 *Physiologische*] 2nd ed., II, 208, 209.

418.28 *Popular*] Pp. 294-295.

419.16 Lotze] *Medicinische Psychologie*, p. 510. In Lotze, James's fourth segment precedes the other three. Figure 39 is not from Lotze.

420.39 *Psychologie*] Théodule Ribot, *Psychologie de l'attention* (Paris: Alcan, 1889), pp. 32ff.

420.40 *Philosophische*] Nikolai Nikolaevitch Lange (1858-1921), Russian philosopher, "Beiträge zur Theorie der sinnlichen Aufmerksamkeit und der activen Apperception," *Philosophische Studien*, 4 (1887), 390-442; the quotation is from p. 415.

421.36 Marillier] Léon Marillier (1842-1901), French psychologist, "Remarques sur le mécanisme de l'attention," *Revue Philosophique*, 27 (June 1889), 566-587. A copy in James's hand of his letter to Marillier, February 11, 1893, is at Houghton (bMS Am 1092.9 [3189]). Marillier published "La Psychologie de William James," *Revue Philosophique*, 34 (1892), 449-470, 603-627; 35 (1893), 1-32, 145-183.

422.14 Ribot] *Psychologie de l'attention*, pp. 51-52.

422.26 Perez] Bernard Perez (1863-1903), French educator, *L'Enfant de trois à sept ans* (Paris: Alcan, 1886), p. 108.

422.30 Ferrier] 1st ed., pp. 282-287.

422.30 Obersteiner] See note to 409.34.

422.36 Lewes] See note to 166.38.

422.37 Schneider] James's index to Schneider's *Menschliche Wille* includes the following entries: "Schreck als Keim der Aufmerksamkeit, 294" and "N. B. Attention 309."

422.38 Carpenter] Ch. 3, "Of Attention," pp. 130–147.

422.38 Cappie] James Cappie, British physician, "Some Points in the Physiology of Attention, Belief, and Will," *Brain*, 9 (July 1886), 196–206.

422.39 Sully] James Sully, "The Psycho-Physical Process in Attention," *Brain*, 13 (1890), 145–164.

423.24 Herbartian] See pp. 750–751; also James's *Talks to Teachers on Psychology* (New York: Henry Holt, 1899), pp. 155–168.

424.4 *Principium*] Lucretius, *De Rerum Natura*, bk. II, lines 254–255.

425.38 Hermann's] See note to 414.29.

428.2 Bradley] Francis Herbert Bradley (1846–1924), English philosopher, "Is There Any Special Activity of Attention?" *Mind*, 11 (July 1886), 305–323 (reprinted in Bradley's *Collected Essays*, 2 vols. [Oxford: Clarendon, 1935], I, 181–202); the quotation is from p. 318 (I, 196). For the relations between James and Bradley see Perry, II, 485–493. For a note on the correspondence between them see *Some Problems of Philosophy*, WORKS, note to 48.19. Criticism of Bradley can be found in most of James's works, but especially in *Essays in Radical Empiricism*, WORKS; some critical papers are included in *Essays in Philosophy*, WORKS.

428.38 Lipps] Pp. 45–63, 650–678.

430.28 Hobbes] See note to 660.40.

430.34 Ward's] James Ward, "Psychological Principles," pt. III, *Mind*, 12 (January 1887), 45–67; "Mr. F. H. Bradley's Analysis of Mind," *Mind*, 12 (October 1887), 564–575.

432.40 inquiry] Nothing has been found in the James Collection on this topic.

433.4 Scott] J. G. Lockhart, *Memoirs of the Life of Sir Walter Scott, Bart.*, 2nd ed., I (Edinburgh: Cadell, 1839), 128.

436.36 Robertson] George Croom Robertson, "Axiom," *Encyclopædia Britannica*, 9th ed., III (New York: Samuel L. Hall, 1878), 158–162; reprinted in *Philosophical Remains of George Croom Robertson*, ed. Alexander Bain and T. Whittaker (London: Williams and Norgate, 1894), pp. 119–132.

437.37 Hodgson] Pp. 403–413.

437.37 Lotze] Hermann Lotze, *Logic*, trans. B. Bosanquet (Oxford: Clarendon, 1884) (WJ 751.88.10), pp. 19–20.

437.40 Locke's] *Essay*, p. 92. In his copy, next to the passage quoted, James notes "Platonism 383."

438.38 Spencer] II, 406–409.

444.16 Mill] James Mill, *Analysis of the Phenomena of the Human Mind* (1869), ch. 8 (I, 247–293) on "Classification." See below, p. 450.

444.39 *Principles*] Pp. 176 (sec. 7), 177 (sec. 9), 178–179 (sec. 10), 182–183 (sec. 14). On p. 178 of his copy, James has: "What kind of abstraction does Berkeley admit? (—of parts that can exist separate)."

444.40 Rabier] Élie Rabier (b. 1846), French philosopher, *Leçons de philosophie*, I (Paris: Hachette, 1884), 310; vol. I of the *Leçons* is subtitled *Psychologie*.

445.19 *Omnis*] A formula much like this one can be found in St. Thomas Aquinas, *Commentarium in Quatuor Libros Sententiarum*, book I, distinction III, question I, article I, objection 3.

445.35 *Examination*] 4th ed.

445.35 *Logic*] *A System of Logic*, I, 258–262, II, 195–196. On I, 259, James has: "Cf. Exam. of H. p. 393[,] supra p. 170[,] infra vol. II, p. 196." On II, 196, where Mill asserts that there are "such things as general conceptions, or conceptions by means of which we can think generally," James comments, "general, not *abstract*."

445.39 Caird] Edward Caird, *A Critical Account of the Philosophy of Kant* (Glasgow: Maclehose, 1877), p. 553. Preserved is *The Critical Philosophy of Immanuel Kant*, 2 vols. (New York: Macmillan, 1889) (WJ 511.41).

447.21 Bradley] Francis Herbert Bradley, *The Principles of Logic* (London: Kegan Paul, Trench, 1883) (WJ 510.2.2), p. 11.

447.38 Reid's] *The Works of Thomas Reid*, pp. 394–398; the whiteness illustration is on p. 395.

448.31 Bradley] *The Principles of Logic*, p. 4. James's second sentence is from p. 4n. Ch. 1 (pp. 1–39) is titled "The General Nature of Judgment."

448.39 Rosmini's] Antonio Rosmini-Serbati (1797–1855), Italian philosopher and statesman, *The Philosophical System of Antonio Rosmini-Serbati*, trans. and ed. Thomas Davidson (London: Kegan Paul, Trench, 1882) (WJ 841.77), p. 43, from the Introduction by Davidson. Perry reports that Rosmini's *Psychology*, 3 vols. (London, 1884–), with summaries by James in vol. II, was sold.

449.6 Ferrier] James Frederick Ferrier, *Lectures on Greek Philosophy* (Edinburgh: William Blackwood, 1866), pp. 333, 336, 338–339. The *Lectures* were published as vol. I of the *Lectures on Greek Philosophy and Other Philosophical Remains*, ed. Alexander Grant and E. L. Lushington, 2 vols. (Edinburgh: William Blackwood, 1866), and became vol. II of the three-volume *Philosophical Works of the Late James Frederick Ferrier*. The two-volume set is listed among books given to Harvard (bMS Am 1092.9 [4580]), but it has not been located. Perry reports that this set, annotated, was sold, but his 1856 as the date of publication is an error.

450.38 *Analysis*] (1869), I, 264–266.

450.39 *Principles*] Pp. 180, 181. On p. 180 James has: "general, universal, ideas, *vs.* ideas genera*lized*, universa*lized*"; while on p. 181: "No general ideas, but a general *use of* ideas."

451.41 Galton's] In his *Inquiries into Human Faculty*, pp. 340–348, Galton describes "composite portraiture," the process of producing "blended" images by projecting photographs of different individuals upon a screen, so that the photographs blend into a single image. Galton reproduces images blended from as many as 100 cases. On pp. 349–354, Galton discusses "generic images."

452.1 Huxley] See pp. 692–694.

454.39 Hodgson's] James's index to *Time and Space* includes the entry "Skepticism 310," in reference to Hodgson's view that the skeptic refuses to accept the postulate that the results of an inquiry will be truer than its beginnings.

458.30 Martineau] James Martineau (1805–1900), English clergyman, *Essays, Philosophical and Theological* (Boston: William V. Spencer, 1866), pp. 268–273, from the essay "Cerebral Psychology: Bain." A copy of this work, with pp. 268–273 heavily marked, was sold. In later editions additional volumes of essays were added, and the 1866 *Essays* were identified as vol. I.

458.40 *Human*] *Essay*, p. 91. James omits section numbers.

459.43 *Analysis*] James Mill, *Analysis of the Phenomena of the Human Mind*, 2 vols. (London: Baldwin & Cradock, 1829), I, 70–71 (ch. 3, sec. 8).

460.43 *Senses*] Alexander Bain, *The Senses and the Intellect* (London: John W. Parker and Son, 1855), p. 411 (sec. 53).

462.39 Montgomery] Edmund Duncan Montgomery, "Space and Touch," *Mind*, 10 (1885), 227–244 (April), 377–398 (July), 512–531 (October).

464.33 Each] For James's controversy with F. H. Bradley concerning this section of the *Principles* and the subject of immediate resemblance, see *Essays in Philosophy*, WORKS, pp. 65–70, and notes.

467.22 Stumpf] For Stumpf's text see p. 503n.

467.28 Wahle] Richard Wahle (1857–1935), "Bemerkungen zur Beschreibung und Eintheilung der Ideenassociationen," *Vierteljahrsschrift*, 9 (1885), 404–432. In Widener is James's marked copy of *Gehirn und Bewusstsein* (Vienna: Hölder, 1884) (Phil 6132.22).

467.36 Schneider] Georg Heinrich Schneider, *Die Unterscheidung, Analyse, Entstehung und Entwickelung derselben bei den Thieren und beim Menschen* (Zürich: Cæsar Schmidt, 1877), p. 11, "*Unterschiedsempfindungscomplex.*"

468.37 Ward] James Ward, "An Attempt to Interpret Fechner's Law," *Mind*, 1 (October 1876), 452–466.

470.22 Homer] For Homer and Dante see notes to 1156.9 and 1156.10.

470.39 Sully] James's index to *Outlines* contains "Discrimination—'clearness' in sensation 141,–2."

472.39 *Analysis*] James's index to vol. II of *Analysis* includes "Likeness 17."

474.34 Bowne's] Borden Parker Bowne, *Introduction to Psychological Theory* (New York: Harper & Brothers, 1887), p. 28. An annotated copy was sold.

477.39 *Sensations*] James at this point is using the Ellis translation (see note to 416.38).

478.38 Read] Carveth Read (1848–1931), British philosopher, *The Metaphysics of Nature* (London: Adam and Charles Black, 1905), p. 260. In Houghton is James's copy of the second edition (1908) (WJ 575.2). The Hume citation is found on I, 332–333 of the Green and Grose edition. Four letters from Read to James are at Houghton (bMS Am 1092, letters 781–784).

479.37 *Psychology*] On I, 345 of his copy of Spencer, James comments: "We can only discriminate what we have separately experienced. *Properties* are only separately exp.^{d} by the *things in* which they reside being differentiated. They can then be discriminated *as* properties and generalized." Also on I, 345, "Fuller example on p. 464."

481.6 De Morgan] Augustus De Morgan (1806–1871), British mathematician and logician, *A Budget of Paradoxes* (London: Longmans, Green, 1872), p. 380.

482.3 Bridgman] Laura Dewey Bridgman (1829–1889). Her unusual sensitivity was noted by Granville Stanley Hall, "Laura Bridgman," *Mind*, 4 (April 1879), 151, and other writers, many of whom derived their accounts from Mary Swift Lamson, *Life and Education of Laura Dewey Bridgman* (1878).

482.5 Brace] Julia Brace (1806–1884), American teacher of blind deaf-mutes.

484.45 Donders] Franciscus Cornelis Donders (1818–1889), Dutch ophthalmologist, "Das binoculare Sehen und die Vorstellung von der dritten Dimension," *Archiv für Ophthalmologie*, vol. 13, pt. 1 (1867), pp. 1–48.

485.24 Czermak's] Johann Nepomuk Czermak (1828–1873), Czechoslovakian laryngologist-phoneticist. Volkmann refers to Czermak but cites no specific work.

486.34 Volkmann] Alfred Wilhelm Volkmann (1800–1877), German physiologist, "Über den Einfluss der Uebung auf das Erkennen räumlicher Distanzen," *Berichte über die Verhandlungen der königlich sächsischen Gesellschaft der Wissenschaften zu Leipzig* (mathematisch-physische Classe), 10 (1858), 38–69. Fechner contributed an appendix, "Beobachtungen, welche zu beweisen scheinen dass durch die Uebung der Glieder der einen Seite die der andern zugleich mit geübt werden. Zusatz zur vorhergehenden Abhandlung," pp. 71–76.

488.39 *Sensations*] See note to 416.38.

489.19 Purkinje] See note to 734.35.

490.11 Mariotte] Edme Mariotte (1620–1684), French physicist.

491.42 Wadsworth] Oliver Fairfield Wadsworth (1838–1911), American physician, "The Amblyopia of Squint," *Boston Medical and Surgical Journal*, 116 (January 20, 1887), 49–52. Discussion of the paper is reported on pp. 61–62. Hasket Derby (b. 1835), American physician, commented on p. 186 (February 21, 1887), to which Wadsworth replied on pp. 232–233 (March 10, 1887).

494.25 *Metaphysic*] Pp. 457–458.

494.39 *Tonpsychologie*] I, 106–107.

495.14 Tischer] Ernst Theodor Fürchtegott Tischer (b. 1855), "Über die Unterscheidung von Schallstärken," *Philosophische Studien*, 1 (1883), 495–542. James omits the data for three subjects.

495.37 *Physiologische*] 2nd ed.

496.35 *Mind*] See note to 95.40. The six pairs of figures were picked out by James from Cattell, pp. 380, 383, 385, 387.

497.12 "We] Cattell, p. 387.

497.36 Kries] Johannes von Kries and Felix Auerbach (1856–1933), German physicist, "Die Zeitdauer einfachster psychischer Vorgänge," *Archiv für Anatomie und Physiologie*, 1877, pp. 297–378.

497.38 Friedrich] Max Friedrich Friedrich (b. 1856), "Über die Apperceptionsdauer bei einfachen und zusammengesetzten Vorstellungen," *Philosophische Studien*, 1 (1881), 39–77.

497.38 Buccola's] Pp. 249–282.

499.39 Sully] James Sully, "Comparison," *Mind*, 10 (October 1885), 489–511.

499.39 Bradley] Francis Herbert Bradley, "On the Analysis of Comparison," *Mind*, 11 (January 1886), 83–85.

499.39 Bosanquet] Bernard Bosanquet (1848–1923), English philosopher, "Comparison—in Psychology and in Logic," *Mind*, 11 (July 1886), 405–408.

500.24 Bain] See note to 984.15.

501.7 Stumpf] *Tonpsychologie*, I, 122.

501.32 Delbœuf] Joseph Remi Léopold Delbœuf, *Éléments de psychophysique générale & spéciale* (Paris: Baillière, 1883), p. 64.

501.32 Plateau] Stumpf, *Tonpsychologie*, I, 124–126, describes the investigations of Joseph Antoine Ferdinand Plateau (1801–1883), Belgian physicist.

501.42 Blood] Benjamin Paul Blood (1832–1919), American mystic, *The Anæsthetic Revelation and the Gist of Philosophy* (Amsterdam, in New York, America, 1874). James's marked copy, with portions cut out, is preserved along with other pamphlets and clippings sent by Blood to James (bMS Am 1092.9 [4522, 4584], MS Am 1092.9 [4585]). James reviewed the work in the *Atlantic Monthly*, 34 (1874), 627–629. For the relations between James and Blood see the notes to "A Pluralistic Mystic," James's main treatment of Blood's work, in *Essays in Philosophy*, WORKS. To "On Some Hegelisms," *Mind*, 7 (April 1882), 186–208 (*The Will to Believe*, WORKS, pp. 196–221), James added an appendix of notes on difference and likeness made while in a state of nitrous oxide intoxication.

503.29 Stumpf] *Tonpsychologie*, I, 115–116, 117. The quotation in the footnote is from I, 116. In his index, James has "Aehnlichkeit urspringlich 116-7, -9."

504.21 Wundt] I, 84–90.

507.7 "We] I, 91, 91–92.

507.20 "So] I, 98.

508.4 Weber's] Ernst Heinrich Weber, "Der Tastsinn und das Gemeingefühl," in *Handwörterbuch der Physiologie*, ed. Rudolph Wagner, vol. III, pt. 2 (Braunschweig: Vieweg, 1846), pp. 481–588.

509.13 Fechner] Fechner discusses the *Massformel* in chs. 16–17, *Elemente der Psychophysik*, II, 9–39.

509.38 Delbœuf's] Joseph Remi Léopold Delbœuf, *Étude psychophysique. Recherches théoriques et expérimentales sur la mesure des sensations et spécialement des sensations de lumière et de fatigue* (1873), p. 35; a separately paged pamphlet in vol. 23 of the *Mémoires Couronnés et Autres Mémoires, Publiés par l'Académie Royale des Sciences, des Lettres et des Beaux-Arts de Belgique*.

509.39 Elsas's] Adolf Elsas (1855–1895), German physicist, *Über die Psychophysik. Physikalische und erkenntnisstheoretische Betrachtungen* (Marburg: N. G. Elwert, 1886), p. 16.

510.3 Fechner] Fechner discusses the three methods in *Elemente der Psychophysik*, I, 71–129; the threshold of sensation (*Schwelle*) in I, 238–300 and elsewhere; the discrimination of differences in weight in I, 183–201.

511.26 Wundt] Wundt discusses the four methods in *Grundzüge*, 2nd ed., I, 321–334.

512.2 Merkel] Julius Merkel (b. 1858), German psychologist, "Die Abhängigkeit zwischen Reiz und Empfindung," *Philosophische Studien*, 4 (1888), 541–594; 5 (1888), 245–291, 499–557; 10 (1894), 140–159, 203–248, 369–392, 507–522.

512.8 Volkmann] James's summary of investigations of sensitivity to light seems based on Wundt, *Grundzüge*, 3rd ed., I, 358–360. Wundt provides references to the works of Alfred Wilhelm Volkmann, Hermann Aubert (see note to 738.19), A. Masson (unidentified), Helmholtz, and Emil Kraepelin (see note to 775.6).

512.8 Helmholtz] *Handbuch*, pp. 309–336.

512.20 König] Arthur König (1856–1901), German physiologist, and Eugen Brodhun (b. 1860), "Experimentelle Untersuchungen über die psychophysische Fundamentalformel in Bezug auf den Gesichtssinn," *Sitzungsberichte* (Berlin), 1888, no. 37, pp. 917–931.

512.28 Delbœuf] James's account of Delbœuf's work and of the criticisms of it by Alfred Lehmann and Hjalmar Neiglick seems based on Wundt, *Grundzüge*, 3rd ed., I, 362–363. Wundt provides references.

512.32 Lehmann] Alfred Georg Ludwig Lehmann (1858–1921), Danish psychologist, "Über die Anwendung der Methode der mittleren Abstufungen auf den Lichtsinn," *Philosophische Studien*, 3 (1886), 497–533. Preserved is *Die Hauptgesetze des menschlichen Gefühlslebens* (Leipzig: O. R. Reisland, 1892) (WJ 749.39). James in the *Psychological Review*, 3 (1896), 113, discusses a review of Lehmann's book. He treats Lehmann's work on telepathy in the *Psychological Review*, 3 (1896), 98–99, and in three letters to *Science*: n.s. 8 (1898), 956; n.s. 9 (1899), 654–655, 752–753.

512.38 Dobrowolsky] Wundt, *Grundzüge*, 3rd ed., I, 364, provides references to the works of W. Dobrowolsky (Vladislav Ivanovich Dobrovolski [b. 1838]) and S. Lamansky (unidentified).

513.8 Jastrow] Joseph Jastrow, "The Psycho-Physic Law and Star Magnitudes," *American Journal of Psychology*, 1 (November 1887), 112–127. Jastrow uses tables compiled by Edward Charles Pickering (1846–1919), American astronomer, director of the Harvard observatory.

513.25 Weber] Wundt, 3rd ed., I, 367, gives a similar account of Weber's results.

513.31 Hering's] This account of work in Ewald Hering's laboratory seems based on pp. 189–204 of G. E. Müller (see below).

513.40 Müller] Georg Elias Müller, *Zur Grundlegung der Psychophysik. Kritische Beiträge* (Berlin: T. B. Grieben, 1878), pp. 189–204. An annotated copy was sold.

514.15 Müller] Pp. 205–217 (secs. 74–80).

514.37 *American*] Joseph Jastrow, an untitled contribution to the "Studies from the Laboratory of Experimental Psychology of the University of Wisconsin," *American Journal of Psychology*, 3 (January 1890), 43–58.

516.28 Stumpf] The quotation is from I, 399.

516.31 Kries] Johannes von Kries, "Über die Messung intensiver Grössen und über das sogenannte psychophysische Gesetz," *Vierteljahrsschrift*, 6 (1882), 257–294.

516.34 Tannery] Jules Tannery (1848–1910), French mathematician, writing to Émile Alglave, in Delbœuf, *Éléments de psychophysique*, pp. 132–139.

516.34 Ward] See note to 468.37.

516.35 *Metaphysic*] Pp. 453–455.

516.36 Brentano] In his copy of the *Psychologie*, on p. 9, James refers to p. 88, while on p. 88, to p. 9.

516.36 Merkel] See note to 512.2.

517.28 Delbœuf] See for example *Éléments de psychophysique*, p. 65.

517.28 Bernstein] In "An Attempt to Interpret Fechner's Law" (see note to 468.37), Ward discusses the notion of irradiation in the writings of Julius Bernstein (1839–1917), German physiologist.

517.30 Ebbinghaus] Hermann Ebbinghaus (1850–1909), German psychologist, "Über den Grund der Abweichungen von dem Weber'schen Gesetz bei Lichtempfindungen," *Archiv für Physiologie*, 45 (April 1889), 113–133.

518.13 'idol] Francis Bacon, *The New Organon*, bk. I, p. 42.

518.29 "And] From "The Battle of Blenheim" by Robert Southey (1774–1843), English poet and historian, *The Poetical Works of Robert Southey*, VI (Boston: Little, Brown, 1863), 140.

520.18 Renouvier] Charles Renouvier, *Traité de logique générale*, 2nd ed., 3 vols. (Paris: Bureau de la *Critique Philosophique*, 1875) (WJ 765.61.2), II,

493–516, appendix to ch. 40 titled "Sur les facultés humaines et l'association des idées." This work is the first of the *Essais de critique générale*.

521.38 Locke] James could be referring to bk. II, ch. 33 of the *Essay* (pp. 283–288).

522.9 Hartley] See p. 529n.

524.36 " 'Lost] From Tennyson's "The Ancient Sage," *The Works of Alfred Lord Tennyson*, p. 551.

525.25 Valentin] The remark was not found in several works of Gabriel Gustav Valentin.

526.21–22 Cattell] James McKeen Cattell, "The Time It Takes to See and Name Objects," *Mind*, 11 (January 1886), 63–65. James omits paragraph numbering.

526.39 *Physiologische*] 2nd ed.

526.41 Galton] Section on "Psychometric Experiments."

526.41 Trautscholdt] Martin Trautscholdt (b. 1855), "Experimentelle Untersuchungen über die Association der Vorstellungen," *Philosophische Studien*, 1 (1882), 213–250. The work was done in Wundt's laboratory.

528.1 Cattell] James McKeen Cattell, "Experiments on the Association of Ideas," *Mind*, 12 (January 1887), 68–74. The association times are on p. 72, the averages and the quotation on p. 71.

528.20 Webers] Wundt (2nd ed., II, 286) cites Wilhelm Eduard Weber and Eduard Friedrich Wilhelm Weber, *Mechanik der menschlichen Gehwerkzeuge* (Göttingen, 1836), pp. 77, 254.

528.31 Tschisch] Woldemar von Tschisch, "Über die Zeitdauer der einfachen psychischen Vorgänge bei Geisteskranken," *Neurologisches Centralblatt*, 4 (May 15, 1885), 217–219. This periodical was edited by E. Mendel.

528.41 Walitzky] Marie Walitzky, "Contribution à l'étude des mensurations psychométriques chez les aliénés," *Revue Philosophique*, 28 (December 1889), 583–595. Walitzky transliterates Tschisch's name as Tchige.

529.31 *Senses*] 3rd ed.

529.32 Hartley's] David Hartley, *Observations on Man, His Frame, His Duty, and His Expectations*, 2 vols. (London, 1749), I, 65.

530.31 Münsterberg] On p. 132 of his copy of the *Beiträge*, pt. I (1889), James has: "Why can't the just past moments be equally well reproduciert?"

530.34 Ward] "Psychology," p. 61. On p. 61 of his copy, next to the quoted text, James has: "association is only of *successives*."

531.24 Descartes] In his index to *Les Passions*, James has "Association 180," a reference to pt. II, article 136.

531.34 *Essay*] P. 284.

531.36 " 'Twou'd] *Treatise*, I, 364–365 (bk. I, pt. II, sec. 5).

532.39 *Op.*] *Observations*, I, 67 (pt. I, ch. 1, sec. 2, prop. 11).

534.38 "I] *The Works of Alfred Lord Tennyson*, pp. 101, 102.

536.38 *Senses*] 3rd ed.

537.4 Hamilton] *Lectures on Metaphysics and Logic*, II, 238. See also note to 559.35.

538.7 Austen's] The quoted text appears in *Emma* (Boston: Houghton, Mifflin, c1957), p. 132.

539.34 *Time*] Pp. 266-267.

539.34 Coleridge] Samuel Taylor Coleridge, *Biographia Literaria; or, Biographical Sketches of My Literary Life and Opinions*, I (New York: Wiley & Putnam, 1847), 244 (conclusion of ch. 7).

540.7 resolution] A resolution offered by Thomas Francis Bayard (1828–1898), Democratic senator from Delaware.

540.30 Hobbes] Since later (p. 553), James refers to *Leviathan* by the date of the first edition (1651), the first edition is used in the present notes. The text quoted is found on p. 9.

541.5 Hodgson] *Time and Space*, pp. 267-268.

541.34 Göring's] In a letter dated Leipzig, December 27, [1879], Granville Stanley Hall mentions the suicide of Carl Theodor Göring (1841–1879), German philosopher (Perry, II, 18). James's copy of the *System der kritischen Philosophie* (1874–1875) is unknown.

543.18 Dumas] Earlier translations of Alexandre Dumas (1802–1870), *Les Trois mousquetaires* appeared under the title *The Three Guardsmen.*

543.38 Wahle] See note to 467.28.

544.21 Hamilton] *Lectures on Metaphysics and Logic*, I, 352–353.

545.37 Ehrenfels] Christian von Ehrenfels (1859–1932), Austrian philosophical writer, "Über 'Gestaltqualitäten'," *Vierteljahrsschrift*, 14 (1890), 249–292.

545.40 Höffding] Harald Höffding (1843–1931), Danish philosopher, "Zur Theorie des Wiedererkennens. Eine Replik," *Philosophische Studien*, 8 (1892), 86–96. For the relations between James and Höffding consult the notes to James's Preface to Höffding's *Problems of Philosophy*, reprinted in *Essays in Philosophy*, WORKS. In his letter to Höffding of October 23, 1893 (bMS Am 1092.9 [999]), James responded to the charge of inconsistency: "I cannot admit that I am inconsistent. I believe that the only associations by similarity that exist are those where the resemblance *is* compound. Between simple qualities I see no ground for supposing that association by similarity takes place. One degree of heat as such doesn't remind us of another degree of heat as such, though it may recall the total situation where we experienced the other heat, and then, secondarily, *that*." James continues with a reference to the Ehrenfels paper.

547.25 Hobbes's] See pp. 559–560.

548.10 Bagehot] Walter Bagehot (1826–1877), British economist and essayist, *Physics and Politics; or, Thoughts on the Application of the Principles of 'Natural Selection' and 'Inheritance' to Political Society* (1872; rpt. New

Notes

York: D. Appleton, 1879), p. 120.

548.14 Stephen] Perhaps James Fitzjames Stephen (1829–1894), English jurist, but the remark was not found.

548.20 Lowell's] James Russell Lowell (1819–1891), American poet and essayist, *Among My Books* (Boston: Fields, Osgood, 1870), p. 293, from the essay "Lessing."

553.38 *Leviathan*] Pt. I, ch. 3.

554.4 "The] *The Theory of Practice*, I, 394–395.

554.34 Bain] 3rd ed., pp. 376–377.

555.24 Mill] *A System of Logic*, bk. III, ch. 8, "Of the Four Methods of Experimental Inquiry," I, 448–471. On I, 448, James comments: "Mill treats these as if they were mainly methods of *discovering* causes. 9 times out of 10 they are used merely for *testing* causes hypothetically conceived."

556.30 Rabier] *Leçons de philosophie*, I, 187ff.

556.30 Paulhan] Frédéric Paulhan, "À propos du rapport de ressemblance," *Critique Philosophique*, 2nd series, vol. 1 (1885), pp. 458–460.

556.31 Rabier] Élie Rabier, "À propos de l'association par ressemblance," *Critique Philosophique*, 2nd series, vol. 1 (1885), pp. 460–466.

556.31 Pillon] François Pillon (1830–1914), French philosopher, "Reponse aux observations de M. Rabier sur l'association par ressemblance," *Critique Philosophique*, 2nd series, vol. 2 (1885), pp. 55–66. The correspondence between James and Pillon is at Houghton (bMS Am 1092.9 [470–482, 3494–3514]).

556.33 Wahle] See note to 467.28.

556.34 McCosh] James McCosh (1811–1894), Scottish-born philosopher, *Psychology: The Cognitive Powers* (New York: Charles Scribner's Sons, 1886), p. 130.

558.37 Bain] While Bain begins the discussion on p. 564 of *The Senses and the Intellect*, 3rd ed., the sentence paraphrased by James is found on p. 566.

558.37 Mill's] 2nd ed., II, 199n–200n.

559.25 "By] *Leviathan*, pp. 8–10.

559.35 Hamilton's] Appendix D**, pp. 889–910 of *The Works of Thomas Reid*, is titled "Contribution towards a History of the Doctrine of Mental Suggestion or Association," and Appendix D***, pp. 910–914 (in this edition, the appendix is incomplete and breaks off in mid-sentence), "Outline of a Theory of Mental Reproduction, Suggestion or Association." Hamilton claims that Aristotle originated the doctrine of association and cites Aristotle's *De Memoria et Reminiscentia*, 451b–452a, and other writings.

559.36 Ferri] Luigi Ferri (1826–1895), Italian philosopher, *La Psychologie de l'association depuis Hobbes jusqu'à nos jours (Histoire et critique)* (Paris: Baillière, 1883).

559.36 Robertson] George Croom Robertson, "Association of Ideas," *Encyclopædia Britannica*, 9th ed., II (New York: Samuel L. Hall, 1878), 730–

734 (*Philosophical Remains*, pp. 102-118).

562.11 Priestley] Joseph Priestley (1733-1804), English clergyman and scientist, *Hartley's Theory of the Human Mind, on the Principle of the Association of Ideas; with Essays Relating to the Subject of It*, 2nd ed. (London, 1790), p. xxvii of the Introductory Essays. James reverses the order of the two passages.

562.17 Ribot] Théodule Ribot, *La Psychologie anglaise contemporaine (École expérimentale)* (Paris: Ladrange, 1870), pp. 242-244. James is not using the available English translation (London: Henry S. King, 1873).

562.35 *Treatise*] I, 319-321.

565.32 Mill] John Stuart Mill in an unsigned review of Bain's *The Senses and the Intellect* and *The Emotions and the Will*, in the *Edinburgh Review*, 110 (October 1859), 287-321; reprinted in *Dissertations and Discussions: Political, Philosophical, and Historical*, IV (New York: Henry Holt, 1874), 101-156.

565.35 *Principles*] *The Principles of Psychology*, pt. II, ch. 8 (I, 259-271). The quotation is from an earlier chapter on "The Associability of Feelings," I, 256-257 (sec. 115).

566.5 Mill] John Stuart Mill, see especially his note 35 to James Mill's *Analysis* (2nd ed., I, 111n-114n).

568.31 *Time*] *Time and Space*, ch. 5 (pp. 256-294) on "Spontaneous Redintegration"; *The Theory of Practice*, I, 367-445.

568.32 *Psychologie*] James perhaps has in mind the second part of volume I (1824), "Grundlinien der Statik des Geistes" (I, 158-243), but similar discussions can be found throughout both volumes.

568.33 Ribot] *La Psychologie allemande contemporaine*, ch. 1 (pp. 1-34) on "Les Origines: Herbart."

568.34 Beneke] Friedrich Eduard Beneke (1798-1854), German philosopher.

568.35 Stout] George Frederick Stout, "The Herbartian Psychology," *Mind*, 13 (July 1888), 321-338; (October 1888), 473-498.

568.36 Morell's] John Daniel Morell (1816-1891), English philosopher, *An Introduction to Mental Philosophy, on the Inductive Method* (London: Longman, Green, Longman, and Roberts, 1862). The title used in the present text represents a change from James's title of *Outlines of Mental Philosophy*. The latter title appears on the spine of the Widener copy, still in its original binding, but not on the title page. Furthermore, while using the 1862 date, James cites the second edition, but no evidence was found that a second edition was published in that year.

568.38 *Grundtatsachen*] Ch. 6 (pp. 96-125) is titled "Von der Verknüpfung der Vorstellungen."

568.40 Steinthal's] Heyman Steinthal (1823-1899), German philosopher and linguist, *Einleitung in die Psychologie und Sprachwissenschaft*, 2nd ed. (Berlin: Dümmler, 1881). An annotated copy of this work was sold.

568.42 Glogau] Gustav Glogau (1844-1895), German philosopher, *Stein-*

thals psychologische Formeln zusammenhängend entwickelt (Berlin: Dümmler, 1876).

569.24 *Leçons*] I, 183–197.

569.25 Bradley] Bk. II, pt. II, ch. 1 (pp. 273–321) is titled "The Theory of Association of Ideas." On p. 281 of his copy of *The Principles of Logic*, where in reference to the doctrine of redintegration Bradley writes, "Given any presentation X, which has a content such as . . . *a b c d e* . . . , it asserts that the oneness of this presentation is in a certain sense a connection of its content," James comments: "Yes, but in what sense? The associationists say in a mere juxtapositional sense, and Bradley makes no attempt to disprove this. What is connected, whether universals or particulars, is of secondary importance in the debate, tho' B. puts it first. The *manner* of connection, whether inward or outward, is the real question." Attached by a guideline to '*manner*', James adds references to pp. 380, 420, 448. On p. 287, James comments: "In other words the associationist really believes in universals and works with them just as Bradley does. How perverse then are the latters tactics in pinning him down to an outside metaphysical theory of nominalism, which *as associationist* he is in no way bound to, instead of simply accepting his description of the association *phenomena* and reformulating & interpreting them so as to bring out emphatically the implication of universals etc. wh. they contain."

573.7 "Le] Quoted by Hodgson in *Time and Space*, p. 105, without a source.

573.15 Clay] *The Alternative: A Study in Psychology* (London: Macmillan, 1882), pp. 167–169; published anonymously, but usually attributed to Edmund R. Clay.

573.21 Herbart] II, 153.

573.34 Wundt] In his copy of the *Grundzüge*, 1st ed., p. 682, James asks: "Errinerungsbild und associationsbild sind also zweierlei?"

574.29 *Essay*] Pp. 109, 125.

574.29 Reid] *The Works of Thomas Reid*, pp. 348–349.

574.40 Royer-Collard] Pierre Paul Royer-Collard (1763–1845), French statesman and philosopher, "Fragments des leçons de M. Royer-Collard," in *Œuvres complètes de Thomas Reid, chef de l'école écossaise*, ed. Théodore Jouffroy, 2nd ed., IV (Paris: Sautelet, 1828), 363. From the list of page numbers in back, it is clear that James used the copy of volume IV now in Widener (Phil 2240.20).

576.39 *Physiologische*] 2nd ed. Wundt retains the '5 groups' in the third edition (II, 77).

577.25 Estel] Volkmar Estel (b. 1858), working in Wundt's laboratory at Leipzig, "Neue Versuche über den Zeitsinn," *Philosophische Studien*, 2 (1883), 37–65. In his set of the *Philosophische Studien* (WJ 140.70), in vol. 2, p. 50, James has: "Explained by Mehner als accidental results due to insufficient practice."

577.25 Mehner] Max Mehner (b. 1857), working in Wundt's laboratory, "Zur Lehre vom Zeitsinn," *Philosophische Studien*, 2 (1885), 546–602.

577.29 *Ibid.*] 2nd ed.

577.30 *Philosophische*] See note to 385.37.

577.42 Wundt] 2nd ed.

578.10 Savart's] A toothed wheel for producing tones the pitch of which varies with the speed of rotation invented by Félix Savart (1791–1841), French physicist.

578.35 Pflüger's] Pp. 415–420 (see note to 94.2).

578.42 Hall] Granville Stanley Hall and Joseph Jastrow, "Studies of Rhythm," *Mind*, 11 (January 1886), 55–62.

579.26 Gruenhagen] Alfred Wilhelm Gruenhagen, "Versuche über intermittirende Nervenreizung," *Archiv für Physiologie*, 6 (August 1872), 157–181.

579.28 Wittich] Wilhelm Heinrich von Wittich (1821–1884), German physiologist, "Bemerkungen zu Preyers Abhandlung über die Grenzen des Empfindungsvermögens und Willens," *Archiv für Physiologie*, 2 (1869), 329–350. James rounds off the figures.

579.29 Preyer] Wilhelm Thierry Preyer (1842–1897), German physiologist, *Über die Grenzen des Empfindungsvermögens und des Willens* (Bonn: Adolph Marcus, 1868) (WJ 772.25), p. 15. In his copy, on a flyleaf, James writes: "This paper is replied to by *v*. Wittich Pflügers Archiv Bd. 2 1869 p. 329. Between 1000 & 2000 contacts are discriminated by the finger. He found no summation of effects in rapidly interrupted irritations of muscle nerve (Tetanus is the reverse of irritation)[.] Lalanne (Ctes rendus LXXXII, p. 1314) found summation of finger contacts after 13 or 22 repetitions [*illegible*]. The question of summation is treated by Grünhagen (Pflug. Arch. VI) 1872. He finds it when the irritations are very similar = current weak. Says that Tongue can discriminate 10000 shocks a second as interrupted. Heidenhain (Studien d. phys Inst. etc. 1861 also found summation. Engelmann (Pflug. Arch. IV p. 3 1871) H. M. p. 275 seems to have found just what Grünhagen had. See also Brücke H. M. 1861 p. 381. H. M. 1861, 360, 361[;] 1863, 362. 1868 380 p. 81. 1869 256." In addition to papers cited in *Principles*, James is referring to Rudolf Heidenhain (see note to 90.39), "Die Erregbarkeit der Nerven an verschiednen Puncten ihres Verlaufes," *Studien des physiologischen Instituts zu Breslau*, 1 (1861), 1–66 and to Theodor Wilhelm Engelmann (1843–1909), German physiologist, "Beiträge zur allgemeinen Muskel- und Nervenphysiologie," pt. 3, *Archiv für Physiologie*, 4 (1871), 3–33. The 'H.M.' references have not been interpreted.

579.31 Mach] Ernst Mach, "Untersuchungen über den Zeitsinn des Ohres," *Sitzungsberichte* (Vienna), vol. 51, pt. 2 (1865), pp. 133–150.

579.32 Lalanne] Léon Louis Chrétien Lalanne (1811–1892), French scientist, "Sur la durée de la sensation tactile," *Comptes Rendus Hebdomadaires des Séances de l'Académie des Sciences* (Paris), 82 (1876), 1314–1316.

579.39 Pflüger's] See notes to 94.2 and 100.39.

579.41 Tigerstedt] Robert Adolf Armand Tigerstedt (1853–1923), Swedish physiologist, "Über den kleinsten subjectiv merkbaren Unterschied zwischen Reactionszeiten," *Bihang till Kongl. Svenska Vetenskaps-Akademiens Hand-*

Notes

lingar, vol. 8, pt. 2 (1884). Each paper is paged separately.

580.38 *Mind*] Pp. 61–62 (see note to 578.42).

580.39 Estel] See note to 577.25.

580.39 Mehner] See note to 577.25.

580.40 Fechner] Gustav Theodor Fechner, "In Sachen des Zeitsinnes und der Methode der richtigen und falschen Fälle, gegen Estel und Lorenz," *Philosophische Studien*, 3 (1885), 1–37.

581.12 Kollert] Julius Kollert, work done in Wundt's laboratory, "Untersuchungen über den Zeitsinn," *Philosophische Studien*, 1 (1881), 78–89.

581.13 Estel] Pp. 56–57.

581.14 Mehner] P. 595.

581.15 Stevens] Lewis Tebbetts Stevens, "On the Time-Sense," *Mind*, 11 (July 1886), 393–404.

581.23 American] On p. 393, Stevens states that his seven subjects responded by tapping a lever and that his results were confirmed by experiments in the Physiological Laboratory of Henry P. Bowditch in the Harvard Medical School.

581.26 Glass] Richard Glass (b. 1860), "Kritisches und Experimentelles über den Zeitsinn," *Philosophische Studien*, 4 (1887), 423–456. The figures are found on p. 454. In his set of the *Philosophische Studien* (WJ 140.70), James commented critically upon the Glass article.

581.35 *Physiologische*] 2nd ed.

581.38 *Physiologische*] 2nd ed. On p. 286 of his copy, James has "See p. 290."

581.41 *Loc.*] See note to 579.31. Because Mach does not use 'indifference-point', it is not certain which of Mach's figures James is trying to use. He could have derived his figure from data given by Mach on p. 144. However, on p. 142, Mach estimates the "Unterschiedsempfindlichkeit" as .375. This notion is viewed by Edwin G. Boring, *Sensation and Perception in the History of Experimental Psychology* (New York: Appleton, Century, Crofts, °1942), pp. 577–578, as comparable to the indifference-point.

581.42 *Op.*] James is drawing his own conclusions from a table given by Buccola.

582.6 Glass] P. 446.

582.37 *Physiologische*] 2nd ed.

582.37 Hall] See note to 578.42.

583.18 "to] From Tennyson's "The Mystic," one of the suppressed poems, *The Poems of Tennyson*, ed. Christopher Ricks (London: Longmans, 1969), p. 230.

583.37 Wundt] See p. 599.

583.38 P. 19] On p. 19 of his copy of *Der Zeitsinn*, James has a reference to p. 77. Sec. 18 is on pp. 77–83. On the back flyleaf James has: "Adäquate geschwindigkeit der successiven Eindrücke # 18." On p. 112, James has: "i.e. the further back in memory short times lie the longer they seem."

584.18 *Beiträge*] Pp. 1-68 on the "Zeitsinn."

585.22 Hodgson's] See p. 572n.

586.27 *Psychology*] II, 208.

587.12 Holtei's] Karl von Holtei (1798-1880), German poet, playwright, and novelist, *Die Vagabunden* (1851).

587.19 Lazarus] Moritz Lazarus (1824-1903), German philosopher and psychologist, *Ideale Fragen in Reden und Vorträgen* (Berlin: A. Hofmann, 1878), pp. 218-219. The Widener copy (Phil 186.4), acquired May 22, 1880, contains a list of page numbers in back in James's hand, "176, 7, 181, 202, 213, Qu 218-9."

587.42 Du Prel] Carl Ludwig Du Prel (1839-1899), German occultist and philosophical writer, *The Philosophy of Mysticism*, trans. C. C. Massey, 2 vols. (London: George Redway, 1889), I, 87-112, "The Transcendental Measure of Time." James's copy was given to Widener, but has not been found. Additional works by Du Prel from James's library will be listed in the volume of manuscript remains.

588.27 Janet] Paul Janet (1823-1899), French philosopher, "Une Illusion d'optique interne," *Revue Philosophique*, 3 (1877), 497-502. The quotation is from p. 497. Works by Janet from James's library will be listed in the volume of manuscript remains.

589.41 Herbart] II, 155.

590.2 Volkmann] W. Volkmann von Volkmar, *Lehrbuch der Psychologie*, II, 26.

590.34 Romanes] George John Romanes, "Consciousness of Time," *Mind*, 3 (July 1878), 297-303.

590.35 Sully] James is referring to ch. 10, pt. 1 on "Illusions of Time-Perspective" and a portion of ch. 11 on "misrepresentation of future duration."

590.35-36 *Physiologische*] 2nd ed.

590.37 Volkmann's] W. Volkmann von Volkmar, II, 27-36. James's reference to note 3 could be an error for note 2.

590.39 Lindner] Gustav Adolph Lindner (1828-1887), Czechoslovakian psychologist, *Lehrbuch der empirischen Psychologie, als inductiver Wissenschaft*, 3rd ed. (Vienna: Carl Gerold's Sohn, 1872), p. 91.

592.27 Ward] See note to 164.26.

592.37 *Lehrbuch*] II, 12.

592.37 Lotze] *Metaphysik*, pp. 294-296. On p. 294 of his copy, James writes: "Das wissende Subject muss doch zeitlos sein."

594.26 Volkmann] W. Volkmann von Volkmar, II, 14.

595.5 Herbart's] *Psychologie als Wissenschaft*, II, 157; *Lehrbuch zur Psy-*

chologie (Königsberg: Unzer, 1816), pp. 131 (secs. 171, 172), 133–134 (sec. 175) (pp. 131, 133–134 of the English translation).

595.10 Drobisch] Moritz Wilhelm Drobisch (1802–1896), German mathematician and philosopher, *Empirische Psychologie nach naturwissenschaftlicher Methode* (Leipzig: Voss, 1842), pp. 150–152.

595.13 Waitz] Pp. 578–604.

595.15 Volkmann's] W. Volkmann von Volkmar, II, 12–21.

595.30 Guyau's] Marie Jean Guyau (1854–1888), French philosopher, "L'Évolution de l'idée de temps dans la conscience," *Revue Philosophique*, 19 (1885), 353–368.

595.38 Ward] On p. 65 of his clipping, where Ward has: "Nevertheless after each distinct representation *a, b, c, d* there probably follows, as we have supposed, some trace of that movement of attention of which we are aware in passing from one presentation to another," attached by a guideline to 'follows', James writes: "between any two, he means, is represented." Attached to the first 'temporal signs' (595.49), James has the comment: "But they are themselves only feelings. The universe in which they lie is required to make them *successive* and not merely serial." Attached to '*a to b*' (596.16), James has: "This then is the original time sensation—why the d'l does he deny it to be felt as duration?"

596.9 Locke] Ward cites *Essay*, bk. II, ch. 14, secs. 9–12 (pp. 111–112 in James's edition).

596.48 "We] Pp. 65–66.

597.19 Stevens] See note to 581.15.

597.21 *Physiologische*] 2nd ed. The reference to the Webers is inserted by James into Wundt's text from Wundt's footnote. For the reference see note to 528.20.

597.41 *Beiträge*] The quotation is from pp. 105–106.

598.40 *Physiologische*] 2nd ed., II, 263–264.

600.37 Exner] See note to 100.39. Exner uses "primäre Gedächtnissbild."

600.37 Richet] See note to 89.39.

601.3 Baer] Karl Ernst von Baer (1792–1876), German naturalist, *Reden gehalten in wissenschaftlichen Versammlungen und kleinere Aufzätse vermischten Inhalts*, I (St. Petersburg: Schmitzdorff, 1864), 255–268.

601.38 *Psychology*] I, 216.

602.38 Grashey] Hubert G. Grashey (1839–1914), German physician, "Über Aphasie und ihre Beziehungen zur Wahrnehmung," *Archiv für Psychiatrie*, 16 (1885), 654–688. The quotation is from pp. 670, 672, 673.

606.34 Richet] See note to 89.39. James is combining two sentences which in Richet are separated by a paragraph.

607.30 Helmholtz] *Handbuch*, p. 358.

607.35 Fechner] Fechner's term is "Erinnerungsnachbilder." Fechner's account of the four characters of such after-images is found in *Elemente der Psychophysik*, II, 493–495.

608.39   Hermann's] Pp. 281–282 (see note to 100.39).

609.30   Richet] P. 583 (see note to 89.39).

609.42   Cattell] See note to 385.22. The figures are given on pp. 104 and 110.

610.25   Ladd's] In *Elements of Physiological Psychology*, pp. 480–481, Ladd summarizes the investigations of N. Baxt, from St. Petersburg, "Über die Zeit, welche nöthig ist, damit ein Gesichtseindruck zum Bewusstsein kommt und über die Grösse (Extension) der bewussten Wahrnehmung bei einem Gesichtseindrucke von gegebener Dauer," *Archiv für Physiologie*, 4 (1871), 325–336. Helmholtz presented Baxt's investigations to the Prussian Academy, see *Monatsberichte der königlich preussischen Akademie der Wissenschaften zu Berlin*, 1871, pp. 333–337.

613.34   *Psychologia*] *Psychologia Empirica*, p. 76.

613.35   *Analysis*] 2nd ed.

615.38   Bain] *Analysis*, 2nd ed., I, 323 (note 88).

615.42   *Analysis*] 2nd ed., I, 322–324.

622.23   Henkle] William Downs Henkle (1828–1881), American educator, "Remarkable Cases of Memory," *Journal of Speculative Philosophy*, 5 (January 1871), 6–26. Henkle describes the case of Daniel McCartney, then living in Ohio, born in 1817 in Pennsylvania.

625.26   Holbrook] Martin Luther Holbrook (1831–1902), American physician and author, *How to Strengthen the Memory; or, Natural and Scientific Methods of Never Forgetting* (New York: M. L. Holbrook, ᶜ1886). The Widener copy (Phil 5545.14) contains the page numbers 39–40, 68, 100 in James's hand.

625.36   Ebbinghaus] Hermann Ebbinghaus, *Über das Gedächtnis. Untersuchungen zur experimentellen Psychologie* (Leipzig: Duncker & Humblot, 1885), pp. 67, 45. Because Ebbinghaus does not discuss the training of memory, it is difficult to see to what James is referring. Perry reports that a marked copy of this work was sold with "forgetting [sec.] 26, [pp.] 67, 115" on the flyleaf, suggesting that '45' is an error for '115'. James reviewed the work in *Science*, "Experiments in Memory," 6 (September 4, 1885), 198–199.

626.15   Weed] Holbrook does not cite a source for his quotation from Thurlow Weed (1797–1882), American journalist and political figure. The text is found in Thurlow Weed Barnes, *Memoir of Thurlow Weed* (Boston: Houghton, Mifflin, 1884), pp. 26–27.

627.36   Burnham] William Henry Burnham (1855–1941), educator, attended Harvard College from 1878–1882; Edward Staples Drown, clergyman, Harvard College, 1880–1884, graduate school, 1887–1888; Charles Handy Baldwin, lawyer, Harvard College, 1884–1888; Edward Allen Pease, physician, Harvard College, 1884–1888, medical school, 1889–1891.

629.37   Pick] Edward Pick (1824–1899). The quoted text was not found in

Notes

Memory and Its Doctors (London: Trubner, 1888), nor in several other editions of this work. However, one of the copies examined was mutilated and the required pages were missing. The text can be found in Pick's *Lectures on Memory Culture* (New York: E. L. Kellogg, ᶜ1899), p. 13. In an undated preface to the *Lectures*, Pick cites the following by James: "Dr. Pick is a well-known authority on Memory. His lectures are based on solid psychological principles, and there is absolutely no element of charlatanry about them." For additional comments see *Talks to Teachers* (1899), pp. 128–129.

630.2 (Pick)] The text was not found in Pick. It is quoted by Holbrook, pp. 118–119, from an unidentified pamphlet published by Pick in 1862.

630.39 Evans] William Lemuel Evans, *Memory Training: A Complete and Practical System for Developing and Confirming the Memory Adapted to All Kinds of Subjects* (New York: A. S. Barnes, 1889).

631.17 Brierre] Taine, I, 78n, cites Alexandre Jacques François Brierre de Boismont (1797–1881), French scholar, *Des hallucinations ou histoire raisonnée des apparitions, des visions, des songes, de l'extase, des rêves, du magnétisme et du somnambulisme.* In James's annotated copy of this work in Widener, 3rd ed. (Paris: Baillière, 1862) (Phil 7060.14.3), the text quoted is found on p. 376. Also in Widener is an annotated copy of *Du suicide et de la folie suicide* (Paris: Baillière, 1865) (Phil 7150.1.2).

631.41 Paulhan] Frédéric Paulhan, *L'Activité mentale et les éléments de l'esprit* (Paris: Alcan, 1889), p. 70. Perry reports that a marked copy was sold. The copy in Widener (Phil 5255.2) is a gift from the author "through W. James." Paulhan cites no source for the reference to Jean Étienne Esquirol (1772–1840), French psychiatrist; on p. 70n, he cites Luys, *Études de physiologie*, p. 29.

634.20 *Psychology*] I, 450–451.

634.21 Höffding] Harald Höffding, *Psychologie in Umrissen auf Grundlage der Erfahrung*, trans. into German by F. Bendixen (Leipzig: Fues, 1887), p. 188; "Über Wiederkennen, Association und psychische Activität," *Vierteljahrsschrift*, 13 (1889), 420–458; 14 (1890), 27–54, 167–205, 293–316. Preserved is a copy of the English translation, *Outlines of Psychology*, trans. Mary E. Lowndes (London: Macmillan, 1891) (WJ 816.39).

634.31 Lehmann] Alfred Lehmann, "Über Wiedererkennen. Versuch einer experimentellen Bestätigung der Theorie der Vorstellungsassociationen," *Philosophische Studien*, 5 (1888), 96–156.

635.23 Brooke] James Brooke, Rajah of Sarawak (1803–1868), English adventurer.

636.14 Ebbinghaus] In his review of *Über das Gedächtnis* in *Science*, 6 (September 4, 1885), 198, James remarks: "To most people a north-pole expedition would be an easy task, compared with those ineffably tedious measurements of simple mental processes of which Ernst Heinrich Weber set the fashion some forty years ago." According to James, "Ebbinghaus makes an original addition to heroic psychological literature."

636.33 Proctor] Richard Anthony Proctor (1837–1888), British astronomer and popularizer of science, "Our Two Brains," *Knowledge: An Illustrated Magazine of Science Plainly Worded—Exactly Described*, 6 (November 28,

1884), 435-436 (an installment in a long series).

636.34 Ribot] Pp. 149-154.

636.36 *Zeitschrift*] Moritz Lazarus, "Zur Lehre von den Sinnestäuschungen," *Zeitschrift für Völkerpsychologie und Sprachwissenschaft*, 5 (1868), 113-152.

636.38 *Ibid.*] Pp. 74-79.

637.38 *Op.*] Pp. 103-104.

638.12 Ebbinghaus] Pp. 123-139.

638.29 Binet] See p. 202.

639.1 Wolfe] Joseph Jastrow, "Experimental Psychology in Leipzig," *Science*, 8 (November 19, 1886), 459-462, summarizes H. K. Wolfe, "Untersuchungen über das Tongedächtniss," *Philosophische Studien*, 3 (1886), 534-571.

640.40 *Essay*] P. 88.

641.14 Emerson] Perhaps a reference to Ralph Waldo Emerson, *Essays*, 1st series (Boston: Fields, Osgood, 1869) (*AC 85.J2376.Zz869e), p. 309, from the essay on the "Intellect." For other works by Emerson from James's library see the notes to James's "Address at the Emerson Centenary in Concord," *Essays in Religion and Morality*, WORKS.

641.40 Ribot] Pp. 45-46. James does not use the available English translation.

642.31 Carpenter's] *Principles of Mental Physiology*, pp. 437-438, from Samuel Taylor Coleridge, *Biographia Literaria*, 2 vols. (London: William Pickering, 1847), vol. I, pt. 2, pp. 117-119.

642.34 Ribot] In the English translation by William Huntington Smith, *Diseases of the Memory: An Essay in the Positive Psychology* (New York: D. Appleton, 1882), ch. 4 (pp. 174-191) is called "Exaltations of Memory."

642.36 girl] In "Notes on Automatic Writing," pp. 552-554 (see note to 206.39), James includes an account of the case of Anna Winsor. He does not refer to the writing out of an Ingoldsby Legend, one of a number of burlesque poems and stories by Richard Harris Barham (1788-1845), English clergyman and author.

643.33 Kussmaul] Adolf Kussmaul (1822-1902), German physician, *Die Störungen der Sprache. Versuch einer Pathologie der Sprache* (Leipzig: Vogel, 1877), p. 164 (vol. XII of the *Handbuch der speciellen Pathologie und Therapie*, ed. H. von Ziemssen). James's annotated copy is in Widener (Phil 5520.27.2).

643.34 *Lectures*] *Lectures on Metaphysics and Logic*, II, 211-212. James is quoting Hamilton's translation of Heinrich Johann Theodor Schmid (1799-1836), German philosopher, *Versuch einer Metaphysik der inneren Natur* (1834), pp. 231-235. Hamilton does not identify the edition, but the 1834 edition appears to be the only one of this work.

643.35 Delbœuf] Joseph Remi Léopold Delbœuf, *Le Sommeil et les rêves, considérés principalement dans leurs rapports avec les théories de la certitude et de la mémoire* (Paris: Baillière, 1885). James could be referring to pp. 119-

128, on "Le principe de la conservation de la force."

643.35 Verdon] R. Verdon, "Forgetfulness," *Mind*, 2 (October 1877), 437–452.

643.37 Maury] Louis Ferdinand Alfred Maury (1817–1892), French scholar, *Le Sommeil et les rêves: Études psychologiques sur ces phénomènes et les divers états qui s'y rattachent*, 3rd ed. (Paris: Didier, 1865), p. 442.

643.38 Ribot] Pp. 133–134.

644.33 Galton] Francis Galton, *English Men of Science: Their Nature and Nurture* (London: Macmillan, 1874), pp. 107–121.

644.36 *Op.*] In the English translation, ch. 3 (pp. 135–173) on "Partial Amnesia."

645.21 "When] "Forgetfulness," p. 450.

645.32 "Practically] "Forgetfulness," pp. 449–450.

645.34 Huber] Johann Nepomuk Huber (1830–1879), German philosopher, *Das Gedächtniss* (Munich, 1878), pp. 36ff., pt. II of Huber's *Psychologische Studien*.

647.24 Ladd] *Elements of Physiological Psychology*, pp. 556–558. James adds some italics and ignores paragraph divisions. In his copy, on p. 556, James underlines the phrase 'psycho-physics *can*' and in the margin writes "?!!"

649.24 Burnham] William Henry Burnham, "Memory, Historically and Experimentally Considered," *American Journal of Psychology*, 2 (November 1888), 39–90; (February 1889), 225–270; (May 1889), 431–464; (August 1889), 568–622.

649.25 Kay's] David Kay, British geographer and writer, *Memory: What It Is and How to Improve It* (New York: D. Appleton, 1888).

649.26 Fauth's] Franz Fauth (b. 1841), German educator, *Das Gedächtnis. Studie zu einer Pädagogik auf dem Standpunkt der heutigen Physiologie und Psychologie* (Gütersloh: C. Bertelsmann, 1888).

652.44 Herbart] See Johann Friedrich Herbart, *Allgemeine Metaphysik, nebst den Anfängen der philosophischen Naturlehre*, II (Königsberg: Unzer, 1829), 209.

652.45 Meinong] Alexius Meinong (1853–1920), Austrian philosopher, "Über Begriff und Eigenschaften der Empfindung," *Vierteljahrsschrift*, 12 (1888), 324–354, 477–502; 13 (1880), 1–31. For James's comments on this paper see *Essays in Philosophy*, WORKS, p. 87n.

653.29 Condillac's] Étienne Bonnot, Abbé de Condillac (1715–1780), French philosopher. James could be referring to Condillac's *Traité des sensations*, pt. I, ch. 11, sec. 1. Widener preserves the *Œuvres philosophiques de Condillac*, 6 vols. in 2 (Paris: Dufart, 1795) (Phil 2493.21), from the library of Henry James, Sr., given together with James's books.

653.37 Bernstein's] Julius Bernstein, *The Five Senses of Man* (New York: D. Appleton, 1876).

653.39 Hermann's] Vol. III of Hermann's *Handbuch* is titled *Handbuch der Physiologie der Sinnesorgane*, 2 pts. (1879–1880).

654.16 Seth] Andrew Seth Pringle-Pattison (1856–1931), Scottish philosopher, *Scottish Philosophy: A Comparison of the Scottish and German Answers to Hume* (Edinburgh: William Blackwood and Sons, 1885), p. 89: "It is misleading, therefore, to speak as if we ever reached, in actual life, the sensations which we postulate as the signs or occasions of our perceptions." On p. 89 of the Widener copy (Phil 1818.1), where Seth says "we never see colour without seeing it extended," James comments: "after-image is not extended." Seth's letters to James are at Houghton (bMS Am 1092, letters 985–1004). Works by Seth from James's library will be listed in the volume of manuscript remains.

654.18 Dewey] Italics are James's. The text quoted as well as the whole discussion to which it belongs does not appear in the revised (1889) edition of Dewey's *Psychology*.

654.19 Green] Thomas Hill Green, "Mr. Herbert Spencer and Mr. G. H. Lewes: Their Application of the Doctrine of Evolution to Thought," pt. 2 "Mr. Spencer on the Independence of Matter," *Contemporary Review*, 31 (March 1878), 745–769. James's annotated set of the *Contemporary Review* is in Widener (P 141.10). Green, *Prolegomena to Ethics*, pp. 49–51.

654.34 Hering] See note to 414.29.

655.25 Reid] *Essays on the Intellectual Powers of Man*, essay II, chapter 11 (*The Works of Thomas Reid*, p. 291).

655.35 Bain] *The Emotions and the Will*, 3rd ed., p. 568.

656.25 Bradley's] *The Principles of Logic*, pp. 80–81 (bk. I, ch. 2, sec. 42). On pp. 80–81 of his copy, James comments: "Reality according to B. is something we 'directly encounter', 'are in contact with', etc., 'have' as a fact (81) etc. It 'appears' in our presentation, whose 'thisness' is an 'aspect' (67) of its content, to be analyzed out in an idea. But 'this' tho also an idea (77) seems to be the 'hole' (70) of exit, the bridge between all other ideas & reality."

656.37 *Essay*] *Essay*, pp. 213, 200. On p. 213 of his copy, on top of the page, James has: "Relations 'terminate' in what? (200) idea here = conception." Next to sec. 9 he lists pp. 200, 256, 273, 191, 254.

656.38 *Op.*] *Essay*, p. 64. In the margin next to the quoted passage, James has "N. B. 526[,] 74."

658.33 Martineau] James Martineau, *A Study of Religion: Its Sources and Contents* (Oxford: Clarendon, 1888) (WJ 553.78), pp. 192–194.

658.34 Bradley] *The Principles of Logic*, pp. 40–108, "The Categorical and Hypothetical Forms of Judgment."

658.35 "Sense] Ralph Cudworth (1617–1688), English philosopher, *A Treatise Concerning Eternal and Immutable Morality* (London: James and John Knapton, 1731), pp. 85–86.

658.43 *Anaxagoras*] Cudworth in a note quotes a text from Aristotle's *De Anima*, 429^a (bk. III, ch. 4) which, according to Aristotle, expresses a view held by Anaxagoras.

659.12 *Plotinus*] Cudworth cites Plotinus' *De Sensu et Memoria*, ch. 2, that is, ch. 2 of the 6th tractate of the 4th of the *Enneads.*

659.16 *Sense*] Cudworth, pp. 90–91.

659.25 Malebranche] Nicolas de Malebranche, *Entretiens sur la métaphysique*, in *Œuvres de Malebranche*, I (Paris: Charpentier, 1871), 44–45, 47 (WJ 653.49).

659.48 Green] *Prolegomena to Ethics*, pp. 23, 31.

660.17 "Introduction"] "Introduction" to Hume's *Treatise*, I, 125, 153.

660.29 Caird's] *A Critical Account of the Philosophy of Kant*; the quotation is found on p. 394.

660.34–35 *Contemporary*] See note to 654.19. The second excerpt is found on pp. 749–750.

660.37 *Prolegomena*] Pp. 48, 51.

660.39 *Mind*] "On the Function of Cognition," *Mind*, 10 (1885), 27–44; reprinted in *The Meaning of Truth*, WORKS.

660.40 Hobbes's] For the English translation of the complete passage see *The Meaning of Truth*, WORKS, note to 14.30; from the *Elementorum Philosophiæ. Sectio Prima. De Corpore*, pt. IV, ch. 25, sec. 5.

660.42 Mill] *An Examination of Sir William Hamilton's Philosophy*, 4th ed., p. 6, from ch. 2 on "The Relativity of Human Knowledge."

660.42 *Senses*] 3rd ed.

660.43 *Emotions*] 3rd ed. James's index contains "Relativity 551, 568–70–2."

660.43 *Logic*] Alexander Bain, *Logic*, pt. I, *Deduction* (London: Longmans, Green, Reader, & Dyer, 1870), p. 2.

661.20 Bain] Alexander Bain, *Mind and Body. The Theories of Their Relation*, 2nd ed. (London: Henry S. King, 1873), p. 81. James's edition is not identified.

661.36 Hamilton] *Lectures on Metaphysics and Logic*, lecture 9 (I, 153–167), "Explication of Terms—Relativity of Human Knowledge."

661.36 Spencer] On p. 719 of his copy of Spencer's "Replies to Criticisms" (see note to 152.35), James comments: "This is just what Sp. does in his discussion of the 'relativity' of knowledge. Finding so many anomalies in our apparent cognitions he concludes that there is no such thing as cognition at all." Pt. I, ch. 4 (pp. 68–97) of Spencer's *First Principles* deals with "The Relativity of All Knowledge."

662.39 Delabarre] Edmund Burke Delabarre (1863–1945), American psychologist, a graduate student at Harvard in 1888–1890. In his "A Student's Impressions of James in the Late '80's," *Psychological Review*, 50 (January 1943), 125–127, Delabarre does not refer to this collaboration.

663.31 Preyer] Wilhelm Thierry Preyer, "Über den Farben- und Temperatur-Sinn mit besonderer Rücksicht auf Farbenblindheit," *Archiv für Physiologie*, 25 (1881), 31–100.

667.37   Hering] See note to 414.29.

668.22   Hering] Pp. 24–28.

669.10   *Meyer's*] In the *Handbuch*, p. 398, Helmholtz cites the work of H. Meyer, "Über Contrast- oder Complementarfarben," *Annalen der Physik und Chemie*, 95 (1855), 170–171.

669.29   Hering] Ewald Hering, "Über die Theorie des simultanen Contrastes von Helmholtz," *Archiv für Physiologie*, 40 (1887), 172–191; 41 (1887), 1–29, 358–367.

673.33   Exner] Sigmund Exner, "Über eine neue Urtheils-Täuschung im Gebiete des Gesichtssinnes," *Archiv für Physiologie*, 37 (1885), 520–522; the quotation is from p. 521.

673.39   Delabarre] Edmund Burke Delabarre, "Colored Shadows," *American Journal of Psychology*, 2 (August 1889), 636–643. According to a note on p. 636, the paper was written for the "Graduate Course in Psychology" at Harvard, thus for Philosophy 20a for 1888–1889, "Questions in Psychology (with laboratory work).—Lectures.—Study of special subjects by the students."

674.37   Hering] Ewald Hering, "Über den Begriff 'Urtheilstäuschung' in der physiologischen Optik und über die Wahrnehmung simultaner und successiver Helligkeitsunterschiede," *Archiv für Physiologie*, 41 (1887), 91–106.

674.38   *Die*] Johannes von Kries, *Die Gesichts-Empfindungen und ihre Analyse* (Leipzig: Veit, 1882), p. 128n.

675.40   *Vorlesungen*] Wilhelm Wundt, *Vorlesungen über die Menschen- und Thierseele*, 2nd ed. (Hamburg: Voss, 1892), pp. 65–67.

676.8   Fick] Adolf Fick, "Experimentelle Beiträge zur Physiologie des Tastsinnes," *Untersuchungen zur Naturlehre des Menschen und der Thiere*, 7 (1860), 393–400, provides a summary of work done by Arnold Wunderli.

676.20   Weber's] Ernst Heinrich Weber, "Der Tastsinn und das Gemeingefühl," pp. 512–513.

676.21-22   Szabadföldi's] Mihály Szabadföldi, Hungarian physician. Ladd, p. 348, provides no citation; Boring, p. 513, cites "Beiträge zur Physiologie des Tastsinnes," *Untersuchungen zur Naturlehre des Menschen und der Thiere*, 9 (1865), 624–631.

676.24   Hall's] Granville Stanley Hall and Henry Herbert Donaldson (1857–1938), American neurologist, "Motor Sensations on the Skin," *Mind*, 10 (October 1885), 557–572.

676.27   Bleuler] Eugen Bleuler (1857–1939), Swiss psychiatrist, and Karl Bernhard Lehmann (1858–1940), physician, *Zwangsmässige Lichtempfindungen durch Schall und verwandte Erscheinungen auf dem Gebiete der andern Sinnesempfindungen* (Leipzig: Fues, 1881).

676.32   Urbantschitsch] Victor Urbantschitsch (1847–1921), "Über den Einfluss einer Sinneserregung auf die übrigen Sinnesempfindungen," *Archiv für Physiologie*, 42 (1888), 154–182.

678.32   Bain] On p. 364 of his copy of *The Senses and the Intellect*, James asks "What amount of knowledge would be given us by the feeling of colour per se?" and with a guideline attaches this to Bain's remark that "Knowledge or belief in an external or material coloured body, there would be none" (p. 365). On p. 365, James asks "What would the feelings of ocular movement add?" and attaches this to Bain's "a feeling of a definite amount of *action.*" On p. 366, James attaches the question "Which 2 primary attributes does he say cannot be known by sight alone?" to Bain's claim that by sight alone we cannot know the distance of an object from the eye and the object's real dimensions in space. On p. 367, James has "Prove it as to distance?"

679.41 Riehl] On p. 61, Riehl does not provide a reference for Theodor Wilhelm Engelmann. On p. 61 of his copy, James has "From here on this Chap. is unimportant."

680.9 *Intelligence*] Secs. 7 and 8 are found on II, 86–96. The quotation is from sec. 3.

680.28 Schopenhauer] *Über die vierfache Wurzel des Satzes vom zureichenden Grunde*, pp. 57–58.

681.36 Sergi] Giuseppe Sergi (1841–1936), Italian anthropologist, *La psychologie physiologique*, trans. from the Italian by M. Mouton (Paris: Alcan, 1888), p. 189 (sec. 209). A marked copy was sold. Preserved is *Dolore e piacere; storia naturale dei sentimenti* (Milan: Fratelli Dumolard, 1894) (WJ 841.80).

681.37 Liebmann] Otto Liebmann, *Über den objectiven Anblick. Eine kritische Abhandlung* (Stuttgart: Schober, 1869), pp. 67–72. James's index in his copy in Houghton (*AC 85.J2376.Zz8691) contains the entry "Problems of perception 70." Works by Liebmann from James's library will be listed in the volume of manuscript remains.

683.20 Cheselden] William Cheselden (1688–1752), English surgeon. "An Account of Some Observations Made by a Young Gentleman, Who Was Born Blind, or Lost His Sight so Early, That He Had no Remembrance of Ever Having Seen, and Was Couch'd between 13 and 14 Years of Age," *Philosophical Transactions*, 35 (1728), 447–450; the quoted text is on p. 448.

683.38 Weber's] Ernst Heinrich Weber discusses the sense of direction in the head in "Der Tastsinn und das Gemeingefühl," pp. 536–537, but does not mention this experiment.

685.4–5 amputated] See William James, "The Consciousness of Lost Limbs," *Proceedings of the American Society for Psychical Research*, vol. I, no. 3 (December 1887), pp. 249–258; reprinted in *Essays in Psychology*, WORKS.

685.10 Mitchell] Silas Weir Mitchell, *Injuries of Nerves and Their Consequences* (Philadelphia: J. B. Lippincott, 1872), p. 349.

685.26 "lost] P. 352.

687.1 Janet] Paul Janet, "De la perception visuelle de la distance," *Revue Philosophique*, 7 (January 1879), 1–17; the quotations are from pp. 6, 6–7.

687.38 Dunan] Charles Stanislas Dunan (1849–1931), French philosopher, "L'Espace visuel et l'espace tactile," *Revue Philosophique*, 25 (1888), 134–169, 354–386, 591–619.

687.39–40 Abbott] Thomas Kingsmill Abbott (1829–1913), Irish scholar,

Notes

Sight and Touch: An Attempt to Disprove the Received (or Berkeleian) Theory of Vision (London: Longman, Green, Longman, Roberts, and Green, 1864), ch. 10 (pp. 140-162) titled "Cases of Persons Born Blind." Perry reports that an annotated copy was sold.

689.11 Berkeley] George Berkeley, *An Essay towards a New Theory of Vision*, in *The Works of George Berkeley, D. D.*, ed. Alexander Campbell Fraser, 4 vols. (Oxford: Clarendon, 1871), I, 79-81, 87-89.

689.22 Uphues] Goswin K. Uphues (1841-1916), German philosopher, *Wahrnehmung und Empfindung. Untersuchungen zur empirischen Psychologie* (Leipzig: Duncker & Humblot, 1888), pp. 1-41 (Introduction), 51-61.

690.9 Locke's] See p. 656.

690.20 Jastrow] Joseph Jastrow, "The Dreams of the Blind," *New Princeton Review*, 5 (January 1888), 18-34.

692.23 Huxley] Thomas Henry Huxley, *Hume* (New York: Harper & Brothers, 1879), pp. 92-94. Perry reports that a copy of an 1879 edition was sold with "generic images 92" on the flyleaf.

692.39 *Treatise*] I, 326, 327.

692.40 Spinoza] *Œuvres de Spinoza*, ed. Émile Saisset, 3 vols. (Paris: Charpentier, 1861) (WJ 871.82), III, 85-88 (part II, proposition 40, scholium).

695.36 Locke] *Essay*, p. 458 (bk. IV, ch. 7, sec. 9). In his copy on pp. 458-459, James has "What has Locke to say against the importance ascribed to the general ones?"

695.40 *Intelligence*] II, 139-140.

696.13 Fechner] James is summarizing part a of chapter 44, *Elemente der Psychophysik*, II, 469-491.

696.19 "It] *Elemente*, II, 477.

696.23 Galton] Francis Galton, "Statistics of Mental Imagery," *Mind*, 5 (July 1880), 301-318.

696.26 Galton] On the title page of his copy of *Inquiries into Human Faculty*, James has: "Cut out: pp. 83 to 88, 96-103." These pages, corresponding to the long quotation, are either cut out or mutilated. The first portion of the quotation is from pp. 83-88.

696.35 *Principles*] P. 182.

700.12 "It] *Inquiries*, pp. 97-101.

700.39 I] See p. 1088.

702.17 "I] *Inquiries*, p. 96.

702.37 McCosh] James McCosh and Henry Fairfield Osborn (1857-1935), American paleontologist, "A Study of the Mind's Chambers of Imagery," *Princeton Review*, 60th year (January 1884), pp. 50-72.

702.38 London] The *Spectator*, 51 (September 28, 1878), 1208-1209, published an account of the powers of G. P. Bidder, occasioned by his death. This was followed by "An Extraordinary Calculator," *Spectator*, 51 (December 28, 1878), 1631–1632, describing Bidder's powers in more detail, as well as those of members of his family and others similarly gifted. Many letters on the subject followed: 51 (December 28, 1878), 1634–1635; 52 (January 4, 1879), 11–12; 52 (January 11, 1879), 47; 52 (January 25, 1879), 111–112; and others. There is no March 18, 1879 issue of the *Spectator*. The calculators described were often able to visualize large numbers clearly.

703.34 *La Fontaine*] The opening words of lines 45–52 of fable 4 of book 8, *Œuvres de J. de La Fontaine*, ed. Henri Regnier, II (Paris: Hachette, 1884), 232–233.

704.41 Wilbrand] *Die Seelenblindheit*, pp. 43–49, reproduces Jean Martin Charcot, "Un Cas de suppression brusque et isolée de la vision mentale des signes et des objets (formes et couleurs)," *Progrès Médical*, 11 (July 21, 1883), 568–571.

706.35 letter] *Die Seelenblindheit*, pp. 49–51.

707.5 Binet] Alfred Binet, *La Psychologie du raisonnement: Recherches experimentales par l'hypnotisme* (Paris: Alcan, 1886), pp. 25–29.

707.12 Legouvé] Binet cites Bernard, *De l'aphasie*, p. 50, for the exchange between Ernest Wilfried Legouvé (1807–1903), French dramatist and writer, and Augustin Eugène Scribe (1791–1861), French dramatist.

707.32 Galton] *The Oxford English Dictionary* (supplement) does not attribute this term to Galton, but rather cites Joseph Jacobs, review of Binet's *Psychologie du raisonnement*, in *Mind*, 11 (July 1886), 415.

708.4 (Ribot)] Binet, p. 27, cites Ribot's *Maladies de la volonté*, p. 7.

708.7 yield] Binet, p. 27, cites James's "Feeling of Effort"; see *Essays in Psychology*, WORKS.

708.15 Lecoq] Horace Lecoq de Boisbaudran (1802–1897), French painter.

708.19 Galton] *Inquiries*, p. 106.

709.17 (Charcot)] Binet, p. 29, does not cite a source.

709.24 Franz] J. C. August Franz, German physician, "Memoir of the Case of a Gentleman Born Blind, and Successfully Operated upon in the 18th Year of His Age, with Physiological Observations and Experiments," *Philosophical Transactions*, 131 (1841), 59–68.

709.28 Stricker] Salomon Stricker, *Studien über die Sprachvorstellungen* (Vienna: W. Braumüller, 1880); *Studien über die Bewegungsvorstellungen* (Vienna: W. Braumüller, 1882) (see note to 249.29).

709.37 Farges] Farges, unidentified French physician, "Aphasie chez une tactile," *L'Encéphale*, 7 (1887), 545–553.

710.35 Stricker] *Studien über die Bewegungsvorstellungen*, pp. 23–24.

711.26 *Studien*] In *Studien über die Sprachvorstellungen*, the pronunciation of labials is discussed on pp. 9–15; auditory images and words, p. 31; verbal thinking and motor representation, pp. 29–33; silent thinking, pp. 49–50; acoustic images, pp. 69–70.

711.27 *Revue*] The following appeared in the *Revue Philosophique*: Carl

Stumpf, "Sur la représentation des mélodies," 20 (December 1885), 617–618; Frédéric Paulhan, "Images et mouvements," 16 (October 1883), 405–412; Salomon Stricker, "Note sur les images motrices," 18 (December 1884), 685–691; Paulhan, "À propos de la note de M. Stricker," 19 (January 1885), 118–119.

711.41 Hugo's] Victor Hugo, "Le Régiment du baron Madruce," from *La Légende des siècles* (Paris: Gallimard, ᶜ1950), p. 453.

712.40 Meyer] Georg Hermann Meyer (1815–1892), German psychologist, *Untersuchungen über die Physiologie der Nervenfaser* (Tübingen: Laupp, 1843), p. 233.

712.41 Tuke's] Daniel Hack Tuke (1827–1895), English physician, *Illustrations of the Influence of the Mind upon the Body in Health and Disease Designed to Elucidate the Action of the Imagination* (London: J. & A. Churchill, 1872). Ch. 2 (pp. 29–55) on the "Influence of the Intellect on Sensation"; ch. 7 (pp. 122–145) on the "Influence of the Emotions upon Sensation."

714.34 Féré] Charles Féré (1852–1907), French psychiatrist, "Sensation et mouvement," *Revue Philosophique*, 20 (1885), 337–368.

714.34–35 Müller's] Johannes Müller (1801–1858), German physiologist, *Elements of Physiology*, trans. William Baly, 2 vols. (London: Taylor and Walton, 1838–1842), II, 1394.

714.38 Wundt's] 1st ed.

715.41 *Senses*] 3rd ed., pp. 337–338. On p. 337, where Bain writes "What is the probable seat, or local embodiment, of a sensation, or a mechanical feeling, when persisting after the fact, or when revived without the reality?", James asks "What question does he begin with?" On p. 338, connected with a guideline to 715.20–22, James asks "How does he answer it? First set of reasons?"

716.3 Bain's] *The Senses and the Intellect*, 3rd ed., p. 341. On p. 341 of his copy, next to the passage quoted, James has a diagram depicting a flow from S to si to mi to M and outward from M, and the comment: "si might have actual motor consequences, i.e. innervate M, - without occupying S as its seat. Two questions therefore: 1) as to the seat of si; 2) as to what is a sufficient cause of motor consequences."

716.10 Braid] See note to 1107.43.

716.39 Kandinsky] Victor Kandinsky (Viktor Khrisanfovich Kandinskii) (1849–1899), Russian psychiatrist, *Kritische und klinische Betrachtungen im Gebiete der Sinnestäuschungen* (Berlin: Friedländer & Sohn, 1885) (WJ 878. 43), pp. 135ff.

717.25 Binet's] Alfred Binet and Charles Féré, *Le Magnétisme animal* (Paris: Alcan, 1887), p. 188. In the copy in Widener (Phil 6671.7), "after image of hall, 188" and the page numbers 186, 187, 148 are written out in James's hand.

717.26 Parinaud] On pp. 44–45 of *La Psychologie du raisonnement*, Binet quotes Henri Parinaud (1844–1905), French oculist, "Du siége cérébral des images consécutives," *Comptes Rendus des Séances et Mémoires de la Société de Biologie*, 7th series, vol. 4 (1882), pp. 342–347.

717.31 Delabarre] Edmund Burke Delabarre, "On the Seat of Optical After-Images," *American Journal of Psychology*, 2 (February 1889), 326–328. Delabarre's paper, read to the Graduate Course in Psychology at Harvard in January 1889, is a discussion of Binet's *Psychologie du raisonnement*, pp. 43ff. Delabarre writes: "Retinal rivalry has been suggested by Prof. James as a test, and I also have found it reliable."

717.35 Binet] The letter dated February 20, 1890, is preserved (bMS Am 1092, letter 38).

717.44 Lombroso] Cesare Lombroso (1835–1909), Italian sociologist and physician, and Salvatore Ottolenghi (1861–1934), Italian specialist in legal medicine, "L'Image psychique et l'acuité visuelle dans l'hypnotisme," *Revue Philosophique*, 29 (January 1890), 70–72.

719.40 Binet] Alfred Binet, "Sur les rapports entre l'hémianopsie et la mémoire visuelle," *Revue Philosophique*, 26 (1888), 480–488.

720.37 Dufour] *Neurologisches Centralblatt*, 9 (January 15, 1890), 48, contains an abstract of Marc Dufour (1843–1910), physician, "Sur la vision nulle dans l'hémiopie," *Revue Médicale de la Suisse Romande*, 9 (August 20, 1889), 445–451.

722.18 Hamilton's] *Lectures on Metaphysics and Logic*, II, 96–97.

722.22 *Psychology*] II, 253.

723.39 *Analysis*] 2nd ed.

724.30 Reid] *An Inquiry into the Human Mind*, ch. 4, sec. 1, in *The Works of Thomas Reid*, p. 117.

724.39 *Essay*] *The Works of George Berkeley*, I, 57–58.

730.12 *Intelligence*] I, 61–63.

730.13 Lazarus] See note to 636.36. The quotation is on pp. 118–120; "visionäre illusion," on p. 131. Taine is using an off-print. James's p. 19 for "visionary illusions" fits the off-print paging.

731.34 Reid's] *The Works of Thomas Reid*, pp. 334–339.

731.34 Binet] Alfred Binet, "La Rectification des illusions par l'appel aux sens," *Mind*, 9 (April 1884), 206–222.

732.2 Robertson] George Croom Robertson, "Sense of Doubleness with Crossed Fingers," *Mind*, 1 (January 1876), 145–146 (*Philosophical Remains*, pp. 133–134). Robertson cites Aristotle's *Metaphysics*, 1011ª. The *Métaphysique d'Aristote*, ed. Jules Barthélemy-Saint-Hilaire, 3 vols. (Paris: Baillière, 1879) was sold with the note "crossed fingers 69" in volume II.

732.24 Wheatstone's] The pseudoscope is a stereoscope that interchanges the normal perceptions of the two eyes.

734.35 Purkinje] Johannes Evangelista Purkinje (1787–1869), Czechoslovakian physiologist. For Purkinje's writings on vertigo see Boring, *Sensation and Perception*, p. 568.

Notes

734.35 Mach] In later editions of *Beiträge zur Analyse der Empfindungen*, Mach evaluates all of his writings on vertigo; see the English translation by C. M. Williams, *The Analysis of Sensations*, rev. ed. (Chicago: Open Court, 1914), pp. 135–170. In the *Beiträge*, p. 70 (pp. 148–149 of translation), Mach comments on James's "Sense of Dizziness in Deaf-Mutes."

734.35 Breuer] Josef Breuer (1842–1925), Austrian psychoanalyst. For works by Breuer on vertigo see Boring, *Sensation and Perception*, p. 569.

734.36 I] William James, "The Sense of Dizziness in Deaf-Mutes," *American Journal of Otology*, 4 (October 1882), 239–254, reprinted in *Essays in Psychology*, WORKS.

737.37 Berkeley's] *The Works of George Berkeley*, pp. 64–73.

737.38 Lechalas] Georges Lechalas (b. 1851), "L'Agrandissement des astres à l'horizon," *Revue Philosophique*, 26 (July 1888), 49–55.

738.19 Aubert] Hermann Aubert (1826–1892), German physiologist, *Grundzüge der physiologischen Optik* (Leipzig: W. Engelmann, 1876) (WJ 705.7), p. 602. James's copy is dated January 1878. His index contains "Micropsy 601–2."

738.24 FIG. 49] Christine Ladd-Franklin (1847–1930), American psychologist and philosopher, "A Method for the Experimental Determination of the Horopter," *American Journal of Psychology*, 1 (November 1887), 99–111. Figure 49 is from p. 100 (Ladd-Franklin's fig. 2), while figure 50, from p. 102 (Ladd-Franklin's fig. 6). Two letters from Ladd-Franklin to James are at Houghton (bMS Am 1092, letters 269, 270), while James's letters to Ladd-Franklin are in the Columbia University Library. Much of the correspondence concerns illusions of vision and dates just before and after *Principles*.

739.15 "In] Ladd-Franklin, pp. 102–103, 103–104.

741.34 Lazarus] Moritz Lazarus, *Das Leben der Seele in Monographien über seine Erscheinungen und Gesetze*, 2 vols. (Berlin: Schindler, 1856–1857), II, 31–32.

742.41 Meyer] James omits Meyer's section numbering.

743.38 Helmholtz] See p. 852.

744.11 Davy] John Ayrton Paris, *The Life of Sir Humphry Davy* (London: Henry Colburn and Richard Bentley, 1831), p. 172, in reference to potassium. The remark is attributed to George Pearson. In "The Perception of Space," *Mind*, 12 (1887), 331, James identifies the speaker as William Hyde Wollaston (1766–1828), English scientist.

744.39 Taylor] Charles Fayette Taylor (1827–1899), American physician, *Sensation and Pain* (New York: G. P. Putnam's Sons, 1881), pp. 37–38.

745.2 Reid] *Inquiry into the Human Mind*, in *The Works of Thomas Reid*, p. 117.

745.8 Delbœuf's] Joseph Remi Léopold Delbœuf, *Examen critique de la loi psychophysique: Sa base et sa signification* (Paris: Baillière, 1883), p. 61.

745.39 Volkmann's] Alfred Wilhelm Volkmann, *Physiologische Untersuchungen im Gebiete der Optik*, 2 pts. (Leipzig: Breitkopf und Härtel,

1863–1864) (WJ 791.51), pp. 139–180. James's index contains the entries: "Against projection-theory 168" and "Primitive way of feeling field of view 165."

746.13 Hyatt] Alpheus Hyatt (1838–1902), American naturalist, professor at the Massachusetts Institute of Technology and Boston University.

746.39 Hering's] Vol. III, pt. 1, pp. 564–584, "Der Einfluss der Erfahrungs-motive auf die Localisirung" (see note to 414.29).

747.25 Lazarus's] James perhaps is referring to a discussion in "Zur Lehre von den Sinnestäuschungen," p. 134 (see note to 636.36), "Kopf als Sitz des Denkens."

749.5 Reid] For both Reid and Helmholtz see p. 852.

749.17 Sternberg] Maximilian Sternberg (1863–1934), Austrian physician, "Zur Lehre von den Vorstellungen über die Lage unserer Glieder," *Archiv für Physiologie*, 37 (September 1885), 1–6. See also p. 1125n.

749.28 *Proceedings*] See note to 685.4–5.

750.40 Herbart] *Psychologie als Wissenschaft*, II, 209–215.

751.37 Lange] Karl Maximilian Lange (1849–1893), German educator, *Über Apperception. Eine psychologisch-paedagogische Monographie* (Plauen: F. E. Neupert, 1879), pp. 12n–14n.

751.38 Staude] See note to 96.33.

751.38 Marty] See note to 96.35.

751.40 *Problems*] George Henry Lewes, *Problems of Life and Mind*, 1st series, 2 vols. (London: Trübner, 1874–1875), I, 118–124 (Introduction, pt. 2, secs. 6–10).

751.41 *Einleitung*] Steinthal's treatment of apperception is on pp. 166–263.

753.40 *Op.*] James omits paragraph numbering.

754.40 Lange] Pp. 74, 76.

755.30 Schopenhauer] *Über die vierfache Wurzel des Satzes vom zureichen-den Grunde*, pp. 28–96.

755.30 Spencer] II, 117–135.

755.31 Hartmann] I, 301–353.

755.32 Wundt] *Beiträge zur Theorie der Sinneswahrnehmung* (Leipzig: Winter, 1862) (WJ 796.59), pp. 422–436; *Vorlesungen*, 1st ed., I, 41–56, 187–201. James's copy of the *Beiträge* is dated Dresden, June 15, 1868.

755.33 Binet] Pp. 55–94, 143–171.

756.36 *Hamilton*] *Lectures on Metaphysics and Logic*, II, 99.

757.5 Spencer] *The Principles of Psychology*, II, 246–251 (sec. 353). Spencer is commenting upon the passage from Hamilton quoted by James.

758.18 Clouston] Thomas Smith Clouston (1840–1915), Scottish psychiatrist, *Clinical Lectures on Mental Diseases*. James's marked copy is in Widener

(Philadelphia: Henry C. Lea's Son, 1884) (Phil 6952.6B); however, in *Principles* James used the London edition (J. & A. Churchill, 1883), in which the list is found on pp. 87–89.

759.27 "Dr.] On p. 41 of the *Kritische und klinische Betrachtungen*, Kandinsky identifies the subject of the hallucination as "Herr College N. Laschkow."

760.10 Kandinsky] Perhaps the case of Michel Dolinin described by Kandinsky on pp. 44–54.

760.28 *Census*] The census of hallucinations, a continuation of work begun by Gurney, was undertaken in 1889 by a committee headed by Henry Sidgwick. The final report, "Report on the Census of Hallucinations," was published in the *Proceedings of the SPR*, 10 (1894), 25–422.

760.36 Kandinsky] Pp. 40–42.

760.38 *Proceedings*] Henry Sidgwick (1838–1900), British philosopher, "Address by the President on the Census of Hallucinations," *Proceedings of the SPR*, 6 (December 1889), 7–12; "Ad Interim Report on the Census of Hallucinations," pp. 183–185 of the supplement.

760.40 agent] Excerpts from James's letter to Henry Sidgwick, July 11, 1896, the final report of the American figures, were read by Mrs. Sidgwick before the Third International Congress of Psychology, in 1896, *Dritter internationaler Congress für Psychologie in München* (Munich: J. F. Lehmann, 1897), pp. 392–394. James reported 7123 responses. None of the responses received by James are in the James Collection. In a letter to Richard Hodgson, May 25, 1892 (bMS Am 1092.9 [965]), James states that he has delivered two boxes of cases to Hodgson's room. He could be referring to census responses.

763.38 Myers] In the *Proceedings of the SPR*, 12 (1896–1897), p. 170 of the supplement, Frederic William Henry Myers in a glossary of psychical research terms, under hallucination, states that a veridical hallucination is one which corresponds to "real events happening elsewhere."

764.40 Staffa] An island off the coast of Scotland containing Fingal's Cave.

767.38 Maury] Ch. 3 (pp. 35–41), "Des rêves et de la manière dont fonctionne l'intelligence pendant le sommeil"; ch. 4 (pp. 42–79), "Des hallucinations hypnagogiques."

768.36 Taine] "Of the Nature and Reduction of Images," I, 35–74. See *Essays in Radical Empiricism*, WORKS, note to 12.3.

769.15 Jackson's] John Hughlings Jackson, "The Croonian Lectures on Evolution and Dissolution of the Nervous System," *British Medical Journal*, vol. I for 1884 (March 29), pp. 591–593; (April 5), 660–663; (April 12), 703–707; Charles Mercier, "Inhibition," *Brain*, 11 (October 1888), 361–385, discussion by Jackson, pp. 386–393.

770.8 Maury's] *Le Sommeil*, p. 132.

770.11 Descartes] *L'Homme de René Descartes* (Paris, 1664) (*AC 85. J2376.Zz664d), p. 102 (sec. 102). Descartes speaks of a *mouche.*

Notes

771.10 *point*] *Le Magnétisme animal*, p. 167.

771.19 *Binet's*] See the English translation, *Animal Magnetism* (New York: D. Appleton, 1888), p. 244: "Hallucination must, therefore, be a disease of external perception."

771.29 Binet's] Alfred Binet, "L'Hallucination," *Revue Philosophique*, 17 (1884), 377–412; *Animal Magnetism*, ch. 9 (pp. 211–276) on "Hallucinations."

772.10 prism] *Animal Magnetism*, p. 228.

772.12 Tuke] Daniel Hack Tuke, "Hallucinations, and the Subjective Sensations of the Sane," *Brain*, 11 (January 1889), 441–467.

772.14 Gurney] Edmund Gurney, "Hallucinations," *Mind*, 10 (April 1885), 161–199; "Supplementary Note on Hallucinations," *Mind*, 10 (April 1885), 316–317.

773.22 Meyer] For both Meyer and Féré see pp. 713–714.

773.37 Gurney's] Following the publication of *Phantasms of the Living*, controversy arose concerning the veridical character of the hallucinations. A. Taylor Innes, "Where Are the Letters? A Cross-Examination of Certain Phantasms," *Nineteenth Century*, 22 (August 1887), 174–194, claimed that all of the supposed veridical hallucinations in *Phantasms* rested upon the memory of the witnesses, that there was not a single case in which contemporary documents had been produced, even in cases where such documents were alleged to exist. Gurney replied in "Letters on Phantasms. A Reply," *Nineteenth Century*, 22 (October 1887), 522–533, claiming that the book mentioned at least three cases in which the required contemporary evidence was produced.

773.39 *Mental*] Pp. 136–137.

775.6 Kraepelin] Emil Kraepelin (1856–1926), German psychiatrist, "Über Trugwahrnehmungen," *Vierteljahrsschrift*, 5 (1881), 204–228, 349–369. Widener preserves *Psychiatrie: Ein Lehrbuch für Studirende und Ärtze*, 5th ed. (Leipzig: J. A. Barth, 1896) (Phil 6960.5).

775.8 Ireland's] William Wotherspoon Ireland, *Through the Ivory Gate: Studies in Psychology and History* (Edinburgh: Bell & Bradfute, 1889).

775.11 Myers] See note to 378.13.

777.34 Jastrow] Joseph Jastrow, "The Perception of Space by Disparate Senses," *Mind*, 11 (October 1886), 539–554; Joseph Jastrow and Frederick Whitton, "The Perception of Space by Disparate Senses," *American Journal of Psychology*, 3 (January 1890), 49–54.

778.39 *Philosophical*] P. 66 (see note to 709.24).

778.40 Hermann's] See note to 414.29.

779.41 *Loc.*] Pp. 572–573.

780.20 Hering] In "The Perception of Space," *Mind*, 12 (1887), 5, for this quotation James cites Ewald Hering, "Der Temperatursinn," in Hermann's *Handbuch*, vol. III, pt. 2 (1880), pp. 436–437. Without citing a source, Hering

Notes

attributes this view to Ernst Heinrich Weber.

780.24 Foster's] Michael Foster, *A Text Book of Physiology*, from the 3rd English edition, with notes by Edward T. Reichert (Philadelphia: Henry C. Lea's Son, 1880), pp. 816–828, "The Mechanisms of Co-ordinated Movements." James's reference fits several of the numerous editions of this work.

781.11 tympanic] The *Boston Medical and Surgical Journal*, 101 (August 7, 1879), 199–200, gives an account of James's report before the Boston Society of Medical Sciences, February 18, 1879, of experiments on the function of the tympanic membrane in the perception of space. James studied inmates of the Perkins Institution for the Blind and healthy persons.

783.1 FIG. 51] Figures 51 and 52 do not appear in "Der Tastsinn und das Gemeingefühl," but could have been intended to represent experiments described in that work.

784.12 Classen] August C. Classen (1835–1889), German physician, *Physiologie des Gesichtssinnes zum ersten Mal begründet auf Kant's Theorie der Erfahrung* (Braunschweig: Vieweg, 1876) (WJ 713.5), p. 114.

785.2 Panum] Perhaps Peter Ludwig Panum (1820–1885), Danish physiologist.

785.24 Cheselden] Pp. 449, 450 (see note to 683.20).

786.40 Brown] *Lectures on the Philosophy of the Human Mind*, p. 139.

789.28 Nunneley's] Thomas Nunneley (1809–1870), British surgeon, *On the Organs of Vision: Their Anatomy and Physiology* (London: John Churchill, 1858), pp. 31–32.

791.3 Story's] Perhaps William Wetmore Story (1819–1895), American sculptor and essayist.

792.29 Kant] *Prolegomena zu einer jeden künftigen Metaphysik die als Wissenschaft wird auftreten können* (Riga, 1783) (*AC 85.J2376.Zz783k), p. 59.

794.42 'Empfindungskreis'] Ernst Heinrich Weber divides the skin into circles, holding that two stimuli falling within the same sensory circle are felt as one. For references to Weber's work see Wundt, *Grundzüge*, 3rd ed., II, 13.

795.38 Vierordt] Karl von Vierordt, *Grundriss der Physiologie des Menschen*, 5th ed. (Tübingen: Laupp, 1877), pp. 326, 436. The copy in Widener (KF 4657) is a gift from James, with a few annotations. On p. 326 James has a reference to p. 332.

796.31 Wundt] *Beiträge zur Theorie der Sinneswahrnehmung*, pp. 54–55.

796.37 Hall] See note to 676.24.

798.12 Berkeley] *An Essay towards a New Theory of Vision*, sec. 17, in *The Works of George Berkeley*, I, 39.

798.27 Reid] *Inquiry into the Human Mind*, ch. 4, sec. 3, "Of Natural Signs," in *The Works of Thomas Reid*, pp. 121–122.

798.34 Sully's] James is referring to the section on "Local Character" of Sully's *Outlines of Psychology*. On p. 119 of his copy, where Sully writes "local *interpretation*," James has, "Local *character*? Is this the same with felt *locality*?"; while on p. 120, where Sully claims that differences of local character are found only in touch and sight, James has, "Are any senses without local character?"

798.35   Erdmann] Benno Erdmann (1851–1921), German philosopher and psychologist, "Zur Theorie der Apperception," *Vierteljahrsschrift*, 10 (1886), 306–345, 391–418.

798.39   Kries] See note to 497.36.

800.20   Weber] Ernst Heinrich Weber, "Der Tastsinn und das Gemeingefühl." For additional references see Boring, *Sensation and Perception*, p. 513.

802.40   Lamansky] S. Lamansky, "Bestimmung der Winkelgeschwindigkeit der Blickbewegung, respective Augenbewegung," *Archiv für Physiologie*, 2 (1869), 418–422.

803.15   So] This note was criticized by E. Ford, "The Original Datum of Space-Consciousness," *Mind*, n.s. 2 (April 1893), 217–218; James replied in "The Original Datum of Space-Consciousness," *Mind*, n.s. 2 (July 1893), 363–365, reprinted in *Essays in Psychology*, WORKS.

804.8   se] In "The Perception of Space," *Mind*, 12 (1887), 27, there is a note containing a quotation from Carl Stumpf, *Über den psychologischen Ursprung der Raumvorstellung* (Leipzig: S. Hirzel, 1873) (WJ 783.89.2), pp. 121–123, with the remark to see also pp. 143–153. In James's copy, the quoted passage is marked with "From here" at the beginning of the quotation, and "to here" at the end, perhaps instructions for a copyist or translator. James's copy is dated July 1876.

806.10   pass] In "The Perception of Space," *Mind*, 12 (1887), 183, James in a note referred to James Ward's "Psychology" in the *Encyclopædia Britannica*, pp. 46, 53.

807.36   Binet] Alfred Binet, "De la fusion des sensations semblables," *Revue Philosophique*, 10 (September 1880), 284–294.

808.44   article] "The Spatial Quale," *Journal of Speculative Philosophy*, 13 (January 1879), 64–87, reprinted in *Essays in Psychology*, WORKS. The quotation is from pp. 84–85 of the *Journal*.

809.10   Czermak] James perhaps is referring to Johann Nepomuk Czermak, "Zur Lehre vom Raumsinn der Haut," *Untersuchungen zur Naturlehre des Menschen und der Thiere*, 1 (1857), 183–205.

809.10   Klug] Nandor (Ferdinand) Klug (b. 1845), Hungarian physiologist, "Zur Physiologie des Temperatursinnes," *Arbeiten aus der physiologischen Anstalt zu Leipzig*, 11 (1877), 168–176.

809.24   Rutherford's] William Rutherford (1839–1899), Scottish physiologist, "A New Theory of Hearing," *Journal of Anatomy and Physiology*, 21 (October 1886), 166–168; a report of a lecture before the British Association for the Advancement of Science, September 6, 1886.

809.29   Stepanoff] E. M. Stepanoff (Yevgenij Mikhailovich Stepanoff) (b. 1855). An abstract of his "Zur Frage über die Function der Schnecke im Gehörgang des Menschen," *Jahresbericht*, vol. 15, pt. 2 (1888) (covering the literature of 1886), pp. 404–405.

809.32 Donaldson] Henry Herbert Donaldson, "On the Temperature-Sense," *Mind*, 10 (July 1885), 399–416; see note to 676.24.

809.32 Goldscheider] Alfred Goldscheider, "Neue Thatsachen über die Hautsinnesnerven," *Archiv für Anatomie und Physiologie*, 1885, pp. 1–110 of the supplement.

809.33 Blix] Magnus Blix (1849–1904), Swedish physiologist, "Experimentelle Beiträge zur Lösung der Frage über die specifische Energie der Hautnerven," *Zeitschrift für Biologie*, 20 (1884), 141–156; 21 (1885), 145–160.

809.33 Ladd's] Pp. 345–352.

810.19 Czermak] On p. 161 of the paper cited below, Exner makes a similar remark about Czermak and cites Czermak's "Ideen zu einer Lehre vom Zeitsinn," *Sitzungsberichte* (Vienna), 24 (1857), 231–236.

811.7 *Exner*] Sigmund Exner, "Über das Sehen von Bewegungen und die Theorie des zusammengesetzten Auges," *Sitzungsberichte* (Vienna), vol. 72, pt. 3 (1875), pp. 156–190. The figures are on p. 161.

811.23 *Vierordt*] Karl von Vierordt, "Die Bewegungsempfindung," *Zeitschrift für Biologie*, 12 (1876), 226–240.

812.25 Schneider] Georg Heinrich Schneider, "Warum bemerken wir mässig bewegte Dinge leichter als ruhende?" *Vierteljahrsschrift*, 2 (1878), 377–414. The figures are on p. 397.

813.19 Exner] "Über das Sehen von Bewegungen," p. 185.

813.37 Fleischl] Ernst Fleischl von Marxow (1846–1891), Austrian physician, "Physiologisch-optische Notizen," pt. 2, *Sitzungsberichte* (Vienna), vol. 86, pt. 3 (1882), pp. 8–25.

814.17 Czermak] See p. 485.

814.34 Brown] See p. 826.

814.34 Bain] See for example *The Senses and the Intellect*, 3rd ed., pp. 94–100. James's index contains "3 kinds of musc. feeling 97."

814.34 Mill] *An Examination of Sir William Hamilton's Philosophy*, 4th ed., ch. 13 (pp. 265–313), "The Psychological Theory of the Primary Qualities of Matter."

814.34 Wundt] See pp. 836n, 906–908.

814.34 Helmholtz] See pp. 836n, 908–910.

814.34 Sully] *Outlines of Psychology*, pp. 173–174.

814.35 Dunan] See note to 687.38.

817.26 Ruskin] John Ruskin (1819–1900), English critic and essayist, *The Elements of Drawing*, letter 1, sec. 5, in *The Works of John Ruskin*, ed. E. T. Cook and Alexander Wedderburn, XV (London: George Allen, 1904), 27n.

818.12 Spencer's] In *The Principles of Psychology*, I, 358 (sec. 163), Spencer claims that all impressions must be translated into tactual impressions before they can be known. He then remarks: "The mother tongue must be as copious as the foreign; otherwise it cannot render all the foreign meanings."

818.31 Jastrow] Pp. 53–54 (see note to 514.37).

822.39 Shand] Alexander F. Shand (1858–1936), British psychologist, "Space and Time," *Mind*, 13 (1888), 339–355.

823.38 Bain's] This does not appear to be a direct quotation but something put together by James using Bain's terms. Thus, on p. 371 of *The Senses and the Intellect*, 3rd ed., James has marked "extension means a given movement of body or limb." In ch. 13 of *An Examination* (see note to 814.34), Mill quotes Bain extensively, including the passages cited by James in the present context.

826.17 Brown] See especially lecture 23, pp. 140–148.

826.19 Delbœuf] Joseph Remi Léopold Delbœuf, "Du rôle des sens dans la formation de l'idée d'espace: Pourquoi les sensations visuelles sont étendues?" *Revue Philosophique*, 4 (August 1877), 167–184.

826.35 Münsterberg's] James's copy of pt. 3 of the *Beiträge* (1890) is inscribed to him by Münsterberg. The inscription is dated 1890.

828.35 Lewinski] L. Lewinski, "Über den Kraftsinn," *Archiv für pathologische Anatomie und Physiologie und für klinische Medicin*, 77 (1879), 134–146.

828.37 Duchenne] Guillaume Benjamin Amand Duchenne (de Boulogne) (1806–1875), French physician, *De l'électrisation localisée et de son application à la pathologie et à la thérapeutique*, 3rd ed. (Paris: Baillière, 1872), 767–770. That James is not using either of the earlier editions is indicated by the fact that some of the observations James seems to have had in mind were made by Duchenne in 1871.

828.37 Leyden] Ernst Viktor von Leyden, "Über Muskelsinn und Ataxie," *Archiv für pathologische Anatomie und Physiologie und für klinische Medicin*, ed. Rudolph Virchow, 47 (1869), 321–351.

828.39 Eulenburg] Albert Eulenburg (1840–1917), German physician, *Lehrbuch der Nervenkrankheiten*, 2nd ed., 2 vols. (Berlin: A. Hirschwald, 1878), pt. I, sec. 3 (I, 110–118) on "Sensibilitätsstörungen der Gelenke und Knochen."

829.19 Goldscheider] Alfred Goldscheider, "Untersuchungen über den Muskelsinn," *Archiv für Anatomie und Physiologie*, 1889, pp. 369–502. A summary of this paper appears on pp. 540–543 among the reports of the physiological institute at the University of Berlin.

834.37 Pflüger's] Georg Elias Müller and Friedrich Schumann (1863–1940), German psychologist, "Über die psychologischen Grundlagen für die Vergleichung der gehobener Gewichte," *Archiv für Physiologie*, 45 (1889), 37–112.

835.39 *Problems*] 1st series, II, 478–479.

836.17 Hering] Ewald Hering, *Beiträge zur Physiologie* (Leipzig: W. Engelmann, 1861–1864) (WJ 737.76). The work was published in five parts, with special titles for the parts, but with a continuous numbering of pages. James is referring to pts. 1 and 2. James's index contains "Nachbild bei Schwindel 31" and "Convergence & feeling of depth 140."

836.23 Lipps] Theodor Lipps, *Psychologische Studien* (Heidelberg: Weiss, 1885) (WJ 750.71.2). On p. 18 of his copy, James comments: "Die innervations gefühle sind in keinen Verhaltnisses mit den durchlaufenen Netzhautstrecken." James reviewed this work in *Science* (October 9, 1885), 308–310.

836.29 Münsterberg's] The number of observations is found on p. 154 of pt. 2 (1889) of the *Beiträge*.

837.41 Weber's] See p. 676.

837.46 *Archiv*] See note to 829.19.

838.5 Bell] Charles Bell (1774–1842), British physiologist and anatomist. In *Sensation and Perception*, p. 565, Boring gives several references to Bell on the muscle sense, but emphasizes Bell's "On the Nervous Circle Which Connects the Voluntary Muscles with the Brain," *Philosophical Transactions*, 1826, pt. 2, pp. 163–173.

838.20 'mental] An allusion to John Stuart Mill, see note to 163.32.

838.20 'synthesis'] An allusion to Wundt, see p. 907. Wundt comments on this remark in *Grundzüge*, 3rd ed., II, 40n.

839.33 Levy] William Hanks Levy (d. 1874), British organizer of workshops to provide the blind with jobs, *Blindness and the Blind: Or, A Treatise on the Science of Typhlology* (London: Chapman and Hall, 1872), pp. 64–65, 66.

840.40 Kilbourne] Frank H. Kilbourne.

841.40 Dunan] See note to 687.38.

842.11 Franz] The locket incident is not found in Franz's "Memoir" (see note to 709.24). It is found in Cheselden's "An Account" (see note to 683.20), p. 449.

843.12 Hamilton] William Hamilton, *Lectures on Metaphysics and Logic*, II, 174; John Stuart Mill, quoting Hamilton, *An Examination of Sir William Hamilton's Philosophy*, 4th ed., p. 284. Hamilton cites Ernst Platner (1744–1818), German philosopher, *Philosophische Aphorismen*, 2nd ed. (1793), vol. I, pp. 439ff.

843.25 Dunan] See note to 687.38.

845.6–7 Molyneux] William Molyneux (1656–1698), Irish philosopher, in Locke's *Essay*, p. 84.

845.22 Cheselden's] Quoted by William Hamilton, *Lectures on Metaphysics and Logic*, II, 178, and others, from Cheselden (see note to 683.20), p. 448.

845.35 *Philosophical*] Pp. 64–65 (see note to 709.24).

845.35 Abbott's] See note to 687.39–40.

845.38 Dufour] Marc Dufour, *Guérison d'un aveugle-né: Observation pour servir à l'étude des théories de la vision* (Lausanne: Cobraz, 1876). Dunan (pp. 376–381) quotes Dufour, pp. 9–10, for the observation that the patient could not distinguish motion.

Notes

845.39 Naville] Ernest Naville (1816-1909), philosopher, "La Théorie de la vision," *Revue Scientifique*, 19 (March 31, 1877), 943-952.

847.37 Müller] J. J. Müller, German physiologist, "Über den Einfluss der Raddrehung der Augen auf die Wahrnehmung der Tiefendimension," *Berichte über die Verhandlungen der königlich sächsischen Gesellschaft der Wissenschaften zu Leipzig* (mathematisch-physische Classe), 23 (1871), 125-134.

848.17 Reid] Ch. 6, sec. 9, "Of the Geometry of Visibles," in *The Works of Thomas Reid*, pp. 147-152.

848.42 Schopenhauer] Arthur Schopenhauer, *Die Welt als Wille und Vorstellung*, 3rd ed., 2 vols. (Leipzig: F. A. Brockhaus, 1859) (*AC 85. J2376.Zz859s), II, 44, quotes the account from *Neue Notizen aus dem Gebiete der Natur- und Heilkunde*, vol. 7, no. 133 (July 1838), columns 1-5. The periodical was edited by Ludwig Friedrich von Froriep.

849.35 *Berkeley*] See especially *An Essay towards a New Theory of Vision*, sec. 16, in *The Works of George Berkeley*, I, 38-39.

852.8 Reid] *The Works of Thomas Reid*, p. 175.

853.7 next] In his copy of *The Principles of Psychology*, opposite this passage, James notes that he meant the earlier chapter on perception, especially pp. 80ff. (pp. 726ff. in WORKS).

853.13 Stumpf] In "The Perception of Space," p. 333, from which the present text is taken, the *"op. cit."* refers to Stumpf's *Über den psychologischen Ursprung der Raumvorstellung* (see note to 804.8).

853.38 later] See pp. 908-910.

854.38 Stumpf] James appears not to be quoting directly, but putting together several passages from *Über den psychologischen Ursprung*, p. 194.

855.8 Sully] James Sully, "The Question of Visual Perception in Germany," *Mind*, 3 (January 1878), 1-23; (April 1878), 167-195. In James's annotated set of *Mind* (Phil 22.4.6*), the Sully article is marked, but there is only one brief annotation (p. 7).

855.13 Panum] Peter Ludwig Panum maintains this in *Physiologische Untersuchungen über das Sehen mit zwei Augen* (Kiel: Schwerssche Buchhandlung, 1858) and elsewhere.

855.16 Lipps] On the bottom of p. 69 of *Psychologische Studien*, James comments "Ferrier's objection."

855.17 Ferrier] *Lectures on Greek Philosophy and Other Philosophical Remains*, II, 291-347, "Berkeley and Idealism," a review of Samuel Bailey, *A Review of Berkeley's Theory of Vision* (see note to 912.6). On II, 331, Ferrier states what he takes to be Berkeley's position that objects are not seen as external to the eye itself.

855.47 Dougall] James Dalziel Dougall (1818-1891), British writer on weapons, "Two-Eyed Rifle Shooting," *Times* (London), February 8, 1884, pp. 2-3.

857.17-18 people] See Helmholtz, *Handbuch*, pp. 612-613, for this experiment.

857.24 Helmholtz] In the *Handbuch*, pp. 611–612, Helmholtz discusses the cyclopean eye in reference to Hering's view and cites Hering's *Beiträge zur Physiologie*, pp. 254–256.

859.16 haploscopic] James could be referring to experiments with the haploscope, an instrument for presenting to each eye a field invisible to the other.

859.37 Wheatstone] Charles Wheatstone, "Contributions to the Physiology of Vision. —Part the First. On Some Remarkable, and Hitherto Unobserved, Phenomena of Binocular Vision," *Philosophical Transactions*, 1838, pt. 2, pp. 371–394.

860.14–15 Helmholtz] Helmholtz identifies the two questions in the *Handbuch*, p. 736, while discussing Wheatstone.

860.33 Nagel] Albrecht Eduard Nagel (1833–1895), German ophthalmologist, *Das Sehen mit zwei Augen und die Lehre von den identischen Netzhautstellen* (Leipzig: Winter, 1861) (WJ 758.32), pp. 78–82.

860.34 Volkmann] Alfred Wilhelm Volkmann, "Die stereoskopischen Erscheinungen in ihrer Beziehung zu der Lehre von den identischen Netzhautpunkten," *Archiv für Ophthalmologie*, vol. 5, pt. 2 (1859), pp. 1–100.

860.35 Hering] *Beiträge zur Physiologie*, pp. 81–107; see note to 414.29.

860.36–37 Aubert] Hermann Aubert, *Physiologie der Netzhaut* (Breslau: E. Morgenstern, 1865), p. 322. Perry reports that a copy of this work was sold.

860.37 Schoen] Wilhelm Schoen (b. 1848), German physician, "Zur Lehre vom binocularen Sehen," pt. 2, *Archiv für Ophthalmologie*, vol. 24, pt. 1 (1878), pp. 27–130.

860.38 Donders] See note to 484.45.

861.32 Le Conte] Joseph Le Conte (1823–1901), American scientist, *Sight: An Exposition of the Principles of Monocular and Binocular Vision* (New York: D. Appleton, 1881). Because the work contains a number of similar laws, it is difficult to establish which of these James had in mind. If the reference to pt. II, ch. 3 (pp. 120–144) is correct, one of the laws would be the law stated on p. 124, but it is not clear what would be the second law. James reviewed the work in the *Nation*, 32 (March 17, 1881), 190–191. One letter from Le Conte to James is at Houghton (bMS Am 1092, letter 494).

862.4–5 Aguilonius] François d'Aguilon (1566–1617), Belgian scholar.

863.26 Donders] Franciscus Cornelis Donders, "Die Projection der Gesichtserscheinungen nach den Richtungslinien," *Archiv für Ophthalmologie*, vol. 17, pt. 2 (1871), pp. 1–68.

865.2 Zöllner's] In *Sensation and Perception*, p. 260, Boring gives a brief history of the illusion first described by Johann Carl Friedrich Zöllner in 1860. Several forms of the illusion exist: the lines are sometimes very thick and usually the parallel lines are vertical. James's form is like that in Zöllner's *Über die Natur der Cometen*, fig. 1 of table 9.

865.7 FIG. 61] This figure is known as Hering's figure and was first published by him in *Beiträge zur Physiologie*, p. 74.

866.1 FIG. 62] The circle and square figure is fig. 141 in Wundt's *Grund-züge*, 2nd ed., II, 104; the other is fig. 138, II, 101.

866.19 Volkmann] See figure 70, p. 884.

867.6 Wheatstone] Charles Wheatstone, "Contributions to the Physiology of Vision. —Part the Second. On Some Remarkable, and Hitherto Unobserved, Phenomena of Binocular Vision," *Philosophical Transactions*, vol. 142, pt. 1 (1852), pp. 1–17.

867.25 Donders] Franciscus Cornelis Donders, *On the Anomalies of Accommodation and Refraction of the Eye*, trans. William Daniel Moore (London: New Sydenham Society, 1864), p. 155 (vol. 22 of the New Sydenham Society Publications).

867.37 author] Hermann Helmholtz, "Über die Bedeutung der Convergenz-stellung der Augen für die Beurtheilung des Abstandes binocular gesehener Objecte," *Archiv für Anatomie und Physiologie*, 1878, pp. 322–324.

868.34 Aubert] On p. 627 of his copy of Aubert's *Grundzüge*, James marks the text with two exclamation points.

868.39 Charpentier] Pierre Marie Augustin Charpentier (1852–1916), French physicist, "Illusion relative à la grandeur et à la distance des objets dont on s'éloigne," *Comptes Rendus Hebdomadaires des Séances de l'Académie des Sciences*, 92 (1881), 741–742; an abstract appeared in *Jahresbericht*, 1882 (covering the literature of 1881), pp. 430–431.

868.41 Revue] Wilhelm Wundt, "Sur la théorie des signes locaux," *Revue Philosophique*, 6 (September 1878), 217–231. See also p. 1104.

869.32 Wundt] See p. 907.

869.32 Helmholtz] See p. 852.

872.14 Berkeley] From Berkeley's *Alciphron: Or, the Minute Philosopher*, 4th dialogue, sec. 12, in *The Works of George Berkeley*, II, 154.

872.25 Reid] *The Works of Thomas Reid*, p. 135.

876.5 "On] *Handbuch*, p. 442. In Helmholtz, 'Raumempfindungen' is in italics and enclosed by quotation marks. The italics in 'overcome' are James's.

877.11 FIG. 64] In *Sensation and Perception*, pp. 592, 605, Boring notes that the waterfall illusion is sometimes attributed to James. The illusion appears as figure 4 of plate 18 in Henry Pickering Bowditch and Granville Stanley Hall, "Optical Illusions of Motion," *Journal of Physiology*, 3 (1882), 297–307, with no reference to James.

878.11 FIG. 65] In *Sensation and Perception*, p. 592, Boring identifies a similar figure as Plateau's Spiral (1850). James's version seems based on Bowditch and Hall, figure 2 of plate 18.

878.26 Dvořák] V. Dvořák, "Versuche über die Nachbilder von Reizverän-derungen," *Sitzungsberichte* (Vienna), vol. 61, pt. 2 (1870), pp. 257–262. Dvořák notes that the work was performed in the laboratories of Prague University with the encouragement of Mach.

879.5 FIG. 66] This figure seems based on Helmholtz, *Handbuch*, p. 569.

879.25 Helmholtz] Helmholtz discusses the Zöllner figure in the *Handbuch*, p. 566.

880.12 Zöllner] See p. 171n.

880.19 FIG. 67] Helmholtz, *Handbuch*, p. 565, and Wundt, *Grundzüge*, 2nd ed., II, 105; both give similar figures and attribute them to Ewald Hering.

880.21 Delbœuf] Joseph Remi Léopold Delbœuf, *"Note sur certaines illusions d'optique;* essai d'une théorie psychophysique de la manière dont l'œil apprécie les distances et les angles," *Bulletin de l'Académie Royale des Sciences, des Lettres et des Beaux-Arts de Belgique*, 2nd series, vol. 19 (1865), pp. 195–216.

881.1 FIG. 68] This figure seems based on Wundt's figures 135 and 136, *Grundzüge*, 2nd ed., II, 100.

881.33 *Revue*] See note to 868.41.

882.10 Hering's] See note to 414.29.

882.16 FIG. 69] James's fig. 69 seems based on fig. 1 in Lipps, *Grundtatsachen des Seelenlebens*, p. 527. In Lipps the segments mp and mb are on the left, mb is shorter than in James, and the segments are not identified by letters. In James's copy the letters are added by hand.

883.1 Vierordt's] See pp. 811–812.

883.29 Hering] James's index to Hering's *Beiträge zur Physiologie* contains the entry "His skill in seeing double images 107, 337," and on the line just below, "51, (also [space, perhaps to indicate that subject is repeated] 322, 334."

883.29 Le Conte] In *Sight*, p. 91, Le Conte begins his treatment of binocular vision with the remark that he has acquired "an unusual voluntary power over the movements of the eyes."

884.7 FIG. 70] Alfred Wilhelm Volkmann, *Physiologische Untersuchungen im Gebiete der Optik*, p. 253.

884.22 *Archiv*] See note 860.34.

884.26 Schweigger] Carl Ernst Theodor Schweigger (1830–1905), German ophthalmologist, *Klinische Untersuchungen über das Schielen* (Berlin: A. Hirschwald, 1881).

884.27 Javal] Émile Javal (1839–1907), French ophthalmologist, "De la vision binoculaire," *Annales d'Oculistique*, 85 (1881), 217–229.

884.30 Kries] Johannes von Kries, "Wettstreit der Sehrichtungen bei Divergenzschielen," *Archiv für Ophthalmologie*, vol. 24, pt. 4 (1878), pp. 117–138.

885.28 *Physiologische*] Ch. 5 is the essay mentioned on p. 745n.

886.13 FIG. 73] This figure appears based on Victor Egger, "Sur quelques illusions visuelles," *Revue Philosophique*, 20 (1885), 485–498; figures are on pp. 488, 489.

887.12 FIG. 74] In *Sensation and Perception*, p. 269, Boring identifies this figure as Schröder's stairs (1858), after H. Schröder. Similar figures appear frequently in the literature cited by James.

887.12 FIG. 75] Several similar figures appear in Julius Bernstein, *The Five Senses of Man*, p. 139.

887.13 FIG. 76] This figure appears based on Hering's figure 63 in "Der Raumsinn," p. 580 (see note to 414.29).

888.31 Loeb] Jacques Loeb, "Über die optische Inversion ebener Linear-zeichnungen bei einäugiger Betrachtung," *Archiv für Physiologie*, 40 (1887), 274–282.

888.33 Helmholtz's] James omits Helmholtz's reference to Hering.

893.41 Hermann's] See note to 414.29.

894.10 FIG. 77] Alfred Wilhelm Volkmann, *Physiologische Untersuchungen im Gebiete der Optik*, p. 150.

895.20 *Bulletin*] See note to 880.21.

896.1 FIG. 79] This figure is based on figure 61 in Hering's "Raumsinn," p. 579 (see note to 414.29).

898.36 *Physiologische*] The quotation is on pp. 549–550.

901.10 Brown] *Lectures on the Philosophy of the Human Mind*, p. 145.

901.14 Mills] For James Mill see p. 723.

901.24 Bain] In his copy of *The Senses and the Intellect*, 3rd ed., p. 183, attached by a guideline to the text quoted, James comments: "Suppose we move a limb in vacuo—What ought this to make us acquainted with? besides our own expended energy?"

902.9 Stumpf] James's index to Stumpf's *Über den psychologischen Ursprung* contains the entry "Psychischer Reiz theorie 28." On p. 28 Stumpf discusses Kant's view of space.

902.14 Mills] See note to 163.32.

902.21 Sully] James's index to Sully's *Outlines of Psychology* contains the entry "Space perception 198." On p. 198, apparently in reference to Sully's remark that at an "early age" a child learns to connect a sound with a corresponding movement, James asks: "How come we to identify the seen with the felt orange, the heard with the touched bell?" Next to Sully's claim that "the perception of a thing as the sum of coexisting qualities arises much in the same way as the perception of a surface as made up of coexisting points," James comments: "but then why the colossal difference in the result? see 159." In reference to Sully's remark that the quality of an object is referred to "a substance in which it is said to inhere," James asks: "What is the *substance* of the thing?" On p. 199, James continues the same questioning: "If you see a hat foreshortened, and still identify it, what is the *real* hat with which you make the identification?"

902.22 Spencer] The italics are added by James. On II, 187 of his copy, attached by a guideline to 'coexistent position' in "Let us return now to the above-described state of the retina as occupied by an image or by a cluster of images. Relations of coexistent position like those we have here considered in respect to a particular linear series, are established throughout countless such series in all directions over the retina," James remarks: "Here the illegitimate child is born. The limits of the linear series are not yet known as *spatially* separated, only as *serially* separated, whatever that may mean. In his discussion of non spatial consciousness on p. 152, he insists that a mere series (of sounds) does not as a series involve spatial perception." By a guideline attached to 'p. 152', James adds "see also p 172." Also on p. 187, James has "Represent the series, yes! but not represent it necessarily as spatial unless the series as such be intrinsically spatial," " 'graduated coexistence' is all he can fairly say," and " 'complexity of graduated coexistences.' His words beg the whole question, which is how they here are felt as spatial."

906.21 Lotze] See p. 798.

906.29 *Logik*] I, 457–458 for the quotation.

906.34 *Psychologie*] II, 127.

906.35 *Psychologie*] II, 133–137.

906.36 Volkmann's] II, 1–156.

907.11 Wundt] *Logik*, I, 453.

907.14 "It] *Logik*, I, 458–459.

910.10 Hering] In his review of Le Conte (see note to 861.32), James makes a similar comment about Hering's terminology, but cites no source.

910.27 Hodgson] This distinction is emphasized in some of Hodgson's pamphlets, for example in *The Method of Philosophy* (see note to 329.8).

910.33 'aggregate] This appears to be a paraphrase from Spencer's *Principles of Psychology*, II, 177 (sec. 329), 184 (sec. 331).

910.37 *Grundtatsachen*] Near the bottom of p. 591 of his copy of *Grundtatsachen*, James has "N B 480." On p. 14 of *Psychologische Studien*, James has: "The spatial *quale* an ultimate fact."

910.39 *Psychology*] Sec. 328.

911.34 *Senses*] "*Scope for movement*" is on p. 375. In his copy, next to this phrase, James refers to p. 186, while on top of the page, he asks: "What do we *mean* by empty space? What *kind* of movements, passive or active? (369)."

911.35 Hall] See note to 676.24.

911.36 Sully] See note to 855.8.

911.38 Wundt] In James's copy of the *Grundzüge*, 1st ed., the quoted passage is marked "N B?"

912.6 Bailey] Samuel Bailey (1791–1870), British economist and philosopher, *A Review of Berkeley's Theory of Vision, Designed to Show the Unsoundness of That Celebrated Speculation* (London: James Ridgway, 1842). For a work by Bailey from James's library see *A Pluralistic Universe*, WORKS, note to 8.9.

912.7 Mill's] John Stuart Mill, *Dissertations and Discussions: Political, Philosophical, and Historical*, II (New York: Henry Holt, 1873), 162–197, "Bailey on Berkeley's Theory of Vision," reprinted from the *Westminster Review* (October 1842).

912.8   Ferrier] See note to 855.17.

912.9   Bain] *The Senses and the Intellect*, 3rd ed., pp. 321–456, ch. 1 of section on "Intellect" titled "Retentiveness—Law of Contiguity."

912.9   Spencer] *The Principles of Psychology*, II, 178–206, 216–231, chapters on "The Perception of Space" and "The Perception of Motion."

912.10   Mill] See note to 814.34.

912.12   Abbott] See especially p. 75.

912.14   Fraser] Alexander Campbell Fraser (1819–1914), Scottish philosopher, "Berkeley's Theory of Vision," *North British Review*, 41 (1864), 199–230. Works by Fraser from James's library will be listed in the volume of manuscript remains.

912.15   review] James perhaps has in mind T. Collyns Simon, "Can We See Distance?" *Macmillan's Magazine*, 13 (March 1866), 429–442, in the main a review of Bailey.

912.15   Sully] Pp. 147–218, on "Perception."

912.18   'discussion'] George Croom Robertson, "The Psychological Theory of Extension," *Mind*, 13 (July 1888), 418–424; James and James Ward responded in *Mind*, 14 (January 1889), "'The Psychological Theory of Extension'," pp. 107–109 for James, pp. 109–115 for Ward. James's response is reprinted in *Essays in Psychology*, WORKS.

913.17   Bagehot] See p. 936.

914.34   Bradley's] Pp. 109–120, on "The Negative Judgment."

914.37   *Mind*] James is referring to the appendix on nitrous-oxide intoxication of his "On Some Hegelisms"; see *The Will to Believe*, WORKS, pp. 217–221.

915.40   Clouston] Pp. 43–44.

915.41   Berger] Oscar Berger, German physician, "Die Grübelsucht, ein psychopathisches Symptom," *Archiv für Psychiatrie*, 6 (1876), 217–248.

917.37   Marty] Anton Marty, "Über subjectlose Sätze und das Verhältniss der Grammatik zu Logik und Psychologie," *Vierteljahrsschrift*, 8 (1884), 56–94, 161–192, 292–340.

918.22   *Ethics*] *Œuvres de Spinoza*, III, 102, 103. James adds italics and ignores paragraph divisions.

920.21   Taine's] See p. 768n.

921.35–36   Swedenborg's] Emanuel Swedenborg (1688–1772), Swedish religious writer. James's father was a Swedenborgian; see James's Introduction to *The Literary Remains of the Late Henry James* in *Essays in Religion and Morality*, WORKS.

922.21   'idols] Francis Bacon, *The New Organon*, bk. I, aphorism 41.

922.33   Thackeray] A reference to Thackeray's burlesque novel, *Rebecca and Rowena*.

924.39   *Inquiry*] *Essays Moral, Political, and Literary*, II, 42.

Notes

925.11 Kant] *Immanuel Kant's Critique of Pure Reason*, pt. 2, containing Kant's *Critique*, trans. by F. Max Müller (London: Macmillan, 1881) (*AC 85.J2376.Zz881k), pp. 515–516 (B627=A599–B629=A601).

925.41 *Treatise*] I, 394–395.

926.22 Lipps] *Grundtatsachen des Seelenlebens*, p. 400. In James's copy, the passage is marked with three N.B.'s and a reference to p. 446. James used this as a motto in "The Psychology of Belief," *Mind*, 14 (1889), 321.

927.36 Griesinger] Pp. 83–84, 170. On p. 84 of his copy of *Die Pathologie*, James has cross-references to pp. 170, 219, 228.

928.4 Hume's] Perhaps an allusion to *A Treatise of Human Nature*, I, 399 (bk. I, pt. 3, sec. 8).

932.20 Tylor] Edward Burnett Tylor (1832–1917), British anthropologist, *Researches into the Early History of Mankind and the Development of Civilization*, 2nd ed. (London: John Murray, 1870), pp. 108–111. James's edition has not been identified, but his reference fits this edition and not several others. Tylor provides references to the works of James Backhouse (1794–1869), and Adolf Bastian (1826–1905), German anthropologist.

932.40 *Treatise*] I, 420, 401–402, 410, 400 (bk. I, pt. 3, secs. 10, 8, 9, 8).

933.17 Fichte] James perhaps is remembering Fichte's letter to Marie Johanne Rahn, his fiancée, May 14, 1790: "sie sagen Nichts, Auge fehlt, Ausdruck der Miene fehlt, Farbe fehlt, alle die holden Grazien fehlen, die auf Deinem Gesichte wohnen" (Johann Gottlieb Fichte, *Gesamtausgabe*, ed. Reinhard Lauth and Hans Jacob, vol. III, pt. I [Stuttgart: Frommann, 1968], p. 117).

934.26 Aristotle] James could be referring to *De Anima*, bk. III, ch. 12.

934.40 *Essay*] *The Works of George Berkeley*, I, 60–61.

935.18–19 Emerson] Ralph Waldo Emerson, *Essays*, 1st series, p. 244, from the essay on "The Over-Soul."

935.29 *Essay*] P. 395.

935.41 *Ibid.*] *Essay*, pp. 486–487.

936.12 Bagehot] Walter Bagehot, *Literary Studies*, ed. Richard Holt Hutton, 2nd ed., 2 vols. (London: Longmans, Green, 1879), II, 412–414, from the essay "On the Emotion of Conviction." The verses are from Walter Scott, "The Lady of the Lake," canto IV, stanza 6.

937.5 "A] Bagehot, *Literary Studies*, II, 413, 415. The country girl example is used to support the claim that a belief may exist even when there is no possibility of acting upon it.

937.12 Renouvier] *Traité de psychologie rationnelle*, 2nd essay of the *Essais de critique générale*, 2nd ed., 3 vols. (Paris: Bureau de la *Critique Philosophique*, 1875) (WJ 675.61.4), II, 1–54; on p. 12 Renouvier introduces the "théorie du vertige mental."

937.39 Reid] *The Works of Thomas Reid*, p. 113.

938.5 Stanley] Henry Morton Stanley (1841–1904), British explorer,

Through the Dark Continent, 2 vols. (London: Sampson Low, Marston, Searle & Rivington, 1878), II, 384–386. James's edition has not been identified.

941.32 Horwicz] See *The Will to Believe*, WORKS, note to 72.13.

943.3 Emerson's] See *The Will to Believe*, WORKS, note to 74.19.

944.39 Royce] Josiah Royce, *The Religious Aspect of Philosophy* (Boston: Houghton, Mifflin, 1885) (WJ 477.98.4), pp. 316–317, 357. James's index contains "Law of attention 316." James reviewed this work in the *Atlantic Monthly*, 55 (June 1885), 840–843, reprinted in *Collected Essays and Reviews* (New York: Longmans, Green, 1920).

945.36 *Religious*] James's index contains "The *will to have* an external world 304, 403."

945.42 Royce's] Pp. 291–383, on "The World of the Postulates" and "Idealism."

947.39 Bain] On p. 511 of James's copy of *The Emotions and the Will*, 3rd ed., next to the opening words of the passage quoted, James has a reference to p. 536. James ignores paragraph numbering.

949.10 Hume] I, 394–423.

949.10 Bain] *The Emotions and the Will*, 3rd ed., pp. 505–538, part on "Belief"; pp. 20–23, sec. 20 on "The Influence of Feeling on Belief" and sec. 21, titled "The Emotions Affect the Judgment of True and False. Deep-Seated Corruption of the Intellect."

949.11 Sully] James Sully, *Sensation and Intuition: Studies in Psychology and Æsthetics* (London: Henry S. King, 1874), pp. 73–162, on "Belief: Its Varieties and Its Conditions."

949.12–13 Renouvier] Pt. 2, on "La certitude," begins on II, 129 and ends on III, 107 of *Traité de psychologie rationnelle*; and in *Esquisse d'une classification systématique des doctrines philosophiques*, 2 vols. (Paris: Bureau de la *Critique Philosophique*, 1885–1886) (WJ 675.61), II, 1–126, on "L'évidence, la croyance."

949.14 Newman] John Henry Newman (1801–1890), Roman Catholic cardinal, *An Essay in Aid of a Grammar of Assent* (New York: Catholic Publication Society, 1870) (WJ 559.95). Writings by Newman from James's library will be listed in the volume of manuscript remains.

949.15 Venn] John Venn (1834–1923), British logician, *On Some of the Characteristics of Belief Scientific and Religious* (London: Macmillan, 1870). Works by Venn sold from James's library will be listed in the volume of manuscript remains.

949.15 Brochard] Victor Charles Louis Brochard (1848–1907), French philosopher, *De l'erreur* (1879); in the 2nd ed. (Paris: Alcan, 1897), pt. II, ch. 6 (pp. 126–165) titled "De la croyance," ch. 9 (pp. 213–238), "Des causes psychologiques de l'erreur." "De la croyance," *Revue Philosophique*, 18 (July 1884), 1–23.

949.16 Rabier] Pp. 266–276, "De la croyance, sa nature, ses modes, ses degrés, son origine."

Notes

949.17 Ollé-Laprune] Léon Ollé-Laprune (1839–1898), French educator, *De la certitude morale* (Paris: Eugène Belin, 1880).

949.17 Stout] George Frederick Stout, "The Genesis of the Cognition of Physical Reality," *Mind*, 15 (January 1890), 22–45.

949.18 Pikler] Julius (Gyula) Pikler (1864–1937), Hungarian sociologist and philosophical writer, *The Psychology of the Belief in Objective Existence* (London: Williams and Norgate, 1890).

949.19 Mill] James seems to be referring to James Mill, *Analysis of the Phenomena of the Human Mind*, 2nd ed., I, 342–393. Bain criticizes Mill along the lines indicated by James in his note, *Analysis*, I, 393–402.

949.26 Sully] In essay 4 of *Sensation and Intuition*, especially pp. 76–83, Sully criticizes Bain's conception of belief. The two questions quoted by James are not there, although they fairly represent the general tendencies of Sully's criticism. Sully's description of belief is a quotation from p. 83.

949.34 Stephen] Leslie Stephen (1832–1904), English philosopher and critic, "Belief and Conduct," *Nineteenth Century*, 24 (September 1888), 372–389. Stephen's letters to James are at Houghton (bMS Am 1092, letters 1030–1035); an additional letter is in James's copy of *The Science of Ethics* (London: Smith, Elder, 1882) (WJ 583.24). Perry reports that *The English Utilitarians* (1900) was sold.

949.39 Census] See p. 760.

953.11 them] In "Brute and Human Intellect," *Journal of Speculative Philosophy*, 12 (July 1878), 239, James has at this point several paragraphs with quotations from Bain's *Mental and Moral Science*, pp. 85, 127.

954.14 Romanes] *Mental Evolution in Man*, ch. 3 (pp. 40–69) on the "Logic of Recepts"; ch. 4 (pp. 70–84) on the "Logic of Concepts." On p. 68 of his copy, James has references to pp. 187, 353.

954.33 Binet] P. 126.

955.18 Darwin] Romanes, *Mental Evolution in Man*, pp. 51–52, is quoting Darwin, *The Descent of Man, and Selection in Relation to Sex*, new ed. (New York: D. Appleton, 1879), pp. 76, 83. Darwin, for the Texas story, is quoting Jean Charles Houzeau (1820–1888), French scientist, *Études sur les facultés mentales des animaux* (1872).

955.39 *Loc.*] Pp. 49–50.

957.35 Locke] P. 391.

958.45 *Logic*] *A System of Logic*, I, 438–439; bk. IV, ch. 2 (II, 195–210), "Of Abstraction, or the Formation of Conceptions."

960.15 Warner] Charles Dudley Warner (1829–1900), American author, "How I Killed a Bear," *In the Wilderness* (Boston: Houghton, Osgood, 1878), p. 14.

961.13 Locke] James could be referring to Locke's *Essay*, p. 343 (bk. III, ch. 6, sec. 51). On p. 343 of his copy, James has: "The intuition at the bottom of his whole argument agst. essences is that of the *continuity of nature* wh. the pedantic scholastic use of species broke up & violated. See also pp. 365–6[,] 438[,] 457."

961.38 Whewell] William Whewell (1794–1866), British philosopher and historian of science, *History of Scientific Ideas*, 3rd ed., 2 vols. (London: John W. Parker, 1858), II, 103–104.

961.40 article] In *The Analysis of Sensations*, p. 310n, Mach writes: "With regard to the idea of concepts as labor-saving instruments, the late Prof. W. James directed in conversation my attention to points of agreement between my writings and his essay on 'The Sentiment of Rationality'." Mach could be referring to his meeting with James in 1882 (see *Letters*, I, 212).

962.17 Ueberweg's] *System of Logic*, p. 139. For Ueberweg's text see *Essays in Philosophy*, WORKS, note to 34.33.

962.24 Hartmann] *Philosophy of the Unconscious*, I, 303. For the German reference see *Essays in Philosophy*, WORKS, note to 35.7.

963.7 Clay] Edmund R. Clay, *The Alternative*, pp. 85–86.

964.34 Lotze] *Metaphysik*, pp. 117–118, 132–134. On p. 117 of his copy, James has: "Kein a priorisches Verstandniss der Thatsache dass dieselbe Ursache immer dieselbe Wirkung haben muss." On p. 118, a reference to p. 132 and: "Gegenseitige Beeinflussung heterogener Wesen muss am Ende als letzte synthetische Form des Seins anerkant, aber (von uns) nicht aufgeklärt, werden." On p. 132, a reference to sec. 58 and: "Bei der prästabilirten Harmonie ist die *Uniformität* der Causalen Verknüpfung sinnlos."

965.31 Black] Ralph Waldo Black (b. 1862), attended Harvard College from 1882–1883, 1884–1886. In a letter to Ralph Barton Perry, June 2, 1931 (bMS Am 1092.10 [7]), Black states that his paper was written for Philosophy 9, James's advanced psychology course, probably in 1885–1886. James found the paper publishable and asked for permission to keep it. Black was surprised, many years later, to find his paper used here.

969.26 Kingsley] Charles Kingsley (1819–1875), English clergyman and author.

971.23 Mill's] See note to 555.24.

972.26 Bain's] Alexander Bain, *On the Study of Character, Including an Estimate of Phrenology* (London: Parker, Son, and Bourn, 1861), pp. 322–344. Perry reports that a marked copy of this work (1861), was sold. James appears to be referring to pp. 511–543 in ch. 2 of "Intellect" in *The Senses and the Intellect*, 3rd ed. His index contains "Qu Reasoning, discrimination of fertile character, etc. 494–499, 510, 527."

973.15 Darwin] *The Descent of Man* (1871), I, 46, citing Isaac Israel Hayes (1832–1881), American explorer.

976.37 Romanes's] See note to 954.14.

977.21 Strümpell] Ludwig Adolf Strümpell (1812–1899), German philosopher, *Die Geisteskräfte der Menschen verglichen mit denen der Thiere. Ein Bedenken gegen Darwin's Ansicht über denselben Gegenstand* (Leipzig: Veit, 1878), pp. 39–41.

979.25 *Coriolanus*] From Shakespeare's *Coriolanus*, act 5, scene 4, lines 29–30.

979.30 Schumann] Th. Schumann, "Gescheidte Thiere," *Daheim: Ein deutsches Familienblatt mit Illustrationen*, 14 (February 9, 1878), 312.

979.42 Morgan] Conwy Lloyd Morgan (1852–1936), British biologist and philosopher, "On the Study of Animal Intelligence," *Mind*, 11 (April 1886), 174–185. Perry reports that marked copies of Morgan's *Habit and Instinct* and *Animal Life and Intelligence* were sold. James's copy of *Psychology for Teachers* (London: Arnold, 1894) was given to Widener, but has not been found. One letter from Morgan to James is at Houghton (bMS Am 1092, letter 565).

981.33 Bleek] Wilhelm Heinrich Immanuel Bleek (1827–1875), South African linguist and folklorist, *On the Origin of Language*, trans. by Thomas Davidson (New York: L. W. Schmidt, 1869), pp. 48–49.

982.1 Howe] Samuel Gridley Howe (1801–1876), American educator and philanthropist, Laura Bridgman's teacher.

982.39 Wright] Chauncey Wright, *Philosophical Discussions*, ed. Charles Eliot Norton (New York: Henry Holt, 1877), pp. 199–266.

982.39 Romanes] See in particular *Mental Evolution in Man*, pp. 190, 397.

984.15 Bain] *On the Study of Character*, p. 327.

985.8 Homer] *Odyssey*, bk. XXII, lines 381–389; *Iliad*, bk. IV, lines 141–147. The text as quoted by James is different from that in George Herbert Palmer (1842–1933), American philosopher, James's colleague at Harvard, *The Odyssey of Homer* (Boston: Houghton, Mifflin, 1891), p. 354. In the surviving correspondence between them (bMS Am 1092.9 [426–456, 3366–3369]), there are no references to this translation.

985.29 Taine] *De l'intelligence*, 1st ed., I, 44.

987.40 Renouvier] Charles Renouvier, "De la ressemblance mentale de l'homme et des autres animaux selon Darwin," *Critique Philosophique*, 5th year, vol. 2 (October 19, 1876), pp. 184–191 (anecdote on p. 191). Renouvier cites no source for David Livingstone (1813–1873), British explorer and missionary. James uses the anecdote in "Brute and Human Intellect," *Journal of Speculative Philosophy*, 12 (July 1878), 271; while Renouvier comments on James's use in "De la caractéristique intellectuelle de l'homme, d'après M. Wm. James," pt. 3, *Critique Philosophique*, 8th year, vol. 2 (August 13, 1879), p. 22n.

991.41 Whately's] Richard Whately (1787–1863), British clergyman and philosopher.

992.8 Lazarus] Moritz Lazarus, *Das Leben der Seele*, 2nd ed., 2 vols. (Berlin: Dümmler, 1876–1878), II, 229.

992.20 Bowditch] Nathaniel Bowditch (1773–1838), American mathematician. The remark is attributed to Bowditch by his son, Nathaniel Ingersoll Bowditch, in the latter's "Memoir of the Translator" in Laplace's *Mécanique céleste*, trans. Nathaniel Bowditch, IV (Boston: Charles C. Little and James Brown, 1839), 62.

995.40 *Emotions*] 3rd ed. James changes the order of passages.

996.13 Haller] Albrecht von Haller (1708–1777), Swiss scientist.

996.20 Couty] Louis C. Couty, French physiologist, and Pierre Marie Augustin Charpentier, "Recherches sur les effets cardio-vasculaires des excitations des sens," *Archives de Physiologie*, 2nd series, vol. 4 (1877), pp. 525–583. James's figure 81 is on p. 560.

996.38 Féré] Charles Féré, *Sensation et mouvement: Études expérimentales de psycho-mécanique* (Paris: Alcan, 1887), p. 56. Féré does not cite a source for Haller.

996.39 Féré] Pp. 102–115.

996.40 *Revue*] Charles Féré, "Note sur les conditions physiologiques des émotions," *Revue Philosophique*, 24 (1887), 561–581. James's figure 82 is figure 7 (p. 570) in Féré; figure 83 is figure 2 (p. 566); figure 84 is figure 3 (p. 567).

998.11 Tarchanoff] A summary by Christine Ladd-Franklin, *American Journal of Psychology*, 2 (August 1889), 652–653, of Ivan Romanovitch Tarchanoff (d. 1908), Russian physiologist, "Über die galvanischen Erscheinungen in der Haut des Menschen bei Reizungen der Sinnesorgane und bei verschiedenen Formen der psychischen Thätigkeit," *Archiv für Physiologie*, 46 (1889), 46–55.

998.16 Danilewsky's] B. Danilewsky (Vasilii Iakovlevich Danilevskii) (b. 1852), "Gehirn und Atmung," *Biologisches Centralblatt*, 2 (January 15, 1883), 690–699.

999.3 Sander] Wilhelm Sander (1838–1922), German physician. James's first reference is to a remark made by Sander during a discussion at the Berliner Medicinisch-Psychologische Gesellschaft, *Archiv für Psychiatrie*, 7 (1877), 652–653; the second, is to Sander's article in the same *Archiv*, 9 (1879), 129–146, "Über die Beziehungen der Augen zum wachen und schlafenden Zustande des Gehirns und über ihre Veränderungen bei Krankheiten."

1000.6 Mosso] Angelo Mosso and P. Pellacani, "Sulle funzioni della vescica," *Atti della R. Accademia dei Lincei*, 3rd series, *Memorie della classe di scienze fisiche, matematiche e naturali*, 12 (1881–1882), 3–64; reported in *Jahresbericht*, 10 (1882), 92–95 (literature for 1881).

1000.34 Féré] *Sensation et mouvement*, p. 42.

1000.40 Féré] Pp. 90–97, "Sur la physiologie du fœtus."

1001.14 Féré] In ch. 6 (pp. 32–50) "Excitation produite par les hallucinations, par les excitations sensorielles.—Excitation des divers sens.—Peptogènes. —Rôle du tabac, de l'alcool, etc."

1001.23 FIG. 85] *Sensation et mouvement*, p. 43.

1001.27 Mitchell] Silas Weir Mitchell and Morris J. Lewis, "Physiological Studies of the Knee-Jerk, and of the Reactions of Muscles under Mechanical and Other Excitants," *Medical News* (Philadelphia), 48 (February 13, 1886), 169–173; (February 20, 1886), 198–203.

1001.27 Lombard] Warren Plimpton Lombard (1855–1939), American physician, "The Variations of the Normal Knee-Jerk, and Their Relation to the Activity of the Central Nervous System," *American Journal of Psychology*, 1 (November 1887), 5–71.

1001.30 Féré] *Sensation et mouvement*, p. 26.

1002.24 Schneider] Georg Heinrich Schneider, "Zur Entwicklung der Willensäusserungen im Tierreiche," *Vierteljahrsschrift*, 3 (1879), 176–205, 294–307.

1002.32 Bowditch] Henry Pickering Bowditch, "The Reinforcement and Inhibition of the Knee-Jerk," *Boston Medical and Surgical Journal*, 118 (May 31, 1888), 542–543.

1004.23 Chadbourne] Paul Ansel Chadbourne (1823–1883), American educator, *Instinct: Its Office in the Animal Kingdom, and Its Relation to the Higher Powers in Man* (New York: Geo. P. Putnam & Sons, 1872), p. 28. James's annotated copy is in Widener (Phil 5812.1.2).

1006.14 Schneider] Georg Heinrich Schneider, *Der thierische Wille; Systematische Darstellung und Erklärung der thierischen Triebe und deren Entstehung, Entwickelung und Verbreitung im Thierreiche als Grundlage zu einer vergleichenden Willenslehre* (Leipzig: Ambr. Abel, [1880]) (WJ 779.39.2). James's copy is dated Lausanne, August 1880.

1012.37 Darwin's] Charles Darwin, *On the Origin of Species* (London: John Murray, 1859). James's copy, probably of this edition, was sold. James could be referring to ch. 7 (pp. 207–244) on "Instinct."

1012.38 Romanes's] *Mental Evolution in Animals*, pp. 159–255, chapters on instinct. The Appendix (pp. 353–384) on instincts is by Darwin.

1012.39 Lindsay's] William Lauder Lindsay (1829–1880), Scottish physician, *Mind in the Lower Animals in Health and Disease*, 2 vols. (New York: D. Appleton, 1880) (WJ 550.59). Vol. II, ch. 5 (II, 62–66) is titled "Perversions of the Natural Affections," while ch. 20 (II, 276–290), "Individuality."

1012.40 Semper's] Karl Gottfried Semper (1823–1893), German zoologist, *The Natural Conditions of Existence as They Affect Animal Life* (London: C. K. Paul, 1881). The American edition is titled *Animal Life As Affected by the Natural Conditions of Existence*.

1014.19 Spalding] Douglas Alexander Spalding, "Instinct. With Original Observations on Young Animals," *Macmillan's Magazine*, 27 (February 1873), 282–293. On p. 289, Spalding writes that in the case of animals "any early interference with the established course of their lives may completely derange their mental constitution." Romanes quotes this passage in *Mental Evolution in Animals*, p. 170.

1018.16 Spalding] "Instinct," p. 289.

1019.24 Schmidt] Henry D. Schmidt (1823–1888), American physician, "On the Structure of the Nervous Tissues and Their Mode of Action," *Transactions of the American Neurological Association*, 1 (1875), 71–141; quotation from pp. 129–130.

1020.34 Lewes] 1st series, vol. I, p. 238n.

1020.39 Stebbing] Thomas Roscoe Rede Stebbing (1835–1926), British zoologist, *Essays on Darwinism* (London: Longmans, Green, 1871), p. 73. The Widener copy (S 7900.82) is a gift from James, October 23, 1902. There are no markings by James.

1022.35 Preyer] Wilhelm Thierry Preyer, *Die Seele des Kindes. Beobacht-ungen über die geistige Entwickelung des Menschen in den ersten Lebensjahren* (Leipzig: Th. Grieben, 1882), p. 147. An annotated copy was sold.

1023.14 Schneider] James's index to *Der menschliche Wille* contains "Boy's & girl's instincts 205, 224" and attached to this "See Thierische Wille 180+."

1023.40 Preyer] In *Die Seele des Kindes,* Preyer frequently mentions this, for example, on pp. 156, 177, 189, but no comparisons with chimpanzees were found.

1025.15 Spalding's] Douglas Alexander Spalding, "Instinct and Acquisition," *Nature*, 12 (October 7, 1875), 507–508.

1027.8 Preyer] *Die Seele des Kindes*, p. 177.

1028.21 Faust] *Faust*, p. 41 (lines 1112–1113).

1029.26 Bain's] *The Emotions and the Will*, 3rd ed., p. 121.

1029.30 Spencer's] *The Principles of Psychology*, pt. VIII, ch. 5 (II, 558–577) on "Sociality and Sympathy."

1030.26 Fowler] Thomas Fowler (1832–1904), British philosopher, *The Principles of Morals*, pt. II *(Being the Body of the Work)* (Oxford: Clarendon, 1887). Ch. 2 (pp. 67–104) is titled "On the Sympathetic Feelings."

1030.44 *menschliche*] Pp. 224–225.

1031.7 Rochefoucauld] François La Rochefoucauld (1631–1680), French moralist. James seems to have in mind one of the suppressed maxims, see *Maximes*, ed. Jacques Truchet (Paris: Garnier Frères, [1967]), p. 139.

1031.33 Tuke] Daniel Hack Tuke, "Case of Moral Insanity or Congenital Moral Defect, with Commentary," *Journal of Mental Science*, 31 (October 1885), 360–366. The first part of the quotation is from p. 362, from the records of the case in the Kingston Asylum, Ontario, Canada; the second, p. 364, from Tuke's commentary. George Henry Savage (1842–1921), British psychiatrist, was a physician in the Bethlem Royal Hospital.

1032.26 Pomeroy] In September of 1872, Jesse Harding Pomeroy, then 14 years old, pleaded guilty to the mutilation of young boys in the Boston area. For an account of the case see the *New York Times*, September 22, 1872, p. 5.

1032.39 Guyau] Marie Jean Guyau, *Esquisse d'une morale sans obligation ni sanction* (Paris: Alcan, 1885), p. 210, quoting Charles Laurent Bombonnel (1816–1890), French hunter and adventurer, *Bombonnel le tueur de pan-thères* (1860).

1034.6 'like] From Tennyson's "Lotos-Eaters," *The Works of Alfred Lord Tennyson*, p. 56.

1034.15 Perez] Bernard Perez, *La Psychologie de l'enfant (les trois premières années)*, 2nd ed. (Paris: Baillière, 1882), pp. 72, 74, 75. In back of the Widener copy (Educ 2068.82), pp. 96, 72, 74, 296, 317, 322 are listed in James's hand.

1035.34 Hartmann] Robert Hartmann, *Anthropoid Apes* (New York: D.

Appleton, 1886), p. 265; quoting Julius Ferdinand Falkenstein (1842–1917). No citation is provided.

1036.7   Preyer] *Die Seele des Kindes*, p. 106.

1036.39   *Der*] The paragraph division is James's.

1037.12   Mosso] Angelo Mosso, *La Peur: Étude psycho-physiologique*, trans. Félix Hément (Paris: Alcan, 1886).

1037.15   Bain] See for example *The Emotions and the Will*, 3rd ed., p. 158; *Mental and Moral Science*, pp. 232–238, on "Emotion of Terror."

1037.37   Brooks] William Keith Brooks (1848–1908), American naturalist.

1038.22   Lindsay] P. 526. James's index contains "immobility etc. 526."

1038.28   Romanes] In *Mental Evolution in Animals*, p. 156, Romanes gives several stories, including one from Darwin's *Descent of Man* (I, 67) about a dog barking at a parasol moved along a lawn by wind.

1038.30   Sanford] Edmund Clark Sanford (1859–1924), American psychologist, "The Writings of Laura Bridgman," *Overland Monthly*, 8 (October 1886), 577–586; the quotation is from p. 362.

1040.39   Hall] Granville Stanley Hall, "A Study of Children's Collections," *Nation*, 41 (September 3, 1885), 190; using responses to questionnaires collected by Sara Eliza Wiltse (b. 1849), American educator.

1041.31   Silliman] Lindsay, *Mind in the Lower Animals*, II, 151–152, cites no source for Benjamin Silliman (1779–1864), American chemist, or Benjamin Silliman, Jr. (1816–1885), American chemist.

1043.37   Flint] Robert Flint (1838–1910), British philosopher and theologian, "Association and the Origin of Moral Ideas," *Mind*, 1 (July 1876), 321–334. James Sully comments on this paper in "The Associationist Theory of Avarice," *Mind*, 1 (October 1876), 567–568. Works by Flint from James's library will be listed in the volume of manuscript remains.

1045.39   Bain] *The Emotions and the Will*, 3rd ed., pp. 220–224, entitled "Emotions of Action—Pursuit."

1046.36   Lazarus] Moritz Lazarus, *Über die Reize des Spiels* (Berlin: Dümmler, 1883), p. 44.

1048.4   Darwin] Charles Darwin, *The Expression of the Emotions in Man and Animals* (New York: D. Appleton, 1873), pp. 330–332. A marked copy was sold.

1048.33   Bain] *The Emotions and the Will*, 3rd ed., p. 162.

1049.2   Darwin] *The Expression of the Emotions*, p. 332.

1050.30   Thackeray] *Roundabout Papers* (Boston: Estes & Lauriat, 1896), p. 126.

1052.39   Waitz] Theodor Waitz, *Anthropologie der Naturvölker*, I (Leipzig: Fleischer, 1859), 358.

1054.15   Darwin] James perhaps is referring to *The Descent of Man*, I, 96, in ch. 4 on the "moral sense."

Notes

1056.9 Schneider] *Der thierische Wille*, pp. 91-93.

1056.29 phrenologists] George Combe (1788-1858), Scottish phrenologist, in *The Constitution of Man Considered in Relation to External Objects*, 5th American ed. (Boston: Marsh, Capen & Lyon, 1835), vol. 7 of the Phrenological Library, pp. 52-55, distinguishes between feelings and intellectual powers and divides feelings into propensities and sentiments. Adhesiveness, described as attachment to friends, and acquisitiveness, the desire to possess, are classed among the propensities, while love of approbation, among the sentiments.

1056.31 Fortlage] Karl Fortlage (1806-1881), German philosopher, *System der Psychologie als empirischer Wissenschaft aus der Beobachtung des innern Sinnes*, 2 vols. (Leipzig: F. A. Brockhaus, 1855), II, 33-112, ch. 5 titled "Von den vegetativen Trieben."

1056.33 Santlus] Jacob Christoph Santlus (1809-1873), German physician, *Zur Psychologie der menschlichen Triebe* (Neuwied and Leipzig: J. H. Heuser, 1864), pp. 2-4.

1059.14 Lange] Carl Georg Lange (1834-1900), Danish physiologist, *Über Gemüthsbewegungen. Eine psycho-physiologische Studie*, trans. H. Kurella (Leipzig: Theodor Thomas, 1887) (WJ 816.48), pp. 13-16.

1061.8 author] *Über Gemüthsbewegungen*, pp. 16-17.

1061.16 Henle] Jakob (Friedrich Gustav Jakob) Henle (1809-1885), German anatomist, *Anthropologische Vorträge*, 2 vols. (Braunschweig: Vieweg, 1876-1880), I, 54-55. In the Widener copy of vol. II (Phil 5247.7), on the back endpaper, "Qu 13" appears in James's hand.

1062.1 "The] *Über Gemüthsbewegungen*, p. 17.

1062.37 'Obstupui] Virgil, *Aeneid*, bk. II, line 774.

1062.40 Curtis] Thomas B. Curtis (1842-1881), American physician, "A Case of Hydrophobia: With Remarks on the Pathological Physiology of the Disease," *Boston Medical and Surgical Journal*, 99 (November 7, 1878), 581-590; (November 14, 1878), 619-627. James Jackson Putnam's comments appeared in the same journal, 99 (November 21, 1878), 650-653, "The Physiological Pathology of the Hydrophobic Paroxysm."

1063.7 *huc*] Virgil, *Aeneid*, bk. IV, line 363.

1063.13 Hagenauer] F. A. Hagenauer of Lake Wellington, a missionary in Australia, was one of several persons who observed aborigines for Darwin.

1063.18 Mantegazza] Paolo Mantegazza (1831-1910), Italian physician and anthropologist, *La Physionomie et l'expression des sentiments* (Paris: Alcan, 1885), p. 140. Mantegazza lists the effects in tabular form. In back of the Widener copy (Phil 6022.1), pp. 70, 71, 110, 111 are listed in James's hand.

1065.14 *Mind*] "What Is an Emotion?" *Mind*, 9 (April 1884), 188-205; for James's response to critics see "The Physical Basis of Emotion," *Psychological Review*, 1 (September 1894), 516-529. Both papers are reprinted in *Essays in Psychology*, WORKS. The distinction between the coarser and the subtler emotions could be a response to criticism such as Edmund Gurney's in " 'What Is an Emotion?' " *Mind*, 9 (July 1884), 421-426.

1070.21   Lange] *Über Gemüthsbewegungen*, p. 52.

1070.35   Höffding] *Psychologie*, p. 342. On p. 343, Höffding comments on James's "What Is an Emotion?"

1071.3   Winter's] Georg Winter (1856–1946), German physician, *Ein Fall von allgemeiner Anaesthesie* (Heidelberg: Winter, 1882). In "What Is an Emotion?" *Mind*, 9 (April 1884), 204, James quotes part of a letter from Winter to James in response to questions about the case. No letters between James and Winter have been found.

1071.6   Strümpell] See note to 355.29. In "What Is an Emotion?" *Mind*, 9 (April 1884), 204n–205n, James quotes from Strümpell's letter to him about the case. No letters between James and Strümpell have been found.

1071.27   Janet] The letter from Janet was not found. On p. 215 of *L'Automatisme*, Janet comments on "What Is an Emotion?"

1073.17   Bain] *The Emotions and the Will*, 3rd ed., ch. 7 of "The Emotions" (pp. 124–150) on "Tender Emotion."

1075.27   Schwartzer] Otto Schwartzer (1853–1913).

1075.42   Bucke] Richard Maurice Bucke (1837–1902), British physician and writer, *Man's Moral Nature: An Essay* (New York: G. P. Putnam's Sons, 1879), pp. 96–97. Annotated copies of this work and Bucke's *Cosmic Consciousness* (1901) were sold.

1075.43   Lange] Pp. 60–61. James ignores paragraph divisions.

1077.38   *Op.*] *Anthropologische Vorträge*, I, 71–72.

1077.38   Lange] Pp. 53–59 for the effects of alcohol and other drugs.

1078.24   Burke] Edmund Burke (1729–1797), British statesman and writer, *A Philosophical Enquiry into the Origin of Our Ideas of the Sublime and Beautiful*, pt. IV, sec. 4, about Tommaso Campanella (1568–1639), Renaissance scholar, quoted by Dugald Stewart, *Elements of the Philosophy of the Human Mind*, ed. William Hamilton, III (Edinburgh: Constable, 1854), 140n–141n (vol. IV of *The Collected Works of Dugald Stewart*, ed. William Hamilton).

1079.6   Archer] William Archer (1856–1924), British critic and journalist, "The Anatomy of Acting," *Longman's Magazine*, 11 (January 1888), 266–281; (February 1888), 375–395; (March 1888), 498–516; the quotations are from pp. 392–394; reprinted as *Masks or Faces? A Study in the Psychology of Acting* (London: Longmans, Green, 1888). Archer's work is in part based upon the responses of leading British actors. Howe is Henry Howe and Coleman, John Coleman. More complete names for those mentioned in Coleman's response are W. C. Macready, Samuel Phelps, G. V. Brooke, and Charles Dillon. Bob Acres is a character in Richard Brinsley Sheridan (1751–1816), *The Rivals*, while Joseph Surface is in Sheridan's *The School for Scandal*.

1079.34   Fechner] Gustav Theodor Fechner, *Vorschule der Aesthetik* (Leipzig: Breitkopf und Härtel, 1876), pp. 156–157.

1080.9   Sikorsky] Ivan Aleksandrovich Sikorsky (b. 1845), Russian psychiatrist, "Die Bedeutung der Mimik für die Diagnose des Irreseins," *Neurologisches Centralblatt*, 6 (November 1, 1887), 492–496.

1081.1 Dante] James perhaps is referring to *Purgatorio*, canto XXXIII, line 74.

1081.5 Bain] *The Emotions and the Will*, 3rd ed., p. 361.

1083.12 'banquet] Perhaps from Thomas Moore (1779–1852), Irish poet, "Oft, in the Stilly Night," from *National Airs*, in *The Poetical Works of Thomas Moore*, IV (Boston: Houghton, Mifflin, ᶜ1855), 212.

1083.14 Guyau] Frédéric Paulhan, *Les Phénomènes affectifs et les lois de leur apparition: Essai de psychologie générale* (Paris: Alcan, 1887), p. 84; quoting Marie Jean Guyau, *Les Problèmes de l'esthétique contemporaine* (Paris: Alcan, 1884), p. 63. An annotated copy of Paulhan's book was sold.

1083.23 Ingersoll] Robert G. Ingersoll (1833–1899), American orator and controversialist, *The Letters of Robert G. Ingersoll*, ed. Eva Ingersoll Wakefield (New York: Philosophical Library, ᶜ1951), p. 478. While not identified as such, the letter was published in an unsigned article on "Whiskey" in the *Nation*, 47 (July 19, 1888), 44.

1083.33 Gurney's] See note to 1065.14. The quotation is from pp. 425–426.

1085.39 Ruskin] In the essay "St. Mark's" from *The Stones of Venice*, in *The Works of John Ruskin*, ed. E. T. Cook and Alexander Wedderburn, X (London: George Allen, 1904), 124–125.

1088.7 Bain] *The Emotions and the Will*, 3rd ed., p. 92. In his copy, attached by a guideline to 'being always incorporated' James has "How can the Emotions be so easily revived?" "Ideal Emotion" is ch. 5 of "The Emotions" (pp. 89–110).

1088.25 Galton] See p. 256.

1088.27 I] See p. 700.

1089.34 Höffding] *Psychologie*, p. 357. The Goethe passage is taken from the *Briefe aus der Schweiz*. Ch. 6, sec. E (pp. 348–377) is titled "Die Gültigkeit des Gesetzes der Beziehung für die Gefühle."

1089.41 Bain's] 3rd ed., pp. 78–88.

1090.12 Hamilton] *Lectures on Metaphysics and Logic*, II, 440.

1090.18 nitrous-oxide] See the appendix to "On Some Hegelisms," *The Will to Believe*, WORKS, pp. 217–221.

1090.31 *Phénomènes*] P. 41.

1091.33 Mantegazza's] Pp. 1–19, "Esquisse historique des études sur la physionomie et la mimique humaines."

1091.34 Darwin's] *The Expression of the Emotions*, ch. 1 (pp. 27–49) on "General Principles of Expression."

1091.34 Bell's] Charles Bell, *Essays on the Anatomy of Expression in Painting* (1806); the revised edition appeared as *The Anatomy and Philosophy of Expression as Connected with the Fine Arts* (1844).

1091.35 Piderit's] Theodor Piderit (1826–1898), *Wissenschaftliches System der Mimik und Physiognomik* (Detmold: Klingenberg, 1867).

1091.36 Duchenne's] Guillaume Benjamin Amand Duchenne, *Mécanisme de la physionomie humaine ou analyse électro-physiologique de l'expression des passions*, 2nd ed. (Paris: Baillière, 1876).

1091.38 Sully] *Sensation and Intuition*, pp. 23–36 on "New Theories of Emotional Expression."

1092.19–20 Darwin] *The Expression of the Emotions*, pp. 253, 282–284.

1092.28 Spencer] *The Principles of Psychology*, II, 548 (sec. 498).

1092.32 Mantegazza] *La Physionomie*, p. 78.

1092.33 Wundt] Wundt discusses reddening in the *Grundzüge*, 2nd ed., II, 420–421 and crying, in II, 421.

1092.36 Darwin] *The Expression of the Emotions*, p. 176.

1092.40 *Psychology*] I, 482–483.

1093.6 Darwin] *The Expression of the Emotions*, pp. 225–226.

1093.13 Hecker] Ewald Hecker, German psychiatrist, *Die Physiologie und Psychologie des Lachens und des Komischen* (Berlin: Dümmler, 1873), pp. 13–15.

1093.30 Mosso] *La Peur*, pp. 123–125.

1093.36 Gratiolet] Pierre Gratiolet (1815–1865), French zoologist, *De la physionomie* (1865), quoted by Darwin in *The Expression of the Emotions*, p. 242.

1093.38 Mosso's] On p. 123 of *La Peur*, Mosso cites his "Sui movimenti idraulici dell'iride e sulla azione dei mezzi che servono a ditatore, od a restringere la pupilla," *Giornale della Reale Accademia di Medicina di Torino*, 38 (November 30, 1875), 483–502.

1094.6 Wundt] Wundt, *Grundzüge*, 2nd ed., II, 423, discusses the "Princip der Association analoger Empfindungen." In II, 424, Wundt cites Piderit's *Wissenschaftliches System* (1867), p. 69.

1094.34 *Physiologische*] 2nd ed.

1094.35 Henle] *Anthropologische Vorträge*, I, 14–15.

1094.39 Piderit] *Wissenschaftliches System*, pp. 77–78, section titled "Der prüfende Zug."

1095.34 *Loc.*] *The Principles of Psychology*, II, 542–545.

1095.37 Bell] In the revised edition (1844) of *The Anatomy of Expression*, instead of an essay by Bell which Bell had marked for revision, there appeared an Appendix, "On the Nervous System," by Alexander Shaw (1804–1890), British surgeon, summarizing Bell's views of the nerves involved in respiration and their role in expression.

1096.26 Bain] See note to 1037.15.

1096.28 Darwin] *The Expression of the Emotions*, p. 28.

1097.35 Bain's] James is referring to part B of the Appendix (pp. 591–602) on "Classifications of the Emotions."

1097.36 Mercier's] Charles Mercier, "A Classification of Feelings," *Mind*, 9 (July 1884), 325–348; (October 1884), 509–530; 10 (January 1885), 1–26.

1097.36 Stanley's] Hiram Miner Stanley, "Feeling and Emotion," *Mind*, 11 (January 1886), 66–76.

1097.36 Read's] Carveth Read, "Mr. Mercier's Classification of Feelings," *Mind*, 11 (January 1886), 76–82.

1100.21 Bastian] *The Brain as an Organ of Mind*, p. 543.

1101.14 Strümpell] See note to 355.29. The quotation is from pp. 327–328.

1102.32 Landry] O. Landry, French physician, "Mémoire sur la paralysie du sentiment d'activité musculaire," *La Lancette Française, Gazette des Hôpitaux*, 28th year (June 7, 1855), p. 262; (June 12, 1855), pp. 269–271; (June 19, 1855), pp. 282–283; (July 10, 1855), pp. 318–319; (July 19, 1855), pp. 334–335.

1102.34 Takács] Andreas Takács, "Untersuchungen über die Verspätung der Empfindungsleitung," *Archiv für Psychiatrie*, 10 (1880), 527–533.

1102.37 *Proceedings*] "Report of the Committee on Hypnotism," *Proceedings of the American Society for Psychical Research*, 1 (July 1886), 95–102, signed by James and Gouverneur M. Carnochan, a student at Harvard from 1881–1886.

1102.39 Strümpell] P. 339.

1103.2 Strümpell] See note to 355.29. Quotation is from p. 335.

1103.8 Landry] P. 271.

1103.15 Bell's] Charles Bell, *The Nervous System of the Human Body: As Explained in a Series of Papers Read Before the Royal Society of London*, 3rd ed. (London: Renshaw, 1844), p. 245.

1103.31 Binet] Alfred Binet, "Le Problème du sens musculaire d'après les travaux récents sur l'hystérie," *Revue Philosophique*, 25 (1888), 465–480.

1103.36 Müller] See note to 834.37.

1103.40 Janet's] James's index to *L'Automatisme psychologique* contains "Proof that anaesthesia entails amnesia 97, 99."

1103.43 Bastian's] Charlton Bastian, "The 'Muscular Sense'; Its Nature and Cortical Localisation," *Brain*, 10 (April 1887), 5–89; discussion of the paper with Bastian's response is on pp. 89–137. The paper was first published as a pamphlet. An annotated copy of it, inscribed "with the author's compliments," from James's library is in Widener (Phil 5649.12).

1104.32 Wundt] Wundt commented on this discussion in the fourth edition of *Grundzüge*; James responded in "Professor Wundt and Feelings of Innervation," *Psychological Review*, 1 (January 1894), 70–73, reprinted in *Essays in Psychology*, WORKS. In "The Feeling of Effort," in *Anniversary Memoirs of the Boston Society of Natural History* (Boston: Published by the society, 1880), reprinted in *Essays in Psychology*, WORKS, James quotes Wundt, Bain, Helmholtz, and others on innervation; James's notes provide additional references.

Notes

1104.36 Beaunis] Henri Étienne Beaunis, *Les Sensations internes* (Paris: Alcan, 1889), the Appendix (pp. 253–256) on "Une Expérience sur le sens musculaire."

1105.18 Mach] In *The Analysis of Sensations*, pp. 173–180, Mach discusses the feeling of innervation and comments upon James's treatment.

1107.32 Manouvrier] Léonce Manouvrier (1850–1927), French anthropologist, "Mouvements divers et sueur palmaire consécutifs à des images mentales," *Revue Philosophique*, 22 (August 1886), 203–207.

1107.41 Townsend] A case described by George Cheyne (1671–1743), Scottish physician, in *The English Malady* (1733), pt. III, ch. 4.

1107.42 Tuke] Pp. 344–350, on "The Influence of the Will upon the Involuntary Muscles and the Organic Functions."

1107.43 Braid] James Braid (1795?–1860), British hypnotist, *Observations on Trance: Or, Human Hybernation* (London: John Churchill, 1850).

1107.45 Pease] Edward Allen Pease, American physician, "Voluntary Control of the Heart," *Boston Medical and Surgical Journal*, 120 (May 30, 1889), 525–529.

1108.38 Harless] Emil Harless (1820–1862), German physiologist, "Der Apparat des Willens," *Zeitschrift für Philosophie und philosophische Kritik*, n.s. vol. 38 (1861), pp. 50–73; 'ein Effektbild' is found on p. 66. The *Zeitschrift* was edited by Immanuel Hermann Fichte.

1110.27 Wundt] Wilhelm Wundt, "Neuere Leistungen auf dem Gebiete der physiologischen Psychologie," *Vierteljahrsschrift für Psychiatrie in ihren Beziehungen zur Morphologie und Pathologie des Central-Nervensystems, der physiologischen Psychologie, Statistik und gerichtlichen Medicin*, vol. I, no. 1 (1867), pp. 23–56. The Widener copy (Phil 31.2) is from James's library. It is dated Berlin, 1868; the Wundt article is annotated.

1110.34 Jaccoud] Sigismond Jaccoud (1830–1913), Swiss-born physician, *Études de pathogénie et de semiotique. Les Paraplegies et l'ataxie du mouvement* (Paris: Delahaye, 1864).

1110.38 Fouillée] Alfred Fouillée (1838–1912), French philosopher, "Le Sentiment de l'effort et la conscience de l'action," *Revue Philosophique*, 28 (December 1889), 561–582. Works by Fouillée from James's library will be listed in the volume of manuscript remains.

1112.35 Souriau] See note to 291.38.

1112.35 Müller] See note to 834.37. Quotation is found on pp. 46–47. The Hering quotation is found on pp. 58–59 and comes from Hering's letter to Fechner, from Fechner's *In Sachen der Psychophysik* (Leipzig: Breitkopf und Härtel, 1877), pp. 49–50.

1113.33 Bernhardt] Martin Bernhardt (1844–1915), German neurologist, "Zur Lehre vom Muskelsinn," *Archiv für Psychiatrie*, 3 (1872), 618–635.

1113.39 Sachs] Carl Sachs (1853–1878), German physician, "Physiologische und anatomische Untersuchungen über die sensiblen Nerven der Muskeln," *Archiv für Anatomie, Physiologie und wissenschaftliche Medicin*, 1874, pp.

175–195. The *Archiv* was edited by Carl Bogislaus Reichert and Emil Du Bois-Reymond.

1113.41 Mays] Karl Mays, German physiologist, "Histo-physiologische Untersuchungen über die Verbreitung der Nerven in den Muskeln," *Zeitschrift für Biologie*, 20 (1884), 449–530.

1113.42 *Functions*] 1st ed.

1113.43 *Vorlesungen*] James ignores a paragraph division.

1114.9 Vulpian] Ferrier cites no source.

1114.34 Bastian] Charlton Bastian, "Remarks on the 'Muscular Sense', and on the Physiology of Thinking," *British Medical Journal*, vol. 1 for 1869 (May 1), pp. 394–396; (May 15), pp. 437–439; (May 22), pp. 461–463; (June 5), pp. 509–512.

1117.37 *Physiologische*] *Handbuch*, pp. 600–601.

1117.41 Graefe] Alfred Karl Graefe (1830–1899), "Motilitätsstörungen" in *Handbuch der gesammten Augenheilkunde*, VI (Leipzig: W. Engelmann, 1880), 18–19.

1118.11 Graefe] Graefe does not cite a source for Albrecht von Graefe (1828–1870), German ophthalmologist.

1119.27 explanation] In "The Feeling of Effort," pp. 10–14.

1119.28 Mach] Mach comments upon James's failure in *The Analysis of Sensations*, p. 129. The putty experiment is discussed in the correspondence between James and Christine Ladd-Franklin, especially her letters to James of February 1 and 21, 1889 (bMS Am 1092, letters 269, 270) and James's letters of February 3 and 28 (Columbia University Library, Franklin Collection).

1120.2 Graefe] *Handbuch*, VI, 21.

1120.13 Adamük] E. Adamük, "Über die Innervation der Augenbewegungen," *Zentralblatt für die medizinischen Wissenschaften*, 8 (1870), 65–67.

1120.22 Hering] See especially Ewald Hering, *Die Lehre vom binocularen Sehen* (Leipzig: W. Engelmann, 1868). An annotated copy was sold.

1120.23 Helmholtz's] In the translation, some of the references to the figure which accompanies Helmholtz's text are omitted.

1122.39 *Beiträge*] Pp. 65–66. On p. 144 of *The Analysis of Sensations*, Mach notes James's treatment. The oil-cloth experiment is discussed in the correspondence between James and Christine Ladd-Franklin (see note to 1119.28).

1123.28 Drown] See note to 627.36.

1124.4 Gley] Eugène Gley and Léon Marillier, "Expériences sur le 'sens musculaire'," *Revue Philosophique*, 23 (1887), 441–443. In the original, the experiments are numbered.

1124.21 Gley] Eugène Gley, "Le 'Sens musculaire' et les sensations musculaires," *Revue Philosophique*, 20 (1885), 601–610; citing A. M. Bloch,

"Expériences sur les sensations de contraction musculaire," *Comptes Rendus Hebdomadaires des Séances et Mémoires de la Société de Biologie*, 8th series, vol. 1 (1884), pp. 31-33.

1125.5 Sternberg] See note to 749.17. Exner's suggestion was made personally to Sternberg.

1125.29 *Proceedings*] See note to 684.4-5.

1125.30 Loeb] Jacques Loeb, "Untersuchungen über die Orientirung im Fühlraum der Hand und im Blickraum," *Archiv für Physiologie*, 46 (August 1889), 1-46. The quotation is on p. 2.

1126.30 Loeb's] Jacques Loeb, "Untersuchungen über den Fühlraum der Hand," part I, *Archiv für Physiologie*, 41 (September 1887), 107-127.

1126.36 Müller] See note to 834.37.

1127.33 Maine de Biran] François Pierre Maine de Biran (1766-1824), French philosopher and statesman, emphasized the importance of an "effort voulu" in knowing. Preserved are the *Œuvres philosophiques de Maine de Biran*, ed. V. Cousin, 4 vols. (Paris: Ladrange, 1841) (WJ 653.41). For references see "The Feeling of Effort" (1880), p. 16n.

1127.33 Royer-Collard] In his "Fragments," IV, 329 (see note to 574.40), Royer-Collard emphasizes the role of touch in sensation and perception.

1127.33 Herschel] John Frederick William Herschel (1792-1871), British astronomer and physicist, in *A Preliminary Discourse on the Study of Natural Philosophy*, new ed. (Philadelphia: Lea & Blanchard, 1839), p. 66 (sec. 77), asserts that "This impression which we receive of the nature of force from our own effort and our sense of fatigue, is quite different from that which we obtain of it from seeing the effect of force exerted by others in producing *motion*."

1127.33 Carpenter] In *Principles of Mental Physiology*, p. 11, Carpenter claims that we know matter as force through our "Tactile Sense" which includes the "Mental Sense of Effort."

1127.33 Martineau] James perhaps has in mind James Martineau, "Modern Materialism: Its Attitude towards Theology" (1876), reprinted in *Essays, Reviews, and Addresses*, IV (London: Longmans, Green, 1891), especially pp. 241ff.

1127.38 Bertrand's] Alexis Bertrand (1850-1923), French philosopher, *La Psychologie de l'effort et les doctrines contemporaines* (Paris: Alcan, 1889), especially in the chapter on "L'effort musculaire," pp. 96-125.

1129.13 Bowditch] Henry Pickering Bowditch and William Freeman Southard, American physician, "A Comparison of Sight and Touch," *Journal of Physiology*, 3 (January 1882), 232-245.

1129.24 Bastian] See note to 1103.43.

1129.24 Binet] See note to 1103.31.

1129.32 Binet] Alfred Binet and Charles Féré, "Recherches expérimentales sur la physiologie des mouvements chez les hysteriques," *Archives de Physiologie*, 3rd series, vol. 10 (1887), pp. 320-373.

1130.37 Janet] See pp. 199–208.

1131.3 Carpenter] In sec. 3 on "Ideo-Motor Action" of ch. 6 (pp. 279–315) of *Principles of Mental Physiology*.

1131.33 *Medicinische*] *Medicinische Psychologie*, pp. 293–294. In his copy on p. 311, opposite the passage quoted, James asks: "Warum denn nicht alle beide, da wir doch auch der Willensimpulse bewusst sind?" James is quoting from sec. 26, "Von den Bewegungsgefühlen" of ch. 3, bk. II, "Von den Bewegungen und den Trieben."

1132.39 Féré] Pp. 8–25.

1133.19 Lotze] *Medicinische Psychologie*, p. 293.

1133.35 Carpenter] Ch. 6 (pp. 220–315), "Of Ideation and Ideo-Motor Action."

1133.37–38 Cumberland's] Stuart C. Cumberland, mind-reader and critic of spiritualism, "A Thought-Reader's Experiences," *Nineteenth Century*, 20 (December 1886), 867–885.

1133.39 Gley] Eugène Gley, "Expérience relative au pouvoir moteur des images ou représentations mentales," *Bulletins de la Société de Psychologie Physiologique*, 5 (1890), 30–33.

1141.39 Everett] Charles Caroll Everett (1829–1900), professor of theology at Harvard. Four letters from Everett to James are in Houghton (bMS Am 1092, letters 177–180).

1144.16 Clouston] *Clinical Lectures*, p. 317.

1145.31 Dudley] Albertus True Dudley (1866–1955), American educator and author, "The Mental Qualities of an Athlete," *Harvard Monthly*, 6 (April 1888), 43–51; the quotation is from pp. 45, 46.

1148.16 Ribot] Ch. 4 (pp. 111–122) of *Les Maladies de la volonté*.

1148.40 *Maladies*] Pp. 77–79, quoting Louis Florentin Calmeil (1798–1895), French psychiatrist, *Traité des maladies inflammatoires du cerveau*.

1149.39 Maudsley's] Henry Maudsley, *Responsibility in Mental Disease* (New York: D. Appleton, 1874), pp. 133–170 on "Impulsive Insanity." James reviewed this work in the *Nation*, 19 (July 16, 1874), 43 and the *Atlantic Monthly*, 34 (September 1874), 364–365.

1149.40 Winslow's] Pp. 138–246.

1150.12 Alfieri] Vittorio Alfieri (1749–1803), Italian dramatist, *Life of Vittorio Alfieri*, with an essay by William Dean Howells (Boston: James R. Osgood, 1877), pp. 192–196. James omits paragraph divisions and section numbers.

1150.40 Burr] George Burr (1813–1882), American physician, "On the Insanity of Inebriety," *Psychological and Medico-Legal Journal*, n.s. 1 (December 1874), 341–365; the quotations from Reuben Dimond Mussey (1780–1866), American physician, and J. E. Turner are from pp. 355–356. Burr does not cite any sources.

1152.37 Cowles] Edward Cowles (1837–1919), American psychiatrist,

"Insistent and Fixed Ideas," *American Journal of Psychology*, 1 (February 1888), 222–270. In Widener is an annotated copy of *Neurasthenia and Its Mental Symptoms* (Boston: Clapp, 1891) (Phil 6952.10.2).

1152.38 Knapp] Philip Coombs Knapp (1858–1920), American physician, "The Insanity of Doubt," *American Journal of Psychology*, 3 (January 1890), 1–23.

1153.3 *"Video]* From Ovid's *Metamorphoses*, bk. VII, lines 20–21.

1153.39 Ribot] *Les Maladies de la volonté*, pp. 38–39, quoting Joseph Guislain (1797–1860), Belgian psychiatrist, *Leçons orales sur les phréno-pathies*.

1154.8 Restif] Nicolas Edme Restif (Restif de la Bretonne) (1734–1806), French novelist.

1156.9 Dante] *Inferno*, canto 5, line 121.

1156.10 Homer] *Odyssey*, bk. XV, lines 400–401. The translation used by James is unknown.

1158.33 *Emotions]* 3rd ed. In James's copy of *The Emotions and the Will*, on these pages, there are numerous markings and several cross-references. On p. 132, next to Bain's "why should a more lively feeling" (1157.34–35), James has "associationist mode."

1159.18 Spencer] Herbert Spencer, *The Data of Ethics* (New York: D. Appleton, 1879) (WJ 582.24), p. 83: "Sentient existence can evolve only on condition that pleasure-giving acts are life-sustaining acts."

1160.32 *Emotions]* In James's copy, the quoted passage is marked with a question mark.

1160.35 P.] Pp. 354–355.

1163.4 Hamlet] Shakespeare, *Hamlet*, act I, scene 5, lines 189–190.

1163.31 Hume's] *Essays Moral, Political, and Literary*, II, 11n.

1163.39 Sidgwick] Henry Sidgwick (1838–1900), British philosopher, *The Methods of Ethics* (London: Macmillan, 1874), pp. 30–42, "Pleasure and Desire." Perry reports that annotated copies of this work and of the *Outlines of the History of Ethics* (1886) were sold. The correspondence between James and Sidgwick is at Houghton (bMS Am 1092.9 [615–618, 3760–3767]), and at the Society for Psychical Research in London.

1163.41 Carpenter] See note to 1133.35.

1163.41 Martineau] James Martineau, *Types of Ethical Theory*, 2 vols. (Oxford: Clarendon, 1885) (WJ 553.78.2), II, 65–69, on "Objects of Prudential Judgment," and II, 297–301, on "Meanings Given to the Word 'Pleasure'." In James's copy, on II, 300, there are cross-references to pp. 68–69 and p. 69, as well as the remark "Moth & flame."

1163.42 Stephen] *The Science of Ethics*, pp. 50–51 (see note to 949.34). In James's copy on p. 50, there is a cross-reference to p. 47.

1164.37 Spencer] *The Data of Ethics*, pp. 26–46.

1164.37–38 Thompson] *A System of Psychology*, II, 503–570, on "Volitional and Ultimate Integrations"; "The *Summum Bonum,*" *Mind,* 6 (January 1881), 62–81.

1164.38 Bain] While Bain does on pp. 342–344 of *The Senses and the Intellect,* 3rd ed., discuss pleasure and pain, he treats the same topics on pp. 338–344 of *Mental and Moral Science.*

1170.38 Aristotle's] Alexander Grant, *The Ethics of Aristotle Illustrated with Essays and Notes,* 2nd ed., 2 vols. (London: Longmans, Green, 1866), I, 212–219. Both volumes of this edition were sold. Also sold was the *Nicomachean Ethics* in the French translation of Jules Barthélemy-Saint-Hilaire.

1171.25 Another] Pp. 122–123.

1174.6 Paris] For James's brief note on this Congress, see *Mind,* 14 (October 1889), 614–615.

1176.22 "*dazu*] Goethe, *Faust,* p. 55 (line 1650).

1176.26 genius] Jules Lequier (1814–1862), French philosopher, *La Recherche d'une première vérité: Fragments posthumes,* ed. Charles Renouvier (Saint-Cloud: Belin, 1865), p. 90.

1176.37 lecture] Reprinted in *The Will to Believe,* WORKS.

1179.34 Spencer's] On I, 503 of his copy, in reference to Spencer's 'nonsense', James writes: "Nonsense yourself! Psychology don't pretend to be a quantitative science. Free will is solely a question of ['the' *deleted*] *quantity* ['of' *deleted*] in motives. The motives are as to their possible *kinds* always determined. Out of several possibles liberty chooses one. But Psychology is the science of the possibles, of the *classes* of representations. To claim more wd. be to make it a knowledge not of general laws but of all the particular details of all future history."

1180.12 Fiske's] II, 180–181, 184, 186–187.

1181.9 'searching] Psalms, VII, 10.

1182.38 Hall] Granville Stanley Hall, "The Education of the Will," *Princeton Review,* 58th year (November 1882), pp. 306–325.

1183.39 *Emotions*] 3rd ed., pp. 303–320 on "The Primitive Elements of Volition."

1184.28 Golgi] Camillo Golgi (1843–1926), Italian histologist.

1185.4 Janet] *L'Automatisme psychologique,* pp. 56–57.

1185.9 Charcot] See p. 1203.

1187.27 Herbart] See for example the *Lehrbuch zur Psychologie,* pp. 101–102 (secs. 124–125) (pp. 9–10 of the English translation).

1191.32 Lange's] See note to 99.1 and pp. 409–410.

1191.37 Münsterberg] Hugo Münsterberg, "Die Association successiver Vorstellungen," *Zeitschrift für Psychologie und Physiologie der Sinnesorgane,* vol. 1, no. 2 (1889), pp. 99–120. No article by James in response to Münsterberg is known and this part of the discussion is not reproduced in *Psychology: Briefer Course* (1892).

1194.2 'hypnotic'] For James's own study of hypnosis, see notes to 103.5 and 1102.37.

1194.7 Braid] James Braid describes his method of hypnotizing in *Neurypnology; Or, the Rationale of Nervous Sleep, Considered in Relation with Animal Magnetism* (London: John Churchill, 1843), p. 27.

1194.22 Liébeault] Ambroise Auguste Liébeault (1823–1904), French physician and hypnotist. James reviewed Liébeault's *Du sommeil et des états analogues, considérés surtout au point de vue de l'action du moral sur le physique* (1866), in the *Nation*, 7 (July 16, 1868), 50–52. A marked copy of *Thérapeutique suggestive* (1891) was sold. Liébeault describes how he came to use the method of verbal suggestion in part I of his "Confession d'un médecin hypnotiseur," *Revue de l'Hypnotisme*, 1 (1887), 105–110.

1195.4 Liégeois] Jules Liégeois (1833–1908), French jurist, *De la suggestion et du somnambulisme dans leurs rapports avec la jurisprudence et la médecine légale* (Paris: Octave Doin, 1889), pp. 730–731.

1195.12 Pitres] Albert Pitres, *Leçons cliniques sur l'hystérie et l'hypnotisme faites à l'hôpital Saint-André de Bordeaux*, II (Paris: Octave Doin, 1891), 97–116 on "zones hypnogènes."

1195.19 Gurney] For a note on Gurney's hypnotism experiments see *The Will to Believe*, WORKS, note to 229.4.

1195.22 Liébeault] James's source for this percentage is unknown. In *Le Sommeil provoqué et les états analogues* (Paris: Octave Doin, 1889), p. 19n, Liébeault claims that in 1887 and 1888, he succeeded to some degree in slightly more than 95 percent of the cases.

1195.23 Wetterstrand] The *Revue de l'Hypnotisme*, 3 (1889), 144–147, published a critical review by F. Van Eeden of Otto G. Wetterstrand, a physician in Stockholm, "Om hypnotismens anvandande i den praktiska Medicinen" (1888), likely the source used by James.

1195.32 Bernheim] Hippolyte Bernheim, "L'Hypnotisme et l'école de Nancy," *Revue de l'Hypnotisme*, 2 (1888), 322–325.

1196.14 Moll] Albert Moll (1862–1939), German psychiatrist, *Der Hypnotismus* (Berlin: Fischer's medicinische Buchhandlung, 1889) (WJ 756.51), p. 25. Also preserved is James's copy of *Der Rapport in der Hypnose: Untersuchungen über den thierischen Magnetismus* (Leipzig: Ambr. Abel, 1892) (WJ 756.51.2).

1196.29 Moll] *Der Hypnotismus*, p. 163.

1196.37 Despine] Prosper Despine (b. 1812), French psychiatrist, *Étude scientifique sur le somnambulisme, sur les phénomènes qu'il présente et sur son action thérapeutique dans certaines maladies nerveuses, du rôle important qu'il joue dans l'épilepsie, dans l'hystérie et dans les névroses dites extraordinaires* (Paris: F. Savy, 1880), pp. 286–289. The Widener copy (Phil 6673.7) has an index in what appears to be James's hand, but it is too faded to read. In Widener is James's copy of *Psychologie naturelle*, 3 vols. (Paris: F. Savy, 1868) (Phil 5243.6), with vol. I inscribed to Matthew Arnold from the author.

1197.16 Charcot] In "Magnetism and Hypnotism," *Forum*, 8 (January

1890), 566–577, Jean Martin Charcot distinguishes three hypnotic states, lethargy, catalepsy, and somnambulism. An essay by J. Babinski, of the Salpêtrière, "Grand et petit hypnotisme," appears in the *Œuvres complètes de J. M. Charcot*, IX (Paris: Aux bureaux du *Progrès Médical*, 1890), 505–537.

1197.31 Charcot] Many of the terms describing hypnotic states used by James appear in Charcot's *Œuvres*, IX, 300–304, in the paper "Essai d'une distinction nosographique des divers états nerveux compris sous le nom d'hypnotisme."

1198.21 Heidenhain] Rudolf Peter Heinrich Heidenhain, *Animal Magnetism: Physiological Observations*, trans. L. C. Wooldridge (London: C. Kegan Paul, 1880), pp. 78–79. In the Widener copy (Phil 6677.2), the following page numbers are listed in James's hand: 12, 17, 19, 22, 30, 37, 38, 44–6, 47, 48, 49, 60, 61, 65, 78, 79, 83, 86, 88, 89, 90, 91, 92.

1202.23 Delbœuf] Joseph Remi Léopold Delbœuf, "La Mémoire chez les hypnotisés," *Revue Philosophique*, 21 (May 1886), 441–472.

1203.22 Charcot] Charcot discusses simulation in *Œuvres*, III, 109–111, in lesson 8 of the *Leçons sur les maladies du système nerveux.*

1205.12 Delbœuf] Joseph Remi Léopold Delbœuf, *Le Magnétisme animal à propos d'une visite à l'école de Nancy* (Paris: Alcan, 1889), p. 106.

1206.20 Binet] James perhaps is referring to a case described in *Animal Magnetism*, p. 312, except that the persons involved are identified by different initials.

1208.26 Bergson] Henri Bergson, "De la simulation inconsciente dans l'état d'hypnotisme," *Revue Philosophique*, 22 (November 1886), 525–531. For notes on the relations between James and Bergson see the notes to "Bergson and His Critique of Intellectualism," *A Pluralistic Universe*, WORKS, pp. 101–124.

1208.31 Taguet] Frederic William Henry Myers, "Note on Certain Reported Cases of Hypnotic Hyperæsthesia," *Transactions of the SPR*, 4 (May 1887), 532–539, on p. 537 mentions a report from a Dr. Taguet of Bordeaux whose patient was able to read words reflected upon a card. Myers notes that when the patient was examined later, she did not have the power.

1208.32 Sauvaire] C. Sauvaire, "Observations d'hyperesthésie des sens dans l'état hypnotique," *Revue Philosophique*, 23 (March 1887), 333–335.

1209.25 Gurney's] See for example the "Second Report of the Committee on Mesmerism," by Gurney and others, in the *Proceedings of the SPR*, 1 (December 1883), 251–262.

1209.40 Proceedings] This literature can be located through the *Combined Index* to the *Proceedings*, *Journal*, and other publications of the Society for Psychical Research. On p. 128 of the *Combined Index* (1904), numerous references are listed under "Hypnotisation at a Distance."

1210.29 Beaunis] *Recherches expérimentales*, II, 29–30.

1210.29 Berjon] Augustin Berjon (b. 1859), French physician, *La Grande hystérie chez l'homme* (Paris: Baillière, 1886), pp. 36–39.

1210.29 Bernheim] *Suggestive Therapeutics*, pp. 75–76.

1210.29 Bourru] The main work on this subject by Henri Bourru and Prosper Ferdinand Burot is *La Suggestion mentale et l'action à distance des substances toxiques et médicamenteuses* (Paris: Baillière, 1887), but their experiments are often cited in the literature, for example, by Bernheim, *Suggestive Therapeutics*, p. 76.

1210.29 Charcot] References to Charcot are very numerous in the literature; in "On Telepathic Hypnotism, and Its Relation to Other Forms of Hypnotic Suggestion," *Proceedings of the SPR*, 4 (October 1886), 151n, Myers lists several papers by Charcot.

1210.29 Delbœuf] Joseph Remi Léopold Delbœuf, "De la prétendue veille somnambulique," *Revue Philosophique*, 23 (February 1887), 113–142; (March), 262–285.

1210.30 Dumontpallier] Victor Alphonse Amédée Dumontpallier (1827–1899), French physician, "De l'action vaso-motrice de la suggestion chez les hystériques hypnotisables (seconde note)," *Comptes Rendus Hebdomadaires des Séances et Mémoires de la Société de Biologie*, 8th series, vol. 2 (1885), pp. 458–459, reports that he was able to raise the body temperature of his subjects by suggestion. He is cited to this effect by Bernheim, *Suggestive Therapeutics*, p. 76, who also adds that Dumontpallier failed to raise blisters.

1210.30 Focachon] In *Suggestive Therapeutics*, pp. 75–76, Bernheim states that Focachon, "an apothecary at Charmes," raised blisters in two cases, on persons Focachon had taken to Nancy for purposes of demonstration. Focachon's work is discussed at greater length by Liébeault, *Le Sommeil provoqué*, pp. 299–303.

1210.30 Forel] August Forel (1848–1931), Swiss psychologist, *Der Hypnotismus: Seine psycho-physiologische, medicinische, strafrechtliche Bedeutung und seine Handhabung*, 2nd ed. (Stuttgart: Ferdinand Enke, 1891). The first edition was published in 1889. Preserved in Widener is James's copy of *Gehirn und Seele*, 5th and 6th eds. (Bonn: Emil Strauss, 1899) (Phil 6115. 21.4), inscribed to James by the author.

1210.30 Jendrássik] András Jenö Jendrássik's experiments, performed in 1887 in connection with the medical society in Budapest, are described by Richard von Krafft-Ebing (see below), pp. 24–27.

1210.30 Krafft-Ebing] Richard von Krafft-Ebing (1840–1902), German neurologist, *Eine experimentelle Studie auf dem Gebiete des Hypnotismus* (Stuttgart: Ferdinand Enke, 1888). Krafft-Ebing relies heavily upon Jendrássik's work. Works by Krafft-Ebing from James's library will be listed in the volume of manuscript remains.

1210.30–31 Liébeault] *Le Sommeil provoqué*, ch. 4 (pp. 41–218), "Du sommeil profond ou somnambulisme provoqué."

1210.31 Liégeois] *De la suggestion*, p. 293. In some of his investigations, Liégeois was associated with Liébeault and Focachon.

1210.31 Lipp] Eduard Lipp, an Austrian dermatologist, served as an observer in some of Jendrássik's investigations; see Krafft-Ebing, p. 59.

1210.31 Mabille] H. Mabille, director of the Insane Asylum at Lafond, France, "Note sur les hémorrhagies cutanées par autosuggestion dans le somnambulisme provoqué," *Progrès Médical*, vol. 2 for 1885 (August 29), pp. 155–156. Mabille's work is discussed by Bernheim, *Suggestive Therapeutics*, pp. 76–77.

1211.3 Delbœuf] "De la prétendue veille somnambulique," p. 266.

1211.36 Liégeois] *De la suggestion*, p. 128.

1213.21 Gurney] The planchette is used in experiments described by Gurney in "Peculiarities of Certain Post-Hypnotic States" (see note to 206.12).

1214.8 Moll] Albert Moll, *Hypnotism* (London: W. Scott, 1890). The earliest American edition located was published in 1893.

1214.12 Dessoir] Max Dessoir (1867–1947), German psychologist, *Bibliographie des modernen Hypnotismus* (Berlin: Carl Duncker, 1888). In Widener is James's copy of *Das Doppel-Ich* (Leipzig: E. Günther, 1890) (Phil 7042.2), while Houghton preserves a pamphlet by Dessoir (WJ 700.5).

1214.16 Gurney] Edmund Gurney, in vol. 9 of *Mind*: "The Stages of Hypnotism" (January 1884), 110–121; "The Problems of Hypnotism" (October 1884), 477–508.

1214.20 In] The chapter on hypnotism was published in the *Religio-Philosophical Journal*, n.s. 1 (August 23, 1890), 196; (August 30, 1890), 212; (September 6, 1890), 228–229; (September 13, 1890), 245–246; (September 20, 1890), 260. The remainder of this note was substituted for the following references which appear in the *Journal* (p. 260): J. W. Cadwell, *Full and Comprehensive Instructions How to Mesmerize*, 2nd ed. (Boston: The author, 1882); C. Lloyd Tuckey (1855–1925), *Psycho-Therapeutics; Or, Treatment by Hypnotism and Suggestion* (London: Baillière, Tindall, and Cox, 1890); Fredrik Johan Björnström (1833–1889), *Hypnotism: Its History and Present Development*, trans. Nils Posse (New York: Humboldt Publishing Co., 1889); John Gray McKendrick (1841–1926), British physiologist, an article on animal magnetism in the *Encyclopædia Britannica*, 9th ed., which has not been identified.

1214.21 Mitchell] John Kearsley Mitchell (1793–1858), American physician and physiologist, *Five Essays*, ed. Silas Weir Mitchell (Philadelphia: J. B. Lippincott, 1859). Perry reports that a copy of this work was sold.

1216.38 Darwinian] James develops similar notions in "Great Men and Their Environment," *The Will to Believe*, WORKS, pp. 163–170.

1218.10–11 Spencer's] *The Principles of Psychology*, I, 424 (sec. 189); I, 460 (sec. 205); I, 466–471 (sec. 208). On I, 460 of James's copy, attached to '*frequency*' (1219.1 in WORKS), James has the comment, "not *persistence*. See p 408[,] 464, 463, 500, 466." On I, 469, 'infant's' (1220.40 in WORKS) is underlined and James comments, "better an animal's."

1223.29 Spencer's] *The Principles of Psychology*, I, 387 (sec. 173). For James's criticism of Spencer on this point see "Remarks on Spencer's Definition of Mind as Correspondence," *Essays in Philosophy*, WORKS.

1224.16 Darwin] See p. 1275.

1225.31 *Principles*] I, 432–463.

1225.39 Loeb] See note to 44.23. On p. 300 Loeb mentions Goltz, but does not cite a specific source. For Goltz's work on dogs see note to 22.32.

1228.30 Allen] Grant Allen, "Idiosyncrasy," *Mind*, 8 (October 1883), 487–505. In James's set of *Mind* (Phil 22.4.6*), the article is marked but not annotated. Allen's "The Genesis of Genius," *Atlantic Monthly*, 47 (March 1881), 371–381, is a criticism of James's "Great Men and Their Environment," see *The Will to Believe*, WORKS. James responded to Allen in "The Importance of Individuals," *The Will to Believe*, WORKS.

1231.20 Mill] *A System of Logic*, I, 437–438.

1232.37 Hodgson] Ch. 5 (pp. 288–372) on "Percept and Concept."

1232.38 Lotze] *Logik*, pp. 550–572.

1232.38 Sigwart] Christoph Sigwart (1830–1904), German philosopher, *Logik*, 2 vols. (Tübingen: Laupp, 1873–1878), II, 3–27, 591–603. For a note on James's copy of this work and Sigwart's influence on James see *The Will to Believe*, WORKS, note to 20.14.

1232.39 "Great] Reprinted in *The Will to Believe*, WORKS, as "Great Men and Their Environment."

1236.16 Hodgson] See note to 1232.37.

1236.25 Layard] Austen Henry Layard (1817–1894), British archeologist and diplomat, *Discoveries among the Ruins of Nineveh and Babylon* (New York: Putnam, 1853), pp. 663–664.

1239.38 Locke's] *Essay*, p. 92. In his copy, next to the passage quoted, James has "Platonism 363."

1241.39 Bradley] Bk. II, pt. 1, ch. 1, secs. 3–4.

1243.36 Bradley] Pp. 235–239.

1246.38 Wundt] 2nd ed.

1248.34 Mill] *A System of Logic*, I, 296. In his copy, James has "The same numbers can be apprehended or composed in many ways."

1248.36 Grassman] Perhaps Robert Grassman (1815–1901), German mathematician.

1248.38 Helmholtz's] Hermann Helmholtz, "Zählen und Messen erkenntnisstheoretisch betrachtet," *Philosophische Aufsätze. Eduard Zeller zu seinem fünfzigjährigen Doctor-Jubiläum gewidmet* (Leipzig: Fues, 1887), pp. 17–52.

1249.38 Mill's] *A System of Logic*, I, 292–298. On I, 297, opposite Mill's claim that arithmetic involves an assumption ("which may be false") that "1=1; that all the numbers are numbers of the same or of equal units," James comments: "This gives away the whole case about abstract concepts. —How can there be pure number per se in the mind, and any certain equality if number be an 'exact' copy of originals themselves vague." James makes additional critical comments both in the above section and in bk. III, ch. 24, sec. 5 (II, 149–154).

1250.1 Mill] James is paraphrasing *A System of Logic*, I, 293.

1250.7 "We] *A System of Logic*, I, 293. In his copy, attached with a guideline to 'so divided', James comments: "This shows the idea of a unit to come rather from our manner of carving out things than from their sensible appearance."

1250.21 Lavoisier] Antoine Laurent Lavoisier (1743–1794), French chemist.

1251.22 separate] On II, 149 of his copy of Mill's *System of Logic*, James comments: "*lines* which intersect each other need not continue to diverge, only when they do not, we *refuse to call them straight*."

1254.40 De Morgan] Augustus De Morgan, *Syllabus of a Proposed System of Logic* (London: Walton and Maberly, 1860), pp. 46–56.

1255.20 Locke's] *Essay*, p. 132.

1255.23 Kant's] In his copy of the Adickes edition of the *Critique*, opposite p. 46 (B11=A7), James writes: "See my psychol. II, 661, Synthetic j. expresses a relation between 2 data at least. Distinction can't be made sharp."

1255.42 Spir's] Afrikan Spir (1837–1890), Ukrainian-born philosopher, *Denken und Wirklichkeit. Versuch einer Erneuerung der kritischen Philosophie* (Leipzig: J. G. Findel, 1873), pp. 205–210. Perry reports that an annotated copy of this work was sold from James's library.

1256.2 Locke's] *Essay*, pp. 385, 452–453, 412, 489 (bk. IV, ch. 1, sec. 9; ch. 6, sec. 13; ch. 3, sec. 31; ch. 11, sec. 14). On p. 452, James writes: "[Note diff. between philos. quâ large & grand but loose view, & phil. quâ fine & exact work]." This, and several other similar comments, appear to have been made with teaching in mind.

1257.40 Book] *Essay*, pp. 474, 465, 435–436, 465 (bk. IV, ch. 9, sec. 1; ch. 7, sec. 14; ch. 4, sec. 6; ch. 7, sec. 14).

1257.41 Book] *Essay*, pp. 443–445.

1258.38 Spir] *Denken und Wirklichkeit*, p. 13.

1259.32 Berkeley's] P. 254.

1260.35 Helmholtz] Hermann Helmholtz, *Über die Erhaltung der Kraft, eine physikalische Abhandlung* (Berlin: G. Reimer, 1847), pp. 2–3, 4–5, 5, 6.

1260.40 Gay-Lussac] Joseph Louis Gay-Lussac (1778–1850), French chemist and physicist.

1263.27 Liberatore] Matteo Liberatore (1810–1892), Italian Roman Catholic theologian, *Compendium Logicae et Metaphysicae*. No copy of the third edition was examined, but in the fifth edition (Prato: Giachetti, 1885), the quoted text is found on p. 259.

1264.37 Riehl] Vol. II, pt. 1, pp. 215–218.

1266.35 Hamond] Henry Crabb Robinson (1775–1867), British writer, *Diary, Reminiscences, and Correspondence*, ed. Thomas Sadler, 2 vols. (Boston: Fields, Osgood, 1869), I, 424–425; quoting from letters and diaries of Elton Hamond (1786–1819). Robinson describes Hamond as a merchant who fired his whole staff so that "he might not be interfered with in his plans," and explains this action as one of "those extravagances" resulting from "insanity" (I, 417). Robinson quotes Hamond as follows: "It is provoking that the secret of rendering man perfect in wisdom, power, virtue, and happiness should die with me" (I, 424). Hamond committed suicide.

1266.37 Sidgwick] Pp. 357–360. James's third formula is a paraphrase of a view attributed by Sidgwick (p. 358) to Samuel Clarke (1675–1729), British theologian and philosopher.

1267.39 Aurelius] *The Thoughts of the Emperor M. Aurelius Antoninus*, pp. 164–165.

1268.23 Spencer's] See pp. 1218–1222.

1270.21 Lamarck's] Jean Baptiste Pierre Antoine de Monet de Lamarck (1744–1829), French naturalist, *Philosophie zoologique*, new ed., 2 vols. (Paris: F. Savy, 1873), II, 293–298, a section titled "De l'instinct des animaux" of ch. 5.

1270.29 Lewes] *Problems of Life and Mind*, 1st series, vol. I, pp. 140–141.

1270.34 Spir] P. 257.

1270.37 Spencer's] I, 432–443.

1270.38 Romanes] Pp. 256–272, "Examination of the Theories of Other Writers on the Evolution of Instinct, with a General Summary of the Theory here Set Forth."

1273.23 Knight] Thomas Andrew Knight (1759–1838), British naturalist, "On the Hereditary Instinctive Propensities of Animals," *Philosophical Transactions* for 1837, pt. 2 (vol. 127), pp. 365–369. This paper is cited by Ribot, *L'Hérédité psychologique*, p. 26.

1273.24 Darwin] Ribot, p. 26, attributes this remark to Darwin and cites *On the Origin of Species*, ch. 8 (p. 212 in ch. 7 in 1859 ed.).

1273.38 Spencer] Herbert Spencer, *Illustrations of Universal Progress; A Series of Discussions* (New York: D. Appleton, 1864), pp. 310–311, 315–316. James omits paragraph divisions.

1273.40 Ribot] Théodule Ribot, *L'Hérédité psychologique*, 2nd ed. (Paris: Baillière, 1882), pp. 26–27.

1274.7 Darwin] While Darwin does not refer to orphans, in *The Expression of the Emotions*, pp. 265–267, he does discuss the shrugging of shoulders by French children brought up outside France.

1274.11 Brown-Séquard] In *The Variation of Animals and Plants under Domestication*, II, 24 (see below), Darwin discusses Brown-Séquard's experiments on guinea pigs and cites Brown-Séquard, "Hereditary Transmission of an Epileptiform Affection Accidentally Produced," *Proceedings of the Royal Society*, 10 (1860), 297–298.

1275.33 Carpenter] William Benjamin Carpenter, "On the Hereditary Transmission of Acquired Psychical Habits," *Contemporary Review*, 21 (January 1873), 295–314; (April 1873), 779–795; (May 1873), 867–885.

1275.34 Spencer] I, 184–200, 238–291, 432–463.

1275.35 Darwin] Charles Darwin, *The Variation of Animals and Plants under Domestication*, 2 vols. (London: John Murray, 1868) (WJ 516.78), II,

1–84. James's copy is dated Teplitz, March 1868. James reviewed the work in the *Atlantic Monthly*, 22 (July 1868), 122–124, and in the *North American Review*, 107 (July 1868), 362–368.

1275.36 Butler] Samuel Butler (1835–1902), British novelist, *Life and Habit*, 2nd ed. (London: Trübner, 1878). James cites the second edition in his manuscript note to p. 131.

1275.37 Dupuy] Eugène Dupuy, "On Heredity in Nervous Diseases," *Popular Science Monthly*, 11 (July 1877), 332–339.

1275.38 Papillon] Fernand Papillon (1847–1873), French writer, *Nature and Life. Facts and Doctrines Relating to the Constitution of Matter, the New Dynamics, and the Philosophy of Nature*, trans. A. R. Macdonough (New York: D. Appleton, 1875), pp. 330–363, chapter on "Heredity in Physiology, in Medicine, and in Psychology." James reviewed this work in the *Nation*, 20 (June 24, 1875), 429.

1275.38 Crothers] Thomas Davison Crothers (1842–1918), American physician, "New Facts in Alcoholic Heredity," *Popular Science Monthly*, 34 (February 1889), 524–535.

1275.41 *Origin*] P. 209.

1277.39 *Principles*] II, 560–561 (sec. 504).

1278.13 *Ibid.*] II, 623 (sec. 532).

1278.13 Weismann] August Weismann (1834–1914), German biologist, *Über die Vererbung* (Jena: Gustav Fischer, 1883); English translation appears in *Essays upon Heredity and Kindred Biological Problems*, ed. Edward B. Poulton, Selmar Schönland, Arthur E. Shipley (Oxford: Clarendon, 1889).

1278.37 Essay] August Weismann, *Die Continuität des Keimplasmas als Grundlage einer Theorie der Vererbung* (Jena: Naumburg, 1885); reprinted in *Essays upon Heredity*.

1279.6 Bernoullis] A family of Swiss mathematicians prominent in the 17th and 18th centuries.

1279.26 Spencer] Herbert Spencer, *The Factors of Organic Evolution* (New York: D. Appleton, 1887) (WJ 582.24.2), pp. 13–17.

Appendixes

Appendix I

Extracts from Collated Journal Articles

The following extracts from collated journal articles are not printed in the Historical Collation because of their length.

CHAPTER XIV: ASSOCIATION

Extracts from "The Association of Ideas" (P29), which are variant or omitted in (I).

520.1–31 terms ... them.] [¶] Two great philosophic efforts to this end have been made. The one is called the associationist philosophy of England, the other the Herbartian system of Germany. Professor Bain's books are generally regarded as the most successful expression of the first movement. Volkmann's "Psychology" is perhaps the most finished utterance of the last. These schools differ as to their theoretic basis (the one being ontological and the other phenomenal), but they agree in almost all besides; especially in the attempt to show how all the different kinds of mental activity (such as memory, judgment, reasoning, self-consciousness, desire, etc., etc., which were formerly classed as distinct and original "faculties") may be explained as *resultants* of the manner in which, by the working of two or three simple elementary laws of revival between images, these latter are grouped ·into certain characteristic forms.

In fact, the easiest way of describing the entire industry of these schools would be to say that they seek to explain the forms of consciousness by means of its materials.

Now, to another class of minds any such attempt seems so preposterously absurd that they pour out the child with the bath, and disdain even a modest ambition which should content itself with tracing out in the jungle of the mind a few of the trails by which its *materials* are brought together. As this article is born of the latter ambition, and as its author thinks he has succeeded in making the trails broader and smoother than previous writers have left them, it behooves him to defend himself and his purpose by a few preliminary words addressed to this class of critics. They are recruited mainly from the school of Hegel, but we find even as fertile and acute a writer as Lotze sharing their prejudices and negations in this respect.

The intuition they start from is that thought is not a sand-heap of juxtaposed images with associating links outside of them and between them. It is a unitary *continuum* of which the items, and the logical relations between the items, form alike integral parts, equally imbedded, equally essential, equally interdependent. *Any* relation may carry us from one item to another, and according as we follow one or the other relation we shall traverse the field of thought in this way or in that, have one train of images or its opposite. But all the relations are *logical*, are relations of *reason*. A thing may suggest its like, or its opposite, its genus or its species, its cause or its effect, its means or its purpose, its habitual neighbors in space or in time, its possibilities or its impossibilities, its changes or its resistance to change—in short, it *may* call up every consideration to which it can have a possible logical relevancy, and call up each in its turn. And the only summary formula that can be applied to all these infinite possibilities of transition is that, as transitions of Thought, they are all alike *acts of Reason*. This monotonous appeal to "Thought" with a capital T and Reason with a capital R is apt to irritate the ear of him bent on analysis, very much as the stereotyped "Allah is great" of the Mussulman irritates the ear of the scientific traveler. It is true enough, but sterile. And, when it interdicts discrimination and the search for secondary causes, it performs as obstructive a function as that of our dear old friend the dog in the manger.   P29 (577.12–578.36)

522.10–523.2 and . . . facts.] but failed to dispose of the difficulty which comes in when we notice that in the *highest* flights of Reason habit does not seem the link between one item and the next. Rather are the transitions of genius distinguished by their express defiance of all that is habitual.

This led to the erection of other laws to supply the gaps in explanation left by the law of habit alone. No sensible man now considers the habit-philosophy of Hartley, Priestley, and James Mill to be adequate to its task. Professor Bain, reverting to Hume's standpoint, supplements the law of Contiguity by that of Similarity, and, in a subordinate degree, by that of Contrast. *All* the materials of thought, without conception, are in his psychology pushed or drawn before the footlights of consciousness by the working of these laws and by them alone.

Mr. Hodgson, ablest of recent (if not of all) English philosophers, supplements Bain's laws by an important principle, that of Interest.

And every one before whose consciousness, when falling asleep, trains of faces and other disconnected images are wont to pass, and who, moreover, after his attention has once been called to the subject, surprises vestiges of the same process at work during his waking hours, in the form of a sort of meteoric shower of random images, visual or verbal, which cross the main current of thought, but are so faint that they ordinarily arrest no attention and are forthwith forgotten*—every such person, I say, will plead for the admission of a principle of spontaneity or accidental arousal, along with the principles already mentioned.

In the pages that follow I accept all these laws save that of contrast; and that I do not reject, but simply ignore and disregard on the present occasion. I try to show how they all may follow from certain variations in a fundamental process of activity in the brain. In particular I reduce Contiguous and Similar Associations to one, by exhibiting their most pronounced forms as mere extremes of a common mode. But the reader is requested to remember that in thus trying to explain, by laws of matter, what ideas shall be presented to consciousness at any moment, I expressly repudiate the pretension to explain the form of consciousness itself. Consciousness, as I understand it, is always in the midst of the present aware of the past as that from which the present came; and, out of the materials which the present furnishes, she is always comparing one part with another, to select that which most fits her

*See Maury's classic work, "Le Sommeil et les Rêves."

ends. These peculiarities of consciousness were referred to above, when it was spoken of as a "presiding arbiter." I am wholly unable to picture this strange discriminating industry, this bringing of things together in order to keep them apart, this setting of ends and choosing from equal possibilities, in terms of any physical process whatever. The laws of association to be treated of here might, for aught we can see, be true in a creature wholly devoid of memory or comparison. Each of his ideas would vanish in the act of awakening its successor; his mind (if such it could be called) would be shut up to the punctiform instant; he would obey, without noticing, the current which swept him on; drift to his conclusions, but never know why; and act upon the suggestions of experience with a fatality which would be inwardly all the blinder in proportion as it was the more rational to outward semblance. I simply *assume* for his benefit the possession of a consciousness. I *beg* that much from the reader's liberality; and limit my ambition to showing (the consciousness being granted) with what objects it is at any given moment most likely to be filled.   P29(579.44–581.9)

523.10–531.19 With . . . arousal.] Not only poems, but the multiplication-table, Greek verbs, and formulas of gibberish like "*ana, mana, mona, mike,*" etc., cohere in the self-same order in which they have once been learned. If we have blundered once in a certain place, we are prone to repeat the mistake again. The higher and the lower nerve-centers, then, are subject to one and the same law; and the reason of the law must be in both cases the same. The fact that there are isolated tracts of conduction in all the centers, and that as we pass from below upward the different centers have in the main different characteristic functions, leads to the notion that each function, ideational or motor, is dependent on a certain tract localized somewhere, which tract when once excited may propagate the excitement to other outlying tracts.
                P29(581.19–31)

549.5 thinking.] thinking. Professor Bain, more profusely and cogently than any one else, has illustrated the truth that the leading fact in what we call genius in every department of life is a high development of the power of Similar Association. I therefore refer the reader to his work on the "Study of Character," Chapter XV., and to Chapter II., sections 25 to 45, of the portion entitled "Intellect" of his treatise on "The Senses and the Intellect."
   Into the study of voluntary trains of thought there is no space to enter. The student will find in Hodgson's "Theory of Practice," vol. i., pp. 394–400, the best account with which I am acquainted. Meanwhile he will no doubt admit that the promise with which this article set out has been fulfilled, and that the processes of spontaneous association have become already a little more intelligible to his mind.   P29(593.22–35)

CHAPTER XIX: THE PERCEPTION OF 'THINGS'

Extract from "The Perception of Space (III)" (P24), which is omitted in (I).
743.21 disappears.] disappears.[1]
   Taste is a sensation; yet there are but few people, in tasting wine, butter, oil, tea, meats, &c., who are not liable, temporarily at any rate, completely to misjudge the quality of what is in their mouth, through false expectation, or in consequence of some authority in such matters, standing by and dog-

matically declaring the article to be different from what it is. In the matter of taste, it seems to me that most men are normally nearer to the trance-state than in respect of their other sensations. 'Suggestion' influences them more easily. The trance-subject's peculiarity is that *all* sensations are falsified and overpowered by the imagination. In all men *some* sensations are. And between the two extremes there are exemplifications of every intermediate degree.

P24(331.26–29;332.1–9)

Chapter XX: The Perception of Space

Extracts from "The Perception of Space" (P24—all four parts), which are variant or omitted in (I).

803.14 awakening.[27]] awakening.[1] | [1]Notice that all these tracing motions, as we describe them, are supposed to awaken sensibility by the lines they draw on the *sensitive surfaces*, by moving these over objective points, lines which for an instant are felt through their whole extent. They are not supposed to be perceived by the muscular organs, as so much space moved through, along which the surface-sensations are distributed like beads upon a string. We shall later see reason to think that all the muscular sensations have a certain largeness; they never can give rise in the mind to anything as distinct as the feeling of a *line*, with its direction and length. Only a sensitive *surface* is competent to that. Most English psychologists, however, assume that when muscles contract their sensation is that of the line traversed by the extremity which they move. Undoubtedly muscular contractions do break space up for us into lines; they dissect it in a way impossible without their aid, but only because they *draw* lines for us upon our sensitive surfaces. P24(25.34–48)

804.8 *in se?*ₐ] *in se?*[1] | [1]How strong the temptation to admit this may become is well seen in the following quotation from Stumpf's *Psychologischer Ursprung der Raumvorstellung* (p. 121), a work which seems to me to give on the whole the most philosophical account of the subject yet published. Stumpf says: "We hold a sheet of paper before us and ask: Can different positions be distinguished, in and of themselves, when of precisely the same colour? They can, without doubt, and indeed in the same way and in the same sense in which two colours can be distinguished one from the other. It makes a difference in our experience, we notice, whether red is presented in this place or the other, just as it makes a difference whether green or red is offered. We recognise in both cases by simply looking at them that we have before us different species of the same genus. Red and green are both colours, but *different* colours as our sight assures us. Here and There in the field of vision are both positions, but *different* positions, as again our sight proves to us. Here, There, In that place, are specified differences of place, as green, red, blue, are of colour. So then separate positions are plainly distinguished as such in representation. Indeed they are so very distinct that identity never occurs between them (we cannot imagine two positions the same), and the same colours can be recognised as two only through the difference of their positions. To depict this difference I am naturally unable, for it is no qualitative difference; but notwithstanding that it is a real difference and can be *felt*. I can moreover as little *define* it as I can that of the two colours (as sensations namely, not ethereal vibrations). But I can *point it out*, and upon him who does not know it, or denies it, force conviction. In short, then, what is the meaning of 'Two things are different in representation,' other than 'They can as such be distinguished, belong to a particular class of distinguish-able contents'? I know not in what other sense we can talk of the difference of colours. This criterion however is just as applicable to positions; nor do I know how difference of colours is distinguished from difference of positions. See also pp. 143–153.   P24 (27.21–51)

804.32 occurs.ˍ] occurs.[1] | [1] The reader will please remember that when we began to give our account of the matter, we said nothing of association, which is a psychic law, but spoke only of the "law of habit in the nervous system". This might easily bring it about, that a point, positionless through nerve-process (1), should appear embedded in a line through nerve-process (2), and finally should start out from a particular part of that line through nerve-process (3).   P24 (28.41–46)

806.11 THE . . . SPACE] IN previous sections I sought to show that the primitive experience, which lies at the bottom of our knowledge of space, is the quality of bigness or extensiveness which all of our sensations possess.[2] I showed, moreover, that if an original sensation of extent were subdivided into parts by discriminative attention, these parts must come to be perceived, through processes of association, in definite relations of mutual position and order. I said nothing, however, of the combination of one sensible space-total with another, the inquiry to which we must now turn.   P24 (183.2–11, 29–37)

820.37 touch.ˍ] touch.[1] | [1] It might, indeed, seem incredible that life-long association should be so rapidly undone. Were there any truth at all in the prevalent modern doctrine that ancestral habits engender fixed instincts in the progeny, one would say that the connexion with each other of the space-directions given by different senses ought to be congenital, inseparable and unconquerable. The facts cited might be taken to show that this modern doctrine, however it may be verified for lower forms, fails in its application to man. It must be remembered, however, that the association of particular body-movement directions with particular visual directions is not so constant as the objection assumes, even in creatures ignorant of mirrors, prisms and lenses. Every time we move one end of a lever towards the right we see the other end move towards the left. Every time we pull down a rope or vine hanging over a tree branch, the other end of it is seen to rise. And thus even in infra-human creatures a certain indeterminateness of connexion between visual and tactile directions of movement may be kept up. The topic is one which might repay evolutionist philosophers for more minute study.
         P24 (194.36–47; 195.37–41)

820.38–824.13 The . . . these.] [¶] The general principles of the baby's action in all this have now to be examined. As we found a little while ago

---

[2] *Consensus* is such a precious thing in the present state of psychology, that I cannot refrain from reminding the reader that in this, the fundamental and indispensable, part of my thesis, I have an ally in Mr. James Ward, whose article "Psychology" in the edition still publishing of the *Encyclopædia Britannica*, seems to me, on the whole, the deepest and subtlest collective view of the subject which has appeared in any language. *Extensity* is Mr. Ward's name (see pp. 46, 53, of the article) for this primitive quality of sensation, out of which our several perceptions of *extension* grow.

that the different seen magnitudes are reduced to representatives of one real one, through the intermediation of an *object* judged to be the same in all, so we shall now find that the continuity and identity of the different sense-spaces rest on the same *objective judgment*. This is what gives order to the chaos.

Any group of different feelings always experienced (or at will to be experienced) together, are simplified by the mind's holding them for so many attributes or aspects of the same outer reality—which reality is always held to be represented by one of them more truly and essentially than by the rest. Space-feelings follow this law. *If two or more sensible spaces always do or always may occur at the same time or vary concomitantly, we take them for two modes of appearance of the same real space. That one whose content is most interesting is judged to be the truest representative of this, the others become its mere associates, properties or signs.*[1]

Thus, when a baby looks at its own moving hand, its retina gets a certain movement-feeling whilst its hand and arm become the seat of another movement-feeling. The baby holds the two movements to occupy the same space. The result is that the arm-space, more interesting than the retinal space by reason of the important skin-sensations to which it may lead, and therefore judged more real, is equated with a certain part of the retinal space, which, in becoming its sign, fixes to a certain extent the absolute space-values of the rest of the retinal field.   P[24] (195.34-36;196.1-26)

830.7-9 *We ... joints.*] The tip is indubitably localised at the successive points of its path by incoming sensations produced by the slipping over each other of the cartilages on which it turns; and the whole phenomenon, instead of refuting, most brilliantly corroborates the view that localisation is exclusively a surface-affair. *Muscular contraction is only indirectly instrumental in giving us space-feelings, by its objective effects on surfaces.* In the case of skin and retina, it produces a motion of the stimulus upon the surface; in the case of joints it produces a motion of the surfaces upon each other—such motion being by far the most delicate manner of sensibly exciting the surfaces in question. One is tempted to doubt whether the muscular sensibility as such plays even a subordinate part as *sign*, of these more immediately geometrical perceptions which are so uniformly associated with it as effects of a common cause—the contraction objectively considered.[1] | [1] The admirably judicious A. W. Volkmann says (*Untersuchungen im Gebiete der Optik*, Leipzig, 1863, p. 188): "Muscular feeling gives tolerably fine evidence as to the *existence* of movement, but hardly any direct information about its extent or direction. We are not aware that the contractions of a *supinator longus* have a wider range than those of a *supinator brevis*; and that the fibres of a bipenniform muscle contract in opposite directions is a fact of which the muscular feeling itself gives not the slightest intimation. Muscle-feeling belongs to that class of general sensations which tell us of our inner states, but not of outer relations; it does not belong among the space-perceiving senses." See also *Ibid.*, p. 189, and Hering, *Beiträge*, pp. 31, 240. Weber (Article "Tastsinn") also calls attention to the fact that muscular movements as large and strong as those of the diaphragm go on continually without our perceiving them as motion. See also Lewes, *Problems*, vol. ii., p. 478. But the final crushing defeat of the muscular-sense as the chief agent in space-perception is given by Prof. Lipps in a few pages (6 to 27 of his *Psychologische Studien*, 1885), which I advise all students to read.

Nevertheless certain facts may still be brought up against our surface-theory. When we move the wings of the nostrils, the external ear and, to a certain degree, the tongue, the feeling we get is distinctly one of movement, but it involves anatomically no such passage of anything over a surface as, according to our text, it should. The explanation is that we have learned the movement-significance of these movement-feelings and skin-stretchings, by producing them "passively," by manipulating the parts on former occasions with our fingers. A personal experience, made since the text was written, seems to me strongly to corroborate this view. For years I have been familiar, during the act of gaping, with a large, round, smooth sensation in the region of the throat, a sensation characteristic of gaping and nothing else, but which, although I had often wondered about it, never suggested to my mind the motion of anything. The reader probably knows from his own experience exactly what feeling I mean. It was not till one of my students told me, that I learned its objective cause. If we look into the mirror while gaping, we see that at the moment we have this feeling, the *uvula* or hanging palate *rises* by the contraction of its intrinsic muscles. The contraction of these muscles and the compression of the palatine mucous membrane are what occasion the feeling; and I was at first astonished that, coming from so small an organ, it could appear so voluminous. Now the curious point is this—that no sooner had I learnt by the eye its objective space-significance, than I found myself enabled mentally to *feel* it as a movement upwards of a body in the situation of the uvula. When I now have it, my fancy *injects* it, so to speak, with the image of the rising uvula; and it *absorbs* the image easily and naturally. In a word, a muscular contraction gave me a sensation whereof I was unable during forty years to interpret a motor meaning, of which two glances of the eye made me permanently the master. To my mind no further proof is needed of the fact that muscular contraction, merely as such, need not be perceived directly as so much motion through space.   P24 (200.44–201.51;202.36–47)

832.1–838.7 The . . . be.] [¶] Such examples open up the whole subject of Extradition, one of the most difficult problems which can occupy the space-philosopher. We shall see later in the special section on vision that the third dimension, or depth, has always been the stumbling-block of theorists. Here, however, it behoves us to note that the seeming migration we have just studied, of a feeling from a joint to a finger-tip, with concomitant enlargement of size, seems to differ in no essential respect from those migrations beyond the skin with greater enlargement still. Closer examination will corroborate this essential identity of the two cases, and the examination will be much facilitated by recalling a few general principles at the start. We saw that all sensations are voluminous or contain the third dimension in a vague way. Projection, which is localisation of an impression at a determinate distance in this dimension, involves three factors: (1) feeling, the extent of the dimension as a whole; (2) discriminating a partial sensation within it; (3) measuring the distance of that sensation from one of the extremes.

It would appear therefore that, in the first instance at any rate, a sensation can be projected or extradited, only if it form part of a space-volume felt all at once, or in continuous succession. The mind in projecting would seem to identify its own position with that of one part of this volume, as a *here*, and detach from itself the other part, as a *there*. Now the centre the mind has thus chosen for its own felt habitation is undeniably sometimes within the head, sometimes within the throat or breast—not a rigorously fixed spot there, but a region within which it seems to itself to move,[2] and from any portion of which it may send forth its various acts of attention. Extradition from either of *these* regions is the common law under which we perceive the whereabouts of the north star, of our own voice, of the contact of our teeth with each other, of the tip of our finger, the point of our cane on the ground, or a pain in our elbow-joint. The appearance of a feeling in the joint is as much a projection or a migration as its appearance in the north star would be. Amputations show how, owing to central excitement, limbs no longer existing are felt in their old site, or somewhat retracted. But the fact of extradition is the same when the limb is there[1] as when it is not. Extradition obtains, then, even of such sensations as we locate on the exact sensory surfaces where the nerves terminate. Could we feel our *retinal* pictures *where they are*, this would involve a dealing with the third dimension quite as thorough as does our feeling them across the room. The distinction so often made between our primitive spatial perception as that of a surface, and our perception of the third dimension as subsequent and acquired, is utterly baseless. For to feel any surface, *as such*, involves all three dimensions.

The only difference between primitive and acquired in this department of consciousness is the difference between vague and unbroken on the one hand, and subdivided and measured on the other. It is conceivable that the *subdivision* of either dimension might be earlier and more accurate than that of the two others, but it is inconceivable that either dimension should appear out of relation to the others, inconceivable that the very earliest apprehension of space should not be that of space cubic, as it really exists. Those philosophers therefore who hold that the *prius* of all external perception is the vague consciousness of the body as cubically extended must be held to be essentially in the right.[2]

To return now, after this theoretic digression, to our special facts. *For a joint to be felt in situ, the entire intervening mass of tissue between it and the brain must be susceptible of becoming one continuous object of perception.* The existence of this intervening space-object is the *conditio sine qua non* of the joint's 'projection' to the farther end of it. To say nothing of other ways in which this space may be felt (as by the eye or the exploring hand), it is felt by means of its *own* nerves, whose local-signs pass gradually into those in and about the joint, and give us, whenever they awaken together, a unitary

---

[2] The reader is reminded of the facts mentioned in sec. 1.

[1] In a purely subjective account, its 'being' there means, of course, only the presence of other feelings than the one in question, projected 'there' just as it is.

[2] Of late years the doctrine has been revived by I. H. Fichte and Ulrici that the soul itself is a cubically extended substance pervading the body, and that the latter becomes the "immediate object" in perception through the fact that the perceiving subject is coextensive with it. And this view has been defended in a recent American work of unusual critical ability—*The Perception of Space and Matter*, by J. E. Walter, Boston, 1880. (Cp. Noah Porter's *Human Intellect*, p. 130.) But it is not necessary that we should commit ourselves either to the theory of an extended soul-substance or to that of the body as "immediate object". I only cite these theories to illustrate the need which coerces men to postulate *something* tridimensional as the first thing in external perception.

massive space. For the finger-tip to be felt where it is, a still longer intervening *continuum* must be sensible, with the feeling lodged at its end.

But how, when the space between the brain and the point of projection has no nerves (which is the case with spaces beyond the body's limits), is it to be felt as an intervening *continuum* at all? Simply by forming *with* the mass of sensitive tissue and surface beyond which it extends a *new object for some other sense.*

Suppose the cane held in my right hand and its point pressed against the wall. I can, by paying attention, feel the whole solidity of my arm, the sensations in its joints as they move, and the pressure of the fingers upon the cane. But I also feel the wall where the cane touches it a yard away from my hand. Now this yard forms with the arm a common object, either for the exploring motion of my left hand (which may pass first down the right arm, and then down the cane it holds, by a combination of continuous movements); or for the skin of the body and leg, against the length of which both arm and cane may be applied.[1] This common objectivity of arm and cane gives the space of the projection as a whole, the first of those three factors which we saw extradition to involve.

The next factor is the particular kind of sensation to be extradited. This can be nothing else than the feeling of the hardness or softness of the wall as it would affect our exploring hand. The similarity of the cane's actual pressure to this ideal pressure makes it seem as if the actual feeling of the hand had migrated into a new place. Most probing and palpating instruments are rigid, and communicate without alteration the feeling the hand itself would receive if it took the place of their farther extremity. Finally, the last factor is the precise distance within the total depth at which the sensation shall be lodged. In the case of the rigid stick this offers no difficulty. Easy experiences teach us that the cane's tip is the point from which diverge all the pressures it exerts upon our hand. Thither accordingly we send our image of the resisting thing we feel. When the cane is flexible, its own changes of shape become important, and we lodge the feeling of resistance partly in its tip, partly along its whole length. If we move the cane's tip through the air, instead of letting it touch the wall, all we need do is to multiply our hand-movement sensations by a certain factor corresponding to the cane's length. This gives us the distinct image of a large path traversed by the tip.

P24 (205.3–207.45)

853.4–13 But . . . *thing*.] The wisest order of procedure seems this: first, Reid's and Helmholtz's principle for distinguishing between what is sensible and what is intellectual, must be disproved by showing cases of other senses than sight in which it is violated; secondly, we must review the further facts of vision to which the principle is supposed to apply (—this will be the longest segment of our task); and thirdly, it must be shown that the facts admit of another interpretation completely in accordance with the tenor of the space-theory we have ourselves defended hitherto. I think we shall, without extreme difficulty, make good all the parts of this perhaps presumptuous-sounding program.[2]

(*b*) *Suggested Feelings can overpower Present Feelings.*

First, then, is it impossible that actual present sensations can be altered by suggestions of experience? In the case of hallucinations, we perfectly well

[1] Again I omit all mention of the eye, so as to account for the blind man.

know that the retinal image of the side of a room can be blotted out of view by an over-excitement of the cerebral sight-centres. And, as Stumpf remarks (*Ursprung der Raumvorstellung*, 210), hallucinations shade gradually into the illusions of everyday life. The filling-out of the blind spot is a permanent hallucination. Faces, colours, shapes, change in the twilight, according as we imagine them to represent this or that object. Motionless things appear to move under the same circumstances. The colour of the marginal field of view is seen like that of the central in the absence of any reason why we should judge it different (as in looking at the blue sky or a white wall), though a small marginal patch seen alone would be quite different. Colour is surely a sensation!

But leave the optical realm, where everything has been made doubtful.
P24(328.17-28;329.1-9;330.1-10)

876.17-18 But . . . *groups*.] [¶] Helmholtz's (and Wundt's) argument in brief is this, that since our spatial interpretation of certain optical sensations is altered by ideas or other sensations alongside of the former, this spatial interpretation could never have been an original element of the sensations as such, but must always have been what it proves itself now to be, an *inference*, *made unconsciously* from a number of premisses.

Profitably to conduct the somewhat tedious discussion, I must divide the instances into groups. But the room vouchsafed me in this number of MIND is already exhausted, and the discussion of the facts relied on by these authors had best form the opening section of my fourth and final article.

5. *The Intellectualist Theory of Space (continued).*

LET me remind the reader of where we left off. I had spoken of the difference which frequently obtains between the form and size of an optical sensation and the form and size of the reality which it suggests; and I had tried to make it clear that, in all common cases, the form and size which we attribute to the reality mean nothing more than certain other optical sensations, now absent, but which would be present under different conditions of observation. I then referred to a residual class of cases on which much stress is laid by such authors as Helmholtz and Wundt. These are cases of *illusion*, cases in which a *presented* form and size are not felt at all, the only thing cognised being what these authors consider to be a demonstrably *inferred* form and size. Were the presented form and size themselves sensations, the authors say, they could not be annulled by inferences; no instance of the suppression of a real sensation by the inferred image of an absent one being known.

I am utterly unconvinced of the truth of this thesis, and of the theory which would explain most of the illusions in point by inferences unconsciously performed. But profitably to conduct the discussion we must divide the alleged instances into groups. P24(353.38-50;516.1-22)

CHAPTER XXIV: INSTINCT

Extract from "Some Human Instincts" (P29), which is variant in (I).

1022.18-1028.18 Let . . . consider.] IT is generally considered that a cardinal *differentia* of the human race is its poor endowment in the way of instincts. Brutes need instincts, it is supposed, because they have no reason. But man, with his reason, can do without instincts. "Instinctive actions," says Professor Preyer, in his careful little work, "Die Seele des Kindes," "are in man few in number, and, apart from those connected with the sexual passion, difficult to recognize after early youth is past. So much the more attention," he adds, "should science pay to the instinctive actions of young children."

I believe this doctrine to be a great mistake. Instead of having fewer, man has more instincts than any other mammal. He has so many that they bar one another's path, and produce an indeterminateness of action in him, supposed to be incompatible with that automatic uniformity which, according to popular belief, characterizes all instinctive performances. Popular belief is here in error. The more carefully instincts have been studied of late years, and the more clearly their mechanism has been laid bare, the more evident has it become that their effects are liable to be modified by various conditions. Instincts are due, at bottom, to the organization in the nerve-centers of certain paths of discharge, or reflex-arcs, as they are technically called. The disturbance produced in the way of sound, light, or other sensible emanation, by some object in the environment, runs in at an animal's senses, and then out through his muscles. Each special sort of disturbance or stimulus affects a special set of muscles, and makes the animal act in a special way, he knows not why, except that it seems the only natural way to act at the moment. Witness the fear of a natural enemy, the love of the opposite sex, the pursuit of a natural prey. Some of these reflex-arcs are transient. Some of the environing objects stimulate more than one arc at once (as when the presence of a strange dog awakens timorous, pugnacious, and sociable movements, all at the same time, in another dog), and then small accidents determine the resultant path of discharge. Finally, habits are formed of reacting on one particular object of a kind, and inhibit the application of the instinct to other individuals (limitation of the sexual instinct to one mate, etc.). In an article published elsewhere,* I have tried to trace these complications and variations, and to show that the presence of too many instincts in a creature, some of them transient, some of them tending in opposite ways, some of them inhibited in their application by the habits earliest formed, must needs produce a life, as unautomatic and ununiform in its outward aspect, as human life has ever been claimed to be.

In this article and a later one, I will run over the human instincts in detail, commenting with fullness only upon such as are interesting enough to repay the pains.

The line to be drawn between simply reflex and instinctive actions is an entirely arbitrary one; so I can see no objection, on the score of principle, to including under the title of instincts Professor Preyer's whole list of the gradually evolving propensities to action of the human babe: *Sucking, biting, spitting, making grimaces, clasping, pointing, making sounds expressive of desire, carrying objects to the mouth, averting head and body, sitting up, standing,* are all accomplishments which come in due order, and lead us to the locomotor age. Each is irresistibly called forth by some appropriate stimulus, and finally becomes subject to the conscious will.

Locomotion is more interesting. Until the walking impulse ripens in the nerve-centers, the legs remain limp and indifferent, no matter how often the child may be hung with his feet in contact with the ground. No sooner,

*"Scribner's Magazine," March, 1887.

however, has the standing instinct come, than the child stiffens his legs and presses downward as soon as his feet feel the floor. In some babies this is the earliest locomotor reaction. In others it is preceded by the impulse to *creep*. Yesterday, the baby sat contentedly wherever he was put. To-day, it is impossible to keep him sitting at all, so irresistible is his impulse to throw himself forward on his hands. Usually the arms are too weak, and the ambitious little experimenter falls on his nose. But his perseverance is dauntless, and he soon learns to travel in the quadrupedal way. The *walking* instinct may awaken with no less suddenness, and its entire education be completed within a week's compass, barring a little "grogginess" in the gait. The common belief that a baby *learns* to walk is, strictly speaking, untrue. The reflex machinery, as it begins to ripen, prompts him to its use. But, as it is imperfectly organized, he makes mistakes. If, however, a baby could be prevented from getting on his feet at all for a fortnight or so after his first impulse to do so had manifested itself, and then restored to freedom, I have little doubt of his then being able to walk perfectly, or almost perfectly, "from the word 'go.' " A small blister on each foot-sole would do the business; and it is much to be desired that some scientific widower, left alone with his infant at the critical moment, should repeat on the human species the brilliant observation of Mr. Douglas Spalding on various small birds, which he kept till they were fully fledged, and then found to fly with absolute perfection the first time he allowed them to spread their wings. Usually, birds start to fly before either the central or peripheral apparatus is quite ripe. And so do we, to walk.

Of *vocalization* I will say nothing except that it is instinctive in both of its forms, singing and speech, and that the propensity to speak often ripens in a child with almost startling suddenness. A few significant sounds are gradually acquired, but the vocabulary is very small until the impulse of imitating sounds awakes. When its awakening is abrupt it is impossible to talk with the child. His condition is that of *echolalia:* instead of answering, he repeats the question. His whole energy may for a few days be poured into this channel, and during those days the foundations of his future vocabulary are laid.

Imitation is a human instinct which has other fields of application than the vocal one. Say what one will of monkeys, man is the imitative animal. Civilization, in fact, depends on the trait. *Nil humani a me alienum*, is the motto of each of us, and we are uneasy when another shows any power or superiority, till we can exhibit it ourselves as well. Much might be said of this propensity, as well as of the impulse to *rivalry* which is akin to it, and equally instinctive; but I must hasten on to—   P29(160.1–162.16)

Appendix II

James's Annotations of His Private Copy
of The Principles of Psychology

This appendix contains transcripts of all the autograph markings that James made in his specially interleaved private copy preserved in the James Collection in the Houghton Library, Harvard University (*AC85.J2376.890p [v 1–4]). The first page-line reference is to the present edition; the second, within parentheses, is to the original 1890 volumes. The lemma is that of the first printing. Page-line references preceded by an asterisk identify entries made on the text page itself. Otherwise, if no indication is provided, the entries have been transcribed from the interleaved blanks opposite the passage suggested by the lemma. The exact text referred to is not always to be identified precisely, this being especially true of general notes placed at the head of a page. Underlines and marginal lines have not been recorded. Professor Skrupskelis has provided what annotations seem useful as an aid to the reader; reference is also made to other entries in the Appendix and to the Notes.

There are numerous inconsistencies in spelling and in what would appear to be typographical errors in James's notes which have been retained in their original form. Missing letters in words have been supplied in square brackets.

21.31 (I,8.30) In the lengthy] [*penc.*] E.g. when it is argued from animals' acts (Lubbock, G. Allen) that they possess *colour*-preferences like or unlike our own,

> John Lubbock (Baron Avebury) (1834–1913), British banker and naturalist, discusses color preferences, particularly those of bees, in *On the Senses, Instincts, and Intelligence of Animals with Special Reference to Insects*, 2nd ed. (London: Kegan Paul, Trench, 1889). Grant Allen treats this question in *Physiological Æsthetics*, pp. 155–156. Allen also treats the color preferences of insects in *The Colour-Sense: Its Origin and Development* (London: Trübner, 1879).

*22.10 (I,9.12) stock instance] [*penc.*] *hyphen insrtd.*

50.10–11 (I,39.15) But the left-brainedness] [*pasted-in clipping*] [¶] Concerning the different periods at which different motor activities become manifested in the human infant, it is well to remember that the voluntary motor tract is not completely developed in the human being until after the end of the first year (Flechsig), and that the fibres developing from the occipital cortex only begin to appear between the second and third months of extrauterine life. Up to the latter period, motor activities following visual stimulation must be considered as reflex; but the use of the right hand predominantly, or at a later period from conscious choice, is a consequence of the pre-existing better nutrition, and hence readier functional activity, of the left

cerebral hemisphere. | JOSEPH T. O'CONNOR, M.D. | 51 West 47th Street, New York, Dec. 3.
　　Clipping taken from "Right-Handedness" in Letters to the Editor, *Science*, 16 (Dec. 12, 1890), 331–332.

50.39 (I,40.37) *Nothnagel und Naunyn] [*ink*] Lichtheim on Aphasia, Brain, Jan. 1885.
　　Ludwig Lichtheim (1845–1928), German physician, "On Aphasia," *Brain*, 7 (Jan. 1885), 433–484.

59.1 (I,48.26) tracts.‡] [*penc.*] Henschen (Brain *1893, [*comma insrtd.*] p. ['p.' *ov. closing paren*] 177) limits it to *cortex ['c' *ov.* 's'] of calcarine fissure. [*entry brought ov. by guideline to follow* 'tracts.‡' *on text page, evidently intended as addition to fn.*]
　　S. E. Henschen, see note to 59.1.

59.5 (I,48.27) A most interesting] [*ink*] Vitzou: Archives de Physiol. Oct. 1893 finds permanent blindness from loss of both occipital lobes in dog.
　　Alexandre Vitzou, see note to 59.2.

*61.38 (I,51.44) p. 74.] [*ink*] See also Binet in Rev. Phil. XXVI, 481
　　Alfred Binet, see note to 61.38.

64.34 (I,56.1) aphasia which he was] [*ink*] In Henschen's Pathologie des Gehirns there are a lot of first rate plates of Aphasic & other lesions
　　Salomon Eberhard Henschen, *Klinische und anatomische Beiträge zur Pathologie des Gehirns*, 8 vols. (1890–1930).

*79.22 (I,71.36) led to them] [*ink*] and Memory is only a matter of paths. [*mrgn. entry positioned by guideline aft.* 'them']

91.32 (I,85.2) met in the dark] [*ink*] We can't enjoy smoking in the dark— we must also *see* the smoke.

91.33 (I,85.3–4) Street-hawkers well know] [*ink*] Effects of continued *teasing*

99.3 (I,92.11) In the '*extreme*] [*penc.*] See letter on rifle shooting from Mr Stevens (Senior) who appears to use the muscular method, *think* of the trigger, but not pull till he sees the mark

103.16 (I,97.27) The next point] [*penc.*] See a prize Essay by one MacKenzie (?) in J.ⁱ of Mental Science (or Brain) 1891 for facts about brain circulation during sleep etc. | Also Cappie's book
　　John C. Mackenzie, "The Circulation of the Blood and Lymph in the Cranium during Sleep and Sleeplessness, with Observations on Hypnotics," *Journal of Mental Science*, 37 (Jan. 1891), 18–61.
　　James Cappie, *The Intra-Cranial Circulation and Its Relation to the Physiology of the Brain* (Edinburgh: James Thin, 1890).
　　James's annotated copy of the book is in Widener (Phil 6112.24).

124.37 (I,120.22) "Habit a second] [*ink*] D.ʳ *Jno. H [*intrl.*] Lowman of Cleveland writes of an old German *soldier [*intrl.*], with anaemia of the brain, excessively tardy response to questions, and impaired locomotion. Making him stand against a walk, and suddenly calling "March!" he straightened himself, and marched instantly *& firmly [*ab. del. doubtful* 'acr'] across the room, everyone present being struck with the performance. (letter to Jas. F. Rhodes of Cambr.).

James Ford Rhodes (1848–1927), American author. One letter (1907) from Rhodes to James is at Houghton (bMS Am 1092, letter 787).

129.29 (I,125.33–34) The habit of] [*ink*] Cf Taylor's Nat. Hist. of enthusiasm, p 17.

Isaac Taylor (1787–1865), English author, *Natural History of Enthusiasm* (New York: Jonathan Leavitt; Boston: Crocker & Brewster, 1831). James's edition of this work is unknown, but his reference fits the edition cited.

130.27 (I,127.1) daily inured] [*ink*] Maine de Biran: Influence de l'Habitude sur la faculté de Penser. | Dugald Stewart: Elements: Chap II. | A. Bain: Intellect Ch. I. Will: Chap IX. | W. B Carpenter: Mental Physiology: VIII; IX. | Sam. Butler: Life & Habit, 2nd Ed. 1878. | J J. Murphy: Habit & Intelligence 1st ed. '69 Chap XV, 2nd ed. '79, chap. IX | P. Radestock: die Gewohnung, 1882

Dugald Stewart, *Elements of the Philosophy of the Human Mind*, in *The Collected Works of Dugald Stewart*, ed. William Hamilton, IV (Edinburgh: Thomas Constable, 1854), 120–143.

Alexander Bain, *The Senses and the Intellect*, 3rd ed., pp. 1–9.

————, *The Emotions and the Will*, 3rd ed., pp. 321–339.

William B. Carpenter, *Principles of Mental Physiology*, pp. 337–375, 376–413.

Samuel Butler, see note to 1275.36.

Joseph John Murphy (1827–1894), *Habit and Intelligence*, 2 vols. (London: Macmillan, 1869), I, 167–186; 2nd ed. (London: Macmillan, 1879), pp. 87–112, on "Habit and Variation."

Paul Radestock, German educator, *Die Gewöhnung und ihre Wichtigkeit für die Erziehung* (Berlin: L. Oehmigke, 1882).

131.15 (I,127.30) If he keep faithfully] [*ink*] Murphy. vol I, Chap XV | [*penc.*] In Kröner's "Das Korperliche Gefühl' Chap. XIX, the best 'philosophy' of habit which I know is contained

Eugen Kröner (b. 1861), *Das körperliche Gefühl, ein Beitrag zur Entwicklungsgeschichte des Geistes* (Breslau: E. Trewendt, 1887).

132.0 (I,128.0) THE AUTOMATON-THEORY.] [*ink*] This theory contends that human life can be *entirely explained by Physics.* If ['the' *del.*] Physics ['P' ov. 'p'] itself can't be explained ['by' *del.*] without Psychics (as Idealism holds) then this theory is *ultimately* false. It may be true however relatively to the ['phy' *del.*] *psychics of the individual consciousness* for possibly they themselves may have a relation to the absolute Psyche similar to that of the details of physics—i.e. an individual soul may be a fact *coordinate* with its individual body, and, incapable of interference with ['of' *del.*] or guidance of it, both being explained by the deeper Psyche. | [*short rule*] S. H. Wilder: Natural Law & Spiritual Agency New Englander, Oct. 1874. "Christian Thought" Sept. 1883 (this latter on Spencer.)

M. A. Wilder, "Natural Law, and Spiritual Agency," *New Englander*, 33 (Oct. 1874), 674–702.

S. H. Wilder, "The Spencerian Philosophy: A Misinterpretation of the Doctrine of the Correlation of Forces," *Christian Thought*, 1st series, 1 (Sept. 1883), 65-93.

134.6 (I,130.9) To Descartes] [*penc.*] Spinoza | Leibnitz (Janet) I, 583-4. [*added later*] Erdmann II p 430
> Johann Eduard Erdmann, *Versuch einer wissenschaftlichen Darstellung der Geschichte der neuern Philosophie*, vol. II, pt. 2 (Leipzig: Vogel, 1842), p. 430.

*141.28-29 (I,138.18) *state of psychology.*] [*penc. fn.*] Cf. infra vol II, 583-4 [*ed.*, 1185-1186]

148.0 (I,145.0) CHAPTER VI.] [*ink*] Make it clear to the class that the express purpose of the M. S. theory is to deny any Soul or consciousness *additional* to that of the elements, and to prove that the consciousness that appears, though unlike that of the elements yet *consists* of it. | ['If the f' *del.*]

153.2 (I,150.7) Some of this duty] [*ink*] Cf. Leibnitz (Janet) *I [*in penc. ab. del.* 'II']. 519 [*closing paren penc. del.*] [*penc.*], 586-7

156.38 (I,154.1) REFUTATION] [*cut reproduced; see opposite page*]

158.19 (I,155.31) Blow through] [*ink*] Blow a spark—you increase it; but increasing the blowing blows it "out."

*159.26 (I,157.31-32) What . . . is no doubt] [*ink*] 'no doubt' *intrl. w. caret aft.* 'What'; 'no doubt' *del. aft.* 'is'

161.18 (I,158.26) In other words] [*ink*] Cf. Spinoza, Ethics, Pt. II. Def. VII. | [*penc.*] Leibnitz Janet, II. 369, 519 | [*ink*] Kant: K.d.r.V. 1st Ed. 2nd paralogism, beginning
> Spinoza, *Œuvres de Spinoza*, III, 50.
> Kant, *Critique of Pure Reason*, A 351 ff.

162.29 (I,159.32) *In defence of*] [*penc.*] Stumpf: Tonpsych. II | Dauriac in Rev. Phil. XXII, 545 | [*ink*] On mental chemistry, see Mill's Logic, II, 441-2 | Bixby, ['in' *del.*] "The Monistic theory of the Soul" in the New World for December 1892 (Vol I. p. 724) | Conybeare in Monist, II. 209; Montgomery, ib. 338.
> Lionel Alexandre Dauriac (1874-1923), French philosopher, "Un Problème d'acoustique psychologique," *Revue Philosophique*, 32 (Dec. 1891), 545-570.
> James Thompson Bixby (1843-1921), American clergyman and educator, "The Monistic . . . ," *New World*, 1 (Dec. 1892), 724-748.
> Frederick Cornwallis Conybeare (1856-1924), British Armenian scholar, "Professor Clifford on the Soul in Nature," *Monist*, 2 (Jan. 1892), 209-224.

165.25 (I,163.22) thousand?] [*ink*] ['x' *added in text aft.* 'thousand?'] [x]If the sensation of *pitch* be ignorant of all such things as *taps*, what sense is there in the declaration that it consists of nothing ['by' *del.*] but things that know taps exclusively?

166.39-40 (I,164.42) Baldwin . . . chap. IV.] [*ink*] Cesca: Vierteljrsch IX, 288
> Giovanni Cesca (1858-1908), Italian philosopher and educator,

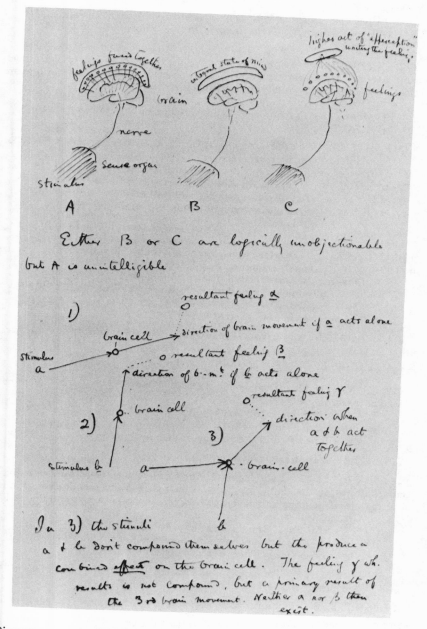

Diagrams opposite 154.1 [*ed.*, 156.38] of James's marked copy of *The Principles of Psychology* (*courtesy Houghton Library, Harvard University, Barry Donahue, photographer*)

"Über die Existenz von unbewussten psychischen Zuständen," *Vierteljahrsschrift für wissenschaftliche Philosophie*, 9 (1885), 288–301.

172.5 (I,170.20) *Tenth Proof.*] [*penc.*] But see Kulpe's defense of Verschmelzung *against the "Einheitstheorie" [*intrl.*] in his Psychol. p. 290+ | Compare also Stout's discussion Analytic Psychol., I, p. 56+

> Ostwald Külpe (1862–1915), Latvian-born psychologist, *Grundriss der Psychologie* (Leipzig: Wilhelm Engelmann, 1893) (WJ 747.51).

174.1 (I,172.30) Take the latter] [*ink*] Cf. D.ʳ Worcester's letter of Dec 24.

> William Leonard Worcester (1845–1901), American physician. Three letters from Worcester to James are at Houghton (bMS Am 1092.9 [712a]) (bMS Am 1092, letters 1183–1184). Letter 1183 is the letter of December 24, 1890. Worcester developed his criticism in "Observations on Some Points in James's Psychology," *Monist*, 2 (April 1892), 417–434; 3 (Jan. 1893), 285–298; 4 (Oct. 1893), 129–143.

176.17 (I,175.12) *The text was] [*penc.*] Cf. also, Rehmke's Allg. Psych. p. 197–8 ("Butter-taste" example)

> Johannes Rehmke (1848–1930), German philosopher, *Lehrbuch der allgemeinen Psychologie* (Hamburg: Voss, 1894) (WJ 755.39). For works by Rehmke from James's library see *Essays in Radical Empiricism*, WORKS, note to 3.12.

*181.20 (I,181.16) occurrences] [*penc.*] *aft. del.* 'the manifold' *and bef. del.* 'that go on'

*195.37 (I,197.9) *psychologist'*] [*penc.*] 's' *added*

*212.37–38 (I,215.39) Fechner . . . XXXVII.] [*added in penc.*] A. Lemoine: l'Ame et le Corps

> Albert Lemoine (1824–1874), French philosopher, *L'Âme et le corps* (Paris: Didier, 1862). Works by Lemoine from James's library will be listed in the volume of manuscript remains.

*213.14 (I,217.14) likely to wrong] [*ink*] 'be' *intrl.*

*214.36–37 (I,219.5) by . . . mind.] [*penc. underl. w. penc. note in mrgn.*] Carelessly put, so that Fullerton Psych. Rev. I, 124–5 finds a mare's nest in it, accusing me of denying knowledge to be a relation betw. mind & thing. Silly!

> George Stuart Fullerton (1859–1925), American philosopher, "The Psychological Standpoint," *Psychological Review*, 1 (March 1894), 113–133. For the relations between James and Fullerton, see *Some Problems of Philosophy*, WORKS, note to 93.46.

225.39–40 (I,231.26) The grass] [*ink*] Cf. D.ʳ Worcester's letter of Dec 24. See entry for 174.1 (I,172.30)

*227.38 (I,233.36) common;] [*ink*] *exclm. mk. subst. in mrgn. for semicolon*

*237.6–7 (I,244.9) crystal . . . crystal] [*ink*] ¹'crystal' *del.*; 'flake' *insrtd. in mrgn. for del.* ²'crystal'

259.35 (I,269.34) Quoted by] [*penc.*] Romanes: Tho't & Language Monist Oct. 1891 | Sully (same subject XIXth Century same date

George J. Romanes, "Thought and Language," *Monist*, 2 (Oct. 1891), 56–69.
James Sully, "Is Man the Only Reasoner?" *Nineteenth Century*, 30 (Nov. 1891), 735–745.

263.39 (I,273.37) Revue Philosophique] [*ink*] Compare Harless on ether intox.^{n} in Lotze: Med. Psych., 502
  Lotze quotes Emil Harless (1820–1862) and Ernst von Bibra (1806–1878), German naturalist, *Die Wirkung des Schwefeläthers* (Erlangen: Heyder, 1847), p. 24.

264.13 (I,274.1) Many philosophers] [*ink*] Cf. Spinosa (Saisset) III. 309
  Spinoza, *Œuvres*, III, 309, a reference to *On the Improvement of the Understanding.*

*264.22–265.1 (I,274.12) think] [*ink*] 'ing' *added in mrgn.*

*265.5 (I,274.17) known it] [*ink*] 'O' *subst. in mrgn. for del.* 'it'

*273.21 (I,284.15) tock] [*ink*] *acute accent added ov.* 'o'

279.0 (I,291.0) CHAPTER X.] [*ink*] Illingworth: Personality Human & Divine Bampton Lectures, 1894
  John Richardson Illingworth (1848–1915), British clergyman and educator, *Personality, Human and Divine* (London: Macmillan, 1894).

280.16 (I,292.14) (*a*) The body is] [*penc.*] See Lutoslawski's Seelenmacht, 30. The man's pen, his rifle, his rifle bullet, the horse he rides, are only extensions of his bodily self
  Wincenty Lutoslawski (1863–1954), Polish philosopher and writer, *Seelenmacht: Abriss einer zeitgemässen Weltanschauung* (Leipzig: Wilhelm Engelmann, 1899). For the relations between James and Lutoslawski see the notes to James's Preface to Lutoslawski's *World of Souls* reprinted in *Essays in Religion and Morality*, WORKS.

281.3 (I,293.4) An equally instinctive] [*ink*] The things for which we are *responsible*—e.g. magazine articles in our own *Fact* vs. those on other subjects possibly more interesting *per se*. I collect & put away the former—the latter——!

*285.31 (I,298.19) become] [*ink*] 's' *added*

*286.24 (I,299.15) *Now can we*] [*ink*] *square bkt. placed bef.* 'Now' *in text and closing bkt. aft.* 'nature may be.' (I,305.29–30 [*ed.*, 292.8]); *square bkt. placed bef.* 'I think' *in text and then del.* (I,299.19 [*ed.*, 286.28]); *on interleaf:* [From here to Self Feeling on p. 305 ought to be removed from the text, which it sadly interrupts, into a note, or appendix to the Chapter.] | [*penc.*] Criticized in Stout, Analytic Psychology, I, *148 ['4' *ov.* '8'] (about)
  See note to 286.25 for marginal comments by James.

*290.30 (I,303.29) mental act,] [*ink*] *comma del.*

*290.6–7 (I,304.7) there . . . fact] [*penc.*] Bewusstheit *in mrgn. opp. this line*

291.6 (I,304.23) The sciousness] [*ink*] "The Witness"—(E. D. Fawcett)—the Bewusstsein überhaupt (Kant)

Appendix II

Edward Douglas Fawcett (1866-1960), English writer and adventurer. For a note on the relations between James and Fawcett, see *Essays in Philosophy*, WORKS, note to 55.38.

291.32 (I,305.12-15) suppose.] *bef. penc. del. text*: At the conclusion of the volume, however, I may permit myself to revert again to the doubts here provisionally mooted, and will indulge in some metaphysical reflections suggested by them.

292.8 (I,305.29-30) nature may be.] [*ink*] See p. 299] *referring to closing square bkt. added aft.* 'be.' *See entry above*, *286.24 (I,299.15).

*293.24 (I,307.19) noticean, d] [*ink*] *vertical stroke separates words but comma is not alt.*

*298.41 (I,313.39) Emotion] [*penc.*] 's' *added*

302.30 (I,318.1) called unselfish] [*ink*] Toute individuality, au point de vue scientifique est une sorte de patrie provisonè pour nous. Toute patrie, d'autre part, est une sorte *de grand ['e grand' *intrl.*] individu | Guyau. l'irréligion de l'Avenir, 460
　　M. Guyau, *L'Irréligion de l'avenir* (Paris: Félix Alcan, 1887).

*317.35-36 (I,334.28) pale-appearing] [*ink*] *underl.; in mrgn. qst. mk. ab.* 'F. W. H. M'
　　Frederic William Henry Myers

*327.24-25 (I,345.27) second, of one] [*penc.*] 'a brain' *subst. in mrgn. for del.* 'one'

*329.13 (I,347.23-24) mitigated, spiritualistic,] [*ink*] *both commas del.*

*330.22-24 (I,348.37-39) 'substance, . . . itself,] [*ink*] *comma aft.* ' 'substance' *del. and sg. qt. subst. in mrgn.; comma aft.* 'itself' *del.*

*335.5 (I,353.25) *A after B*] [*ink*] *B after A*

*335.18 (I,354.5) pretended] [*penc.*] *del. and* 'asserted' *subst. in mrgn.*

*335.21-22 (I,354.8) existance] [*ink*] *corr. to* 'existence'

*335.23 (I,354.10) wholly] [*ink*] *alt. to* 'widely'

*336.5 (I,354.31) touch] [*ink*] *corr. to* 'touches'

336.13 (I,355.1) "All states] [*penc.*] Ladd. Phil. of M. *p. 163 [*intrl.*] assumes that I
　　On p. 163 of his *Philosophy of Mind* Ladd writes: "And to such a statement as this we have the assent of another writer on psychology who speaks disparagingly of 'Kantian machine-shop,' and who deliberately discards all 'mind-stuff' theory. 'This,' says Professor James (referring to Mr. Thompson's elusive Ego), 'is exactly our judging and remembering present "Thought," described in less simple terms.' But neither in the heavens above nor in the earth beneath nor in the waters that are under the earth, nor in consciousness, . . . 'lies' any such Ego as this." In his copy, James comments: "Upon my word this is sassy! Cf. 201"; "Does Ladd deny the *existence* of the passing thought? And what means then all his talk about the self being more than 'Content'. Cf. 55,

58, 84–6." On the top of the same page, James has "Thompson and James's ghost-philosophy."

341.14 (I,360.24) THE TRANSCENDENTALIST THEORY.] [*penc.*] "The "mind" as "combiner" of ideas, see Lockes Essay; II, XII, §1
    Essay, pp. 96–97.

358.13 (I,379.14) 2. The phenomenon] [*ink*] Case of gradual substitution of secondary (hypnotic) personality for primary one, but Jules Janet, in P. J.'s E. M. des Hyst. ['the' *del.*] les Accidents, p. 210.
    Pierre Janet, *État mental des hystériques: les accidents mentaux* (Paris: Rueff, 1894).

358.31 (I,380.1) At the age] *Clipping pasted in* "—In a recent number . . . obvious convulsion."; *In mrgn. vertically*, WJ *wrote in ink*: Science, Jan. 22'–92
    Science, 19 (Jan. 22, 1892), 45, a summary of H. Grandjean, "Un Cas d'automatisme comitial ambulatoire," *Revue Médicale de la Suisse Romande*, 11 (June 20, 1891), 354–358.

371.36 (I,392.46) who kept it.] [*ink*] ['x' *added in text aft.* 'it.'] ˣThe ladies were traced later by Dᴿ Newbold and full corroboration obtained of the boarding-house episode.
    "Report by Mr. Wm. Romaine Newbold," *Proceedings of the Society for Psychical Research* (London), VII (July 1891–92), 250–253.

*378.40 (I,400.39) for 1889.] [*added in ink*] Also B.–Séquard, Forum Aug. 1870
    See note to 378.39.

379.39 (I,401.38) But that carries] [*ink*] L. Dumont: Théorie Scient. de la Sensibilité, Pt. I, ch. VI.
    Léon Dumont, *Théorie scientifique de la sensibilité* (Paris: Germer Baillière, 1875), pp. 85–101. A marked copy of this work was sold.

380, 382 (I,402, 404) CHAPTER XI.] [*ink*] *H. C. Bastian*: | The Neural processes *underlying ['un' *ov.* 'at'] Attention & Volition, Brain, pt. I. 1892. (Reprint in Neurology shelves) | *Pilzecker*: Lehre von sinnl. Aufmksmkeit 1889 | Bertels: Versuche über Ablenkung der A.ᵏᵗ (Both in *Pamphlet ['l' *ov.* 'e'] case "Psychology") | "W. J.'s discussion of Attention" by H. M. Stanley, in Monist III, 122 (Oct. 92) | Féré: Note sur la Physiol. de l'A. Rev. Phil. XXX, 392 | Uhl: Attention (Johns Hopkins dissertation containing the history) | Cogswell: Phil. Rev. III. 462 | H. M. Stanley: Evolutionary Psychology, Ch. XIV. | [*printed clipping*] *Lecture Notes on Attention. An Illustration of the Employment of Neurological Analogies for Psychical Problems.* By C. L. HERRICK. [*ink*] J'l of Comp. Neurology, Mch. 1896 | Shand: an analysis of Attention. Mind. N. S. III. 449 | Lingard: Carpenters Theory of A. . *Mind*, II., 272. | Bain: on Sully's theory, Brain XIII, 348 [*cont. opp. p.* 404] Griffing: Visual perception & At.—Am. J. of P., VII, 227. | Münsterberg: Intensifying effects. Psych. Rev. I. 39 | Stanley: Reply to the same, ibid. II., 53. | Heinrich—proves accommodation in marginal field—report in Am. J. of P. VII. 429. | Hylan: fluctuations, Psych. Rev. Jan. 96 | Swift: Disturbance of At.— Am. J. of P. V., 1. | Hibben: Case of girl deaf when not attending. Psych.

Rev. II. 369 | Stumpf: *Tonpsychologie ['T' *ov.* 'P'], I. 67. | Alf. Lehmann: Die Hypnose, 26. Vasomotor theory

Henry Charlton Bastian, "On the Neural Processes Underlying Attention and Volition," *Brain*, 15 (1892), 1–34.

Alfons Pilzecker (b. 1865), *Die Lehre von der sinnlichen Aufmerksamkeit* (Munich: F. Straub, 1889).

Arved Bertels, see note to 409.36.

Hiram Miner Stanley, "Some Remarks upon Professor James's Discussion of Attention," *Monist*, 3 (Oct. 1892), 122–124.

Charles Féré, "Note sur la physiologie de l'attention," *Revue Philosophique*, 30 (Oct. 1890), 393–405.

Lemon Leander Uhl (b. 1848), American clergyman, *Attention: A Historical Summary of the Discussions Concerning the Subject* (Baltimore: Johns Hopkins Press, 1890).

George A. Cogswell, "Attention: Is It Original or Derivative?" *Philosophical Review*, 3 (July 1894), 462–469.

Hiram M. Stanley, *Studies in the Evolutionary Psychology of Feeling* (London: Swan Sonnenschein, 1895) (WJ 483.4), pp. 225–250.

Clarence Luther Herrick (1858–1904), American naturalist and psychologist, "Lecture Notes on Attention," *Journal of Comparative Neurology*, 6 (March 1896), 5–14.

A. F. Shand, "An Analysis of Attention," *Mind*, n.s. 3 (Oct. 1894), 449–473.

Jno. T. Lingard, "Dr. Carpenter's Theory of Attention," *Mind*, 2 (April 1877), 272–273.

A. Bain, "Remarks on Mr. Sully's Paper on the Psycho-Physical Process in Attention," *Brain*, 13 (1890), 348–355.

Harold Griffing (1869–1900), "On the Development of Visual Perception and Attention," *American Journal of Psychology*, 7 (Jan. 1896), 227–236.

Hugo Münsterberg, "The Intensifying Effect of Attention," *Psychological Review*, 1 (Jan. 1894), 39–44.

Hiram M. Stanley, "Attention As Intensifying Sensation," *Psychological Review*, 2 (Jan. 1895), 53–57.

Wilhelm Heinrich, "Die Aufmerksamkeit und die Funktion der Sinnesorgane," *Zeitschrift für Psychologie und Physiologie der Sinnesorgane*, 9 (1896), 342–388, noticed by Arthur Allin (1869–1903), Canadian-born psychologist, *American Journal of Psychology*, 7 (April 1896), 429–430.

John Perham Hylan, "Fluctuations of the Attention (I.)," *Psychological Review*, 3 (Jan. 1896), 56–63.

Edgar James Swift (1860–1932), American psychologist, "Disturbance of the Attention During Simple Mental Processes," *American Journal of Psychology*, 5 (Oct. 1892), 1–19.

John Grier Hibben (1861–1933), American philosopher, "Sensory Stimulation by Attention," *Psychological Review*, 2 (July 1895), 369–375. Three letters from James to Hibben are in the Princeton University Library.

Alfred Georg Ludwig Lehmann, *Die Hypnose und die damit verwandten normalen Zustände* (Leipzig: O. R. Reisland, 1890).

In back of the Widener copy (Phil 6681.3), pp. 59 and 65 are noted in James's hand.

383.9 (I,405.12) TO HOW MANY] [*ink*] Binet: Concurrence des Etats psychol. Rev. Phil. XXIX, 138

A. Binet, "La Concurrence des états psychologiques," *Revue Philosophique*, 29 (Feb. 1890), 138–155.

*383.38 (I,405.40) con usion] [*ink*] *corr. to* 'confusion'

391.6 (I,414.1) Wundt's pupil] [*ink*] Wundt P. P. 3rd Ed. II. 254 considers that apperception takes between 0.4″ & 8″ to ripen. He bases his conclusion upon Dietzes metronome expts. (supra 407 note [*ed.*, 385]) there occurring no synthesis of the strokes when these time limits were exceeded for a pair.

*398.11 (I,421.9) let] [*ink*] *corr. to* 'lets'

403.17 (I,426.27) The subject is] [*penc.*] Münsterberg (Psychol. Rev. I. 39) found that sensations fully attented to were estimated ['as' *del.*] *smaller* than when the attention was distracted.

See entry for 380, 382 (I,402, 404).

418.9 (I,441.31) Again, writing] [*ink*] See Also H. on Pseudoscope, P. O. p. *647 ['47' *ov. illeg. numbers*]

Helmholtz, *Handbuch*, p. 647.

*418.25 (I,442.10) e] [*ink*] *corr. to* 'we'

423.21 (I,447.15) Second, *a teacher*] [*ink*] "Give them something to attend *with!*" [*exclm. mk. ov. qst. mk.*]

*425.26 (I,448.39) fact,] [*penc.*] 'however,' *insrtd. aft.* 'fact,'

430.12 (I,455.1) INATTENTION.] [*ink*] "La distraction," apud Janet: Autom. psych. 185, 237

*438.16 (I,463.25) can always tell] [*ink*] 'always' *del.*

*439.26 (I,464.29–465.1) theempirical] [*ink*] *vert. stroke separates the words; in mrgn. an* 'x' *to call attention to the error*

443.1 (I,468.10) 'ABSTRACT' IDEAS.] [*ink*] The conceptualist position *is [*intrl.*] argued by Fullerton (The Conception of the Infinite [*closing paren del.*] Chap. *VI) [*paren ov. comma*] much in my way, and Meinong's)

George Stuart Fullerton, *The Conception of the Infinite, and the Solution of the Mathematical Antinomies* (Philadelphia: Lippincott, 1887). Chapter VI is entitled "The Conceivability of the Infinite."

444.13 (I,470.1) The note, so] [*ink*] Cf. Ribot, Enquête s. 1. Idées generales, in Rev. Phil. *XXXII 376 1891 [*intrl.*] | Noël: Noms et Concepts, Rev. Phil. XXXI, 463

Théodule Ribot, "Enquête sur les idées générales," *Revue Philosophique*, 32 (Oct. 1891), 376–388.

Georges Noël, "Noms et concepts," *Revue Philosophique*, 31 (May 1891), 463–482.

*444.33 (I,470.23) out] *corr. to* 'our'

445.24-25 (I,471.15) self-transcendent function] [*penc. underl. w. penc. comment on interleaf*] Caird says this contradicts p. 369 [*ed.*, p. 349] & is an essentially hegelian conception
Edward Caird, *A Critical Account of the Philosophy of Kant.*

445.31 (I,471.21-22) All that a state] [*ink, completed on interleaf for p. 474*] Both schools, believing that an "image" is an absolutely determinate singular entity, and believing also that for a thing to be known, it *suffices that it should be *in* [*ab. del.* 'must somehow get *into*'] the mind, see no difficulty in *singular* objects being known by images ['that are' *del.*] since the latter are as it were so identical with them[', that they are' *del.*] as to be their duplicates *in* the mind. But when *the [*ov.* 'an'] object is unlimited or abstract, or when it is a whole class of entities, this *duplication [*ab. del.* 'relation'] does not hold, and another explanation of the knowledge must be found or | [*opp. p.* 472] else the possibility of the knowledge denied altogether. The conceptualists affirm a higher spiritual act (E.g. Maher: Psych. Chap XV) the nominalists deny *actual* ['intuition' *del.*] knowledge of every-[*ab. del.* 'all knowledge of any'] thing but singulars, and say *that what we take for [*ab. del.* 'our apparent'] knowledge of universals and abstracts is ['due to extra-mental relations of association between the thoughts in the mind and is' *del.*] the *potentiality* which some of our singular images have (through the *names* with which they are associated) of leading to either *one [*intrl.*] of a large number of other singular images, or of having some one of their parts emphasized. [¶] The whole quarrel is outflanked when we admit three facts [[¶] '1) the vagueness of our images;' *del.*] [¶] 1) that most images are intrinsically vague; [¶] 2) that intrinsically they represent no | [*opp. p.* 473] thing, all representative function on their part being a question of what they *lead to*, so that the same ['image' *del.*] blurred image intrinsically undetermined to any object will be "of" a singular, a general, ['or' *del.*] a concrete or an abstract reality, according to its associates. [¶] 3) That the associates, ['wh' *del.*] even while nascent, form a "fringe" which we feel, and so may be said to be aware of the universal or particular tendency of our ['sta' *del.*] mental state, before it has worked itself out. [¶] Thus the ['nom' *del.*] conceptualists, right in claiming this last awareness are | [*opp. p.* 474] wrong in insisting that no associationist account of it can be given but that our idea itself must *be* universal or abstract like its object. [¶] And the nominalists, ['are' *del. intrl.*] right in saying that knowledge is made to have a universal function by external association, are wrong in denying that *awareness [*ab. del.* 'consciousness'] of this function is itself ['directly' *del.*] a direct property of the mental state in so far *as it is [*smudged as if for deletion*] "fringed."
Michael Maher (1860–1917), Jesuit philosopher and psychologist, *Psychology* (London: Longmans, Green, 1890), pp. 290–304.

447.10 (I,473.5) After abstractions] [*ink*] Good example of a general idea in an infant in Perez, quoted by Maillet, *487-8 ['87-8' *ab. del.* '88-89']
Eugène Maillet, *Éléments de psychologie de l'homme et de l'enfant appliquée à la pédagogie* (Paris: Belin, 1890). Quotes Bernard Perez but does not cite a source.

455.15 (I,482.1) There is nothing] [*penc.*] See the Symposium on "the Concept" in the successive numbers of the "Public School" (Harris, Dewey)

etc *) [*closing ov. opening paren*] tucked into Dewey's Psychol.
John Dewey, "How Do Concepts Arise from Percepts?" *Public-School Journal*, 11 (Nov. 1891), 128–130.
William Torrey Harris (1835–1909), American philosopher and educator, "A Letter from Dr. Harris," *Public-School Journal*, 11 (Dec. 1891), 179.

*457.20 (I,483.21) hereafter?] [*ink*] *period subst. in mrgn. for del. qst. mk.*

*458.39 (I,484.32) and the with then] [*ink*] 'the' *del. and* 'then' *alt. to* 'their' *but then to* 'the'

*464.29 (I,490.32) Chapter XX] [*penc.*] 'XX' *corr. to* 'XXVIII'

*465.24 (I,491.30) x + 2d] [*ink*] 'x' *corr. to* 'X'

*473.17–18 (I,500.17) When I recognize] [*ink in mrgn.*] Starke, Merkel & Lehmann experimenting (Phil. Studien [*closing paren del.*] VII. 204) on sounds & their comparison all find a tendency in the earlier sound to appear less strong in retrospect than it was in reality. The discrepancy becomes less after 6 sec. interval (ib. p. 207.
Paul Starke (b. 1861), "Die Messung von Schallstärken," *Philosophische Studien*, no. 2, 3 (1886), 264–304.
Julius Merkel, "Das psychophysische Grundgesetz in Bezug auf Schallstärken," *Philosophische Studien*, no. 1, 4 (1887), 117–160.
Alfred Lehmann, "Kritische und experimentelle Studien über das Wiedererkennen," *Philosophische Studien*, no. 2, 7 (1891), 169–212.

475.28 (I,503.8) The consequence is] [*penc.*] Catalepsy

478.31–32 (I,506.23) *concomitants.*] [*ink*] ['x' *added in text aft.* 'concomitants.'] [x]Attributed to Hume, by Carveth Read, Treatise, Bk I, Pt I, §7 esp[ly] last 2 ['§§' *del.*] ¶¶. (Metaph. of Nature, 260)
See note to 478.38.

*482.3–4 (I,509.36–37) has so . . . once has] [*ink*] *both* 'has' *alt. to* 'had'

*496.29 (I,525.32) and 10.10] [*ink*] '10.10' *corr. to* '0.110'

*496.41 (I,525.39) 3] [*ink*] *corr. to* '379'

503.7 (I,533.1) less of the identical] [*ink*] HÖFFDING contends for the same view, 4tljsch. XIV, 49, 167 ff. | Discussion betw. Bradley and W. J. in Mind, vol. | W. J. criticized by Stout in Proc. Aristot. Soc. Vol II, No 1 p. 116
Harald Höffding, "Über Wiederkennen, Association und psychische Activität," *Vierteljahrsschrift für wissenschaftliche Philosophie*, 14 (1890), 27–54, 167–205, 293–316.
Francis Herbert Bradley, "On Professor James' Doctrine of Simple Resemblance," *Mind*, n.s. 2 (January 1893), 83–88; "Professor James on Simple Resemblance," *Mind*, n.s. 2 (July 1893), 366–369; both papers reprinted in Bradley's *Collected Essays*, I, 287–300. James's responses, "Mr. Bradley on Immediate Resemblance" and "Immediate Resemblance," are reprinted in *Essays in Philosophy*, WORKS.
George Frederick Stout, "A General Analysis of Presentations

as a Preparatory to the Theory of Their Interaction," *Proceedings of the Aristotelian Society*, 2 (1892), 107–120.

508.24 (I,538.20) To take an example] [*penc.*] $a^2+2ab+b^2$ | $A+2Ar+r^2$ | $A+2r$

508.30 (I,538.27) A $(1+r)$] [*penc.*] $A+Ar$ | $A+$

*510.4 (I,540.11) (1) *The Method*] [*penc. in mrgn.*] "minimal changes"

515.5 (I,545.30) const.] [*ink*] [*asterisk added in text aft.* 'const.'] *Explain this: *As ['A' *ov.* 'a'] stimulus grows we feel "more"; then again "more" etc. Fechner says *all [*ab. del.* 'each of'] these mores are equal (i.e. "constant") and each of them consists of a little *bud of sensation*. By bud after bud the sensation grows and equals the original Sensation + the sum of the buds.
Fechner (no reference found).

*515.15–16 (I,546.5) is what] [*penc.*] is really what

515.32 (I,546.25) Compound *things*] [*ink*] [*asterisk added in text bef.* 'Compound' *and aft.* 'things'] *A line is a compound thing—you take take away one part and treat it by itself. In *lines* the lesser is *part* of the greater. But in other objects not so by introspection—taking advance in the line of pitch an acute note does n't contain a grave one;—in the line in light a white colour does n't contain a gray etc—

516.9 (I,547.1) that in most sensations] [*ink*] Wundt, (Vorles^{gn} 2nd Ed. 67; P. P. 4th Ed. I, 393, -6, -7*-8 [*intrl.*] calls Weber's 1. a law of Apperception. The *pure* [*intrl.*] sensations may be prop! to the stimulus (Merkel's results wd. seem to speak for this) but the excitability of the *apperceptions organ* may differ from one sense to another and produce the logarithmic law. The com['apr' *del.*]pared sensations are *appercipirte* Empfindungen—no *pure ones [*ab. del.* 'others'] do we know. W's whole doctrine seems to me like the wriggling of a worm on the hook He is vainly trying to twist language into some appearance of a formula which shall sound intelligible. *What* is it that grows logarithmically ['? No' *del.*] now, according to W.? Not the stimulus, not the "pure" sensation (whatever that may be), not the act of "apperception" itself, but the apparent *object* of our judgment which seems to *us to [*intrl.*] have increased by a step of addition when it has really increased by a step of multiplication. This, according to W., because of our "*relativen* Schätzung" der Empfindungstärken. The only sense such a vague expression can have (*vague [*intrl.*] since *all* measurement and estimation must neccessarily be in its nature relative, *relative [*intrl.*] to *some* term of comparison or standard) in the present context, seems to be this, that our mind in comparing things can *observe* only *their [*intrl.*] quotients and ratios, but is impelled to *call* these quotients & ratios "differences." But such a universal "*relativitätsprinzip* as this is grotesque. All our comparisons are of course perceptions of ['the' *del.*] relations. But we perceive *relations of [*intrl.*] difference['s' *del.*] as well as ratios, and perceive them fairly correctly when we try to. The talk about the "apperceptions organ" is fearful. To what does it react? To both single sensations, and pairs, or *higher ['er' *intrl.*] groups. It *can* react therefore to something less than $s+\frac{s}{r}$; and we must say that its reaction to $\dfrac{s}{s+\frac{s}{r}}$ (a ratio of "pure" sensations) ['is' *del.*] is our perception of difference. It responds to *an ['n' *insrtd.*] objective [*intrl.*] ratio by a feeling of difference. But how different a conception [*opp. p.* 548] is this *objective ratio* from that of the *Reiz* ordinarily talked of in these discussions, and how queer to speak as Wundt does *on p. 398 [*intrl.*] of its *Schwellenwerth!* An Apperceptions centrum with so many different classes of function, and so many different sorts of threshold is not a clearly represented organ.

 Wundt, see note to 675.40.

517.11 (I,548.9–10) *Weber's law*] [*ink*] Cf. Cattell: On errors of observation (a radical criticism of Weber's law, J. of Am. P. Vol V. [Reprint in Psychophysic Pamphlet C

 James McKeen Cattell, "On Errors of Observation," *American Journal of Psychology*, 5 (April 1893), 285–293.

519.0 (I,550.0) CHAPTER XIV.] [*ink*] For proof that the operative link in association may be subconscious, take the hysteric anaesthetics described by Binet and Janet who *see* *their ['ir' *ov.* 'se'] limbs moved, who react determinately when touched in special ways, who hande objects, etc. Janet, Etat Mental etc. p. 47+

*521.26 (I,552.33) droopping] [*penc.*] *corr. to* 'dropping'

*522.2 (I,553.11) preprocessions] [*ink*] *partly corr. to* 'preposessions'

522.20 (I,553.31–32) I believe that] [*ink*] Perhaps I ought to say in a note that no explanation is intended ['of' *del.*] either of *thought* or of any of its forms, (such as that of seeing that two things are similar, or that the same thing is meant once again). We assume thought and the sorts of relation it can cognize, and simply seek to show, by cerebral conditions, what *things* at any moment come to be known in any of these relations.

534.10 (I,566.28) Let us then assume] [*penc.*] Lotze Micr. (Eng. tr.) I, 218

*535.38 (I,568.30) however] [*penc.*] *comma added*

*540.7–9 (I,573.12–13) clock called . . . . He suggested] [*ink*] clock had called . . . . He had suggested

542.11 (I,575.24) Excitement of] [*penc.*] The fact that we are apt to *dream* of matters connected with some insignificant impression of the day, shows that cells are left hyperexcitable for some time after *a [*ov.* 'an'] recent [*intrl.*] excitement

*545.6 (I,579.2) *like.*] [*ink*] ['x' *added in text aft.* '*like.*' *w. guideline bringing down mrgn. note*] Ehrenfels: 4tl.jsch. XIV, 282 admits this and suggests that if there *be* any pure Ass^n by similarity it ['is limited to' *del.*] applies to forms of combination only (Gestaltqualitäten) and not to elements. | [*penc.*] See also Lotze: Microc. Eng tr. I, p. 217

 Ehrenfels, see note to 545.37.

545.11 (I,579.9) mind.] [*ink*] ['x' *added in text aft.* 'mind.'] [x]Hoffding forgets this passage when in Phil Studien VIII, p. 96, he accuses me of inconsistency in maintaining both that there is immediate resemblance and that *association* by resemblance is through a common part. Only *such [*intrl.*] like things *as [*ab. del.* 'that'] have a common part, or at least a common associate, will call each other up.

 Harald Höffding, see note to 545.40.

548.18 (I,582.13–14) It is subtler] [*penc.*] Mark Twain: While the angels were hauling in the slack of it [viz. the minister's long grace] the guests sat wondering whether they were ever going to begin to eat.

557.4 (I,592.1–2) how can this occur] [*penc.*] Wundt espouses this view squarely in Philos. Studien, VII, 341, -4, -58. Also in Lectures, 291–2, 297 | Höffding: Psychol, 124, 126, 157 | J. S. Mill, in Note to J. M.'s Analysis I, p. 112. Bain: S & I. 458. Rabier, & Ward in Mind II. denying it. Stout ditto: Analyt. Psych I. 278 | [*ink*] Cornelius, Psychologie, 32–3, 39.

    W. Wundt, "Bemerkungen zur Associationslehre," *Philosophische Studien*, 7 (1891), 329–361.

    ———, *Lectures on Human and Animal Psychology*, tr. J. E. Creighton & E. B. Titchener (London: Swan Sonnenschein; New York: Macmillan, 1894) (WJ.796.59.10).

    Höffding, *Outlines of Psychology*, trans. Mary E. Lowndes (London: Macmillan, 1891) (WJ 816.39).

    Bain, *The Senses and the Intellect*, 3rd ed.

    Rabier: James could have in mind the essay by Rabier on association cited on p. 556n.

    James Ward, "Assimilation and Association," pt. I, *Mind*, n.s. 2 (July 1893), 347–362.

    Hans Cornelius (1863–1947), Monacan-born philosopher, *Psychologie als Erfahrungswissenschaft* (Leipzig: Teubner, 1897) (WJ 714.77.2). For an additional work by Cornelius from James's library see *The Meaning of Truth*, WORKS, note to 43.6.

*557.8 (I,592.7) similarity] [*penc. underl. in text w. note in upper mrgn.*] 'Gleichheit (Wundt)'

562.29 (I,597.32) Hobbes, Hume] [*penc.*] Descartes *on Man §73 [*intrl.*] & Spinoza, Eth. II, 18 III, 14–17.

    René Descartes, *L'Homme*, pp. 76–78. On p. 76, WJ has "Association."

    Spinoza, *Ethics*, pt. II, prop. 18; pt. III, props. 14–17. In *Œuvres*, III, 72–73, 123–126.

564.15–16 (I,599.15) Hearing the same] [*penc.*] The *great* associationist achievement is the explanation of the *impulsive [*ov.* 'instinctive'] and emotional life by the association of *bodily ['bo' *ov.* 'pl'] pleasures & pains with the ['huma' *del.*] objects which produce them

569.25 (I,604.35) Mr. F. H. Bradley] [*penc.*] Max Offner: Philos. Monatshefte, Bd 28, 385, 513 1892 | [*ink*] Scripture: Philos. Studien, VII, 50 | Cattell & Bryant, Mind, XIV, 230 | Bourdon: Rev. Phil. June 1891 (31.561) | [*penc.*] " " [*ditto mks. under* 'Bourdon'] 1895

    Max Offner (1864–1932), German philosopher, "Über die Grundformen der Vorstellungsverbindung," *Philosophische Monatshefte*, 28 (1892), 385–416.

    Edward Wheeler Scripture (1864–1945), American psychologist, "Über den associativen Verlauf der Vorstellungen," *Philosophische Studien*, 7 (1891), 50–146.

    J. McK. Cattell & Sophie Bryant (1850–1922), "Mental Association Investigated by Experiment," *Mind*, 14 (April 1889), 230–250.

Benjamin Bourdon (1860–c.1943), French psychologist, "Les Résultats des théories contemporaines sur l'association des idées," *Revue Philosophique*, 31 (June 1891), 561–610.

————, "Observations comparatives sur la reconnaissance, la discrimination et l'association," *ibid.*, 40 (Aug. 1895), 151–185.

571.25 (I,606.23) *The knowledge*] [*ink*] Cf. C. S. Peirce, in Monist II, 535–7, 545–7 (July 1892

Charles S. Peirce, "The Law of Mind," *Monist*, 2 (July 1892), 533–559.

575.27 (I,611.1) ACCURACY] [*ink*] Spinosa (Saisset) III. 187
See entry for 264.13 (I,274.1).

577.3 (I,612.22) Wundt and his] [*penc.*] Bolton, Am. J. of Psych. VI, 219, found that in the *subjective ['su' *ov.* 'gr'] grouping of rapidly succeeding clicks, whatever the rapidity was, the groups remained at about one second. Is this the specious present? (Woodworth).

Thaddeus Lincoln Bolton (b. 1865), "Rhythm," *American Journal of Psychology*, 6 (Jan. 1894), 145–238.

Robert Sessions Woodworth, see entry bel., 592.36 (I,630.3).

582.2–3 (I,618.1) as the interval of time] [*ink*] Meumann Phil. Stud. VIII, IX, X. | Münsterberg, Beiträge IV, 89 (filling) | Psychol. Rev. I. 51 ″ ″ [*ditto mks. under* 'filling'] | Schumann: Ztsch. f. Psychol. I. 75 | IV. 1 | Strong: Psychol. Rev. III. 149

Ernst Meumann (1862–1915), German psychologist, "Beiträge zur Psychologie des Zeitsinns," *Philosophische Studien*, 8 (1892), 431–509.

————, "Beiträge zur Psychologie des Zeitsinns," *ibid.*, 9 (1893), 264–306.

————, "Untersuchungen zur Psychologie und Aesthetik des Rhythmus," *ibid.*, 10 (1894), 249–322, 393–430.

Charles Augustus Strong (1862–1940), American philosopher and psychologist, "Consciousness and Time," *Psychological Review*, 3 (March 1896), 149–157.

Friedrich Schumann (1869–1940), German psychologist, "Über das Gedächtnis für Komplexe regelmässig aufeinander folgender, gleicher Schalleindrücke," *Zeitschrift für Psychologie und Physiologie der Sinnesorgane*, 1 (1890), 74–80.

587.1 (I,624.1) From this we] [*penc.*] M–g finds the more interestingly filled times are more often judged *shorter* than the others Psych. Rev. I. 51. Explains by attention being distracted from muscular processes.

Hugo Münsterberg, "Optical Time-Content," *Psychological Review*, 1 (Jan. 1894), 51–56.

592.36 (I,630.3) lines in a plane] [*penc.*] "As the vertical line sweeps along the time line it scrapes off one infinitesimal element after another and these elements crowding into the coexistent line retain for a time the order in which they were scraped off." (R. S. Woodworth Thesis, 1896.)

Robert Sessions Woodworth (1869–1962), American psychologist, attended Harvard College in 1895–1896, graduate school in 1896–1897. The thesis would have been written in connection with one of several psychology courses given by James.

596.25 (I,634.4–5) if I understand Mr. Ward] [*ink*] Do Ward's "movements" of attention come with a later and an earlier end? If so do they give order to our images by contrasting adhesions of their ['f' *del.*] earlier end to one, of their later end to another. If so they are the originals of our time sense

605.0 (I,643.0) CHAPTER XVI.] *clipping pasted on interleaf beginning report in* Science, 11 (June 8, 1888), 271, *describing the results of tests on the memories and receptive powers of school-children performed by* Harlan Hoge Ballard (1853–1934), *American librarian, originally published in* Journal of Education, May 3, 1888.

*605.0 (I,643.0) CHAPTER XVI.] [*penc. at top*] Explained by Descartes, de Homine §72 | " " [*ditto mks. under* 'Explained by'] Spinoza Ethics, II 17, also Saisset, III, 331–2, 238–9
     Descartes, *L'Homme*, pp. 74–75. On p. 74 of his copy, James has "memory."
     Spinoza, *Ethics*, pt. II, prop. 17 (*Œuvres*, III, 69–72); *Œuvres*, III, 331–2, a reference to *On the Improvement of the Understanding*; *Œuvres*, III, 238–9, *Ethics*, pt. IV, prop. 62.

*605.9 (I,643.10) painted on the latter] [*ink*] 'former' *subst. in mrgn. for* 'latter'

*607.10 (I,645.11) throught] [*ink*] *corr. to* 'through'

*607.22 (I,644.37) cause] [*ink*] *corr. to* 'caused'

607.33 (I,645.31) after-images] [*penc.*] Article from Prag lab, *on [*ov.* 'in'] positive aft. Im. *in [*ov.* 'un' *or* 'an'] Pfluger's Archiv, in Lib, June 1891
     Carl von Hess (1863–1923), German ophthalmologist, "Untersuchungen über die nach kurzdauernder Reizung des Sehorgans auftretenden Nachbilder," *Archiv für Physiologie*, 49 (1891), 190–208.

609.8 (I,647.13) When we] [*ink*] Horwicz remembers sensorially the events of a three day's festival when a student (P. A. 1. 303
     Adolf Horwicz, *Psychologische Analysen auf physiologischer Grundlage*, I (Halle: Pfeffer, 1872) (WJ 739.78).

*627.42 (I,667.24) maximum . . . minimum] [*ink*] minimum . . . maximum

634.12 (I,673.36) That nascent] [*ink*] Baldwin (Phil. Rev. II, 402) accounts for recognition of a thing as having already formed part of *our* experience, by the greater ease in attending to what we already have dealt with. The reinstatement of the old motor adjustments give the sense of familiarity. | Compare also Steinthal: Einleitung in die Psych. 191–2
     J. Mark Baldwin, "Internal Speech and Song," *Philosophical Review*, 2 (July 1893), 385–407.
     Heymann Steinthal, *Einleitung in die Psychologie und Sprachwissenschaft* (Berlin: F. Dümmler, 1881).

*634.21 (I,674.6) Professor Höffding] [*ink*] Höffding replies in Phil. Studien, VIII, 86. claiming that he is nearer my position than ['he' *del.*] I seem to think (93) & that all he means by the awaken "images of the past self" is a "disposition the potentiality of an idea (*sit venia verbo*) which under other conditions would become an ['image' *del.*] independent image" (90) [*rule*] Lehmann in Phil. St. VII, 169 Does expts. with sounds & smells wh. he thinks corroborate those on tints. Only seven % of the smells were ['ref' *del.*] recognized without distinct revival of associates. After 10 seconds ['the' *del.*] recognition of the sound grows very uncertain. The later sound tends to be overestimated, i.e. identified with a louder preceding one. L. also calls attention to the fact that the recognition *takes time* in the case of simple sensations. | [*penc., top of p.* 674] Wundt gives similar explanⁿ. Phil. Stud. VII, 351–3 | [*top p.* 675] Ward (Mind, N S., II., 347) argues against the resuscitated past identical; and yet seems to favor Hoffding's view (360–1) He vacillates.

Harald Höffding, see note to 545.40.
Alfred Lehmann, see entry for *473.17–18 (I,500.17).
James Ward, see entry for 557.4 (I,592.1–2).

636.3 (I,676.1–2) I have over] [*ink*] "Paramnesia"—see my abstracts in Psych. Rev., vol I. | [*penc.*] On paramnesia & the sense of recognition or "Known-again feeling" Cf. Allin in *Am ['A' *ov.* 'P'] J. of P., 235–73. A. seems to make the *facility* of the process the chief sign by which we class things as already met

William James, Review of A. Lalande's "Des Paramnésies," *Psychological Review*, 1 (Jan. 1894), 94–95.
Arthur Allin, "The Recognition-Theory of Perception," *American Journal of Psychology*, 7 (Jan. 1896), 237–248.
————, "Recognition," *ibid.*, pp. 249–273.

638.27 (I,678.26) All the inferences] [*ink*] Cf. J. A. Krieger in Sͭ Louis Courier of Medecine, April 1890. "If I. W's hand is made anaesthetic &c p. 230

J. A. Krieger, "Novel Manifestations in Hysteria," *St. Louis Courier of Medicine*, 2 (1890), 226–231.

646.22 (I,686.25) then when we] [*penc. caret bef. del.* 'then' *in text*] [*penc.*] ‸ what we need for remembering hereafter is that the path 1–2 should be deepened. Obviously when etc.

646.22–23 (I,686.25) inward effort,] [*penc. w. guideline bringing entry ov. into text and caret aft.* 'effort,'] this is the path this is now used *and [*ab. del.* 'again'] consequently also deepened for future use,

649.7 (I,689.3) The result is] [*penc.*] See Ladd's retort in the Philosophic Review, I, 44

George T. Ladd, "Psychology As So-Called 'Natural Science,' " *Philosophical Review*, 1 (Jan. 1892), 24–53.

649.22 (I,689.20) For a history] [*ink*] *J. Ross* on M. in Brain *vol 14 [*penc. intrl.*] No 2. 1891 | Meinong: Zur Erkentnisstheoretchen Würdigung d͡e͡s Ged͡s 4tel. jsch. X. 7. | [Ladd *entry in penc.: see ab.*] J. *Jastrow* on Memory & Association in Educational Review, Dec. 1891, and in New Review about same time. | *Dugas*: la M. brute et la M. organisée, Rev. Phil. XXXVIII, 449 | [*penc.*] Dorpfeld: Thought & Memory 1896

James Ross, "On Memory," *Brain*, 14 (1891), 35–50.
Alexius Meinong, "Zur erkenntnisstheoretischen Würdigung des Gedächtnisses," *Vierteljahrsschrift*, 10 (1886), 7–33.
Joseph Jastrow, "A Statistical Study of Memory and Associ-

ation," *Educational Review*, 2 (Dec. 1891), 442–452.

————, "A Study in Mental Statistics," *New Review*, 5 (Dec. 1891), 559–568.

Ludovic Dugas (1857–1943), French psychologist, "La Mémoire brute et la mémoire organisée," *Revue Philosophique*, 38 (Nov. 1894), 449–464.

Friedrich Wilhelm Dörpfeld (1824–1893), German psychologist, *Denken und Gedächtnis* (1884). James could be referring to the adaptation by Herman Tyson Lukens, *The Connection Between Thought and Memory: A Contribution to Pedagogical Psychology on the Basis of F. W. Dörpfeld's Monograph "Denken und Gedächtnis,"* with an introduction by G. Stanley Hall (Boston: Heath, 1896 [first printing 1895]).

651.0 (II,[1.0]) CHAPTER XVII.] [*ink*] *Bloch*: on pressure & traction on skin, Archives de Physiol. Avril 1891 | Sensation cognitive because synthetic, Baldwin: Handbook, II, 94–5

   A. M. Bloch, "Recherches expérimentales sur les sensations de traction et de pression cutanées," *Archives de Physiologie*, 3 (April 1891), 322–333.

   J. Mark Baldwin, *Handbook of Psychology: Feeling and Will* (New York: Henry Holt, 1891).

*656.9 (II,6.25–26) sensations are . . . things] [*penc.*] *all underl. except* 'first', *and marked* 'ital' *in mrgn.*

*657.23–24 (II,8.13) (See above] [*penc.*] 'Vol I' *subst. for* 'above'

*659.4 (II,10.4–5) gnarls of relations] [*penc.*] *alt. to* 'snarls of relations'

662.1 (II,13.3) THE LAW] [*ink*] A. M. Mayer: Studies of the phenomena of simultaneous Contrast-color. Am. J. of Sc. July 1893 [with Herings' reprints]

   Alfred Marshall Mayer (1836–1897), American physicist, "Studies of the Phenomena of Simultaneous Contrast-Color; and on a Photometer for Measuring the Intensities of Lights of Different Colors," *American Journal of Science*, 46 (July 1893), 1–22.

666.11 (II,18.1) We have sufficient] [*penc.*] According to Helmholtz the induced *colour [*ab. del.* 'sen'] is not a *sensation ['s' *ov.* 'p'] or *first psychical thing* but a logical inference or a last psychical thing, the first psychical thing having been *another* colour and the intermediary psychical things a number of ideas etc, all subconscious. Wundt expresses this by saying (since the induced colour may also under other conditions be a true sensation) that "mechanism & logic are identical."–(M. u. Th. Seele, I. 200)

672.32 (II,25.4) Brief mention] [*penc.*] Ragona-Scina's

*675.9 (II,27.32) their knowledge] [*ink*] *alt. to* 'the sensation's knowledge'

*675.36 (II,28.35) *allgemeiner*] [*penc.*] *alt. to* '*allgemeines*'

*675.38 (II,28.37) contrast‸] [*penc.*] ' "feeling," ' *insrtd.*

*675.39–40 (II,28.39) why does] [*penc.*] *alt. to* 'why need'

*675.40 (II,28.39) when it thus feels] [*penc.*] *alt. to* 'in order thus to feel'

*675.40 (II,28.39) in relation?] [*added in ink*] See Vorlesungen 2nd Ed.

p. 65+ & P. P. 4th Ed. I, 397

676.1 (II,28.24)   *There are many*] [*penc.*] Compare the examples on pp. 80–82 [*ed.*, 726–727]

677.7 (II,30.3)   Smell, taste] [*clipping pasted in*] —A Brooklyn Times correspondent says: "I telephoned to a friend the other day, and after he learned who wanted him he said: 'Wait a minute.' I waited, and then he said: 'Well, go ahead.' I said what I had to say and then asked why he had told me to wait, and he replied: 'I wanted to put on my glasses.' I laughed and asked him what his glasses had to do with the telephone. He said: 'My hearing is perfect, but my sight is poor. You know I always wear glasses when reading or writing. Now, I find that I can hear better over the wire if I have my glasses on. It may seem strange, but it it is true.' " Theatre goers have perhaps noticed that opera glasses are a help in hearing.

*677.29 (II,30.28)   chord, it is] [*ink*] *alt. to* 'chord; but it is rather'

*680.7 (II,33.7–8)   sensation | is projected] [*ink in mrgn. w. guideline drawn to point betw. the lines*] w. l.

*681.11 (II,34.13)   elsewhere.] [*added in ink*] Psychologist's fallacy.

681.29 (II,35.1–2)   He does not feel] [*penc.*] Cf. Lipps Grundtatsachen pp 70–71

688.2 (II,42.1)   We think of] [*penc.*] "In the mind"—what do you mean by that? Where is the mind? If the *mind ['in' ov. 'es'] is wherever its object is, of course the object is in it, but then it *never gets *projected* ['j' ov. 'd'] *out of it.* If the mind is in the head, and most of the extraditers really mean this, then the assertion is false, for our visual sensations never either are or appear *in* the head, and *therefore ['t' ov. 'a'] can never be projected out of it.

690.20 (II,44.26)   Prof. Jastrow] [*ink*] Hitschmann: ueber den *Traumleben ['leb' ov. 'be'] des Blinden, Ztsch. f. Psychol., VII, 387. | [*space*] The blind painter Anastasi tells Th. Gautier (Jl. des Goncourt V. 17) that he had no memory for colours "mais qu'il la retrouvait dṢ les rêves de son sommeil: Les choses dṢ la nuit éternelle où A. est plongé se rappelent à lui seulement par un contour et un modelage, mais il ne les voit plus colorées." (T. S. P.)
        Friedrich Hitschmann, "Über das Traumleben des Blinden," *Zeitschrift für Psychologie und Physiologie der Sinnesorgane*, 7 (1894), 387–394.
        Théophile Gautier (1811–1872), French writer, in an article in the *Journal des Goncourt*, 5 (Paris: Charpentier, 1891), about Auguste Paul Charles Anastasi (1820–1889), French painter.

692.21 (II,46.22)   writers.] [*penc.*] ['x' *added in text aft.* 'writers.']
ˣSpinoza sets forth the blended image theory in his Ethics II, 40, schol.
        See footnote at 692.40.

*696.16 (II,50.9)   results of a most] [*ink*] 'most' *del.*

702.28 (II,56.8–9)   I have myself] *clipping laid in fr. the* Sun, Dec. 5, 1896, *headlined* 'THE OLD BEECHER STOVE FOUND.', *headed in ink and underl.* 'Imagination.' *in* WJ's *hand. Also laid in is clipping of article* "Imagination and Conception," Saturday Review (Sept. 30, 1871), 425–426.

*712.34 (II,65.41) to lie together] [*ink*] *comma added aft.* 'lie'

714.34 (II,68.35) That of Dr.] [*penc.*] Gruithuisen

*714.41 (II,68.43) my students.] [*added in ink*] Remember Prof. Scott's letter to me from Ann Arbor.—Also Mr. Smith's account. Washburn's Acct.
    Perhaps Fred Newton Scott (1860-1930), American educator. Neither Smith nor Washburn have been identified.

719.9 (II,73.3) After occipital] [*penc.*] Separate seats for image & sensation are defended by J. Ward in Mind, N S., III. 509
    James Ward, "Assimilation and Association, pt. II," *Mind*, n.s. III, 19 (Oct. 1894), 509-532.

*722.0 (II,76.0) CHAPTER XIX.] [*penc.*] Royce's criticism that in this Chapter I have ignored too much (as elements of the secondary processes to which the sensation leads) the processes of muscular reaction and adaptation, which determines the object in a vital way.

727.26 (II,82.2) The sensation] [*penc.*] Compare the facts of contrast, and the examples given above on pp. 28-31 [*ed.*, 676-678]

*728.26 (II,83.2) grave] [*ink*] *alt. to* 'the *gravest* ['st' *ov.* 'er']'

*729.5 (II,83.21) *resemble those*] [*ink*] 'sensations' *subst. in mrgn. for* 'those'

732.13 (II,87.9) There is a] [*ink*] Two good articles on Stereoscope, by Leconte Stevens in Pop. Sci. M. May (?) June, 1882
    Walter Le Conte Stevens (1847-1927), American physicist, "The Stereoscope: Its History," *Popular Science Monthly*, 21 (May 1882), 37-53.
    ———, "The Stereoscope: Its Theory," *ibid.*, 21 (June 1882), 197-205.

734.30 (II,89.32) Giddiness is] [*ink*] Parker on Vertigo: Brain Jan. 1885
    George Parker, "On Vertigo," *Brain*, 7 (Jan. 1885), 514-528.

736.21-22 (II,91.28-30) But with . . . to be.] [*penc.*] *Three lines of text vertically lined in both mrgns. w. line running across to interleaf*: This sentence is too compressed (complained of by Stevens)

740.24 (II,96.7) As with game] *pasted-in clipping fr.* Science, 18 (Aug. 14, 1891), 91 "When the Crystal Palace . . . to judge." [*In the great fire when the menagerie was rescued, a writhing ape on the roof was reached with difficulty, but the ape turned out to be a piece of canvas.*]

*747.36 (II,103.27) These images] [*added in penc.*] 'either'

*748.20 (II,104.14) If B . . . has] [*penc.*] 'But if B in turn have,'

*748.32 (II,104.27) habitual,] [*penc.*] 'and fluent' *insrtd. bef. comma*

*749.3 (II,104.38) chapter)] [*penc.*] 'p. 231 ff.' *insrtd. bef. paren*

*750.12,15 (II,106.11,15) foot . . . toes.] [*penc.*] *fn. indicator for second fn. on page del. aft.* 'foot.' *and subst. aft.* 'toes.' *for third indicator. The third indicator is correctly printed on this page aft.* 'found.' [*ed.*, 750.24]. *The corresponding footnotes in the present edition are* 26-28.

*754.7 (II,110.14) Old-fogyism] [ink] On Old fogyism Cf. Paulhan's Activité mentale, etc. p. 131 ff.

765.12 (II,122.1) complete anatomy] [penc.] Hallucinations of the muscular sense—Lane's paper with Tamburini's cases—Lehmann etc etc.

Wilmot Burkemar Lane (b. 1871), *Space-Threshold of Colours and Its Dependence on Contrast Phenomena* (Toronto: The University Library: published by The Librarian, 1898). It has not been established which papers by Augusto Tamburini (1848–1919), Italian psychologist, and Alfred Lehmann James has in mind.

767.2 (II,123.35) Let water] [ink] Descartes, L'Homme, CII. Descartes, see note to 770.11.

773.24 (II,131.24) But until these] [ink] On centrifugal optic paths to retina see Engelmann in Helmholtz Festschriften, quoted by Wundt P. P. 4th Edition, I, 319–20. Also pp. 130, 323. —Monakow also.

Theodor Wilhelm Engelmann in *Festschrift zur Feier des Siebzigsten Geburtstages von Hermann von Helmholtz* (Hamburg: Voss, 1891).

776.0 (II,134.0) CHAPTER XX.] [ink] Guy Tawny: Pschol. Rev. II. 585 | Symposium by Carr, Muirhead, & Stout, in Proc. Aristotelian Society, Vol 3. p. 119 | Crude extensity in all the senses amply and distinctly defended by ['Du' del.] J. P. Durand (de Gros): Essais de Physiologie philosophique, 1866, p. 363 ff.

Guy Allan Tawney (b. 1870), "The Perception of Two Points Not the Space-Threshold," *Psychological Review*, 2 (Nov. 1895), 585–593.

Herbert Wildon Carr (1857–1931), British philosopher; John Henry Muirhead (1855–1940), British philosopher; and G. F. Stout, "Symposium—Is the Knowledge of Space *A Priori*?" *Proceedings of the Aristotelian Society*, 3 (1895), 119–133.

Joseph Pierre Durand (de Gros) (1826–1900), French philosopher, *Essais de physiologie philosophique* (Paris: Baillière, 1866). The chapter cited is entitled "La Propriété de sensation figurative et ses causes organiques."

*778.39 (II,136.38) (1841).] [added in ink] p. 66

*781.28 (II,139.36) either case wc] [ink] 'wc' *corr. to* 'we'

781.33 (II,140.1) The tympanic] [ink] F. B. Dresslar: Am. J. of. Psychol. V. No 3. found by expt that increasing pressure in meatus required from *3.9 ['3' ov. doubtful '5'] to 0.6 mm. of mercury before it was noticed. Stopping ears with cotten stopped the perception, shielding rest of face did not. He concludes that the perception is due to feeling of variation in outer sounds due to nearness of screen or object.

Fletcher Bascom Dresslar (1858–1930), American educator, "On the Pressure Sense of the Drum of the Ear and 'Facial Vision,'" *American Journal of Psychology*, 5 (April 1893), 344–350.

785.24 (II,143.27) The celebrated boy] [ink] Franz's pt.

791.5 (II,149.28) But just as, in] [*penc.*] The same retinal or cutaneous impression may give a['n' *del.*] space-[*intrl.*] relation or a term, according to the way in which the mind takes it, or attends to it.

791.21 (II,150.6) If these relations] [*penc.*] The intellectualists insist on a first in the shape of a non spatial sensation—purely 'intensive' or qualitative. They don't mean chronologically separate in experience, but an *element* lower than all the rest, of unextended light or colour or touch. I call this an artificial hypothesis, since all we perceive is *already* extensive. If the word 'sensation' offend when applied to anything extensive, drop it. Then all that I say is that the first experience gives an object which, when later identified, located, sub-divided and otherwise 'related' has to undergo no such intrinsic change or transformation of appearance as the intellectualist claim (that it becomes extensive then for the first time) would seem to require.

805.3 (II,165.1-2) We have also shown] [*ink*] ['Two sounds *a* & *β* may be' *del.*] One may pass from sound *c* to sound *g* through *sounds [*intrl.*] d e f and through muscle-feelings, but the intervening sensations are not felt as *extents* ['of' *del.*] separating *c* and *g*. ['But when in skin or retina we pass' *del.*] *They give us [*ab. del.* 'It is'] a "distance" only in Stumpf's sense of the word, an amount of difference, or else ['it is' *del.*] a time interval. But when we pass over *skin* or *retina* from a contact ['c' *del.*] or seen point *c* to another *g*, *and [*intrl.*] there similarly intervene points d e f, and ['a' *del.*] muscular *feelings ['s' *added*] ['yet' *del.*] here *what ['w' *ov.* 'is'] intervenes is directly seen or felt as an *extent*, not only *realized [*intrl.*] as a *difference ['c' *ov.* 't'] or time-interval. We can't explain this difference between our organs; but we *can* say that *unless* we suppose *the [*intrl.*] skin and retinal intervals natively to carry with them the extensive quality, no later associations into which they enter | [*opp. p.* 166] will enable us to account for their acquiring this quality.

*805.10 (II,165.21) But note now] [*ink*] Cf. W. J. in Mind N. S. II p. 364
   William James, "The Original Datum of Space-Consciousness,"
   Mind, n.s. 2 (July 1893), 363–365.

808.5-7 (II,168.33-35) strong . . . member] [*penc.*] *qst. mk. in mrgn.*

814.1 (II,175.1) Enough has now] [*penc.*] Ztschr. f. Psychol. II. 91 (Raehl-mann) Cf. what he says about his blind boy at first *counting* by movements of head, altho he could from the first see "mehrere" things to be there. *94 ['4' *ov.* '8']–5 | Franz's p! otherwise.
   Eduard Raehlmann (b. 1848), "Physiologisch-psychologische Studien über die Entwickelung der Gesichtswahrnehmungen bei blindern und bei operierten Blindgeborenen," *Zeitschrift für Psychologie*, 2 (1891), 53–96.

815.38 (II,176.42) Motion does this] [*penc.*] The eye too clings to points & boundaries

821.28-29 (II,184.8) The sensation chosen] [*ink*] "J'entends un jour un bruit sec produit ['by' *del.*] par un *fragment [*ab. del.* 'morceau'] de charbon qui dans mon foyer se dètache brusquement d'un morceau de charbon, et en même temps ma pendule sonner une demie; immediatement je songe que [*illeg. letter del.*] q chose s'est brisé dṣ ma pendule au moment où elle sonnait. Si, au moment où je pose le pied par terre, un ['p' *del.*] bruit se

produit, ma première pensée est que c'est la pression de mon pied qui l'a produit." Bourdon, in Rev. Phil. XXXI, 596. He refers to Wundt's Physiol. Psych. II. 237 | See also cases in J A. McLellan, Applied Psychol. p. 33
Bourdon, see entry for 569.25 (I,604.35).

Wundt, *Grundzüge*, 3rd ed.

James Alexander McLellan (1832-1907), *Applied Psychology: An Introduction to the Principles and Practice of Education* (Boston: Educational Publishing Company, 1889).

826.19-20 (II,189.22) consciousness of active] [*penc.*] On muscular sense see Charpentier in Archives de Physiol. Jan. 1891 | Ags! Sachs, see Tschiriew, ibid, Nos. 2, 3, 4. (?)

A. Charpentier, "Analyse experimentale de quelques éléments de la sensation de poids," *Archives de Physiologie*, 5th series, 3 (Jan. 1891), 122-135.

Sergei Ivanovich Tschirew, *Archives de Physiologie*, 2nd series, 6 (1879); "Sur les terminaisons nerveuses dans les muscles striés," 89-116; "Étude sur la physiologie des nerfs des muscles striés," 295-329; "Lésions de la moelle épinière et de la peau dans un cas de lépre anesthésique," 614-623.

Sachs, see note to 1113.39.

828.4 (II,191.12) It has long] [*penc.*] Case where muscles were a fatty mass incapable of contraction *([*paren ov. comma*] yet sense of position preserved ['?' *del.*]) in Stern, Arch. f. Psychiat. XVII, 509

Bolko Stern, "Über die Anomalien der Empfindung und ihre Beziehungen zur Ataxie bei Tabes dorsalis," *Archiv für Psychiatrie und Nervenkrankheiten*, 17 (1886), 485-517.

839.19-20 (II,204.2) So it seems] [*ink*] Sizeranne: The blind through blind eyes. (Mr. Hackett's thesis showed that fog diminishes the ['j' *del.*] ear judgment of sound-variation from distance. He thinks the blind conceive of large supra tactile spaces by a summary symbol, as we do of "South America" etc.

Maurice de La Sizeranne (1857-1924), French writer on blindness, *The Blind As Seen Through Blind Eyes*, trans. F. Park Lewis (New York: G. P. Putnam's Sons, 1893).

Possibly Henry Seavey Hackett (1875-1915) (Harvard class of 1897) who studied English and Philosophy.

840.29 (II,205.11) Certainly in this] [*ink*] Mr. Perry's letter.—Mr Steeley's case in Religio Phil J. May 2. 1890

Religio-Philosophical Journal, n.s. 1 (May 2, 1891), 774-775.

846.39 (II,211.40) still (p. 9).] [*ink*] Monck: Mind, VII, 107. | Raehlmann: Ztsch. f. Psych. etc II, 53 | [*penc.*] Heller: Studien zur Blinden-Psychol. Phil. Stud. XI | [*ink*] Hitschmann: Begründung einer Blindenpsychologie, Ztsch. f. Psychol. III., 388.

William Henry Stanley Monck (1839-1915), "Observations on Cases of Couching for Cataract," *Mind*, 7 (Jan. 1882), 107-110.

Raehlmann, see entry for 814.1 (II,175.1).

Theodor Heller, "Studien zur Blinden-Psychologie," *Philosophische Studien*, 11 (1895), no. 2, 226-253; no. 3, 406-470; no. 4, 531-562.

Friedrich Hitschmann, "Über Begründung einer Blindenpsychologie von einem Blinden," *Zeitschrift für Psychologie und Physiologie der Sinnesorgane*, 3 (1892), 388–397.

847.33–35 (II,213.25–26) the parts . . . seem] [*penc.*] *Two lines of text vertically lined in both mrgns. w. line running across to interleaf:* False! Corrected by Margaret Washburn in Mind, 1894

> Margaret Floy Washburn (1871–1939), American educator, "The Perception of Distance in the Inverted Landscape," *Mind*, n.s. 3, 19 (July 1894), 438–440.

853.8–10 (II,219.11–13) but if the reader . . . mind.] [*penc.*] By this the Chapter on Perception was meant. Cf. p. 80+ above [*ed.*, 726+]

853.11 (II,219.14) *actually* FEEL *different*] [*penc.*] Compare the facts, above, of contrast etc. pp. 28+ [*ed.*, 675+], also 80–82 [*ed.*, 726–727].

*853.12 (II,219.16) *that*] [*penc.*] 't' *underl. and marked* 'ital' *in mrgn.*

*859.23–25 (II,226.20–22) The former . . . difficulty.] [*penc.*] *in mrgn.* 'Badly expressed.'

*861.16 (II,228.23) Fig. 50] [*penc.*] Fig. 55

*863.3 (II,230.16) eyes, alter] [*penc.*] eyes alters

*865.8 (II,232.20) Fig. 52] [*ink*] Fig. 62

*873.24 (II,241.34) are necessary conditions] [*ink*] is a necessary condition

*882.25–26 (II,251.15–16) *discarding his*] [*penc.*] *discarding this*

*884.2 (II,253.7) Fig. 65] [*penc.*] Fig. 70

890.21 (II,260.2) In no other class] [*penc.*] Remember, too, that all that the "imagination" does here is to alter the relative extent-value of of different seen patches, and this is what it everlastingly and incessantly has to do whenever things are discerned to be at different distances.

906.10 (II,276.9) The obvious objection] [*penc.*] Leibnitz (Janet 2, 660 etc) defines S. very well as a mere ideal "order [*closing db. qts. del.*] of coexistence."

*909.11 (II,279.16) space,] [*ink*] 'of' *added*

*911.27 (II,282.11) *soi-distant*] [*penc.*] *soi-disant*

913.0 (II,283.0) CHAPTER XXI.] [*ink*] See Comments on this *Chapter [*ab. del.* 'article'] by D.^r W L. Worcester in the Monist. April 1892, vol 2. p. 321. [*Bel. is a clipping from an article by* Charles Bradlaugh *discussing* James's "Psychology of Belief," Mind, 14 (July 1889), 321–352, *substantially reprinted as Chapter XXI. The clipping is completed opp. p. 284.*]

> Charles Bradlaugh (1833–1891), British critic of religion, "Belief," *National Reformer*, n.s. 54 (Sept. 15, 1889), 161.
> For the Worcester reference, see the entry for 174.1 (I,172.30).

*913.7 (II,283.8) every] [*penc. underl. in text w. mrgn. note*] correct verbally

*917.38 (II,287.38) VII. 161 ff.] [*ink*] VIII. 161 ff.

918.22 (II,288.33) its existence."] [*ink*] Cf. also *Saisset's ['S' ov. 's']

Œuvres' paging contains *Ethics*, pt. II, prop. 17. See entry for 264.13 (I,274.1).

919.27 (II,290.4) *all propositions*] [*penc.*] Blind boy (Raehlmann) tries with his *real ['r' *ov.* 'o'] hand to take hold of his nose in the looking glass— discovers that if he takes *hold ['h' *ov.* 'l'] of real nose the looking glass nose is grasped, but then only by the looking glass hand.
    See entry for 814.1 (II,175.1).

924.1–3 (II,294.22–24) which . . . consider] [*penc. w. guidelines to marked-off passage and mrgn. note*] Make clearer

924.11–12 (II,295.10) reality with simple] [*ink*] Reality-perfection Spinosa (Saisset) III. 50
    See entry for 161.18 (I,158.26).

*924.13 (II,295.12) *simply*] [*penc.*] 'y' *underl. and marked* 'ital' *in mrgn.*

*927.36 (II,298.43) Griesinger] [*penc. bel. fn.*] See also Lotze: Med. Psych. p. 251

*928.12 (II,299.17) *stronger*] [*penc.*] 'contradicting' *added, marked by caret; in next line a penc. caret appears betw.* 'relation' *and its comma and in penc. opp. on the interleaf is the word* 'which', *apparently the aborted start of an insrtd. clause.*

*934.26 (II,306.16) Berkeley has] [*penc.*] Aristotle and Berkeley have

*935.17 (II,307.13) Moral and religious] [*penc. in mrgn.*] See "letter from Mazzini in Mathilde Blind's article about him in Fortnightly Review May (or April) 1891 | [*ink*] Cf. also Griesinger's psych. kk^{tn} p. 28
    Mathilde Blind (1841–1896), German-born writer, "Personal Recollections of Mazzini," *Fortnightly Review*, 55 (May 1891), 702–712. The letter starts on p. 709.
    Wilhelm Griesinger, *Die Pathologie und Therapie der psychischen Krankheiten.*

937.12 (II,309.9) M. Renouvier] [*penc.*] To conceive is to believe, even without passion: See the effect of often repeated advertisements praising articles of which we have no other information than what the advertisement gives—it is hard not to believe that the article in question is what it is cracked up to be—*provid*ed of course that the blackguardly style of the advertisement does n't make it smack to palpably of humbug.

*940.19–20 (II,312.37) problem of 'good.'] [*ink*] 'problem of good.'

*945.11 (II,317.23) What is beyond] [*penc.*] 'beyond' *underl. and marked* 'ital' *in mrgn.*

*948.3–5 (II,320.32–34) this difference . . . goes.] [*penc.*] *qst. mk. in mrgn.*

*948.28 (II,321.21) If belief] [*penc. in mrgn.*] Guard against misapprehension of my meaning here.

949.31–32 (II,322.29–30) *our belief . . . fact.*] [*ink*] *underl. in text; on interleaf* 'This needs correction'

*950.46–47 (II,323.50) xperience] [*penc.*] experience; *also in same line faultily inked* 'c' *in* 'presence' *underl. and marked w.* 'x' *in mrgn.*

Appendix II

952.0 (II,325.0) CHAPTER XXII.] [*penc.*] Story

*952.20-953.1 (II,325.23-24) contiguities, or similarities,] [*penc.*] *commas del.*

954.6 (II,327.6) In these first] [*penc.*] "Constructs," Lloyd Morgan 312, 339 | Say *hereabouts [*intrl.*] that particular *concrete [2'c' *ov.* 's'], and sharply conceived abstract universals were the only *named* sorts of ideas until a few years ago. Between them are various intermediaries which now that infants and brutes are *being ['be' *ov. doubtful* 'now'] studied need equally to be named. "Construct" and "predominant" are attempts.

954.31 (II,327.30) I see no need] [*ink*] "Influent" Briefer Course, 348
    William James, *Psychology: Briefer Course* (New York: Henry
    Holt, 1892).

957.13 (II,330.19) if it suggests] [*penc.*] "isolate"

*963.24 (II,337.26) repugance] [*penc.*] repugnance

*966.8 (II,340.20) of the new lines.] [*penc.*] 'special' *in mrgn. w. wrongly placed caret aft.* 'of'; 'which serve his purpose.' *added w. caret ov. period aft.* 'lines'.

972.18 (II,348.1) If so much] [*ink, written later*] Brutes only abstract *sensible parts* of present situations, and are led from them to expect *immediate* consequences to which they adapt their acts. They do not think of part and consequence in the form of a general proposition, but simply *obey* the connection, with their consciousness confined to the present single case. Men abstract not only sensible but "metaphysical parts, think them as ['usin' *del.*] universals by coupling them with the consequences in [*doubtful* 'a n' *del.*] a general proposition, and then proceed to the present single case.

973.12 (II,348.24) I will first try] [*penc.*] Story in Dᴿ Worcester's letter of squirrel gnawing nuts smaller to make them *get [*ov.* 'run'] into hole.
    See entry for 174.1 (I,172.30).

974.36-37 (II,350.19) 'recept'] [*penc.*] "predominant" (Morgan) | "influent"?

980.1-2 (II,355.29-356.1) language is assuredly] [*ink*] Cf. R. L. Garner, the Simian Tongue, (New Review, June 1891).
    Richard Lynch Garner (1848-1920), American naturalist,
    "The Simian Tongue," *New Review*, 4 (June 1891), 555-562.

992.17 (II,369.37) The reason] [*penc. in mrgn.*] Helmholtz

992.35 (II,370.20) an ordinary] [*penc.*] a common

1004.0 (II,383.0) CHAPTER XXIV.] [*ink*] Chapter on I. in *W. [*ov.* 'H']
A. Hammond on Insanity, 1891.
    William Alexander Hammond, *A Treatise on Insanity in Its
    Medical Relations* (New York: Appleton, 1891).

1005.19 (II,384.14) appeart] [*ink*] appears

1017.1 (II,397.1) Their case was] [*letter tipped in*] McCormick Theological Seminary, 1060 N. Halsted Street. Chicago, Feb. 20 1896 | Prof. William James, Harvard University, Dear Sir: I have read with great interest your works on Psychology— If you will permit me I will mention one instance which seems to contradict, to a certain extent your argument from The *Law of Transitoriness of Instinct.* Vol II page 399 psychology— Speaking of the argument from sucking calves—'I remember this incident, which came under my observation on a ranch in my native state Texas—A certain cow had a calf which was two years old This calf had ceased to suck [*comma del.*] when about eight months old. Its mother had her second calf since this two year old | The two year old had a calf when about thirty months old—and after this time began to suck its own mother again. It was no uncommon occurrence for a calf to be *weaned, when six months old and after, six or eight months,* when its mother had another calf, to *begin sucking again* It would seem here that the Instinct of sucking was not entirely extinct, unless you say the second case of sucking is "Inhibition of instinct by habits" or perhaps the old habit was called back by seeing the new calf suck— [¶] Allow me, again to express to you my appreciation of your works on psychology,— as a young student they have been very helpful to me. | Very truly | John L Kell

1018.18 (II,398.28) "A chicken] [*ink*] A teacher after one of my lectures on pedagogic psych. told me that in his family they had allowed kittens to follow them (as kittens will do) and that the habit had persisted in the cats, who followed them abroad like dogs. Older cats could not be taught this habit

1019.26 (II,400.1) "I may cite] [*penc.*] See in my Psychology drawer the case of Grace Harrington child of deaf mutes taught to talk after the normal age—result not conclusive—only slow and difficult learning.

1025.2 (II,406.1) Bain has tried] [*penc.*] "Deferred instincts" Morgan

1028.12 (II,409.20) *Emulation or*] [*ink*] False views of Rousseau about emulation in Maillet, 108–9
    See entry for 447.10 (I,473.5).

*1028.14 (II,409.22) Nine-tenth] [*ink*] Nine-tenths

1028.19 (II,409.27) *Pugnacity; anger*] [*ink*] Attraction of danger: panther story etc., *Guyau: M. ŝ. O. ni S. [*intrl.*] 210 | [*tipped in on same interleaf is a clipping fr. a newspaper headlined* 'NEARLY KILLED BY A PANTHER.' *and datelined* 'JUNO, Fla., March 11.' *describing ferocious attack of a mother panther on two hunters who had killed her young.*]
    Guyau, see note to 1032.39.

1029.3 (II,410.16) *Sympathy* is] [*penc.*] Explained Spinoza III. 27 (also 11) | It is really *pity* that I *here [*ov.* 'hear'] speak of. | Sympathy proper is based on imitation & exemplified in massacring as much as in aiding.
    Ethics, pt. III, prop. 27 (*Œuvres,* III, 132–134).

*1030.26 (II,411.26) by Thos. Fowler] [*penc. in mrgn.*] Also Spencer, Psychology VIII, v.
    Herbert Spencer, *The Principles of Psychology,* pt. VIII, ch. 5 (II, 558–577) on "Sociality and Sympathy."

1033.26 (II,415.22) *Fear* is a] [*ink*] Ferrero: la Crainte de la Mort, Rev. Scientif. 23 Mars, 1895. 32me Année p. 361 | Sully on Children's fears, Pop. Sci. M. *July. 1895 [*intrl.*]
    Guillaume Ferrero, "La Crainte de la mort," *Revue Scien-*

tifique, 4th ser., 3 (March 23, 1895), 361–367.

James Sully, "Fear," *Popular Science Monthly*, 47 (May 1895), 1–11; (July 1895), 340–353. Secs. VIII and IX of a series, "Studies of Childhood."

1035.22 (II,417.23) The first time he] [*ink*] Fear of a fur carriage cloth in my Tweedy, aged 8 months—would n't touch it, etc.—Similar example in *Richet ['i' ov. 'e']: l'Home & *l[ov. 'I']'Intel. p. 482

 L'Homme et l'intelligence cited in text; see note to 89.43.

1041.19 (II,424.2) Better to live poor] [*ink*] Extract from Ste. Beuve's Port Royal, about *nun's [¹'n' ov. 'a'] putting all things in common, in Maillet, Psychol. de l'Home et de l'Enfant, pp. 105–6

 Charles Augustin Sainte-Beuve (1804–1869), French writer, from his *L'Histoire de Port-Royal*. Maillet does not give page numbers.

 Maillet, see entry for 447.10 (I,473.5).

1041.31 (II,424.16) Professor Silliman] [*ink*] Cf. Case of John Elwes in Hammond's Treatise on Insanity, p. 409

 See entry for 1004.0 (II,383.0).

 John Elwes (1714–1789), English miser.

1047.11 (II,430.21) *Sociability and*] [*ink*] See Maillet (Psych de l'H. et l'Enfᵗ) 111–9 especially about *camaraderie*.

 See entry for 447.10 (I,473.5).

1048.30 (II,432.3) As Mr. Darwin] [*ink*] A. Kielblock: "Stage Fright," Boston 1892

 Adolph Kielblock, *The Stage Fright or How to Face an Audience* (Boston: George H. Ellis, 1891).

1058.0 (II,442.0) CHAPTER XXV.] [*ink*] Review of Lange by Hoffding, in 4tljsch. XII, 357 | Review of this Chapter by W. L. Worcester in Monist, III, 285 (Jan. '93) | On the emotional brain-centres see Brissaud: "Rire et Pleurer Spasmodiques" in Rev. Scientif. 13 Janvier, 1894 | Review by Irons in Mind, Jan. 1894 | Worcester shows well that the particular idea-combinations in diffᵗ individuals have very different emotional results, and concludes that here the *first* result ought to be supposed ideal, not physical | [*short rule*] | Reply to criticisms, by W. J. in Psychol. Rev. Sept. 1894, ['p. 5' *del.*] Vol I p. 516 | [*short rule*] | Sollier in Rev. Phil. XXXVII, 241 | [*penc.*] Aristotle, Descartes | Volkmann, II. 314 | [*opp. p.* 443] [*ink*] G. M. Stratton, Psychol. Rev. II. 173 | *H [ov. 'C']. N. Gardiner: Philos. Rev. V, 102 | A. E. Wright: on the Nature of the Physiological Element in ['Br' ov. 'St' *del.*] Emotion, Brain, vol 17.

 Harald Höffding, Review of Dr. Carl Lange's *Über Gemüthsbewegungen: Eine psycho-physiologische Studie*, Autorisirte Übersetzung von Dr. H. Kurella in *Vierteljahrsschrift für wissenschaftliche Philosophie*, 12 (1888), 357–366.

 Edouard Brissaud (1852–1909), French neurologist, "Le Rire et le pleurer spasmodiques," *Revue Scientifique*, 3rd series, vol. 1 (1894), 38–46.

 David Irons (1870–1907), Scottish psychologist, "Prof. James' Theory of Emotion," *Mind*, n.s. 3, 19 (Jan. 1894), 77–97.

W. James, "The Physical Basis of Emotion," *Psychological Review*, 1 (Sept. 1894), 516–529.

Paul Auguste Sollier (1861–1933), French psychologist, "Recherches sur les rapports de la sensibilité et de l'emotion," *Revue Philosophique*, 37 (March 1894), 241–266.

For Aristotle and Descartes, see entry for 1065.21 (II,449.28).

W. F. Volkmann von Volkmar, *Lehrbuch der Psychologie*, II, 314.

George Malcolm Stratton (1865–1957), American psychologist, "The Sensations Are Not the Emotion," *Psychological Review*, 2 (March 1895), 173–174.

Harry Norman Gardiner (1855–1927), English-born American philosopher, "Recent Discussion of Emotion," *Philosophical Review*, 5 (Jan. 1896), 102–112. The correspondence between James and Gardiner is at Houghton (bMS Am 1092.9 [157–159, 911–925]).

Almroth Edward Wright (1861–1947), English bacteriologist, "On the Nature of the Physiological Element in Emotion," *Brain*, 18 (1895), 217–226.

1065.21 (II,449.28) obvious and strong.] *[ink]* *['x' added in text aft.* 'strong.'] ˣ—and which Lotze had to all practical intents and purposes fully expressed in his Med. Psych. in 1852 (See p. 518 of that work). Aristotle also, de Anima Bk I, Ch. 1, and Descartes, des Passions, *Art ['A' ov. 'B'] XLVI.

*1068.38 (II,453.20) deep, pure, worthy,] *[ink]* *commas del.*

*1068.40 (II,453.22) deep, pure, spiritual,] *[ink]* *commas del.*

1070.27 (II,455.16) A positive proof] *[ink]* Dᵣ H. J. Berkley of Baltimore *reports 2 [ab. del. 'has'] cases of general anaesthesia in Brain 1892. In reply to Dᵣ W. L. Worcester he writes that in one case "there was no departure from a normal psyche. She would show anger, smile, laugh, and talk. Never the slightest apathy after the first few days of febrile movement." In the other case, apathy, but she has laughed heartily. There has been (in *first [ab. del. 'this'] case?) no feeling of hunger or thirst for 2 years. Face flushes in laughing—says she perceives no difference between the act now and some years ago. She also shows fear, shame, grief. "My own impressions," Dᵣ B. writes, is that all mental emotional sensibilities are present, and only a little less vivid than in the normal state, and that emotions are approximately natural, and not at all coldly dispassionate." (March 10. 1892).

Henry Johns Berkley (1860–1940), American physician, "Two Cases of General Cutaneous and Sensory Anaesthesia, without Marked Psychical Implication," *Brain*, 14 (1891), 441–464.

*1074.16 (II,459.20) this most distressing] *[penc.]* 'evil' *subst. for del.* 'distressing'

1090.9 (II,477.7) organs.] *[penc.]* *['x' added in text aft.* 'organs.'] Cf. Meynert, Psychiatrie, 180–1

*1096.14 (II,483.26) inefficacy] *[ink]* in efficacy

*1097.13 (II,484.36) have already traced] *[ink]* shall have to trace

*1097.13 (II,484.36) origin.] *[ink]* origin.‡ | *fn. added* '‡ *Vide infra*, p. 627'

[*fn.* 33a *this edition*]

1097.16 (II,485.1)   This is all] [*ink*] See Wundt, in Philos. Studien VI, 335
   Wilhelm Wundt, "Zur Lehre von den Gemüthsbewegungen,"
   Philosophische Studien, 6 (1890), 335–393.

1102.38 (II,491.11)   In reality] [*ink*] Pitres (Les Clin. s. *l'Hystérie, [*comma
aft. del. closing paren] I. 116–9, tells of a case where the man could *continue*
a movement with his eyes shut, but not *begin* one. If the movement were
made on a sensitive surface (['playing' *del.*] drumming with finger on thigh)
he could do it with eyes shut, but not when made in the air. Similar case
quoted from Lasègue. In another man closing eyes weakened *all* movements,
esp.ᵞ on side of closed eye. It also weakened understanding of words whis-
pered in ear on that side. | Pitres found his *amblyopic [*ab. del.* 'hemiaopic']
patients blind of one eye able to see with that eye when the other was also
opened. | "Syndrome de Lasègue," Janet E. M. les Stigmates, 174
   Albert Pitres, *Leçons cliniques sur l'hystérie et l'hypnotisme,*
   (see note to 1195.12).
   Janet, see entry for 519.0 (I,550.0) referring to Ernest Charles
   Lasègue (1816–1885), French physician, *Études Médicales* (1884).

1109.2–3 (II,498.1)   processes in the brain-cortex] *laid-in slip on ruled paper
in strange hand*; *top center, printed* 'H. W. Stevens.' *and to right the note*
'Page 305 Lord Bacon's necessity to address him to something to unfold his
thoughts—see Essays Conversation I think.' *The text reads*: Perhaps it is
grübelei but a new-born mind must be sought earlier than the period of birth
must it not? Isn't the *pre*-natal mind somewhat educated by experience while
yet in the mother? [¶] The discussion in the class about the changing relations on the retina and those in the outer world seems to me to rest on a half
view of what was really done. As far as I can see, the man turning round is
supposed to keep looking now from his true eyes and now from the back of
his ['neck' *del.*] head. As far as I see, this oversight is the cause of all the
seeming trouble. | *at bottom and to the right the word* 'over' [*verso of slip,
headed* 'p. 299'] [¶] Vaguely in my mind there seems a difference between
the primitive savage's mind and the child's. You speak of the "jungle of
hallucinations, dreams, superstitions, conceptions and sensible objects flour-
ishing alongside of each other unregulated except &c". But taking the North
American Indians, everything in nature speaks to them of the supernatural.
He "sees God in whirlwind and wind," birds, fluttering leaves &c are deified-
but this multitudinous incarnation does not mean nature-worship only the
vaguely apprehended occult powers apprehended through these natural
objects. The doctrine of *correspondences[*final* 's' *doubtful*]-nature has a
language that fits the moods of the soul. The lightening darts across the sky
and kills with its forked fangs, so the rattlesnake becomes sacred, but there
is no real confusion in their minds—in the minds of the ordinary Indian—as to
the sensible objects. Superstitions and conceptions. Perhaps *these [*alt. fr.*
'this'] extremely sensitive, imaginative races are not ['not' *del.*] typical
savages.
   Also laid in is a sheet of unruled white paper in a different hand: On p.
498 [*ed.,* p. 1109] you say that Wundt claims that the feeling of innervation
is the "mental cue," i.e. it does exactly what your ideas of movement do,
viz. determine which action shall occur, as well as its ['stru' *del.*] amount and
direction. [¶] On the same page lower down also you say: "It is impossible

to see how a mind with its idea vaguely conceived could tell out of a lot of innervationsgefühle, were they never so sharply differentiated, *which one fitted that idea exactly*, and which one did not." This passage also seems to imply that the feeling of innervation determines the action as well as its amount and direction. [¶] On p. 500 [*ed.*, p. 1110] however, you say that W. admits that these feelings are used by the mind "not as guides of *which* movement, but of *how strong* a movement." Has W. shifted his position? If these innervation feelings do not de['r' *del.*]termine for Wundt *which* action shall occur, what does? Ideas of the movement? [*rule*] Another question not connected with the above, "What is the difference between the idea of a movement which you will to execute and one which you will not to execute? The same idea must be present [*verso*] in both cases. Would W. say that in the former instance there was the feeling of innervation and not in the latter?

    Hermon Weed Stevens graduated from Harvard in 1889 and took his M.A. in 1891.

1118.5 (II,508.1) the paretic eye] [*penc. on tipped-in slip*] Eye must try to move— 2 distance of false image for real grows as effort grows. 3 direction of false from true image lies in the projection outward of the path described by the eyeball under the influence of the affected muscle. p. 22. ['u' *ink del.*] G. | Gehen wir . . . aus dem Gebiete des Einfachsehens in das des Doppeltsehens uber, so gehört dasjenige Bild welches nahezu in der Richtung der Objectbewegung der letzteren voraneilt offenbar dem affizirten Auge an den das vorauseilen des Bildes ist gleichbedeutend mit dem zuruckbleiben des Auges oder besser noch mit der beginnenden Manifestation der fehlerhaften Projection. ['p. 37' *del.*] Dies Gesetz hat eine ganz allgemeine Gultigkeit, se[l]bstredend auch dann noch wenn das paretisch Auge fixirt u. das Gesunde in die Secundäre Ablenkung rückt, nur würde im letzteren falle das vorauseilen des Scheinbildes um so rapider ergehen. *A [*ov.* 'p']. ['v.' *ink del.*] G. in G. in S. p. 37 | Es ist ferner beim einseitigen Gebrauch des kranken Auges zu bemerken dass, sowie das Gesichtsobject sich bei seiner bewegung von rechts nach links der centralen Blickfeldregion nähert, dasselbe in irrthümlicher Weise nach links hinüber projicirt wird. Diese abnorme Projection . . . . is[t] ganz unabhängig davon ob noch central oder bereits excentrisch fixirt wird, ob überhaupt irgend eine reale Drehung im Bereich des Abducens erfolgt oder nicht; es handelt sich einfach um ein Missverhaltniss d. Anstrengung zu der realen Stellung des Auges [*in left mrgn. beg. w.* 'Es ist ferner beim einseitigen Gebrauch' *is the note*: [*ink*] Alb. v. [*penc.*] Graefe Symptomenlehre p. 95

    Alfred Graefe, "Motilitätsstörungen," *Handbuch der gesammten Augenheilkunde*, ed. A. Graefe and Theod. Saemisch, vol. 6, pt. 1 (Leipzig: Engelmann, 1880), 22, 36–37.
    Albrecht von Graefe, *Symptomenlehre der Augenmuskellähmungen* (Berlin: H. Peters, 1867), 95.

1120.16 (II,511.5) function] [*penc.*] 'act' *subst. in mrgn.*

1126.25 (II,517.22) in infancy] [*penc.*] at a certain period of infancy

1127.33 (II,518.32) Roger] [*ink*] Royer

1129.32 (II,521.22) MM. Binet and] [*ink*] Binet: les Altérations, p. 148+ | Cf. *J. M. [*intrl.*] Charcot: Oeuvres III. p. 464 | H. C. Bastian: Various forms of hysterical or functional paralysis, pp 22–50 | A. Grafé: Etude s. qq.

Paralysies d'Origine psychique Bruxelles, 1889. | P. Janet, les Stigmates, 174 | Pick, Ztsch. f. Psych. IV, 161.

Alfred Binet, *Les Altérations de la personnalité* (Paris: Baillière, 1892).

Jean Martin Charcot, *Œuvres complètes*, III (Paris: Lecrosnier et Babé, 1890). The reference is to the chapter "Les Notions du sens musculaire et le mouvement volontaire" in *Leçons sur les maladies du système nerveux*.

Henry Charlton Bastian, *Various Forms of Hysterical or Functional Paralysis* (London: H. K. Lewis, 1893).

Alfred Grafé, *Étude sur quelques paralysies d'origine psychique* (Brussels: F. Hayez, 1889).

Janet, see entry for 1102.38 (II,491.11).

A. Pick, "Uber die sogenannte Conscience musculaire (Duchenne)," *Zeitschrift für Psychologie*, 4 (1893), 161–210.

1130.14 (II,522.4) IDEO-MOTOR ACTION] [*ink*] Example in Janet, E. M. d. H, I. 180

See entry for 1102.38 (II,491.11).

1131.14 (II,523.1) but the perception] [*ruled paper slip tipped in, in strange hand*] [¶] The following incident occurred to the knowledge of my brother who is with the Forbes Lithographic company in whose factory it transpired. [¶] The foreman of the works at Chelsea was showing some ladies a machine which he said had recently cut off a finger of one of the operators. He described somewhat carefully just how the accident had happened. The story had such an effect on one of the ladies that she could not resist the impulse to thrust in her finger which was immediately cut off. | R T Greene '96.

Russell Thomas Greene, Jr., Harvard College, 1892–1896, graduate student 1896–1897, 1899–1903.

1133.37 (II,525.35) For a full account] [*penc.*] Hold your watch by its chain etc.

*1137.15 (II,529.29) come in either] [*ink*] 'any one' *subst. in mrgn. for* 'either'

1140.28 (II,533.23) The whole scale] [*penc.*] "We see things in their true relations"

1144.26 (II,538.1) temperaments] [*ink*] What a tremendous nullifyer of the vivacity and interest of social intercourse is our anglo-saxon inability to lie. Compare the mendacious and treacherous social life of France in the XVIII century, or of Italy in the renaissance with *the sodden [*intrl.*] social life of *New England. [*tr. w. guideline fr. bef.* 'social' *and added period*] The difference is largely due to the inhibition in N. E. of all mendacious impulses.

1151.25 (II,545.1) "The only good] *tipped-in clipping by* James Mark Baldwin, "Origin of Right or Left Handedness," Science, 16 (Oct. 31, 1890), 247–248. *In sec. 7 of the clipping* James *has underlined in ink* 'Why did . . . hand?' *(lines 6–8) and drawn a vertical stroke from this underline to* 'hand responds, or both.' *in line* 21. *In line* 20 James *corrected* 'efferent' *to* 'afferent' *and in line* 22 'afferent' *to* 'efferent'.

James replied to Baldwin in "The Origin of Right-handedness," *Science*, 16 (Nov. 14, 1890), 275 (McD 1890:7); Baldwin replied to James in "Right-handedness and Effort," *Science*, 16 (Nov. 28, 1890), 302–303.

*1153.37 (II,547.21) as far] [*penc.*] 'so' *subst. in mrgn. for* 'as'

1154.19 (II,548.3) We now see] [*penc.*] W. L. Worcester (*Monist [*ov.* 'Open Court'] vol IV, p. 135+) shows that the opposition between ideals & propensities is too narrow a statement, & that there is effort, often, in turning the lower way *([*paren ov. comma*] Galieo's case) effort when we renounce any good.

1156.11 (II,550.5) But as present] [*ink*] The hedonist has to account for our sternness towards present pleasures by the perception that they will if indulged frustrate future pleasures. But can the tho't of future pleasure awaken the stern mood? To me it seems unnatural that any mere calculus of pleasure should produce the impulse to give *pain*, present and actual. We may it is true be nerved to giving pain now by the fear of ['future' *del.*] worse future pain, if we don't. Therefore *pain*-philosophy seems more congruent with the facts than pleasure-philosophy.

1156.30 (II,550.27) Important as is] [*penc.*] H. R. *Marshall ['s' *ov.* 'c'], Instinct & Reason Chap. XXII, argues very forcibly and successfully for my thesis.

Henry Rutgers Marshall (1852–1927), American architect and writer, *Instinct and Reason* (New York and London: Macmillan, 1898). Chapter XXII (pp. 531–549) is entitled "Ethics and Hedonism." Four letters from Marshall to James are at Houghton (bMS Am 1092, letters 546–549).

1160.13 (II,554.30) Pleasures and pains] [*penc.*] Cf. Bain in Mind XVI, 253 ff.

Alexander Bain, "Notes on Volition," *Mind*, 16 (April 1891), 252–258.

1162.13–14 (II,557.1) *with mere pleasure*] [*penc.*] Cf. Kant: K. d. prakt. V. p. 254, 152

Critique of Practical Reason; the page numbers fit the edition by Karl Rosenkranz and F. W. Schubert, *Sämmtliche Werke*, VIII (Leipzig: Voss, 1838).

1163.16 (II,558.9) therefore no steamer] [*penc.*] See Schmidkunz, Psychol. d. Suggestion, who distinguishes between desire κατ' αὐτό & κατά συμβηβηκός. In sugar I want the sweetness, but I never have it without the whiteness, therefore on might say I sought it for the whiteness sake. (p. 192)

Hans Schmidkunz (1863–1934), German psychologist, *Psychologie der Suggestion* (Stuttgart: Ferdinand Enke, 1892). In Schmidkunz the phrase is κατά συμβεβηκός. James's copy in Widener (Phil 7140.8.5) contains a letter from the author to James.

*1165.5 (II,560.4) neura] [*ink*] *corr. to* 'neural'

*1165.38 (II,560.36) am I able energetically] [*ink*] 'energetically' *del.*

1166.2 (II,561.8) It does so] [*penc.*] Cf. John Dewey: The Psychology of Effort, in Phil. Rev. VI, 43

Philosophical Review, 6 (Jan. 1897), 43–56.

1167.5 (II,563.1) Certainly there is] [*ink*] Julia's letter wooden

*1168.8 (II,563.28–29) mid-career. "*Hæc tibi erit janua leti,*" we feel.] [*penc.*] ' "*Hæc* . . . feel.' *del.*

*1168.20 (II,564.3) congerers] [*ink*] *corr. to* 'congeners'

*1168.36 (II,564.21) in] [*ink*] within

1172.12 (II,568.8) It is unqualifiedly] [*penc.*] Will*ing*ness vs. volition— | Voluntas *complacentiae*

*1178.17 (II,575.6) reflex] [*ink*] *comma added*

1183.23 (II,581.3) How is a fresh] [*penc.*] Excuse all this *that [*ov.* 'by'] follows by quoting Lange G. d. M. II 190

1191.35 (II,590.25) Even as the proofs] [*ink*] Bradley "Why do we remember forwards & not backwards? Mind XII 579
     F. H. Bradley, "Why Do We Remember Forwards and Not Backwards?" *Mind*, 12 (Oct. 1887), 579–582.

1193.8–9 (II,592.1) should establish itself] [*ink*] Ch. Sigwart: Kleine Schriften, 2te Reihe, p. 115–211
     Christoph Sigwart, *Kleine Schriften*, Zweite Reihe (Freiburg und Tübingen: Mohr, [1881]). The chapter is entitled "Der Begriff des Wollens und sein Verhältnis zum Begriff der Ursache."

*1206.36 (II,607.26) had actively] [*ink*] 'had' *alt. to* 'has'

*1210.11–12 (II,611.16) only finds it] [*penc.*] 'it' *del.*

*1210.18 (II,611.24) French ones,] [*penc.*] *comma alt. to semicolon*

1210.28–29 (II,612.7) Messrs. Beaunis] [*ink*] Also Bechterew, Neurol. Cbl. 1893, 758
     Wladimir Bechterew, "Über die Bedeutung der Hypnose als eines Heilmittels," *Neurologisches Centralblatt*, 12 (Nov. 1, 1893), 757–758.

*1211.3–4 (II,612.13–14) experiments after . . . suggestion,] [*penc.*] *comma added aft.* 'experiments' *and del. aft.* 'suggestion'

1216.5 (II,618.3) 2) That there is] [*ink*] G. H. Lewes: Problems, vol I. Chaps. XI to XIV
     George H. Lewes, *Problems of Life and Mind* (1st series). The chapters are respectively, "Intuition and Demonstration," "Axioms and Their Validity," "Necessary Truths," and "Mathematics an Empirical Science."

1217.5 (II,619.11) WHAT IS MEANT] [*laid-in piece of wove paper in hand of Mrs. Alice James*] [*ink*] Mill's Logic Bk. 3, chap 5. §6. 8th Ed vol I. p. 390. | [*penc.*] Sensational & à priori hypotheses Prob. 1. Chap 2 of Lewes's Problems | Consciousness everywhere Prob. 4. vol III. | Spencer on Adaptation vs. spontaneous variation Principles of Biology vol II, part 3, chapters XI & XII.
     A System of Logic, I, 390–395 (Bk. III, ch. 5, sec. 6).
     Lewes, *Problem*, I, Chap. II (1st ser., I, 207–248) is entitled "The Sensational and A Priori Hypotheses," Problem IV in Third

Series, 3, 441-500, has the general title of "The Sphere of Intellect and Logic of Signs."

Herbert Spencer, *Principles of Biology*, 2 (London and Edinburgh: Williams and Norgate, 1864), 432-463. The chapters are entitled "Direct Equilibration" and "Indirect Equilibration" under the title for Part III of "The Evolution of Life."

On the interleaf ab. the clipping is written in a strange hand of a librarian: 'Letter removed given to Ms. Division 3-28-51'.

1225.10 (II,627.25) It has no] [*penc.*] "Ticklishness" is another of these useless complications of our nature.

*1238.2 (II,642.12) sequnce] [*ink*] *corr. to* 'sequence'

1238.11 (II,642.22) But the advocate] [*ink*] Cf. Stallo, Modern Physics, p. 140

John Bernard Stallo (1823-1900), German-born American philosopher of science, *The Concepts and Theories of Modern Physics* (New York: D. Appleton, 1882) (WJ 483.3).

*1258.28 (II,665.13) of sensible] [*penc.*] 'supposing' *insrtd. w. caret aft.* 'of'

1258.32 (II,664.38) Kant] [*ink*] Malebranche: Entretiens p. 122-3
Œuvres de Malebranche, vol. I, pp. 122-123.

*1260.10 (II,667.1) *only* facts] [*penc.*] 'only' *underl. and marked* 'roman'

1263.3 (II,670.1) Such principles] [*ink*] Compare Kant's Appendix to the transcendental Dialectic.

On "The Regulative Employment of the Ideas of Pure Reason" and "The Final Purpose of the Natural Dialectic of Human Reason."

1266.18 (II,674.1) in not being themselves] *clipping laid in of a review by* P. Jensen *of* Wilhelm Fliess, Der Ablauf des Lebens, *from* Deutsche Literatur Zeitung, no. 15 (April 13, 1907), 951. *Passages* 11.15-20 (nämlich ... [*first line of formula*]), [*opp. p.* 675] 11.26-30 (werden ... 97).), *and* 11.32-36 (so kommen ... Nachdruckes,) *are marked in mrgn. in red pencil. Beneath the column, in lead pencil, is written in a strange hand*: 'This may interest you as it amused me.'

Wilhelm Fliess (1858-1928), German psychologist.

*1269.9 (II,676.38) transactions] [*penc.*] *alt. to* 'transitions'

*1276.29 (II,684.35) air.] [*ink*] air, an adaptation which the stiffer thorax of the first imported ['dogs' *del.*] adult ['cou' *del.*] dogs could not undergo.

1278.6 (II,686.12) I leave my text] [*ink*] C. Lloyd Morgan: Weis['s' *del.*]mann on Heredity & Progress, in Monist, IV. 20 (Oct. 1893). | H. Spencer: The Inadequacy of Nat. Sel., Contemp. Rev. Feb., March 1893.—Also Dec. 1893 | Romanes: The Spencer-Weissman Controversy, ibid. July, 1893 | A Weissman: The all-sufficiency of Nat. Sel. ibid. Sept., Oct., 1893 | J. Mc K. Cattell: Survival of the fittest and sensation-areas, Mind, Oct 1893. NS. 2. 505 | T. Eimer: Organic Evolution [v. 3084] | Sutton: Evolution & Disease | J. A. Thompson: Proceedings Royal Physical Soc. Edinb. IX, 1885-8 p. 446 [23.101 (?)] | H. F. Osborn: Difficulties etc. American **Naturalist**, 1892,

537 | M. Miles: Heredity of Acquired Characters, *ibid*, 887. | Nutting: ibid, 1009 | G. J. Romanes: Darwin & After Darwin | Weissman's Romanes lecture | Baldwin in Science, Mch. 20 '96 (vol *III [*ov.* 'iii'], p 439) | Panmixia, by Romanes, Contemp. R. vol 63, p 610– | Weismann: Heredity once more. Ibid. 68, p. 400 | Spencer: ditto, ibid p. 608. | [*cont. on verso, facing p.* 687] Lloyd Morgan: Science, IV, *734 ['3' *ov.* '2'], also in | " " " [*ditto mks. under* 'Lloyd Morgan'] Habit & Instinct, Chap. XII. | J. M. Baldwin: Science, V., *633 [²'3' *ov.* '4']; IV, 724. | Weismann: Germinal Selection, Monist VI, 250. | Morgan on Weismann's theories, ibid. IV. 20.

Conwy Lloyd Morgan, "Dr. Weismann on Heredity and Progress," *Monist*, 4 (Oct. 1893), 20–30.

Herbert Spencer, "The Inadequacy of 'Natural Selection,'" *Contemporary Review*, 63 (Feb. 1893), 153–166.

―――, "A Rejoinder to Professor Weismann," *ibid.*, 64 (Dec. 1893), 893–912.

George John Romanes (With a Note by Herbert Spencer), "The Spencer-Weismann Controversy," *Contemporary Review*, 64 (July 1893), 50–53.

August Weismann, "The All-Sufficiency of Natural Selection. I. A Reply to Herbert Spencer," *Contemporary Review*, 64 (Sept. 1893), 309–338.

J. M. Cattell, "Survival of the Fittest and Sensation-Areas," *Mind*, n.s. 2 (Oct. 1893), 505–518.

Eimer, see entry for 1278.10 (II,686.17).

John Bland-Sutton (1855–1936), British surgeon, *Evolution and Disease* (London: Walter Scott, 1890).

J. Arthur Thomson, "Synthetic Summary of the Influence of the Environment upon the Organism," *Proceedings of the Royal Physical Society*, 9 (1885), 446–499.

Henry Fairfield Osborn (1857–1935), American naturalist, "The Difficulties in the Heredity Theory," *American Naturalist*, XXVI (July 1892), 537–567.

Manly Miles (1826–1898), "Heredity of Acquired Characters," *American Naturalist*, XXVI (Nov. 1892), 887–900.

Charles Cleveland Nutting (1858–1927), American zoologist, "What Is an 'Acquired Character?'" *American Naturalist*, XXVI (Dec. 1892), 1009–1013.

Romanes, *Darwin, and After Darwin*, 2 vols. (London: Longmans, Green, 1892–1895).

August Weismann (Romanes lecture), *The Effects of External Influences upon Development* (London: H. Frowde, 1894).

J. M. Baldwin, "Heredity and Instinct," *Science*, n.s. III (March 20, 1896), 438–441.

Romanes, "A Note on Panmixia," *Contemporary Review*, 64 (Oct. 1893), 611–612.

Weismann, "Heredity Once More," *Contemporary Review*, 68 (Sept. 1895), 420–456.

Herbert Spencer, "Heredity Once More," *Contemporary Review*, 68 (Oct. 1895), 608.

C. Lloyd Morgan, "On Modification and Variation," *Science*, n.s. IV (Nov. 20, 1896), 733–740.

————, *Habit and Instinct* (London: E. Arnold, 1896).
Baldwin, "Organic Selection," *Science*, n.s. V (April 23, 1897), 634–636.
————, "On Criticisms of Organic Selection," *ibid.*, n.s. IV (Nov. 13, 1896), 724–727.
Weismann, "Germinal Selection," *Monist*, 6 (Jan. 1896), 250–293.

1278.10 (II,686.17) Whether acquired] [*ink on tipped-in wove slip*] You will find on | p. 91, sbs. of color in cave animals (*Infl of [*intrl.*] darkness | p. 92 Infl. of increased nutrition | p. 93–103, *151–153 [*insrtd.*] " " [*ditto mks. each time under* 'Infl. of'] climate | p. 104, *149–151 [*insrtd.*] " " quality of food | p 104, 105 " " density (saltiness) of water. | *p. 116–126 | p 131–135 [*connected by brace*] " " temperature on Lepidoptera | [*vert. in left mrgn. ab. line fr. p. 93 to p. 116*] 'Eimer'
Gustav Heinrich Theodor Eimer (1843–1898), German zoologist, *Organic Evolution as the Result of the Inheritance of Acquired Characters According to the Laws of Organic Growth*, trans. by J. T. Cunningham (London and New York: Macmillan, 1890).

1279.18 (II,687.29) theory of *panmixy*] [*ink*] Panmixia, cessation of selection. Romanes on, Nature Mch. 13. 1890 (XVI, 437)
George J. Romanes, "Panmixia," *Nature*, 16 (March 13, 1890), 437–439.

1279.28 (II,688.1) Since, says Mr. Spencer] [*penc.*] Biol. bbl. Zacharias VII, 575, Doderlen | ibid 720, " " " [*ditto mks. under* 'Zacharias'] VIII 204, Dingfelder | " [*ditto mks. under* 'ibid'] 210 — Also Bd VII, Nr 14, | Kollmann, ibid. Nr 17 (Hereditary mutilations). | Neumayer: Die Stämme des Thierreichs, 1889 (approves Lamarkism).
Emil Otto Zacharias, "Schwanzloses Katzen-Pärchen," *Biologisches Centralblatt*, 7 (Nov. 15, 1887), 575–576; "Zur Frage der Vererbung von Traumatismen," 8 (June 1, 1888), 204–210.
Ludwig Heinrich Philipp Döderlein (1855–1936), German zoologist, Summary of "Über schwanzlose Katzen," *Biologisches Centralblatt*, 7 (Feb. 1, 1888), 720–721.
Johann Dingfelder, "Beitrag zur Vererbung erwobener Eigenschaften," *Biologisches Centralblatt*, 8 (June 1, 1888), 210–217; 8 (Sept. 15, 1887), 427–432.
Julius Constantin Ernest Kollmann, German anatomist, *Biologisches Centralblatt*, 7 (Nov. 1, 1887), 531–533.
Melchior Neumayr (1845–1890), *Die Stämme des Thierreiches* (Vienna: Tempsky, 1889).

p. 1284 (II,692.Index) Blind, the,] [*ink*] 'their facial perception, 204;' *insrtd. aft.* 'their space-perception, II. 202 ff.;'

p. 1285 (II,693.Index) Darwinism] [*ink*] 'reputation' *corr. to* 'refutation'

p. 1287 (II,695.Index) 'Fringe' of object] ', II, 49' *added aft.* '478'

p. 1287 (II,695.Index) Grübelsucht] [*penc.*] *corr. to* 'Grübelsucht'

Appendix III

James's Preface to Ferrari's Italian Translation

In a letter of June 13, 1898, James granted Giulio Cesare Ferrari permission to translate *The Principles of Psychology* into Italian, and on July 27 (or 29—the last digit is uncertain), he agreed to write a word of recommendation for the translation. On September 15, 1900, he tried to back out of this agreement, alleging not only his bad health but also his puzzlement at what to say. Nevertheless, the Preface was written within the next month, for on October 28, 1900, James mailed it to Ferrari. (For the details of this correspondence, see The Text of *The Principles of Psychology* under Section I: "The History.") The text below represents a diplomatic transcript of James's manuscript (printed here for the first time), which Ferrari translated into Italian for his edition. Permission is gratefully acknowledged to C. A. Ferrari di Valbona of Rome, Italy, the present owner of the manuscript.

Author's Preface.

It is with much pleasure that I respond to the invitation of Dr Ferrari to contribute a short preface to his translation of my Principles of Psychology. I feel how great an honour it is, to an American writer to have his book adopted, as it were, into italian literature; and as I have read portions of each successive fasciculus of the translation, it has seemed to me that my poor thoughts received an increase of dignity from being clothed in the noble and sonorous italian tongue. Having been a traveller for more than a year, and far from libraries, I have not had an opportunity of confronting the translation with the original, but all that I have read of it gives me an impression of its being superiorly done. The omissions are judicious; and the additions and notes will make the work more useful to the student than the original is at this date.

We live at a time of transition and confusion in psychology as in many other things. The classic spiritualistic psychology using the Soul and a definite number of distinct ready-made faculties as its principles of explanation, was long ago superseded by the school of association. But it still lingers. It is taught in Italy and other Catholic countries from scholastic compendiums, in England and America it is taught in manuals deriving their inspiration from the scottish school of common sense. Scholasticism is after all only Common sense made systematic, the the 'school of common sense' is only scholasticism in informal shape.

The older associationism itself retained a half-scholastic character. Recognizing no general evolution of the human species, it took the mind too statically, as something whose peculiarities were absolute and not to be explained. Moreover it was purely intellectualist, and did justice neither to our impulses and passions nor to the cooperation of our will with our intellectual life.

Within our generation Darwinism has come and added its new insights to these older tendencies. It has cast a flood of light upon our instinctive and passional constitution, and has brought innumerable attempts at explaining psychological facts genetically in its train. Later still exact & ingenious studies of sense-perception and illusion began to be made in physiological laboratories; higher intellectual operations themselves were conpared experimentally and their duration measured; the modern physiology of the brain next *fêted* its triumphs; and finally the study of mental defect and aberration and other abnormal states of consciousness began to be carried on in an intelligent and psychological way.

All these different tendencies, the classic tradition, the associationist analysis, the psychogenetic speculations, the experimental methods, the biological conceptions, and the pathological extensions of the field, have introduced a period of chaotic fermentation of which some writers have profited by developing one sided crudities in a very confident way. Unfortunately orthodoxy and tradition are not the exclusive proprietors of narrowness of view.

Such being the general condition of the time in which my book has been written, I fear that it may bear some traces of the prevalent confusion. I confess, however, that my aim in writing it, was to help to make the confusion less. I thought that by frankly putting psychology in the position of a natural science, eliminating certain metaphysical questions from its scope altogether, and confining myself to what could be immediately verified by everone's own consciousness, a a central mass of experience could be described, which everyone might accept as certain, no matter what the differing ulterior philosophic interpretations of it might be. I therefore assumed uncritically an external world, I assumed the existence of states of consciousness, and I assumed that the states of consciousness might "know" both the external world and each other. On this simple basis of natural experience I tried to reach a harmony by giving to each of the different tendencies of which I have spoken its just voice in the result. The harmony involves some compromise, and possibly no party will be absolutely contented. My hopes lie with the unprejudiced reader, and the newer generation.

The book is really more systematic and complete than a glance at the table of contents may suggest. I have expressly avoided the outward appearance of doctrine and system, the definitions, classifications, subdivisions, and multiplication of technical terms, because I know that these things tend to substitute an artificial schematism for the living reality, and it was the living reality with which I wished to bring my reader into direct concrete acquaintance, whether he should have technical names to call its parts by or not.

So instead of starting with the mind's supposed elements (which are always abstractions) and gradually building-up, I have tried to keep the reader in contact throughout as many chapters as possible, with the actual conscious unity which each of us at all times feels himself to be. This unity is what the classic spiritualism has always fought for against the associationist doctrine that the mind is a mere collection of 'ideas.' But as I wished to disentangle psychology as far as possible from any close alliance with ultimate questions of metaphysics, I have limited my contention of unity to what is empirically verifiable, namely to the unity each passing wave or field of consciousness, and left the problem of the Soul's existence to be treated by general philosophy.

The analysis of consciousness into 'ideas' and their association, I have retained on condition of its undergoing a certain transformation. No one can possibly be blind to the enormous services which the associationist explanations have rendered to mental science. The whole concrete course of an individual's thinking life is explicable by the cooperation of his interests and impulses, his sensational experiences, his associations, & his voluntary acts of choice. Only in this account one must take the word association broadly and practically, and not in that half-metaphysical sense of a mental chemistry of 'ideas' which is oftenest suggested by the word. It is either *objects thought of*, or it is *brain processes*, which are associated. On condition of this re-interpretation we reap all the benefits of detail of the associationist doctrine, and we escape criticisms to which it has never been able to reply.

I have sought to do ample justice to the recent discoveries in the physiology of the brain and senses, and I have made report of the more important facts brought out by psychological experimentation up to 1890, when the book was published, whilst D.r Ferrari's additions have brought these portions of the matter up to date. I have been mindful of the more important psychogenetic speculations; and have made use of the biological point of view which now so dominates psychology, to vindicate, as against the pure passive sensism which has so often characterized the empiricist tendency in mental science, the native activity which is also an irreducible element of the life of the mind. The materials of our thought come from without, but the form which the individual gives to them is almost entirely due to his personal spontaneity.

Here again I have offered a compromise in which each school may find that the essential truth which it contends for has been recognized. In sum, then, my effort has been to offer in a 'natural science' of the mind a *modus vivendi* in which the most various schools may meet harmoniously on the common basis of fact. The intention is a good one, whether it be successfully carried out or not. I must confess that in the years which have intervened since the book's publication I have realized more and more the difficulty of treating psychology without introducing some positive philosophic doctrine. It may be that attempts at compromise like that which now is offered to the italian reader are doomed to be provisional, and that a finally satisfactory treatment of psychology must wait until our general metaphysic of experience and our theory of knowledge have themselves come into a more developed and satisfactory state.

Appendix IV

Notes for The Principles of Psychology

In the Houghton Library of Harvard University, the James Collection under the general call number of bMS Am 1092.9 contains various folders of miscellaneous manuscript material, certain of which represent notes and drafts for portions of *The Principles of Psychology* or for the journal articles subsumed in various chapters and hence not elsewhere reprinted in the WORKS. The list of these articles is provided in the textual discourse, with a detailed accounting of the relationship of articles to book chapters. It is sometimes difficult to demonstrate whether the manuscripts relate to the composition of article or of book; but the strong presumption is that most of this material lies in back of the article form, even though, usually, the article was written with the intention to print it later (in revised form) in the *Principles*. Since these folders were assembled from James's miscellaneous papers by Ralph Barton Perry, no authority resides in the arrangement; hence portions of some folders will relate to *Principles* but other portions not. In such cases only the pertinent section of a folder is transcribed here, the remainder being reserved for the volumes devoted to James's manuscripts planned for these WORKS. The bracketed number above an item refers to its position in the folders as presently constituted. The headnotes to the folders' manuscripts will attempt a general identification of the chapters in this edition to which the transcribed material relates, although a certain amount of the material seems to have formed part of the background of *Principles* and so is not readily identified either in the book or in the underlying articles.

There are numerous inconsistencies in spelling and in what would appear to be typographical errors in James's notes which have been retained in their original form. Missing letters in words have been supplied in square brackets.

MISCELLANEOUS

Various notes from bMS Am 1092.9 (4410) are now preserved within the covers of a folder intended for an early form of Chapter X (see "The Documents" in the textual discourse). The notes seem to bear no particular relation to Chapter X and were perhaps placed within the empty folder covers for the chapter by Ralph Barton Perry who was sorting out James's miscellaneous papers. With the exception of items 1 and 7, the paper for the series of references is the same, a probable indication that the notes were made at approximately the same time. The same page number 311 on items 2, 5, and 6 would indicate that items 5 and 6 probably were intended to follow item 2, as if at the end of a chapter. The relationship, if any, of page 311 to the pagination 123–169 listed on the cover for present Chapter X is unknown, but the high number 311 might suggest that the sheets of paper originally formed part of a book and not of an article manuscript. The references in these notes cannot be identified with any single chapter, and some of the items are not utilized in *Principles*; nevertheless, they appear to form part of its background.

[1]

[wove leaf, 10 x 8", watermarked Library Bureau Boston; verso blank]
Locke says our conception of an object is a lot of characteristics which somehow became united.
The *qualities ['q' ov. 'ch'] of the thing must have some glue to hold them together, otherwise they would be a mere jumble.
Empiricist says our idea of ['som ['m' *doubtful*] ' *del.*] triangle is ['composed of a' *del.*] made up, not of one thought, but of the idea of three sides and three angles. Empiricist says you must first get an idea of the three sides of a triangle before you get one of the whole triangle, whereas you get the idea of the *whole triangle [*words represented by ditto marks*] first and then pick out the sides.
The state of mind thinking 3 sides & 3 angles is totally different from the *state ['ta' ov. 'at'] of mind thinking a triangle.

[2]

[thin laid piece, 5 11/16 x 8 1/2", watermarked fleur-de-lys with crown; numbered 311 in upper right corner; verso blank]
REFERENCES. The literature is very extensive. I only subjoin what is either very important or easily accessible to the English *reader, [*comma alt. fr. period*] *very roughly classed. [*intrl.*]
*Constituents of the *Self.* ['S' ov. 's'] J. F. Herbart: *Psychol. ['s' ov. 'h'] als Wissenschaft, § 132–138. M. *Lazarus: [*comma erased; colon ov. semicolon*] Das Leben der Seele, Essay entitled "Ehre u. Ruhm." ['H. Lotze: Mikrok' *del.*] W. Wundt: Vorlesungen uber Menschen u. Thier Seele, vol. I. *289['2' ov. '1']–97. J. Delboeuf. *Psychol. ['yc' ov. 'cy'] comme Science Naturelle, Chap I. §III,IV.

[3]

[thin laid paper, 8 1/2 x 6 7/8", watermarked fleur-de-lys with crown; verso blank]
Lotze, *Psychology* Pt II
    Mikrokosmus Book II
    Metaphysics, Bk III Ch I.
James Mill's *Analysis*, (J. S. Mill's Edition) Ch. X (Memory) Ch. XIV. § 7 (Identity) with Notes.
*J. S. Mill Exam. Ch. XII & Appendix. [*insrtd.*]
J. Locke's Essay, Ch. XXVII, Identity.
H L Mansel: *Metaphysics*, Chapter on "the Real in Psychology."
J. F. Ferrier: "The Philosophy of Consciousness," in Works vol II—
Wundt: Logik II, 502–7.

[4]

[thin laid paper, 10 3/4 x 8 1/2", watermarked fleur-de-lys with crown; verso blank]
Ego-Theory

Notes for The Principles of Psychology

I. Kant: *Critique ['C' ov. 'P'] of Pure Reason, "of the Deduction of the pure Concepts of the Understanding" "Of the Paralogisms of pure Reason." Also the ['en' del.] paraphrasers of Kant, ['in such as E. Caird['s' del.]' del.] e.g. E. Caird, J. Watson, J. H. Stirling, K. Fischer, J. P. Mahaffy, W. H. S. Monck, *G. S. Morris. [insrtd.]–C. C. Everett: Fichte.–G. W. F. Hegel: Encyclopadie etc. § 413–481. –K. Rosenkranz: Psychologie, 2ter Th. 2ter Abschnitt.–J. E. *Erdmann: [colon ov. semicolon] Grundriss *d. [alt. fr. 'der'] Psychol. 2ter Theil. Psychol. Briefe, IX, X, XI.–T. H. Green: Prolegomena to Ethics, *Bk. [alt. fr. 'Book'] I.

A. Bain: The Emotions & the Will, Chapter on Consciousness at *end [ab. del. 'End'] of Book.

[5]
[thin laid paper, 10 3/4 x 8 1/2", watermarked fleur-de-lys with crown; numbered 311 in upper right corner; verso blank]
*Self-feeling. ['S' ov. 's'] A. Bain: Emotions & Will, Part I. Chap. XI. A. Horwicz: Psychologische *Analysen ['s' ov. 'z'] 2te Theil, 2te Hälfte, 3tes Buch, 11). H. Lotze, Mikrokosmus, Bk II, Chap. V.

*Soul-Theory. [period alt. fr. colon] Radical; [intrl.; 'R' ov. 'r'] Any scholastic text-book, such as A. Stockl: *Lehrbuch [2'h' ov. 'k'] d. Philos. § 123–*45, [comma ov. period]
*A [ov. 'a']. Rosmini, Psychology, ['Bo' del.] Part I. [intrl.] Mitigated; *T. Reid: Essay III "on Intellectual Powers," chaps IV, V, VI. T. Brown, Lectures, XII. [intrl.] N. Porter: Human Intellect, Introduction. J. McCosh: Intuitions of the Mind, Part II Book I, Chap I, § VI. *Th. Jouffroy, Nouveaux Mélanges, "De la legitimité de la distinction etc. [intrl.] H. L. Mansel: Prolegomena Logica, pp. 137–145; Metaphysics, ['Pt II' del.] Chapter "of the *Real ['R' ov. 'r'] in Psychology." A. W. Momerie: Personality the Beg. & End of Metaphysics. 2nd Ed. 1883. H. Lotze: Mikrokosmus, Bk. II. Chaps. I, II; *Metaphysics ['M' ov. 'm'], Bk. III. Chap. I. ['Th. Jouffroy' del.] C. Jeanmaire: L'Idée de la Personnalité dans la Psych. moderne, 1882. F. Brentano: Psychologie, ['Bd. I.' del.] Bk I. Chap. IV.

[6]
[thin laid paper, 10 3/4 x 8 1/2", watermarked fleur-de-lys with crown; numbered 311 in upper right corner; verso blank]
['Ego theory' del.]
J. S. Ferrier: Institutes of Metaphysic, Chaps. I, VIII, IX; *Lectures & [intrl.] Philosophical Remains, [' "Philo' del.] vol II. pp. 29–30, 66–9, 80, 84, 102–14, 119, 129–['36' del.]147, 155, 175–181.

['J. Butler: Disserta' del.]
J. Locke: Essay conc. Hum. Und. Bk. II. Ch. 27.
J. Butler: Dissertation on Personal Identity.

D. Hume: Treatise on Human Nature Pt IV, § 6 & Appendix. – J. Mill: Analysis of *Human ['H' ov. 'M'] Mind, (J. S. Mill's edition,) Chaps. X, & XIV "Identity."–J. S. Mill: Exam. of Hamilton, Chap. XII.–H. Taine: On Intelligence, Pt. I. Bk IV, Chap. *III [ov. '3'] Pt. II. Bk III. Chap. I.–S. H. Hodgson Time & Space, § 18–27.–F. Paulhan: Revue Philosophique, vol X,

p. 491 *(1880) [*final paren ov. period*].

[7]

[laid paper, 11 1/4 x 8 5/8", no watermark, vertical chainlines; numbered 6
after deleted 74 in upper right corner; verso blank]
various sensations and their copies, and devoid of any other *use [*ab. del.*
'content, or use,'] or specification save that it is "not in time." "There must
be something other than the manifold things themselves, which combines
them without effacing their severalty. With such a combining agency we are
*familiar"ˣ [*db. qts. and* ˣ' *insrtd.*] ['in [*doubtful*] our intelligence;"ˣ . . .
If it were not for the action of something which is not either of them or both
together, there would be no alternative between their separateness and their
confusion. . . . A unity in which' *del.*] [*opening db. qts. del.*] Only in virtue
of the presence to feelings of a subject which distinguishes itself from them
do they become related *objects;"† [*semicolon ov. period*] [' "But the presence of consciousness to itself, though . . . . it is the condition of the observation of events in time, is not such an event itself;"*‡ [*insrtd.*] *etc etc, etc,
ad libitum."' del.*] Etc., etc., *ad ['d' ov. doubtful 't'] libitum.*

To ourselves, however, the atomistic

ˣT. H. Green: Prolegomena to Ethics: §§ 28-*9: [*colon ov. semicolon*]
†*Id. [*intrl.*] "Introduction to Hume, ['p. 2' *del.*] § 318.
['‡*Ibid.*, § 142.' *del.*]

Chapter XX: The Perception of Space

Notes from bMS Am 1092.9 (4411) relating to the article "The Perception
of Space," *Mind*, 12 (January, April, July, October 1887), 1-30, 183-211,
321-353, 516-548 (McD 1887:4) on which Chapter XX is based. However,
the inclusion of a clipping of an article from *Science* of February 3, 1888,
indicates that James kept the folder current after the writing of the article
with a view to its revision in the book.

[1]

[piece of wove paper, 3 5/8 x 6 5/8", no watermark, verso blank; below
inscription is a card advertising a 'CURIOUS OPTICAL ILLUSION' adver-
tising Thomas Hall, Electrician and Optician, 19 Bromfield Street, Boston]
Schön 1874 Bd XX. 2. 171, 308., XXIV. 1
Schweigger.
Volkmann V. 2. 1 1859
Donders ['IX' *del.*] XIII. 1 XXVII. 2

[2]

[piece of thin wove unwatermarked paper, 5 1/4 x 8 5/8", verso blank; top
rough torn]

ˣ "Were the end of a wire brought into contact with the hand of a person
blind or blindfold, could he tell its length? It might be but a short knitting-
wire; it might be an Atlantic cable: the touch of the end would indicate no
difference of length. So a ray of light may come from a neighboring gas-lamp,
or from a star countless millions of miles away; it is merely the termination

of the ray that strikes the eye." J. C. MURRAY: Psychology, London & Montreal, 1885, p. 161.

[3]

[leaf of wove paper, 11 5/8 x 7 1/2", partial watermark 'STON'S LINEN 1881'; upper part, now a revised paste-on, lower part representing remains of original leaf; verso blank]

1. Confusion: neither discrimination nor in the proper sense of the word identification of objects. Mutual indifference of the parts of the two retinae.

2 Develop! of fovea *& [*intrl.*] pari-passu with *it [*intrl.*] selective attention, and binocular fixation. *An [*ab. del.* 'Object'] [*end paste-on*] Object, once noticed, is ['pa' *del.*] brought to foveae of two eyes and at the same time *located* at the intersection of optic axes and perceived as one. ['Vestiges of this state in Donders. Aguilonius Exp! Arch vii p 44–6.' *del.*] This [*ov. doubtful* 'Then'] the one *distance* we ['are acu' *del.*] then are aware of, and even now this distance tends to invade the rest of the field. (Donders lo. ct)

4 Other objects *are [*intrl.*] noticed both with relation to their lateral distance & their depth-distance from this one. This involves ['lateral' *del.*] discrimination ['on *ea [*intrl.*] retina' *del.*] of points on *each* retina ['without' *del.*] whilst ['corresponding' *del.*] points on the *two* retinæ *must [*ab. del.* 'should'] not be felt as two. Our ordinary untrained condition.

[4]

[piece of laid unwatermarked paper, 6 7/16 x 4", verso blank]

Als [*intrl.*] Secundäre Urtheils Taüschung
    Small size of moon in telescope.
Pseudoscopy, treppenfigur etc.
    Arundel societies' cast mould. Carrie Cranch's mask. (monocular)
Treat [*ov.* 'Take'] first of 3rd dimension
Taine ii. 85
    "   " 108, Quotation fm Weber

[5]

[leaf of laid paper, 10 x 8", watermarked Royal Irish Linen; written in pencil; on verso is pencil sketch of seated woman in hat and vertical inscription 'NB | Aubert 599, 603, 608']

Disprove identical points by ster[e]oscopic looking at figures like
    | | | |, | | | | etc.

Donders says (Bd. 13. 1867) that double images of this indistinguis[h]able shape, (as when we view 1 2 & see $\cdot^a_{\cdot b}$ but a & b belong now to r., Now to l. eye. according as we fixate 1 or 2) show clearly our inability to distinguish the *sensations* of the 2 retinae. The basis of his essay is the fact that we cant *feel* on which eye ['the' *del.*] any particular element of a compound picture falls. When the elements are interchanged, the "sinnliche empfindung remains unaltered, but the *Vorstellung ['V' *ov.* 'v'] changes. How is this possible? Das problem scheint unlösbar, except by the supposition of a "verschiedenheit des Auftretens" of the elements, which thus work differently on *the [ov. 'a'] Vorstellungsorgan, wh. thus works independently of *feeling*, and is not the organ of Schlüsse, bewusst or unbewusst. "Verschiedenheit der Vorstellung ist möglich *bei [alt. fr. 'by'] gleich heit der directen empfindung. p. 45

On p. 47, he makes some *observations ['ob' ov. doubtful 're'] to show that the retinal figures do not give an infallible impulse ['zum con' del.] to the proper convergence, *but ['b' ov. illeg. letters] may hesitate (hollow mirror, outline stereoscope figures if we fixate one point. Weak prism before one eye wh. doubles image, slight hesitation often how to make it single.) "The social Instinct of the eyes" Tourtual

[6]

[piece of heavy wove unwatermarked paper, 7 x 4 1/2", written in pencil]
[*recto*]
P.O. 551, 662 (Hering 550)
Kuster A. f. O XXII 1 Abth. p. 149
Hering Hb. 538-9
    Pflügers Arch XIII 373
Scheinbewegungen bei Engelmann
    Jena Ztsch. III. S 443. 1867
    Platner Annal de Phys. in Ch. LXXX. 1850. p. 289
    Oppel ibid XCIX 1856 p. 540
    Dvořák Wien Stzb. LXI, 1870 p 257
    Kleiner. Pflugers Arch. XVIII, 1878 p ['443' del.] 573
[*verso, vertical*]
Volkmann A f. O V, 63, how we come to neglect doppelbilder 67-8

 don't melt

|| use of Donders law Hering *B. [*intrl.*] 256.

[7]

[wove unwatermarked paper, 7 5/8 x 4 5/9", vertical blue rules]
[*recto*]
Schweigger, Klin. Unters. üb. *dass [*false start of* 's' *undel. in error*] Schielen. Berlin 1881.
"Man kann nichts lernen, was man nicht auch wieder verlernen kann." p. 73.

He says Seeing depends on a chain of inferences. The first depends on binocular fixation & is that the images of the two foveae ['b are' del.] refer to ['sp' del.] same *point ['o' insrtd.] of space. This causes Verwirrung in squinting for 2 difft objects are thus referred, and the Pt's consciousness may stop here. For double vision the further inference is required, that in two difft parts of space *lies ['i' ov. 'a'] the same object. Where double vision fails in squinting the explanation is that binocular fixation [*verso*] has ['h' ov. 'e'] either never occurred, or has been unlearned. Nur aus der bin fix. *kann ['k' ov. 'C'] sich die normale Verschmelzung der Gesichtsfelder entwickeln, & und doppelsehen ist nur dann möglich wenn irgend eine art ['for' del.] von binoc. ['fix.' del.] Verschmelzung vorhanden ist. p. 73

[8]
[leaf of laid paper, 10 x 8″, watermarked Royal Irish Linen]
[*recto*]
Blinden mit *gelahmter ['hmter' *ov.* 'mhten'] Netzhaut projiciren bilder bestim̃t nach aussen, showing the absurdity of Brewster's theory. Donders p. 8.
Accom[m]odation to abnormal circumstances: Prismatic ablenkung. Clavierspielen mit breiteren tasten
Fiddles—size of handwriting with specs. ibid 22
Bei directem sehen: ['Werden objecte' *del.*] The direction of the object is in the Richtungs linien, the distance is measured by the impulse to converge. Infant fixirt at *birth ['i' *ov.* 'e'] 34 [*alt. fr.* '35']
Impulse to ['f' *del.*] bring to fovea ['ex' *del.*] measures [*final* 's' *ov.* 'd'] sideward distance of object since when motion made object does not seem to move 33
More distant spark seen single when instantaneous
    double *when continuous.* 43.
[*vert. penc. in mrgn.*] Donders lays much stress on Giraud Teulon's observation (Helmholtz p. 607)
[*penc., horizontal*]
Projection theory *empiristisch ['stisch' *ov.* 'cal'] because object *is* single only when at intersection. If we think it *there* we think it aright, and single, elsewhere wrong & double. Experience must then have taught us to make see things single as much as possible in order to see them right, and we have learned to do so by thinking them at *that* distance.
[*verso, on left half of folded leaf, ink*]
"—Vorstellungen, welche anfanglich durch Urtheil und Schluss nur schwer aus den Empfindungen abgeleitet werden, bei der Wiederholung spontan entstehen, und fürhen ['f' *ov.* 'w'] uns zur Annahmen dass jeder Vorstellungsprozess in Vorstellungsorgane eine Modification hinterlässt, welch dasselbe in unmittelbarere Verbindung bring mit den Processen der directen Empfindung. *Donders [*intrl.*] 13.(1)45.
[*reversed on opposite half of verso fold, in* Mrs. James's *hand, trial forms of her maiden name (*Gibbens), *in combination with first names, and then below, in* WJ's *hand,* 'Perception of *Motion,* Rabier p. 448, 449, notes. Solve the difficulty by brain scheme of fringe!']

[9]
[leaf of wove paper, 12 5/16 x 7 3/8″, partial watermark 'L. W']
[*recto*]
Note to p. 179, cont'd.
Note to p. 179, cont'd.

ly c with what happens in the skin. The *optical [*insrtd.*] illusion ['is well known.' *del.*] produced in fig—is well known. We can easily make the figure an object for the skin by pricking with a thick needle holes in *the [*insrtd.*] paper close together. ['and following the lines,' *del.*] We ['W' *ov.* 'w'] thus [*ab. del.* 'shall'] get on the reverse side of the sheet, a series of small eminences which the finger-|tip can follow, and out of its sensations ['perceive the' *del.*] read the figure. ['ˣOne' *del.*] [A still easier way of making the drawing is by one of the little sharp toothed stencil-wheels ['used by' *del.*] mounted on a handle and used by dress-|makers for ['cutting' *del.*]

tracing patterns.] Now to the eye, ['it is' *del.*] the right hand ['si' *del.*] (upper) half of the *fine [*ab. del.* 'single'] line ['that' *del.*] seems *highest.* To the finger it seems *lowest.* This is one of the illusions which, according to Helmholtz, *may **fail['s' *del.*] to [*intrl.*] disappear when the eye is fixed. The finger ['can only' *del.*] gets ['s' *added*] the perception *only [*intrl.*] when it moves along the fine line. With more complicated patterns, ['such as Zöllners figure' *del.*] the perception is too confused for a ['deaf in' *del.*] definite
[*verso*]

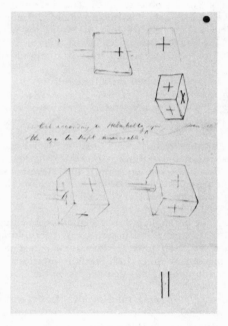

[10]
[leaf of laid unwatermarked paper, 9 x 6 3/8"]
[*recto*]

☞ E. Seguin Psycho-physiol. education of an idiots eyes. Arch. of Med. IV (1880) Dec. p. 217.

☞ Donders Essay in Pflüger on genetic explanation of motions.

☞ The same, reviewed by Giraud Teulon in Annales d'Oculistique LXXXIV, (12.s.IV) 3/4 p. 138. Bullet. de. l'Acad. de Med. 1880, IX, 37. 908-*924 ['9' *ov.* '3'].

☞ Schön in Jbr. *VII [*alt. fr.* 'VIII']. 156–60
[*fist del.*] Fialla, "couching," ibid 164

☞ Javal, "Double centre" Soc. de Biol. 4 mai, 1878. Progrès med. 19, p. *359 [*ab. del.* '35']
[*verso*]

☞ Backhouse, Physiol. Opt.
☞ Leconte Stevens, thereupon

Silliman's J. XXVI (1883) *p 305 [*intrl.*] 399
Leconte, ib. XX, 83.
☛ Oughton, Lancet, *1881, II. 17 [*intrl.*] 1882, 134, 1068.
   Trans. ophth. Soc. of United Kingdom. *1. Oct 13. [*insrtd.*]
☛ Doppelbilder u. Tastsinn. Schön in Arch. f. Ophth. XXIV. 1. 1878. S. 108. 8.
   *Fleischl. Med. Jbch. 1882. p. 91 Jsbr. XI. .166 [*circled*]
☛ Javal (like Schweigger) Annales d'Oculistique LXXXV, (12.s.V) 5/6 p. 216

Against this: Kries Jbr. VII, 162

[11]
[leaf of heavy wove slightly bluish paper, 9 1/2 x 7 1/2", partial watermark STON'S LINEN 1881; verso blank]

*Note to p. 78 [*penc.*]
   "The perception of the position of a limb depends on the cooperation of many ['factors,' *del.*] sensations, of which *those [*alt. fr.* 'the'] ['sen' *del.*] in muscles & tendons *claim [*ab. del.* 'have particular'] especial importance. In active movement we do not neccessarily attend to the feelings of position which come to us from the moved limbs, but are accustomed to consider the movement executed as soon as the volitional impulse is given."
Sternberg, Pflügers Arch. XXXVII; 4. A ['very' *del.*] complete bibliography of the perception of performed movement and position of limbs is appended to the article.
   Cf. *Siphr, [*doubtful*]

[12]
[two leaves of STON'S LINEN 1881 paper as in #11; versos blank]
[*fol.* 1]
   Helmholtz first drew attention to *certain [*ab. del.* 'the'] harmonies ['ies' *ov.* 'y'] between the *habits [*ab. del.* 'laws'] of motion of the eyeball, and the way in which, when the eyeball is at rest, we judge of the direction of lines that appear *on [*ov.* 'in'] the outskirts of *its [*ab. del.* 'our'] field ['f' *ov.* 'v'] of view. ['The judgments in question are erroneous ones.' *del.*] The *habits [*ab. del.* 'laws'] of motion of the eyeball are expressed in two formulas known as the laws of Listing and of Donders. The upshot of them ['is, that' *del.*] popularly expressed, *is [*insrtd.*] that ['when the there is a certain' *del.*] the eyeball ['habit' *del.*] which might conceivably *perform [*ab. del.* 'in'] its rotations ['*illeg. word*] are about' *del.*] and carry its line of sight from *any [*intrl.*] one point to another of the visual field in an indefinite number of ways, by ['using' *del.*] turning upon a variable succession of axes passing through its centre, actually [*fol.* 2] does nothing of the kind, but uses ['a small number of ax' *del.*] a *single ['s' *ov.* 'd'] definite axis for every ['definite excursion' *del.*] glance it makes from one object to another. There is a certain position of the *eye [*ab. del.* 'line of sight'] called the primary position, *or normal position of ease. [*ab. del.* 'In ['all almos' *del.*] all eyes it looks direction'] An eye in this position looks directly forward, and more or less downward['s' *del.*], according to the person to whom it belongs, and when it passes out of this position to look at something to the right or left, above or below, it does so in such a way as not to revolve in the least degree about the *optic axis [*intrl.*] line of sight. ['The consequence of this absence

of twist is that ['any l' *del.*] the picture of any line in the field of view drawn'
del.] That is, if in the ['pos' *del.*] primary position meridians

[13]
[leaf of wove unwatermarked paper, 10 1/4 x 8 1/4"]

Space

Javal. Annale d'Oculist. Mai & Juin 1881. Tome LXXXV, p. 217
De la *Vision ['V' *ov.* 'v'] Binoculaire ['B' *ov.* 'b']. Declares himself in favor
of the "theorie empiristique des points identiques."
"Jamais aucun strabique ne perçoit le relief *binoculaire, [*comma ov. period*]
Du moins je *n'en ['e' *ov.* 'a'] ai pas rencontré [*illeg. letter del.*] un qui le
vit sur près de 200 que j'ai examiné, a ce point de vue, et la th. empiristique
des projections exigerait que certain strabiques puissent percevoir le relief
stereoscopique['s' *del.*]." p. 227

Case 1.   10 yrs. old. Squints since 2 years. Exercises in binocular vision have
taught her to combine stereoscopic views. Ink spots dispersed on the views
are infallibly referred each to its proper eye—refuting identical points
(?)
Case 2.   11 years old, squint[s] since 3, inwardly.

Pt. sees *both* window *and*
Javal each in its own place,
not superposed.

['G. T.' *del.*]
Javal

[*verso*]
Case 3.   To obviate objection that Case *2 [*ov.* '1'] is one of incongruence of
the retinae, J. quotes a Pt. who formerly saw like *Case ['Ca' *ov.* '2,'] 2, and
whose strabismus was cured by double internal tenotomy, and the Pt. *immediately* saw simple binocularly.[x] [This seems in favor of projection theory,
but] J. explains by saying that for *each eye*, the Pt. had a habit of estimating
position *with reference to the* ['fix' *del.*] point fixated [which alternated
apparently] Now, as both eyes fixate the same point, it is seen simple because
it is now the ['sam' *del.*] point of fixation for both.

Case 4.   21 years, squints inwardly since 3. Double tenotomy, suppressing
squint, but instead of restoring simple vision, Pt. now see double in such wise
that the images on the left eye seem to the right of those on the right eye.
['Same relative position in which images, ['of corr' *del.*] not of same *things*,
but of things cast on *corresponding points*, seemed before the operation. Two
prisms with bases inwards so refract the rays *from any one thing [*intrl.*] as
to throw them onto the old' *del.*]
Unintelligible!

---

[x]Javal says this is a rare case

[*vert. in mrgn.*] J. insists on the part played by "neutralization" or suppression of one image, & says "le neutralization laisse toujours persister celle des
2 images qui *nous [*intrl.*] donne la notion la plus *complète* de l'object dont
nous nous occupons." p. 227

[14]
[two leaves of wove paper, 10 x 8″, watermarked Library Bureau Boston, each containing a single full-page diagram drawn in india ink with a vertical pencil notation '3 1/2 inches'; versos blank]

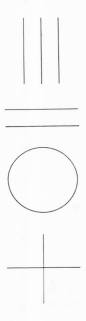 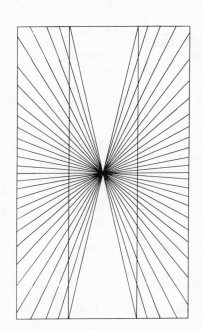

[15]
[leaf of wove unwatermarked paper, 10 1/8 x 8 1/8″, folded horizontally to make four pages; written in a strange hand]
Experiments on Optical Vertigo.
April 20-27. 1880.
[*signed*] Francis Almy

[16]
[six leaves of unwatermarked wove paper, 8 5/8 x 7 1/8″, versos blank, headed 'Space'; for a transcript see WORKS, volumes of manuscript transcripts]

[17]
[leaf of laid unwatermarked paper, 11 1/8 x 8 5/8″, verso blank]
L. Hermann (editor): Handbuch der Physiologie. Leipzig 1878–82.
W. Wundt: Grundzüge der Physiologischen Psychologie, 2te Auflage. Leipzig 1880. (1st edition, 1874)
R. H. Lotze: Medicinische Psychologie, oder Physiologie der Seele. Leipzig, 1852.
['H. Dohrn: Das Problem der Aufmerksamkeit, Schleswig, 1876' *del.*]

Appendix IV

[18]

[six clippings from *Science*]
anonymous, "The Sense of Touch, and the Teaching of the Blind," March 19, 1886, pp. 271–272
W. H. Pratt, "Stereoscopic Vision," December 31, 1886, pp. 631–632.
J. H. Hyslop, "Binocular Combinations upon Disparate Retinal Points," February 3, 1888, pp. 59–61
W. T. Harris, "Wasp-Stings," February 3, 1888, p. 62
J. H. Hyslop, "Experiments in Vision Again," May 4, 1888, pp. 217–218
W. LeConte Stevens, "Disparate Vision," May 18, 1888, p. 241

Chapter XI : Attention

A portion of bMS Am 1092.9 (4412) applies in detail to Chapter XI. The brief table for statistics from Wundt, Hirsch, Hankel, and Exner was used in Chapter III, p. 101.

[2]
[leaf of laid paper, 8 1/2 x 5 5/8", right edge ragged, watermarked 1887; verso blank; see opposite page for diagram]

[3]
[two sheets of laid paper, indeterminate watermark, 8 1/4 x 10 1/4", folded horizontally and quired to make a notebook of four leaves; part of a letter in a strange hand to WJ, acknowledging his articles on Time and Space and discussing the problems of terminology in percept, idea, sensation, emotion, and the like; the letter is preserved only in part, without beginning or ending, and has an internal date of February 29, which would establish it as written in the year 1888; not transcribed]

[4]
[six leaves of thick laid unwatermarked paper, a sheet measuring 12 7/8 x 8 15/16", two sheets folded vertically to make a quired fold of four leaves, with two separate leaves, the first with torn inner and the second with torn outer edge, laid in after the first leaf of the outer fold]
[*fol.* 1^r]

Psychic times.
[*del.* 'Process of Apperception

Attention, involuntary & voluntary.
"Notice"
Inner field of view & point of sight
Impossible to notice without assimilating.
   In some cases at any rate *Notice [*ab. del.* 'voluntary attention'] consists in nothing but presence of assimilating image. Over tones—can't see a thing until we *have* seen it, then wonder why we could n't. Hearing speech, reading print. Impression wd. not be noticed s̄. assimilating idea. Foreign language. Proof-reading.
   In general we *notice [*ab. del.* 'hear'] only what we have a matrix prepared for. Lover—sportsman—theif—ghost seer. Difficulty of ['good' *del.*] ']
[*fol.* 1^v] finding good observers.—Layman in library or museum. etc.

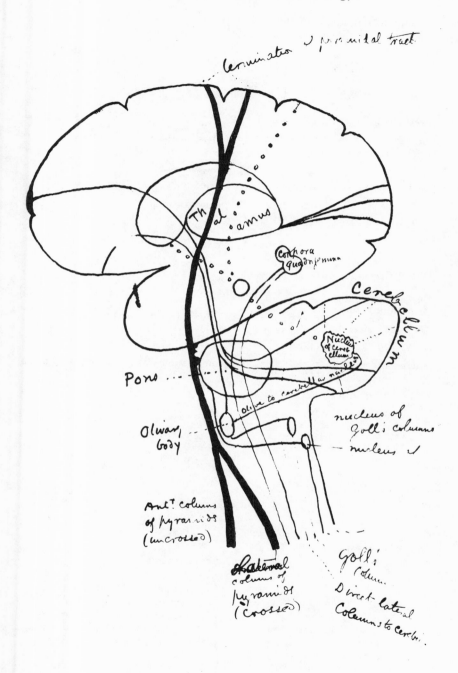

Time measurements of the process of *noticing [*alt. fr.* 'notice'].
['Con' *del.*] Simple ['p' *ov.* 'e'] [*ab. del.* 'Complete'] reaction time:

(Wundt p. 223

	Wundt	Hirsch,	Hankel	Exner
Sound	0.167	0.149	0.1505	0.1360
Light	*0.222	0.200	0.2246	0.1506
[*ab. del.* '0.149']				
Electric skin.	0.213	0.182	0.1546	0.1337

Vary according to place *& sense [*intrl.*] & to strength of stimulae
Great part due to central process.

Sensory conduction, *impression [*intrl.*] notice, will, motor conduction.

Modified by Expectation (Signal)

Wundt (p. 238)	without Signal	0.253 } 1
	with	0.076 }
	without	0.266 } 2
	with	0.175 }

[*fol.* 2^r (*separate leaf*); *verso blank*]

	Simple time.	black,	Time of white	*mean [*ab. del.* 'avera'] delay for discrimination
M. F.	0.133	0.176	0.190	0.050
E. T.	0.182	*0.224 [²'2' *ov.* '3']	0.235	*0.047 ['7' *ov.* '8']
W. W.	0.211	0.286	0.295	0.079

where *the [*alt. fr.* 'there'] ['we' *del.*] impression was to be identified out of
4 still more delay. 0.157, 0.073, 0.132

Assimilation with choice.

	with discrimin	choice to rest or move	Diff.
M. F.	0.185	0.368	0.183
E. T.	0.240	0.424	0 184
W. W	0.303	0.455	0.152

	to move this or that	Diff.
	0.514	0.331
	*0 510 ['5' *ov.* '0']	0.284
	0.479	0.188

[*fol.* 3^r (*separate leaf*)]

Psychic time measurements

Reaction time *may ['ma' *ov.* 'in'] in *include ['in' *added; final* 's' *del.*] all these times

1) motor Nerve conduction
2) Sensory centre process
*3 [*ov.* '2']) idea centre process
      (assimilation, classification)
*4 [*ov.* '3']) Choice process
5) Will process
6) Motor Nerve conduction.

In *simple reaction-time*, *3 [*ov.* '2'], 4, & 5 are left out. It is almost a reflex action a sensori motor process. This proved by fact that we react to wrong *signal [*ab. del.* 'stimulus'], often; and by prolongation of time when assimilation is made.

It varies according to sense, to place of organ [*fol.* 3ᵛ] and to strength of stimulus.

Safe to say that most of it is occupied by 2). Table in Wundt. p. 223

It may be shortened ['to 0' *del.*] by a preliminary warning. 3) becomes then active through the warning, and 2) is excited *from ['f' *ov.* 'b'] above so that 2) discharges the very instant, or even before, *1 [*ov.* 'is']) is complete. In the latter case the ['discharge occurs' *del.*] reaction time is zero, ['and' *del.*] the discharge *occurring [*alt. fr.* 'occurs'] so [*ab. del.* 'in order'] that the signal and the sensory nerve processes of completed reaction may reach sensorium *of patient [*intrl.*] at same moment.

Will takes no time *here. [*intrl.*] Discharge occurs [*fol.* 4ʳ]

"Apperception" & Psychic time. p. 3.

---

even if no signal or wrong one is made and we know it—we can't help recording.

Reaction time delayed by *complicating* the signals—surprise in their quality or accompanying noise which distracts. (Wundt p. 244)

Simple *assimilation* delays—and the delay increases *with [*ab. del.* 'where'] the ['possible vari-' *del.*] variety of possible signals. p. 248. and the complication of each one. *p. [*intrl.*] 257 [*fol.* 4ᵛ]

Assimilation with *simple choice* to react or not as this or that signal is recognized ['also' *del.*] delays still more.

Assimilation with *choice to react with this or that hand* most of all.

These two last varieties differ from the simple one only in a greater complication of the idea to be awakened. *The [*insrtd.*] Concept of the signal must itself awaken *a further concept, [*ab. del.* 'one of 2 alternatives of action'] in the *first ['i' *ov.* 'r'] case that of acting uberhaupt, in the 2nd. that of acting in a specific way. No need of any will process additional to these ideas.
[*fol.* 5ʳ, *see diagram opposite*]

[*fol.* 5ᵛ]
Notice (W's apperception) is all that is involved in the simple sensori-motor reaction time.
It may occur without assimilation. Usually it entails assimilation.
Generally only that which is assimilable *can* be noticed. Only what there is a matrix prepared for. Hard to find

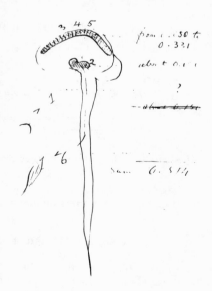

good observers. Often the idea dominant assimilates every impression—lover—sportsman—ghost seer etc.

In very faint impressions, ['notice due' *del.*] voluntary attention due wholly to presence of anticipatory assimilating image. Over tones—Wonder why we cd n't see a thing, after it has been pointed out.
Wundts field of *view ['v' *ov.* 'f'] & point of sight [*fol.* 6r] The impression was the fall of a ball the signal its escape. ['If the fall' *del.*] in 1 the fall was 25 cm in 2, 5 cm. The greater time allows the central process to reach a higher point.
This anticipatory tension or preparation of the idea may *reduce ['d' *ov.* 'g'] reaction time to zero. or even make it negative. The idea is *equivalent* to the impression.
Negative case explained: We strive *not only [*intrl.*] to make time short, but to make ['sound &' *del.*] impression and reaction objectively *simultaneous [¹'s' *ov.* 'as']. We anticipate *both*.

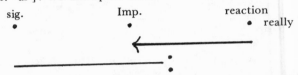

| sig. | Imp. | reaction |
| • | • | • really |

Will and notice are one—we can't help recording—even if a false impression comes & we know it.
[*fol.* 6v] Modified by perplexity:
Alternation of strong & weak impressions—suddenly interposing a weak one, &c, prolongs time

Accompanying noises.

	1	2	3	
without	0.189	0.158	0.222	1, moderate sound as impression
with	*0.313	0.203	0.300	2, strong sound
	['1' *ov.* '0']			3, light

(Wundt p. 244

Delay.
0.073————————unexpected strong sound
0.071————————un   "   ly weak   "
0.045————————Disturbance *of [*ov.* 'by'] sound by sound
0.078————————   "   "   "   light   " *sound
                                        [*bel. del.* 'lig']

So ['o' *ov.* 'ou'] a loud noise either before or after delays.

———————————

Assimilation delays.
Identification of an impression before reacting (Wundt p. 248)

CHAPTER II: THE FUNCTIONS OF THE BRAIN

Two items in bMS Am 1092.9 (4413) relating to Chapter II, chiefly pp. 51 ff. The cover reads 'On Sensation | *and [*ab. del.* 'Free'] Will ['W' *ov.* 'w'] |

p.o.t.o.a.t.o.t.w. | Tennyson'. A note ascribed to R. B. Perry reads 'Apparently notes for the *Principles*'.

[1]

[leaf of laid paper, 7 x 4 5/8" (left edge torn), partial watermark 'TINGS | NDARD'; verso blank]

*Brown, VII, 145 [*insrtd.*]

Luciani   Sight

amblyopia vs. psychical blindness.

visual disturbance *(hemiopic) [*intrl.*] follows *large* [*intrl.*] lesion *anywhere*, even cornu ammonis, *permanent* only in occip. & part. lobes.

dog   ang. gyri less concerned & occip. lobes.

incomplete decussat^n in dog's chiasma.

even bilateral lesions ['of sl small partial' *del.*]

if "circumscribed" in occip. temp. & par. lobes give transient symptoms.

---

occip. l. destroyed completely on one side gives hemiopia—transient—reproduced by farther ablation.

in   extensive ablation of occipito-temp. area gives transient *sensory

apes   [*intrl.*] blindness, followed by psychic blindness *this alone remains [*insrtd.*]

visual sensation takes place in crp quad.

[2]

[six leaves of wove paper, 10 x 8", watermarked Library Bureau Boston]
[*fol. 1, verso blank*]

Seat of sensation

Luciani explains *(rather lamely?) [*intrl.*] klinical amaurosis ['etc. as' *del.*] from cortical disease as collateral effect of lesion. Permanent effects are psychic p. 405

Vulpian

Bechterew in Ferrier 414 finds emotional expressions during irritation & nothing but reflex cries after ablation of thalami

In dogs ant. crp. quad. Luciani 152

[*fol. 2, verso blank*]

Sight

*Monkeys [*added vert. in mrgn.*]

Schaefer ['S' ov. 'T'] *total & [*intrl.*] permanent *sensorial (does n't say how long animal lived. [*intrl.*] blindness fm destruct^n of both occipital lobes *(Brain X. 368) [*intrl.*]

Ferrier & Yeo [*ditto marks under* 'permanent . . . lobes'] plus [*insrtd.*] ang. gyri.

Luciani ['not' *del.*] *permanent* blindness only *psychic*

Schaefer, (Brain X. 365) *complete* destruction *cauterz [*intrl.*] of both angular gyri, with *no* appreciable ocular disturbance. In another monkey hemiopia frm *deep* scooping out of ang. gyrus—explained by vascular changes in occip. lobe—Also temporary hemiopia fm. temp. lobe (371

"   "   Movements of eyes fm. occip. lobe.

Appendix IV

" " When small portion of occip. lobes is left, blindness *incomplete [ab. is del. intrl. '& trans'] and transient Sch. explains thus Ferrier's results.

Terrible discussion in Brain vol XI betw. Schaefer & Ferrier., F. accusing S. of falsifying facts as to am͟t of ablation. ['of' del.]

Ferrier (Functions 273) removes "the greater portion" of both occip͟t͟l lobes without slightest appreciable defect of vision.

Exner (Pfluger) XL, 62, found crossed hemiopia in 11 dogs out of 14 in which the motor region was destroyed. Disappeared within a month.

Chaufford & Bouveret report 4 cases of *double* occipital lesion with total blindness (Brain XII, 98)

[fol. 3, verso blank]

Hearing

*Monkey [added vert. in mrgn.]

Ferrier & Yeo found bilateral destruction of *sup͟r [intrl.] temporo-*speroidal [ab. del. 'occipital lobes to c'] convolution to cause *permanent* deafness, without other defect. *(Brain XI, 13)ˣ ['ˣ' connected by WJ guideline to 'ˣ & denies . . . (ib. 152)' (ed., 1502.28)]

Schaefer (Brain X, 374) finds *complete* *destructionˣ ['ˣ' connected by WJ guideline to 'ˣ Ferrier . . . it,' (ed., 1502.27)] of *both* sup͟r temp͟l gyri to produce *no* disturbance of hearing.

*Monkey [added vert. in mrgn.]

Temporal lobes largely destroyed ['gave' del.] on both sides gave semi-idiotic condition, transient, explained by circulation disturbed.—Neither smell nor taste interfered with—*No* deafness.—After idiocy ceased animals seemed normal.

ˣ Ferrier (Brain XI, 10) denies completeness; Schaefer (ib. 147) reaffirms it,
ˣ& denies deafness in Ferrier's & Yeo's case as above (ib. 152)

Ferrier (ib. 24-6) gives case of monkeys seeing well *two hours ['almost immediately' del.] [intrl.] after destruction of both occip. lobes.

[fol. 4, verso blank]

Corpora Striata.

Hemiplegia ['H' ov. 'P'] from lesion is temporary (Charcot in Ferrier 409
Excitable Ferrier 407, 265
Not-so   Franck, 22, 384, 280
Connected with cortex (Meynert)
Doubtfully so (Ferrier 404)
Ablation of nucl. caud. does n't stop movements fm. cortical irritation (Carville et Duret, in F.-Fk. 280)
Not connected with cortex (Wernicke
Connected   Obersteiner   340
[fol. 5ʳ]

*Touch ['T' ov. 't']

Schaefer (Brain X 379) found contralateral hemianaesthesia, persistent fm ablation of *gyrus fornicatus* in monkey.

Centres of common sensibility are situated in the falciform lobe, and to produce permanent & absolute anaesthesia, it is necc. to destroy the whole of this lobe, callosal as well as hippocampal division. (343 Ferrier)

Clinical observation does not support (does not *dis*prove *either [intrl.])

Ferrier's theory (Luciani 323) Doch! disproves, 324.
Removal of one or both angular gyri doesn't affect in the least the sensibility of the conjunctivæ (against Munk) Brown & Schaefer Ph. Tr. 324
Luciani found *hyperaesthesia* with cortical motor disorder (in dog?) the hyp. being result-of cut cord. Shows (he thinks) independence of both symptoms. 235
Goltz produced hyperaesthesia of entire body frequently from ablating frontal lobes, once from ablating motor zone without frontal lobes in dog. Pflug. A. 34, 471
Horsley & Schaefer Cbl 622
Not [*illeg. word del.*] hippocampal Luciani 152 note
Delicate sensibility after motor zone gone, Goltz, in Pflüger 34, 468
[*fol.* 5ᵛ]

Restitution of Function.

Not through other hemisphere, Loeb, Pfluger XXXIX, *297, [*intrl.*] 299
Independent of exercise   ibid, 276, 289
Possible [*false start of letter del.*] ibid 329
not by collateral innervation, *Schrader ['Sc' *ov.* 'ibi'], ibid 44, p. 218
[*fol.* 6ʳ]

Rolandic zone

Destruction followed by descending degen *of pyramids [*intrl.*] : Ferrier & Yeo
Hitzig & Nothnagel ascribe muscular sensibility
Schiff ['& Herzen' *del.*] tactile and Herzen thermic.
Schiff resects posterior columns, and finds 5 days later that motor cortex is no longer excitable. Horsley explains by degeneration of lateral columns near posterior (Brain. IX)
Schiff insists (agsᵗ motor theory) on recovery of *voluntary* movemᵗˢ later and on strength of moveᵗ always
Sensibility not lost fm. destruction, Ferrier & Yeo, Goltz, Bechterew
Abundant cases of hemiplegia without either musc. or tactile anaesthesia in human subject disproves sensory functions of this part. Ferrier (functions etc. 379–60
Bechterew Pfluger XXXV, 1885, p. 137 denies *any* anaesthesia in cat after loss of sigmoid gyrus
Schiff "I have not found one motor centre in cortex—no motor paralysis even after a complete section of int. caps. of one side." (Brain IX. 298)
Goltz finds (in dog with one hemisphere entirely destroyed) ['*hyperaesthesia*' *del.*] no symptoms after some months.—Destruction on both sides of *entom. [*doubtful*] antʳ brain, with *hyperaesthesia*, no particular *paralysis*, but incoordination & loss of voluntary power. Explains by disturbances of conduction.
Luciani explains restitution by lower ganglia assuming function.
['Permanent' *del.*] *Goltz quoted by L. [*ab. del.* 'Lu'] says hemisph. have *naught* to do with simple sensation. 242
Lesions of inner capsule in man produce *lasting [*intrl.*] hemiplegia without exception 243
Dog J had no restitution, & crp striat were found serous cyst. p. 275
     L thinks motor & sensory regions coincide, the latter involving the 2 parietal convolutions in man *(muscular sense) [*first paren ov. comma*]

Hitzig's zone being *for [*intrl.*] touch proper (327) Not easy to discriminate points for diff⁞ parts of body (335)
In *monkeys* no restitution, but contracture
[*fol.* 6ᵛ]
Secondary loss of excitability of whole centrum ovale ['and [*illeg.*]' *del.*]
  after ablation of whole motor zone, after 96 hours in dogs and of whole
  inner capsule later. Fçs Frk. 276
Crp. striat. inexcitable directly ibid 22, 384, *Ferrier finds them excitable
  [*intrl.*] 408
Ablation of nucl. caud. does n't interrupt motor excitability of cortex, 280
Anatom. relation c̄. cortex 280
Termination *of [*ov.* 'in'] pyramidal fasciculus in the cellules of ant⁞ cornu:
  proved by contractures consecutive degeneration and by degeneration
  not reaching nerves
Circumvallation of a motor centre destroys its function (Marique)
  Not so Fcs. Fck. 370. Not so (except under explained circumstances)
  Paneth, Pflüger, 37, 535
Suppléanc: Herzen Jbr. XV, 38 proved on *a [*intrl.*] puppy that left sigm.
  gyrus does n't take on function of right.

CHAPTER XXVI: WILL

Heavy buff folder and miscellaneous separate leaves from bMS Am 1092.9
(4418). Inside the front cover is a piece of laid paper, 3 x 5 5/8″, with partial
watermark 'Paper', written in pencil on the back of part of a leaf containing
an inventory of kitchen effects and food in Mrs. Alice James's hand. In
James's hand are two titles: 'Musical Devotees & Morals And Jan. 1887' and
'Genesis of Genius Atlantic March 1881'. At a later time a hand, probably
James's, wrote in ink above the first 'Scudder' and above the second 'Grant
Allen'. This leaf has no relation to Chapter XXVI. Instead, the Scudder article
is referred to in Chapter IV, footnote 18; that by Allen in Chapter XXVIII,
footnote 4.
[cover]
On the recto of the front cover James wrote in ink 'Will' double underlined.
In the upper left corner in his hand is 'Fig. on p. 39'.
On the verso of the back cover is written the following in ink:

"Imperative conception"
Bain on spontaneity as basis etc

Qu. Effects of habit on	Sully	Idea of
power—of will	Schneider	pleasure
Martineau S. of R. II. 113	Sigwart	not pleasant
	Richet	nessun maggior

Everett on change of level—so that things get a diff⁞ worth perspective—
my decision about going to Europe.
Easy & strenuous moods.
Muskelsinn *Goldscheider Hall's J. II, 656 [*penc. ab. del.* 'Froschhirn']
lebl. [*doubtful*] 1888, 16, 281 Lagegefühl fully preserved ['whilst'*del.*] in
complete cortical paralysis. Nothnagel Localization 15. Also Leyden 26

Education of will by reflex performance depositing idea of its motor effects which *idea [*intrl.*] thenceforward serves as motor cue, labors under paradox—why should what is *1st [*ab. del.* 'second'] in original occurence become ['1st in' *del.*] second in reproduced occurrence?

[1]

[single leaf of heavy wove unwatermarked paper, 8 x 10", written in blue-black ink on recto and verso]
[*recto*]

Free-will [*circled*]

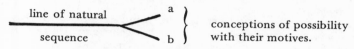

line of natural
sequence
a
b
conceptions of possibility
with their motives.

a and *b* are natural facts about which there is no element whatever of chance.
['Either' *del.*] The character of actuality ['I' *del.*] may come to either.
This character however is, if free will be true, accidental with respect to
['nature' *del.*] the rest of nature. But is *it ['i' *ov.* 'a'] an accident *absolutely*?
What is an accident? That which is utterly disconnected, external, independent. An absolute accident is a fact *external—[*dash doubtful*] to *every* other fact.
Now the character of actuality which comes, suppose, to *a* rather than *b*, is not external to the consciousness of the doer. That doer at the moment of deciding, adopts *a [*ov.* 'b'], identifies himself with it, and makes of *b [*ov.* 'a'] an accident inessential and external to himself. But he believes he could, mutatis mutandis ['do the same to *b [*ov.* 'a']' *del.*], reverse the operation.
[*verso*]
Nowhere in the process is there a point at which any existence is absolutely accidental. The conceptions of possibility grow from the natural order, and are accidents neither for the world nor for the individual mind. The reality of *a* is an accident for the world, but not for the mind. The reality of *b [*ov.* 'be'] ['becom' *del.*] *would be* an accident for the mind which disowns it, only this reality don't exist. The *conception* of *b* is an accident for neither world nor mind. Ergo no absolute accident *exists. It is [*intrl.*] useless to say, the reality of *a* was the *only* possible reality. This is a *brutum fulmen*, a *machtspruch*, based on the ['notion' *del.*] utterly gratuitous and baseless assumption that [*breaks off in mid-line about two-thirds down on page*]

[2]

[sheet of heavy laid unwatermarked paper, 8 3/4 x 12 1/2", folded to make two leaves of 6 1/4 x 8 3/4", written in black ink with a slight blue tinge]
[*fol.* 1ʳ]

Freedom

is opposed 1) *to constraint. 2) to indetermination. [*the two categories exchanged by a guideline*]
Monists keep saying that determination is no obstacle to freedom provided the agent himself be an accomplice of, acquiesce or find himself at home in

the only one possible course. His freedom is at the maximum in fact when he most vividly conceives that no other course is even possible. Complete *neccessity [^{1}'c' ov. 's'] is thus complete freedom. Only the dream of ['an' *del.*]other *possibility ['ility' ov. 'les'] mars the purity of the freedom of the course taken. [*fol.* 1^V] ['Inanimate ['I' ov. 'i'] Nature should thus be free, and' *del.*] The ['T' ov. 't'] servitude of man *must thus [*intrl.*] be exactly proportionate to the flexibility of his imagination to conjure up alternatives. For then he feels *constraint [*alt. fr.* 'constrained'], feels at least loss, feels that the path taken murders other chances,—['and' *del.*] feels *finally [*intrl.*] regret.

[*in left mrgn. of paragraph is penc.* 'Locke p. 171, 168'] [¶] Against this ['f' *del.*] view that what *men [*alt. fr.* 'man'] care for when they argue for free will is the mere absence of conscious constraint, I urge first this: The phrase "free to do" as practically used by anyone, always assumes tacitly that "not to do" is already free as a matter of course. It never means simply "obliged to do," as the monists ['make out.' *del.*] would have it. [*fol.* 2^r] *Even if there is no temptation not to do. [*insrtd.*] [¶] It is a gift, an addition to a state already conceived as independently possible. "You are free to eat your dinner" may indeed *be [*alt. fr.* 'by'] said to one whom you intend to feed with a stomach pump if he does n't *exert **his [ov. 'its'] freedom as you desire [*ab. del.* 'wish his dinner, and'] just as to one who ['h' *del.*] is ravenous with hunger. The phrase is grammatical and courteous to the ears of both. But it derives all its inward meaning and sweetness from its contrast with *another ['nother' *insrtd.*] notion in the mind of each, in the first "I *am [ov. *doubtful* 'wi'] free not to eat it," in the 2nd. "I might ['still' *del.*] not ['have' *del.*] be [*alt. fr.* 'been'] free to eat *it. [*period insrtd.*] ['still.' *del.*]"

[*fol.* 2^V] [¶] The Monistic view is incompatible with anything but an absolute optimism. The only cases in which the notion of freedom can ever arise are those in which an alternative possibility has occurred to the imagination, *the [*ab. del.* 'an alternative e'] possibility *either [^{1}'e' ov. 'o'] of ['constraint to do the thing un another tem' *del.*] constraint, restraint, or of another tempting course.

Oftenest it occurs that in the moment of doing the act the alternative possibility was far from the mind and only *arises [*alt. fr.* 'arose'] later when the consequences turn out bad. Then we say I might have acted otherwise. There was indetermination & I took the wrong side.

[3]
[leaf of heavy wove unwatermarked paper, 10 x 8″, partly in James's and partly in Mrs. Alice James's hand]
[*recto*]

*Cause & Will [WJ *penc.*]

[*page in* AJ's *hand*] No difficulty whatever in conceiving ourselves to experience things arising from or passing into nothing, absolutely appearing or disappearing. Difficulty comes in when we put ourselves in['to' *del.*] the position of the thing itself and try to understand how it does it. This difficulty evidently due to continuity of our own consciousness, in which nothing becomes actual without being called up by what preceded it or disappears without calling a successor. Sudden interruptions are referred to outward existences. In our volitions the antecedent is in *material [*intrl.*] quality identical with the consequent. The actual is foreshadowed by the consciousness of its potentiality. All this would be violated by an outward "chance" ['creation' *del.*] or "absolute" commencement.

[*verso, vertically in upper left in* AJ's *hand*] Simplest case of volition: disagreeable experience—shall I accept it or resist it? Be resigned and quiet or shriek and struggle? Question of willingness; willingness to find myself, to know myself, to keep myself, in one attitude or another.

[WJ, *penc., horizontally*]

M & M^1 ['are' *del.*] and their relation are the cause If the *act ['a' *ov.* 'e']
R occurs M^1 is the cause, if L, M. The combined action is suspense. One
may say the act comes about through the cessation of M leaving the causality
of M^1 to act alone. Or one may say it comes about through the reinforcement
of M^1,—by what? the ego? the mind? By a choice? by a suddenly arising
effort. Then the determinists say, Irrational! the mind must contain *already*
a reason for its choice, or effort. Forgetting the *semblance ['b' *ov.* 'p']
['that' *del.*] to the mind the ['the' *del.*] M^1 ['M' *ov.* 'm'] is reinforced by
a dead heave, a new ['f' *del.*] beginning, a determination of *being*. Nothing is
to the living sense more rational than this. Only when we demand that it shall
be expressed in a [*broken off*]

CHAPTER XV: THE PERCEPTION OF TIME

A separate leaf from bMS Am 1092.9 (4418) relating to the book, which in
turn is based on "The Perception of Time," *Journal of Speculative Philosophy*, 20 (October 1886), 374–407 (McD 1886:3).

[4]
[leaf of heavy fine quality wove paper, 8 3/8 x 6 7/8″, right edge irregular,
medallion watermark with cross]
[*recto*]

Time!

['April' *del.*]
Bibliography.
    ['Fragment X de la Durée in' *del.*] Jouffroy's
['Reid vol 4' *del.*]
Dugald Stewart Elements i 350 to 428 first rate practical remarks on Memory.
[*del.* 'NB!
☛ Supply to time chapter a criticism of Wundt ['on' *del.*] p. 263, (vol II)
NB. Don't forget my enlarged time-perspective when dropping asleep.
NB "Sense of recency" a temporal sign *of [*ov.* 'in'] memory experiences
not far very far outside the limits of direct time-intuition']
[*deleted verso*]
                Minimum of time subjectively perceived.

Tigerstedt (Bihang till Kongl. *Svenska ['v' *ov.* 'w'] Vetenskaps-*Akademiens
['k' *ov.* 'c'] Handlingar. ['Attonde' *del.*] Bd. 8. Häfte 2. Stockholm 1884)
revising Exner (Pfl. Arch. VII esp.Y pp. 613, 615, 639) (whose figures don't
bear out his conclusions) shows that the subjective judgment *(in 2 observers)
[*intrl.*] almost always rightly appreciated *as "longer" or "shorter" [*intrl.*]
a time difference *greater than [*insrtd. for del.* 'amounting to' *ab. del.* 'greater
that'] 0″.05 or 0″.06. More than half the time the interval was rightly judged
['when' *del.*] (as longer or shorter) when it *amounted ['a' *ov. poss.* 'ex']
to 0″.03. Judging a longer time shorter & vice versa (inverting the difference)
was frequent below 2 or 3 100ths of a second

Notes for The Principles of Psychology

CHAPTER XXVIII: NECESSARY TRUTHS AND THE EFFECTS OF EXPERIENCE

A separate leaf from bMS Am 1092.9 (4418), most of which relates to Chapter XXVIII.

[5]
[leaf of laid unwatermarked paper, 8 3/4 x 6 1/4"]
[recto]

To last Chapter.
['Dont forget to consult Leibnitz on Locke p. 370–*89. ['8' ov. poss. '1']' del.]

☛ [penc.] Pillon on Spencer's theory Crit. Phil. Aug. ['8' del.] 1886
[ink] *New Series [intrl.] vol I, p. 81
[del. 'Spir i, 248 list of relations between ideas.
Thompson II, 278, 282
Sigwart II, 39
Kant Kritik Einleit^g IV–V.
Riehl II, 13
Lotze Metaph. § 58, 67']
[verso; reversed, penc.] *Instead of back door vs. front-door metaphor consider 'brot in at door & born in house [note to right of del. 'Conse']
Amongst the postulates of rationality say this: the world must be so made as to admit of sweeping statements being made about it.

[6]
[piece of heavy buff paper, 1 1/2 x 7 1/4" (irregular), verso blank]
Hereditary neurosis from alcohol in dog
Hall's Journal, II, 173

[7]
[Chapter VIII, p. 208, and Chapter XXVII]
[piece of laid unwatermarked paper, 6 3/8 x 6 1/2" (irregular), verso blank]
Distinction between sensational & apperceptive processes proved by hypnotic blindness to particular things (after-image of unseen red wafer Callere 213) and by such exp^{ts} as are recited by Mitchell pp 205–15
Apperceptions dauer. Tigerstedt. Jahresb. XII, 190

CHAPTER V: THE AUTOMATON-THEORY

A separate leaf (now cut apart) from bMS Am 1092.9 (4418) with references later than "Are We Automata?" Mind, 4 (January 1879), 1–22 (McD 1879:5) and therefore at least in part referring to the book.

[8]
[two pieces of wove unwatermarked paper, originally 8 x 5", now cut apart; relates to Chapter V]

The Conscious Automaton Theory.
[ink] T. H. Huxley. Fortnightly Review, Nov. 1874. *reprinted in Science & Culture [insrtd. in penc.]

W. K. Clifford. Fortnightly Review. Dec. 1874. *Reprint in Lectures & Essays [*insrtd. in penc.*]
W. B. Carpenter. Contemporary Review. Feb. 1875
        "   "   "   May. 1875
Lord Blackford.   "   "   Sept. 1875.
G. H. Lewes. "Physical Basis of Mind." Prob. III.
Nature. 1872-3-4 (?) articles by [*lower piece*] D. A. Spalding
[*insrtd. in penc. to left and right*]
VI. 485   X. 1.82. 520
VII. 298, 357, 377
VIII. 289
IX. 178
[*ink*] *Wm. James.* Mind. Jany 1879
London Spectator 1874-5
    "Automaton Theory," Conscious['cious' *del.*]
    "Automaton Theory," etc in Index
[*penc.*]
XLVII. 2. p. 1394, 1457, 1461, 1492, 1529, 1562.
XLVIII. 1. p. 12, 80, 109, 178, 244, 756, 819, 979.
[*ink*] J. J. Murphy: Habit & Intelligence 2nd Edition
H. C. Wood, Lippincott's Mag. Nov. 1880
[*verso, upper*]
Malcolm Guthrie: On Mr. Spencer's Unification of Knowledge, p. 137, 231-63.
[*penc.*] Morton Prince, Human Automatism.
Alfred Barratt, Physical Metempiric.
[*lower, ink*]
Munsterberg W. H.

[9]

[*resume* Chapter XXVI]
[leaf of laid paper, 11 x 8 1/2", watermarked L. L. Brown, paged in upper
right corner deleted '22, 23', and then '39' over '26'; left margin torn as if
it had been glued before removal; verso blank]

[*penc.*]   Optical vertigo
        Mach.
        Gley, Rev. Phil. Dec. 88, p. 605
        Gley & Marillier
                 XXIII, 441
[*ink*] Julia's letter wooden.

Fatal word escapes, *irrevocable! [*exclm. mk. ov. period*] unforgettable.

Have a paragraph making it plain how the only result of effort is to delay or
intensify processes the nature of which is determined mechanically.

CHAPTER XXVIII: NECESSARY TRUTHS AND THE EFFECTS OF EXPERIENCE

Quired notebook from bMS Am 1092.9 (4419, folder 1), of six thick laid-
paper sheets, 8 13/16 x 12 3/8", no watermark, folded vertically.

Notes for The Principles of Psychology

[*fol.* 1] (headed by '[Original of note pp. 674–75 of *Principles*. R. B. Perry] ', blue-black ink)

Examples of logic from Science

Nerve and muscle action = "discharge."
What Hitzigs exp^{ts} involve as to *property* of centres in question?
Jenner's observation of immunity of milkers—method of agreement.
Buried pottery & arrow heads.
[*black ink*]
Mortality.
Tides—law of coincidence with moon's culmination diff^t from causal explanation.
Alkaloids bitter, coal tar compounds colored
[*fol.* 1^V, *black ink*]
Day ['D' *ov.* 'd'] and night case of rotation of sphere.
Water rises in Cambridge reservoir because it seeks *sea ['a' *ov. doubtful* 'e']
   ['level' *del.*] & reservoir lies between Fresh pond & the sea
Herodotus: "*Cold ['Co' *ov. doubtful* 'se'] drives Sun over Libya.
[*fol.* 2, *black ink*]
   The best possible equipment in the struggle for existence is a hard heart.
   The mephistophelian point of view—pure rationalism—complete immunity from superstitious prejudice—treating ['in cold blooded equality' *del.*] the country of your birth, the house of your fathers, the mother who bore you, on a naked equality with all other species of their respective genera, is always possible. It shows the world in a clear naked frosty light from which all fuliginous | [*fol.* 2^V *blank*] | [*fol.* 3] mists of affection, all ['swap' *del.*] swamps of sentimentality, that perturb straight and immediate action are absent. We may take it if we will. But the question always remains, are not the swamps & mists *worth* retaining? Shall we not add those superfluities, and fight for their retention?
   The illogical preference for certain species of a genus is what has made the drama of human history. The arbitrary assertion that tweedledum is better than tweedledee | [*fol.* 3^V] is the bone & marrow of life. Look at the intensity of the scotch, with their miserable clan factions, & dogmatic sectarian disputes,—*get ['ge' *ov. doubtful* 'ke'] men of genius to espouse them, & poets to sing them and they become a classic heritage to the race, altho' there's neither rhyme nor reason in them intrinsically. Look at the Jews with their Judaea worship & their exclusiveness, look at the Greeks. A thing is important if any one *think* it important. The process of history consists in certain folks ['perceiving' *del.*] becoming possessed with the mania that certain things are important; & other folks forthwith becoming possessed of the mania of keeping the first ones from securing | [*fol.* 4] what they want. | [*fols.* 4^V–12^V *blank*]

CHAPTER XV: THE PERCEPTION OF TIME

Continuation of bMS Am 1092.9 (4419, folder 1).
[leaf of laid paper, 11 x 8 1/2", plus 1 1/4" extension pasted on top, no watermark]

Appendix IV

[*fol.* 1, *black ink*]
['0.71, in Mach 0.35.ˣ' *del.*]

Time.

['ˣ*Loc. cit*, p. 14' *del.*]
['ˣLoc. cit. p. 144' *del.*]
[*fol.* 1ᵛ, *begin paste-on*]

In the first place there is always a ['maxim' *del.*] point of maximum accuracy, or as Vierordt calls it, an "indifference-point," *a time which we [*ab. del.* 'at which we neither'] tend to ['var' *del.*] estimate ['the time' *del.*] as neither longer nor shorter than it really is. But this [*end paste-on*] time varies from one observer to another, as the following table will show. The time *being [*ov.* 'was'] noted by the ear, [*doubtful* 'in ind' *del.*] the *indifference-points ['s' *added*] ['was for' *del.*] (given in seconds) were for

['Mehner (*2nd indif. pt. [*alt. fr.* '1 Indif. Pt.']) . . . . . 5 ['seconds' *del.*]' *del.*]

Vierordt & his *pupilsˣ ['ˣ' *connected by* WJ *guideline to* 'ˣDer . . . p.' (*ed.*, 1512.31)]	3.5 to 1.5	
Kollert†	0.75	
Estel (constructively)	0.75	
Mehner (['1st. indif. pt.' *del.*])	0.*71 [*aft. del.* '70']	
Stevens‡ (average of seven men) . . .	0.71	
Mach§	0.35	
Buccola¶	(about) 0.40 ‖	
*Wundt **(7 [*ov.* 'ˣˣ'] men)ˣˣ	0˙70 to 0˙76 [*insrtd.*]	

(Note) ‖ Curious discrepancies exist between ['some of' *del. insrtd.*] the german and ['all' *del. intrl.*] the american observers. ['With' *del.*] The ['T' *ov.* 't'] former, [*ab. del.* 'latter,'] in reproducing intervals shorter than the indifference-point, made them too long; in reproducing longer ones, *they [*ov.* 'it'] made them too short. Mehner alone found a second indifference-point See next p.[*to left in mrgn.* 'Print this note *after* the others!']

ˣDer Zeitsinn, ['18' *del.*] 1868, p.   † Philos. Studien, I, 86. ‡Mind ['M' *triple underl.*], XI, 400. § *Loc. cit.* p. 144. ¶*Op. cit*, p. 376. ˣˣPhysiol. Psych. 2nd E. II, 286, 290

[two sheets of wove paper, 8 3/8 x 7 5/16", no watermark, inscribed on rectos only in black ink; the first leaf is foliated 9, the second 23]

[*fol.* 9]
i.e leading on to another *cerebro-[*intrl.*] mental modification C, c. *it [*insrtd.*] strengthened the tendency to recurrence of the particular series A. B. C. by all that proneness to make themselves actual which we know is the peculiarity of agreeable as distinguished from neutral or unpleasant states. The first explanation, that from *habitual [*intrl.*] passive experience, and the second, that from preserving life are applicable to the physical train a, b, alone. If ['no ment' *del.*] there were no accompaniment *in [*ab. del.* 'of']

consciousness of that train, it would still be intelligible & satisfactory. But the third explanation, from pleasure, brings in another element, that of ['the' *del.*] *quality* of ['the' *del.*] feeling, as a determinant, and *as [*alt. fr.* 'at'] ['least it has' *del.*] it has been expressed so far at least, brings it into the explanation

[*fol.* 23]
Coalescence from utilities, coalescence from similarity which gives rise to abstraction, *form [*ov.* 'from'] the foundation of this explanation. And the rationality of the subject's future tho't that peculiar coherence, lucidity and even creative fertility which it may prove to possess is defined to be nothing but ['the' *del.*] its correspondance with the things that it denotes. *If ['f' *ov.* 't'] it unearths new properties in them—this is because the *qualities [*in penc. ab. del.* 'abstractions'] that the past *enabled ['a' *ov.* 'e'] ['us' *del.*] him to ['form' *del.*] *abstract from things have certain general associations with each other valid through all experience, and their conjunction in his partial experience was strong enough to work thus. [*in penc.*]

CHAPTER XVIII: IMAGINATION

A single leaf abstracted from bMS Am 1092.9 (4419, folder 2), which relates directly to footnote 22.

[3]
[leaf of thin laid unwatermarked paper, 10 x 8″, written in the hand of Mrs. James; numbered '57' in upper right corner by WJ, who also wrote the heading 'Note to page 56']

Note to page 56
['*Dr. S. Stricker* page 49–50' *del.*]
I have made inquiries of about 100 people as to the feeling in their lips when silently thinking the letters M, B, P['syc' *del.*] and I found but one who thought he had no sensation of the kind. Shall I not therefore consider the existence of this feeling of the lips in silent thought, as proved? I have moreover asked nearly 60 people about inward articulation in reading. Of these 60, two declared that while reading they were conscious of no such internal process. But is the *fact [*ab. del.* 'truth'] any the less certain that we accompany reading with an inward speech? x x x x x x x
I believe I can venture to say to those who cannot discover these phenomena, *as described, [*intrl.*] in themselves, that *it is ['for' *del.*] only [*ab. del.* 'they fail for'] want of practice and of ['keen' *del.*] acute sense of feeling which hinders them.

Folder 3 of bMS Am 1092.9 (4419) is in part miscellaneous, but some of the items contained in the folder can be pinpointed in relation to specific chapters. Item 1 is closely related to Chapter XVIII, pp. 709–711. Item 2 seems to be miscellaneous jottings that concern (1) Chapter XIX, p. 739; (2) Chapter XX, p. 911 and footnote 144; (3) Chapter XX, footnote 39 or possibly pp. 843–844 in the same chapter; (4) Chapter XIX, pp. 735–736, Chapter XX, or perhaps Chapter XXVI, p. 1121 ff.; (5) Chapter XXVI; (6) Chapter XXII, p. 974 ff.; (7) not located; (8) perhaps Chapter XIV, p. 544, Chapter VII, p. 187 ff., and Chapter XV, p. 603; (9) not located; (10) Chapter XXVI, footnote 29. Item 3 (but not its footnote) is utilized toward the end of the long footnote 45 in Chapter XV. Items 4 and 5 are concerned with Chapter XXVIII, and item 6 seems to have some relation to Chapter X, pp. 346–348 but not as a footnote. Item 7 is not used in *Principles*.

[1]

[leaf of thin laid unwatermarked paper, 10 x 8″, verso blank]
[*in* Mrs. James's *hand*]
Dr. S. Stricker
"When I represent to myself the B-sound, I only find there, however carefully I fix my attention upon it, the consciousness of the feeling of the lips. x x x x (p. 27)

"The pure verbal image *arises [*ab. del.* 'consists'] then in me out of nothing other than the knowledge that something is happening in the muscles of speech. And this process must be excited by the psychic activity of representation. For only as I represent to myself the word, can I awaken those feelings." (28)
[*space*]
Studien über die Sprachvorstellungen, pp. 27–8.

[2]

[piece of heavy wove unwatermarked paper, 6 7/8 x 4 1/2″ (irregular)]
[*recto*]

PERCEPTION OR SPACE: the Christine Ladd Illusion

Sensations of movement in SPACE chapter—remember Hall & Donaldson in Mind.

SPACE Remember Dunan & Shand.

PERCEPTION Illusion of landscape moving and we at rest in Mach Beiträge, also Mind.

Belief Bring in the talk in Feeling of Effort about *muscular [*ab. del.* 'forces'] sense not being peculiarly force-sense.: Volitional character of belief—Renouvier's pur enfantillage.

Attention: dog in the place about Logic-lesson in the Scribner-article.
[*verso*]
Effect on sensation on *belief* shown by the inability to believe that the rain is not over, if the sun comes out for a moment.

In *classification* use as example the Grundeintheilung of the psychic operations, Hamilton, Brentano, Herbart, Turner etc. quite futile dispute!

Belief. Act! allez en avant, and you'll believe.

SPACE Loeb's Fuhlraum der Hand. Put in Deaf-mutes under water.

Notes for The Principles of Psychology

[3]

[two leaves of laid unwatermarked paper, 11 x 8 1/2″, versos blank; in upper left corner of fol. 1 pencil by WJ 'Mach 1'; fol. 2 has paste-on at foot]
[*fol.* 1, Mrs. James's *hand*]

"Where we find attention, there, in my opinion, we find mechanisms and naturally also feelings, of accommodation. Perhaps our feelings of r[h]ythm come from the organ of accommodation. Imagine the same sound recurring at regular intervals. At each new return it will draw the attention to itself, will be so to speak, fixated, and arouse each time in consequence, *a feeling of fixation*. I can imagine that in the apparatus of accommodation, from the first moment of this process a steady alteration (fatigue? relaxation? rest?) should take place. If the sound recurs a second, third, x x x time it will *strike [ab. del.* 'meet'], according to the length of the interval, the apparatus in so many different states, and call forth from it each time, a *correspondingly [intrl.]* different feeling of fixation. A tone recurring at equal intervals would obviously always call forth the same fixation feelings. The simplest *agreeable* rhythm would then naturally be based on repetition of similar sensations, like the sym[m]etry of forms and the accord of tones.ˣ
[*fol.* 2]
*Mach (notes) [WJ *pencil*]

ˣMach adds ['a' *del.*] some ['s' *ov.* 'p'] philosophic reflexions which are so memorable that I cannot refrain from copying them in a note: Physics endeavors to represent each phenomenon as a function of time. To measure time the *swing [alt. fr. doubtful* 'move'] of the pendulum is employed. *Physics ['P' *ov.* 'p' *aft. period ov. comma*] therefore expresses every phenomenon as a function of the pendulum's position x x x x When *we [*ov.* 'it'] shall succeed in formulating all phenomena, both physical and psychical, as functions of the phenomenon of the pendulum's movement, this will only prove that all phenomena are so connected that each may be represented as a function of every other. Time is, therefore, physically, the susceptibility of each phenomenon to ['appear as' *del.*] be expressed as the function of every other. And psychologically as well, time will reduce itself to this, that certain *feelings [ab. del.* 'ideas'] (such as sounds) are in such a way bound up with certain others (such as sensations of accommodation) that they may be regarded, [*paste-on*] so to speak, as functions of the latter." (loc sit. page 149–50)——Mach of course, uses the word function in its mathematical sense.

[4]

[sheet of heavy unwatermarked laid paper, 12 3/4 x 8 7/8″, folded to make two leaves]
[*fol.* 1ʳ]

Mill's logical axioms Logic vol i, p. 203
(coexistences of attributes)
    mark of a mark [*opening db. qt. del.*] same operations on same ideas as
      give the same results.
"Gleiches, auf gleicher Weise verandert, gibt Gleiches." Schmitz-Dumont.
    Vierteljsch. vol V, p. 394—That is if it *giebt überhaupt etwas*; whether
    it do that depends on what the ideas are.

Equals + equals = equals }   Bain Logic i, 224 calls these the
Equals of equals are equal }   only 2 axioms of mathematics

Appendix IV

Action & reaction equal & contrary
Every event has a cause—a uniform antecedent
Sum of matter cannot be altered
Kinds of things have definite differences, & these depend on Elementary
    composition.

Wheadl. Phil. of Disc. p. 477

Future will resemble past
"Force is persistent."
Nature is simple & invariable
Axiom of sufficient reason
Lange's ['L' ov. 'A'] Ax. *von ['v' ov. 'd'] der Begreiflichkeit der Welt
No number of zeros added together can make a quantity.
[fol. 1ᵛ]
*Quicquid est in effectu debet esse in causa. **Nemo [ink ov. 'Nihil'] dat
    quod non habet. ***Nemo [ink insrtd. for del. 'Nihil'] potest ****su-
    pra [ab. del. 'praeter'] seipsum. [insrtd. in pencil]
Causa aequat effectum, (also resembles)
Change presupposes s'thing unchanged
("Nur das Beharrliche kann sich verändern.")
"Omnia quae sunt, vel in se vel in alio sunt." Spinoza
"A thing can only work where it is."
"A thing can only effect another of its own kind.
"Cessante causa, cessat effectus."
"Folge der Folge ist Folge des Grundes" Sigwart i, 375.
*Ex nihilo nihil [penc.]
The principle of things is One.
Two different [doubtful 'pro' del.] ideas can refer to the same object.
The same object can appear under different forms (Identisches kann ver-
    schieden vorkommen.)
Attributa non separantur a substantiis (See Lotze, Metaph. § 56.
*Nature makes no leaps. [penc.]
*Leibnitz Nouv. Ess. p. 370, **421,-5,-9,-34-44 [penc.]
Every palpable is visible, every hard sonorous, ['co' del.] je suis, God is
    veracious.
Nature agit par plus courtes voies. [written vert. in mrgn.]
[fol. 2ʳ]

Synthetic apriori judgments   *B [penc.]

Nothing real can exist indeterminate (Rosmini 219)
All resistents are extended
['There can be no' del.] All motion is of something moved.
Straight is short.
Every concave line is also convex.
No tho't without a content (& vice versa?)
   (emotion)   (object)
No being without quality.
No feeling without time.
No change without time
*So sensation without a degree of intensity. [insrtd.]
A thing can't be in two places at once.
3 geometrical axioms
Arithmetical ones

*Dictum de omni et nullo. [*brown ink*]

Ex [*penc.*]

[*fol.* 2ᵛ]

Even God can't change the past.

Nothing can be right for me which wd. not be right for another in identical circumstances

The fulfilment of my desires cannot be regarded as intrinsically *more ['m' *ov.* 'l'] desirable than the equal gratification of anyone else.

What is reasonable another shd. do for me is reasonable I shd. in like case do for him

It is right to act rationally

It is right that lower parts of Nature be governed by higher.

Postulate of harmony between universal & individual good.

The truth ought to be believed. *An all-|wise **Creator ['C' *ov.* 'G'] ought to be obeyed. [*insrtd.*]

The good ought to be attained.

The right ought to be done.

Quicquid recipitur recipitur ad modum recipientis.

*Nihil appetimus nisi sub specie boni. [*written vert. in mrgn.*]

[5]

[sheet same as in no. 4 above, folded to make two leaves]

[*fol.* 1ʳ, Mrs. James's *hand*]

Logical

    *Substitution of similars [WJ *insrtd.*]

    Dictum de omni

    *What all are some are [WJ *insrtd.*]

    Nota notae

    What coexists etc.

    Sufficient reason

    Things belong together

    Things in relation to a 3ᵈ thing are in relation to each other.

Ontological

    No thought, but of something

    No thing, but as thought.

    No being without quality

    No feeling without time

    No change   "   "

    No sensation without intensity

    Uniformity of Nature.

    *Attributa non separantur a substantiis [WJ *insrtd.*]

[*fol.* 1ᵛ, Mrs. James's *hand*]

Quantity in general.

*Mediate equality or coincidences Things Equal **to same ***thing ['i' *ov.* 'e'] [*ab. del.* 'or [*doubtful*] equals'] are equal [WJ *insrtd.*]

The ['T' *ov.* '2'] same 2. treated in the same way gives the same result.

Result independent of order of operations.

Every operation can be repeated on its own result.

*more than more is more than less [WJ *insrtd. for* WJ *del.* 'If a > b, & b > c, then a > c']

*Whole is greater than the part. [WJ *insrtd.*]

Arithmetical
　　All combinations of numbers consist of the combinations of their units.
　　The series of numbers is infinite.

Time
　　God can't change the past.
[*fol.* 2^r, Mrs. James's *hand*]
Geometrical
　　Any figure can be moved in space without changing.
　　Two points determine a line
　　Three a plane
　　Through each point only one parallel to a given line is possible.
　　A thing can't be in two places at once.
Mechanical
　　Action and reaction
　　Inertia
　　Composition
Physical
　　Force is persistent
　　Nature simple and invariable
　　All resistants extended
　　All motion of something moved.
[*fol.* 2^v, WJ's *hand*]
Effect must in some way be contained in cause
Nothing evolved which was not involved, etc.

[6]
[leaf of laid paper, 11 1/4 x 8 3/8", watermarked 1874; verso blank]

Note to p. *95 ['9' *ov. doubtful* '1']

ˣThis fallacy runs in exquisite form through all of Professor T. H. Green's writings. He absolutely insists on the confusion, reiterating in every conceivable form that a "feeling consciousness" is as if it were not, ['and that' *del.*] so long as it is not *also [*intrl.*] a fact for itself, a fact about which it knows. Therefore it *is* not, for ['the' *del.*] philosophy ['y' *ov.* 'er'] it exists not. The only real consciousness is a "thinking consciousness" knowing all about itself as a fact related to other facts in a total world. As, at bottom, nothing does this thoroughly but an Absolute Mind, Prof. Green leaves *human [*intrl.*] psychology with no *special [*intrl.*] matter to talk about. It ought to follow from his doctrine that if *he [*ab. del.* 'I'], dosing *me [*ab. del.* 'him'] with, say, *quinine [*ab. del.* 'colocynth'], perceived from *my [*ov.* 'his'] face ['that' *del.*] the fact related to other facts, of *my [*ov.* 'his'] feeling its ['unpleasant' *del.*] bitter taste, that bit of knowledge on *his [*ab. del.* 'my'] part might take the place of *my [*ov.* 'his'] feeling [*comma del.*] in a true *philosophy ['y' *ov.* 'er']. Poor philosophy must be sick indeed if *"feelings" disagree with her so that [*intrl.*] *such* knowledges ['as that' *del.*] are the only pabulum her stomach will ['suf' *del.*] bear.

[7]
[leaf of laid unwatermarked paper, 8 13/16 x 6 1/4"]
[*recto*]

Notes for The Principles of Psychology

March 15. 79

Bowne says the Evolutionist in making time, space, etc to be forms of ancestral experience, postulates the objectivity of the forms. ['Yo' *del.*] He explains time by an explanation which assumes it—(unless he say the Unknowable does it.)

I add, he assumes the faculty of *cognition* on the subject's part. The experiences are *cognized* from the start and end by becoming cognized more & more as what they are.

Bowne then says this is the same thing as admitting inborn ['forms' *del.*] categories in the mind for all possible experience.

Davidson cries: Aristotleism.

[*verso*]

The mind is the potential Cosmos.

[Mrs. James's *hand*]

On the supposition of separate mind and being there are but two possibilities: either the mind knows the being, or it does not. If it does, ['then' *del.*] *de deux chose l'une*

A Note on the Editorial Method

The Text of
The Principles of Psychology

Apparatus
Emendations
Textual Notes
Historical Collation
Word-Division

A Note on the Editorial Method

These volumes of THE WORKS OF WILLIAM JAMES offer the critical text of a definitive edition of his published and unpublished writings (letters excepted). A text may be called 'critical' when an editor intervenes to correct the errors and aberrations of the copy-text[1] on his own responsibility or by reference to other authoritative documents, and also when he introduces authoritative revisions from such documents into the basic copy-text. An edition may be called 'definitive' (a) when the editor has exhaustively determined the authority, in whole or in part, of all preserved documents for the text; (b) when the text is based on the most authoritative documents produced during the work's formulation and execution and then during its publishing history; and (c) when the complete textual data of all authoritative documents are recorded, together with a full account of the edited text's divergences from the document chosen as copy-text, so that the user may reconstruct these sources in complete verbal detail as if they were before him. When backed by this data, a critical text in such a definitive edition may be called 'established' if from the fully recorded documentary evidence it attempts to reconstruct the author's true and fullest intention, even though in some details the restoration of intention from imperfect sources is conjectural and subject to differing opinion.

Not only every different printed version of a work, as between journal and book publication, but every printing of a book during the author's lifetime carries within itself the possibility of authoritative correction and revision which an editor must take into

[1] The copy-text is that document, whether a manuscript or a printed edition, chosen by the editor as the most authoritative basis for his text, and therefore one which is reprinted in the present edition subject only to recorded editorial emendations, and to substitution or addition of readings from other authoritative documents, judged to be necessary or desirable for completing James's final intentions.

account. Hence, after preserved manuscripts and journal publications have been identified, the definitive form of the book text itself is established by the mechanical collation on the Lindstrand Collator of the first printing against some posthumous printing from the same plates, followed by the identification by inspection of the precise impression in which any alteration in the plates was made, with a view to determining its date and authority. (*Principles*, incidentally, is very rich in such plate-changes.) Moreover, the James Collection in the Houghton Library of Harvard University contains various examples of article offprints and personal copies of his books annotated with corrections and revisions, valuable evidence of his post-publication intentions to improve the texts. The richness of the James Collection in James's working manuscripts, including various examples of the actual printer's copy, offers a valuable opportunity for an editor to secure documentary evidence not usually available to assist in the many critical and bibliographical decisions required in the formulation of a critical text.

The most important editorial decision for any work edited without modernization[2] is the choice of its copy-text, that documentary form on which the edited text will be based. Textual theorists have long distinguished two kinds of authority: first, the authority of the words themselves—the *substantives*; second, the authority of the punctuation, spelling, capitalization, word-division, paragraphing, and devices of emphasis—the *accidentals* so-called—that is, the texture in which the substantives are placed

---

[2] By 'modernization' one means the silent substitution for the author's of an entirely new system of punctuation, spelling, capitalization, and word-division in order to bring these original old-fashioned 'accidentals' of the text thoroughly up to date for the benefit of a current reader. It is the theory of the present edition, however, that James's turn-of-the-century 'accidentals' offer no difficulty to a modern scholar or general reader and that to tamper with them by 'modernization' would not only destroy some of James's unique and vigorous flavor of presentation but would also risk distortion of his meaning. Since there is every evidence that, in his books at least, James was concerned to control the texture of presentation and made numerous nonverbal as well as verbal changes in preparing printer's copy, and later in proof, for an editor to interfere with James's specific, or even general, wishes by modernizing his system of 'accidentals' would upset on many occasions the designedly subtle balances of his meaning. Moreover, it would be pointless to change his various idiosyncrasies of presentation, such as his increasing use of 'reform' spellings and his liking for the reduction of the capitals in words like *darwinism*. Hence in the present edition considerable pains have been devoted to reprinting the authoritative accidentals of the copy-text and also by emendation to their purification, so far as documentary evidence extends, from the housestyling to which they were subjected in print, which was not entirely weeded out in proof. For a further discussion, see below under the question of copy-text and its treatment.

but itself often a not unimportant source of meaning. In an unmodernized edition like the present, an attempt is made to print not only the substantives but also their 'accidental' texture, each in its most authoritative form. The most authoritative substantives are taken to be those that reflect most faithfully the author's latest intentions as he revised to perfect the form and meaning of his work. The most authoritative accidentals are those which are preferential, and even idiosyncratic, in the author's usage even though not necessarily invariable in his manuscripts. These characteristic forms convey something of an author's flavor, but their importance goes beyond aesthetic or antiquarian appreciation since they may become important adjuncts to meaning. It is precisely these adjuncts, however, that are most susceptible to compositorial and editorial styling away from authorial characteristics and toward the uniformity of whatever contemporary system the printing or publishing house fancied. Since few authors are in every respect so firm in their 'accidental' intentions as to demand an exact reproduction of their copy, or to attempt systematically to restore their own system in proof from divergent compositorial styling, their 'acceptance' of printing-house styling is meaningless as an indication of intentions. Thus, advanced editorial theory agrees that in ordinary circumstances the best authority for the accidentals is that of a holograph manuscript or, when the manuscript is not preserved, whatever typed or printed document is closest to it, so that the fewest intermediaries have had a chance to change the text and its forms. Into this copy-text—chosen on the basis of its most authoritative accidentals—are placed the latest revised substantives, with the result that each part of the resulting eclectic text is presented in its highest documentary form of authority.[3] It is recognized, however, that an author may be so scrupulous in supervising each stage of the production of a work that the accidentals of its final version join with the revised substantives in representing his latest intentions more faithfully than in earlier forms of the text. In such special cases a document removed by some stages from a preserved manuscript or

---

[3]The use of these terms, and the application to editorial principles of the divided authority between both parts of an author's text, was chiefly initiated by W. W. Greg, "The Rationale of Copy-Text," *Studies in Bibliography*, 3 (1950–51), 19–36. For extensions of the principle, see Fredson Bowers, "Current Theories of Copy-Text," *Modern Philology*, 68 (1950), 12–20; "Multiple Authority: New Concepts of Copy-Text," *The Library*, 5th ser., 27 (1972), 81–115; "Remarks on Eclectic Texts," *Proof*, 4 (1974), 31–76, all reprinted in *Essays in Bibliography, Text, and Editing* (Charlottesville: University Press of Virginia, 1975).

from an early intermediary may in practical terms compose the best copy-text.[4]

Each work, then, must be judged on its merits. In general, experience shows that whereas James accepted some journal styling without much objection even though he read proof and had the chance to alter within reason what he wished, he was more seriously concerned with the forms of certain of his accidentals in the books, not only by his marking copy pasted up from journal articles for the printer but more particularly when he received the galley proofs. Indeed, it is not too much to state that James sometimes regarded the copy that he submitted for his books (especially when it was manuscript) as still somewhat in a draft state, to be shaped by proof-alterations to conform to his ultimate intentions. The choice of copy-texts in the WORKS, therefore, rests on the evidence available for each document, and the selection will vary according to the circumstances of 'accidental' authority as superior either in the early or in the late and revised forms of the text. In this connection, the earlier discussions in the textual analyses for the philosophical volumes of this edition give examples of the evidence and its application to the selection of copy-text that are pertinent to the present psychological volumes.

On the other hand, although James demonstrably made an effort to control the forms of certain of his accidentals in the proofs, even when he had been relatively careless about their consistency in his manuscript printer's copy, he was not always equally attentive to every detail of the housestyling that printers imposed on his work. In some cases he simply did not observe anomalies even in his own idiosyncratic practices; in others he may have been relatively indifferent when no real clash of principles was involved. Thus, when an editor is aware by reason of inconsistencies within the copy-text that certain 'accidental' printing-house stylings have been substituted for James's own practices as established in manuscripts and marked copy, or have been substituted for relatively neutral journal copy that seems to approximate James's usual practice, he may feel justified in emending to recover by the methods of textual criticism as much of the purity of the Jamesian accidentals as of the substantives—both ultimately contributing to the most complete and accurate expression of James's meaning. However, although the texture of James's care-

---

[4] An extensive analysis of specific problems in the mechanical application of traditional theories of copy-text to revised modern works may be found in Bowers, "Greg's 'Rationale of Copy-Text' Revisited," *Studies in Bibliography*, 31 (1978), 90–161.

fully worked-over book copy-text is ordinarily accepted in general detail over earlier documents, not every book variant may be thought of as the direct result of James's own marking whether of copy or of proof. On sufficient evidence, most are taken to have derived from this actual authority; nevertheless a decision on such grounds is impossible to make comma for comma, say, and unless contrary evidence is present the general authority of a revised book copy-text is likely to hold so long as it conforms on the whole to James's practices.

Except for the small amount of silent alteration listed below, every editorial change in the copy-text has been recorded, with the identification of its immediate source and the record of the rejected copy-text reading. An asterisk prefixed to the page-line reference (always to this edition) indicates that the alteration is discussed in a Textual Note. The formulas for notation are described in the headnote to the list of Emendations, but it may be well to mention here the use of the term *stet* to call attention in special cases to the retention of the copy-text reading. Textual Notes discuss certain emendations or refusals to emend. The Historical Collation lists all substantive readings in the collated authoritative documents that differ from the edited text except for those recorded in the list of Emendations, which are not repeated in the Historical Collation. The principles for the recording of variants are described in the headnote to this Collation.

A special section of the apparatus treats hyphenated word-compounds, listing the correct copy-text form of those broken between lines by the printer of the present edition and indicating those in the present text, with the form adopted, that were broken between lines in the copy-text and partake of the nature of emendations. Consultation of the first list will enable any user to quote from the present text with the correct hyphenation of the copy-text.

Manuscript material that is reproduced or is quoted in this edition is transcribed in diplomatic form,[5] without emendation, except for two features. As with many writers, James's placement of punctuation in relation to quotation marks was erratic, sometimes appearing within the marks as in the standard American sys-

---

[5] A diplomatic transcript reproduces exactly the final form of the original, insofar as type can represent script, but with no attempt to follow the lining of the original or visually—by typographical devices—to reproduce deletions, interlineations, additions, or substitutions. It follows that no emendation is attempted in such a transcript and all errors in the text are allowed to stand without correction, although a sparing use of square brackets for addition or clarification has been permitted.

tem for commas and periods, sometimes outside according to the sense as in the British system, and sometimes carelessly placed immediately below the quotation mark. To attempt to determine the exact position of each mark would often be impossible; hence all such punctuation is placed as it would be by an American printer, the system that James in fact seems to have employed himself when he thought of it. Second, the spacing of ellipsis dots has been normalized. As part of this normalization the distinction is made (James's spacing usually being variable and ambiguous) between the closeup placement of the first of four dots when it represents the period directly after the last quoted word and the spaced placement (as in three dots) when the ellipsis begins in mid-sentence and the fourth dot thus represents the final period. According to convenience, manuscripts may be transcribed in their final, or clear-text, form, with all alteration variants recorded systematically in an apparatus list, or on occasion they may be transcribed with a record of their alteration variants placed within the text. An abstract of the major features of the formulaic system for recording alterations, especially when they are described within the transcript of the text, may be found in the headnote to the Alterations in the Manuscripts.[6]

In this edition of THE WORKS OF WILLIAM JAMES an attempt has been made to identify the exact edition used by James for his quotations from other authors and ordinarily to emend his care-lessnesses of transcription so that the quotation will reproduce exactly what the author wrote in every detail. All such changes are noted in the list of Emendations when they concern the sub-stantives. On some occasions James altered quotations for his own purposes in such a manner that his version should be respected. Such readings are retained in the text but recorded in the list of Emendations (with the signal *stet*), and the original form is pro-vided for the information of the consulting scholar. The general principles governing the treatment of emendation within quota-tions are as follows. As a rule, the author's accidentals are silently inserted from the original to replace variants created in the normal course of James's copying without particular attention to such features, or of compositorial styling. For substantives, James faced the usual problem of a quoter in getting at the meat of the quota-tion by judicious condensation. Major omissions he was likely to mark by ellipsis dots. On the other hand, he was by no means

---

[6] For full details of this system, see F. Bowers, "Transcription of Manuscripts: The Record of Variants," *Studies in Bibliography*, 29 (1976), 212–264.

invariably scrupulous in indicating a number of his alterations. Thus to condense a quotation he might silently omit material ranging from a phrase to several sentences. Major omissions that would require excessive space to transcribe in the list of Emendations are indicated in the text by editorially added dots, recorded as emendations. For minor condensing omissions, James's text is ordinarily allowed to stand without the distraction of ellipsis dots, and the omitted matter is recorded as part of a *stet* entry in the list of Emendations. However, James's treatment of quotations could be more cavalier. Sometimes to speed up the quotation, but occasionally to sharpen its application to his own ideas, he paraphrased a word or phrase, or a major part of a sentence. Since alteration of this nature was consciously engaged in for literary or philosophic purposes, James's text in such cases is allowed to stand but the original reading is given as part of a *stet* entry in the Emendations. More troublesome are the minor variants in wording that seem to have no purpose idealogically or as condensations. When in the opinion of the editor these represent merely careless or inadvertent slips in copying, on a par with James's sometimes casual transcription of accidentals, the originals are restored as listed emendations. Within James's quotations, paragraphing that he did not observe in the original has not been recorded and final dots have not been added editorially when he ends a quotation short of the completion of a sentence. Variation from the original in James's choice whether to begin a quotation with a capital or lower-case letter has also not been recorded. Similarly, James's syntactical capitalization or use of lower case following ellipsis has been ignored whenever by necessity it differs from the original. The Notes provide full information about quotations in the text that James did not footnote.

References to McDermott (McD) are to the "Annotated Bibliography," *The Writings of William James*, ed. John J. McDermott (New York: Random House, 1967).

Silent alterations in the text of this work concern themselves chiefly with mechanical presentation. For instance, heading capitals are normalized in the first line of any chapter or section, headings may have their final periods removed, the headlines of the originals may be altered for the purposes of the present edition, anomalous typographical conventions or use of fonts may be normalized including roman or italic syntactical punctuation, which here has been made to conform to a logical system. Finally, James's occasional variation between the usual three or four dots for ellipsis is not recorded, nor are such purely typographical matters as the use of an asterisk instead of a number for a footnote.

For the treatment of footnotes in this edition, see "III. The Editorial Problem" in the textual discourse.

All line numbers keyed to the text include section numbers and subheadings but do not include spaces after titles or subheadings or spaces within the text itself.

The intent of the editorial treatment both in large and in small matters, and in the recording of the textual information, has been to provide a clean reading text for the general user, with all specialized material isolated for the convenience of the scholar who wishes to consult it. The result has been to establish in the wording James's latest intentions in their most authoritative form, divorced from verbal corruption whether in the copy-text or in subsequent printings or editions. To this crucial aim has been added the further attempt to present James's final verbal intentions within a logically contrived system of his own accidentals that in their texture are as close to their most authoritative form as controlled editorial theory can establish from the documentary evidence that has been preserved for each work.[7]

The aid offered by this edition to serious scholars of William James's writings is not confined to the presentation of a trustworthy, purified, and established text. Of equal ultimate importance are the apparatuses and appendixes devoted to the facts about the progress of James's thought from its earliest known beginnings to final publication in journal and book, and continuing to annotation in his private copy of the two original volumes by the record of alterations there that have not previously been made public except in a few of the plate-changes of later printings. Most of the materials here made available for close study of the development and refinement of James's ideas—almost literally in the workshop—have not previously been seen by scholars except in the James Collection of the Houghton Library, and then they could not be studied in detail without tiresome collation (here fully recorded in the apparatus). The refinements of thought between journal articles and book collection are of particular interest; but scholars may find of especial value the corrections, revisions, and general notes from his reading that James made in

---

[7]That is, when the copy-text has been inconsistent, as in the division or non-division of 'every one' or 'everyone', James's preferences have been restored. On the other hand, the printer of *Principles* was consistent in imposing housestyling in some spellings, like the use of 's' for James's 'z' in 'criticise'. In such cases of absolute consistency textual theory does not encourage the restoration of James's own characteristics.

his private interleaved copy, in some part for use in the classroom, but in some part with a view to a revised edition that was never to materialize.

In some few respects, chiefly in the omission in the Historical Collation of most variant accidentals between journal and final book publication, these editions of James's scientific books in the WORKS differ in their methodology from that adopted for the apparatus of his more literary philosophical books. The major points have been mentioned in this Note, but a fuller account will be found under "III. The Editorial Problem" in the textual discourse.

It is the belief of the editors of the WORKS, and the Advisory Board, that this living historical record of the development of James's psychological ideas and their expression, as found in the apparatus and appendixes, is as significant a part of the proposed 'definitive edition' for the purposes of scholarly research as is the establishment of a corrected text closer to James's own intentions than has previously been available.

F. B.

The Text of *The Principles of Psychology*

I. THE HISTORY

What seems to be the earliest reference to *The Principles of Psychology* comes in an undated letter (in early June 1878) from James to Henry Holt, obviously in answer to Holt's invitation to write a Psychology for Holt's American Science Series: "Nothing would please me better than to do the 'Psychology' for your series of American Science books. Your proposal merely gives definiteness to an intention which I have long harbored in my mind but should probably have still longer postponed without this spur. [¶] You say nothing of pecuniary terms. I think it best that everything of that kind should be settled at the outset. [¶] You also say nothing as to time. My other engagements and my health both forbid the attempt to execute the work rapidly. Its quality too might then suffer. I don't think I could finish it inside of two years—say the fall of 1880. Will that suit? [¶] Thanking you for your flattering proposal I am with great respect | truly yours | Wm. James" (typed copy, Harvard bMS Am 1092.1).

To this Holt responded on June 8, 1878:

I am a little staggered by the length of time which you think it would take to write the Psychology and hope that your health will improve and your engagements admit of modifications so that the work can be done sooner. I hope this not only from the obvious considerations, but because I know to my cost that what is generally taught at our higher institutions as "Mental Science" or "Metaphysics" is a great deal worse than nothing at all, and I am eager to see something better within reach.

This delay, however, does not incline me to seek any other author in preference to yourself.

The terms I have offered for the series are 10% of the retail price of each copy sold.

If this is satisfactory, I will send a form of contract covering minor details.

It would be important to have the book done by early Summer so that it could be printed & circulated before studies begin in the Fall, so we'd better say two (?) years from *now* rather than from Fall (Letter Book flimsy, Holt Archives, Princeton University Library [hereafter referred to as LB]; typed copy at Harvard, bMS Am 1092 [406]).

Thus began a story of Holt's tenacity and James's procrastination that was to end not in two but in twelve years' time. In the absence of preserved correspondence we must assume that James at first had agreed to the proposed date for submission of copy as the spring of 1880, which was presumably noted in the contract signed on June 12, 1878, this date on the authority of a signed statement about royalties made by Henry Holt on April 21, 1910 (Holt Archives, Princeton, James folder 1890–1911; see also Holt to Henry James, Jr., on July 6, 1917, Harvard bMS Am 1092.10 [86]). Francis J. Child wrote to James Russell Lowell on August 12, 1878, that "William has already begun a Manual of Psychology—in the honeymoon—but they are both writing it" (Ralph Barton Perry, *The Thought and Character of William James*, II, 28). But a letter from Holt on November 21, 1878, reveals some of James's early misgivings:

> I regret the cause of your mistrust of your ability to finish the Psychology as soon as expected more than I regret the fact itself, much as I regret that. I hope for every reason that your eyes will be better than you expect.
> Of course I cannot say what I may find it best to do regarding a book for the series. My *impulse* is to draw on faith and hope, and wait for yours. At present, at least, I shall do nothing but continue to act as if *the book [*ab. del.* 'you'] were to sometime *go in the series. [*ab. del.* 'finish the book.'] I beg, however, that if you find yourself making any progress, you will occasionally let me know (Harvard, bMS Am 1092 [407]).

In this same correspondence and in answer to a lost letter, James wrote to Holt on November 22: "So far am I from leaving out the environment, that I shall call my textbook 'Psychology, as a Natural Science,' and have already in the introduction explained that the constitution of our mind is incomprehensible without reference to the external circumstances in the midst of which it grew up" (*Thought and Character*, II, 35). Holt continued his encouragement. On November 23, at the end of a long letter about other matters, he concluded, "I enclose a page that ['will' *del.*] represents an average, though varying amounts of matter may necessitate varying it, and I hope that you will be able sooner than you expect, to fill the required number of them" (bMS Am 1092 [408]).

Holt was sufficiently confident of James's ability to produce the work that he advertised it in 1881 among the volumes of the American Science Series listed in H. Newell Martin's *Human Body*.

However, the question that James had once raised (referred to in
Holt's letter of November 21, 1878) whether *Principles* would be
so delayed as to prevent its admission to the Series raised its head
again in Holt's letter of October 10, 1881:

> I suspect the best way for all parties now is for you to give Prof [Granville
> Stanley] Hall to understand that I'm the publisher for his Psychology book,
> and *so vigorously [*moved fr. aft.* 'it'] give him to understand it that the
> book will be offered to me when ready. Then we'll all hold a pow-wow as to
> whether the greatest happiness of the greatest number will be promoted by
> putting it in the Am. Sci. Series, and letting yours stand unique like the Peak
> of Teneriffe or the conception of Napoleon. Perhaps that question may be
> already settled when the time comes, by your book being obviously near
> completion. Then we'll let the other fellow stand for Teneriffe and Napoleon
> (bMS Am 1092 [409]).

Stray comments in letters give glimpses of work on the book.
On February 16 [1879] he dictated a letter to Josiah Royce:
"With me, save for my eyes, things are jogging along smoothly. I
am writing (very slowly) what may become a text-book of Psychology" (bMS Am 1092.9 [3595]), and about a year later, on
February 3, 1880, he deprecated to Royce his too hastily written
article "The Spatial Quale" but continued: "I don't see why its
main doctrine from a psychologic and sublunary point of view is
not sound, and I think I can, if my psychology ever gets writ, set
it down in decently clear and orderly form" (3596). When James
revived the project of moving from Harvard to The Johns Hopkins
University (first broached in April 1877), he wrote President
Daniel Gilman on April 2 [1881], "I forgot to give you my
motives for desiring the year in Europe, whether I stay here or
join your University. Partly, I wish to advance (or finish) a text
book on Psychology which I have promised to a publisher, sooner
than I can in the midst of College work" (Gilman Papers, The
Johns Hopkins University Library). Later, in a letter to his brother
Henry from Venice on October 16, 1882, he remarked that "the
Psychology is the one thing that justifies my trip" (bMS Am
1092.9 [2602]). In December he had "hoped to begin writing
about November 1" but as yet had written only six pages (*Thought
and Character*, II, 38). James was defensive about the European
trip, which he had made alone, and which had produced few concrete results. From London on January 23 [1883], he wrote to
Henry (then in America):

In the first place, I hesitated long whether to take my leave of absence at all;
doubting whether anything material was to be gained by it. What decided me
was the Psychology alone. Then I *long [*intrl.*] doubted whether the better

way would not be to finish that in Cambridge, & not come away; & finally decided that the chance of hygienic benefit & refreshment for me, & undisturbed possession of its mother by the baby, spoke in favor of departure. . . . I have already gained much from Europe in the way of seeing philosophers & races of men; but all that is secondary to my main purpose. . . . I certainly believe, since I have *begun* the experiment, in prolonging it as long as possible, short of the point of absolutely losing the year, which would happen if if the non-psychologising weeks of hitherto extend into the future. . . . The last two days I have written some psychology; & since yesterday noon a dry east wind & cold air has made me feel like a different man . . . . If the Psychology only keeps on as it has now started . . . I certainly shall not think of coming home for a good many weeks to come. . . . Your working power is about three times mine; & what is lost this year on my psychology can perhaps never, or not for 8 years to come, be made up. *All* that I see & do here is futility compared to that (bMS Am 1092.9 [2608]).

Since James used a mechanical printing device in capitals for the above, the capitalization of 'Psychology' is conjectural but probable. On the basis of later references it is unlikely that James had started on the book in any systematic manner but was instead making notes and setting down ideas in brief essay form. Some of these became articles, although they were conceived originally as parts of the book. For instance, R. B. Perry conjectures that in the following excerpt from a letter of February 10, 1883, to his wife James is referring to "On Some Omissions of Introspective Psychology":

Yesterday I was parturient of psychological truth, being in one of my fevered states you wot of, when ideas are shooting together and I can think of no finite things. I wrote a lot at headlong speed, and in the evening, having been appointed, gave an account of it—the difference between feeling and thought—at the Scratch Eight (*Thought and Character*, II, 38).

But the English winter depressed him, and on February 6, a few days before his letter to Alice, he wrote to Henry again: "For some reason or other London does thoroughly disagree with me. I am in a state of acute brain-fag, although I've done a mere minimum of work" (bMS Am 1092.9 [2609]). Pressure also built up from friends in universities who were anticipating early publication; an example is the letter to James from G. Stanley Hall in May 1883: "I am sorry about the psychology, for I had encouraged my men here [Johns Hopkins] to expect an ideal book of its kind for part of our work next year" (bMS Am 1092.9 [170]). (Hereafter correspondence in the bMS Am 1092.9 series will often be identified merely by its letter number.) Only a few months later, on August 5, 1883, James wrote to Renouvier in discouragement: "I understand now why no really good classic manual of psychology exists, why all that do exist only treat of particular points and chapters with any thoroughness. It is impossible to write one at present; so infinitely more numerous are the difficulties of the task than the means ['for' *del.*] of their solution. Every chapter bristles with obstructions that refer one to the next ten years of work for their mitigation.—With all this I have done very little consecutive reading" (3529). And on January 9, 1884, James wrote to Karl Stumpf, "My own work has hardly been advanced at all in the past 6 months,—a most humiliating confession" (3779). This is also the theme of a letter to Théodule Ribot on February 26 in which he remarks that the book is at a complete standstill: "It advances somewhat in my head, but nowhere else" (bMS Am 1092.1, typed copy). However, some preliminary writing must have been done, because he speaks to Ribot of an almost completed chapter on Space (see below). But a systematic and formal start had apparently not been made even eight months later, when on October 14, 1884, he remarked to Henry that he was "hard at work" on the Psychology although his eyes were troubling him. A few days later, on October 18, he added before posting the letter: "College work has begun never for me with so little strain. Only six hours a week so far and subjects I have been over before[.] I hope this will permit me to do something toward my psychology" (2614); but the next month, on November 15, he admitted to Karl Stumpf, "My 'psychology' makes *no [*underl. aft. del. of db. qts.*] progress, literally. But while there's life there's hope" (3780).

The next spring, on April 1, 1885, James wrote to Henry, after rejoicing at the improvement in his eyes ("It has continued gradually so that practically I can use them all I will. It saves my life. *Why* it should come now, when, bully them as I would, it would n't come in the past few years is one of the secrets of the nervous system which the last trump, but nothing earlier, may reveal"); he states, "I have made a start with my psychology which I shall work at, temperately through the vacation and hope to get finished a year from next fall, *sans faute*" (2615). Such language would seem to refer to a formal start on the book itself, and not merely to notes or preparatory writing on appropriate subjects. Shortly, on April 17, he wrote to Thomas Davidson in answer to an invitation: "I can't stop in mid-career to write a ['subject' *del.*] lecture on so remote a subject as ethics. If some of my already written *(not already published, of course) [*intrl.*] stuff on Psychology will suit you I might be able to run on to farmington for a night or two, especially if there is any 'money in it'" (859). The next day,

April 18, in a letter to Henry he repeated his announcement although in more cautious terms, "I am working hard, and very busy and preoccupied with my Psychology, which I hope is at last under way" (2616). Six months later, on October 19, 1885, he seemed more established, as suggested by a side remark to his sister Alice: "I am trying to write, and shall probably get a certain number of pages finished before the year is out. The trouble with my work of that sort is that as soon as I get warmed up and interested in any chapter I have to stop, for bang goes my sleep,— which makes my progress rather halting" (1131). On December 24, 1885, he told Alice: "I am working more successfully than ever this winter and more continuously. But never do you *contract* to do a Psychology! The length of the job makes it terrible" (1132). Finally, on August 8, 1886, once more to Alice: "Subjectively ['I' *del.*] my main problem is to get through my psychology which lags wofully on account of the fact that whenever I get writing a few hours, bang goes my sleep & I have to stop a fortnight. But I have great hopes of next winter. I shan't touch a medium and probably not a mesmeric subject, with the end of a long pole. Psychical Research took up a long time last year" (1135).

The actual progress of composition from point to point is impossible to trace with any continuity owing to the scattered and incomplete references to the work in any detail. Moreover, it is likely that, at the start, James did not compose all the material in its present order of chapters. For instance, on November 8, 1886, he wrote to G. C. Robertson, the editor of *Mind*, about his "Perception of Space" which he had just submitted, "I have had most of it written this 5 years or more" (3542), and on April 28, 1887, he again stated, "I wrote it six years ago" (3545) although ten days before, on April 18, he had stated to Shadworth Hodgson that he was "still gladder you have smiled on my space articles, which were all written out seven years ago. I always supposed myself that they were but a filling out of your 'Time & Space' framework" (980). These references give a range of 1880–81; but following the publication of "The Spatial Quale" in January 1879, James seems to have begun preparation for what was to be Chapter XX on the subject in his book, as indicated in a letter of September 3, 1879, to G. Stanley Hall: "I am composing a chapter on space for my psychology and find I have to re-read about all I ever read on that driest of subjects, which seems an awful waste of precious time" (*Thought and Character*, II, 16). By February 26, 1884, James was promising Théodule Ribot the manuscript of his chapter on space for translation, but on June 29 he had to confess that the chapter was not yet done (bMS Am 1092.1). The use of the word "chapter" on June 29 makes it clear that James believed he was essentially working on a section of his book (even though "The Perception of Space" was published as an article in 1887). Nevertheless, the occasional difficulty of distinguishing work on the book from the writing of articles for their own sake is illustrated by James's remark in a letter to Robertson of March 19, 1887: "The paper on Habit of which you write was a mere pot-boiler which I had long had, written, in my drawer. No new thing in it, so I hardly advise you to read it" (3544), a reference to an offprint of "The Laws of Habit," *Popular Science Monthly*, 30 (February 1887), 433–451 (McD 1887:5). This was reproduced with only minor changes as Chapter IV, "Habit," for which James had received proof in December 1886. From the terms of the reference it might seem that Chapter IV was drawn from an article written considerably earlier than December of 1886 and that the original article was published in 1887 to make James some money; but the case is not altogether clear (see below, the section on "The Documents").

The start of what reconstruction is possible of the growth of *Principles* must be based on the Henry Holt Archives. By the end of 1886, over a year and a half after what seems to have been the 'official' date of setting pen to paper systematically (as suggested by his letter of April 1, 1885, to his brother Henry), James felt confident enough to send the first batch of copy, albeit a small one, to the publisher. This we know from a note by Holt's assistant Vogelius to James on December 2, 1886: "We have your favor of yesterday together with the first thirty seven pages of MS. The proofs will be sent in due course as you direct," to which was attached as postscript, "It would be better if we had a little more of the copy now so as to keep the printer agoing" (LB [Vogelius]). This copy was set up and proofs returned to James by Vogelius on December 7:

> With this we send the first instalment of proofs, pages 1–20.
> We have left the head lines of the odd pages blank for you to fill in.
> When you return these proofs please state whether you wish to see a revise before the matter is electrotyped, or, whether a set of plate proofs will be sufficient? [P.S.] Is there a chapter V to come? If not all the rest of the chapters in copy should be changed (LB [V]).

This was followed on December 17 by a third communication from Vogelius:

> We send to-day proofs of pages 96–170.
> We notice that the printer has put the chapter heads on the odd pages

instead of on the even pages. In the first two batches of proofs you corrected the head lines, so the chapter heads come on the even pages as they should come, and the subject on the odd pages, but on the third batch, pages 42–59 you simply filled in the blanks on the *even [¹'e' *ov.* 'o'] pages. We have corrected this lot to correspond with the previous one. Will you please correct all future lots so that the head lines will be uniform. We have instructed the printer to put the chapter heads on the even pages on future lots (LB[V]).

The allusions in the letter of December 7 can be explained only on the assumption that between the receipt of thirty-seven pages of manuscript copy on December 2 and the return of its proof pages 1–20 on December 7, further copy sufficient to make up proof pages 21–41 had been received but not yet set. By December 17 Vogelius could speak of the return of corrected proof pages 42–59 but not of pages 60–95 which evidently were still with James. On the 17th further proofs for pages 96–170 were sent. Pages 1–20 of Volume I of *Principles* cover the present first chapter, "The Scope of Psychology," and continue into Chapter II, "The Functions of the Brain," as far as *Thus, a tired wayfarer on a hot day throws himself on* (33.11). The proofs for pages 21–41 ([33.11] *the damp earth . . . as when we* [52.11]) continued within Chapter II, as did proofs for pages 42–59 ([52.11] *see a page . . .* fn. 45, the last line of text on p. 59 being *Horsley . . . necessarily* [68.10–11]). Pages 60–95 concluded Chapter II and began Chapter III, "On Some General Conditions of Brain-Activity" ([68.11] *abolished . . .* fn. 26, the last text line being Olfactory *. . . Vintschgau* [101.26]). Pages 96–170 complete Chapter III, cover Chapter IV, "Habit," and Chapter V, "The Automaton-Theory," and carry on well into Chapter VI, "The Mind-Stuff Theory" ([101.26] *Buccola . . .* fn. 25, the last text line being *for we . . . in* [172.19–20]). These identifications can be only approximate, for it is clear (as will be suggested below) that this initial typesetting was distributed and that the book as presently printed was set afresh from the very beginning. Hence, we have no means of knowing the extent to which in the interval between 1886 and 1890 James may have altered these early chapters (except, of course, for Chapter IV, which was firmly fixed by the form of the journal article). Also, of course, the word-count per page may have been different in the early setting from the format that we now know.

Vogelius' query on December 7, "Is there a chapter V to come? If not all the rest of the chapters in copy should be changed," suggests that the manuscript James had sent between, say, December 3 and December 6 in response to Vogelius' P.S. on December 2, contained not only the copy for Chapter IV (present pages

109–131) but also the start, at least, of Chapter VI (present pp. 148 ff.), while copy for Chapter V (omitted at this time) was supplied between, say, December 9 and a few days before December 17. In the book as printed the title *PSYCHOLOGY* is used on the even pages and the chapter titles on the odd.

After this exchange of correspondence in December 1886 about the abortive start of the book the Holt records are silent until 1889, and we have no record of proofs sent out and returned, or even whether more than Chapter VI had been put into Holt's hands but had not been typeset by December 17. Probably Chapter VI was the last copy received. Moreover, we have no information why James stopped sending copy to be typeset except for a casual remark in a letter from Holt to Henry James, Jr., on July 6, 1917: "I remember that he had a good deal of difficulty in getting started, and told me one day when he luncht with me at the Brunswick in Boston, that he had got to do it all over again; but I cannot fix the date" (bMS Am 1092.10 [86]). Even this recollection may not refer to James's abrupt disengagement from the printing of the book, of course, although the reason can only have been his dissatisfaction with what had been done and his determination to improve the work. The decision could not have been a traumatic one, for only a few months later he was dictating a letter to Henry, on March 10, 1887, that was optimistic: "I have been writing with something more like continuity this winter, and shall to all appearance, have the book finished a year from now" (2632). On April 12, 1887, he wrote to Henry again:

I never did my work so easily as this year, and hope to write two more chapters of psychology ere the vacation. That immortal work is now more than two-thirds done. To you, who throw off two vols. a year, *I [*ov.* 'it'] must seem despicable for my slowness. But the truth is that (leaving other impediments out of account) the "science" is in such a confused and imperfect state that every paragraph presents some unforeseen snag, and I often spend many weeks on a point that I did n't foresee as a difficulty at all (2633).

The same theme is repeated in another letter to Henry, this of September 1, 1887, from Cambridge:

This summer I have lived in such a chaos, trying to do some writing and oversee house construction at one and the same time, that letters were impossible, especially as the *ailing ['a' *ov.* 's'] condition of the baby made it impossible for Alice to help by writing under my dictation. . . . [*continued* September 19 *from* Tamworth Iron Works] Alice has taken charge of the carpenters and graders & hired man, and I have a clear morning at my desk. I am awfully impeded by not being able to write at night; and the all but complete stoppage of my intellectual work this summer has much depressed my spirits. But the exigency is temporary . . . . I *hope* to finish the *MS. ['M' *ov.* 'm'] of my book by Christmas time, if things run smoothly. Anyhow I shall finish it this winter; and then a great load will be taken off me. It must seem amusing to you, ['to' *del.*] who can throw off a chef-d'oeuvre every 3 months, to hear of my slowness. But my time is altogether ['by' *del.*] taken up by other things, and almost every page of this book of mine is against a resistance which you know nothing of in your resistless air of romance, the resistance of *facts*, to begin with, each one of which must be bribed to be on one's side, and the resistance of other philosophers to end with, each one of which must be slain. It is no joke slaying the *Helmholtzes ['es' *ov.* 's'] as well as the Spencers. When this book is out I shall say adieu to Psychology for a while and study some other things, Physics a little, and History of Philosophy, in which I'm awfully in arrears (2634).

Fortunately, other evidence is available that 1887 was a fruitful year for James, and that his boast to Henry on April 12, 1887, that the book was over two-thirds done was accurate in that he had just about completed the article form of Chapter XX, "The Perception of Space," by that date. In the preface to *Briefer Course* James defends the structure of his *Principles* and concludes (p. v):

But whether the critics are right, or I am, on this first point, the critics are wrong about the relation of the magazine-articles to the book. With a single exception all the chapters were written for the book; and then by an after-thought some of them were sent to magazines, because the completion of the whole work seemed so distant.

The "single exception" that James remarks was undoubtedly "Brute and Human Intellect," *Journal of Speculative Philosophy*, 12 (July 1878) 236–276 (McD 1878:4), which he utilized almost completely in Chapter XXII, "Reasoning" (with a small portion used earlier in Chapter XIII, "Discrimination and Comparison"). This was the earliest article revised for use in *Principles*. Since the contract with Holt was signed on June 12, 1878, and there is no indication that James had been planning a book on psychology before Holt suggested one for his American Science Series, this article could have had no connection with a *Principles* chapter.[1] Other early articles that James used in the preparation of *Principles* cannot conform literally to his statement in *Briefer Course* or to his more general statement in the preface to *Principles*, "The completion of the book has been so slow that several chapters have been published successively in Mind, the Journal of Specula-

---

[1] See below for similar doubts about two later articles, "Are We Automata?" and "The Feeling of Effort," as well as "On Some Omissions of Introspective Psychology."

tive Philosophy, the Popular Science Monthly, and Scribner's Magazine." After James had actually started to write the book in the spring of 1885, it is true that on occasion he wanted to see his ideas in print before the uncertain completion of the whole work. Hence, he published in journals certain articles that undoubtedly had their origin in an already written chapter. But even in this later period a fine line might exist between an article written on the subject of a proposed chapter with the intention to utilize it when the chapter came to be written, and (what James intended the reader to believe) an article that was a version of an already written chapter but published in anticipation of the book.

Before the 1885 date marking the formal start of the composition of *Principles*, a strong question may arise as to whether James's early articles were written with the possibility of their later use in the book in mind. For example, his article "Are We Automata?" *Mind*, 4 (January 1879), 1–22 (McD 1879:5), was accepted by the editor G. Croom Robertson on November 20, 1878 (bMS Am 1092.9 [505]). But an earlier form of the article, James stated to Royce, went back to 1877 (bMS Am 1092.9 [3595]), which would place its draft before the signing of the contract for the book. However, this piece might technically come into the fold on the basis of its post-contract revision, even though there is no indication that, so early on, James had made any move about the book except possibly for planning appropriate chapters. This article was used, in part, in Chapter V, "The Automaton-Theory," and in Chapter IX, "The Stream of Thought." Another early article, and one so completely reworked in Chapter VI, "The Mind-Stuff Theory," as to suggest that when it was written the book was not in James's mind (or at the very least that the chapter was a thorough revision of the article) is "The Feeling of Effort," *Anniversary Memoirs of the Boston Society of Natural History* (1880), pp. 3–32 (McD 1880:3). The chapter was sent to Holt in December 1886. Another that could not have been a chapter when composed, whatever ultimate plans James may have had for it, was "On Some Omissions of Introspective Psychology," *Mind*, 9 (January 1884), 1–26 (McD 1884:1). On May 2, 1883, in a dictated letter to Thomas Davidson, James remarked: "I have half engaged to give some lectures at the Concord School—Jonah among the prophets. [¶] I send you a bill of fare which may interest you. My own subject must be something in the way of an analysis of consciousness into its factors, object, ego, and stream of feelings, but my own thoughts are all muddled and clotted, and if I can't work them into lecturable shape, it is agreed that I shall back out" (850). His thoughts became unclotted, however, and on August 1 he mentioned to Henry, "t'is a solid comfort to have so unexpectedly got off an article for Mind" (2612). More valuable detail comes in a letter to Charles Renouvier on August 5:

The most rapid piece of literary work I *ever [¹ 'e' *ov.* 'd'] did was completed 10 days ago, and sent to *Mind* where it will doubtless soon appear. I had promised to give three lectures at a rather absurd little "Summer School of Philosophy" which has flourished for 4 or 5 years past in the little town of Concord, near Boston, and which has an audience of from 20 to 50 persons, including the lecturers themselves,—&, finding at the last moment that I could do nothing with my much meditated subject of the Object and the Ego, I turned round and lectured "*on some omissions in Introspective Psychology*," and wrote the *substance of the [*intrl.*] lectures out immediately after giving them—the whole occupying 6 days.

Earlier in the letter James had written about his originally proposed subject for the summer school lecture(s): "I floundered round in the morasses of the theory of cognition,—the Object & the Ego,—tore up almost each day what I had written the day before, and altho I am inwardly of course more aware than I was before of where the difficulties of the subject lie, outwardly I have hardly any manuscript to show for my pains" (3529). The article "On Some Omissions" was worked in bits and pieces into Chapter VII, "The Methods and Snares of Psychology," Chapter IX, "The Stream of Thought," and Chapter XII, "Conception." Finally, the date of "What Is an Emotion?" *Mind*, 9 (April 1884), 188-205 (McD 1884:2), parts of which are scattered through Chapter XXV, "The Emotions," almost certainly prevents any suggestion that it was drawn from an already composed chapter, again without precluding the possibility that James was anticipating such a chapter in the future. The date of its composition can be established from a letter of December 20, [1883], to Thomas Davidson: "I am tougher than I was last, can walk more, see better, & sleep better. I sent off to day a sort of a squib to *Mind* ['M' *ov.* 'm'], to prove that we are sorry because we cry, angry because we strike etc, instead of vice versa" (853).

One reaches firmer ground with "The Perception of Time," *Journal of Speculative Philosophy*, 20 (October 1886), 374-407 (McD 1886:3), which was reprinted, substantially complete, as Chapter XV, "The Perception of Time." The first notice we have of this is a letter addressed to W. T. Harris, editor of the *Journal*, on October 21, 1886:

Should you like to look at a psychological article on "the Perception of

Time" which I have just written. Possibly it might be fit to publish in the Journal of Spec. Phil.

I can claim no special originality for it; but it brings together a lot of information in the shape of opinions from recent authors and experimenters, and so may be useful to some readers. If you would like to see it I will send it to you ("Pragmatist to Publisher: Letters of William James to W. T. Harris," ed. Wallace Nethery, *The Personalist*, 49 [Autumn 1968], #25, p. 500. Quotation is made from the originals in the Hoose Library, University of Southern California.)

In response to a lost reply, James sent the article off on October 24: "I send you herewith the MS, which I am afraid you will find too long for insertion in a single number. It can be curtailed a good deal by omitting quotations. Please let me know after looking at it how you should prefer to have it, or if you care to have it at all—I don't want you to buy a pig in a poke—and I will do what is required" (#26, p. 500). On an undated postcard postmarked October 29, 1886, James wrote: "I am very much pleased with your appreciation, and delighted you can print the stuff *in extenso* and so soon. You will of course let me have a proof" (#27, p. 501). On another postcard, postmarked November 23: "Before sending my MS. on Time to the printer I had better see it again. I want to add a paragraph, and possibly shorten it a bit elsewhere" (#28, p. 501, dictated). On February 6, 1887, there is another postcard that James is sending the proof (#29, p. 501), and, finally, on October 2, 1887, a postcard of inquiry why he has not received complimentary copies of the *Journal* containing his article (#30, p. 501). On November 9, 1887, he wrote to G. C. Robertson:

I published a paper on "the ['Sensa' *del.*] Perception of Time" in the last Journal of Spec. Philos. (the one yclept October 1886) which possibly you may be interested to read. Much of it is mere compilation; but the core of the thing is a view I have nowhere seen, that our *intuited* ['sensations of' *del.*] time is only a few seconds long, and is a genuine sensation, due to a nerve-process which I try to adumbrate hypothetically (bMS Am 1092.9 [3547]).

The writing of this article on Time preceded by two or more months James's first dispatch of copy to Holt. From Vogelius' note of December 17, 1886, enclosing proofs up to page 170, we know that Chapter VI had been written by that date, but information is wanting whether the copy James had submitted in December extended as far as this "Perception of Time," Chapter XV. Whether it did or not, the fact that it represents the chapter so substantially, combined with James's willingness to cut it for journal publication, suggests strongly that James's manuscript had progressed as far as Chapter XV by October 1886, and even beyond, always allowing for the possibility that all of the chapters need not have been written in strict order. For instance, on April 22, 1888, James wrote to Théodule Ribot: "I am ashamed to say that I know your articles on Attention only through the resumé of one of my students. I have been postponing the reading of them till next winter, when I shall have to revise a chapter of my own on attention, written last year" (bMS Am 1092.1). If this is literally true, Chapter XI (which should have been included in the initial proof) had not been written for the first stage of the book; but of course James may instead be referring to such a markedly different version of an early chapter that he could consider that he had, instead, written it in 1887. The matter is obscure. In other respects what was already a chapter and what an article (actual or planned) later to be made into a chapter, may be at this time a doubtful point. For instance, Chapter XXIV, "Instinct," is referred to in quite specific terms in a letter to George Croom Robertson on October 4, 1886: "In looking at my 'Space' I found it would take up certainly more than 100 of Mind's pages—how much more I can't say. So since you seemed dependent on something I looked over my other MSS, and after first choosing, and then rejecting on account of its length & lack of novelty a very *readable* paper on Instinct, concluded to send you the 1st half—the 2nd will be ['if any' *del.*] a little shorter by my computations, of a chapter on the Ego" (3540). In a later letter to Robertson on March 19, 1887, James referred again to the work on Instinct, now published: "The same is less true[2] of an article on Instinct I sent you a fortnight since, ['an' *del.*] which will soon be followed by some others in the Pop. Sci. These are parts of chapters written for my book, but out of which I meanwhile turn an honest penny.—If I ever get writing again I ['shall' *del.*] suppose I shall have to alternate my contributions" (3544). The reference is to "Some Human Instincts," *Popular Science Monthly*, 31 (June, September 1887), 160–170, 666–681 (McD 1887:8), or at least to one of its parts, which can therefore be assigned as an article derived from a chapter composed before October 1886.[3]

[2]The preceding sentences in the letter had been: "The paper on Habit of which you write was a mere pot-boiler which I had long had, written, in my drawer. No new thing in it, so I hardly advise you to read it."

[3]James does not mention to Robertson "What Is an Instinct?" *Scribner's Magazine*, 1 (March 1887), 355–365 (McD 1887:6), also drawn from the chapter. The first reference, on October 4, 1886, in speaking of the length of the paper on Instinct, appears to refer to both parts.

On the other hand, the earlier Chapter XX, "The Perception of Space," *Mind*, 12 (January, April, July, October 1887), 1-30, 183-211, 321-353, 516-548 (McD 1887:4), which was discussed in the March 1887 letter mentioning "Instinct" as existing as a chapter, was vaguely associated in James's mind as a book chapter when it was originally started, about 1881, as a revision of some ideas in "The Spatial Quale" of 1879. Several references suggest at least two layers of revision of the original matter with a book chapter in mind. One of these references comes in a letter of November 8, 1886, to Robertson rejoicing that he had accepted "Space" instead of an article on the Ego James had first sent and, in course, James wrote: "I bungled the matter from the first. Had I supposed you would print a thing in so many parts, I should have sent it to you two years ago—not to speak of the other day" (3542). The two years perhaps came to James's mind because of a revision that made something of a proposed book chapter which in early 1884 James almost sent abroad to Ribot to make and publish a French translation (see below). Perhaps acting on this stimulus, James must have continued his work on the subject, for a still later state of revision seems to be represented by his statement in a letter to Robertson on April 28, 1887, "Most of No IV [i.e., *the fourth section of the article*] was writ last year, and is *freer ['ee' ov. 'es'] and more entertaining" (3545). This would put the shaping of the earlier material, and a major addition, within the period of activity that led to his submission of initial copy (but not including "Space") to Holt in early December 1886. Thus it seems clear that the chapter on Space Perception in its book form, at least, followed on the final writing of the article for *Mind*, and not vice versa.

If the article on the Ego that he first submitted to *Mind* in a letter of October 4, 1886, is to be related to what was subsequently to become part of Chapter X, "The Consciousness of Self," after much revision, then it is clear that this chapter had by no means taken final form by October 4, 1886, and was most unlikely to have been part of the copy sent to Holt in early December of the same year. In the October 4 letter to Robertson after announcing that he had sent the first part of "a chapter on the Ego" James continued:

Much of it is altogether *banal* & hackneyed, but there is no time to change. In the *2nd ['2' ov. 's'] part I review the "theories" of the Ego, and strive to give a clearer *statement ['st' ov. 'ac'] than any yet pub^d of the purely phenomenalistic *conception [¹'c' ov. 'a'] thereof. This 2nd part is the more important but it leaned on the 1st so that I *could ['ou' ov. 'an'] not without much reediting, send it alone.

I regard the whole treatment *(so far as not merely descriptive) [*parens ov. commas*] as provisional, on account of the problem left unsolved on p. 136ᵇ. I *am [*ov.* 'was'] tempted to ask you to publish it anonymously, but conclude on the whole to leave my name. Having got the thing once into print in this shape, I can start to revise it far better than if it were not thus objectified. I find that printing a thing *dispossesses* me of it in a surprising way, and leaves me free to go against it as I otherwise should not be.

I doubt whether there be time for a proof. But please return me the MS as soon as you have done with it. I may need it for my class before January arrives. I will forward the 2nd part whenever you need it (3540).

On November 8, 1886, James heard of Robertson's acceptance of "The Perception of Space" (offered on October 17 [3541]) and wrote: "To tell the truth, I had vastly rather print the space than the Ego. The 2nd half of the latter is, though original, still unripe. The half already printed [i.e., *he assumes, already set in type by* Mind] is quite commonplace." A little later in the letter he queried, "Can't you stereotype the *Ego ['E' *ov.* 'e'] already printed and keep it thus indefinitely?" The next day James added a second section to the letter in which he informed Robertson: "Meanwhile your card has come this AM. expressing further doubts, and urging me not to fail to send the ego. As that is already gone, it will be all right so far. But I do hope you will see your way to the space instead" (3542). On December 27, 1886, after expressing his pleasure that "The Perception of Space" would substitute for his article on the Ego, James added:

I am very sorry, too, that the "composition" of the Ego article is a dead loss, and since the whole thing grew out of my own personal shilly shallying I insist on paying that bill, and confidently expect you to send it to me. Don't prevaricate—there is no possible reason for its being anyone's loss but mine. Work of that kind *costs [*ov.* 'is'] so much less with you than here that I cannot guess at the amount, or I'd send you an order at a venture. Remember, I count on this; and am glad to get off so cheap—for, sooth to say, the [*doubtful* 'mo' *del.*] Ego *as a whole* is not yet ripe for treatment at my hands—or rather I am not ripe for treating it (3543).

Even as late as November 4, 1888, the material on the Ego does not seem to have been worked into the final form of Chapter X, for in a letter of that date to Robertson James added the postscript: "The Ego business is unfinished still, and had better be left to the very last, when my wisdom shall be at its unsurpassable climax!" (3550). Whether any of this material was worked into "The Hidden Self," *Scribner's Magazine*, 7 (March 1890), 361–373 (McD 1890:1) is not to be demonstrated but is possible since James was likely to turn such available popular material into money. One may refer back to his description to Renouvier on

August 5, 1883, of his difficulties with this material on the Ego, quoted in the letter concerning "On Some Omissions of Introspective Psychology" above.

If these extracts make it clear that Chapter X, "The Consciousness of Self," could not have been a part of the manuscript sent to Holt in December of 1886, the case is even clearer for Chapter XX, "The Perception of Space," the history of which is worth quoting from various letters. This article had its inception in "The Spatial Quale," published in the *Journal of Speculative Philosophy*, 13 (1879), 64–87 (McD 1879:6), which James confessed to Royce in 1880 had been "dashed off for a momentary purpose and published for another" (3596). But in the same letter he sturdily asserted that the basic ideas were sound and if his Psychology were ever to get written he would set them down in clear and orderly form. That he had worked on this favorite subject as a prospective chapter is clear from a letter of February 26, 1884, to Théodule Ribot, editor of the *Revue Philosophique*:

> As for my Psychology bad eyes and nerves, and lots of other work, keep it at a complete standstill, so that I am ashamed I ever spoke of it. It advances somewhat in my head, but nowhere else. . . . You ask for a chapter to translate. I am much obliged for the honour. I have now a chapter all but finished which I should be glad to see translated or published in any way in advance of the (only possible) book. It is on *the perception of space* and would probably take up 60–70 of your pages, perhaps even a few more. It is thoroughly empirical, has a good many new points, and having worked over it a great deal, it seems to me the best thing I have so far written (bMS Am 1092.1, typed copy).

However, on June 29, responding to Ribot's offer to publish the article sight unseen, James wrote:

> I received your letter a couple of weeks ago and felt much flattered at your willingness to accept my long lucubration on Space. I had to wait many days before looking it over . . . but when . . . I took out my unfinished manuscript to see if it was in a fit state for the honour of a french translation *I feared to send it.* That is, I feared to let the first part go until I was sure of the termination. The number of pages lacking is not great but their content is important, and I will not risk the beginning till the end is sure. I expect to finish the thing in the autumn; and if it turns out well, I will without fail transmit it (typed copy).

The evidence suggests that although James may have continued to work on the material, he never entirely finished it and so never offered it to Ribot. We next hear of the matter in the letter to G. Croom Robertson, editor of *Mind*. On October 4, 1886, as already noted, James passed over his Space and Instinct articles because of their length and sent instead one on the Ego. Second thoughts soon assailed him, and on October 17, 1886, he wrote:

Altho I conscientiously refrained from sending you my Space MS the other *day ['d' *ov.* 's'], my mind has been hovering round the subject ever since, wishing there were some possible way for it to see the light. There is a good deal of labour packed away in it, and the exposition of a part of it rests on, first a statement, and then a confutation by the facts in detail, of Helmholtz's doctrines of unconscious inference['s' *del.*] and of the intellectual character of our perception. It has struck me that if the foul fiend should enter into H. during the preparation of *this ['is' *ov.* 'e'] new edition of his physiol. Optics, and lead him to abandon his old errors and publish a true space-doctrine just to spite me, it would be an ['af' *del.*] awful thing for my "reputation." The world would, it is true be ['withou' *del.*] rid of the duty of reading my stuff, but where should *I* be?

Accordingly I made an exact calculation last night of the number of pages the MS. would occupy of the *smaller* print of Mind, and found it to be just 80—add five for woodcuts and accidents, and you have 85. This I am sure will cover everything.

If, then you care for so long a thing as that, printed in that type,—I am willing to contribute, if desired, funds up to £10″0″0 to pay for extra ['compos' *del.*] cost of [' "composition"' *del.*] "composing"—I *shall ['all' *ov.* 'ould'] be glad to *send ['sen' *ov.* *doubtful* 'ask'] you the MS whenever you are ready. Pray note that I do not ask this of you as a favor, but simply ask ['for' *del.*] your own editorial impulse to manifest itself & set my mind at rest.

The thing seems to me decidedly solid; but of course I am no judge (3541).

On November 8, 1886, acknowledging the receipt of Robertson's card agreeing to the substitution of the Space article, James writes that he has had to spend the day participating in activities celebrating the 250th anniversary of Harvard's founding "though I should rather have been tinker-|[ing] at the text of my *Space*. I am so afraid of getting it to you late, however, that I will despatch it without the *careful [*intrl.*] revision it might perhaps advantageously receive." Then after telling how he had bungled the offer of the Space article from the start (in a passage already quoted), he adds: "I don't mind your putting space into the smaller type a jot. On the contrary I think I should *prefer it*. It is too dry and full of detail for a literary presentation, and 3 instalments are surely better than 4, of anything.—However, I leave that to you." On the next day he continues in the same letter:

I have been revising all the morning (and "cutting" my lecture so to do) and send you herewith (registered) the first 80 pp. of the darned old MS. . . . But I do hope you will see your way to the space instead [*of the Ego article*]. It grows better & better as it advances. I have recomputed the pages, & fear it may be ['four numbers' *del.*] 120, ['pages,' *del.*] even of the smaller type. *So pray don't put it into the larger*. If there are any ['extra' *del.*] damages to pay for extra composition in the *printing['ing' *ov.* 'er's']-office I shall be glad to foot the bill; and I will ['forthwith' *del.*] have the ['the' *del.*] electrotype ['p' *del.*] blocks made for the woodcuts which appear in the later parts and send them to you by express in due time. In the last resort, however, I understand that you must yourself choose—so don't ruin Mind on my account (3542).

Robertson's final decision in favor of "The Perception of Space" is replied to on December 27, 1886: "I am glad you have decided for *Space*—in fact very glad. But very sorry it has caused delay." After offering to pay for the discarded typesetting of the Ego article, he adds: "I send you another installment of Ms. which will more than suffice for the April number, in whichever type you put it. I will get the blocks made for the cuts, which will all be in the July instalment—possibly a few for October, and send you the rest of the MS. betimes. You *will [*intrl.*] have *now* considerably the larger half" (3543).

The correspondence continues with James's letter of March 19, 1887, beginning: "Your letter *of the 7th [*intrl.*] arrives just after I have sent off the end of the Space MS. I am sorry you should have been troubled at the bulk of the last remittance, which was not ['necessarily' *del.*] meant to fit all into No III, but only sent that you might yourself make the most convenient division. Neither III nor IV ought to exceed 30 pages of any sort of type. The reason why I did n't send the whole MS at once was that I was having the latter 3/4 of it copied, as an insurance" (3544). The last sentence suggests the relation between the article and the book, although James was putting the best face on his installment mailings, a major reason certainly being the revision he was making in the copy during the intervals. A letter to Robertson dated April 28, 1887, discusses more details of publication but also comments on the article itself:

I send, registered, herewith, the corrected proofs and the blocks to print the figures, of Space-perception No III. The Proofs are much bescribbled o'er, and would look neater had the printer vouchsafed wider margins to his slips. I made the break only a few lines farther on than the earlier place you suggested. There is a longish addition to the already overlong note, and a MS. addition on a loose sheet, *for [*ab. del.* 'of'] which you will easily find the *proper [*insrtd.*] place. I don't see how there can be any difficulty about placing the figures after my indications. I have marked figs 5 & 6 on the proof as if they were to come in without interrupting the text. I think it will be better to put them in a break with the number of the figure printed under each.

I keep what remains of the proof, to begin article IV, and send back with the remaining blocks and rest of the proof, whenever I shall get the latter. I'm sure No IV will be less than 30 pp., now.

I. The History

In rereading this stuff which I send, I feel that it might be much improved by writing over again. I wrote it six years ago. But its a spiny subject at best, and hard to expound without taxing the reader's attention, so perhaps its not worth while to fret too much about the form. Most of No IV was writ last year, and is *freer ['ee' *ov.* 'es'] and more entertaining (3545).

More tinkering with the text is shown in a letter of May 12, 1887:

I[t] suddenly shoots across me that the *note on the "Feeling of Effort"* (whose place is indicated in the margin of the galley ['la' *del.*] herewith enclosed) ought to be omitted altogether from the article, with so much of the text as belongs with it, or ought to be supplemented by something like what I enclose. I should prefer the latter course. But I am inclined to think it will prove too late for either. In that case, the article must go to press with all its imperfections on its head, and Mach must think me *an['d' *del.*] *oberflächlicher Ausländer.*[4]
I felt in reading the last proof how much a great deal of it would gain in clearness by being all written over again.[5] That's the advantage of seeing *a [*ov.* 'it'] thing in print—it *exteriorates*, and you can judge it as a foreign body.

I am keeping the remaining proof slips to send all together, with the end of the essay, when I get the proofs of it, and the remainder of the blocks (3546).

When the preparation of the essay was in mid-career, James wrote on February 6, 1887, to Karl Stumpf:

I found to my surprise & pleasure that Robertson was willing to print my chapter on Space in Mind even tho' it should run through all 4 numbers of the year. So I sent it to him. Most of it was written 6 or even *7 [*ov.* '8'] years ago. To tell the truth, I am *off* of Space now, and can probably carry my little private ingenuity concerning it no farther than I have already done in this essay; and fearing that some evil fiend might put it into Helmholtz's mind to correct all his errors *& tell the full truth [*intrl.*] in the new edition of his Optics, I felt it was high time that what I had written should see the light and not be lost. It is dry stuff to read, and I hardly dare to recommend it to you. . . . Space is really a direfully difficult subject! The third dimension bothers me very much still.—I have this very day corrected the proofs of an essay on the *Perception ['P' *ov.* 'p'] of Time, which I will send you when it *shall [*intrl.*] appear, in the Journal of Speculative Philosophy for October last. . . . I rather enjoyed the writing of it. I have just begun a Chapter on "Discrimination & Comparison," subjects which have long been stumbling blocks in my path. Yesterday it seemed to me that I could perhaps do nothing

---

[4]It was, in fact, too late, as Part III (p. 347) appeared with the offending footnote to the sentence "I have elsewhere tried to show that the observations by no means warrant the conclusions drawn from them, and that the feeling in question is probably a wholly fictitious entity." In *Principles*, II, 236.34-37 (868.33-869.3) James wrote instead, "I shall elsewhere try to show that . . . entity" with a footnote referring the reader to Chapter XXIV, and not to "The Feeling of Effort."

[5]James's rewriting in *Principles* was fairly extensive.

better than just translate §§6 & 7 of the first *Abschnitt* of your Tonpsychologie, which is worth more than every thing else put together, which has been
written on the subject. But I will stumble on and try to give to it a more
personal form. I shall, however, borrow largely from you (3782).

From the fall of 1886 when James and Robertson agreed that
"Space" would be published in *Mind* until the last letter to Robertson on May 12, 1887, about the publication of "The Perception
of Space," and even in later letters of November 9, 1887 (3547),
and August 22 (3548) and October 7, 1888 (3549)—these latter
two concerned with Robertson's criticism of the Space article and
James's reply, "The Psychological Theory of Extension," *Mind*, 14
(January 1889), 107-109 (McD 1889:1)—no mention of another
article occurs, but only complaints that either his teaching or his
summer work on the farm prevents his writing. The letter of November 9, 1887, seems to contain his last words on the subject of
Space: "To tell the sober truth about the matter, I fancy I have
done all about Space that my poor powers are capable of, in that
little essay. Now that I have 'extradited' it, I feel no longer any
personal connexion with it, and am willing to let it drift and take
its chances in the ['ocean of' *del.*] literary ocean. If it have merit
it will probably float. If it sink 'tis that it will deserve to. And
others may see to it if they will" (3547).

Meanwhile a few references to his work come in family or
professional letters. In a continuation dated September 19 of a
letter to Henry of September 1, 1887 (already quoted), James
hoped to complete the book by Christmas, or at least during the
winter.

On November 24, 1887, he wrote to Henry, in discouragement:

A strange coldness has come over me with reference to all my deeds and
productions, within the past 6 months. I dont know whether it be the passage
under the meridian of 45 years, or *due to [*intrl.*] a more *reparable [*ab.
del.* 'transient'] cause, but everything I've done and shall do seems so
small. . . . Life has been absolutely monotonous since the beginning of the
term. I do my work *tant bien que mal*, try to get a few hours for writing, but
they amount to very few, and see a limited number of people (2635).

And on April 19, 1888, again to Henry, "I am well and plodding
away *in [*ov.* 'at'] my slow fashion, with incessant interruptions
from 'bad days' at my work" (2637). Something of the same tone
is heard in a letter to Théodule Ribot on May 13: "My Psychology,
to which you give such publicity in advance [*in* Revue Philoso-
phique], still lags behind. It is one thing to write chapters,
another to write a book, on a subject of which the first principles
are as yet undetermined." In another to Ribot, July 5, James is

more cheerful: "[I] hope to finish my 'Psychology' in the next couple of months. It will need much revision in passing through the press. It has stuck to my fingers so long that I am quite sick and tired of it, and long to plunge into some other department of study" (bMS Am 1092.1).

However, the summer did not go well and on August 22, 1888, James is full of complaints to G. Croom Robertson: "As ['you' *del.*] usual, the record of my work is a record of frustration and disappointment. I had hoped ere this to have written a certain amount this vacation, but sleep and all *the [*ov. doubtful* 'ot'] other requisites have played me false again, so I've done hardly anything" (3548). And on October 7: "I am teaching Ethics and the Philosophy of Religion for the first time, with that dear old duffer of a Martineau's works as a text. It gives me lots to do, as I only began my systematic reading in that line three weeks ago, having wasted the summer in farming (if such it can be called) and psychologizing. My Psychology will therefore have to be postponed another year, for with as much College work as I have this year I can't expect to write a line of it" (3549). One would expect the "psychologizing" to have been some writing unconnected with the book, but if so (or if it were only making notes) within a month of October 7 he was offering two articles.

On November 4, 1888, James mailed the manuscript for "The Psychology of Belief," *Mind*, 14 (July 1889), 321–352 (McD 1889:4) to Robertson: "Before I sent you 'Space,' you remember you wrote me that you wanted articles more lively and popular than you often got for Mind. I venture to send you part of a Chapter on Belief which I wrote *last ['la' *ov.* 'th'] as possibly less technical than the common run of contributions. It is, as you will readily see, quite unoriginal, and yet I cleared up my own ideas a little in writing it. By putting the ['number' *del.*] numerous quotations in smaller type, it will easily fall within your usual length. It contains, the type writer[6] tells me, 17,500 words" (3550). It is clear that this article, drawn from Chapter XXI, "The Perception of Reality," had not been available in October 1886, just as it seems clear that Chapter XX, "The Perception of Space," hardly existed as a real chapter at that date. In the interval, then, James wrote this Chapter XXI, but just when is uncertain. Unfortunately he seemed about to specify when he started the phrase "I wrote th" (perhaps *this* to be followed by a season, like spring), but before finishing the word he altered it to "last" and then either

---

[6]This is James's usual word for *typist*.

intended this word to stand for the last-composed article or else he inadvertently omitted the time that could have followed. Perhaps James concealed the exact time in order not to admit that he had done more on the book than he chose to state, especially in view of his letter the next day to W. T. Harris. At any rate, he continues to Robertson that his college work takes so much time "that I don't expect to be able to write a single page this year. Meanwhile a considerable psychologic manuscript is rotting on my desk and growing obsolete for mere lack of its complement. Most of the chapters are too long for articles, but by working a few of them off in this way I relieve myself of the burden of so much ['of my' *del.*] dead or dying matter, once a part of my *self ['s' *ov.* 'S']. A published thing is something which one no longer appropriates" (3550). But we now know from a letter of February 15, 1888, to his wife Alice that on that day he was sitting down to write a new chapter, "the perception of reality" (1529). When the chapter was completed has apparently not been recorded; however, the normal inference would be that it need not have taken more than a month or two. Thus whether James had skipped ahead to the last chapter, or whether his writing on *Principles* by late 1888 consisted chiefly of addition and revision, it is true that on November 5, 1888, he offered Harris, editor of the *Journal of Speculative Philosophy*, an article that concerned the subject of Chapter XXVIII, "Necessary Truths and the Effects of Experience":

I have an Essay which might take 50 or 60 pages of print, on the relation of necessary propositions to experience—"Mental Structure & Experience" is its title—which has been the result of a good deal of thinking on my part, and which I imagine would be found instructive by a certain number of readers. I consequently should be glad to see it published—but its length seems to unfit it for any of the reviews. However, I seem to remember certain past articles in your "Journal" which were exceptionally long; and, on the chance that you might possibly consider the matter as feasable, I venture to write this and ask whether it be worth while to send the MS. for your inspection (*Personalist*, #33, p. 502. Quoted from the original in the Hoose Library, University of Southern California.).

On November 6, in a dictated letter, he answered Harris: "Much obliged for your confidence in *blindly* offering to print my long Essay. Won't it be better for me to send you the manuscript when you are ready to have it put into type? I may need to refer to it myself between now and then and don't like to send it to you and ask to have it back again so soon. Still, if you wish to see it before fully making up your mind I will gladly send it" (#34, p. 503). James was well aware of Harris' dilatory publication of the *Journal*, but one may surmise that he was still at work on the chapter proper and had no extra copy of his manuscript. Unfortunately, the *Journal* suspended publication before James's article could appear and thus we have no means of knowing the relationship of the article to the final form of the chapter. There is nothing improbable in speculating, however, that between the spring of 1887 and November of 1888 James had completed some form of Chapters XXI–XXVIII.

That early 1889 found the book well advanced (even though the final touches were not to be made until a year later) is suggested by James having initiated inquiries about English publication, as seen in a letter of April 13, 1889, from Holt who stated that his firm usually handled these rights and divided the profits with the author and that James's contract, to which he should refer, is drawn with that provision. However, if James wishes to handle the matter himself, Holt will agree provided James does not involve Holt and does not interfere with the American market. To this he adds a postscript that he is sending a new contract embodying revisions he has made in this standard form since James first signed over eleven years ago, and ends, "When, as it looks to you now, ought the book to be ready?" (HLB no. 12, p. 285; part copy at Harvard, bMS Am 1092 [412]. From this point, some of the Henry Holt correspondence is known only from typed copies preserved at Harvard which seem to have been transcribed, probably by Henry James, Jr., from Holt's personal business letter books, no longer extant, as distinct from those of the firm that are preserved in the Holt Archives at Princeton. The initials HLB denote these copies, to distinguish them from LB, the Princeton letter books.) On April 17 James replied that he would like to see the improved contract and that Holt should make what arrangements he can for publishing abroad since James is unlikely to be able to do any better himself. He adds, "The book ought *certainly* to be finished by July, 1890" (HLB). The contract was sent on April 18 (HLB no. 12, p. 302; part copy at Harvard bMS Am 1092.1 [413]). According to a Holt memorandum dated April 21, 1910, the royalty on sales to England had been set at 14.3 cents in the original contract of June 12, 1878; but in a letter to James of April 25, 1891, Holt volunteered that justice would be served by an increase to 33 1/3 cents (Holt Archives, Princeton, James folder).

In 1889 a letter of February 3 to Mrs. Christine Ladd-Franklin discusses eyeball movements at length and James sends her a manuscript that he calls "printer's copy" (Columbia).[7] As late as August 12, 1889, in a letter to Ribot from London, he is full of confidence, after attending a Congress in Paris: "I go home quite 'set up' as a psychologist and shall finish my everlasting text book on that subject with infinitely more interest and zeal after finding

[7] The discussion seems to concern Chapter XIX, "The Perception of Things," even though the references to the putty experiment and to Mach are not identifiable. The whole letter is worth quoting for its explication of James's ideas: "You ask for a 'brief word of reply' and I send you a lot of printer's copy! It is easier to send you what I've already written than to write afresh, however briefly, so pray forgive the *inundation. [*ab. del.* '*Ueberschüttung.*'] The first two pages deal with the putty experiment—those from 39 to 41 with another of Mach's proofs, which I confess seemed to me at one time as if possibly convincing (see Mind XII, 347 note), but which, I am now quite *sure, is [*ab. del.* 'convinced, is more naturally'] to be interpreted in a ['quite' *del.*] different way. I trust you may have no difficulty in understanding so many pages of MS. torn from their context.

As for your own remark about the illusion of movement 'when both eyes are pushed up, say, with the fingers,' that does n't stagger me, either. *Primitively,* I take it, any relative movement of retina and object ['is interpreted as' *del.*] makes us see the object as moving. By experience we learn to correct this impression under certain conditions, the usual ones being the *intention* to move our own head or eyes. Even then however the correction is not absolute: I detect an apparent movement of the entire field of view whenever I move my own head and eyes rapidly. Usually however, we *overlook* this apparent movement, *for we [*ab. del.* 'and'] *know* that the objects are at rest. Now the condition of moving the eyeballs by the fingers is an entirely unusual one, unpreceded by the usual condition of moving the eyes (which is *the ['th' *ov.* 'a'] wandering of the attention to another part of the field or point out of the field) and unaccompanied by the usual condition of moving the head (which is muscular sensations in the neck or other part of the body, or knowledge that we are *riding [*ab. del.* 'driving'] through space). What wonder *then [*intrl.*] that the correction usually applied fails? What wonder that the primitive feeling persists unrebuked? A test would be this: Let someone try nudging his eyeball in a uniform manner a [*doubtful* 'once twice' *del.*] number of times a day, for several weeks—Would the illusion finally disappear, or tend to disappear? I should expect it would;^x | **It must be remembered that [*in mrgn.*] but am prevented by my [*doubtful* 'own' *del.*] bad asthenopia from playing any['th' *del.*] tricks at all with my own organs of vision. How should you like to try yourself?

I thank you heartily for taking my opinions so very seriously. Munsterberg's little book, die Willenshandlung 1888, is much the most original and vigorous thing on the will with which I am acquainted. He also discards the *Innervationsgefühl ['I' *ov.* *doubtful* 'i']."

In a letter subscribed merely "Cambridge April 29" James wrote again to Mrs. Ladd-Franklin: "Do you happen by any accident, still to have a letter which I wrote you last year (or possibly earlier) about illusions of motion, and the primitive condition of our sensation of motion being that of the relative motion of background and moving body. I happen to be writing on the subject again, and feel as if what I then said might help me. But it is hardly possible that you should have kept the letter" (both letters in Columbia University Library). Whether this date was 1891 or 1892 is not known, nor is the work which he is writing positively identified, although the odds are that it was *Briefer Course.* Also, whether the presence of the letter among Mrs. Ladd-Franklin's papers at Columbia is an indication that she did not return the letter is unknown.

myself in presence of this large number of persons to whom the subject is a reality" (bMS Am 1092.1). The beginning of 1890 saw James prepared to submit some early copy. On January 11 he informed Holt:

As usual I am late. The chapters I hoped to have finished before the end of the Christmas holiday are hardly done yet. Within a week however they will be completed, possibly within 3 or 4 days, and I shall have some 350 pages of manuscript ready to go to press, and to be followed up by the rest with probably very little delay. Rewriting the first chapter was hard because it made me re-read the entire physiology of the brain again, and like a fool I didn't destroy my original manuscript but tried to patch old and new together with the result of a fearful loss of time. The thing now satisfies me very well (HLB).

This reference to rewriting sounds as if James had revised at this late date the original version of the chapter, presumably in the state in which it had been sent to Holt in December 1886. The letter continues with questions about the manufacture of the cuts that will be required, whether to be made in Boston or in New York, and ends with the plan to come to New York on January 25 "with a good instalment of Ms." A brief note doubtfully dated on the copy January 15, 1890, begins, "All right then—we'll await the Spring for putting the book through the press" (HLB) probably in answer to some lost letters between the two in which James pressed for the start of typesetting of the manuscript he proposed to bring to New York, although the letter would as easily fit in after the New York visit either in answer to a lost Holt letter or to their discussion at the time. The visit was postponed for a few days, seemingly because of a serious illness for one of the James children: on January 28 James wrote to Holt about dining together in New York and the need for him to return promptly; he promises, "I will then dictate my 'epitaph' to you, sign contract, and get the arrangements for printing (page etc. settled) so as to lose no time when the MS. is finished" (HLB).

At some point in this January correspondence, perhaps in response to James's letter of January 11, but certainly before the New York trip, Holt warned James that though he would be glad to see the pages of manuscript that James felt should be used as immediate copy to get the printer started, "don't bring me anything to start making the book before you bring me the MS. complete. When you do that latter, we'll try and dispose all the orbs in the system to make the world roll smoothly" (Charles A. Madison, *The Owl among Colophons* [New York: Holt, Rinehart and Winston, 1966], p. 46). At first James seems to have agreed, but not for long despite the incomplete state of the manuscript.

On March 21, 1890, a chapter remained to be written and five or six to be revised. Yet James is chivvying Holt because Holt will not start typesetting until all copy is in his hands, and because Holt has declined to receive the Harvard Library books for making woodcuts that James proposed to bring to New York during vacation:

As for the MS. I confess I don't know why you need the whole of it en bloc in your own hands, before printing begins. After this week of recess I shall write a chapter which may take 3 weeks at the outside and complete the book. Some 1700 pp. of MS. will then be ready for the printer without another touch from me. There will remain 5 or 6 chapters, some of which need slight retouches and additions, which can be added by me perfectly well in the intervals of correcting proofs, thereby enabling the latter to begin about the first of May. The *whole* work as I said will then be *written*, only those few chapters not *revised*. Time is so precious now that I don't see what possible thing is risked by proceeding to press with the revised mass [?mss]. The rest *could* be printed without revision, but it will be better to go over it again. Write and tell me what is your decree. I want to get forward now with the least possible delay (Holt Archives, Princeton, James folder, typed copy).

His brother Henry is thanked on April 2, 1890, for having sent the electrotype blocks (presumably from "The Perception of Space" in *Mind* [see #2635, November 24, 1887, for the original request]), and James adds, after some discussion of Henry's latest work, "My own book gets on steadily, and August will see it published, at this rate" (2654). On April 2 Holt answered James's letter of March 21 by a patient explanation of the difficulties caused printers by typesetting from incomplete manuscript, with the certain delays that in his experience had always ensued. He writes bluntly, "Your letter makes plain what I took for granted—that your MS. will not be ready as early as May 1." He sends a duplicate of the new contract which James had mislaid, and advises James to complete his manuscript if he wishes to get forward with the least delay. He adds, "I have just seen a contract signed by you to give us that MS. June 12/80 and yet, you, you, you, Brute (2 syllables) revile me for being a demon!" (HLB, no. 14, p. 256; typed copy at Harvard, bMS Am 1092 [414]). James answered on April 5, in part:

How those vermin of authors must have caused you to suffer in your time to wring from you such a tirade! Well, it has been very instructive to me to grasp the publishers point of view. Your fatal error however has been in not perceiving that I was an entirely *different kind* of author from any of those whom you had been in the habit of meeting, and that *celerity*, celerity incarnate, is the motive and result of all my plans and deeds. It is not fair to throw that former contract into my face, when you know or ought to know that when the ten years or a little more from the time of its signature had elapsed I wrote to you that you must get another man to write this book for you, and that, as things were then going, I didn't see how I could ever finish it.[8]

James concluded by protesting against a clause in the contract requiring him to prepare matter for a new edition on demand, and by requesting that a former clause to provide him with twenty free copies be reinstated (Holt Archives, Princeton, James folder). Holt wrote a soothing letter on April 7, pointing out the purely formal status of the matter of a new edition. "And now may you have all the blessings necessary to keep you up to your standard of 'celerity', and a few marginal ones simply as illustrations of the affectionate nature of my prayers for you" (HLB, no. 14, p. 270; typed copy at Harvard, bMS Am 1092 [415]). In a response to Holt of April 8, James returned the signed new contract.

I add as you suggest, the clause about 20 copies; and I leave the clause about new matter for new editions; but I warn you clearly that I shall only consent to furnish such new matter in case it involves no great sacrifice. I can easily imagine myself engrossed in some other work hereafter, and having grown into such a state of disgust for my old psychology-book as to find the rehandling of it an intellectually impossible task. In that case I should calmly fold my arms and say "the book has had its day—let it be republished if at all as an historical monument, not as a sham exhibition of my present opinions." There comes a time in all books when[9] a man can't tinker them; he must write a new work altogether[10] (Holt Archives, Princeton, James folder).

Holt acknowledged receipt of the contract on April 14 and added, "If you don't have your manuscript ready May 1st, let that day be a day of fasting over your sins" (HLB, no. 14, p. 285; typed copy at Harvard, bMS Am 1092 [416]).

The end was approaching, but James did not meet the deadline.

[8]This is a curious statement since in 1888 the book seems to have been going well, James was in the full tide of writing, and he was optimistic about finishing the book in the near future. Certainly there seems to have been an earlier period of discouragement before 1886, but on March 10, 1887, he wrote to Henry that he was writing and hoped to finish in a year. On April 12, 1887, he told Henry that the book was two-thirds done. Of course, there were intervals of depression when his eyes failed him, and he may have written to Holt in one of these. No record seems to be preserved of such a letter.

[9]The remainder of the letter is lost in the autograph but preserved in a typed copy in the same folder.

[10]On the evidence of the interleaved copy of the first printing, James in fact kept in mind the possibility of a second edition and made notes for that purpose (as well as for his teaching from the book) at least as late as 1896 when his interest appears to have stopped. In a letter of March 3, 1892, to Mrs. Ladd-Franklin he remarks that he will take account of her views on Chapter XXVIII "if I ever do revise the book" (Columbia).

On May 7, 1890, he wrote to Holt:

If you will look at our contract I think you will see that it has yet over three weeks to run. I shall however be through in less than two, and as I am anxious, on every account, not to lose a single day, I don't see why we should n't be beginning already to decide on the page. The ms., to my great regret, is panning out bigger than I thought it would. I fear there will be no less than about 460,000 words, which would require 575 words on a page to make a book of 800 pp.[11] I cant poss-|sibly cut this thing down, as it all belongs together; and I trust this bulk will not unfit it for the "series." It is a disappointment to me not to have made a smaller book, that ['being' *del.*] having been my aim all along.

My calculation is n't *close*, as the pages are very irregularly written, & there are many notes, internal headings etc. But I feel pretty confident *now, that [*intrl.*] taking the "Mind" page, or the page of Ladd's Physiol. Psych. (Strange to say they contain each just about the same no. of words *(460) [*insrtd.*] although the Mind p. is so much smaller and handsomer-looking to my eye) my book will hardly fall inside of a 1000 of 'em! What shall be done? Two vols? or publish outside of the series?—or what? let me know please, forthwith. It is only this A.M. that I have been able to make the calculation with any definiteness, owing to the broken up condition of the MS. hitherto.

Meanwhile I send you some of the first sheets, to be used if you wish to make experiments (Holt Archives, Princeton, James folder).

On May 8 Holt responded:

We must get it into one volume,[12] and I think we can do so without having you realize that it looks any worse than Remsen's Chemistry. If fellows will write such long books, however, they must not expect beautiful big margins and wide spaces.

When I was angel enough to give you a month more than you asked for, I did not think you would be demon enough to use it as an excuse for not coming up to the scratch as proposed by yourself. That's the sort of world this is, however, yet I remain, | Faithfully yours (HLB, no. 14, p. 401; typed copy at Harvard, bMS Am 1092 [417]).

To this James responded the next day, May 9:

I was in hopes that you would propose to break away from the famous "Series" and publish the book independently, in two volumes. An abridgement could then be prepared for the Series. If there be anything which I loathe it is a mean overgrown page in small type, and I think the author's feelings ought to go for a good deal in the case of the enormous *rat* which his ten years gestation has brought forth.

In any event, I dread the summer and next year, with two new courses to teach, and, I fear, no vacation. What I wrote you, if you remember, was to send you the "heft" of the MS. by May 1st, the rest to be done in the

[11] The actual count, including index and prefatory matter, is 1412 pages.

[12] Since James had so consistently underestimated the length, the work necessarily appeared in two volumes.

intervals of proof-correcting. You however insisted on having the entire MS. in your hands before anything should be done. It seems to me that this delay is, *now* at any rate, absurd. There is certainly less than two weeks' work on the MS. undone. And every day got behind us now means a day of travel and vacation for me next September. I really think, considering the sort of risk I am running by the delay, that I must *insist* on getting to press now as soon as the page is decided on.

No one could be more disgusted than I at the sight of the book. *No* subject is worth being treated of in 1000 pages! Had I ten years more, I could rewrite it in 500; but as it stands it is this or nothing—a loathsome, distended, tumefied, bloated, dropsical mass, testifying to nothing but two facts: *1st,* that there is no such thing as a *science* of psychology, and *2nd,* that W. J. is an incapable (*The Letters of William James,* ed. Henry James, Jr., I, 293–294).

Holt refused to be moved, and on May 10 he answered: "I wonder what has destroyed your confidence in me! Haven't I told you twice, and given you long strings of reasons based on our experience hundreds of times as large as you can possibly have in such matters, that I am not going to set any of that book until I have it all? You may think that if I were to turn tail and do it, you would still have some faith in me, but you wouldn't, and I wouldn't have any in myself. I call the first of these results a serious disaster as well as the last" (HLB, no. 14, p. 413; typed copy at Harvard, bMS Am 1092 [418]).

One point should be mentioned here. Since by December 17, 1886, 170 pages of proof had been sent to James, it may seem odd that on May 7, 1890, James should be discussing a page size for the book. The answer is conjectural but reasonably certain. Especially in the days of hand-set type, the cost of keeping type standing for several years would have come to a considerable sum. Moreover, as James gave up active writing and then on resuming would have wished to revise thoroughly what he had already written, it may have been that at some point Holt decided that it would be cheaper to distribute the type and start from scratch when the final copy was handed him than to hold already set matter in type for an unknown and obviously lengthy period, with the possibility always present that the book might never be finished. If this were not what happened, it is odd indeed to find James discussing the page size, for on the evidence of Vogelius' references to proofs, the 1886 copy had been set directly into page proof and there is no indication at all that James was thinking of breaking up these pages into a different format. Indeed, the terms of James's discussion do not sound as if he were making calculations on the basis of text in type but instead of his manuscript against Ladd's *Elements of Physiological Psychology* and *Mind.*

Finally, his sending some of the first sheets of the manuscript for Holt to make experiments would have been useless if the type-setting (or plates) of the early chapters from 1886 had been available. It is a practical certainty, therefore, that the 1886 setting had been scrapped and that *Principles* was set up as a unit from final copy.

The exact date of James's completion of the manuscript can be pinpointed. On May 17, 1890, he wrote to his wife Alice: "Wrote hard pretty much all day . . . . 'Psychology' will certainly be finished by Sunday noon!" (*Letters*, I, 294–295). The next day, May 18, he wrote to Alice again: "The job is done! All but some paging and half a dozen little footnotes, the work is completed, and as I see it as a unit, I feel as if it might be rather a vigorous and richly colored chunk—for that kind of thing at least!" (*Letters*, I, 295). Also on May 18 he officially announced to Holt the completion:

My MS. is now finished and occupies (418 + 2552 =) 2970 pp., many of them pages of print. It will hardly go into 1000 pp. of the usual 8vo size. I base my calculation on the fact that it took just 90 pp. of my MS. to cover 30 of the Journal of Speculative Philosophy when my chapter on Taine appeared therein, which is now to be reprinted with hardly any addition or change.

I expect to ship it to you tomorrow or next day with the list of woodcuts carefully made out and the books from which the photographs are to be made. I shall then wash my hands of all farther responsibility except for the proofs, which I trust will be furnished at the utmost rate of velocity which the printing office can command. I shall be ready to give my whole time to correcting them from tomorrow on until they are done (HLB).

On May 19 he addressed Mrs. Christine Ladd-Franklin: "Congratulate me! I have this day finished the manuscript of a 'Principles of Psychology' which ought to be out in September, and which has been sticking to me like an old man of the sea for the last 8 or 9 years. I feel like a barrel with its hoops gone! and shall grow young again" (Columbia University). To his wife James wrote on May 22: "I sot up till two last night putting the finishing touches on the MS., which now goes to Holt in irreproachable shape, woodcuts and all. I insured it for $1000.00 in giving it to the express people this A.M. That will make them extra careful at a cost of $1.50" (*Letters*, I, 295). On May 24 he was relaxing:

I came home very weary, and lit a fire, and had a delicious two hours all by myself, thinking of the big *étape* of my life which now lay behind me (I mean that infernal book done) . . . . The joke of it is that I, who have always considered myself a thing of glimpses, of discontinuity, of *aperçus*, with no power of doing a big job, suddenly realize at the *end* of this task that it is the biggest book on psychology in any language except Wundt's, Rosmini's and Daniel Greenleaf Thompson's! Still, if it burns up at the printing-office, I shan't much care, for I shan't ever write it again!! (*Letters*, I, 295).

James wrote to his brother Henry on June 4:

The great event for me is the completion at last of my tedious book. I have been at my desk with it every day since I got back from Europe, and up at 4 in the morning with it for ['every da' *del.*] many a day of the last month. I have written every page 4 or 5 times over, and carried it "on my mind" for 9 years past, so you may imagine the relief. Besides I am glad to appear at last as a man who has done something more than make phrases and projects. I will send you a copy, in the Fall I trust, though H. Holt is so inert about starting the proofs that we may not get through till midwinter or later. *As Psychologies go*, it is a good one, but psychology is in such an ante-scientific condition that the whole present generation of them is predestined to become unreadable old mediaeval lumber, as ['firs' *del.*] soon the first genuine tracks of insight are made. The sooner the better, for me! (bMS Am 1092.9 [2655]).

His own delays ignored, James could not understand why proof had not been sent him immediately, although the completed manuscript had been dispatched only on May 22 and Holt had vowed not to start work until the whole had been received. On June 3, notifying Holt that proofs should be sent to him at Tamworth Iron Works, New Hampshire, he complained: "It is now a month or more since I sent you the opening pages of my MS. with a statement of excellent reasons why I wished to insist on getting the work immediately under way. It is a fortnight since the entire Ms. was forwarded. [¶] Under these conditions I feel no farther responsibility whatever about having the thing published by October. I shall take the vacation which I shall sorely need in September, in the form of a journey somewhither, no matter in what condition of forwardness the proofs may be at the time. After the beginning of the college year my duties will be so unusually heavy that the proofs must take whatever spare time they can get. I won't even promise to touch them at all until the following summer. I say this that there may be no misunderstanding on your part as to what you have a right to expect of me, and that you may govern your present treatment of the MS. accordingly" (HLB). On June 5 he responded to a lost letter from Holt:

I'm truly glad to find that you are still in so merry a humor over the delay. My solicitude to get ahead fast has been wholly due to what I supposed were my responsibilities to your interests. For myself, now that the Ms. is once done, the longer it is with[h]eld from the hands of my own students the better. For delay means ready-made stuff to lecture on, whilst publication means so much more work in providing new material. I hold therefore strictly to what I said in my last, about reserving the month of September and making no pledges for next year; and you can take your measures accordingly.

The mysteries of your trade are unknown to me, but I confess it surprises me that the time of nearly three men for a fortnight should need to be employed in counting the number of words in a Ms. before a specimen page can be chosen. The total number is pretty certainly between 1000 and 1200 pp. of the size of that of Mind or of the J. of Spec. Phil. (I forget now just how many words that means) and I should think that the size of page which would be good on the estimate of 1000 could not be so very bad on the estimate of 1200. But of course you know this part of the business best; and indeed it may have more to do with forcasting the price than determining the page.

I'm sorry the manuscript is so bad. We can't all furnish copy like John Fiske's. This is the sort of stuff I have always furnished to the printers, and I have never yet heard any murmurs from them, or found that the proofs suffered from the copy's illegibility (HLB).

Proofs must have started to arrive on or shortly before June 21, for on that date he addressed Holt in a different tone: "All's well that ends well; so let's have no more recriminations nor apologies. Vive la horseplay, in secla seclorum! [¶] As for your dear delightful invitation [*to visit*], it would be very pleasant, but how do you expect me to correct proofs and to go gadding simultaneous? . . . it had better be in September when the proofs are non-existent. I have settled down for June, July and August on a working basis here" (HLB). A few days later, on June 26, James reported to Henry: "My proofs have only just begun coming in; but they promise to come thick and fast. I take little pride or pleasure in the accursed book, which has clung to me so long, but I shall be glad to have it out, just to show that I *can* write one book" (2656). He complained to James Sully on July 8, 1890, "My book ought to be out in October, but the printers are dawdling fearfully with the proofs and I fear it may not be out till the new year" (*Thought and Character*, II, 113). After returning from his summer home to Cambridge, James wrote to his sister Alice on July 23:

I snatch a breathing space between two batches of proofs to send you a word which I have long meant to write, and which I ought to have sent you long ago had I been physically able to get to it. . . . I, as you doubtless know, found it neccessary to come here a couple of weeks since and correct my proofs. The printers are bent on overwhelming me and making me cry mercy now, (I having complained of slowness at first) so that every mail, four times a day, is apt to ['f' *del.*] bring a big bundle. I have stood it so far, but its bad for head and stch. I carry the last ones in at night to mail in the Boston P. O. and often don't get at my dinner till 9 o'clock[.] . . . But here comes the postman with the proofs, which I've *just ['j' *ov.* 's'] opened—40 pages *in [*ab. del.* 'of'] galley and 56 of page-proof! I ought to get it all mailed tonight—it's now half past 3—but of course I can't (1150).

I. The History

And the next day, July 24, to Mrs. Sarah Whitman:

And now 10,000 thanks for your kind words about the proofs. The pages I sent you are probably the most *continuously* amusing in the book—though occasionally there is a passing gleam elsewhere. If there is aught of good in the style it is the result of ceaseless toil in re-writing. Everything comes out wrong with me at first; but when once objectified in a crude shape, I *can [*intrl.*] torture and poke and scrape and pat it till *it offends me [*ab. del.* 'I can do'] no more.—I take you at your word and send you some more sheets—only, to get something pithy and real, I go back to some practical remarks at the end of a chapter on Habit, composed with a view of benefitting the *young*—['*Si vieillesse pouvait*, they might be an inspiration even now.' *del.*] May they accordingly be an inspiration to *you*!

Most of the book is altogether unreadable from any human point of view, as I feel only too well in my deluge of proofs (3899).

Pasted on the second page of this letter is the only known part of the proof for *Principles*, a clipping from the proof of footnote 17 in Chapter XXII, "Reasoning." The following variants appear in the proof from the printed text:

977.31 are] were   977.37 routine] concrete routine
977.36 They (*no* ¶)] ¶   977.37 get] get very

It is probable, however, that this piece of the proof has been attached to the wrong letter, since it seems to be referred to in his next letter, of August 1, 1890, to Mrs. Whitman:

You must be altogether parched and dried up with thirst for "proofs" by this time; and indeed after your so handsome reception of the earlier batch, I ought to be ashamed at sending you no more. But the plain truth is that although I have never for a moment forgotten you or your needs and requirements, I actually haven't met with a page, in all the last fortnight of correcting, that seemed in the least degree worthy of your royal highness'es perusal. The book, I grieve to say, except in gossipy parts of the second vol about instinct and the like which are too newspapery to send, is an irredeemable waste of dulness from the human and literary point of view. Occasionally a gleam, of course, a sentence, a paragraph.ˣ | ˣFor example, the note which I enclose from today's lesson | But it dies away; and for the rest
         "—boundless and bare
        The lone and level sand stretches far away."
I am pretty well tired out with the heat and my ceaseless application of 8, 9, 10 hours a day (3900).

By July 27 James was able to report proudly to Holt from Cambridge: "The proofs go on bravely now and the first volume is all in page. I suppose you'll be going to press with it any day, and wish to ask whether 100 copies or so may not be printed in *black* ink [*presumably for presentation copies*], I mean real black, not the gray substance which is usual nowadays. I suppose it would be too much to claim that for the whole edition, although they do do it for elementary school books—E. G. Trowbridge's New Physics and Allen and Greenough's Caesar which my boy is now reading" (HLB). A letter of August 1, 1890, from Vogelius in Holt's office refers to proofs in different stages:

> We will not disturb the present arrangement between you and the printer, as on the whole it has worked very well.
>
> We have instructed Drummond [*the printer*] to send one set of proofs under cover of letter postage, and we hope it will enable you to get your dinner at a more seasonable hour.
>
> We have often wondered how you could keep up your end so well in the proof-reading, during this hot weather.
>
> Drummond's *chief [*intrl.*] proof-reader, (Herr Neu) is very much interested in your book, so much so, that he will not let any other reader touch it, but stays after hours, so he can read it himself.
>
> Enclosed we return part of your plate proofs. We have transferred the corrections to our set, and will wait until we have them all, before correcting plates, as it will be more economical and will also insure better work.
>
> The diagrams will print all right when they are made ready on the press. We presume you are at work on the index? . . . Drummond has not missed a day, but if he does, he'll send a card (bMS Am 1092.9 [235]).

A suggestion (see below) was made to Holt on August 7: "I want to do something for Bundy Editor of the Religio. Philosophical Journal of Chicago, who has been very helpful to us in the S. P. R. and is a sterling good fellow, who is trying to build his paper up into something better than it has been. I suppose you can have no objection to my sending him the proofs of my chapter on Hypnotism to print ere the book comes out, with acknowledgement of its source. It will of course help to advertize us. But I wont send it until I hear from you." The note ends with the significant sentence, "Thank God the final Galley is in my hands!" (HLB).

The chapter appeared complete as "Hypnotism: Modes of Operating and Susceptibility" under a section called "The Open Court" in the *Religio-Philosophical Journal*, n.s. 1 (1890), August 23, p. 196; August 30, p. 212; September 6, pp. 228–229; September 13, pp. 245–246; September 20, p. 260. The first section was unnamed, the second was given the subheading "Suggestion," and the third through the fifth (the fourth and fifth incorrectly numbered 'III.' and 'IV.'), "The Symptoms of Trance." Each section was prefaced by the bracketed note: "From the Chapter on 'Hypnotism' in Prof. James' forthcoming work, 'Principles of Psychology,' printed from the author's duplicate page proofs with the permission of the publishers, Henry Holt & Co., New York."

The substantive variants between the unemended *Principles*

book text and the version in the *Religio-Philosophical Journal* are as follows:

1194.5 relax] relaxes	1208.20 I] *om. with* space (*typo*)
1194.20 methods] method	
1194.20 and] or	1210.14 not] no *with* space (*typo*)
1194.23 his] the	
1195.39 *must not* have] must stop having	1210.27 or] *om.*
	1211.11 assures] assured
1197.6 *animal-magnetism theory*] first of these theories	1211.23 forehead] foreheads
	1211.30 remain] remains
1197.11 with.ˌ] ~.†	†Gurney, Liébault, etc.	1211.33 patients] patient
	1212.27 really] *om.*
1197.17 admit] admits	1213.31 the] *om.*
1198.8 expectation] expectations	1214.5 ²the] this
	1214.15 (*twice*) 1889] 1890
1198.14 hemisomnambulic] hemisomnambulistic	1214.16-20 —In . . . -274.]

1198.31 what] that
1202.10 earlier] early
1202.35 alterations] alternations
1203.12 for] for an
1203.13 subject's] patient's
1203.33 by] of
1204.14 or a] or
1204.39 ¹by] be (*typo*)
1205.29 of] to
1206.17;1208.10 subjects'] subject's

1214.16-20 —In . . . -274.] To which may be added J. Cadwell, "How to Mesmerize." C. Lloyd Tackey [*i.e.*, Tuckey], "Psycho-Therapeutics," Second Edition 1890. Bjornström, "Hypnotism: its History and Present Development," 1890. J. G. McKendrick, article Animal Magnetism in Encyclopedia Britannica, 9th Edition, (Reprinted).

By normal expectation one might assign the sources of these *Journal* reprint variants to three possible categories: (1) errors, sophistications, and other unauthoritative departures in the reprint from the text of the proofs; (2) original readings in the state of the proofs used as copy for the reprint but altered by James in his own set of book proofs; and (3) independent annotations of the proofs sent to the journal which for one reason or another were not transferred to James's proofs and hence did not appear in the book. It would be daring to attempt to assign each of the variants positively to one of these categories, but at least some examples may be chosen for reasons that may prove acceptable. For instance, the singular 'relaxes' in R-P at 1194.5 seems to be a sophistication in the light of the parallelism of the book's subjunctive 'relax' with preceding 'close'. At 1198.14 'hemisomnambulistic' in R-P is a palpable attempt to correct or normalize the rare book form 'hemisomnambulic'. At 1197.17 R-P 'admits' for 'admit' creates an error by associating a singular verb with a plural subject; and 'alternations' at 1202.35 is a popular copying mistake for correct 'alterations'. The R-P singular 'remains' at 1211.30 represents a grammatical error and can be discarded. Its plural 'expectations' at 1198.8 and, less clearly so, its singular 'patient' at 1211.33 appear to be unauthoritative changes largely governed by the context. That context has caused the authoritative 'by' at 1203.33 to be changed to R-P 'of' seems evident from a scrutiny of the exact meaning of what was produced by the 'suggestion', and so with the R-P parallelism introduced by the change of 'of *comment*' to 'to *comment*' at 1205.29. The effect of context is presumably exhibited again at 1211.23 where R-P reads 'foreheads' for the book's 'forehead': despite the plural 'sides' that precedes, James in tracing stigmata as appearing on hands and feet is referring to the multiple wounds of the nails appearing in a single person's two members, so that the singular 'forehead' is required to associate these stigmata with such an individual. The R-P reading is seemingly thus an error, not the book.

The second and third categories involve one of two forms of authority in the R-P readings; that is, if R-P reproduces an original reading in the proof-copy that James corrected or revised in a later stage of the book proof, then the R-P reading would stand as a testimony to an authentic Jamesian reading even though one that James subsequently discarded, whereas any Jamesian addition or alteration in the proofs he sent to R-P for its copy would possess superior authority to the reading of the book if James had neglected to transfer this reading to his own set of Holt proofs. (This last would hold, of course, only if it were taken that the R-P variant had not been intended by James to appear only in the journal as more suitable for its audience than for the book's.) In fact, the distinction between the two categories may be difficult to make on the available evidence. For example, the short footnote keyed to 'with.' at 1197.11 which appears in R-P but not in the book is not in itself at all demonstrable as an addition in the journal or a subtraction in the book. Its casual notation is not necessarily characteristic of the book, but whether that is an indication of its deletion in James's Holt proof or a brief addition to the journal copy is arguable. The motivation, and the direction of change, in the alteration that took place in the final reference footnote at 1214.14 is obscure in some details but not beyond speculation in others. For instance, it is important to notice that both forms of the footnote start out identically in agreement with the statement in the text that 'other writings most recommendable are subjoined in the note.' Then, instead of continuing in series, R–P reads 'To which may be added' before listing four more titles. It could be suggested that this 'To which may be added' indicates a supplementary listing written-in the copy by James, and it may be that the misspelling 'Tackey' for 'Tuckey' could suggest setting from handwritten copy. It is also interesting that the date 1890 for the Björnström *Hypnotism* is a mistake for 1889. However, objections may be raised, since in the duplicated part of the footnote R–P also gives the date 1890 for the Bernheim *Suggestive Therapeutics* and the Liégeois *De la suggestion*, whereas in the book the correct date 1889 is printed for each. This linked error does not necessarily suggest the inscription of the three titles at different times. Moreover, the question then arises not just that the R–P addition is missing from the book footnote but also that the book's continuation of the duplicated part of the note beginning '—In the recent revival of interest' is not present in R–P although there would seem to be nothing in its contents to warrant its absence.

The evidence suggests either of two hypotheses: (1) the four titles found uniquely in R–P were a handwritten addition in the copy sent to the journal, or (2) the four titles were an original part of the proofs but in a later stage of the book proofs James deleted them.

Something can be said in favor of each speculation. In favor of the first is the error in Tuckey's name, suggesting handwritten copy, as well as the formula 'To which may be added', which is appropriate for an insertion. Against this hypothesis is the similar error in dating three books, two in the original note and the other in the supposed addition. Moreover, this hypothesis almost requires one to take it that the Mitchell part of the book's note was not present in the proofs sent to R–P, for it is difficult to argue that any reason existed for James to cancel this statement, if it had been present, either independently or in favor of the supplementary listing. A rather complicated mechanical explanation does not seem to work. If, for instance, R–P sent James proofs (and we have no evidence whether J. C. Bundy, its editor, did or did not—the numerous errors in the text suggest that he did not) and if James had added the extra titles to R–P proofs that contained his remarks on Mitchell, and if Bundy by the time the proofs were returned had already made up his pages so that there was no room for the addition before the start of the next article on his three-column page, he might have substituted the addition for the concluding part of the original footnote, believing that the extra titles were of more significance than the historical estimate of Mitchell's book. The mechanical difficulty, however, is that this procedure would have saved him two lines of type; but the extra space thus gained is not present in the make-up of the page because the following article starts with only the single line of white space below its predecessor that is normal for R–P's typography. This attractive hypothesis, therefore, must apparently be abandoned since it is not supported by the physical evidence of the typography.

To the present editor, the R–P error in dating two books 1890 in the shared part of the reference footnote, followed by the similar error in a third book given in the unique addition, is the most significant evidence we have that both parts of the list were present in the proofs that James sent to Bundy. The misspelling 'Tackey' for 'Tuckey' in the unique section must then be explained either as the R–P compositor's error, or, more probably, as an error in the duplicate proofs that needed correction such as was given in the book when the dates for the first two '1890' books were altered in the Holt proofs to the correct 1889. The status of the book's own unique section of the footnote praising Dr. John Kearsley Mitchell's work, with a citation going back to 1859, then comes in question. Since space limitations do not seem to have dictated its removal in R–P, the inference follows that it was not present in the duplicate proofs. If so, the further inference then follows that it was a handwritten addition in the Holt proofs that substituted for the extra listing of the more recent books that at some point in his working over of this chapter James had added to his original footnote entry to bring the chapter bibliographically up to date. The obvious weak point in this attempted reconstruction is the question why the addition in praise of the early work of Mitchell (in its nature almost certainly an afterthought) should in the book have substituted for the four titles to his first list that are preserved only in the R–P reprint. No mechanical reason is possible for the excision of the four titles in the book since the final page of the chapter on which the footnote is continued below three lines of text (II, 616) is only a quarter full. Thus if the hypothesis is to hold, one is driven to the conclusion that for reasons of his own, not now to be fully penetrated, James felt that the new addition about Mitchell that he made in the Holt proofs should be a substitute and not a supplement to the footnote as it stood in proof in the form now represented in R–P. Speculation is possible, of course, that he did not want to admit to too many recent works not considered in the chapter, or that he felt that the extra four titles were not of sufficient importance, after all, to mention to the readers of his book, a guess that might apply to the Britannica article especially. If something like this is so, then the formula introducing the four titles 'To which may be added' need not, after all, represent the start of an addition, but instead may merely separate a primary list from what James regarded as a secondary list. In favor of this hypothesis is, first, the coincidence of the 1890 error in books in both parts of the list, and, second, the interesting fact that none of these four titles is mentioned in the annotations and additions of bibliographical references in James's own private copy of *Principles* which, for a time, seems to have been made up not only as a teaching aid but also as a help in revising a possible second edition. If James then came to feel, in the last stage of the Holt proofs, that the secondary list of four titles represented works not important enough to be mentioned, he could have been led to the substitution of the retrospective survey of an author who had indeed been of sufficient importance, though mostly overlooked.

Since the above working hypothesis explains the triple error of 1890 dating in both sections of the list, and the absence of the four titles from James's annotated copy, it seems preferable to another hypothesis that does not include the explanation, which is that the original proofs ended with the reference to Gurney but that James at different times independently added the four titles to the R–P copy (or proofs sent to him) and the praise of Mitchell to the Holt proofs. If the hypothesis be credited, it has some textually significant implications, for it would seem to suggest that James sent his duplicate proofs to Bundy without having marked them with corrections and revisions found in the Holt proofs and thus in the book. But since the evidence is not entirely solid in this respect, for the Mitchell substitution could theoretically have been made in Holt proofs after the R–P proof copy (whether or not otherwise marked) had been sent off, further analysis of certain variants is necessary to determine whether they appear to fall in the second category of original Jamesian readings altered in the Holt proofs or whether they suggest, instead, James's revisory annotations in the R–P copy that he did not transfer to the Holt proofs. Three readings may be especially selected as authoritative variants not to be assigned to the first category of R–P departures from copy. The first is particularly significant since it reveals a typical sharpening of meaning in the book version. The initial footnote in the chapter concluded with the statement that headache, languor, and other symptoms that 'sometimes follow the first trance or two, must be banished at the outset, by the operator strongly assuring the subject that such things *never* come from hypnotism, that the subject *must not* have them, etc.' (1195.37-39). In R-P the reading is, instead, 'must stop having them'. The book corrects an original imprecision as found in the R-P version. In the book, patients who do not have the symptoms are included with those who do in the operator's assurance that hypnotism is not responsible, whereas in R-P patients without symptoms are told by the operator at the outset that they must stop having them. If the order of this revision is relatively certain, then it affects our view of another seemingly authoritative variant in the same footnote earlier at 1194.20-22 where the book reads 'It should be said that the methods of leaving the patient to himself, and that of the simple verbal suggestion of sleep . . . seem, wherever applicable, to be the best'. R-P, on the contrary, reads 'method' and 'or that of'. It would seem that James wanted the plural 'methods' and so was forced to make the consequential grammatical change of 'or' to 'and'. The third clearcut variant with authority on both sides is the alteration at 1197.6 of R-P 'the first of these theories' (which requires reference back to an antecedent list) to the more immediately clear 'the *animal-magnetism theory*', which then parallels in its form the introduction of the discussion of the other two listed theories in subsequent paragraphs by their italicized titles.

Other variants that may or may not have authority can be mentioned briefly. At 1194.23 R-P 'straining the eyes' for the book's 'straining his eyes' may or may not reproduce an original reading sharpened in the book; at any rate, the order of change is effectively suggested by analysis of the other two variants in this footnote already considered. Something of the same sort may be said of R-P 'In the early stages of hypnotism' versus the book's 'earlier stages' (1202.10), which seems to agree better with the subsequent 'deeper condition' resulting from 'successive sittings'. At 1203.13 the odds may favor James's revision in the book proofs as against R-P compositorial or editorial sophistication when R-P 'patient's side' becomes book 'subject's side'. The term 'patient' had been used early in the same paragraph at 1203.6 but thereafter James employs 'subject' as at 1203.15, and it seems probable that he changed 'patient's' at 1203.13 to his preferred term. In the same sentence R-P 'for an example' becomes in the book 'for example' (1203.12), a neutral enough variant but the direction certainly in conformity with the 'patient-subject' change. Whether the omission of 'really' in R–P at 1212.27 is authorial or whether the book's phrase 'The only really mysterious feature' is a case of following copy may be moot; but considering other omissions in R–P that are more certainly errors, such as at 1211.11 and 1213.31, the book's readings at least cannot be doubted as being final. Such an indifferent variant as R–P's genitive singular 'subject's' but the book's plural in 'When one of the subjects' own limbs is made anæsthetic' (1206.16–17) might create some doubt about a book misprint corrected in R–P, whether or not by James. The plural seems odd in view of the preceding singular use of 'subject' in the discussion. However, an exactly similar variant later at 1208.10 should be sufficient to show that the book represents James's intention and that the R–P singular is either a natural normalization or, less likely perhaps, a reading in the original altered in the Holt proofs.

This examination has shown no R–P variant that is demonstrably a revision that James would need to have written in the proof sent to Bundy. It may follow, then, that it is a relatively safe working hypothesis to take it that the duplicate proofs were sent to the journal in an uncorrected state. (A few surviving proofs of portions of articles seem to show that James did not ordinarily transfer to his own set of proofs the changes he had made in the proofs returned to the publisher, and indeed this is the evidence of the small part of a proof of *Principles* that James sent to Mrs. Sarah Whitman.) However, the same examination has revealed some examples of R–P faithfully following the duplicate proof readings that James had changed in the Holt proofs and thereby giving us some insight into his proofreading of *Principles*. Since no R–P reading has final authority, then, we may decide the difficult case of the brief footnote at 1197.11 as one original in the book proofs but removed by James before publication. The same holds true for the four titles in the final footnote found only in R–P. Given the working hypothesis, then, that only the book text has final or primary authority since it contains James's last intentions as represented by the changes made in the Holt proofs, the secondary authority of the original proof readings, insofar as they can be identified among the R–P variants, must yield to the book version. It follows that James's deletion of the brief footnote and, in the final footnote, his substitution of the statement about Mitchell for the secondary list of four titles that the reader could consult, must be followed in an 'established' text of *Principles*. However,

Professor Skrupskelis' commentary Notes on the deleted titles will be found keyed to the proper page-line references.

To George B. Dorr, James writes from Cambridge on August 12, 1890: "The psychology is now done, all but the Index, and a sacred peace descends. By next Monday I shall be at Chocorua again, able to see a little of my family, and doomed to get up my new courses of lectures for next year" (bMS Am 1092.1).

James reports to Holt on August 12: "Nothing remains now but the index—hallelujah! The printing office did nobly, and so (though I say it as should not) did I, for I rarely got my dinner before 9 P.M. when I took the stuff into Boston to the late mail. My fears about not getting through before September were grounded on what you had told me in the winter, that the printers could not be expected to do more than 15 or 16 pages a day. What do you mean to ask for the book? I get a good many notes inquiring about it" (HLB). Again to his sister Alice, on the next day August 13, James mentioned: "My book has come out—that is the last proofs are corrected, and nothing but the index to do. I'll send you a copy when it appears. I've worked like a whole gang of niggers for 6 weeks past, and accomplished the feat of correcting 1400 pp. of proof" (1151). A week later, on August 20, he boasted to W. D. Howells, "I have been in Cambridge six weeks and corrected 1400 pages of proof" (*Letters*, I, 298–299). On August 22 he wrote to Henry:

I finished and post[ed] my index yesterday, so my mind is free to turn to the Universe receptively again. A wondrous boon. I have been six weeks in Cambridge all alone in the house, until the last week when Alice came down, and cooked and helped, and corrected 1400 pp. of proofs, much of them in small type. I almost never got away from my writing-table till 9 P.M. and then used in a starving condition, to go booming along through the sultry night on the front seat of an electric car, the finest locomotion in the world, to get my dinner *between 9 & 10 [*intrl.*] at Young's or Parker's after mailing the proofs in the Boston P.O. to catch the late N.Y. mail. It was hard on the digestive organs, but it has left no bad effects, and I look back to the month and a half of it as a most delightful period of time—only one thing to thing about, and great strides of ['daily' *del.*] progress in that every day (2657).

James reported to Henry on September 28, 1890: "My book appeared two days since, and I've ordered the publisher's to send a copy to you. Most of it is quite unreadable, but you may find some pages in the second volume that will go. Also the earlier pp. of the Chapter on Consciousness of Self. The infernal thing is too long to sell well I'm afraid. . . . I have given away already $450.00 worth *(including postage) [*parens ov. commas*] so my gains *on [*ab. del.* 'with'] the ['f' *del.*] book are not likely to be immense" (2658). Later, on November 23, 1890, James apologized to Henry: "I am mortified about my book, which Henry Holt & Co., contrary to my most express and repeated orders, never sent to its english *destinataires* until Macmillan should take charge. I supposed that you were having it 6 weeks ago. I shan't make aught by it, I fear. I owe Holt 300 dollars for presentation copies, and I know not how much more for extra type corrections" (2660).

The date of September 26 for the receipt of copies coincides roughly with a letter of September 22 from Vogelius:

> Your Psychology will be ready on Wednesday the 24th inst. We judge that the price will be $7.00 for the 2 vols. but are not quite sure yet. We always prefer to see the complete book before fixing the price definitely. How does $7.00 strike you?
>
> We have several orders for the Psychology and have promised the book on the 25th. Shall we hold it back for a few days, (including 40 copies ordered by Sever of Cambridge) so as to give you a chance to get the circulars ready? (LB, Princeton).

Vogelius wrote again, on September 25:

> We have fixed the retail price of the "Psychology at $6.00. As a rule the retail dealer sells to his customers at a discount of 20%, so that would bring it less than $5.00.
>
> We regret very much to see that some of the printers points show on the top margin.[13] Its a serious blemish to so otherwise handsome book. If we had time, we would surpress the entire edition. To print a new one now, would take fully from 4 to 5 weeks, as paper has got to be made for it specially.
>
> Your 20 copies go by express to-day. The complimentary & individual copies will go in due course (Holt Archives, Princeton, James folder; original at Harvard, bMS Am 1092.1 [419]).

James, then, would have received his copies on September 26, two days before he wrote to Henry on the 28th.

Holt arranged for Macmillan to publish *Principles* in England and supplied the sheets with a special English title page containing on its verso the New York copyright notice. Some sheets with the American title page, or bound books, seem to have been imported by Macmillan. The English philosopher Shadworth H. Hodgson wrote to James on December 13, 1890, that he had received a copy from the New York publishers through Macmillan (bMS Am 1092.9 [207]), and the British Library has a (rebound) copy

---

[13]These 'points' are pins that hold the sheet on the flat-bed press as it is being printed, creating small holes that would usually be trimmed off in the binding if they had been set close enough to the edge of the sheet.

of the New York edition date-stamped April 14, 1891 (8468.k.20). The British Library copy of the Macmillan edition is date-stamped March 25, 1891 (2236.f.9), but the Bodleian Library's deposit copy is stamped January 30, 1891 (2645.e.1138=S. Psych. 15ᵇ/1 [690]). The Bodleian's stamping of its received copies is sometimes several weeks late, whereas the British Library usually stamped copies on the actual day of receipt. Thus whether Macmillan published *Principles* in late December 1890 or in January 1891 is not altogether certain, although the title page reads 1890. According to a Holt royalty statement to James dated April 25, 1891, for sales as of December 31, 1890, 250 sheets were sent to England initially, on which James received a royalty of 33 1/3 cents each.[14] Between July 1 and December 31, 100 additional sheets were sent across (LB, January 6, 1892), presumably those with the date 1891 on the title page. The British Library also has a copy of the Macmillan edition dated 1910 (2021.e), rebound; the London Library has copies of 1901 and 1907; and the Bodleian Library that of 1901 and an undated copy. According to the dust jacket for the 1901 edition, the British price was 25 shillings.

The details of the early Holt printings in the United States are obscure since Holt never added an impression notice to the verso of the title page and did not alter the date on the title in any printings before 1893. The size of the first printing is not recorded. A second printing was called for early in 1891, referred to in a letter from James to Holt on February 1, 1891: "Since you are printing off a new 'edition' how would it do to do a little advertising of work's 'edited by the same author' by printing on a fly leaf the titles of Maude's Unfortunate Foundations of Ethics and of my Father's Literary Remains: 'The Literary Remains of the late Henry James, edited with an Introduction, by William James. Pp. 471, and steel engraved likeness. Houghton, Mifflin & Co. 1885. Judge thou!'" (HLB). Holt complied in the second volume of the new printing. James had not been able to make all the corrections in the second printing that he had wished, as indicated by a letter on November 4, 1891, from Vogelius: "We are making preparations for printing a new edition of your 2 vol Psychology. Will it be convenient now to let us have the list of corrections which for lack of time you could not give us when we printed last?

---

[14] In a letter of the same date, April 25, 1891, Holt wrote to accompany the royalty statement that the original contract would have given James only 14.3 cents royalty on English copies but that he thinks 33 1/3 cents is fair (Holt Archives, Princeton, James folder, typed copy). All royalty-statement data come from the Letterbooks at Princeton.

We are anxious to make this book as perfect as possible" (LB). On April 25, 1892, James was billed as of December 31, 1891, for $52.64 for "alterations in plates of 3ᵈ edition large Psychology" (LB). Thus it can be established that a second printing was made, probably in early February 1891, and that a third printing was completed probably in late November 1891, for on December 6 Vogelius wrote James that the correction he had sent in for page 354 of volume I was too late since "The edition is worked off" (LB).[15]

The early royalty statements sent to James assist in a conjectural reconstruction. On April 25, 1891, 544 copies were listed as sold between publication in September and December 31, 1890; on October 24, 1891, 310 copies were reported sold between January 1 and June 30, 1891; on April 25, 1892, 513 copies were reported sold between July 1 and December 31, 1891. In a letter of January 6, 1892, this was amended to 516 copies, to which were added 100 sheets for England. Between publication in late September 1890 and December 31, 1891, thus, 1370 copies had been sold in the United States and 350 sets of sheets to Macmillan. Allowing for copies for review, James's personal 20 copies, and the various gifts he made, something like a total of 1800 copies appear to have been printed and distributed. Thus if the initial printing had been 1,000, about 850 copies of this would have been distributed by December 31, 1890, and a second printing of, say, 800 was required, since by June 30 the total distribution would have reached at least 1200. Thereafter the National Union Catalogue reports editions dated 1893, 1896, 1899, 1902, 1905, 1907, 1908, 1910, 1913, an undated edition, and an undated with a 1918 copyright by Alice James, each of these editions representing a new printing from the plates.

In 1900 an Italian translation *Principii di psicologia* by Giulio Cesare Ferrari, working under the general review of Professor A. Tamburini, was published in Milan by the Società editrice libraria. The chief interest here lies in the writing by James of a special preface, which was also translated into Italian, and in the correspondence with Ferrari concerning it. The autograph manuscript of the preface, in English, has been preserved and is transcribed for the first time in Appendix III.

---

[15] For details of the identification of these printings, see Section II, "The Documents." The correction that James sent in was perhaps 'widely' for 'wholly' at I, 354.10 (335.23) although it could also have been the correction of the misspelling 'existance' in I, 354.8 (355.21-22).

James responded on June 13, 1898, to a lost letter from Ferrari:

I am naturally much flattered at your demand concerning an Italian translation of my Psychology. I agree with you entirely that the two-volume work is too big, whilst the Briefer Course may be a little too small, and, moreover, contains too much exclusively physiological material.

I shall gladly authorize so well known a man of Science as yourself to translate such portions of the two works as seem best to you by combining them according to your own judgment of the needs of your own people. The Chapter on Hypnotism present[s] itself immediately as one to be omitted. The Chapter on Space in the smaller book (which contains the principles of my theory more clearly and without details) might possibly be substituted for the Chapter in the larger book.

Personally I am fond of the very last Chapter of all and should like to see that preserved, but I leave that to you![16]

You ask for notes bringing the matter down to the latest discoveries. I regret to say that that is for me impossible. I cannot undertake so difficult a labor for you, when I have long since determined never to do it for the english "Principles." In two or three years I shall rewrite the briefer Course, to make it sell still better as a college text book. It will thus become shorter rather than longer, and simpler rather than more complex, and so will in no way interfere with your translation. I shall never rewrite the Principles, though I may many years hence write a new book exclusively on the speculative problems of Psychology, entirely different from the predecessors.[17]

On July 27 (or 29—the last digit is uncertain) James enclosed to Ferrari Holt's permission for a translation and added: "I will gladly look over your notes, especially if you send them to me in proof; and I will write a word of recommendation of the translation if it seems to me recommendable,—as I feel sure it will,—after seeing it in proof."

From Bad-Nauheim James wrote Ferrari on September 15, 1900, stating that his ill health

[16] That this Chapter XXVIII was a personal favorite is indicated in a letter of March 3, 1892, to Mrs. Ladd-Franklin: "Thank you for your continued indulgence as to the Psychology. The last chapter however is the one for which I mainly craved your approval as a logician & mathematician, and now it turns out to be the one which you chiefly disapprove. The unfathomable ways of woman! If I ever do revise the book you shall go in with the horopter. I did n't mention *that [*ab. del.* 'it'] because it seemed to me to have much more mathematical than psychological interest—in fact hardly any of the latter except what your illusion gave it" (Columbia). For further comment on this chapter, see James to Ferrari on September 15, 1900, below.

[17] Letters to Ferrari are quoted by courtesy of C. A. Ferrari di Valbona, Piazza di Spagna 29, 00187 Rome, Italy. The letter of June 13 and July 27, as well as a note from Holt to James of July 26, 1898, granting permission for the translation, are preserved only in a transcription, but the remaining correspondence is in James's autograph. James's letter of September 15, 1900, exists also in a typed copy at Harvard. Not quoted here is a note to Ferrari from James on January 9, 1899, stating that he is writing to Holt "to let you have the *clichés* [i.e., cuts] which you desire, if it be possible."

makes me say immediately, though to my great regret, that I had better not look at your translation of my last Chapter at all until it appears in print. All the pages of your work which I have examined have seemed to me so accurate that I am sure that last chapter will no more need my revision than the others have needed it. To be sure, I have not read a great many pages, and I have not confronted your work with the original, of which I brought no copy to Europe with me, but I have a firm impression that your work has been well done.

I congratulate you most heartily on having finished the manuscript part of your colossal ['work.' *del.*] labor. I am surprised to find so little abridgment. I expected a great many more excisions than I can discover *(using my memory) [*parens ov. commas*] in the published parts of the translation.

I confess I am not sorry that the final Chapter will appear *in toto*. Perhaps the Italian learned public will appreciate it better than it has been appreciated at home! I feel however as if I owed you damages for the terrible drudgery you have taken upon yourself. The fact is that I look back with a sort of horror on the obsession of that psychology when I was writing it and the thought of anyone reading it all through, still more translating it, makes me feel like an *inimicus generis humani*.

This is one reason why I am troubled about the preface which you ask me to write. I should do so with the greatest pleasure, and at some length, if I knew what to say. But of late I have become exclusively occupied with metaphysics, and to some extent with sociology *(to say nothing of health and the salvation of my soul (?) in case my body gives out) [*opening and closing parens ov. commas*] and all that psychology belongs so much to a past epoch of my life, that I feel out of connexion with it, and nothing occurs to me in the way of a message to your italian compatriots, with which it might be suitable for me to preface it. Can't you suggest to me some points? I shall be delighted to write the stuff, if I only can decide what to say. Better still, can't you write the preface for me yourself, and let me sign it? I will gladly do that. . . . Of course I am pleased at what you say of the translation's success, so far. But I hope that you won't ever have the labor of correcting the proofs of a second edition.

On October 28, 1900, James enclosed the preface in a brief note to Ferrari mailed from Florence. In connection with the second Italian edition of 1908–9, James wrote on December 4, 1907:

I just receive[d] your letter of November 21st, & hasten to reply to the questions of the *Società editrice*. I am leaving the english edition of my Principles unaltered, and shall never alter it. Therefore let the italian edition *be reprinted as it stands*. If you wish to suppress, change, or add to your annotations at the ends of the chapters, I give you leave to do so (!)—follow your own preference in this regard. It pleases me well that the italian demand continues; but it is not practically possible that I should spend a single hour on *the [*ab. del.* 'its'] revision of the book.

II. THE DOCUMENTS

The manuscript of *The Principles of Psychology* has been lost except for one page, known only in a reproduction found in Bird T. Baldwin's "William James' Contributions to Education," *Journal of Educational Psychology*, 2 (1911), 371. This leaf is stated to have been loaned to Baldwin by E. L. Thorndike, who was a Professor of Psychology at Columbia University and one of James's numerous correspondents. The Thorndike papers were presented to the Library of Congress by Mrs. Frances Thorndike Cope but James's manuscript was not a part of them (nor were his letters to Thorndike) and cannot be traced. The preserved page, numbered 2207, contains text included in Chapter XXVI, "Will," in volume II, 543.29–544.5 (1150.9–22). The first paragraph, James's own composition, is normally revised. The second paragraph, beginning a quotation from Howells' translation of Alfieri, shows the sort of small variation that James was likely to make in copying; but interestingly some of the divergences have been set right in the book whether by accident or design. Not all of the pages would have been in James's holograph, of course, for a number of chapters utilize as printer's copy in whole or in part clippings of his articles in journals that would have been marginally annotated by revisions. It is also possible that some of the extensive quotations in the book were set from clippings pasted on sheets[18] and had not been copied either by James or by his wife, Alice, who helped him in transcribing notes of quotations that might have been pasted-in as well. As suggested in "The History," the first 170 pages that had been set in proof by December 17, 1886, were scrapped, and the typesetting that began in 1890 was made from different copy; for example, it is clear that Chapter IV, "Habit," pp. 109–131, was set not from holograph but from an annotated copy of the article "The Laws of Habit" in the *Popular Science Monthly* for February 1887.[19] The odds

[18]Quotations set from clippings may sometimes be conjecturally identified by a fidelity to the original that is less usual in the copied quotations.

[19]Unfortunately we do not find mention of the writing of "The Laws of Habit" or of its offer to *Popular Science Monthly* in James's letters; thus an outside chance exists that in December 1886 it was set from the proofs for the magazine and that the present chapter could represent the initial typesetting. However, the references quoted in "The History" that point to a new typographical design for the 1890 book indicate otherwise, and it is perhaps a red herring even to mention the possibility of standing type. Given Holt's later uncertainty whether James ever would finish, the expense of keeping 170 pages in standing type for an indefinite period (actually three and a half years) probably caused him to have the first typesetting distributed. It had probably never been plated.

2207

The passion of love may be called a monomania to which all of us are subject, however otherwise sane. It can coexist with contempt and even hatred for the object which inspires it, and whilst it lasts the whole life of the man is altered by its presence. Alfieri then describes the struggles of his unusually powerful inhibitory power with his abnormally excited impulses towards a certain lady:

"Contemptible in my own eyes, wearing my disgraceful fetters, I fell into such a state of melancholy as would, if long continued, have inevitably have led to insanity or death. I continued to wear my disgraceful fetters till towards the end of January 1775 when my rage, which had hitherto so often been restrained within bounds, broke forth with the greatest violence. On returning one evening from the opera (the most insipid and tiresome amusement in

From a portion of the manuscript of James's *Principles of Psychology*, II, p. 543 [*ed.*, p. 1150].

that the early chapters of the 1890 book represent the typesetting of December 1886 are long, therefore. But we have no information whether James used any of these initial 1886 proofs as basic printer's copy, annotated and expanded, for the final setting or whether he had so reworked them in the interval that such a plan was impracticable. His letter to Holt of January 11, 1890, about his reworking the first chapter remarks, "like a fool I didn't destroy my original manuscript but tried to patch old and new together," a statement that could scarcely have taken this form if James had revised the early proofs for this chapter. Indeed, the complete disappearance of these proofs and of all mention of them once James took the decision in 1886 to abandon any attempt at printing the book in its form at that time suggests that he had discarded them and that they have no part in the history of the present text.

Although we know anything of the final manuscript only from the facsimile page of Baldwin's article, various folders in the James Collection contain notes that bear on material used either in *Principles* or, more often, in the articles antecedent to it. Mention may be made here only of two items. These are related and offer an interesting insight into James's original plan to divide his work into a number of books. Folder bMS Am 1092.9 (4412), as presently constituted,[20] has a strong buff-colored paper folder (back cover blank), on the front cover of which is written in ink:

Book II.
[short rule]
Chapter ['II' *del.*] VIII
[short rule]
The External Relations of Minds
['A General Description of Consciousness' *del.*]
[short rule]

[*illeg. erased pencil words, to right*]
*External relations of minds
   1) to time — are we ever truly unconscious
   2) to space — "the seat of the soul."
   3) to other objects — the function of knowing [*penc.*]

---

[20]The present folders with new call numbers were made up in 1977 out of the original assembly of materials which were in so-called 'boxes' chiefly the arrangement of Ralph Barton Perry. The two folders bMS Am 1092.9 (4410) and (4412) came from previously catalogued Box A, envelope 13. Their contents are not necessarily those within the original buff covers, for Perry may have rearranged the material.

In pencil in the upper left corner is a '2'.

The three divisions correspond to the three found in *Principles*, Chapter VIII "The Relations of Minds to Other Things," but the contents concern Chapter XI "Attention" and are so transcribed in Appendix IV.

Folder 4410 is more informative, chiefly because of what is written on its buff front cover. This reads, in ink:

Book II. Chapter ['IV' *del.*] X
[short rule]
*The Consciousness of Self [*db. underl.*]
[short rule]
A. The *Empirical Self or Me. ['E', 'S', 'M' *ov.* 'T', 's', 'm']
Its definition, ['123' *del.*] and *constituents [*ab. del.* 'divisions'] 123–5
The material self, 125–7
The social self, 127–9
The spiritual self, 129
Self-feeling, 129
Self-seeking, ['131' *del.*] and its varieties, 129–35.
Conflict of different selves, 135.
Self-feeling due to relation between *the [*intrl.*] self-claimed & the self realized, 137
Hierarchy of the selves, 138½
What is the object regarded in self love & selfishness? 144
It is one or other of the constituents of the empirical Self, & not the pure Ego, 145
Proof of this in detail: ['146' *del.*] Bodily selfishness 146; Social egoism 148; Spiritual Self-regard 151
Why we ['should' *del.*] love all these ['s' *del.*] constituents of the Self 153
Why we care so much for our own possessions, (Horwicz) 160
*Judicial ['Ju' *ov.* 'Sel'] self-estimation 167 (note about Bain, 169)

The pencil number '4' appears in the upper left corner. On the outer back cover is written in ink:

See A. F. Shand, Mind April 1888
*Paulhan: [*insrtd.*] La Perception Interne, Rev. Scientifique May 18. 88
*Show that the synthesis, or combining that the ego is invoked to account for is only *Knowing*. [*penc.*]
Binet: Rev. Phil. Feb. 89
Don't forget to notice Ladd's Argument.

The sixteen subheadings correspond closely to the Chapter X present subheadings or else to the order of its discourse. The contents of the folder for the developed chapter are disappointing in that they have only slight specific connection with the book's Chapter X, although some are generally related. These manuscripts, whether or not completely relevant, are reproduced in Appendix IV. Two letters laid in the folder, not reproduced, are pertinent to

Chapter X, however. The first is dated December 23, 1887, on the letterhead of the McLean Asylum, Somerville, Massachusetts, signed by James W. Babcock, and concerns an Irishwoman 'who had so far lost her Ego as to believe that she was a rat'; the letter is in response to a remark by a Doctor Tuttle to the writer that James was searching for a case of lost personality. The second letter, dated December 26, 1887, on the letterhead of the Tewksbury, Massachusetts, State Almshouse, from C. Irving Fisher, identifies the woman and describes some of her symptoms.

The connection of these two folder covers is an intimate one since each has had its chapter number altered by the same ratio from an earlier and lower number to that now found in *Principles*. Each cover indicates that it is a part of a Book II. It would seem to be a reasonable hypothesis that each cover was originally prepared to hold the manuscript (and possibly antecedent notes) for an early stage of the book's manuscript. If the contents and the order of chapters were the same as at present in this earlier stage (an hypothesis impossible to prove), it would seem that Book I could have been composed of what are now the first six chapters, ending with "The Mind-Stuff Theory," and Book II could have begun with its first chapter "The Methods and Snares of Psychology," which represents something of a natural division.

The page numbering for original Chapter IV (now Chapter X, "The Consciousness of Self") from 123 to 169 cannot represent the pagination of the 1886 proof (this was set only as far as its page 170), for the reference to the subheading "Hierarchy of the Selves" as page 138½ establishes manuscript foliation in James's characteristic system for numbering additions. Moreover, on October 4, 1886, as already described above in "The History," James sent to Robertson, the editor of *Mind*, an article on the Ego which he called the first part of a "chapter," but the subsequent discussion and his withdrawal of the article indicates that he felt the material was still in very provisional shape, at least in respect to its latter half. In this same letter to Robertson, James speaks of an unsolved problem "on p. 136^b" (which according to the table on the folder's cover would be within the section entitled "Conflict of different selves"). This mention of the page number 136^b almost certainly refers to the early chapter manuscript, in some part at least much as described on the cover, for the page number 136^b could scarcely represent the numbering of an article manuscript beginning with 1. Thus it seems a fair guess that James may have started Chapter I of Book II of *Principles* in 1886, or earlier, with what is now Chapter VII "The Methods and Snares of Psychology" and numbered its pages consecutively, starting with 1, so that its Chapter IV on the Ego (now Chapter X) began with page 123. When he sent the manuscript of this chapter shortly before October 4, 1886, to Robertson, the reference in his letter to "p. 136^b" suggests that he had not recopied the book chapter but merely mailed its manuscript for Robertson's consideration. It is unfortunate that the folder for Book II, Chapter II (now Chapter VIII) does not have its three headings paginated so that the hypothesis could be tested.

Only one edition of *Principles* exists, the numerous printings all being made from the original plates. These received their final authorial correction in 1905, but as time passed repairs were needed because of wear and batter, so that a few unauthoritative variants (errors in resetting) and some corrections of misprints occur after 1905. The edition may be described as follows:

title: *AMERICAN SCIENCE SERIES—ADVANCED COURSE* | [rule] | THE PRINCIPLES | OF | PSYCHOLOGY | BY | WILLIAM JAMES | PROFESSOR OF PSYCHOLOGY IN HARVARD UNI-VERSITY | IN TWO VOLUMES | VOL. I [II] | [publisher's device] | NEW YORK | HENRY HOLT AND COMPANY | 1890

collation: Vol. I. [unsigned: 1-44^8], 352 leaves, pp. [2] [i-iv] v-vii [viii] ix-xii, [1] 2-689 [690]

contents: Vol. I. p. π1: blank; p. π2: 'THE | AMERICAN SCI-ENCE SERIES | FOR SCHOOLS AND COLLEGES. | [9 items] | HENRY HOLT & CO., PUBLISHERS, NEW YORK.'; p. i: title; p. ii: 'COPYRIGHT, 1890, | BY | HENRY HOLT & CO. | ROBERT DRUM-MOND, | *Electrotyper and Printer*, | New York.'; p. iii: 'TO | MY DEAR FRIEND | FRANÇOIS PILLON, | AS A TOKEN OF AFFECTION, | AND AN ACKNOWLEDGMENT OF WHAT I OWE | TO THE | CRITIQUE PHILOSOPHIQUE.'; p. iv: blank; p. v: 'PREFACE. | [short rule]', subscribed on p. vii: 'HARVARD UNI-VERSITY, August 1890.'; p. viii: blank; p. ix: 'CONTENTS. | [short rule]'; p. 1: text with HT 'PSYCHOLOGY. | [short rule]'; on p. 689: 'END OF VOL. I.'; p. 690: blank. [NOTE: in 1910 a plate change substitutes a period after 'PILLON' for the battered comma of the 1908 printing.]

collation: Vol. II. [unsigned: 1^4 2-45^8], 356 leaves, pp. [2] [i-ii] iii-vi, [1] 2-689 [690] 691-704, ^{2}[1] 2-8

contents: Vol. II. p. π1: blank; p. π2: adv. as in vol. I; p. i: title;

p. ii: copyright notice and printer's imprint; p. iii: contents; p. 1: text with HT; on p. 689: 'THE END.'; p. 690: blank; p. 691: 'INDEX. | [short rule] | Authors the titles only of whose works are cited are not, as a rule, referred to in | this index.', ending on p. 704.

paper and binding: white wove unwatermarked paper, leaf measuring 8½ × 5½", top and bottom edges cut, fore-edge rough cut; recto of endpapers coated dark brown on white, single flyleaf of text paper front and back. Dark green buckram. On spine in gilt: 'PSYCHOLOGY | VOL. I. [II.] | JAMES | AMERICAN | SCIENCE SERIES | [short rule] | ADVANCED COURSE | HENRY HOLT & CO.' A band in blind at head and foot of spine; front and back covers blank.

 copies consulted: 1890 (*first printing*) Harvard (1) *AC9.H7375. Zz 890j; (2) Phil 5249.2; (3) Andover-Harvard Theological Seminary Library

 1890 (*second printing*, February 1891) Harvard *AC85.J2376. 890pa; University of Virginia BF121.J2/1890

 1890 (*third printing*, November 1891) University of Virginia Barrett *PS2129/J15/P8

 1893 (*fourth printing*) Union Theological Seminary PP35/J29/ 1893; Montana State University BF121/J2/1890 (1893 on the title page)

 1896 (*fifth printing*) University of British Columbia

 1899 (*sixth printing*) Harvard; University of Cincinnati

 1902 (*seventh printing*) University of Michigan; The Library of Congress

 1905 (*eighth printing*) Bowdoin College; University of Michigan; University of Cincinnati

 1907 (*ninth printing*) University of Virginia

 1908 (*tenth printing*) University of Virginia

 1910 (*eleventh printing*) John Carroll University; Ohio Wesleyan University; University of Virginia

 1913 (*twelfth printing*) University of British Columbia; The New York Public Library

 [undated, copyright 1890] (*thirteenth printing*) University of Virginia

 [undated, copyright 1918 by Alice H. James] (*fourteenth printing*) University of Virginia

It was advertised in *Publishers' Weekly* on September 27, 1890, and again on October 11, 1890.

II. The Documents

The early printings between the first and third, all dated 1890, pose something of a problem. The initial printing can be identified by the typography of the advertisement facing the title pages of both volumes. In this printing the eighth item, the notice of James's *Principles*, reads in bold-face italic, '*The Principles of Psy-|chology.*' and the next line ends with 'Professor of'|. The standard identification in the text has been the misprint on I, 307.19 (293.24) which reads 'noticean, d'; but a more accurate reading in volume I is I,10.9–10 (23.4) 'the seat of intellectual power' and in volume II,101.20 (745.29) 'object of sensation'. The second printing reads in the text 'not the sole seat of intellect', and simply 'sensation' (omitting 'object of'). In the second printing's advertisement page facing the title in the first volume, the title '*Psychology.*' is on one line and the second line breaks at 'Professor' |. In the second volume the advertisement page is boxed and contains two items headed 'Works Edited by William James.' The third printing, still dated 1890, is externally identical with the second but its text has undergone further plate alteration. In I,21.10 (33.17) the error 'catarral' in the first two printings is corrected to 'catarrhal' and in I,134.17 (138.3) the reading is 'means. And' instead of 'means; and'. The misprint on I,307.19 (293.24) of 'noticean, d' is corrected in this printing to 'notice, and'. In II,83.2 (728.26–27) the reading is 'Only in the gravest lesions does he become' whereas the earlier printings read 'It is only in grave lesions that he becomes'. A printing dated 1893 in the title appears to be the fourth impression, with further plate changes. Only one of these is substantive, the substitution at I,354.10 (335.23) of 'widely' for 'wholly'. The rest correct misprints such as 'existance' to 'existence' at I,354.8 (335.21–22) and 'Fowler.' to 'Fowler:' at II,411.26 (1030.26). The impression of 1896, the fifth printing, shows no plate changes, but that of the 1899 sixth printing alters 'fondnesses' to 'fondness' at II,634.43 (1231.30). The 1902 seventh printing has no plate-variants, but that of the 1905 eighth printing attacks more of the errors, as illustrated in its alteration of '*A after B*' to the correct '*B after A*' at I,353.25 (335.5) and in the correction of the reference to Figure 70 changed from Figure 65 at II,253.7 (884.2). There were no corrections of errors in the 1907 ninth printing (although some errors were introduced at this time, probably the result of resetting lines of worn type), nor in the tenth printing of 1908. However, a few misprints were corrected in the 1910 eleventh printing, authority uncertain. Even so late as 1913 (the twelfth printing) and 1918 (the fourteenth) scattered misprints were altered in the plates. The undated printing (designated the thirteenth) shows no corrections of misprints. The fourteenth, in 1918, makes two changes, one at II,89.32 (734.30) where 'exatly' is corrected to 'exactly' and the other at II,531.16 (1138.31) where the error of the single quote missing after ' 'reasons' is corrected to ' 'reasons' '. From 1910 on, repairs of plate batter continued to introduce errors, as in the mistake 'Angloise' introduced in 1910 for the correct 'Anglaise' at I,598.44 (563.42). In fact, errors had been introduced earlier, in authoritative rounds of correction, as in the wrong substitution of a single for a double quotation mark at I,162.36 (164.37) made in the second printing and never changed.

The difficulty of determining the exact number of printings dated 1890 and whether more than one was printed from uncorrected plates, or from plates in some identified state of alteration, stems from what interpretation one can make of Vogelius' letter to James of November 4, 1891 (see "The History"): "We are making preparations for printing a new edition of your 2 vol Psychology. Will it be convenient now to let us have the list of corrections which for lack of time you could not give us when we printed last? We are anxious to make this book as perfect as possible" (LB). At first this could be taken to mean that James had written promising a list of corrections but that Holt could not wait and had run off another printing to satisfy the demand, possibly a second printing hard on the heels of the first, which would thus have been identical. On the other hand, this letter comes over a year after publication, and it seems inconceivable that in the interval James had not provided at least one list of necessary corrections, given the number of misprints and positive errors that had escaped his proofreading for the first impression. Moreover, from James's letter of February 1, 1891, we know that a second printing was about to be ordered, and collation of the plates identifies some corrections that James had made in this printing. Hence it would seem that Vogelius' reference was not to a first list that James had provided too late for inclusion in the second printing (this list in fact having been incorporated) but instead to a second list, which we now find made in the third printing, still dated 1890. Some corroborative evidence is present for this conclusion. The first round of plate alterations in what we may call the second printing consists of only five changes in volume I and five in volume II.[21] Obviously James had had little time to survey

[21] These occur at I,10.9–10 (23.4), I,38.fig. 10 (48.8+), I,92.12 (98.18–19), I,162.36 (164.37) (a mistaken 'correction'), I,332.41 (315.42); II,101.20 (745.29), II,101.26

the volumes before February 1891 and he must have relied for these few corrections on his chance inspection and possibly on suggestions from friends. It is clear that he either had accompanied these with a note that there were others that would be provided later, or else had written later asking to be informed when the next printing was due so that he could add more corrections. It is odd that for a second printing, in February 1891, he had not included the errors provided him on January 12 by his friend Frederic W. H. Myers ("I index a list of misprints in Vol. I some mere defects of printing and none important" [413, typed copy]), but perhaps the mails were slow or he had mislaid this list; at any rate, it found a place among the extensive 59 changes in volume I and 59 in volume II made in the second round (and in response to Vogelius' letter) for the third printing.

Here another letter from Vogelius to James, this a little over a month after his first request for corrections, informs James that the correction he has sent in for page 354 of volume I was too late since "The edition is worked off" (LB). Two corrections occur on this page, for the first time, in the third round of plate corrections found in the fourth or 1893 printing. These two plus one change in volume II are the only corrections found in this printing.[22]

The history of the printings, then, seems to have been somewhat as follows. A second printing was ordered in February 1891; but at the time only a handful of corrections, sent in previously by James, was available; these were made in the plates and the sheets rushed through the press. James had some notice of the intention to print a second impression and it is evident that he wanted to prepare a more extensive list than the few changes he had ordered, and informed Holt of his intention, but, as Vogelius wrote him, the second printing had to be made before he was ready. However, by the time that Vogelius warned him on November 4, 1891, of the imminence of another impression (the third), he was able to furnish a list that performed the really major correction of the

---

(745.34), II,372.0 (994.0), II,654.37 (1248.37), II,685.45 (1273.38). Details may be found in the list of Emendations.

[22]The record of plate alterations was recovered by machining on the Lindstrand Collator the first printing of 1890 against the undated fourteenth printing with a change in copyright to Alice James dated 1918 on the verso of the title, and then identifying by inspection the different rounds of correction and revision in other printings. Because of damage to the plates various resettings were made here and there of lines in some printings starting with 1907, which resulted in unauthoritative differences (chiefly the commission of errors). The complete record of plate changes is to be found in the list of Emendations.

plates, and one of singular importance. However, fresh errors kept turning up, probably including the misspelling in I,354.8 (335.21–22) which he had sent in early in December 1891, but too late. These three printings, although the second and third were made in early 1891 and late in the same year, were all published with the 1890 date unchanged on the title pages. Thereafter, James had no further opportunity to make corrections before the fourth printing was published in 1893. It is theoretically possible that before 1893 Holt published an unobserved fourth printing still dated 1890 in which the third round of correction (now observed in 1893) first appeared. Except for the single alteration in the sixth printing, 1899, of 'fondnesses' to 'fondness' at II,634.43 (1231.30) in a quotation from himself (which perforce must be accepted as authoritative), James did not again attempt to improve the edition until 1905.

As already noted, Holt sold 250 sheets to Macmillan in England, who issued these in two volumes as the English 'edition' with the title page:
THE PRINCIPLES | OF | PSYCHOLOGY | BY | WILLIAM JAMES | PROFESSOR OF PSYCHOLOGY IN HARVARD UNI-VERSITY | IN TWO VOLUMES | VOL. I [II] | London | MACMILLAN AND CO. | 1890
The verso of the title page is the same as in the American edition. The Bodleian Library's date stamp of arrival is 30 January 1891 (2645.e.1138), but the British Library is later on 25 March (2236.f.9). The London Library has a 1901 copy and a 1907; the British Library (2021.e) has a 1910 title page, and the Bodleian (2645.d. $\frac{439}{1}$) an undated title page. A Bodleian copy of the 1901 issue (2645.e.1131), date-stamped 11 June 1901, though rebound has preserved the spine of the dust jacket, reading: 'PRINCIPLES | OF | PSYCHOLOGY | WILLIAM JAMES | VOL I | TWO VOLUMES | 25/–NET. | MACMILLAN & C?'

Shortly after publication James had a copy of the first printing of *Principles* interleaved and rebound in four volumes, now preserved in the James Collection at Harvard (*AC85.J2376.890p). On various of these interleaves, and occasionally in the margins of the book pages, he entered two general categories of notes. The first consisted of the correction of misprints and errors but also revisions and additions to the text. Certain of these appear as plate changes but many do not, these presumably being changes entered after the major round that appeared in the 1891 third printing (still dated 1890), or else alterations impracticable to insert in the plates because of length. These markings give every indication of preparation for a possible second edition, a hypothesis supported by the nature of the numerous notes and annotations not intended for insertion in their form as written, some of which, however, may have been intended for use in his classes. This second category consists of a few notes to himself to improve certain pages, records of disagreements by different writers, and lists of books and articles bearing on the matter at hand, both pre- and post-1890, either not consulted or not utilized. Some few clippings of articles are pasted in or inserted. Except for a laid-in clipping from the *Deutsche Literaturzeitung* for April 13, 1907, which had been sent to James, his own gleanings and notes seem to stop at the end of 1896, at which point it would appear that he lost interest in or hope of a revised edition. These various annotations are transcribed in Appendix II, with added commentary Notes by Professor Skrupskelis.

In different chapters of the book James made use of various of his earlier-published journal and magazine articles. "The History" records what is known about their composition and date and examines James's statement in the Preface to *Briefer Course*, "With a single exception all the chapters were written for the book; and then by an after-thought some of them were sent to magazines, because the completion of the whole work seemed so distant," a statement not always to be taken literally as the composition of the journal form of "The Perception of Space" sufficiently indicates.

These journal articles, however, were utilized—often in much revised form—as printer's copy for portions of the book; hence they qualify as documents to be listed, with an indication of the sections of the book that depend upon them.

The first three chapters of *Principles* are independent of any journal article by James. The fourth chapter, "Habit," reprints with minor differences[23] "The Laws of Habit," *Popular Science Monthly*, 30 (February 1887), 433-451 (McD 1887:5). Because the journal form of this article can be recovered from the apparatus attached to the present edition, it is not reprinted elsewhere in the WORKS.

Chapter V, "The Automaton-Theory," draws on portions of

---

[23] For example, see the addition in the book of "If . . . disappear." (112.11-30) and the added footnote 18 (130.1,39-40).

"Are We Automata?" *Mind*, 4 (January 1879), 1-22 (McD 1879: 5), as follows:

 138.6-30 (I,134.20-135.8) "Mental . . . be feared." P^{24}, pp. 2-3
 142.27-143.28 (I,139.19-140.26) "But this . . . problem." P^{24}, pp. 5-6
 145.7-147.15 (I,142.13-144.35) "Consciousness . . . common-sense." P^{24}, pp. 16-18.

This article is reprinted complete in *Essays in Psychology* in the WORKS.

Chapter VI owes nothing to a journal, but Chapter VII, "The Methods and Snares of Psychology," takes a brief passage from "On Some Omissions of Introspective Psychology," *Mind*, 9 (January 1884), 1-26 (McD 1884:1):

 189.24-190.17 (I,189.36-191.2) "And as in . . . conscious-ness.'" P^{24}, pp. 1-2.

This article is reprinted complete in *Essays in Psychology*.

Chapter VIII, "The Relations of Minds to Other Things," makes extended use of "The Hidden Self," *Scribner's Magazine*, 7 (March 1890), 361-373 (McD 1890:1):[24]

 200.9-29 (I,202.11-203.2) "One . . . disturbed." P^{37}, p. 363
 200.30-201.2 (I,203.3-13) "These . . . sensibility" P^{37}, p. 364
 201.16-24 (I,203.28-37) "'When Lucie . . . auditors.'" P^{37}, p. 364
 202.1-208.9 (I,204.14-211.17) "This *proof* . . . fact." P^{37}, pp. 368-371.

This article, also utilized in Chapter X, will be found in *Essays in Psychology*.

Chapter IX, "The Stream of Thought," draws from two articles already noted. The first is "On Some Omissions of Introspective Psychology":

 228.30-229.3 (I,234.32-235.5) "And (to . . . feel." P^{24a}, p. 12
 229.4-20 (I,235.6-24) "Ever some . . . brain?" P^{24a}, p. 12
 236.15-237.24 (I,243.13-244.30) "As we . . . stream." P^{24a}, pp. 2-3
 238.16-239.7 (I,245.24-246.20) "There is . . . on." P^{24a}, pp. 5-6
 243.1-247.23.(I,250.9-256.18) "Suppose three . . . be." P^{24a}, pp. 13-17

---

[24]Here as in various other articles only the parts are noted in which the printed article could have served as the printer's copy. It is to be understood that James would frequently expand or condense article passages by paraphrase that would need to have been written out independently. These passages are not recorded here.

253.21-32 (I,262.32-263.2) "Usually the . . . thought." P[24a], pp. 19-20

265.28-266.6 (I,275.22-276.2) "But the *Object* . . . meaning." P[24a], pp. 22-23.

In addition, passages are taken from "Are We Automata?":

273.29-274.20 (I,284.23-285.17) "To begin . . . fact." P[24b], pp. 9-10

274.39-277.15 (I,285.39-288.30) "In like . . . on." P[24b], pp. 11-13

277.22-33 (I,288.38-289.12) "We may . . . crab!" P[24b], p. 14.

Chapter X, "The Consciousness of Self," utilizes passages from two articles. The first, already drawn on in a major way for Chapter VIII, is "The Hidden Self":

364.1-365.17 (I,385.5-386.26) "But one day . . . back." P[37], pp. 364-365

365.22-367.23 (I,386.32-388.37) "One stage . . . master.'" P[37], pp. 366-367.

A passage from "Notes on Automatic Writing," *Proceedings of the American Society for Psychical Research*, 1 (March 1889), 548-564 (McD 1889:3) is also quoted:

373.5-374.37 (I,394.31-396.19) "As an example . . . style.'" P[31], pp. 556-557.

Essays in Psychical Research in the Works will reprint this article.

Chapter XI, "Attention," owes nothing to James's articles, but Chapter XII, "Conception," quotes one passage from "On Some Omissions of Introspective Psychology":

451.35-453.38 (I,477.39-479.44 [fn. 17]) "'Why may we . . . contempt.'" P[24], pp. 18-19.

Chapter XIII, "Discrimination and Comparison," draws freely on "Brute and Human Intellect," *Journal of Speculative Philosophy*, 12 (July 1878), 236-276 (McD 1878:4) but in the form of paraphrase,[25] so much rewritten that collation is impracticable except for:

478.37-479.18 (I,506.29-507.8) "Mr. Spencer . . . so on.'" P[21], pp. 253-254 (quotations from Spencer and Martineau)

479.19-480.7 (I,507.9-37) "*Why* . . . consists in." P[21], p. 255. This article is reprinted in *Essays in Psychology*.

---

[25]The reworked passages are chiefly 474.30-475.13 (I,502.15-30) "The components . . . found." (free use of "Brute and Human Intellect," P[21], 254.9-25 "In other words . . . testify."); 478.19-25 (I,506.9-16) "We may . . . accommodation." (free use of P[21], 254.30-255.3 "We may . . . prisms."); 478.31-479.18 (I,506.22-507.8) "One might . . . so on.'" (free use of P[21], 253.13- 254.8 "This process . . . by one.'" except for quotes from Spencer and Martineau drawn from P[21]).

Chapter XIV, "Association," substantially reprints in revised form "The Association of Ideas," *Popular Science Monthly*, 16 (March 1880), 577–593 (McD 1880:1), with expansions. Since the text of the article is recoverable through the present apparatus, it is not reprinted elsewhere in the WORKS. The following passages are utilized:

519.13–520.1 (I,550.15–27) "The manner . . . terms." P^{29}, p. 577

520.32–522.10 (I,551.33–553.20) "But as . . . thoughts," P^{29}, pp. 578–579

523.3–9 (I,554.17–25) "The laws . . . concerned." P^{29}, p. 581

531.20–549.5 (I,563.31–583.6) "*The* . . . thinking." P^{29}, pp. 581–593.

The same is true for Chapter XV, "The Perception of Time," which fully utilizes "The Perception of Time," *Journal of Speculative Philosophy*, 20 (October 1886), 374–407 (McD 1886:3). Chapter XVI, "Memory," is independent of an article. Chapter XVII, "Sensation," utilizes a passage by James's pupil, E. B. Delabarre at 662.5–674.20 (II,13.7–27.3) "Nowhere . . . shadow." and draws on "The Perception of Space (II)," *Mind*, 12 (April 1887), 183–211 (McD 1887:4): 683.32–684.25 (II,37.9–38.8) "If one . . . at once.^{42}" P^{24}, pp. 204–205. Chapter XVIII owes nothing to a journal.

Chapter XIX, "The Perception of 'Things,'" draws one passage from "The Perception of Space (III)," *Mind*, 12 (July 1887), 321–353 (McD 1887:4): 743.15–745.21 (II,99.3–101.11) "When we . . . chase.'^{23}" P^{24}, pp. 331–332 (744.3–4 [II,99.29–30] is found on pp. 330–331 of the article).

Chapter XX, "The Perception of Space," subsumes "The Perception of Space," *Mind*, 12 (January, April, July, October 1887), 1–30, 183–211, 321–353, 516–548 (McD 1887:4); the text of the article being recoverable from the present apparatus is not reprinted in the WORKS. The chapter also draws, although slightly, on "The Spatial Quale," *Journal of Speculative Philosophy*, 13 (January 1879), 64–87 (McD 1879:6):

776.4–9 (II,134.4–10) "We . . . lumbago;" P^{21}, p. 70.28–33

785.17–23 (II,143.19–26) "The . . . parallax." P^{21}, p. 75.38–43

788.7–11 (II,146.18–22) "The . . . other." P^{21}, p. 67.6–10

791.34–792.2 (II,150.20–26) "If . . . blue." P^{21}, pp. 74.38–40, 75.25–26

807.5–15 (II,167.26–168.4) "Granted . . . subdivisions." P^{21}, pp. 77.31–78.5

807.21–25 (II,168.10–16) "In . . . intense." P^{21}, p. 77.14–18

(variants recorded in the Historical Collation)

807.26–32 (II,168.17–24) *"The* . . . withdrawn." P²¹, pp. 79.33–80.3

808.24–33 (II,169.15–25) "even . . . surface." P²¹, pp. 76.27–77.1

809.16–24 (II,169.39–170.18) " 'excited . . . membrane.' " P²¹, pp. 84.38–85.10

810.7–811.22 (II,171.7–172.27) *"The* . . . results." P²¹, pp. 72.31–74.15 (variants recorded in the Historical Collation as well as the P²⁴ variants in this passage).

"The Spatial Quale" is reprinted entire in *Essays in Psychology* in the WORKS. Chapter XXI, "The Perception of Reality," in expanded form takes in all of "The Psychology of Belief," *Mind*, 14 (July 1889), 321–352 (McD 1889:4), which therefore is not reprinted elsewhere. In addition, Chapter XXI at 940.10–943.26 (II,312.27–315.36) " 'A philosophy . . . given him.' " quotes directly from "Rationality, Activity and Faith," *Princeton Review*, 2 (July 1882), 64–69 (McD 1882:2), an article that James in 1897 linked with "The Sentiment of Rationality" of 1879 (original text reprinted in *Essays in Philosophy* in the WORKS) to form in *The Will to Believe* a new essay entitled "The Sentiment of Rationality." The full text of "Rationality, Activity and Faith" is recoverable from *The Will to Believe* text and apparatus and so has not been independently reprinted.

Chapter XXII, "Reasoning," makes use of three articles. The major source is "Brute and Human Intellect," *Journal of Speculative Philosophy*, 12 (July 1878), 236–276 (McD 1878:4), which had earlier been levied from in Chapter XIII. As in the earlier chapter, "Reasoning" makes free use of paraphrase,[26] but printer's-copy revised text is found at:

966.15–967.15 (II,340.27–341.32) "Suppose . . . now." P²¹, pp. 247–248

967.16–970.29 (II,341.33–345.25) "reasoning involves . . . brutes." P²¹, pp. 249–253

971.1–991.32 (II,345.37–369.18) "What does . . . cope with." P²¹, pp. 258–276.

In 961.41–962.28 (II,335.31–336.22, fn. 10) James quotes directly from his "Sentiment of Rationality," *Mind*, 4 (July 1879), 317–

---

[26]The paraphrased passages are chiefly 952.7–19 (II,325.8–22) "Much . . . alphabet, etc." (from P²¹, 237.29–238.22 "To say . . . alphabet."); 959.5–29 (II,332.21–333.10) "Every reality . . . ignored." (from P²¹, 248.15–38 "Every phenomenon . . . plans."); 966.10–14 (II,340.22–26) *"First . . . came."* (from P²¹, 247.6–10 "first . . . evidence.").

346 (McD 1879:7) " 'What is . . . accidents.' " P[24], pp. 318–319. In 975.22–976.36 (II,351.9–48) part of footnote 16 ("If a sheet . . . sagacity.") is drawn from James's (with G. M. Carnochan) "Report of the Committee on Hypnotism," *Proceedings of the American Society for Psychical Research*, 1 (July 1886), pp. 98–100 (McD 1886:1), an article separately printed in *Essays in Psychology*.

Chapter XXIII, "The Production of Movement," has no article source but Chapter XXIV, "Instinct," in its first part (1004.1–1022.16 [II,383.1–402.39]) reprints with considerable fidelity and a minimum of revision "What Is an Instinct?" *Scribner's Magazine*, 1 (March 1887), 355–365 (McD 1887:6), an article not reproduced separately, therefore, in the WORKS. The second part of the chapter reprints "Some Human Instincts," *Popular Science Monthly*, 31 (June, September 1887), 160–170, 666–681 (McD 1887:8), also not separately reproduced. The early pages 1022.18–1028.18 (II,403.2–409.26) "Let us . . . consider." P[29], pp. 160–162, are a paraphrase. However, *Principles* then uses as printer's copy, revised:

1028.19–1029.2 (II,409.27–410.15) *"Pugnacity . . .* unharmed." P[29], p. 163

1029.3–1030.4 (II,410.16–411.22) *"Sympathy . . .* gone." P[29], pp. 162–163

1030.5–1057.17 (II,411.23–441.24) *"The hunting . . .* bringing-up." P[29], pp. 163–170, 666–681.

Chapter XXV, "The Emotions," makes considerable use of "What Is an Emotion?" *Mind*, 9 (April 1884), 188–205 (McD 1884:2):

1065.27–1066.12 (II,449.31–450.20) "Our natural . . . truth." P[24], pp. 189–190

1066.18–1068.26 (II,450.27–453.6) "The various . . . ago." P[24], pp. 192–194

1072.2–1073.32 (II,456.17–458.34) "Let me now . . . suppose." P[24], pp. 196–197

1073.33–1074.22 + fn. 11 (II,458.35–459.26 + fn. 11) "The best proof . . . depart.[11]" P[24], p. 199

1077.9–1078.6 (II,462.19–463.21) "If our theory . . . thaw!" P[24], pp. 197–198

1080.26–1081.24 (II,466.8–467.7) *"Reply . . .* child." P[24], pp. 198–199

1081.24–38 (II,467.8–24) "It is true . . . proceeds." P[24], p. 198

1082.1–1087.31 (II,467.26–474.11) "If our . . . exist." P[24], pp. 201–203.

II. The Documents

"What Is an Emotion?" is reprinted complete in *Essays in Psychology*.

Chapter XXVI, "Will," reworks parts of two articles. The first is "What the Will Effects," *Scribner's Magazine*, 3 (February 1888), 240–250 (McD 1888:1):

1099.13–17 (II,487.9–14) "The other . . . face." P[37], p. 241

1099.17–23 (II,487.14–21) "I have . . . foreseen" P[37], p. 241

1132.23–1133.9 (II,524.15–525.6) "We know . . . volition." P[37], p. 242

1135.12–39 (II,527.14–528.6) "It may . . . kind." P[37], pp. 243–244

1167.5–1169.16 (II,563.1–565.2) "Certainly there . . . will!" P[37], pp. 245–247

1175.13–34 (II,571.23–572.7) "It certainly . . . impossible." P[37], p. 248

1181.33–40 (II,579.4–11) "He can . . . edge." P[37], p. 250

1182.5–8 (II,579.17–20) "The prophet . . . his own." P[37], p. 250. Passages are taken from "The Feeling of Effort," *Anniversary Memoirs of the Boston Society of Natural History* (1880), pp. 3–32 (McD 1880:3):

1101.36–1102.15 + fn. 4 (II,490.5–23) "Or we read . . . limb.'4" P[42], pp. 20–21

1107.7–1109.37 (II,496.7–498.40) "that consciousness . . . cues." P[42], pp. 5–6

1107.21–1107.26 (II,495.37–42) " 'It is possible . . . perspiration.' " P[42], p. 19

1110.22–1112.7 (II,499.29–501.25) "Whoever says . . . farther on." P[42], pp. 7–8

1112.8–1113.8 (II,501.26–503.6) "Now the reader . . . existed." P[42], pp. 17–18

1113.9–1120.20 (II,503.7–511.10) "Since . . . the right." P[42], pp. 8–13

1120.20–1121.10 (II,511.11–22) "It takes . . . we see." P[42], p. 13

1131.24–32 + fn. 34 (II,523.12–20) " 'We see . . . thought.'34" P[42], pp. 16–17

1133.20–29 (II,525.18–27) " 'The spectator . . . action.' " P[42], p. 16

1154.29–1155.37 (II,548.14–549.29) "When outer . . . least." P[42], p. 28

1165.6–1166.3 (II,560.6–561.10) "whether the act . . . before.61" P[42], pp. 19–20

1167.24–33 (II,562.22–32) "These feelings . . . *real*." P[42], p. 25

1167.37-44 (II,562.37-45) "Exhausted . . . morning." P⁴², pp. 21-22

1170.9-16 (II,566.1-9) "The exhausted . . . still." P⁴², p. 23 (*paraphrase*)

1170.19-31 (II,566.12-26) "If a patient . . . reality!'" P⁴², pp. 23-24 (*paraphrase*)

1171.25-44 (II,567.22-43) "*The Duality . . . it.*'" P⁴², p. 24

1176.20-31 (II,572.31-573.13) "He who . . . creed." P⁴², p. 29. Both articles are reprinted in *Essays in Psychology.*

Chapter XXVII, "Hypnotism," draws one passage from the "Report of the Committee on Hypnotism," *Proceedings of the American Society for Psychical Research*, 1 (July 1886), 95-102 (McD 1886:1):

1207.1-1208.3 (II,607.28-608.35) "Make a stroke . . . remains aware." P³¹, pp. 96-97.

Finally, in Chapter XXVIII, "Necessary Truths and the Effects of Experience," James quotes an extensive passage from "Reflex Action and Theism," *Unitarian Review*, 16 (November 1881), 389-416 (McD 1881:3):

1231.24-1232.37 (II,634.35-635.48) "'The conceiving . . . ends.'" P³⁸, pp. 395-396. This article has been reprinted in *The Will to Believe*, WORKS; the quoted passage appears there on pp. 94-96.

III. THE EDITORIAL PROBLEM

For reasons discussed in A Note on the Editorial Method, the first printing of *The Principles of Psychology* (1890) becomes the copy-text. Despite the fact that a number of chapters draw on or were printed from clippings of articles published before 1890, James revised such basic copy so thoroughly that (although closer to James's autograph) the articles have lesser and only a collateral textual authority. On the other hand, verbally they are key documents for any scholarly historical study of the development of James's thought between their publication and the revision for the book, as shown by the record of their substantive variants in the Historical Collation. Textually, however, they are useful chiefly as emending agents for occasional errors in the book and (in their accidentals) as partial witnesses to the nature and extent of the book printer's housestyling.

The relationship of *Briefer Course* (1892) to *Principles* introduces a vexed editorial problem. In producing a one-volume textbook from *Principles* James ruthlessly excised almost all footnotes and quotations and removed many passages from his own text while condensing others by paraphrase. In the interests of shortening the exposition even simple phrases within an otherwise untouched sentence might be deleted or more succinct substitutes inserted. However, the passage of two years had altered some of James's views so that *Briefer Course* in the midst of its redaction displays occasional true revision of his psychological ideas as well as a considerable amount of alteration in pursuit of sharpness and precision, simple felicity, and ease of expression. The case could be argued that substantive revision in *Briefer Course*, aimed at revising and improving the parallel text, is as much a part of *Principles'* textual history as is the treatment that James gave to his basic articles when composing the book text of *Principles*. To the extent that a general reader of *Principles* could be genuinely interested in the further development of its text as found in *Briefer Course*, and a close student would be required to acquaint himself with the differences between the two in their parallel parts in order to comprehend the final exposition of James's psychology,[27] the argument is a valid one. However, the problem presented itself as to the most convenient place for this record of differences. Granting that any concerned reader of *Principles* might wish to have the apparatus record of these changes keyed to the *Principles* text and in the same set of volumes, three objections were powerful enough to enforce the placement of this record in the *Briefer Course* volume instead. The first was a practical one in that extensively revised passages in *Briefer Course* would need reference to its text in the WORKS, else a quite extravagant amount of quoting would have proved necessary. Second, the question of which variants were matters of improvement and revision and which were chiefly motivated by the need for condensation (this of lesser concern to the critic of *Principles*) is not ordinarily a simple matter of automatic decision. Third, a student of *Briefer Course* in its own right—and it deserves such study—will require the record of its variation from the text of *Principles* just as much as a student of *Principles* requires the listing of variation from the source

---

[27]It seems likely that scholars have been thrown off by James's disclaimer in the foreword to *Briefer Course* that about three-fifths of it was a scissors and paste job. It is true that James pasted up some pages of *Principles* and marked them to serve as printer's copy. But the impression he chose to give that he had done little more is quite erroneous, for *Briefer Course* exhibits a significant amount of rewriting and revision and cannot be neglected in any serious study of James's psychology.

journal articles. The Historical Collation of *Briefer Course* contains all this information keyed to its text, but for the convenience of interested students of *Principles*, the major divergences in the two texts also list the page-line references to *Principles* in this edition of the WORKS.

The first part of the problem of the two texts concerned their apparatus. The second part, by analogy, brought into question the status of the *Principles* text when revised by *Briefer Course*, and whether an 'ideal text' of *Principles* might not be constructed that would contain the final form of James's psychological ideas and their presentation, when this was the intent of the variation in *Briefer Course* from the text of *Principles*. The theoretical aspects of this question would require a fuller discussion than is warranted here. Suffice it to say that the practical matter of deciding precisely what emendations to make to *Principles* from ostensible revisions and what to reject as simple condensation or paraphrase, as well as the more subtle point of what had been altered less for revision of *Principles* than in view of the changed purpose and audience of *Briefer Course*, proved too difficult to negotiate. With only a handful of exceptions, therefore, the substantive readings of *Principles* are not emended from *Briefer Course*, except in the correction of error, and *Principles* is edited as a closed historical document except for the post-publication revision and correction that James made in its own text.

The problem of distinguishing pinpointed revision from the results of textbook condensation and presentation that affect the wording, or substantives, has no bearing on the so-called 'accidentals' of the punctuation as an aid to meaning. Such differences between the two texts as occur in spelling or in word-division, say, or in the matter of single versus double quotation marks, may in general be imputed to different compositorial styling, even though both books were printed by the same firm. Concept capitalization or reduction is too closely related to meaning to be classed as a simple matter of accidentals. But punctuation as a part of stylistic texture and as a relatively pure 'accidental' feature of the text proved to be another matter. Tests made by collation of quotations in the two books (where James's own interference in *Briefer Course* would have been absent) demonstrated an admirably close reproduction of the accidentals of the *Principles* copy, and this fidelity of the *Briefer Course* compositors was further attested by the results of collation when there were stretches of parallel text for a number of pages in which James had made few or no substantive changes. On the other hand, in pages where James concerned himself with small substantive alterations, the incidence of change in the punctuation also rises markedly, indicating that when James paid little attention to the wording he was likely to leave the *Principles* punctuation alone; but when he was reading the copy carefully for the revision of wording, he was more scrupulous in improving the punctuation. (This matter is discussed in some detail in The Text of *Psychology: Briefer Course* in that volume of the WORKS.) Outside of certain relatively identifiable compositorial stylings in the punctuation, it seems evident that the considerable majority of the punctuation differences in parallel text in *Briefer Course* were consciously designed by James. Since these do not come under the strictures that prevented the textual editor from attempting to emend the substantives of *Principles* from variants in *Briefer Course*, those changes most readily assignable to James's marking of copy have been adopted in the present text and are, of course, noted in the list of Emendations.

The changes made in the plates of various impressions between the 1891 second printing (title dated 1890) and the 1910 printing, made in the last year of James's lifetime, constitute an important source for James's corrections and revisions of the text. The figures for these plate-changes are interesting as illustration of the errors in the initial typesetting that James was at pains to remove as he observed them or as they were pointed out to him.

Printings	*Plate Changes*
2nd (February 1891)	9 (1 resetting error)
3rd (November 1891)	118 (3 resetting errors)
4th (1893)	3
5th (1896)	no plate changes
6th (1899)	1
7th (1902)	no plate changes
8th (1905)	17
9th (1907)	4 (all resetting errors)
10th (1908)	no plate changes
11th (1910)	12 (9 resetting errors)

Since Holt was as concerned as James to correct mechanical errors, we cannot be certain that every such change has James's own authority. However, the source of correction of obvious error is of small importance; for example, the correction of misprints in 1910 probably did not result from his initiative, but since they (and later changes) were not revisory the question is not crucial, for the text must be corrected either by publisher or by editor. The specific authority of the alterations in the earlier printings, especially in the third of late 1891, and also in 1893, cannot be challenged; but even the single plate change found in the 1899 impression appears to have originated with James. Indeed, many of the earlier corrections and revisions in the plates, as in 1891, are confirmed by the markings in James's interleaved annotated copy of the first printing preserved at Harvard (*AC85.J2376. 890p). Various annotations in this marked copy represent notes for classroom reference or for later use in a possible revised edition; a number by their nature, corroborated by James's markings for insertion in the text itself, reveal themselves as textual revisions that James intended to be made either in the plates of later printings or in a reset later edition. Some of these markings postdate the major round of plate-changes that was made in 1891 and thus they may appear for the first time in the text of the present edition. The list of Emendations records whether these marked alterations are independent of plate-changes or else confirm them. The full list of James's annotations in his marked copy has been transcribed in Appendix II, including the readings adopted as emendations of the copy-text first printing. Slight differences may appear between James's rough jottings of proposed emendations (particularly in his added or revised bibliographical references) and the forms that have been editorially adopted for consistency; hence the exact notes of emendation that James made may need to be recovered from their listing in Appendix II rather than from the forms adopted in the list of Emendations, which may provide fuller titles and so on.

Owing to the large number of quotations and the considerable discrepancies that may develop between the degrees of fidelity to the original authors in James's reproductions, a full record of all variation in the accidentals of quotations would have required space considerably in excess of the value of the information. A working compromise was therefore adopted as follows. Quotations that represent James's translations from the German or French are reproduced faithfully as in the copy-text, with any significant discrepancy between the original and the translation indicated in Professor Skrupskelis' Notes, although occasional errors have been corrected and noted in the Emendations. Quotations in English have ordinarily been reprinted in the accidental texture of their originals,[28] without record of the copy-text's variation except for such semi-substantive matters as cases of concept capitalization.

---

[28]That is, the 'accidentals' of the text—the spelling, punctuation, word-division, capitalization, etc. of the originals—reproduce the forms of the originals that James copied, not the forms found in *Principles*, which may represent a combination of James's variants in copying and the printer's housestyling.

On the other hand, editorial discretion has been applied to the problem of the variant substantives, or wording. As a general rule when the verbal differences in the book appear to be indifferent and to stem from James's inadvertent changes in the process of transcription, the original wording has been restored and the fact recorded in the list of Emendations. However, when the variants appear to have been consciously made, James's intentions in the treatment of the quotation have usually been respected and his version has been retained, in which case the list of Emendations records the fact with a *stet* entry that provides the actual reading as found in the quoted author. Substantive variants in English-language quotations, therefore, whether adopted from the originals or retained in their book form, are always noted in the Emendations list. Variant accidentals for the most part are silently substituted from the originals for the book's unauthoritative alterations. A Note on the Editorial Method contains a further discussion of James's treatment of quotations and of the editorial method adopted to deal with the problems that are raised.

James's footnotes in *Principles* pose a special problem. The profuseness of his reference is not matched in the philosophical writings, nor do any of these bear comparison in sheer magnitude with *Principles*; thus the editorial treatment given elsewhere to footnotes will not work in the present text. A distinction has been made, therefore, between the minutiae of bibliographical reference (largely in the typography and in the accidentals) and questions of substantive fact or importance. The first are dealt with silently; the second are recorded in the list of Emendations. The footnotes in the copy-text are often inconsistent in form and method even for reference to the same titles, and their citation of dates of the editions and of page numbers is not always complete or accurate. It has seemed best to aid the reader as much as possible by smoothing reference to the works cited even when this assistance has involved some alteration in the form of James's citations. First and most obvious, the minutiae of the accidentals have not been regarded as emendations or as rejected readings but have been silently normalized to current usage. For example, book titles are italicized without record from whatever form was present in the copy-text, as within single or double quotation marks or without any marks at all; missing punctuation is silently inserted where required and the forms of abbreviations are made consistent; the use of roman or italic fonts is normalized, as is the general system of punctuating bibliographical references. For instance, James, in text and in footnotes, frequently omitted the comma after such a reference as '*ibid.*, p. 42', or 'e.g., p. 89', and he often used periods instead of commas to separate a volume number from the paginal reference that followed. In all such cases commas are supplied or substituted. James frequently gave a partial title in footnotes. On first use such shortened titles are silently expanded to their full form although the shorthand versions are allowed to stand thereafter unless in need of emendation. Variants editorially introduced but not treated as listed emendations comprise largely mechanical matters such as the expansion to 'Über die Localisation' when James had written simply 'Die Localisation', and so with omitted initial 'De' in French titles. The supplying of omitted words within a title is ordinarily treated also as a silent editorial duty. On the other hand, correction of errors in wording and in spelling within titles is everywhere recorded in the list of Emendations, as for instance the emendation of James's title *Cerveau Moteur* (58.19) to the correct *Fonctions motrices du cerveau*. True misspellings like *Elements* for *Elémens* (239.40) are recorded, but trivial errors or Jamesian inconsistencies in dealing with older and with modern spellings are silently corrected.

Dates and page numbers are corrected by recorded emendation. In any given footnote James's own system of paginal reference is allowed to stand although in corrected form. That is, James might refer to a quotation as occurring on pp. 108–10, or he might simply give the first page in his source on which the quotation started without concern for its end, as in p. 108. If in the latter case he made a mistake and noted the quotation as, say, p. 109, the editorial correction would preserve the system of the original and alter it to p. 108, not expanded as 108–10 unless that had been the system used in the entry. Professor Skrupskelis' Notes are to be taken as the ultimate authority in all cases of identification, however. As is to be expected at the time, no consistency holds in the use of the German umlaut like 'ü' or the equivalent 'ue'. All 'ue' and other such forms of umlauted vowels have been silently altered to the umlaut version except in personal names where an attempt has been made to preserve the form customarily used by the author. This silent treatment of footnotes extends to those added from James's annotated copy (WJ/I). The exact forms in this copy will be found not in the list of Emendations but instead in the listing in Appendix II. If an error occurs in WJ/I, it is corrected accordingly in the text and Emendations.

Within the text an attempt is also made, but less drastically, to reduce in the Emendations list the record of bibliographical minutiae. In fact, unless there is a specific note, any italicized book title in the text may be taken automatically as altering a roman title in the copy-text with or without quotation marks. Similarly, the titles of articles, poems, and the like, are enclosed in double quotation marks without record. An exception to the silent normalizing of double or single quotation marks is made for quotations, however, since in at least some cases the distinction of single versus double marks is a Jamesian intention. Abbreviated titles are usually retained, but abbreviated names, like 'Chas.' for 'Charles' are silently expanded. All ampersands are silently expanded wherever they occur.

The Historical Collation handles the substantive (verbal) variants between the article and book form of the material. A major distinction is drawn between articles that are so completely utilized in the chapters that they will not be printed independently in the WORKS and those that are drawn upon, even to a major extent, but that possess sufficient separate interest in their full article form as to warrant reprinting in other volumes of the WORKS, mainly in the collected *Essays in Psychology*. In the first instance the Historical Collation is complete so that the entire article in full detail can be reconstituted from a comparison of the book text with the apparatus, including the reprinting in Appendix I of extended passages omitted or paraphrased in the book. In the second instance the Historical Collation covers only those parts of the article that in authorially revised form served as setting copy for the book, presumably as annotated clippings. No indication can be given in the Historical Collation of parts of these articles not thus directly utilized in the book copy-text even though the book may paraphrase the article material. The passages in the copy-text that are collated from the articles in the Historical Collation are listed above in Part II, "The Documents."

As has been the custom in the philosophical volumes of the WORKS, the Historical Collation records the unadopted substantive variants from the book copy-text in the antecedent articles. However, the practice in the present volumes of silently altering the accidentals of quotations to agree with their originals has served to emphasize the lack of essential authority both in articles and in book for such accidentals as against their originals; and indeed no case can be made for James in his revision of the articles for the book printer's copy having referred back to the sources of his English-language quotations in order to insure greater fidelity to their accidentals. Hence all such variation between articles and book is either the result of James unauthoritatively (from the point of view of the originals) altering the accidental texture of the quotations according to his own notions or else of the normal variation that derives from compositorial resetting. For this reason, because of the silent editorial reconstitution of the source accidentals in the quotations from English-language sources, variation in these respects between article and book is not listed in the Historical Collation, just as it is ignored in the list of Emendations.

The case is altered in the variation in accidentals between the text of a source article and the revised book text, for these differences represent a mixture of James's own alterations with changes produced by printer's housestyling. Since the two categories are not always clearly distinguishable except in some formal routine aspects, in the philosophical volumes where the data could be handled—and especially in cases of preserved manuscripts—it has been the custom to record all accidental as well as substantive variation within the series of authoritative documents. However, the vast mass of the psychological documents that are associated with *Principles* effectively precludes any such attempt at recording within the Historical Collation the interesting but not always significant variation in accidentals except for a few specific categories mentioned in the headnote to that section of the apparatus. Moreover, it has been taken that in James's scientific as distinguished from his more literary philosophical works, the readers of the psychology volumes will be less concerned with the minutiae of accidental variation between articles and book, but keenly interested in the really crucial matters (from their point of view) of James's verbal, or substantive, alterations in the process of revision. In contrast to the philosophical volumes, therefore, pre-copy-text accidental variation has not been recorded in the Historical Collation, which is thus confined to the variant substantive readings save for a few selected important accidental categories of specific interest.

CORRECTION

Page 1542: The letter of James to Royce (bMS Am 1092.9 [3595]) about a draft piece in 1877 does not refer to "Are We Automata?" but to "The Sentiment of Rationality." No earlier form of "Are We Automata?" is known before 1878.

Emendations

Every editorial change from the copy-text is recorded for the substantives, and every change in the accidentals as well save for such silent typographical adjustments as are remarked in A Note on the Editorial Method. The reading to the left of the bracket, the lemma, represents the form chosen in the present edition, usually as an emendation of the copy-text. (A prefixed superior 1 or 2 indicates which of any two identical words in the same line is intended.) The sigil immediately following the bracket is the identifying symbol for the earliest source of the emendation, followed by the sigla of any later agreeing documents. Readings in parentheses after sigla indicate a difference in the accidental form of the source from that of the emended reading to the left of the bracket. A semicolon follows the last of the sigla for emending sources. To the right of this semicolon appear the rejected readings of the copy-text and of any other recorded documents, followed by their sigla. The copy-text is (I), the first-edition typesetting as represented by the first printing from the plates. If no indication of printing is given, the assumption is that the reading in (I) is invariant in all impressions from the original plates. A superior number identifies the exact printing in case of need, as I^1 for the 1890 first printing and I^4 for the 1893 fourth printing. Emendations marked as H (Harvard) are editorial and are not drawn from any authoritative document. The word *stet* after the bracket calls special attention to the retention of a copy-text reading. It may be employed to key a Textual Note, as marked by an asterisk before the page-line number. In a quotation it may indicate that James's version (differing from the source in some respect) has been retained in the edited text. It may also be used in rare instances to indicate that a possibly questionable or unusual reading has been retained in the text.

For convenience, certain shorthand symbols familiar in textual notation are employed. A wavy dash ($\sim$) represents the same word that appears before the bracket and is used exclusively in recording punctuation or other accidental variants. An inferior caret ($_\wedge$) indicates the absence of a punctuation mark (or of a footnote superscript) when a difference in the punctuation constitutes the variant being recorded, or is a part of the variant. A vertical stroke ($|$) represents a line ending, sometimes recorded as bearing on the cause of an error or fault. A hand symbol (☛) before a page-line reference draws attention to the parenthetical listing of additional lines where the forms of emendation are identical. Quotations within the text are identified in Professor Skrupskelis' Notes. The sigil WJ/ followed by the appropriate symbol (as WJ/I and WJ/BC) indicates James's autograph revisions found in his private copies of books.

Emendations

CONTENTS

10.6 knowledge-] H; ∼∧ I

CHAPTER I: THE SCOPE OF PSYCHOLOGY

The copy-text for Chapter I is (I), the 1890 first printing of *The Principles of Psychology*. An emendation adopted from James's marked copy of the first edition found at Harvard is noted as WJ/I.

15.2 of] I³; *om.* I¹⁻²
15.18 Hume,] H; ∼∧ I
15.19 Britain,] H; ∼∧ I
18.16 mental life] H; mentallife I (*error*)
18.23 psychologist] H; pyschologist I (*error*)
22.10 stock-] WJ/I; ∼∧ I

*23.4 not ... power] H; the seat of intellectual power I¹; not the sole seat of intellect I²
24.14 *Comparative* ... Co.)] H; 'Comparative Anatomy and Dissection of Mammalia' (Longmans) I

CHAPTER II: THE FUNCTIONS OF THE BRAIN

Reference is made to WJ/I. Emendations taken from the 1892 first printing of *Psychology: Briefer Course* are given the sigil BC.

*25.6 system,] BC; ∼∧ I
25.15 animal∧] BC; ∼, I
25.22 "All aboard!"] H; *sg. qts.* I
27.21 them–] BC; ∼; I
28.17 fore-paws] H; ∼∧∼I (forepaws BC)
28.17,25;31.8;91.14 hind-] BC; ∼∧ I
28.19 back∧] BC; ∼, I
28.24 fore-] BC; ∼∧ I
28.37 skin-] BC; ∼∧ I
*30.5-10 He ... person] *stet* I
30.32 -legs, ... frog,] BC; ∧∼∧ ... ∼∧ I
30.33 touched;] BC; ∼, I
30.40-31.1 incalculable–we] BC; ∼. We I
33.17 catarrhal] I³,BC; catarral I¹⁻²
34.19 water∧] BC; ∼, I
*34.29-35.3 And ... alone.] *stet* I
35.20 and,] BC; ∼∧ I
37.15;727.10 upwards] H; upward I
☛37.15 downwards] H; downward I (*also* 104.6;133.28;1024.18)
41.15 J.] H; *om.* I
41.16 lowest ... highest] *stet* I; lowest spinal centres to the very highest centres Jackson
41.19 rest of the] Jackson; *om.* I

41.19 *can*] *stet* I; can Jackson
41.39 344] H; 345 I
43.37 pp. 523-61] H; p. 528 I
☛44.24 anyone] H; any one I (*also* 54.21;148.11;149.32;153.38;171.5; 214.13;217.9;224.35;294.22;329.31, 32;370.7;424.35;569.2;654.35; 1068.31;1094.40;1232.7;1267.29)
45.21 *et seq. this chap.* Schäfer] H; Schaefer I
*46.13 167] Exner; 169 I
48.8+ (*in* Fig. 10) the Face] I²; Sight I¹
53.38 pp. 175-238] H; p. 176 I
53.38 *Sitzungsberichte*] H; Sitzungsberichte I (*error*)
55.26 *et seq. this chap.* Seppilli] H; Seppili I
55.28-29 VII ... -188)] H; VII, VIII, pp. 113-121 I
55.30 VII] H; VII, VIII I
57.37-38 108-10, 420-22] H; 108-420 I
58.18 pp. 83, 88-125] H; p. 83 I
58.19 *Fonctions ... cerveau*] H; Cerveau Moteur I
59.1-4 Henschen ... dogs.] WJ/I; *om.* I
*59.15-16 or of] BC; or I

59.35 Central] H; Cerebral I
60.42 481] H; 581 I
61.36 above] I³; below I¹⁻²
61.38 See . . . 481.] WJ/I; *om.* I
61.39 III . . . (1883)] H; II . . . (1881) I
62.30 145] H; 147 I
63.11 M.] H; *om.* I
63.12-14 collected (cases . . . him),] BC; ~, ~. . . ~, I
65.8 'faculty'] BC; ₍~₎ I
66.7 above] H; below I
66.9;71.37 1889] H; 1888 I

67.37 289] H; 298 I
69.39-40 Charles . . . etc.,] H; Starr, *loc. cit.* I
74.37 W.] H; T. I
77.37 *Text-Book . . . Medica*] H; Pharmakology and Therapeutics I
77.39 Hermann] H; Herman I (*error*)
79.22-23 and Memory . . . paths] WJ/I; *om.* I
80.36 (1888-1889)] H; (1889) I
81.40 1529] H; 1530 I
85.29 1858-59] H; 1859 I

CHAPTER III: ON SOME GENERAL CONDITIONS OF BRAIN-ACTIVITY

Reference is made to BC.

89.13 *alone*),] H; ~)₍ I
89.32 1874 . . . 372)] H; 1875, p. 372 (Journal of Physiol., 1875) I
89.36 ¹II] H; I I
89.38 Bd. II, Thl. II] H; Thl. I I
89.38-39 Bd. I, Thl. I] H; vol. I I
90.36 (supplement)] H; *om.* I
91.21 noticed] Lewes; noted I
91.24 Thomson . . .] H; ~₍ I
91.38 478] H; 479 I
92.35 proves seldom] Fowler; seldom proves I
92.37 will] Fowler; wull I (*error*)
92.38 question] *stet* I; *om.* Fowler
93.16,23 FIG. 21a] H; Fig. 21 I (*error*)
96.34 *Philosophische*] I³; Psychologische I¹⁻²
☛96.35 *Vierteljahrsschrift*] H; Vierteljahrschrift I (*also* 516.31;652.45;775.6; 1002.39)
98.18 minimum] I³; *om.* I¹⁻²
98.19 0.0471] I²; 0.471 I¹
98.19 ¹(*ibid.*] I³; as a minimum (*ibid.* I¹⁻²
98.21 VIII] H; VII I
☛98.23 Everyone] H; Every one I (*also* 134.35;149.26;150.8;173.12;185.8; 220.21;296.22;330.31;354.1;381.36; 501.23;505.13;523.23;554.1;631.1; 677.10,18;735.28;742.27;1061.13; 1065.18;1138.5;1159.34;1196.16; 1235.11)

98.33 think] *stet* I; think however Cattell
98.34 the . . . willing] *stet* I; these processes Cattell
98.35 effort . . . comes],] *stet* I; effort, the time taken up by which could be determined, Cattell
100.40 *German . . . To-day*] H; Contemp. Germ. Psych. I
101.36-37;103.9 Orschansky] H; Orchansky I (*error*)
102.5 0″.234] H; 0″.334 I (*error*)
102.17 0″.332] H; 0.332″ I
102.20 v.] H; V. I
102.20-21 [supplement]] H; *om.* I
103.9 368] H; 468 I
103.10 185] H; 1885 I (*error*)
103.30 Sphygmographic] BC; Sphymographic I (*error*)
104.5 legs] Mosso,BC; arms I
*104.27 blood-supply] *stet* I¹⁻¹⁰; ~₍~ I¹¹(*resetting error*)
105.2 the] Martin; *om.* I
105.3 basis] Martin; foundation I
105.10 sleep,] *stet* I¹⁻¹⁰; ~₍ I¹¹ (*resetting error*)
105.36 Faculty] H; Society I
107.7 alleged] BC; *om.* I
107.12 PO₅] BC; PO I
107.39 1872] H; 1871 I
107.40 1884] H; 1887 I

CHAPTER IV: HABIT

Reference is made to P[29], "The Laws of Habit," *Popular Science Monthly*, 30 (February 1887), 433–451 (McD 1887:5), and to BC.

110.32 Everyone] H; Every one P[29], I (*also* 123.25;1041.27;1050.7;1055.17)

111.9 so‸] Dumont,BC; ∼, P[29],I

111.39 323] H; 324 I

112.15 Nature] BC; *l.c.* I

114.33 indicated] *stet* P[29],I; indicated alike Carpenter

115.3;116.7,9,33;121.26(*twice*) whilst] Carpenter; while P[29],I

115.15 2of] Carpenter; or P[29],I

115.17 surfaces] *stet* P[29],I; surfaces (§ 72) Carpenter

115.23 Now] *stet* P[29],I; 278. Now Carpenter

115.24–25 manifested] *stet* P[29],I; already shown to be manifested Carpenter

115.36 *et seq. this quote* him] *stet* P[29],I; him (§§ 191–194) Carpenter (*internal references in* Carpenter *not quoted*)

115.42 Beneden's] P[29]; Benedens' I (*error*)

116.18 What] *stet* P[29],I; 279. What Carpenter

116.42 associations] Carpenter; association P[29],I

117.19 fore-arm] P[29](∼- | ∼); forearm I

117.40;124.11;534.35 towards] H; toward P[29],I

118.31 even of an] Maudsley; of any P[29],I

118.31 secondary] Maudsley; secondarily P[29],I

118.34 efforts ... produce] Maudsley; effort ... produces P[29],I

118.40 154] H; 155 P[29],I

121.41 "‸With] P[29]; " '∼ I (*error*)

122.10 my] Carpenter,P[29]; the I

122.14 'sensations.'] BC; ‸∼·‸ P[29],I

122.31 trains] Carpenter,P[29]; train I

123.1 a] Carpenter; an P[29],I

123.39 19] H; 20 P[29],I

124.39 pp. 438, 439–40] H; p. 439 P[29],I

125.39 *Lessons* ... XI] H; "Elementary Lessons in Physiology," ... xii P[29];I (*sg. qts.*)

127.26 never] *stet* P[29],I; never, if possible, Bain

127.32 mental] *stet* P[29],I; moral Bain

128.38 (1879)] H; (1878) I

128.39 zur] H; zu P[29],I

129.40 afterwards] H; afterward P[29],I

130.39–40 The ... Devotees] H; Musical Devotees and Morals I

CHAPTER V: THE AUTOMATON-THEORY

Reference is made to P[24], "Are We Automata?" *Mind*, 4 (January 1879), 1–22 (McD 1879:5), and to WJ/I.

134.33 vol. I, p. 416 ff.] I[3]; vol. , p. I[1-2]

135.5 upon] Huxley; on I

135.6 *indicative* ... *cause*] *stet* I; *rom.* Huxley

135.9 struck.] Huxley; ∼. . . . I

135.9–10 to ... [1]the] H; to the I

135.30 utterly] *stet* I; two utterly Clifford

135.34 nonsense. . . .] H; ∼ ·‸ I

135.38 which] Clifford; that I

135.42 we] *stet* I; we quite naturally Clifford

136.1 mental] *stet* I; mental facts Clifford

136.8 Will] Clifford; will I

136.15 made] Clifford; made up I

137.9 common-] H; ∼‸ I

138.2 ways:] I[3]; ∼, I[1-2]

138.3 means. And] I[3]; ∼; and I[1-2] [*begin* P[24]]

138.24;820.23 anyone] H; any one P[24],I [*end* P[24]]

139.17 an ... word!),] I[3]; a 'concomitant,' I[1-2]

139.20 notion] Mercier; very notion I

139.22 meditations] *stet* I; meditations on the subject Mercier
139.30 *why*] *stet* I; why Mercier
139.36 surmounted] *stet* I; already surmounted Mercier
139.39 8] H; 9 I
139.40 10] H; 11 I
140.8,24 beef-steak] H; beefsteak I
141.23 which . . . exist] I3; *om.* I1-2
141.23-24 of . . . forces] I3; by physio-

logical forces of these in paths I1-2
141.28-29 *psychology.*4a] WJ/I; ~.∧ (*om. fn.*) I
144.22 idealistic . . . ancient] I3; idealistic-modern as well as ancient schools I1-2
[*begin* P24]
146.28 *a*] H; *à* P24,I
[*end* P24]

Chapter VI: The Mind-Stuff Theory

Reference is made to WJ/I and to BC. An emendation taken from James's marked copy of the 1892 first printing of *Psychology: Briefer Course* is given the sigil WJ/BC.

149.1 MIND-] H; ~∧ I
149.34 oscillation] Spencer; oscillations I
149.34 represented] *stet* I; represented in consciousness Spencer
150.13-14 the one] Tyndall; one I
150.28 *without break*] *stet* I; *rom.* Spencer
151.27 *raw material*] *stet* I; *rom.* Spencer
151.28 *implication*] *stet* I; *rom.* Spencer
152.6 very] *stet* Marryat, I1-2; little I3 (*resetting error*)
152.6 little] Marryat; small I
152.7 little] I3; small I1-2
152.28-29 *there . . . consciousness*] *stet* I; *all rom.* Spencer
152.32 *evolves . . . consciousness*] *stet* I; *all rom.* Spencer
152.35 n.s.,] H; *om.* I
153.10,42 1864] H; 1862 I
154.29 On] Spencer; In I
154.31 a] Spencer; *om.* I
154.39 of the tone] Spencer; *om.* I
156.38 INSUFFICIENCY] I3; REFUTATION I1-2
157.4 Where?-] I3; ~- I1-2
157.10-11 Figure 25] H; Figure 25, on the previous page, I
159.2+ (*in* Fig. 26) 1x] I3; *om.* I1-2
159.26 no . . . 1is] WJ/I; really occurs is no doubt I
160.35 tastes;] BC; ~, I
160.39;363.23 cannot] H; can not I
161.17 in] Montgomery; on I
161.34 and for] Royce; *om.* I

161.37 mass] *stet* I; thing Royce
162.24-25 *Grundzüge der Psychologie*] H; Outlines of Metaphysics I
162.26 G.] H; J. I
162.33 F.] H; H. I
162.34 *Ethics*] H; Ethic I
162.35 126] H; 129 I
163.15 *a*, . . . are] WJ/BC; *a* + idea of *b* is I
164.30 itself,'] Bain; ~,∧ I (*error*)
164.32 contradiction] *stet* I; self-contradiction Bain
164.37 fact] Bain; the fact I
164.37 fact."] *stet* I1; ~.' I2 (*resetting error*)
164.46 fact] H; the fact I
165.25 thousand?17a] WJ/I; ~.∧ (*om. fn.*) I
166.36 429-] H; 428- I
169.5 the left, out] Maude; left, or out I
169.6 that] Maude; *om.* I
169.8 left] *stet* I; to the left Maude
169.8 your] Maude; the I
169.9 when] *stet* I; when you know that Maude
169.14 distinctly . . . or] *stet* I; *om.* Maude
169.37 II] H; I I
171.39 *Über . . . Grunde*] H; Satz vom Grunde I
171.40 425.] H; ~∧ I (*error*)
176.45 Pp. 37-8] H; P. 38-9 I
177.18 159] H; 23 I (*i.e.*, 156)
177.22 73] H; 158-9 I (*i.e.*, 65)
181.20 occurrences] WJ/I; the manifold occurrences that go on I

Emendations

CHAPTER VII: THE METHODS AND SNARES OF PSYCHOLOGY

Reference is made to WJ/I.

184.38   XI] H; IX   I
187.6   ¹the] Ueberweg; a   I
187.10   outside] Ueberweg; outside of   I
187.37   I . . . I . . . 2, 3] H; II . . . III . . .
          1, 2   I
187.38   34–7] H; 34–8   I
188.1   necessity] H; neccessity   I (*error*)

189.41   482] H; 432   I
190.28   alike?] I³; ∼. I¹⁻²
191.5   mind?] I³; ∼. I¹⁻²
195.37   *psychologist's*] WJ/I,I³;
          psychologist' I¹⁻²
196.26   vocabulary] H; vocabu. | lary   I
          (*error*)

CHAPTER VIII: THE RELATIONS OF MINDS TO OTHER THINGS

Reference is made to P³⁷, "The Hidden Self," *Scribner's Magazine*, 7 (March 1890), 361–373 (McD 1890:1), and to WJ/I.

198.36   XIII, 337] H; X. 338   I
199.34   pt. I,] H; *om.*   I
199.35   Wolff] H; Wolf   I
199.39   Inquiries] H; Researches   I
199.41   *Metaphysic* . . . p. 533] H;
          Metaphysics, § 533   I
[*begin* P³⁷]
201.16   anyone] P³⁷; any one   I
[*end* P³⁷]
201.38–39   July 25 . . . November 7,
          1889] H; July, August and November,
          1889   I
[*begin* P³⁷]
202.16–17;205.3;364.31   Salpêtrière-]
          P³⁷ (∼ₐ); Salpétrière-   I
205.3;364.32   Witt.] H; ∼ₐ P³⁷;Wit.   I
205.5   Cessez] *stet* P³⁷ (*ital.*);I; cesser

Janet
206.40   May] *stet* I¹⁻¹⁰; ∼, I¹¹ (*resetting*
          error)
[*end* P³⁷]
211.21   liver,] H; ∼ₐ I (*error*)
212.17   the body] I³; its body I¹⁻²
212.37   *Grundzüge der Psychologie*] H;
          Outlines of Psychol.   I
213.14   be] WJ/I,I⁸; *om.* I¹⁻⁷
215.12   recognizes] Bowne; knows   I
215.14   this] *stet* I; The   Bowne
215.15   owe it] *stet* I; owe the thought
          Bowne
215.16   never] Bowne; not   I
215.20   in] Bowne; within   I
216.25   This] Bowne; this I (*error*)
216.40   403–] H; 407–   I

CHAPTER IX: THE STREAM OF THOUGHT

Reference is made to P²⁴ᵃ, "On Some Omissions of Introspective Psychology," *Mind*, 9 (January 1884), 1–26 (McD 1884:1), to WJ/I, and to BC.

220.26   'thought'] BC; ₐ∼ₐ   I
221.28   peculiarities] H; peculiaritities   I
          (*error*)
222.34   someone] H; some one I (*also*
          270.35;315.34;419.13;420.5;483.22;
          744.11;770.15;959.17;1079.38;1174.3;
          1182.4;1232.10;1266.2)
223.36   pp. 317–18] H; p. 318   I
223.37   *d'hystéro-démonopathie*] I³;

d'hystero-demonopathie I¹⁻²
223.38   di] H; d'   I
224.25   my] *stet* I; *om.*   Hodgson
224.26   any] *stet* I; *om.*   Hodgson
224.31   parts] *stet* I; part   Hodgson
224.33   consciousness] *stet* I; conscious-
          ness in redintegration   Hodgson
224.33   *differents*] *stet* I; Differents
          Hodgson

226.2   another] BC; arother I (*error*)
226.30   winter;] BC; ∼, I
227.38   common!] WJ/I,I³;BC (∼!−);
   ∼;I¹⁻²
232.7   discontinuous] I³; continuous I¹⁻²
*232.7   time-sense] *stet* I¹⁻²; sense I³
234.30   XXI (1848)] H; XXI, part I
   (1846) I
234.34   very] Wills; *om.* I
234.41   strictly] Wills; recognized as
   strictly I
234.41   *as*] Wills; as I
235.35   lights. . . .] H; ∼.ᴧ I
235.35   Our . . . states] *stet* I; The essential
   character out of which their most apparent use arises, is that to which I have
   mainly pointed your attention,−that
   they Wills
235.37   single whole] *stet* I; *ital.* Wills
235.38   so . . . apprehended] *stet* I; *all ital.*
   Wills
[*begin* P²⁴ᵃ]
237.6   snowflake] WJ/I; snowflake-crystal
   P²⁴ᵃ; ∼ᴧ ∼ I
237.7   flake] WJ/I; crystal P²⁴ᵃ,I
[*end* P²⁴ᵃ]
237.33   exist;] BC; ∼, I
238.36   VIIᴧ] H; ∼, I
239.9   change−] BC; ∼,− I
239.40   *Élémens*] H; Eléments I
241.15   susceptibility] *stet* I; susceptibility
   of the mind, Brown
241.32   Relations] Spencer; *l.c.* I
241.48   Relation] *stet* I; *l.c.* Spencer
242.35   feeling] Spencer; feelings I
[*begin* P²⁴ᵃ]
243.40   feeling: it] BC; feeling. It
   P²⁴ᵃ,I
244.4   Everyone] H; Every one P²⁴ᵃ,I
245.6;922.14;937.33   someone's] H;
   some one's P²⁴ᵃ,I
[*end* P²⁴ᵃ]
249.35   by] *stet* I; by means of   Maguire
249.42   ¹to] I³; *om.* I¹⁻²
250.15   thoughts'] I³; thought's I¹⁻²
252.30   both] Campbell; *om.* I

252.31   it. . . .] H; ∼.ᴧ I
252.37   themselves] Campbell; by
   themselves I
*253.4   genius] *stet* Campbell 1850,I;
   genus   Campbell 1873
254.17-18   organism."²²] I³ (organism."†); ∼."ᴧ I¹⁻²
254.32   "prosodic] H; ᴧ∼ I
256.13   simply] H; simple I (*error*)
258.10   now] Ballard (Porter); *om.* I
258.28   two] Ballard (Porter); *om.* I
260.29   until] Lewes; till I
261.3   Suppose] *stet* I; But now suppose
   that neither sees, smells, hears;   Lewes
261.4   At] *stet* I; and at   Lewes
261.4   To] *stet* I; Whereas to   Lewes
261.9   a lion] Lewes; the lion I
261.29   ²things] *stet* I (∼,); things in my
   mind   Lewes
261.32   Thought] *stet* I; *l.c.*   Lewes
261.34   *recognition*] *stet* I; *rom.*   Lewes
261.35   &c."] Lewes (∼.ᴧ); and so forth.ᴧ
   I (*error*)
261.41   chaps. V, VI] H; chap. VI   I
262.10   4)] H; 4.   I
264.4   quiet] *stet* I; quiet was   Spencer
264.22-265.1   thinking] WJ/I; think I
264.32   cognisance] Ferrier; knowledge I
264.32   itself] *stet* I; *ital.*   Ferrier
264.34-35   ¹*We . . . really*] Hamilton;
   all rom. I
264.36   '*Non . . . sentire.*'] H; 'ᴧ∼ . . . ∼;ᴧ
   Hamilton; ᴧ∼ . . . ∼.ᴧ I
264.37   materials . . .] H; ∼ᴧ I
264.38   mine] *stet* I; *mine*   Mansel
264.42   consciousness . . .] H; ∼ᴧ I
264.43   No] Green; Not I
265.5   known O] WJ/I,I³; known it I¹⁻²
266.38   a] Brown; the I
266.38   must] Brown; *om.* I
267.12   is] *stet* I; *om.*   Brown
267.41   pp. 160-164] H; pp.   I
269.5   *The . . . table*] I³; *normal spacing
   after 'pack', 'cards', and 'on'* I¹⁻²
270.32   V and VI] H; VI and VII   I
273.21   ²-tóck] WJ/I,BC; -tock I

Emendations

CHAPTER X: THE CONSCIOUSNESS OF SELF

Reference is made to P³⁷, "The Hidden Self," *Scribner's Magazine*, 7 (March 1890), 361–373 (McD 1890:1), to P³¹, "Notes on Automatic Writing," *Proceedings of the American Society for Psychical Research*, 1 (March 1889), 548–564 (McD 1889:3), to WJ/I, and to BC.

279.16 material; the] BC; ~. The I
280.15+ *space*] BC; *no space* I
281.10 gold;] BC; ~, I
282.39 mercy"; "As] BC; ~ₐ; ₐ as I
283.24 or] Locke; and I
283.28 most] *stet* I; perhaps most Locke
283.29 law] Locke; laws I
283.32 *their*] *stet* I; *rom.* Locke
283.34 of] Locke; in I
284.7 'section'ₐ] H; '~'* (*no fn.*) I (*error*)
285.31 becomes] WJ/I; become I
286.40 amongst] H; amonst I (*error*)
290.30 actₐ] WJ/I,I³; ~, I¹⁻²
291.19 common-] H; ~ₐ I
291.32 suppose.] WJ/I; suppose. At the conclusion of the volume, however, I may permit myself to revert again to the doubts here provisionally mooted, and will indulge in some metaphysical reflections suggested by them. I
291.38 P.] H; J. I
291.39 que la conscience] *stet* I; qu'elle Souriau
293.24 notice, and] WJ/I(~ₐ);I³,BC; noticean, d I¹⁻²
296.37 *fanciest*] Carlyle; *rom.* I
297.18 thou hast] Carlyle; hast thou I
297.19 wisest] *stet* I; *cap.* Carlyle
297.20 renunciation] *stet* I; Renunciation (*Entsagen*) Carlyle
297.20 life] *stet* I; Life Carlyle
297.34 die; well, but] *stet* I; die, and Higginson
297.35 too? . . .] H; ~?ₐ I
297.35-36 I will . . . reply,] *stet* I; "And I must speak what appears to me to be right."—"But if you do, I will put you to death."— Higginson
297.36 'Then . . . death,'] BC; ₐthen . . . ~,ₐ I
297.39 untroubled.' . . .] H; ~.'ₐ I
297.39 We] *stet* I; What is in my power? To Higginson
297.40 the hour] *stet* I; the day, the hour Higginson

298.1 belongs] *stet* I; belongs to another, Higginson
298.3 submit] *stet* I; I submit Higginson
298.4 of] *stet* I; *om.* Higginson
298.37 pp. 6, 10, 105] H; p. 105 I
298.38 disappointment] *stet* I; disapprobation Bain
298.41 *Emotions*] WJ/I; Emotion I
302.4 in] Job (King James); *om.* I
303.21 premise] H; premiss I
307.21 'self-] H; ₐ~- I (*error*)
311.39 *Analysen*] I³; Analyzen I¹⁻²
312.34 Perhaps (*no ¶*)] *stet* I; ¶ 5. Perhaps Bain
312.39 forth] Bain; forth perhaps I
312.43 towards] Bain; to I
313.9-10 Constructivenessₐ] H; ~, I
313.22 ourselves] Bain; *om.* I
313.28 the other] Bain; other I
313.29-30 *in . . . person*] *stet* I; *all rom.* Bain
314.8 postponed] I³; posponed I¹⁻²
315.29-30 *einem . . . Vorstellungen*] *stet* I; *all rom.* Kant
315.29 mir] Kant; *om.* I
315.30 d. i.] Kant; d. h. I (*error*)
315.42 point] I²; oint I¹
317.6 them;] BC; ~, I
317.11 Western] BC; *l.c.* I
317.12 together,] BC; ~ₐ I
322.25 identityₐ] BC; ~, I
326.23 Wolff] H; Wolf I
327.25 a brain] WJ/I; one I
327.38 word] H; world I (*error*)
329.13 mitigatedₐ] I³; ~, I¹⁻²
329.13 spiritualisticₐ] WJ/I; ~, I
329.18 Mind] *stet* I; mind, as I have remarked, Wayland
329.20 imagines] *stet* I; believes, imagines Wayland
330.22 'substanceₐ'] WJ/I,I¹¹; '~,ₐ I¹⁻²; '~ₐₐ I³⁻¹⁰
330.23 survive;] I³; ~, I¹⁻²
330.24 itselfₐ] WJ/I; ~, I
332.25;334.38;692.39;949.10 of] H;

on I

332.32   *self*] Hume; Self I

332.35   self] Hume; Self I

333.19-20   *nothing . . . perceptions*] *stet* I; *all rom.* Hume

333.28-29   *There . . . different*] *stet* I; *all rom.* Hume (*except 'simplicity' and 'identity'*)

333.33   or] Hume; nor I

333.33   materials] Hume; material I

334.10-11   "connected . . . *all.*] *stet* I (*paraphrase*); connected together by a close relation;2 and this to an accurate view affords as perfect a notion of *diversity*, as if there was no manner of relation among the objects.   Hume

334.12-13   All . . . existences] *stet* I; *all ital.* Hume (*except* 'and')

334.12   All . . . and] *stet* I; *that all . . . and that* Hume

334.14   and] Hume; or I

334.14-15   *did . . . connexion*] *stet* I (*connection*); *all rom.* Hume

334.18   insuperable] *stet* I; absolutely insuperable   Hume

334.19   these] *stet* I; those   Hume

335.5   '*B after A.*'] WJ/I,I8; '*A after B.*' I1-7

335.18   asserted] WJ/I; pretended I

335.21-22   existence] WJ/I,I4; existance I1-3

335.23   widely] WJ/I,I4; wholly I1-3

336.5   touches] WJ/I; touch I

336.13-19   All . . . cognition.] *stet* I; *ital.* Thompson

336.13,15   States of Consciousness] Thompson; *l.c.* I

336.19   cognition."] H; ~.' I (*error*)

337.20   prima facie] Mill; *ital.* I

337.21   Thought] *stet* I; *l.c.* Mill

337.28   myself] Mill; my self I

337.29   as far back] Mill; back as far I

338.8   has yet] Mill; else has I

338.17   *inexplicable tie*] *stet* I; *rom.* Mill

338.28   *something in common*] *stet* I; *rom.* Mill

338.40   174] H; 175 I

338.41   262] H; 263 I

339.3   Matter] H; Mind I

339.9   yet] Mill; *om.* I

339.11   consists] Mill; consist I

339.27,30   Mind] Mill; mind I

339.42   single] Mill; simple I

345.36   toward] Morris; towards I

345.37   *Agent*] *stet* I; *agent* Morris

347.17   and] Green; or I

347.27   . . . which] H; ‸~ I

347.35   therefore] H; therefor I

348.19   action] *stet* I; *rom.* Green

348.20-21   hold . . . *together*] *stet* I; *all rom.* Green

349.33,38;659.2   hegelian] H; *cap.* I

351.13   awakes] Brown; wakes I

351.21   that] Brown; which I

351.24   pursuit] Brown; the pursuit I

351.27   melancholy] Brown; *om.* I

351.31   we] Brown; they I

351.38   gentleness] Brown; tenderness I

351.38   etc.] *stet* I; *om.* Brown

351.39   man] Brown; a man I

351.40   which] Brown; *om.* I

351.41   observe all this] *stet* I; thus observe all that made us one   Brown

352.33   those] Brown; these I

353.5   ‸ whenever they occur‸] BC; ,~~~, I

353.22   writer] Cobbe; *cap.* Carpenter,I

353.24   the assurance] Cobbe; an assurance Carpenter,I

353.24-25   *nobody . . . it*] *stet* Carpenter, I; *all rom.* Cobbe

353.25   1was] Cobbe; being   Carpenter,I

353.25   lady was] Cobbe; lady, though Carpenter,I

353.26   its accuracy, but] Cobbe; the accuracy of her statement,   Carpenter, I

353.27   ago,] Cobbe; previously‸   Carpenter,I

353.27   it] Cobbe; *om.* Carpenter,I

353.29   *the . . . it*] *stet* Carpenter,I; *all rom.* Cobbe

353.29-30   Nothing . . . one] Cobbe; The lady's memory as to all other points Carpenter,I

354.38   *for*] H; of I

355.33-34   *Wenn . . . nicht*] *stet* I; *all rom.* Strümpell

355.33   *dann*] Strümpell (*rom.*); *da* I (*error*)

355.33   BIN] *stet* I; bin Strümpell

355.44   vol. II,] H; *om.* I

356.12-13   be‸ . . . contradictions‸ is, . . . part,] BC; ~, . . . ~, ~‸ . . . ~‸ I

356.15 amongst] BC; among I
356.37 *Die . . . Krankheiten*] H; Mental Diseases I
357.21 live] BC; lived I
357.33 , both . . . therein,] BC; ~ . . . ~ I
358.1 I.] H; J. I
358.4 insane . . . years] Fisher; many years insane I
358.4 and . . .] H; ~ I
358.4-5 her . . . ¹self] *stet* I; herself Fisher
358.5 asking] *stet* I; asks Fisher
358.5-6 Her . . . saying,] *stet* I; She says Fisher
358.7 Dr. F.] *stet* I; Dr Fisher Fisher
358.7 him,' etc.] *stet* I; him &c". Fisher
358.8 back?' . . .] H; ~?' I
358.8 works—] Fisher; works at I
358.8 work and says] Fisher; work, saying, I
358.9 Isn't] *stet* I; *l.c.* Fisher
358.11 buildings, and] *stet* I; building, &c— Fisher
358.11 She] *stet* I; It Fisher
358.30 Félida] I³,BC; Fèlida I¹⁻²
358.40 May 20] H; May 26 I
359.40 by . . . Plumer] H; *om.* I

361.26 Well,"] *stet* I; ~, Mitchell (*error*)
362.11 nor] Mitchell; or I
[*begin* P³⁷]
364.4 asleep.] P³⁷; ~, I (*error*)
366.11 everyone] P³⁷; every one I
366.29 experiences,] P³⁷,BC; ~ I
366.31 woman],] P³⁷('1,'); BC; ~] I
366.37 choice] Janet,P³⁷,BC; ~, I
[*end* P³⁷]
369.30 Witt.] H; Wit. I
369.44 1891] I³; 1890 I¹⁻²
371.36-38 The ladies . . . episode.] WJ/I; *om.* I
[*begin* P³¹]
374.25 *bosh.* . . .] P³¹; ~ . . . I
[*end* P³¹]
376.20 ¹She] *stet* I; and Stevens
376.29 natural] *stet* I; perfectly natural Stevens
377.3 Lurancy] *stet* I; Mary Lurancy Stevens
377.34 1890] I³; 1889 I¹⁻²
378.39 1888] H; 1889 I
378.39-40 Also . . . 1890.] WJ/I (1870);
   om. I
379.6-7 aggregate;] BC; ~, I

Chapter XI: Attention

Reference is made to WJ/I and to BC.

380.22 *and*] H; of I
383.25 Stewart] H; Stuart I
383.28 from] *stet* I; from all Stewart
383.30 figure] *stet* I; figure of the object Stewart
383.31 Adrien Léonard] H; Adrian Leonard I
383.38 confusion] WJ/I,I³; con usion I¹⁻²
383.39 631] H; 632 I
384.15 Mind] *stet* I; mind Hamilton
384.17 Destutt de Tracy] H; Destutt-Tracy Hamilton; Destutt Tracy I
384.18-19 appears] Hamilton; seems I
384.19 experiment] Hamilton; experiments I
385.18 simultaneous] BC; sinultaneous I (*error*)

385.37 2d ed.,] H; *om.* I
388.39 p. 240] H; pp. 238-40 I
391.29 that] Wundt; than I (*error*)
391.32 269] H; 270 I
391.33 no. 4, 603] H; 601 I
392.11 390] H; 411 I (*i.e.,* 412)
396.9 a] Hamilton; *om.* I
396.11 Roman] Hamilton; the Roman I
396.23 whither] Hamilton; whether I
396.37 he has] *stet* I; The writer has himself Carpenter
397.9 everyone] BC; every one I
397.40 held] Cattell; kept I
397.41 one second] *stet* I; 1 sec. Cattell
398.11 lets] WJ/I,BC,I⁸; let I¹⁻⁷
400.32 Helvetius,] *stet* I; Helvetius, whom we have already quoted, Hamilton

400.33   *suivie*)....*patience*).] *stet* I;
    ~.)...~.) Hamilton
400.37   genius.'] Hamilton; ~.$_\wedge$ I
401.37 $_\wedge e$)] H; (*e*) I
404.12   *e*.] H; *e*) I
405.21-22 experiments$_\wedge$ ... same),] H;
    ~, ... ~)$_\wedge$ I
409.28   233] H; 33 I (*error*)
409.36   Bertels] H; Bartels I
411.33   positive] BC,I[11]; pos-|sitive I[1-10]
412.6   seen$_\wedge$] H; ~, I
☛412.14 forwards] H; forward I (*also*
    440.12;619.32;715.35;716.35;735.29;
    736.17;748.25;766.28,36;768.30;
    1024.24;1094.25;1103.18;1175.2-3;
    1187.17;1192.28)
412.27   (when ... another)] BC;
    $_\wedge$~. ... ~$_\wedge$ I
412.32   fills. If] PP Vol. II, 138.14 [*ed.*,
    780.9],BC; ~; if I
413.44   pt.] H; *om.* I
413.44   3] H; 2 I
414.25   organs,] BC; ~; I
416.1   392...410] H; 341 ... 373, 377 I
    (*i.e.*, 415 ... 427-429, 433-434)
416.25   resonator] I[3],BC; reasonator I[1-2]

417.39   2nd ed.] H; *om.* I
417.39   208] H; 209 I
418.10   It] *stet* I; Hence the retinal
    rivalry Helmholtz (Atkinson)
418.11   upon] Helmholtz (Atkinson); on I
418.11   or] *stet* I; on Helmholtz (Atkin-
    son)
418.15-16 [1]*we ... appear*] *stet* I; *all rom.*
    Helmholtz (Atkinson)
418.25   we] WJ/I,I[3],BC; e I[1-2]
418.28   *Popular ... Subjects*] H; Popular
    Scientific Lectures I
418.28   294] H; 295 I
420.8   kindergarten-] BC; ~$_\wedge$ I
422.30   (1876),] H; *om.* I
422.34   1873] H; 1874? I
423.11   Then] H; Second I
424.1   on] I[3]; or I[1-2]
425.26   however,] WJ/I; *om.* I
425.42   place.$_\wedge$] I[3]; ~." I[1-2]
426.9   unnoticed] H; unnoticd I (*error*)
426.23   agent.] H; ~, I
427.17   of] H; of of I (*error*)
428.37   Any] H; a I
431.40   127] H; 128 I
432.5-6 without] H; with | out I

Chapter XII: Conception

Reference is made to P[24], "On Some Omissions of Introspective Psychology," *Mind*, 9 (January 1884), 1-26 (McD 1884:1), to WJ/I, and to BC.

436.25   matter-for-thought] BC;
    ~$_\wedge$~$_\wedge$~ I
436.39   relations] *stet* I; relations of both
    Robertson
437.7   another:] BC; ~, I
437.40   distinct] *stet* I; clear and distinct
    from the idea of sweet Locke
438.14   obtain. But] BC; ~, but I
438.16   tell] WJ/I; always tell I
438.20   Round-] BC; ~$_\wedge$ I
438.24   things$_\wedge$] H; ~. I (*error*)
439.22   strychnin] I[3]; strychuin I[1-2]
439.26   the empirical] WJ/I; theempirical
    I (*error*)
441.2-3 successively] H; sucessively I
    (*error*)
442.7   ways.] H; ~, I (*error*)
443.27   have] *stet* I; have indeed
    Berkeley

443.41   abstract notions] *stet* I; *ital.*
    Berkeley
444.26   formation] *stet* I; formation,
    therefore, Mill
444.32   thinking] Mill; meaning I
444.33   our] Mill,WJ/I,I[3]; out I[1-2]
444.34-38 *While ... concept*] *stet* I;
    rom. Mill
444.35   *lasts*] *stet* I; actually lasts Mill
444.39   7, 9,] H; *om.* I
445.2-4 *attend ... thoughts*] *stet* I;
    all rom. Mill
445.6-7 *exactly ... conceive*] *stet* I;
    all rom. Mill
446.30   picture$_\wedge$] BC; ~, I
447.35   connection ... object] Dewey;
    particular connection with the object I
447.38   Cf.] H; C. F. I (*error*)
448.32   content,] *stet* I; content (original

or acquired), Bradley
448.33 'and ... subject;'] Bradley;
$_\wedge$~ ... ~;$_\wedge$ I
449.1 awakened] I^{12}; awakend I$^{1-11}$
449.13 the] Ferrier; *om.* I
449.20 phenomenon] Ferrier; *om.* I
449.25 additional] *stet* I; outstanding Ferrier
449.27 instances] *stet* I; *ital.* Ferrier
449.28 by any possibility] Ferrier; possibly I
449.33 universal] Ferrier; a universal I
449.39 333-39] H; 33-39 I (*error*)
450.17 up] Mill; *om.* I
450.17-18 forms ... ^{1}idea] Mill; forms a species of complex idea of them I
450.18 degree] Mill; extent I
450.19 *comprehends*] *stet* I; *rom.* Mill
450.20-21 the main] Mill; a main I
450.26 indistinct] Mill, I^3; distinct I$^{1-2}$

450.30 several] Berkeley; many several I
450.31 mind. ...] H; ~.$_\wedge$ I
[*begin* P^{24}]
451.36 a word] *stet* I; the word P^{24}
452.3 thing] P^{24}; thng I (*error*)
452.12 may reveal] *stet* I; reveals P^{24}
452.16 -excitements] *stet* I; -excitements of an effective degree of strength P^{24}
452.19 then,] *stet* I; *om.* P^{24}
452.22 combine the poles] *stet* I; combine past and future, the north pole and the south, P^{24}
452.28 may grasp] *stet* I; grasps P^{24}
452.29 ^{1}truth] *stet* I; universal truth P^{24}
452.47 an] P^{24}; *om.* I
452.47-48 as ... course] *stet* I; for granted P^{24}
[*end* P^{24}]
*453.12 Plato and Aristotle] *stet* I

CHAPTER XIII: DISCRIMINATION AND COMPARISON

Reference is made to P^{21}, "Brute and Human Intellect," *Journal of Speculative Philosophy*, 12 (July 1878), 236-276 (McD 1878:4), to WJ/I, and to BC.

457.20 hereafter.] Locke, WJ/I; ~? I
458.33-34 'Association,'] *stet* I; "Association," "Suggestion," Martineau
458.39 then with the] Martineau; the with then I; with the WJ/I
459.4 one] Martineau; one I
459.12 $_\wedge$The 'idea] Martineau; '~$_\wedge$~ I
459.29 name, idea] Mill (Martineau); name of the idea I
459.40 the new] Bain (Martineau); new I
459.43 70] H; 71 I
460.27 foreground] Martineau; foregronnd I (*error*)
463.3 psychologist's] H; psychologists I (*error*)
464.29 XXVIII] WJ/I, I^3; XX I$^{1-2}$
465.24 ^{2}X] WJ/I, I^8; *x* I$^{1-7}$
467.40 *Unterschiedsempfindungs-complexe*] Schneider; *Unterschieds-empfindungs-Complexe* I
469.25 wines$_\wedge$] BC; ~, I
470.36 ^{1}of] Sully; or I
470.38 most] *stet* I; *om.* Sully

472.28 forsooth?"] H; ~?$_\wedge$ I
474.2 3)] H; 3) and I
474.37 *gathering* ... ^{2}*it*] *stet* I; *rom.* Bowne
474.38 cannot] I^3; can not I$^{1-2}$
476.5 *object*$_\wedge$] BC; ~, I
476.17 *imagine*$_\wedge$] BC; ~, I
476.23-24 XI$_\wedge$ ... reproduction$_\wedge$] BC; ~, ... ~, I
477.8 Hence] *stet* I; Hence in this case also, Helmholtz
477.10 constituents] *stet* I; constituents to be added Helmholtz
477.11 their ... them] *stet* I; the sum into those parts Helmholtz
477.21 notes ... notes] *stet* I; tones ... tones Helmholtz
477.27-28 *a*$_\wedge$ ... *abcd*$_\wedge$] BC; ~, ... ~, I
477.30 *aefg*$_\wedge$] BC; ~, I
478.31-32 *concomitants.*^{16a}] WJ/I; ~.$_\wedge$ (*om. fn.*) I, BC
478.34 total$_\wedge$] BC; ~, I

[*begin* P21]
479.1 If the] *stet* P21,I; The Spencer
479.2 and again] *stet* P21,I; there along Spencer
479.14-16 *color . . . form*] *stet* P21,I; *each rom.* Martineau
479.18 and then] Martineau; then P21,I
[*end* P21]
481.11 cannot] De Morgan; and of course cannot I
482.3 had] WJ/I,I3; has I1-2
482.4 had] WJ/I,I3,BC; has I1-2
487.23 pressure or a] Helmholtz; pressure, I
487.26 *when . . . knowledge*] *stet* I; *rom.* Helmholtz
488.1 other things] *stet* I; others Helmholtz
488.3 we] *stet* I; *om.* Helmholtz
488.5 becomes] *stet* I; is Helmholtz
488.5 work to] H; work at Helmholtz; workto I (*error*)
488.5-6 investigate] *stet* I; investigating Helmholtz
488.6-7 seek . . . understand] *stet* I; at more completely understanding Helmholtz
488.9-10 *two . . . sensation*] *stet* I; *all rom.* Helmholtz
488.11 in which] *stet* I; where Helmholtz
488.15 circumstance in] *stet* I; relation of Helmholtz
488.17 and] Helmholtz; *om.* I
488.40 VI] H; V I
492.12 example,] H; ~ᵥ I
493.34 is] *stet* I; is on the other hand Lotze
493.39 seems] *stet* I; seems to me Lotze

493.40 has really] Lotze; really has I
494.28-29 consciousness (or ᵥif . . . unconscious, . . . soul)] Stumpf; ~, ~ (~. . . ~) . . . ~ᵥ I
494.38-39 peppermint] H; pepperment I (*error*)
494.40 106] H; 107 I
495.38 4,] H; *om.* I
496.11 C.).] H; ~.)ᵥ I
496.29 0.110] Cattell,WJ/I,BC,I8; 10.10 I1-7
496.38 also] Cattell; *om.* I
496.41 379] WJ/I,I8; 3 I1-7
497.2 appeared):] H; ~)ᵥ I
497.7 -the] BC; ᵥThe I
497.12 perceive] Cattell; distinguish I
497.13 to] Cattell; in I
497.37 1877] H; Bd. I I
☛ 497.38 *Philosophische*] H; Psychologische I (*also* 498.38;526.42;609.42; 639.35)
497.38 *La*] H; Le I
506.16 unnoticeable] H; unnoticable I (*error*)
511.29 interval] H; intervals I
512.9 Kraepelin] H; Kräpelin I
512.23 apparently ᵥ] H; ~, I
513.1 neither stands] I3; stands neither I1-2
513.40 *Grundlegung*] H; Grandlegung I
515.5 const.] *see* Appendix II *for a poss. fn.*
515.15 really] WJ/I; *om.* I
515.32 Compound *things*] *see* Appendix II *for a poss. fn.*
518.12 *Massformel*] H; *Maasformel* I
518.28 *science,*] I3; ~ (!). I1-2
518.34 But . . . victory.] Southey; I3 (victory!); *ital.* I1-2(*victory!*)

CHAPTER XIV: ASSOCIATION

Reference is made to P29, "The Association of Ideas," *Popular Science Monthly*, 16 (March 1880), 577-593 (McD 1880:1), to WJ/I, and to BC.

[*begin* P29]
521.26 dropping] P29,WJ/I; droopping I (*error*)
522.2 prepossessions] P29,BC; preposessions WJ/I; preprocessions I (*error*)

523.6 afterwards] H; afterward I
[*end* P29]
526.24 drum,] *stet* I; drum (a physiological kymograph) Cattell
526.26 one, letter ᵥ] BC; ~ᵥ ~, I

526.35　all of them] Galton; *om.* I
526.36　alternatives] Galton; alternations I
527.1　When . . .] H; ∼‸ I
527.11　I] *stet* I; (2) I　Cattell
527.17　them] Cattell; *om.* I
527.33　The] *stet* I; (3) The　Cattell
527.42　name."] BC; ∼·‸ I
528.25　2d ed.,] H; *om.* I
528.32　4] H; 3　I
528.36　0.7"] H; 0.7′　I
529.5　5+7] Cattell; 7+5　I
529.6,7　of a second] *stet* I; sec.　Cattell
529.7　1/10] Cattell; 1/20　I
[*begin* P^{29}]
531.29　*trains . . . spirits*] *stet* I; *all rom.*　Locke;P^{29} (*except 'animal spirits'*)
531.30　*processes*],] Locke (spirits,); P^{29}; ∼]‸ I
534.38;535.2　*the ages*] *stet* P^{29},I; *rom.*　Tennyson
535.2　Yet] Tennyson; For P^{29},I
535.4-5　follows‸ . . . *ages*‸] BC; ∼, . . . ∼, P^{29},I
535.6　memory‸] BC; ∼, P^{29},I
535.38　however,] WJ/I,I^3,BC; ∼‸ I$^{1-2}$
536.11　used‸] BC; ∼, P^{29},I
536.38　-555] H; -556　I
539.3　itself] P^{29},BC; it self I
539.14　and] Hodgson; *om.* P^{29},I
539.18　interest] *stet* I; interest, that is, those which are attended by a representation of pleasure or pain,　Hodgson, p29
539.37-38　contemporaneity or . . . of] H; contemporaeity or of I
539.38　*continuity*] Coleridge; *contiguity* I (*error*)
539.40　*Literaria*] H; Litteraria I
539.40　VII] H; V　I
540.8,9　^{1}had] WJ/I; *om.* P^{29},I
540.32-39　In . . . quick.] Hobbes; *modernized in* P^{29},I
541.6　the decaying] *stet* P^{29},I; that Hodgson
541.7-8　they . . . time] Hodgson; at any time they have P^{29},I
541.11　*habitually*] *stet* P^{29},I; *rom.* Hodgson
541.20　spontaneous] Hodgson; *om.* P^{29}, I

541.28　throat-] P^{29},BC; ∼‸ I
541.37-38　volume . . . it] BC; volumes . . . them P^{29},I
543.36　540] H; 586 P^{29};I (*i.e.*, 573)
543.39　414] H; 144　I (*error*)
544.27　ideas,] BC; ∼‸ P^{29},I
545.37-39　21aEhrenfels . . . 217.] WJ/I; *om.* I
545.40-43　21bHöffding . . . up.] WJ/I; *om.* I
547.25　downwards] H; downward P^{29},I
548.6　revery] H; reverie P^{29},I
[*end* P^{29}]
550.15　nature-] BC; ∼, I
550.22　right,] BC; ∼‸ I
551.5　end‸] BC; ∼, I
551.28　*a propos*] H; *à propos* I
552.1-2　related‸ . . . up‸] BC; ∼, . . . ∼, I
552.25-553.38　Sometimes . . . rime.] Hobbes; *modernized in* I
553.28-29　we . . . beforehand,] *stet* I; we know beforehand‸　Hodgson
553.29　intention,] *stet* I; intention, what we want to find,　Hodgson
553.34　mind . . . .] H; ∼·‸ I
553.38　1651] H; 165　I (*error*)
554.4　The] *stet* I; This　Hodgson
554.4-5　reasoning;] Hodgson; reason. I
554.5　but] H; that Hodgson; But I
554.20　circumstances] *stet* I; circumstances in speculative reasoning, and indeed in voluntary redintegration generally,　Hodgson
554.34　376] H; 377　I
554.37　attention, or] Bain; ∼‸ on I
554.38　on] Bain; upon I
556.35-36　*a . . . things*] *stet* I; *rom.* McCosh (*by inversion of fonts*)
559.2　elements‸ and,] BC; ∼, ∼‸ I
559.5　its] BC; it I (*error*)
559.13;1180.11　free-] H; ∼‸ I
559.25-560.40　By . . . cause.] Hobbes; *modernized in* I
559.25　*Consequence*] Hobbes; consequence I
560.17　it is] Hobbes; is it I
560.36　Discourse] *stet* I (*l.c.*); Disconrse Hobbes (*error*)
560.38　call] Hobbes; called I
561.16　out] Hume; *om.* I

562.13   law] *stet* I; property   Priestley
562.13   only] *stet* I; only that   Priestley
562.13-14   intellectual . . . pains] *stet* I;
   all ital.   Priestley
562.14   but] *stet* I; but that   Priestley
562.14-15   memory . . . reasoning] *stet*
   I; *all ital.*   Priestley
562.16   only] Priestley; but I
563.24   gravity,] H; ∼∧ I
563.42   *anglaise*] *stet* I^1-10 (Anglaise);
   Angloise I^11 (*resetting error*)
564.6-7   "transferring . . . it."] H; *sg. qts.*
   I
564.18   Conscientiousness] H; Conscien-
tiouness I (*error*)
565.26   one; . . .] H; ∼;∧ I
565.32   Oct.] H; Oct. 1   I
565.38-39   "the . . . feelings,"] H; *sg. qts.*
   I
568.32   I, part] H; *om.* I
568.33   *German . . . of To-day*] H;
   'Contemporary German Psychology,' I
568.36   Morell's] H; Morrell's I
568.36   *An . . . to*] H; Outlines of I
568.36   (London] H; (2d ed., London I
568.38   *Seelenlebens*] H; Bewusstseins I
568.42   *Steinthals . . .* (1876)] H;
   Steinthal's . . . (1886) I

Chapter XV: The Perception of Time

Reference is made to P^21, "The Perception of Time," *Journal of Specula-tive Philosophy*, 20 (October 1886), 374-407 (McD 1886:3), and to BC.

571.1   excepting] Mill; except P^21, I
572.25   *et seq. this fn.*   Past, Present, and
   Future] Hodgson; *l.c.* P^21, I
572.29   the minimum] Hodgson, P^21;
   a minimum I
573.2;588.24;985.34   anyone] H;
   any one P^21, I
574.38-39   *there . . . mind.*] *stet* P^21, I;
   all rom.   Reid
574.40   Royer-] P^21 (ROYER-); ∼∧ I
575.10,36   afterwards] H; afterward P^21, I
576.5   upwards] H; upward P^21, I
576.39   54] H; 54, 55   P^21, I
577.29   215] H; 213   P^21, I
579.17   *time-*] P^21 (*rom.*); ∼∧ I
579.39   Hermann's] P^21; Herrmann's I
   (*error*)
579.40   Thl. II] H; i Thl. P^21; I Thl.   I
580.12   Inserting] *stet* P^21, I; So, too,
   inserting Hall
580.18   0.355".] H; 0".355. P^21; ∼." I
581.29   respectively), and thought] H;
   ∼∧, ∼ (∼ I (*error*)
581.32   indifference-] *stet* P^21, I^1-10;
   ∼∧ I^11 (*resetting error*)
582.34   seconds] P^21; second I (*error*)
583.18   to hear] *stet* I; hath heard
   Tennyson
583.19   creeping] Tennyson; moving I
583.24   important;] BC; ∼, P^21, I
586.17   time-] BC; ∼∧ P^21, I
586.18   events∧ . . . time,] BC; ∼, . . .
   ∼; P^21, I
587.43   218] H; 219   P^21, I
588.38   497] H; 496   P^21, I
593.1   *et seq. this quote* A . . . E] Ward;
   rom. P^21, I
593.2   of *C*] Ward; *C* P^21, I
593.4-6   In . . . these differences] *stet* P^21,
   I; In presentation, as we have seen, all
   that corresponds to the differences of
   past, present, and future Ward
593.22   just gone,] BC; ∼ ∼∧ P^21, I
594.36   tomorrow] H; to-morrow P^21, I
595.42   may . . . representation] *stet* P^21,
   I; probably follows, as we have supposed, some trace Ward
595.42   *movement of attention*] *stet* P^21,
   I; *rom.* Ward
595.43   object] *stet* P^21, I; presentation
   Ward
595.43-44   reminiscences] Ward, P^21;
   reminiscence I
595.44   intervention;] *stet* P^21, I; inter-
   position, Ward
595.45   , I think,] *stet* P^21, I; strong
   Ward
595.45   of ideas] *stet* P^21, I; *om.*   Ward
595.46   at] *stet* P^21, I; *om.*   Ward
595.46-47   movement . . . changes,] *stet*

P21,I; movements themselves Ward
595.50 These] *stet* P21,I; They Ward
596.1 intensity] *stet* P21,I; intensity and distinctness Ward
596.3 in intensity] *stet* P21,I; *om.* Ward
596.5 where] *stet* P21,I; and, as a matter of fact, where Ward
596.5 -continuum] *stet* P21,I; -train Ward
596.9 to] *stet* I; *om.* Ward
596.9 present,] *stet* P21,I; $\sim_\wedge$ Ward
596.9 perspective] Ward,P21; perceptive I
596.9 Locke] *stet* P21,I; Locke was awake to this point, though he expresses himself vaguely (*Essay*, ii. 14, §§ 9–12). He Ward
596.12–16 *Now . . . b.*] *stet* P21,I; *all rom.* Ward (*except 'A . . . B, B . . . C . . . A . . . B'*)
596.13 on;] *stet* P21,I; $\sim,$ Ward
596.14 *, probably,*] *stet* P21,I; $_\wedge \sim_\wedge$ Ward
596.15 *I*] *stet* P21,I; we Ward

596.22,23 Time] *stet* P21,I; time Ward
596.23 physically conceived] *stet* P21,I; conceived as physical Ward
596.24–25 and . . . perception] *stet* P21, I; *om.* Ward
596.33–34 *a . . . b*] *stet* P21,I; *A . . . B* Ward
596.34 and] *stet* P21,I; or Ward
596.42 over-] *stet* P21,I; overestimated Ward
596.42 I take this] *stet* P21,I; This we may perhaps take Ward
596.51 three fourths] P21; $\sim$-$\sim$ I
597.19 results] P21; result I
597.22 , according to the Webers,] *stet* P21,I; *om.* Wundt
600.38 606] H; 642 I (*i.e.*, 643)
601.27 per] Spencer; a P21,I
601.32 than] *stet* P21,I; than it seems Spencer
601.33 one] *stet* P21,I; a single Spencer
601.34 hasheesh-] H; hashish- I
602.10 dropped] P21,I3; drooped I1-2

Chapter XVI: Memory

Reference is made to WJ/I and to BC.

605.9 former] WJ/I,I8; latter I1-7
607.10 through] WJ/I,I3; throught I1-2
607.22 caused] WJ/I; cause I
607.39 inwards] H; inward I
607.40;680.3 outwards] H; outward I
608.12 made] I3; done I1-2
608.24 IV] H; V I
608.39 281] H; 282 I
610.18 0.006 to 0.0275] H; 0.00275 to 0.006 I
610.21 Baxt] I3; Boxt I1-2
610.26 disk] *stet* I; first Ladd
610.27 2of] Ladd; *om.* I
610.29 0.0336] Ladd; 0.00336 I
611.12–13 sensations,] BC; $\sim_\wedge$ I
☞611.27 backwards] H; backward I (*also* 715.37;716.27;717.9,11 [*twice*]; 735.29–30;1191.24)
611.31 loss.$_\wedge$] BC; $\sim$.- I
613.11 it . . .] H; $\sim$; I
613.37 called up] *stet* I; are called up together Mill

613.39 II] H; I I
614.30 to try] Mill; *om.* I
614.30 that] Mill; *om.* I
614.31 then is it,] Mill; is it, then, I
614.36 1one] *stet* I; *om.* Mill
615.5 2him,] *stet* I; him, the place in which I knew him, Mill
615.8 in] Mill; *om.* I
615.18 sensation . . . idea] Mill; association or idea I
615.22 on] Mill; in I
616.17 or,] BC; $\sim_\wedge$ I
617.17 is a] *stet* I; is simply a Maudsley
618.1–2,22 nerve element] H; $\sim$-$\sim$ I
618.2 substrata] H; substratum I
619.23 *a*– . . .] H; $\sim$– I
620.5 there . . . about] Taine; wavers about there I
620.18 first] *stet* I; has first Taine
620.21 again] *stet* I; has again Taine
620.22 further] Taine; farther I
620.31 the other] *stet* I; one Taine

622.22 v] H; VI I
625.32 effort] Holbrook; efforts I
625.40 L.] H; H. I
626.1 his] stet I; the Holbrook
626.20 politicians. . . ."] H; ~.' I
626.34 very] Holbrook; om. I
626.40 38] H; 39 I
627.21 99] H; 100 I
627.33 perceptibly] H; peceptibly I (error)
627.42 minimum . . . maximum] WJ/I, I^8; maximum . . . minimum I$^{1-7}$
628.1 ^{2}improvement] BC; in- | provement I (error)
628.15 methods$_\wedge$] BC; ~, I
631.7 If] stet I; If, however, Taine
631.35 extraordinary] Taine; extraordinarg I (error)
631.41 mentale] H; mental I
633.4 imagine] H; |magine I (error)
633.40 78] H; 77 I
*635.4 'sense of pre-existence'] stet I; "sentiment of pre-existence" Wigan
635.11 towards] H; toward I
636.32 A.] H; H. I
636.34 28] H; 8 I
639.15,16 whether] Wolfe; when I
639.17 The] stet I; But the Wolfe
639.21 smaller] Wolfe; smaller are I
639.25 and, . . . it recovers] Wolfe; which, . . . recovers I
640.1 in] Locke; of I
640.8 are] Locke; are fast I
641.40 45] H; 46 I
642.11 363] H; 385 I (i.e., 384)
642.22-23 "They . . . nothing,"] H; sg. qts. I
642.40 unconsciously] H; uncon-|consciously I (error)

643.7 mind,] stet I$^{1-10}$; ~. I^{11} (resetting error)
643.9 would] stet I; would in fact Hamilton
643.34 211] H; 212 I
645.9 further] Verdon; longer I
645.21 attention is] Verdon; attention I
645.23 thus may] Verdon; may thus I
645.27 conserved so well] Verdon; so well conserved I
645.33 mind] Verdon; hand I
645.34 J.] H; A. I
646.21-22 what . . . . Obviously] WJ/I; then I
646.21 that] H; this WJ/I
*646.23-25 this . . . use] WJ/I; the path is formed by discharge from 1 to 2, just as it will afterwards be used I
647.28 toward] Ladd; towards I
647.30 sensations;] stet Ladd, I$^{1-10}$; ~, I^{11} (resetting error)
647.31-32 investigate] Ladd, I^{11}; inves-|gate I$^{1-10}$
647.33 sensations are combined] stet I; rom. Ladd
648.3 physical] Ladd; om. I
648.11 the image] Ladd; an image I
648.14 reproduced] stet I; rom. Ladd
648.17 knows] stet I; , of course, knows Ladd
648.18 similarity] stet I; similarity in impressions and processes Ladd
648.19 know] stet I; rom. Ladd
648.21 implying this] Ladd; involving the I
648.27 essence] Ladd; rom. I
648.27 makes] Ladd; makes the I
648.35-36 connecting] stet I; rom. Ladd
649.25 vol. II] H; vols. I and II I

Chapter XVII: Sensation

Reference is made to WJ/I and to BC.

653.30 rather] H; rather | rather I (error)
654.15 postulate] stet I; rom. Seth
654.16 supposed] stet I; rom. Dewey
655.33 multitude] Locke; multitnde I (error)
655.34 terminate in] stet I; rom. Locke
656.3 boundaries] stet I; rom. Locke
656.9 sensations . . . things] WJ/I; BC (except 'FIRST'); all rom. I (except 'first')

656.19 ideas] *stet* I; *ideas* Locke
656.37 ch. XXV . . . § 29] H; ch. XXIII, § 29; ch. XXV, § 9 I
657.2 *terminus*] I³; *teminus* I¹⁻²
658.23 true] Martineau; being true I
658.30 severed] Martineau; several I
658.35–659.9–23 *Sense . . . Knowledges.*] Cudworth; *modernized in* I
658.38 doth] Cudworth; does I
659.4 snarls] WJ/I; gnarls I (*error*)
659.12 or] Cudworth; *and* I
659.14 Cause] Cudworth; reason I
659.45 Théodore] H; Theodore I
660.24 self-] Caird; Self- I
660.27 by] *stet* I; by Caird
660.29 p. 394] H; pp. 393–4 I
660.31–32 *of which . . . No*] *stet* I; *all rom.* Green
660.34 *neither . . . sensation*] *stet* I; *all rom.* Green
660.34 *sensation.*] H; ~ I
660.35 749] H; 750 I
660.43–661.31 *Mind and Body*] H; Body and Mind I
661.20 of] Bain; by I
674.20 shadow.]] H; ~]. I
675.9 the sensation's] WJ/I; their I
675.35 (2nd ed.)] H; *om.* I
675.36 *allgemeines*] WJ/I; *allgemeiner* I
675.38 "feeling,"] WJ/I; *om.* I

675.40 need] WJ/I; does I
675.40 in . . . feel] WJ/I; when it thus feels I
675.40–41 See . . . 397.] WJ/I; *om.* I
677.29 chord; . . . rather] WJ/I; chord, it is I
678.10 Sensations . . . states] *stet* I; *all ital.* Ladd
678.39 '*spread-out.*'] Ladd; ˏspread-out.ˏ I
679.41 *philosophische*] H; Philosophischer I
679.41 pp. 60–61, 54–55] H; p. 64 I
680.18 objects,] *stet* I; ~ˏ Taine (*error*)
680.33 57] H; 58 I
681.29 71° . . . 42°] H; 72° . . . 41° I
681.37 *Über den objectiven*] H; Der Objective I
682.37 sensationsˏ] H; ~, I
683.20; 845.22, 24 Cheselden] H; Chesselden I (*error*)
683.21–23 when . . . Skin] Cheselden; *modernized in* I
685.38 of] H; to I
685.38 349] H; 350 I
686.12 something] H; omething I (*error*)
687.39–40; 845.35 Abbott] H; Abbot I (*error*)
688.33 half-way positions] H; ~ˏ ~-~ I (*error*)

Chapter XVIII: Imagination

Reference is made to WJ/I and to BC.

691.30–31 The . . . each] *stet* I; *all ital.* Hume
691.31 the] *stet* I; *om.* Hume
692.21 writers.³ᵃ] WJ/I; ~.ˏ (*om. fn.*) I
693.23 commonly] Huxley; *om.* I
693.42 by] Huxley; in I
695.7–8 *But . . . accompaniment*] *stet* I; *all rom.* Taine
695.11 But] *stet* I; now Taine
695.14–15 which . . . me] *stet* I; I may be shown Taine
696.4 *he*] *stet* I; he Berkeley
696.9 inˏ] BC; ~, I
696.15 Chapter XLIV] H; chapter XLIV I
696.16 careful] WJ/I; most careful I

696.27 earlier] Galton; early I
696.27 steps . . . .] H; ~.ˏ I
696.29 persons.] *stet* I; persons (see Appendix F). Galton
698.14–16 *the . . . them*] *stet* I; *all rom.* Galton
698.31 it,ˏ etc.'] Galton; ~,' ~.ˏ I
698.34–38 *in . . . colour*] *stet* I; *all rom.* Galton
698.38 cross-] Galton; crossed- I
699.6 the] Galton; *om.* I
700.6–11 *men . . . Academicians.*] *stet* I; *all rom.* Galton
700.28 ¶"I] *stet* I; *no* ¶ Galton
702.36 Osborn] H; Osborne I
703.32 *fleuve*] La Fontaine; *fleur* I

706.17 objects dating] BC; dating objects I
710.9 words₍ₐ₎] BC; ∼, I
710.28 or a] Bain; or I
710.31-32 is . . . recollection] stet I; all
rom. Bain
711.26 69–70] H; 49–50 I
711.31 M,] H; ∼₍ₐ₎ I (error)
711.32 49–50] H; 59–60 I
712.6 spot,] BC; ∼₍ₐ₎ I
712.8 a] H; om. I (error)

712.34 lie,] WJ/I; ∼₍ₐ₎ I
712.42 II₍ₐ₎] stet I[1-8]; II. I[9](resetting
error)
714.33 239] H; 238 I
715.1 Since] stet I; Since, then, Bain
715.6 [2]in the] Bain; om. I
715.13 persisting] Bain; existing I
715.25 reembodied] Bain; embodied I
715.41 337] H; 338 I
720.39 139] H; 129 I

CHAPTER XIX: THE PERCEPTION OF 'THINGS'

Reference is made to P[24], "The Perception of Space (III)," *Mind*, 12 (July 1887), 321–353 (McD 1887:4), to WJ/I , and to BC.

722.6 results] BC; result I
722.20 states of consciousness] stet I; rom.
Spencer
723.17 distance] Mill; shape I
723.39 94–96] H; 97 I
724.1-2 together, and] stet I; ∼. And
Berkeley
724.2 so] stet I; om. Berkeley
724.39 §] H; om. I
725.3 a sense-impression] stet I; it Sully
727.4;771.3-4 upside-] BC; ∼₍ₐ₎ I
727.10 bottom-] BC; ∼₍ₐ₎ I
727.36 724] H; 728 I
*728.26-27 It . . . becomes] WJ/I; It is
only in grave lesions that he becomes
I[1-2]; Only in the gravest lesions does
he become I[3]
729.5 sensations] WJ/I; those I
729.13 Le . . . rêves] stet ital. title I
(Rêves)
730.4 unfolding] stet I; unfolded Goethe
(Müller)
730.4 developing] stet I; developed
Goethe (Müller)
730.5 leaves, not natural] stet I; leaves.
These were not natural flowers Goethe
(Müller)
730.6 and] stet I; although Goethe
(Müller)
730.12 book, On . . . 61),] H; ∼₍ₐ₎ on . . .
∼)₍ₐ₎ I
730.46 an . . . -image] stet I; a consecutive
sensation of sight Taine
730.49 complementary] Taine; comple-

menatry I (error)
731.14 right;] BC; ∼, I
732.8-9 because . . . space] stet I; all ital.
Robertson
732.34 something] H; somothing I (error)
733.20 image.] H; ∼₍ₐ₎ I (error)
734.18 leftwards] H; leftward I
734.19 rightwards] H; rightward I
734.30 exactly] I[14]; exatly I[1-13]
735.9 anyone] BC; any one I
*736.21-22 But . . . be.] stet I
736.23 seem;] BC; ∼, I
736.39 635] H; 365 I
737.38 Revue] H; Reuve I (error)
739.15 Fig. 50] stet I; Fig. 6 Ladd-Franklin
739.16 in] Ladd-Franklin; into I
739.21 have a] Ladd-Franklin; be of I
739.22 passing] stet I; om. Ladd-Franklin
739.26 number . . .] H; ∼₍ₐ₎ I
739.29 apparent] Ladd-Franklin; om. I
739.30 have all] Ladd-Franklin; all have I
739.32 is] Ladd-Franklin; is I
740.24 like.] I[3]; ∼₍ₐ₎ I[1-2]
741.14 perceive,] BC; ∼₍ₐ₎ I
741.15 Greek, and₍ₐ₎ . . . better₍ₐ₎ Hebrew,]
BC; ∼₍ₐ₎ ∼, . . . ∼, ∼₍ₐ₎ I
741.34 p. 31] H; p. 32 I
741.41 -made] BC; ₍ₐ₎∼ I
742.41 242–4] H; 242–3 I
[begin P[24]]
743.29 stress] Taylor; distress P[24],I
744.6 object.] BC; ∼? P[24],I
744.39 1881] H; 1882 P[24],I

745.20;809.7;854.33   no wise] H; nowise
 P²⁴,I
[*end* P²⁴]
745.29   sensation] I²,BC; object of sensation I¹
745.34   no] I²,BC; any I¹
745.34   form] *stet* I¹⁻⁸; from I⁹(*resetting
 error*)
746.40   Th. 1] H; *om.* I
747.36   either] WJ/I; *om.* I
748.1   he] H; *om.* I (*error*)
748.20   But . . . have] WJ/I; If B, on the
 contrary, has I
748.32   and fluent] WJ/I; *om.* I
749.3   , p. 864 ff.] WJ/I (p. 231 ff.); *om.* I
749.17   illusion.²⁵] H; *fn. incorrectly
 keyed to* '1885,' *in* I [749.18]
749.20   XXVI] H; XXV I (*error*)
749.28   p. 255,] H; pp. 253–4. I (*error*)
*750.12   foot.ₐ] WJ/I; ∼.† (*i.e.*, 27) I
750.15   toes.²⁷] WJ/I (∼.†); ∼.‡ (*i.e.*, 28)
 I
752.11   forth?'] H; ∼?ₐ I
*752.17   nearly] H; newly I
752.42   J.] I³; *om.* I¹⁻²

753.40   167–73] H; 166–171   I
754.1   'eggs' . . . and] WJ/BC (*pencil*); his
 'eggs' broken into a glass, and his I,BC
754.41   74] H; 76   I
758.18   *Diseases*] H; *Disease* I
759.23   persecutors. . . .] H; ∼ . . . I
760.11   hasheesh] H; haschisch I
760.37   40] H; 42   I
767.9   consequently] H; conse-|sequently
 I (*error*)
768.28   J.] H; *om.* I
768.36   Work, *On Intelligence*] H; ∼ₐ on
 Intelligence I
769.16   , vol. I] H; *om.* I
769.22   All] *stet* I; By degrees all   Taine
769.23   gradually] *stet* I; *om.*   Taine
769.44   1394] H; 945   I
770.41   126–32] H; 126–8   I
772.37   an] *stet* I¹⁻⁸; as I⁹(*resetting error*)
774.1   an] *stet* I; a positively   Romanes
774.2   *read*] *stet* I; *rom.*   Romanes
774.2   has] Romanes; have I
774.39   whom] Romanes; *om.* I
775.9   (1889),] H; (1890)ₐ I

Chapter XX: The Perception of Space

Reference is made to P²⁴, "The Perception of Space," *Mind*, 12 (January,
April, July, October 1887), 1–30, 183–211, 321–353, 516–548 (McD 1887:4),
to P²¹, "The Spatial Quale," *Journal of Speculative Philosophy*, 13 (January
1879), 64–87 (McD 1879:6), to WJ/I, and to BC.

[*begin* P²⁴(1)]
778.1   everyone] P²⁴; every one I
778.20   living . . . appeared] *stet* P²⁴,I;
 living objects, such as men, horses, &c.,
 appeared to him   Franz
778.39   p. 66] WJ/I; *om.* I
☛779.32   forwards] H; forward P²⁴,I
 (*also* 786.7;831.4;848.29;864.7)
781.28   we] WJ/I; wc I (*error*)
782.14   anyone] P²⁴; any one I
783.3   fore-arm] P²⁴; forearm I
784.5   Hasheesh] H; Haschish P²⁴,I
784.13   vol. II, pt. 1] H; II P²⁴,I
785.25–31   the Things . . . discover] Cheselden; *modernized in* P²⁴,I (all things)
785.25   he thought] Cheselden; *om.* P²⁴,I
786.41   affected] *stet* P²⁴,I; was affected

 Brown
786.43   or] Brown; and P²⁴,I
786.43   fragrance] Brown,P²⁴; fragance I
 (*error*)
789.28   Nunneley's] H; Nunnely's P²⁴,I
791.10   towards] P²⁴; toward I
792.40   § 13] H; § 12 P²⁴,I
☛798.16   *local*ₐ*signs*] H; ∼-∼ P²⁴,I
 (*also* *806.36;807.2,3;808.1,6)
798.35   Erdmann] H; Erdman P²⁴,I
*799.34   *supra*, p. 797] H; *supra*, p. 19
 P²⁴;I (*i.e.*, 156)
[*end* P²⁴(1); *begin* P²⁴(2)]
802.40   II] H; xi P²⁴; XI I
807.17   cannot] P²⁴; canot I (*error*)
[*begin* P²¹]
809.23   corti] P²¹; Corti P²⁴,I

[*end* P[21]]
809.29 Stepanoff] H; Stepano, ff. I (*error*)
809.32 557] H; 577 P[24],I
809.41 running.] P[24]; ~‸ I (*error*)
[*begin* P[21]]
811.13 0.045] Exner; 0.044 P[21,24],I
811.19 0.014] Exner; 0.015 P[21,24],I
[*end* P[21]]
811.23 *attention*] P[24]; *atttention* I (*error*)
811.34 [1]still] P[24]; still | still I (*error*)
811.37 'content'] BC; ‸~‸ I
813.15 13.8] Schneider; 13.3 P[24],I
813.38 Physiologisch-optische] H;
        Physiologische Optische I
816.21-22 Thus . . . be] P[24](*be*); WJ/BC
        (*pencil*); *all ital.* I, BC
816.22 *really smaller*] WJ/BC (*pencil*);
        rom. P[24],I,BC
816.35 surface.] H; ~‸ I
816.41 text.] H; ~‸ I
817.12 eye,] BC; ~‸ I
818.12 mother‸] Spencer; ~- P[24],I
818.12 of thought] *stet* P[24],I; *om.*
        Spencer
818.33 among] Jastrow; amongst I
818.39 *into . . . equivalents*] *stet* I; *all*
        rom. Jastrow
823.31 with)‸] H; ~), I (*error*)
826.13 fore-arm] H; forearm P[24],I
826.33 sont] H; sont-elles I
827.20 space-] P[24]; ~‸ I
830.1 prove,] BC; ~‸ I
830.2 *joint*-] H; ~‸ I
834.19 Volkmann] H; Volkman I (*error*)
835.2 see] *stet* I; see Lewes
835.4 itself] *stet* I; *om.* Lewes
835.4 seen] *stet* I; seen contracting Lewes
836.26 (2nd ed.)] H; *om.* I
838.14 spatial] P[24]; spacial I
840.14-15 'facial perception.'] *stet* P[24],I;
        "*Facial Perception.*" Levy
840.32-33 indentations] Levy, P[24];
        identations I (*error*)
840.40 Kilbourne] H; Kilburne P[24],I
841.19-20 nine pages back] H; on p. 206
        P[24]; ten pages back I
842.22 drop] P[24]; drops I (*error*)
842.30-32 "To . . . seeing."] P[24]; *sg. qts.* I
843.18 time . . . space] *stet* Hamilton,
        P[24],I; *all ital.* Mill
843.19 means] Hamilton,Mill; mean P[24],I

843.20 some other] *stet* Hamilton,P[24],I;
        another Mill
844.28 kinds?] H; ~. I
845.8-13 " 'Suppose . . . cube?' "] H;
        db. qts. I
845.17 friend . . .] H; ~, I
845.18 able] *stet* I; able with certainty
        Locke
845.38 *aveugle-né*] I[3](Aveugle né);
        Aveuge-Né I[1-2]
[*end* P[24](2); *begin* P[24](3)]
847.8-9 vague— . . . ground—] P[24];
        ~,— . . . ~,— I
847.9-10 enthusiastically] P[24]; enthusi-
        astially I (*error*)
*847.34-35 since . . . about] *stet* P[24],I
847.38 1871] H; 1875 P[24],I
847.38 125] P[24]; 124 I
848.34 724] H; 728 P[24],I
851.28 off] H; of P[24],I
852.8 Ch.] H; c. P[24],I
852.8 VI,] H; VI. P[24],I
852.10 a] Reid; *om.* P[24],I
852.13 custom] *stet* P[24],I; ~, long con-
        tinued, Reid
*853.10-13 Meanwhile . . . *thing.*] *stet* I
853.12 *that*] H; *that* I (*error*)
854.4 -feeling.] P[24]; -~, I (*error*)
855.32 lateral] P[24]; literal I (*error*)
855.46 the London] H; *The* P[24]; The
        London I
855.47 Dougall] H; Dougal I
858.20 leftwards] H; leftward P[24],I
860.33 736-9] H; 737-9 P[24],I
860.33 II,] H; *om.* P[24],I
860.36 §§] H; *om.* P[24],I
861.16 Fig. 55] WJ/I; Fig. 50 I (*error*)
863.3 eyes‸ alters,] H; ~‸ alter, P[24],I[3];
        ~‸ alters‸ WJ/I; ~, alter‸ I[1-2]
865.6 Fig.] P[24]; ~‸ I
865.8 Fig. 62] WJ/I; Fig. 52 I (*error*)
868.41 VI] H; iii. 9, P[24];I (III)
869.38 XXVI] H; XXIV I
871.14 starting‸point] H; ~-~ I
872.20-21 *seen . . . apprehended*] *stet*
        P[24],I; *each rom.* Berkeley
872.22 *Alciphron . . . Dialogue*] H;
        Divine Visual Language P[24];I(*rom.*)
872.28 and] *stet* P[24],I; and that Reid
872.31 them . . . for] H; them (the signs).
        For P[24],I; them; for Reid

872.37　chap. VI] H; chap. V　P24,I
873.24　is a . . . condition] WJ/I; are . . . conditions P24,I
874.39　way,] P24; ~ I
875.5-6　"Don't . . . *looks!*"] H; *sg. qts.* P24,I
[*end* P24(3); *begin* P24(4)]
876.22　laid] P24; said I (*error*)
878.22　movement] P24; movements I (*error*)
878.26　Dvořák has] H; Mach and Dvorak have P24,I
*879.19　page 811] H; page 188 P24;I (*i.e.,* 172)
*881.33　XIX] P24; XXI I
881.34　Bd. II] H; *om.* P24,I
881.37　2nd ed., vol. II] H; *om.* P24,I
882.26　*this*] P24,WJ/I; *his* I (*error*)
884.2　70,] WJ/I,I8; 15 P24; 65, I1-7
884.22　vol. V, pt. 2] H; v. 2 P24,I
889.9　ease] P24; case I (*error*)
896.9+　*space*] P24; *top of page* I
899.36-37　"a . . . understanding."] P24; *sg. qts.* I
901.13　the original] Brown; original P24,I
901.17　a line] *stet* P24,I; the line　Mill
901.26　space] *stet* P24,I; Space　Mill
901.28　it] *stet* P24,I; *om.*　Bain
901.28　1 no other] *stet* P24,I; *ital.*　Bain
901.29　*association*] *stet* P24,I; *rom.*　Bain
901.29-30　sensitive and motor] Bain; motor and sensitive P24,I
901.37,39　4th] H; 3rd P24,I

901.37　295] H; 283 P24,I
902.28　a *simultaneous*] *stet* P24,I; the simultaneous　Spencer
902.31　No] *stet* P24,I; Not that such Spencer
902.32　*successive*] *stet* P24,I; *rom.* Spencer
902.33　motion] *stet* P24,I; the motion, Spencer
902.34　distinct] *stet* P24,I; distinct in nature　Spencer
902.34　space . . . time] *stet* P24,I; *init. caps.*　Spencer
905.6　itself . . .] P24; ~, . . .　I
906.2-3　"the . . . space,"] P24; *sg. qts.* I
906.29　I,] P24 (i.); II.　I
908.34　I] H; ii P24; II　I
909.11　of] P24,WJ/I; *om.* I (*error*)
909.25　mean] I3; means I1-2
909.27　therein . . . not] I3; there professed are not to P24,I1-2
910.15　Hering] I3; ~, P24,I1-2
910.15　imagine–] P24,I3; ~,– I1-2
911.23-24　Le Conte] H; Leconte P24,I
911.24　Schoen] H; Schön P24,I
911.27　-*disant*] P24,WJ/I; -*distant* I
911.36　*fallacious assumption*] *stet* P24,I; *rom.*　Sully
912.8　*Discussions*] H; Disquisitions I
912.12　1864] H; 1861　I
912.15　March] H; Aug. I
[*end* P24(4)]

Chapter XXI: The Perception of Reality

Reference is made to P24, "The Psychology of Belief," *Mind*, 14 (July 1889), 321-352 (McD 1889:4), to P30, "Rationality, Activity and Faith," *Princeton Review*, 2 (July 1882), 58-86 (McD 1882:2), and to WJ/I.

[*begin* P24]
913.15　*nature*] P24; ~,　I
913.24　1889] I3; 1869　I1-2
915.11　1that] Mill; *om.* P24,I
915.11　perceive] Mill; see P24,I
915.19　Belief] Mill; *l.c.* P24,I
915.27　told] Clouston; told that P24,I
915.28-29　It is . . . at hand.] Clouston; Is it . . . on hand? P24,I
915.28　probable] Clouston; probable that P24,I

915.32　should] Clouston,P24; thould I (*error*)
915.33-34　*engrossed* . . . *thoughts*] *stet* P24,I; *all rom.*　Clouston
916.3　*Psychologie*] *stet ital. title* P24,I
917.38　VIII] WJ/I,I3; VII　P24,I1-2
918.31-32　*and similar* 919.15-17,20 "That . . . *world*,"] H; *sg. qts.* P24,I
920.20-21　"where . . . dwell."] P24; *sg. qts.* I
922.5-6　*Iliad* . . . *Papers*] *stet ital. titles*

P24,I
*924.1-3 which . . . 2consider] *stet* P24,I
924.13 *reality*] P24;*reality* I (*error*)
924.13 *simply*] P24,WJ/I,I3; *simply* I1-2
924.25 what] Hume; *om.* P24,I
924.26 It] *stet* P24,I; that belief Hume
924.27 ideas] Hume; the ideas P24,I
924.31 *belief*] Hume; *rom.* P24,I
924.32 the mind] P24; themind I (*error*)
924.32 ideas] Hume; idea P24,I
924.33 imagination.11] *stet* P24,I; ~., (*om. fn.*) Hume
924.35 gives . . . passions,] *stet* P24,I; [*out of place*] Hume
924.36 of] Hume; in P24,I
925.1 Belief] Bain; belief P24,I
925.11 contains no] *stet* P24,I; does not contain Kant (Müller)
925.14 1thing . . .] H; ~, P24,I
925.14 added] *stet* P24,I; really added Kant (Müller)
925.16 of] *stet* P24,I; *om.* Kant (Müller)
925.29 515-16] H; 515-17 P24,I
925.31 on,] Hume; of, P24,I
925.34 to] *stet* P24,I; to the idea of Hume
925.35 ideas . . . idea] Hume; idea . . . ideas P24,I
925.39 parts] Hume; facts P24,I
925.39-40 composition] Hume; compositions P24,I
925.40 *manner*] Hume; *rom.* P24,I
927.6 "but] H; '~ P24; I (*error*)
927.32 insanity."] P24; ~., I
927.36 *Die . . . Krankheiten*] H; *Mental Diseases* P24;I(*rom.*)
927.37 See . . . p. 251.] WJ/I; *om.* P24,I
928.12-13 *contradicting*] WJ/I (*rom.*); *om.* P24,I
*928.13 *relation,*] *stet* P24,I; *relation* which, WJ/I
931.7 canals] Hume; channels P24,I
931.16 chain] Hume; train P24,I
931.30 these] Hume; those P24,I
931.31 influence] *stet* P24,I; influence on the vulgar Hume
931.31 *Catholic*] *stet* P24,I (*both rom.*); *Roman Catholic* Hume
931.32 instances] *stet* P24,I; experiments Hume
931.33 excuse of] Hume; excuse for P24,I

931.34 those] Hume; *om.* P24,I
931.36 away] Hume; *om.* P24,I
932.1 'tis] Hume; it is P24,I
932.21 will . . .] H; ~, P24,I
932.23 representing] Tylor; resembling P24,I
932.25 a coach] Tylor; coach P24,I
932.28 child] *stet* P24,I; child with Tylor
932.30 child] Tylor; child's P24,I
932.31 in] *stet* P24,I; in the midst of a Tylor
932.34 grown-up] Tylor; grown P24,I
932.35 reality] *stet* P24,I; reality and definiteness Tylor
932.36 woman] *stet* P24,I; native woman Tylor
932.40 8] H; 7 P24, I
933.8 baby] Tylor; body P24,I
933.8 no] Tylor; an P24,I
933.17-19 "*Die . . . Züge.*"] P24; *sg. qts.* I
933.24 any one] P24; anyone I
934.4 suggesters] P24; suggestions I
934.26 Aristotle . . . have] WJ/I; Berkeley has P24,I
935.4-5 *this . . . misery*] *stet* P24,I; *all rom.* Locke
935.10 XXV] H; XXIV I (*error*)
935.30 in] Locke; into P24,I
935.35 this] Locke; the P24,I
935.37 knowing] Locke; knowledge P24,I
936.13 The Caliph Omar] *stet* P24,I; He Bagehot
936.13 Omar . . .] H; ~, P24,I
936.13 Alexandrian] *stet* P24,I; Alexandrine Bagehot
936.14 those] Bagehot; *om.* P24,I
936.15 the Koran] Bagehot; it P24,I
936.18 came . . . probably] Bagehot; probably came to him P24,I
936.23 proved] Bagehot; found P24,I
936.26 to] Bagehot; of P24,I
936.29 word] Bagehot; words P24,I
936.33 and ages] Bagehot; or ages P24,I
936.41 II,] H; I P24,I
936.41 412-414] H; 412-417 P24,I
937.40 this] Reid; the P24,I
937.40 a size] Reid; size P24,I
938.5 384] H; 388 P24,I
938.7 down] Stanley; *om.* P24,I
938.12 warriors] *stet* P24,I; warriors, armed with muskets, Stanley

938.13 five] *stet* P[24],I; five hundred Stanley
938.16 amongst] Stanley; among P[24],I
938.16 would] Stanley; should P[24],I
938.23 " 'Mundelé,'] P[24]; "~," Stanley; "ᵥ~,' I (*error*)
938.24 -taraᵥ .... ᵥThis] *stet* P[24],I; *db. qts.* Stanley
938.30 friends] Stanley; your friends P[24],I
938.38 note-] Stanley; field- P[24],I
938.45 many] Stanley; my many P[24],I
938.49 Ah-h-h] Stanley,P[24]; Ah-h I [*begin* P[30]]
940.19-20 'problem of good.'] P[30] (*db. qts.*);WJ/I; ᵥ~~ '~.' P[24],I
*940.33 senses] P[30]; sense P[24],I
941.40 end. ...] H; ~.ᵥ P[30,24],I
942.38 wildfire] P[30]; ~-|~ P[24]; ~-~ I [*end* P[30]]
943.41 actually] Royce; *om.* P[24],I
944.3 sights, sounds] Royce; sounds, sights P[24],I
944.7 law] Royce; laws P[24],I
944.9 good] Royce; great P[24],I
944.11 thought is] Royce; thoughts are P[24],I

944.15 is] Royce; *om.* P[24],I
944.39 316-17, 357] H; 317-357 P[24], I
944.40 XXVIII] H; XXVII I (*error*)
945.11 *beyond*] WJ/I; *rom.* P[24],I [*end* P[24]]
945.26 reality?] Royce,I[3]; ~. I[1-2]
945.32-35 *will ... one*] *stet* I; *all rom.* Royce
945.36 pp. 303-4] H; p. 304 I
946.11 present] H; presently I (*error*)
947.27 XXVI] H; XXV I (*error*)
947.34;1137.1;1215.11 tomorrow] H; to-morrow I
*948.28 If belief ...] *stet* I
949.14 *A*] H; The I
949.16 XVIII] H; XXVIII I
949.17 Ollé-] H; ~ᵥ I
949.17 1880] H; 1881 I
949.17 The] H; On I
949.26 Sully,] H; ~; I (*error*)
*949.31-32 *our ... fact*] *stet* I
949.34-35 *Nineteenth ...* Sept.] H; Fortnightly Review, July I
950.46-47 experience] WJ/I; xperience I (*error*)

CHAPTER XXII: REASONING

Reference is made to P[24], "The Sentiment of Rationality," *Mind*, 4 (July 1879), 317-346 (McD 1879:7), to P[21], "Brute and Human Intellect," *Journal of Speculative Philosophy*, 12 (July 1878), 236-276 (McD 1878:4), to WJ/I, and to BC.

952.20-953.1 ᵥ or similaritiesᵥ] WJ/I; , ~~, I
954.20 formed] *stet* I; formed as I say Romanes
954.23 conscious] Romanes; conscous I (*error*)
954.24 *received ... conceived*] Romanes; *each rom.* I
955.5 far] *stet* I; far, then, Romanes
955.9-17 'Houzeau ... animals.'] H; ᵥ~ ... ~.ᵥ I
955.9 relates] Darwin (Romanes); writes I
955.9 whilst] Darwin; while Romanes,I
955.12 These] Darwin (Romanes); The I

955.21 around] Darwin (Romanes); round I
955.22 scent] Darwin; scout Romanes,I
955.34 substance] Romanes; surface I
955.39 p. 49] H; p. 50 I
955.40 P. 51] H; P. 52 I
956.34 this:] BC; ~, I
957.26 *property*ᵥ] BC; ~, I
958.9 thingsᵥ] BC; ~, I
958.42 men] Mill; man I
959.11 *ad*] BC; *in* I
960.10-11 Godᵥ ... abreastᵥ] BC; ~, ... ~, I
961.22 truths ... become] I[3]; truth ... becomes I[1-2]

961.32   class] Whewell; kind I
961.33   character] *stet* I; *Character*
         Whewell
961.36   persuasion] Whewell; conviction I
961.37   on] Whewell; upon I
[*begin* P24]
961.41   What] *stet* I; What now P24
[*end* P24]
963.24   repugnance] WJ/I; repugance I
         (*error*)
964.22   of‿] BC; ~, I
965.11-12 elevation:] BC; ~– I
*965.12-13 bottom ... up] BC; top by
         friction against lintel—press it bodily
         down I
*966.8   special ... purpose] WJ/I; the new
         lines I
[*begin* P21]
966.18   2but‿] BC; ~, P21,I
966.21   dye,] BC; ~‿ P21,I
967.21   ‿ now‿] P21,BC; , ~, I

970.6   because] P21; bcause I (*error*)
970.21   interests‿] P21,BC; ~, I
982.12-13 "accompanied ... joy"] P21;
         sg. qts. I
982.14;987.15;988.36 embedded] H;
         imbedded P21,I
984.15   leading fact] *stet* P21,I; *ital.* Bain
984.15   genius ...] H; ~. P21,I
984.17   an] Bain; *om.* P21,I
984.37   towards] H; toward P21,I
985.22   blood."23] I3; ~."‿ (*om. fn.*)
         P21,I1-2
986.10   1at] I3; from P21,I1-2
987.40   1876] P21; 1879 I
988.23   latter] I3; former P21,I1-2
[*end* P21]
992.21   *céleste*] H; Céleste I
992.22   it is evident] *stet* I; Thus it plainly
         appears Bowditch
992.35   a common] WJ/I; an ordinary I

Chapter XXIII: The Production of Movement

Reference is made to BC.

994.0   XXIII] I2; XXII I1
994.24   diffuse] *stet* I; *ital.* Bain
994.24   freely] Bain; *om.* I
998.14   impressions and sensations] Tar-
         chanoff; sensations and impressions I
999.3   Sander] H; Sanders I (*error*)

999.12   653] H; 652 I
1000.6   Pellacani] H; Pellicani I (*error*)
1001.31 les] Féré; ces I
1001.36 Nov.] H; Oct. I
1002.27 movements‿ ... expansion‿]
         BC; ~, ... ~, I

Chapter XXIV: Instinct

Reference is made to P37, "What Is an Instinct?" *Scribner's Magazine*, 1 (March 1887), 355–365 (McD 1887:6), to P29, "Some Human Instincts," *Popular Science Monthly*, 31 (June, September 1887), 160–170, 666–681 (McD 1887:8), to WJ/I, and to BC.

[*begin* P37]
1005.19 appears] P37,WJ/I,BC,I8;
         appeart I1-7
1006.14 *thierische*] H; Thierische P37,I
1007.18 pond-] WJ/BC; ditch- P37,I,BC
1010.39 pp. 280-3] H; *om.* P37; pp. 282-3
         I
1011.2   hatch] P37; hatched I
1011.30 O,] BC; ~‿ P37,I

1012.3   'inhibited‿'] P37,BC; '~,' I
1012.5   habit;] BC; ~, P37,I
1012.16 reflex‿] BC; ~- P37,I
1012.40-41 *Animal ... Existence*] H;
         Conditions of Existence in Animals
         P37,I
1013.13 ‿ then‿] BC; , ~, P37(*rom.*);I
1014.20 derangements ... constitution]
         stet P37,I; derange their mental

constitution Romanes

☞1014.34-35 *afterwards*] H; afterward P37 (*or* P29);I (*ital.*) (*also* 1021.10; 1034.32; 1043.18)

☞1015.18,27 towards] H; toward P37 (*or* P29),I (*also* 1017.13;1018.13,15-16;1032.29;1035.11;1051.34;1054.23-24,33;1056.19,20)

1016.17 on-lookers] Spalding; lookers-on P37,I

1016.19 miles] Spalding; for miles P37,I

1016.20 I] Spalding; I had P37,I

1016.21 and . . .] H; ~ₐ P37,I

1016.21 their] Spalding; the P37,I

1016.27 these] Spalding; them P37,I

1016.27 ²of] Spalding; to P37,I

1016.30 glass] Spalding; window P37,I

1016.38 organization] Spalding; organizations P37,I

1018.5 all–] H; ~, P37,I; ~,– BC

1018.10 mentionedₐ] BC; ~, P37,I

1018.18 until] Spalding,BC; till until P37,I (*error*)

1019.10 fore-feet] H; forefeet P37,I

1019.21 instinctive] P37,BC; instructive I (*error*)

1019.31 ground] Schmidt,P37; grond I (*error*)

1020.35 tells] *stet* P37,I; also tells Lewes

1021.29 Butₐ] BC; ~, P37,I [*end* P37]

1023.6 *instinctive*] BC; *rom.* I

1023.23 *spitting-*] H; ~ₐ I

1025.26 about] Spalding; some I

1025.32 too] Spalding; *om.* I

1025.38 a . . . experiment] Spalding; similar observations I

1025.40 412-413, 675-676] H; 413-675 I

1027.13 onwards] H; onward I

1027.17 *Humani nihil*] I3; *Nil humani* I1-2

1028.14 -tenths] WJ/I,I8; -tenth I1-7 [*begin* P29 (1)]

1028.21 his] *stet* P29,I; my Goethe

1028.34 tomorrow] H; to-morrow P29,I [*end* P29(1)]

1030.26 Fowler:] I4; ~. I1-3 [*begin* P29(1)]

1031.38 Bethlem] Tuke; Bethlehem P29,I (*error*)

1031.38 ago, . . .] H; ~,ₐ P29,I

1031.41 blood . . .] H; ~ₐ P29,I

1032.39 Guyau] H; Guyan I (*error*)

1035.33 -75] H; -74 P29,I

1036.34 darkness . . . woods] BC; darkness of caverns and woods P29,I

1037.20 It] *stet* P29,I1-8; -~ I9(*resetting error*)

1037.22 psychical-research societies] BC; ~ₐ ~-~ P29,I

1037.34 Anyone's] BC; Any one's P29,I

1038.23 *the Lower*] H; *om.* P29,I

1038.29 1886] H; this year P29; 1887 I

1038.30 Sanford] H; Sandford P29,I (*error*)

1038.32-41 'My . . . confounded.'] H; ₐ~ . . . ~.ₐ P29,I

1038.33-34 Father . . . and] *stet* P29,I (*both* 'father'); Father used to enter his kitchen bringing some killed animals in [It was customary for farmers to do their own butchering.], and Sanford

1038.34 one of] *stet* P29,I; one of [the] Sanford

1038.35 make] *stet* P29,I; make [made] Sanford

1038.39 queer] *stet* P29,I; queer [The little girl was allowed great freedom of observation after her manner] Sanford

1038.40 that] *stet* P29,I; that that Sanford (*error*)

1038.40 [had]] Sanford; ₐhadₐ P29,I

1038.40 vitality.ₐ] H; ~. . . . P29,I

1039.9 someone] BC; some one P29,I [*end* P29(1); *begin* P29(2)]

1040.35 *my*] P29; my I

1040.39 1885] H; 1886 P29,I

1040.41 twenty-seven] H; twenty-nine P29,I

1041.34-1042.6 'I . . . another.'] H; ₐ~ . . . ~.ₐ P29,I

1041.35 symmetry] *stet* P29,I; *ital.* Lindsay

1042.1 among them] Lindsay; with P29,I

☞1044.18+ *no space*] P29; *space* I (*also* 1046.3+;1049.22+;1050.27+;1052.3+; 1053.25+;1055.8+,9+)

1044.40 someone] H; some one P29,I

1045.33 startingₐ] H; ~- P29,I

1046.36 *Spiels*] H; Spieles P29,I

1047.27 little] *stet* P29,I; so little Galton

1047.27 individual] Galton; *om.* P²⁹,I
1047.28 severance] Galton; separation P²⁹,I
1048.4 is] *stet* P²⁹,I; is, indeed, Darwin
1048.23 perfectly] Darwin; quite P²⁹,I
1048.23 the] Darwin; *om.* P²⁹,I
1048.25 dreads] *stet* P²⁹,I; no doubt dreads Darwin
1048.29 throughout] Darwin; through P²⁹,I
1049.4 when] Darwin; *om.* P²⁹,I

1049.5 towards] Darwin; toward P²⁹,I
1050.38 (of servants)] *stet* P²⁹,I; *om.* Thackeray
1051.14 that] P²⁹; than I (*error*)
1052.13 inhibit] P²⁹; inhibit it I (*error*)
1056.18 development‿] BC; ~, P²⁹,I
1056.33 *menschlischen* . . . Leipzig] H; Menschlichen . . . Leipsic P²⁹,I
1057.16 bringing-] BC; ~‿ P²⁹,I
[*end* P²⁹(2)]

CHAPTER XXV: THE EMOTIONS

Reference is made to P²⁴, "What Is an Emotion?" *Mind*, 9 (April 1884), 188–205 (McD 1884:2), to WJ/I, and to BC.

1061.45 54] H; 55 I
1062.19 whether] Darwin; if I
1062.23 or] Darwin; or is I
1062.26 marvellous] *stet* I; marvellous and inexplicable Darwin
1062.34 is a] Darwin; is I
1063.2 may] Darwin; must I
1063.7 *volvens*] Darwin; *volens* I
1063.40 *Expression*] H; Origin I
1065.21-24 —and . . . XLVI] WJ/I; *om.* I
[*begin* P²⁴]
1066.6 bear‿] BC; ~, P²⁴,I
1067.19 people, . . . asked,] P²⁴,BC; ~‿ . . . ~‿ I
[*end* P²⁴]
1068.38 deep‿ pure‿ worthy‿] WJ/I; ~, ~, ~, I
1068.40 deep‿ pure‿ spiritual‿] WJ/I; ~, ~, ~, I
1069.13 each?"–] BC; ~?"‿ I
1069.15 "Just] H; ‿~ I (*error*)
1069.17 others?] *stet* I¹⁻¹⁰; ~. I¹¹(*resetting error*)
1071.6,12 Strümpell] H; Strumpell I
1071.43 felt."] H; ~.' I (*error*)
[*begin* P²⁴]
1072.7 idea.] BC (*idea.*); ~? P²⁴,I
1074.16 evil] WJ/I; distressing P²⁴,I
[*end* P²⁴]
1075.6 painful,] *stet* I; painful, and accompanied by a feeling of extreme distress, Bucke
1075.42 p. 96] H; p. 97 I

1075.43 p. 60] H; p. 61 I
[*begin* P²⁴]
1077.21 Everyone] P²⁴, BC; Every one I
1077.38 p. 71] H; p. 72 I
[*end* P²⁴]
1078.16-18 *if . . . manifestation*] *stet* I; *all rom.* Bain
1078.18 same] *stet* I; very same Bain
1078.21 induction] Bain; action I
1078.26 philosopher] WJ/I; physiognomist I
1078.28 any] Burke (Stewart); in any I
1078.33 this] Burke (Stewart); the I
1078.39 endeavoured] Burke (Stewart); strove I
1078.40 361-3] H; 361-2 I
1079.12 Mr. . . . writes,] Archer; writes Mr. Lionel Brough, I
1079.15 should] Archer; shall I
1079.16 it.' . . .] H; ~.'‿ I
1080.1 Dillon] Archer; Dillion I (*error*)
1080.37 P. 392] H; P. 394 I
[*begin* P²⁴]
*1081.29 law . . . paragraph] *stet* P²⁴,I
1083.40 by] *stet* I; *om.* Gurney
1083.45 -noteness] *stet* I; -noteness Gurney
1083.45 melody] *stet* I; favourite melody Gurney
1083.46 deny] Gurney; deny to I
1083.47 experience] Gurney; expression I
[*end* P²⁴]
1088.8 Emotion] Bain; *l.c.* I

1090.9   organs.²⁴ᵃ] WJ/I; ∼.ᴧ (*om. fn.*) I
1091.38 essay] H; chap. I
1092.30-31 was . . . had] *stet* I; is . . . has
  Spencer
1093.30 *Principles*] I³; Principle I¹⁻²
1093.34 *La* . . . 1st ed.,] H; La Paura I
1095.15 precordialᴧ] BC; ∼' I (*error*)

1096.14 in efficacy] WJ/I,I⁸; inefficacy
  I¹⁻⁷
1097.13 we] *stet* I¹⁻²; *om.* I³(*resetting
  error*)
1097.13 shall . . . trace] WJ/I,I³; have
  already traced I¹⁻²
1097.13 origin.³³ᵃ] WJ/I,I³; ∼.ᴧ (*om.
  fn.*) I¹⁻²

Chapter XXVI: Will

Reference is made to P⁴², "The Feeling of Effort," *Anniversary Memoirs of the Boston Society of Natural History* (1880), pp. 3-32 (McD 1880:3), to P³⁷, "What the Will Effects," *Scribner's Magazine*, 3 (February 1888), pp. 240-250 (McD 1888:1), to WJ/I, and to BC.

[*begin* P³⁷]
1099.23 so called] P³⁷,BC; ∼-∼ I
[*end* P³⁷]
1099.26 powerᴧ] BC; ∼, I
1099.37-1100.2 *possible,* . . . *performance,*] BC; ∼ᴧ . . . ∼ᴧ I
[*begin* P⁴²]
1102.34 Takács] H; Tàkacs P⁴²,I
[*end* P⁴²]
1103.31 explored] H; unexplored I
  (*error*)
1103.33 1001] H; 377 I (*i.e.*, 379)
1105.26 *consequence of*] H; *consequenceof* I (*error*)
1107.43 *upon*] H; on I
1107.45 E.] H; S. I (*error*)
[*begin* P⁴²]
1108.40 *Effektbild*] Harless; *Effectsbild*
  P⁴²,I
1109.25;1115.31 anyone] H; any one
  P⁴²,I
1110.34 *Les*] H; Des P⁴²,I
1111.1 introspection,] BC; ∼ᴧ P⁴²,I
1111.25 If (*no* ¶)] BC; ¶ P⁴²,I
1111.32 ¶There] BC; *no* ¶ I
1112.21 someone] H; some one P⁴²,I
1112.41 are] I³; is I¹⁻²
1113.31 46] H; 47 I
1113.32 pp. 58-59] H; the same page I
1113.39 Bois-Reymond's] H; Bois' P⁴²,I
1113.40 175-195] H; 174-188 P⁴²,I
1113.42 (Am. ed.)] H; *om.* P⁴²,I
1114.5 *altogether*] *stet* P⁴²,I; *rom.*
  Ferrier

1114.40 own] Bastian; *om.* P⁴²,I
1115.40 clenching] H; clinching I
1117.18 *effects*] P⁴²(Helmholtz 'Folgen');
  effect I
1118.13 forefinger] H; ∼ᴧ∼ P⁴²; ∼-∼ I
1119.7 right] P⁴²; sight I (*error*)
1119.28 ᴧProfessor] H; "∼ I (*error*)
1120.6 left],] H; ∼,] P⁴²,I
1120.16 act] WJ/I; function P⁴²,I
1120.23 *vom*] P⁴²(*rom.*); von I
[*end* P⁴²]
1125.32 XLVI] H; XLIV I
1126.25 at . . . ¹of] WJ/I; in I
1126.36 simultaneously] H; sinultaneously
  I (*error*)
1127.17 'resident'] BC; ᴧ∼ᴧ I
1127.18 'remote'] BC; ᴧ∼ᴧ I
1127.33 Royer-] H; Royerᴧ WJ/I,I⁸;
  Rogerᴧ I¹⁻⁷
1128.35 opticalᴧ . . . remote),] BC;
  ∼, . . . ∼)ᴧ I
1130.9 movement,] BC; ∼ᴧ I
1130.33 XXV] H; XXIII I
1130.36 beginning] H; begin I (*error*)
1131.14 do;] BC; ∼, I
1131.14-15 fruit, . . . it,] BC; ∼ᴧ . . . ∼ᴧ I
1133.40 1890] H; 1889 I
1134.13 from, . . . actionᴧ] BC; ∼ᴧ . . . ∼,
  I
1134.16 thought,] BC; ∼ᴧ I
[*begin* P³⁷]
1135.21 brakes] P³⁷; breaks I (*error*)
[*end* P³⁷]
1137.6 patiently] BC; patient I (*error*)

1137.7 inclining,] I³; ~‿ I¹⁻²
1137.10 rupture] I³,BC; rapture I¹⁻²
1137.15 any one] WJ/I,I⁸; either I¹⁻⁷
1138.20 five] BC; four I
1138.31 'reasons'] BC,I¹⁴; '~‿ I¹⁻¹³
1139.29 moment] H; movement I
1139.39 In the] H; *In the* I (*error*)
1140.6 state‿] BC; ~, I
1140.11 agents‿] BC; ~, I
1140.38 us‿] BC; ~, I
1141.5 beam:] BC; ~; I
1141.11,32 four] BC; three I
1141.17-18 delights;] BC; ~, I
1141.19 good‿] BC; ~, I
1141.22 reality;] BC; ~, I
1141.24 former] BC; three former I
1141.31 fifth] BC; fourth I
1142.27 overpassed] BC (~-|~); overpast I
1142.28 another,] BC; ~‿ I
1142.38 (if ... all)] BC; , ~ ... ~, I
1143.11 obey,] BC; ~‿ I
1144.31 greater] BC; greatest I
1145.26 exhaustion,] BC; ~‿ I
1145.37 think] *stet* I; endeavor to think Dudley
1145.38 his] Dudley; the I
1145.41 first-rate] *stet* I; experienced Dudley
1146.4 stopped] *stet* I; stopped or controlled Clouston
1146.5 act.‿] H; ~. ... I
1146.13 child] *stet* I; young child Clouston
1146.13 will] Clouston; will suddenly I
1146.17 before a] *stet* I; suddenly before a sane Clouston
1146.27 these] *stet* I; those Clouston
1146.31 can] *stet* I; can therefore Clouston
1146.36-37 manifestations] Clouston; manifestation I
1147.4 sorts] *stet* I; sorts (moral insanity) Clouston
1147.15 or] *stet* I; it Clouston
1147.16 the man ... be] *stet* I; the will, the man being Clouston
1147.21 a dement] Clouston; dement I
1148.17 caprices] H; *cap.* I
*1148.31 who ... him] H; whom he adored I

1149.27 ¹at] Burr; *om.* I
1149.29 would] Burr; should I
1150.4 tells ... man] *stet* I; relates a case of a gentleman Burr
[*begin* MS]
1150.14 towards] MS; toward I
1150.18 toward] Alfieri (Howells); towards MS,I
1150.21 , the] Alfieri (Howells); (~ MS,I
[*end* MS]
1150.26 and] *stet* I; and even to Alfieri (Howells)
1150.32 this] Alfieri (Howells); the I
1150.36 renewal] Alfieri (Howells); revival I
1151.9 then] *stet* I; *om.* Alfieri (Howells)
1151.19 almost] Alfieri (Howells); *om.* I
1151.20 frenzy; but about] *stet* I; ~. About Alfieri (Howells)
1151.20 period] Alfieri (Howells); time I
1151.25 new] Alfieri (Howells); *om.* I
1151.37 however, ... employed,] Alfieri (Howells); which I employed, however, I
1151.42 similar] Alfieri (Howells); such I
1152.23 inhibition] BC; inhibition of I
1152.36 *Life*] H; Autobiography I
1153.37 so] WJ/I; as I
1153.38 them‿] WJ/BC; ~, I, BC
1153.39 p. 38] H; p. 39 I
[*begin* P⁴²]
1155.6 way,] BC; ~‿ P⁴²,I
[*end* P⁴²]
1157.30 concurring] Bain; concurrent I
1157.33 the omega] Bain; omega I
1158.27 me] *stet* I; me rather Bain
1158.29 throughout. ...] H; ~.‿ I
1159.2 avoids?] BC; ~. I
1160.7 or] Bain; and I
1160.9 *pleasure*] *stet* I; *rom.* Bain
1160.13;1161.3 *genuine*] *stet* I; *rom.* Bain
1160.15 an] *stet* I; some Bain
1160.21-23 "are ... volition."] H; *all sg. qts.* I
1160.22 traverse] *stet* I; traverses Bain
1160.24 *Disinterested ... are*] *stet* I; disinterested impulses, they are Bain
1160.30 Will] Bain; will I
1160.32 *Emotions*] H; Emotion I
1161.3 *regular*] *stet* I; *rom.* Bain
1161.20 accrues] H; acrues I (*error*)

1163.29 objects] I³; object I¹⁻²
1163.31 those ... disciples] H; that ...
disciples' I (*error*)
1163.35 ¹Passion] Hume; passions I
1163.37-38 in ... *Understanding*] H;
om. I
1164.37 11] H; II I
1165.5 neural] WJ/I,BC,I⁸; neura | I¹⁻⁷
[*begin* P⁴²]
1165.38 able] WJ/I,I³; able energetically
I¹⁻²
1165.39 ¹to] I³; *om.* I¹⁻²
1166.3 clenches] P⁴²; clinches I
[*end* P⁴²]
1166.8 Sensation, Association ... Atten-
tion] BC; *l.c.* I
1166.14 Attention] BC; *l.c.* I
1167.5 wise] BC; unwise I
[*begin* P³⁷]
1167.8 mental:] BC; ~; P³⁷,I
1167.10 us,] BC; ~ˏ P³⁷,I
1168.8 There] WJ/I,BC; "*Haec tibi erit
janua leti*," we feel. There P³⁷;I (*Hæc*)
1168.11 says ˏ] P³⁷; ~, I
1168.20 congeners] P³⁷,WJ/I,BC,I⁸;
congerers I¹⁻⁷
1168.23 possession] P³⁷,BC; possesion I
(*error*)
1168.36 within] WJ/I; in P³⁷,I
[*end* P³⁷]
1169.20 -impulsive] BC; -inpulsive I (*error*)
1169.28 refuse. Or] BC; ~; or I

1170.4 , then,] BC; ˏ ~ˏ I
1171.1 'Jesus Christ,'] *stet* I; *Jesus Christ,
Wigan
1171.8 and] Wigan; *om.* I
1171.9 mind.ˏ] H; ~. ... I
[*begin* P⁴²]
1171.25 122] H; 123 P⁴²,I
1171.27 [and being]] H; ˏ~ ~ˏ P⁴²,I
[*end* P⁴²]
1172.39 Self] H; self I
1173.29 -only-one] I³; -one-alone I¹⁻²
1174.2 on rusty] I³; upon its I¹⁻²
1178.7-8 might ... dimensionˏ ...
¹come, ... does] I³; *might* ... ~, ...
~ˏ ... *does* I¹⁻²
1178.10 possibility] I³; *ital.* I¹⁻²
1178.17 reflex,] WJ/I; ~ˏ I
1179.27 XI] H; VI I (*error*)
1179.31 uns] Lipps,I³; us I¹⁻²
1179.31 naturgemäss] Lipps,I³;
naturgemåss I¹⁻²
1179.32 ganzes] *stet* I; *rom.* Lipps
1179.35 ²not] *stet* I; not conform to law
Spencer
1180.11 free-] H; ~ˏ I
1180.26 cherish] H; chersish I (*error*)
1181.17 and the] WJ/BC; and I,BC
1181.35 take] WJ/BC; face I,BC
1186.9 damp] I³; dampen I¹⁻²
1188.5 connate] I³; a connate I¹⁻²
1188.24,26 *Effektbild*] H; *Effectsbild* I
1188.36 IV] H; VI I (*error*)

CHAPTER XXVII: HYPNOTISM

Reference is made to WJ/I and to "Hypnotism: Modes of Operating and
Susceptibility," *Religio-Philosophical Journal*, 1 (1890).

*1194.22 Dr.] *stet* I¹⁻²; *om.* I³
1194.22;1195.22 Liébeault] I³; Liébault
I¹⁻²
1195.22 Dr.] I³; *om.* I¹⁻²
*1195.23 92 per cent] *stet* I¹⁻²; 92% I³
1195.24 19] Wetterstrand; 18 I
1196.7-8 hypnotizable] I³; hypotizable
I¹⁻²
1196.22 *et seq. this chap.* Salpêtrière] H;
Salpétrière I
1197.11 with.ˏ] *stet* I; with. † | † Gur-
ney, Liébault, etc. *Religio-Philosophical
Journal*

1200.6 hypnotized] H; hynotized I (*error*)
1203.29 clenching] H; clinching I
1206.36 ²has] WJ/I; had I
1209.4 subject] H; *cap.* I
1210.12 finds] WJ/I; finds it I
1210.18 ones;] WJ/I; ~, I
1210.30-31 Liébeault] H; Liébault I
1211.3-4 experiments, ... suggestionˏ]
WJ/I; ~ˏ ... ~, I
1212.11 'suggestible'] I³; 'suggestable'
I¹⁻²
1213.14-15 somnambulists] H; somna-
bulists I (*error*)

1214.14 H.] H; A. I (*error*)
1214.15 Liégeois] I³; Liegeois I¹⁻²
1214.16-19 To ... (Reprinted).] *Religio-*

Philosophical Journal; om. I
1214.18 1889] H; 1890 *Religio-Philo-*
sophical Journal

Chapter XXVIII: Necessary Truths and the Effects of Experience

Reference is made to P³⁸, "Reflex Action and Theism," *Unitarian Review*, 16 (November 1881), 389–416 (McD 1881:3), and to WJ/I.

1218.14 *et seq. similar this quote accumulated*] stet I; *rom.* Spencer
1218.33 them. ...] H; ~.ₐ I
1218.38 §§ 189, 205, and 208] H; § 207 I
1219.3 *experience.* ...] H; ~.ₐ I
1219.37-39 *non-ego* ... *ego*] stet each ital. Spencer,I
1220.17 Leibnitz] *stet* I; Liebnitz Spencer (*error*)
1220.31,32 *established*] stet ital. Spencer,I
1221.31 *produced*] stet ital. Spencer,I
1223.1 erelong] I³; ereloing I¹⁻²
1229.10-11 continue ... juxtaposed] I³; and continue to be thought, in the relation in which they exist there I¹⁻²
1229.11-12 time ... memory] I³; time, ditto I¹⁻²
[*begin* P³⁸]
1231.24 faculty works] *stet* I; faculty,— the mind's middle department,— functions P³⁸
1231.24-25 exclusively ... ends] *stet* I; *all ital.* P³⁸
1231.25 ³the ... received] *stet* I; impressions we receive P³⁸
1231.26 subjectivity] *stet* I; subjectivity altogether P³⁸
*1231.30 fondness] I⁶; fondnesses P³⁸, I¹⁻⁵
1231.35 break] *stet* I; *ital.* P³⁸
1231.37 which] *stet* I; that P³⁸
1232.25 ¹break] *stet* I; *ital.* P³⁸
[*end* P³⁸]
1236.28 *My ... Liver!*] stet I; *all rom.* Layard
1236.30 have I] Layard; *om.* I
1237.34 hast] Layard,I³; has I¹⁻²

1237.35 defile] Layard; spit upon I
1237.40 ZADE] Layard; ZADI I
1238.2 sequence] WJ/I,I³; sequnce I¹⁻²
1238.26 necessity] I³; neccessariness I¹⁻²
1238.32 we] H; *we have* I (*error*)
1241.17;1243.32 *d* ...] H; ~ I
1242.14 fills] I³; fill I¹⁻²
1244.29 treat] I³; use I¹⁻²
1246.2 can] I³; n I¹⁻²(*broken* 'ca')
1248.37 *a*+(*b*+1)] I²; *a* (+*b*+1) I¹
1252.4 new] I³; third I¹⁻²
1253.20 greatly ... no] I³; amazingly from one man to another. No I¹⁻²
1256.5 angles] *stet* I; ones Locke
1256.8 agree ....] H; ~ ... I
1256.14 own] Locke; *om.* I
1256.22 by ... only] Locke; only by the contemplation I
1256.24 certain general] *stet* I; general certain Locke
1257.8 These] *stet* I; Those Locke
1257.12 we have] Locke; *om.* I
1257.25 of a triangle] Locke; *om.* I
1257.31 for] Locke; *om.* I
1257.40 IV, 6] H; *om.* I
1257.41 Book IV,] H; *om.* I
1258.19 outer] I³; *om.* I¹⁻²
1258.23 that] I³; *om.* I¹⁻²
1258.24 outer] I³; objective I¹⁻²
1258.28 supposing] WJ/I; *om.* I
1259.28 *kind*'] I³; ~ₐ I¹⁻²
1260.10 only] WJ/I; *only* I
1260.26-27 will ... formed] I³; the eternal cosmic weather will dissipate as carelessly as it has formed them I¹⁻²
1265.39 society] *stet* I; it Robinson
1266.35 Hamond] H; Hammond I
1267.39 must] *stet* I; *om.* Marcus Aurelius (Long)

1267.42 sheeps'] Marcus Aurelius (Long); sheep's I

1267.44 so] Marcus Aurelius (Long); *om.* I

1267.44 all] Marcus Aurelius (Long); *om.* I

1269.9 transitions] WJ/I; transactions I

1270.29–30 lapsed intelligence] *stet* I; *lapsed* or *undiscursive Intelligence* Lewes

1270.32 *eigenen*] Spir; *eignen* I (*error*)

1271.24 administering] Spencer; ministering I

1271.27 emotion.³⁹ . . .] H; ~.³⁹ ₍ I

1271.27 lands] Spencer; islands I

1271.39–40 p. 1039 ff.] H; p. 420 ff. I (*i.e.*, 422)

1272.7 comparatively] Spencer; *om.* I

1272.21 yet] Spencer; *om.* I

1272.31–33 *If . . . throughout*] *stet* I; *all rom.* Spencer

1272.32 *emotion*] Spencer (*rom.*); *the emotion* I

1272.33 If so, we] *stet* I; We Spencer

1273.38 York,] I²; ~ₐ I¹

1273.39 310] H; 311 I

1274.11–13 In the . . . nerve, the] H; The . . . ~. The I (*error*)

1274.37 267] H; 287 I

1275.15 to] Darwin; in I

1275.16 be clearly] Darwin; clearly be I

1275.26 originated] Darwin; arisen I

1275.33 *L'Hérédité*] I³; l'Hérédite I¹⁻² (*broken accent ov.* ³'e')

1275.38 Feb.] H; Jan. (or Feb.) I

1276.29–30 air, . . . undergo.] WJ/I; air. I

1277.6 moreover] I³; however I¹⁻²

1277.25 habit."] H; ~.' I (*error*)

1277.26–27 feeling] *stet* I; pleasurable feeling which joins itself with the sentiment of pity, Spencer

1277.36 has] H; have I (*error*)

1277.39 560] H; 561 I

1278.4 break] H; breaks I (*error*)

1278.37 *Continuität*] H; *Continuitat* I

Textual Notes

23.4 not . . . power] The addition of 'not' in the plates of I² probably made it necessary for the printer to reduce the text in that line and the line below and appears to have forced the change in the plates from 'seat of intellectual power' in I¹ to 'sole seat of intellect' in I². Since it is relatively certain that this change was mechanical and unauthoritative, it has been rejected and the original reading retained.

25.6 system,] This necessary comma is supplied from the corresponding sentence in *Briefer Course*. In I¹ the comma must have fallen out before plating (there is a space for it at the end of the line) but the mistake was not repaired during the plate-changes of any subsequent printing.

30.5-10 He . . . person] In BC¹⁻³ of 1892 this passage is reprinted verbatim; but in the fourth printing, in 1893, James censored it to read: 'He manifests the sexual instinct at the proper seasons, and discriminates between male and female individuals of his own species. He is, in short, so similar in every respect to a normal frog that it would take a person very familiar with these animals to suspect anything wrong or wanting about him; but even then such a person'.

34.29-35.3 And . . . alone.] In BC¹⁻³ of 1892 this passage is reprinted with only one variant; but in the fourth printing, in 1893, James altered it to read: 'It is the same, according to Goltz, with male dogs who have suffered large losses of cerebral tissue. Those who have read Darwin's Descent of Man will recollect what an importance this author ascribes to the agency of sexual selection in the amelioration of the breeds of birds. The females are naturally coy, and their coyness must be overcome by the exhibition of the gorgeous plumage, and various accomplishments in the way of strutting and fighting, of the males. In frogs and toads, on the other hand, where (as we saw on page 94) the sexual instinct devolves upon the lower centres, we find a machine-like obedience to the present incitements of sense, and an almost total exclusion of the power of choice. The consequence is that every spring an immense waste of batrachian life, involving numbers of adult animals and innumerable eggs, takes place from no other cause than the blind character of the sexual impulse in these creatures.' It is possible to speculate that in the 1893 version James was reducing the sexual explicitness of this passage (as well as that at 30.5-10) in view of the high school and college audience aimed at in *Briefer Course*.

46.13 167] Exner, "Sammlung von Krankenfällen," pp. 88–125, lists only 167 cases. James either made a slip or else the printer misread a 7 as a 9 since '169' appeared in (I).

59.15-16 or of] Almost all of the *Briefer Course* substantive revisions have been ignored as affecting the text of *Principles*. However, this is the first of a handful of necessary changes. Without the addition of the second 'of', as in *Briefer Course*, the modification is seriously in question. In the unemended *Principles* text the inference would be that the sight of words would fail to awaken the movement for pronouncing them, whereas in *Briefer Course* it is clear that James intended that the words should fail to awaken the idea of the movement for pronouncing them.

104.27 blood-supply] The omission of the hyphen present in I^{1-10} in the reset line in I^{11} was an error, as was the omission of a comma after 'sleep' in another resetting, in line 105.10. On pp. 104–105 a number of lines were reset in I^{11} to repair batter.

232.7 time-sense] The reading 'sense' in the plates of I^3 represents another example of the printer's unauthoritative alteration (as in 23.4) to fit an authoritative plate-change into the same line, in this case the addition of 'dis' before 'continuous'.

253.4 genius] The evidence is mixed whether James quoted from the 1850 edition of Campbell or from the common 1873, which perhaps had been used as a text-book at Harvard (see Prof. Skrupskelis' Note). The punctuation in James's quote is nearer to that of 1873 than to that of 1850, and at 252.39 James followed 1873 in 'Farther' while 1850 agreed with the 1776 first edition reading 'Further'. However, 1873 at 253.4 has the misprint 'genus' whereas James quotes correctly the 1776 (and 1850) 'genius'. If he used 1873, perhaps he corrected the word. Possibly some edition intermediate between 1850 and 1873 (or later than 1873) had 'Farther' and 'genius'. The quotation in this text has been adjusted to the readings of 1873 ('genus' aside), however, as the most likely candidate.

453.12 Plato and Aristotle] In *Briefer Course* 'Socrates' is substituted for these two.

635.4 'sense of pre-existence'] James here is altering Wigan who had quoted Sir Walter Scott's 'sentiment of pre-existence'.

646.23–25 this . . . use] James's revision of the printed text on the interleaf of his annotated copy was faulty in that the caret in the text and the guide-line drawn to it appear to indicate that he intended 'this . . . use' to be a simple insertion, whereas in fact it must be taken as substituting for text undeleted in error: 'the path is formed by discharge from 1 to 2, just as it will afterwards be used'. Incidentally, in the interleaved revision James by a slip wrote 'path this' instead of 'path that', as printed here.

728.26–27 It . . . becomes] For an explanation of similar cases of unauthoritative compositorial revision see 23.4 and 232.7.

736.21–22 But . . . be.] In James's annotated copy appears the pencilled remark, 'This sentence is too compressed (complained of by Stevens)', but he made no alteration.

750.12 foot.ᵥ] The adjustments that James made in his annotated copy in the footnotes on this page (see also 750.15) were triggered by the repetition in error of his footnote indicator ‡ at 'toes.' at 750.15 which was also used for 'found.' at 750.24. Since he wished footnote ‡ (i.e., present footnote 28) to come after 'found.', he substituted the symbol † (i.e., footnote 27) after 'toes.' (after deleting † from 'foot.' in line 750.12). The second appearance of ‡ (i.e., 28) was allowed to stand now that it was correct in the sequence.

752.17   nearly] The text of all printings reads 'newly', a slip by James or a misprint. (The German reads, 'nächster Beziehung'.) Someone has written 'nearly' in the margin of the Harvard stack copy Phil 5249.2(A), but the authority of the annotation cannot be determined, and it is probably simply a good guess by some reader.

799.34   *supra*, p. 797] In preparing the book text James forgot to adjust the page reference from that in P24, with the result that it refers, like P24, to 'p. 19'. The reference in terms of the book would be to II, 156.22-28, now adjusted to 797.14-20 in the present text.

806.36   local sign] In the book at its first appearance at 796.3, as a noun, '*Local Signs*' is unhyphenated as a subheading (not present in P24 and hence set directly from James's autograph annotation of the P24 copy for the book's printer). The next appearance is at 798.16 where it is hyphenated in the book, after the example of P24, presumably because it is reproducing in translation a German phrase. Thereafter, through part 1 of P24, although 'local-sign(s)' is invariably hyphenated, the book hyphenates only in adjectival use. The sudden start here at 806.36 of nominal hyphenation in the book presumably has nothing to do with the change in the printer's copy for the chapter from part 1 to part 2 of P24, which is consistently styled, but instead seems due to a shift in the book's compositors. The lack of nominal hyphenation having been established earlier as contrasting, in James's usual manner, with adjectival hyphens, the book's altered system for this phrase is regularly emended to remove the noun hyphens.

847.34-35   since . . . about] In James's annotated copy these words are lined in the margin and a guideline drawn to his comment found on the interleaf opposite II, 213: 'False! Corrected by Margaret Washburn in Mind, 1894'.

853.10-13   Meanwhile . . . *thing*.] In James's annotated copy, this sentence is marked and on the interleaf opposite (opp. II, 219) he wrote: 'By this the Chapter on Perception was meant. Cf. p. 80+ above [i.e., 726.3 ff.]. Compare the facts, above, of contrast etc. pp. 28+ [i.e., 676.1 ff.], also 80-82 [i.e., 726.3-727.30].'

879.19   page 811] James inadvertently allowed the P24 reference to page 188 to stand in the book. The reference should have been to II, 172.

881.33   XIX] The book's change here to 'XXI' of P24 'XIX' is odd, since vol. XIX appears to be the correct reference. Volume XXI does contain an article by Delbœuf, but it is in issue no. 5 and on a different topic.

924.1-3   which . . . 2consider] In his corrected copy James marked these lines with the comment 'make clearer', but no revision ensued.

928.13 *relation*,] In James's annotated copy a pencil caret is placed between '*relation*' and the following comma and on the facing interleaf to II, 299, in its left or farther margin, is the pencil word 'which'. Since the insertion of 'which', alone, at this point would destroy the sentence's syntax, one may conjecture that James proposed the addition of a restrictive relative clause beginning with 'which' that he never finished. This conjecture is assisted by the position of 'which' on the interleaf, especially since James would have written it in the margin of the printed page if the word alone had been intended for insertion.

940.33 senses] The plural is the reading of "Rationality, Activity and Faith" at this point, whereas the book follows P24 in quoting the singular.

948.28 If belief . . .] Against the opening of this section James wrote in the margin of his annotated copy: 'Guard against misapprehension of my meaning here.' No change was made in the text, however.

949.31-32 *our . . . fact*] James noted in his annotated copy, 'This needs correction'; but no change was made.

965.12-13 bottom . . . up] There is nothing wrong with James's illustration of the door sticking at the top except that twice later (967.5-6; 968.2-5), the first time with specific reference to the example of the sill, James took it that he had illustrated a door sticking at its bottom. In *Briefer Course* James noted the discrepancy and brought the example into conformity in the manner here adopted, a procedure that is simpler than replacing 'sill' in the later references by 'lintel' and 'raise' by 'lower' and also one that has more authority.

966.8 special . . . purpose] The phrase 'which serve his purpose.' that James in his annotated copy added to the end of the sentence is clearly marked for position. However, a problem arises about 'special'. In the text James inserted a caret after 'of', which produces an impossible reading 'of special the new lines'. The problem resolves itself into the choice whether (a) James simply misplaced the caret (as he sometimes did) and the revision should read 'of the special new lines' or (b) whether 'the' was intended for deletion, although not so marked, and the reading should be 'of special new lines which serve his purpose.' With some hesitation the editor opts for the second alternative, but there can be no conviction in the matter, for either reading is possible.

1081.29 law . . . paragraph] This phrase is repeated in the book from "What Is an Emotion?" (P24), where it refers to text that may be found in the book at II, 462.19-463.21 (1077.9-1078.6).

1148.31 who . . . him] James incorrectly translated the French 'qui l'adorait' into 'whom he adored' rather than into 'who adored him'.

1194.22 Dr.] For an explanation of similar cases of unauthorized compositorial revision see 23.4 and 232.7.

1195.23 92 per cent] For an explanation of similar cases of unauthorized compositorial revision see 23.4 and 232.7.

1231.30 fondness] This being the only plate change in 1899 (I⁶), its normalization of 'fondnesses' to 'fondness' is automatically suspect. Moreover, it is possible that the publisher's reader noticed what he thought was an awkward usage and ordered the change. Nevertheless, the alteration may just as easily represent James's own second thoughts. Although the authority is not demonstrable, the odds may favor an authoritative plate change if someone had queried the reading to James.

Historical Collation

This list comprises the substantive variant readings that differ from the edited text in the authoritative documents recorded for the book. The reading to the left of the bracket is that of the present edition. The rejected variants in the noted documents follow in chronological order to the right of the bracket. Any collated texts not recorded are to be taken as agreeing with the edition-reading to the left of the bracket; only variation appears to the right. The noting of variant readings is complete for the substantives. However, in order to save space, no accidental variants except differences in paragraphing among authoritative documents are recorded save for some linguistic differences such as everyone] every one, cannot] can not, towards] toward, and forever] for ever, which are noted for their intrinsic interest. Differences in concept capitalization between book and journal articles are also recorded as constituting what may be called 'semi-substantives.' Moreover, if in book or journal two independent clauses separated by a comma or semicolon appear as two sentences in the other, this syntactical variation is shown. Variants are not repeated in the Historical Collation when the copy-text has been emended since the details may be found in the list of Emendations.

The headnote to the Emendations list may be consulted for general conventions of notation, and the Note on the Editorial Method outlines types of variants which are not recorded. One special feature appearing in the Historical Collation, as in the Emendations, is the use of *et seq.* When this phrase occurs, all subsequent readings within the chapter are to be taken as agreeing with the particular feature of the reading being recorded (save for singulars and plurals and inessential typographical variation, as between roman and italic), unless specifically noted to the contrary by notation within the entry itself. Readings grouped together with multiple page-line references may also be concerned with only the particular feature being recorded and not with inessential types of variation.

CHAPTER IV: HABIT

The copy-text for Chapter IV is (I), the 1890 first printing of *The Principles of Psychology*, with reference to P[29], "The Laws of Habit," *Popular Science Monthly*, 30 (February 1887), 433–451 (McD 1887:5).

109.0   Habit] THE LAWS OF HABIT. |
BY PROFESSOR WILLIAM JAMES.
p29

109.20 *et seq. this chap.*   cannot] can not P[29]

110.39   inner] molecular P[29]

110.39-40   outer form] that of grosser parts P[29]

111.2-3   [2]the . . . cause] outward

causality P[29] (causalité Dumont)

111.13   time."[2]] ~."$_\wedge$ (*om. fn.*) P[29]

112.11-30   If . . . disappear.] *om.* P[29]

112.30   For, of (*no* ¶)] ¶ Of P[29]

112.34   path in the] reflex arc in the nervous P[29]

112.34   most] more P[29]

112.35   point] neural point P[29]

112.37   paths] arcs P[29]

113.1   only difficult] *om.* P29
113.1   problem] ~, then, P29
113.2   or path] arc P29
113.4   the entire] a P29
113.4   paths] *paths* which the nerve-current follows, P29
113.8   before;3] *fn. follows* 'know,' [113.7] P29
113.15   a mere] not a moving body, but a mere P29
113.16   itself,] itself in the line of the "path," P29
113.23–24   wave of rearrangement] rearrangement of the molecules P29
113.38   action, . . . chapter,] action P29
114.18–19   I . . . it] This P29
114.39   isometric] isomeric P29 (*error*)
114.41   show] appearance P29
114.41   vagueness] lamentable vagueness P29
117.28   more easily] easier P29
118.2   towards] toward P29
118.15–16   But . . . that] In him, P29
118.39   see also] cf. P29
119.2   *acts*] *actions* P29
119.3;120.6,7,17   act] action P29
119.4   etc.,] *om.* P29
119.7   tend to] *om.* P29
119.7   themselves] themselves as possible P29
119.22   cataract] labyrinth P29

120.14   action grown] actions become P29
120.18   whole] *om.* P29
120.18–19   an habitual] a secondarily automatic or habitual P29
120.24   f] *f, g* P29
120.26   be of] be in P29
120.28   the ear] ear P29
122.15   seem] seem inclined P29
123.38   remain] should remain P29
124.1   may] should P29
124.10   turn] turns P29
126.20   *cannot*] *can't* P29
126.22   better-bred] aristocratic P29
126.25–28   *make . . . must*] *om.* P29
126.29   guard] to guard P29
126.32   effortless] infallible and effortless P29
126.39–40   be so] have been so thoroughly P29
127.2   hour] day P29
127.33–128.4   The . . . formed.] *om.* P29
129.1   ¶ No] *no* ¶ P29
129.27   work-a-day] *om.* P29
129.28   him] work-a-day him P29
129.31   a] the P29
130.1   way.18] ~.ₐ (*om. fn.*) P29
130.2   speaking . . . or] the P29
130.2   2one's] of one's P29
130.22   unnerved] unarmed P29
130.24   which] *om.* P29
130.25   2him] him in P29

CHAPTER V: THE AUTOMATON-THEORY

Reference is made to P24, "Are We Automata?" *Mind*, 4 (January 1879), 1–22 (McD 1879:5).

138.10   chasm, and] ~? And P24
138.20   strong.] strong. Nothing is commoner than to hear them speak of conscious events as something so essentially vague and shadowy as even doubtfully to exist at all. P24
142.27–28   But . . . constitutes] It is . . . which constitutes P24
142.31   It] Now it P24
143.1   child] woman's first child P24
143.9–10   , in short,] *om.* P24

143.23   forever] for ever P24
143.28   the] our next P24
145.7   Consciousness . . . only] That consciousness should only be P24
145.8–14   hesitant . . . discharge.] retarded or hesitant, and at its minimum when nerve-action is rapid or certain, adds colour to the view that it is efficacious. Rapid, automatic action is action through thoroughly excavated nerve-tracks which have

not the defect of uncertain performance. All instincts and confirmed
habits are of this sort. But when
action is hesitant there always seem
several alternative possibilities of
nervous discharge. P24

145.15   each . . . -tract] each
nerve-track P24

145.23–24   (*space*) The . . . bit] (*no
space*) The remarkable phenomena
of "vicarious function" in the
nervous centres form another link
in our chain P24

145.25–27   acts . . . acting] functions . . .
functioning P24

145.34   manner.] manner. Why, if its
performances blindly result from its
structure, undirected by any feeling
of purpose, should it not blindly
continue now to throw off inappro-
priate acts just as before its mutilation
it produced appropriate ones? P24

145.36–39   Some . . . take] If we suppose the presence of a mind, not only
taking P24

146.1   also] able P24

146.1   check] inhibit P24

146.2   and] *om.* P24

146.2   it] the nerve-defect P24

146.4   parts] parts of the brain P24

146.9   force.‸] force. 1 | 1This argument,
though so striking at first sight, is
perhaps one which it would be danger-
ous to urge too dogmatically. It may
be that restitution of cerebral function
is susceptible of explanation on
drainage-principles, or, to use Stricker's
phrase, by "collateral innervation".
As I am preparing a separate essay on
this subject, I will say no more about
the matter here. P24

146.9–10   At . . . again. (*space*)] *om.*
P24 (*no space*)

146.11   on] by P24

146.12,27;147.3   efficacy] efficacity
p24

146.12–13   *is . . . fact*] has long been
noticed P24

146.20   and others have] , in the chapter
of his *Psychology* entitled "Pleasures

and Pains," has P24

146.29   automaton-] *cap.* P24

146.30   thrills] a thrill P24

146.31   agony.‸] agony.2 | 2I do not
overlook an obvious objection suggested by such an operation as
breathing. It, like other motor processes, results from a tendency to nervous
discharge. When this takes place immediately, hardly any feeling but the
rather negative one of ease results.
When, however, a nervous discharge is
checked it is a universal law that consciousness of a disagreeable kind is
awakened, reaching in the case of
suffocation the extremity of agony.
An Automatist may then say that
feeling here, so far from playing a
dynamic part, is a mere passive index
or symptom of certain mechanical
happenings; and if here, then elsewhere. It may be replied that even
were this true of completely habitual
acts like breathing, where the nervous
paths have been thoroughly organised
for generations, it need not be true of
hesitant acts not yet habitual; it need
not be true of pains and pleasures,
such as hunger and sleep, *not* connected with motor discharge; and
even in the instance chosen it leaves
out the possibility that the nervous
mechanism, now automatically perfect, may have become so by slowly
organised habit acquired under the
guidance of conscious feeling. P24

146.32   the] this P24

146.37   now be born to] *om.* P24

146.38   only] only very P24

146.39   has] has ever P24

147.6   strong] very strong P24

147.6   brain-action] brain P24

147.9   a] à P24

147.13   quite] more than P24

147.14   causal] *om.* P24

147.14   automaton-]
Conscious-Automaton- P24

147.15   common-sense] Common
Sense P24

CHAPTER VII: THE METHODS AND SNARES OF PSYCHOLOGY

Reference is made to P[24], "On Some Omissions of Introspective Psychology," *Mind*, 9 (January 1884), 1–26 (McD 1884:1).

190.1,2 (*twice*) state] feeling P[24]
190.6 force.[8]] ~.ᴧ (*om. fn.*) P[24]
190.9 had . . . might] have . . . may P[24]
190.11 Mohr.ᴧ] Mohr in a recent little

work.[1] | [1]*Grundlage der empirischen Psychologie*, Leipzig, 1882, p. 47. P[24]
190.13 but] *om.* P[24]

CHAPTER VIII: THE RELATIONS OF MINDS TO OTHER THINGS

Reference is made to extracts from P[37], "The Hidden Self," *Scribner's Magazine*, 7 (March 1890), 361–373 (McD 1890:1).

200.13–14 blind, . . . contracted.] blind, or blind over one half of the field of vision, or the latter is extremely contracted, so that its margins appear dark, or else the patient has lost all sense for color. P[37]
200.17 learned well] well learned P[37]
200.19 recently] lately P[37]
200.29 becoming] being P[37]
200.30 These . . . anæsthesias] The anæsthesias of the class of patients we are considering P[37]
200.32 or] *om.* P[37]
201.1 question.ᴧ] ~.* P[37] (*plus fn.*)
201.16 "When . . . "she] When Lucie stopped conversing directly with anyone, she P[37]
201.17 any other person] anyone else P[37]
201.17 may] might P[37]
202.1 a] the P[37]
202.3 them] them all P[37]
202.9 etc., etc.] etc. P[37]
202.12 towards] toward P[37]
202.18 no wise] nowise P[37]
202.28 thing] things P[37]
202.38 would] could P[37]
203.1 in cases] of the cases P[37]
203.18 She] But she P[37]
203.22 consciousness,ᴧ] upper consciousness, P[37]
203.25 in this spot] here P[37]
203.35 could not] couldn't P[37]
204.1 Colors . . . self,] Similarly the

sub-conscious self perfectly well perceives colors P[37]
204.3 Pricks] Again, pricks P[37]
204.10 them. More . . . still, they] ~, and—more . . . still— P[37]
204.22–23 said . . . only] picked up only those P[37]
205.1 or] and P[37]
205.2–3 well- . . . Salpêtrière,] subjectᴧ P[37]
205.4 he] he had P[37]
205.11 deepest] deeper P[37]
205.25;206.25;207.6,8,11 Whilst] While P[37]
205.25 J.] Janet P[37]
205.38–39 *writing . . . the*] *om.* P[37]
206.2 go.[7]] ~.ᴧ (*om. fn.*) P[37]
206.3 *the so-called*] *om.* P[37]
206.11 possesses the man] comes over him P[37]
206.13 is] was P[37]
206.19 which] *om.* P[37]
206.21 execution.[8]] ~.ᴧ (*om. fn.*) P[37]
207.2 remained] remains P[37]
207.6 3[9]] ~.ᴧ (*om. fn.*) P[37]
207.10 time] time being, P[37]
207.17 exist] obtain P[37]
207.19 hysterical] hysteric P[37]
207.21 it] it all P[37]
207.28 sub-] self- P[37]
207.37 betweenwhiles] between whiles P[37]
208.9 Léonie's normal self] Léonie 1 p[37]

CHAPTER IX: THE STREAM OF THOUGHT

Reference is made to extracts from P24a, "On Some Omissions of Introspective Psychology," *Mind*, 9 (January 1884), 1–26 (McD 1884:1), and to an extract from P24b, "Are We Automata?" *Mind*, 4 (January 1879), 1–22 (McD 1879:5). For a detailed list of which extracts are used from both articles see the discussion under The Text of *The Principles of Psychology*.

[*begin* P24a]

228.30–31 And . . . as] As P24a

229.3 feel.9] ~.ₐ (*om. fn.*) P24a

229.4 Ever . . . are] Some tracts are always P24a

229.5 tension] ~, however, P24a

229.6 any] the discharges P24a

229.6 and] and consequently P24a

229.7 be] be to which the complex *neurosis* corresponds P24a

229.9 are] are really P24a

229.11 the] the distribution of P24a

229.12 like] like the aurora borealis or p24a

229.13 its] the brain's P24a

229.14 and] that its rate of change is coarser-grained, P24a

236.15 As . . . a] When we take a rapid p24a

236.16 this] the P24a

236.17 parts] different portions P24a

236.17 Like . . . it] Our mental life, like a bird's life, P24a

236.27–28 It then appears] We may then say P24a

236.32 another.] another. Of this perhaps more hereafter. P24a

236.33 Now . . . see] Now the first difficulty of introspection is that of seeing P24a

237.20–24 The . . . stream.] If holding fast the transitive parts of thought's stream, so as to observe them, be the first great difficulty of introspection, then its first great fallacy must necessarily be a failure to register them and give them their due, and a far too great emphasis laid on the more substantive parts of the stream. P24a

238.16 There] On the contrary, there p24a

238.29 use.] use. In a later place we shall see how the analogy of speech misleads us in still other ways. P24a

238.35 that] the P24a

238.35–36 2of . . . p. 194)] which in psychology is just as bad, the error, namely P24a

239.1 or anonymous] *om.* P24a

243.4–5 Leaving . . . leaving] Counting . . . counting P24a

243.16 to us] *om.* P24a

244.24 'Who?'] "~?" "What?" P24a

245.22 admit] say P24a

246.16 attention] reader's attention P24a

246.16–17 , as . . . XVIII,] *om.* P24a

246.19–20 Another . . . of] Mr. Spencer has made another in overthrowing P24a

246.21 subjective] *om.* P24a

247.5 process.17] ~. (*om. fn.*) P24a

253.21 Usually the] When we listen with relaxed attention, this P24a

265.28 But . . . really (*no* ¶)] ¶ The object of any thought is P24a

265.37–39 strictly . . . . And] not simply "the sins we commit," nor "the sins we commit as psychologists," nor "the sins we commit as psychologists naming the objects of thoughts". Its object is nothing short of the entire sentence; and P24a

265.40 thus] in full P24a

266.1 but] short of P24a

[*end* P24a; *begin* P24b]

273.29 what] even in the infra-conscious region which Mr. Spencer says is the lowest stage of mentality. What P24b

273.29 very] *om.* P24b

273.37 Nature] *l.c.* P24b

274.6 changes,] changes, in a word, p24b

274.10 Attention] the attention P24b

274.12 work on Optics] immortal work on *Physiological Optics* P24b

274.17–19 know . . . this] know, as Professor William B. Rogers pointed out, on which of our eyes an image falls, until trained to notice the local sensation. So habitually overlooked is this by most men P24b

274.20 never . . . fact.₍] not know it.[1] P24b (*plus fn.*)

274.39 In . . . manner, the] The P24b

275.6 but] not P24b

275.11 for us] *om.* P24b

275.12 what we call] *om.* P24b

275.13 it . . . us] we may happen to get from it P24b

275.13–16 mere . . . rest.₍] themselves sensations pure and simple, susceptible of being fully given at *some* other moment. The spontaneity of the mind does not consist in conjuring up any new non-sensational quality of objectivity. It consists solely in deciding what the particular sensation shall be whose native objectivity shall be held more valid than that of all the rest.[1] P24b (*plus fn.*)

275.20 stand . . . *excellence.*] be the bearers *par excellence* of objective reality. P24b

275.21 of] of the mind's P24b

275.22 things] objects P24b

275.23 empirical thought] *init. caps.* p24b

275.23 things] objects and events P24b

275.25,29 A thing] An object P24b

276.5 a future . . . see] an article on "Brute and Human Intellect" in the *Journal of Speculative Philosophy*, July 1878, p. 236, I have tried to show P24b

276.7 parts] partial factors or elements P24b

276.9 emergency] theoretical or practical emergency P24b

276.12 bill] bill, as it were, P24b

276.14 it.] it? Association by similarity I have shown to be an important help to this breaking-up of represented things into their elements. But this association is only the minimum of that same selection of which picking out the right reason is a maximum. P24b

276.16 [1]the] that P24b

276.16 of the mind.] which appears to be the true sphere of mental spontaneity. P24b

276.17 its . . . department,] the Æsthetic activity of the mind, the application of P24b

276.30 our] *om.* P24b

276.39–40 Characters] *Selves* P24b

276.40 he] his entire empirical *Ego* P24b

277.4 complexion] very complexion P24b

277.5 itself] *om.* P24b

277.6 what] what kind of a P24b

277.11 attention] *cap.* P24b

277.22–23 , if we like,] ₍ even, P24b

277.28 like sculptors,] as the sculptor extracts his statue P24b

277.28–29 certain . . . stuff.] the other portions of the stone. P24b

277.30 monotonous and inexpressive] *om.* P24b

277.31 My] Goethe's P24b

277.32–33 How . . . worlds] Some such other worlds may exist P24b

277.33 cuttle-fish, or crab!] crab and cuttle-fish. P24b

[end P24b]

CHAPTER X: THE CONSCIOUSNESS OF SELF

Reference is made to P[37], "The Hidden Self," *Scribner's Magazine*, 7 (March 1890), 361–373 (McD 1890:1). Reference is also made to P[31], "Notes on Automatic Writing," *Proceedings of the American Society for Psychical Research*, 1 (March 1889), 548–564 (McD 1889:3).

[begin P37]
364.1–4 But . . . not] One day, when

the subject named Lucie was in the hypnotic state, he made passes over her again for half an hour, just as if she were P37

364.6 half an] another half P37

364.7 thitherto] hitherto P37

364.12 became] was P37

364.26 to . . . to be] *om.* P37

364.27 touch.] touch—of course I state summarily here what appears in the book as an induction from many facts. P37

364.28 and . . . personality] *om.* P37

364.30 and his] and, best of all, his P37

364.35 individuality.56] modification of the personality., (*om. fn.*) P37

364.36–37 these . . . turned] the subjects are transformed P37

364.38 grew] grow P37

364.38–365.1 extensive, . . . generalization.] extensive; and here comes in M. Janet's first great theoretic generalization, which is this: P37

365.1 , he says,] *om.* P37

365.10–14 consequences . . . 1as] effects of this law of M. Janet's upon the patient's recollections would necessarily be great. Take things touched and handled, for example, and bodily movements. All memories of such things, all records of such experiences, being normally stored away in tactile terms, would have to be incontinently lost and forgotten so P37

365.17–19 Now . . . trance.] *om.* P37

365.19–20 that . . . and] such an enlargement of their power of recollecting that P37

365.21–22 otherwise . . . life] of their peculiarities which would else be inexplicable P37

365.23 crisis] attack P37

365.23 , for example,] *om.* P37

365.23 French] the French P37

365.24 1the] *la* P37

365.29;366.7,36 whilst] while P37

365.30–31 the deeper trance] her state of Lucie 3 P37

365.31 crisis] crises P37

365.37 recollected] recollects P37

365.39 touch.] ~, and when awake her feelings of touch and movement disappeared. P37

365.40 M. Janet's subject] the case of P37

365.40 is . . . best] is the most interesting, and shows beautifully P37

366.6 upwards] upward P37

366.13 when] than P37

366.31 [as . . . woman]] *om.* P37

366.35–36 children; but] ~. But P37

367.1 it] since it P37

367.4 or deepest] *om.* P37

367.17 A] Dr. Perrier, a P37

[*end* P37; *begin* P31]

373.5–6 ¶ As . . . by] (*no* ¶) The first is from P31

373.20 tracing.,] ~.1 P31 (*plus fn.*)

374.2 appended.,] ~.1 P31 (*plus fn.*)

[*end* P31]

CHAPTER XI: ATTENTION

Reference is made to PP, *The Principles of Psychology*, Chapter XX, "The Perception of Space."

412.14 sidewise] sideways PP 779.32

412.16 and] wherefore PP 779.34

412.16–17 accordingly] *om.* PP

412.18 oscillates] vibrates PP 779.36

412.18 ear; and the] ear. This PP 779.36

412.24 apprehend] grasp PP 780.2

412.28 several external] *om.* PP

CHAPTER XIII: DISCRIMINATION AND COMPARISON

Reference is made to P21, "Brute and Human Intellect," *Journal of Speculative Philosophy*, 12 (July 1878), 236–276 (McD 1878:4).

478.37 Mr. . . . says] As Spencer says p21

479.8-9 ¶ And . . . writes:] (*no* ¶) As expressed still better by Mr. Martineau, p21

479.14 contrast] contract P21

479.22 is . . . of] must here be left P21

479.22-25 One . . . active.] *om.* P21

479.25-26 ²that . . . is] of its being P21

479.27 such] *om.* P21

479.27-28 that . . . ensue] equivalent

to the accent derived from interest p21

479.29 This] This, at first sight, P21

479.30 For it] It P21

479.33 arrest the] succeed in arresting our P21

479.37 *Psychology*, I, 345.] Spencer: Psychology, vol. 1, p. 345. P21

480.7 more familiar] often-repeated p21

CHAPTER XIV: ASSOCIATION

Reference is made to P29, "The Association of Ideas," *Popular Science Monthly*, 16 (March 1880), 577–593 (McD 1880:1).

519.0 Association] THE ASSOCIATION OF IDEAS. | BY WILLIAM JAMES, M. D., | ASSISTANT PROFESSOR OF PHYSIOLOGY IN HARVARD COLLEGE. p29

519.18 links] links of thought P29

519.20 all] every living man P29

519.22 philosophers] philosophers to try P29

520.1 simpler] somewhat simpler P29

520.1-31 terms . . . them.] *for variant* P29 *text, see* Appendix I

520.32-33 But . . . and] For P29

520.33;521.7;522.2 reason] Reason P29

520.34;521.2,35;522.2 thought] *cap.* p29

521.9,13 thought] pure Thought P29

521.14 truth] *cap.* P29

521.16 The contrary] Such P29

521.33 hegelian] *cap.* P29

522.8 also] *om.* P29

522.9-10 a . . . thoughts] an all-sufficient explanation P29

522.10-523.2 and . . . facts.] *for variant* P29 *text, see* Appendix I

523.8 inveterate] inveterate, like the manipulations of certain trades, the balancings of the body in standing or

walking, the varying pressure of the legs in response to the swayings of a horse's gait, P29

523.8 automatically] automatically while the mind concerns itself with far other affairs P29

523.9 the objects . . . concerned] thoughts P29

523.10-531.19 With . . . arousal.] *for variant* P29 *text, see* Appendix I

531.20-23 The . . . themselves] The reason for the law of habit would, then, seem to be that the propagation occurs P29

531.30 understand . . . *processes*] understand by the words *neural process* P29

534.11 this] the following P29

534.11-14 *elementary* . . . elementary] *brain tracts or processes have occurred together or in immediate succession, any one of them, on reoccurring, tends to propagate its excitement into the other.* [¶] Now, as a matter of fact, things in the brain are much less simple than this. Every elementary tract or P29

534.15 processes] tracts or processes P29

534.19 ¹fact] undeniable fact P29
534.19 ²on . . . of] the P29
534.21 resultant.¹⁵ The process *b*,]
~;ₐ *b* (*om. fn.*) P29
534.28 *accompanied*] *coexisted with* P29
534.30 *point*] *locality or process* P29
534.33-34 Let . . . only] This will now be seen; but the reader will bear in mind that our limits only allow us to p29
534.36 shall . . . later] must be postponed to another opportunity P29
535.15 '*I* . . . *ages*,'] "So I doubt not through the ages‸" P29
535.16-17 the last . . . then] *om.* P29
535.18 '*In*' . . . '*one*'] "One" . . . "in" p29
535.21 ¹is] is just P29
535.21-23 It . . . 'fringe.'] *om.* P29
535.24 But if] In case of P29
535.25 had] having P29
535.26 if] in case P29
535.27 were] was P29
535.28 millionaire] millionaire or leave him penniless P29
535.37-38 He . . . places.] *om.* P29
535.38 however,] *om.* P29
536.5 his] my P29
536.9;538.11;547.6;548.34 cannot] can not P29
536.18 repeated.¹⁶] ~.‸ (*om. fn.*) P29
536.19 *et seq. this chap. Impartial Redintegration*] *om. headings* P29
536.35 also] *om.* P29
536.37 fig. 40, p. 537,] the diagram P29
537.19 Let . . . *redintegration.*] I prefer to discard the word "redintegration" altogether, and to give to this unobstructed process the name of Complete Association by Contiguity. P29
537.20 an] this P29
538.33-34 impartial redintegration] "complete" Association by Contiguity p29
538.35 *equally*] equally and impartially p29
539.4 reproduction] reproduced representation P29
539.5 an equal] the same P29
539.5 are] *om.* P29

539.23 ¶ Only] *no* ¶ P29
539.31 some] a P29
539.32 traced] traced out P29
539.32 ever falls on] irradiates always P29
539.34-40 Compare . . . VII.)] *om.* P29
540.1 so often] commonly P29
540.6 (1879)] *om.* P29
540.6 a] Senator Bayard's P29
540.7 in the Senate] *om.* P29
540.17-18 disappointment] disappointment and perplexity P29
540.20 clocks] it P29
540.29 ORDINARY . . . ASSOCIATION] Partial or *Mixed Association* P29
541.10 ¶ Mr.] *no* ¶ P29
542.17 thought.¹⁹] ~.‸ (*om. fn.*) P29
543.2 intense.²⁰] ~.‸ (*om. fn.*) P29
543.11 it] it equally P29
543.12 thoughts] thoughts in general P29
543.21-22 of which . . . guilty] which . . . guilty of P29
544.1 ²had] has P29
544.3 with] with the excitement of others by the general aspect of P29
544.5 ²into] *om.* P29
544.12 mixed association] *init. caps.* P29
544.13 impartial redintegration] Pure Association by Contiguity P29
544.18 partial . . . association] *init. caps.* P29
544.18 supposed] supposed that P29
544.19-20 to be . . . and to be] was . . . was P29
544.21 , for instance,] *om.* P29
544.25-26 as . . . it,] *om.* P29
544.29 thus] *om.* P29
544.29 impartial redintegration] in the way we have seen complete contiguous association P29
544.35 continue] excited P29
544.38-39 thought's . . . thought] thought and the faded one P29
545.1 *Similarity*.'²¹] Similarity."‸ (*om. fn.*) P29
545.2-15 The . . . common.] To make this perfectly plain we must understand exactly what constitutes similarity between two things. P29
545.17-18 compound] *om.* P29

545.22 attribute.] attribute. Objects are really identical with each other in that point with respect to which they are called similar. P29

545.22 , in compounds,] *om.* P29

545.27 X's] Vanderbilt's P29

546.8 impartial redintegration] Complete Contiguous P29

546.8–9 similar association] *init. caps.* P29

546.9 ordinary . . . association] Partial Association P29

546.10 impartial redintegration] Pure Contiguous P29

546.11,14 mixed] *cap.* P29

546.11 similar association] Similar, Association P29

546.12 'impartial,'] "Contiguous," P29

546.15 'similar,'] "Similar," P29

547.7 To . . . that] *Thus* P29

547.10–11 *comes.* But] ∼, but P29

547.12 The (*no* ¶)] ¶ P29

547.12 the . . . object] B P29

547.14 the . . . object] A P29

547.15 of . . . elements] (*supra,* p. 583) P29

547.17 redintegrative, associative,] contiguous P29

547.22 , into . . . unwittingly,] *om.* P29

548.18–23 It . . . it is] It becomes P29

548.25–26 *blotting-paper* voices] voices like *blotting-paper* P29

548.31 objects,] ideas‸ P29

548.31 its brain-tract] it P29

548.32–33 isolable . . . as] accentuated in consciousness P29

548.33–34 and . . . idea.'] attract the attention to itself and be abstracted. P29

548.37 is] it P29 (*error*)

548.40 impartial redintegration,] Pure Contiguity‸ P29

549.1 similarity] Similarity P29

549.5 thinking.] thinking. (*for completion of* P29 *text, see* Appendix I)

Chapter XV: The Perception of Time

Reference is made to P21, "The Perception of Time," *Journal of Speculative Philosophy*, 20 (October 1886), 374–407 (McD 1886:3).

570.21 If] *above in* P21 *is epigraph:* "Qu'on ne cherche point la durée dans la succession; on ne l'y trouvera jamais; la durée a précédé la succession; la notion de la durée a précéd é la notion de la succession. Elle en est donc tout-à-fait indépendante, dira-t-on? Oui, elle en est tout-à-fait indépendante." ROYER-COLLARD.

571.28–29 as . . . concrete] is a pure fiction, and all our experienced P21

573.1 *et seq. this chap.* THE SENSIBLE . . . DURATION] *om. headings* P21

574.39–43 "Qu'on . . . indépandante."] *om.* P21 (*used as* P21 *epigraph*)

575.3 come to] *om.* P21

575.3 shall] *om.* P21

575.4 regard.‸] ∼.1 | 1Cf. an essay, entitled "The Spatial Quale," in this Journal for Jan., 1879 (vol. xiii, p. 64). P21

575.14 temporal order] time-succession P21

576.5 extents] extensions P21

578.17 President] Prof. G. S. P21

579.21–22 *between . . . perceive*] we can perceive *between two times* P21

579.32 Lalanne] Sulanne P21

579.41 *Svenska*] Fvenska P21 (*error*)

581.4 or] nor P21

581.18 2the] *om.* P21

581.20 Germans] Germans all P21

581.26–31 Glass . . . follow.] *om.* P21

582.1 odd] remarkable P21

582.3 Odder] More remarkable P21

582.5–7 and . . . observations] *om.* P21

582.8–9 -sense, . . . next.] -sense. What can the explanation of such a phenomenon be? We can better turn to this question after going through the rest of our facts. P21

582.15 Mehner] ~, in the interesting paper we have quoted, P21
583.18 time] the time P21
584.16 volition.31] ~.∧ (*om. fn.*) P21
586.12 longer] later P21
587.3 *experiences*] ~, objects which rivet attention, vivid feelings, etc., P21
587.19 (from . . . quotation),] *om.* P21
587.22-42 All . . . § 1.] Idiots, too, are said sometimes to possess this faculty in a marked degree. P21
588.27 ¶ So] *no* ¶ P21
588.27 Paul] *om.* P21
588.29 an interval] a time-interval P21
589.7 contentless] mere contentless P21
589.42 —Compare . . . p. 41.] *om.* P21
591.19 arouse] are the stimulus arousing P21
592.25 of,∧] ~,2 | 2As this object has parts, we ought, in order to symbolize the facts thoroughly, to schematize the stream as a body of three dimensions. The time-thought-of would be represented by a section across this stream's length; the portion of the object most distinct in consciousness (the "nucleus of the thought") would be figured by the highest part of the section, on either side of which the section would fall away to symbolize the parts of the object present to consciousness in a vague or "nascent" way. P21
592.25 all . . . is] which is all P21
593.7 objects] *om.* P21
593.8 wide landscapes] a wide landscape P21
593.14,15 *fairly*] *pretty* P21
593.15 feature in] element of P21
593.16 *feature*] *element* P21
593.29 once completely] *om.* P21

593.30 rearward end] immediately intuited past (or rearward and P21 (error)
593.31-32 direct . . . past] lingering in the specious present P21
593.33 -sense; . . . latter] -sense. It P21
593.34 to] to the duration of P21
593.35 Time . . . recall.] *om.* P21
593.38 perceiving, . . . perceived!] perceiving as distinguished from the object perceived. P21
594.2-3 present . . . future] present, or some other P21
594.22 correlative feeling] product P21
594.24 what they may] sensible qualities, or logical relations, or spaces intuited, or pleasures and pains P21
594.27-28 as . . . duration,] *om.* P21
597.5 (See . . . -92.)] *om.* P21
598.33-34 past . . . conceived] simply recollected and conceived past P21
599.16 consciousness."48] ~."∧ (*om. fn.*) P21
599.20 would appear] is P21
599.20 to be] *om.* P21
600.18 thus] then P21
600.19 meanwhile] *om.* P21
600.23 Exner] Professor Exner P21
600.23 Richet] Professor Richet P21
600.25 which] *om.* P21
600.27 length of that] longer P21
600.30 2in] of P21
600.33 *conceive*] *feel* P21
600.34 it which is] it, P21
600.38 See . . . -608.] *om.* P21
602.43 a] *om.* P21
603.4 to] *om.* P21
603.32 conjecturally] *om.* P21
604.1-2 changes . . . being] changes; for the intuition is P21
604.3 must] and must P21

Chapter XVII: Sensation

Reference is made to P24, "The Perception of Space (II)," *Mind*, 12 (April 1887), 183-211 (McD 1887:4).

683.32 If] *(e) Extradition.* [¶] It is now necessary to carry our study of the imaginary projection of feelings still further, and to follow out those cases where we seem to perceive directly by the sense of touch what happens at distances far removed from any sensory surface of the body. Take first a few more facts. [¶] If P24

684.15 path . . . tip] cane's path P24
684.16–17 , without . . . finger] ˄ formerly we seemed to feel the path described by the finger P24
684.38 Lotze] Cp. Lotze P24

CHAPTER XIX: THE PERCEPTION OF 'THINGS'

Reference is made to P24, "The Perception of Space (III)," *Mind*, 12 (July 1887), 321–353 (McD 1887:4).

743.15 When] Smell is a sensation; yet who does not know how a suspicious odour about the house changes immediately its character the moment we have traced it to its perhaps small and insignificant source? When P24
743.21 disappears.˄] ∼.1 | 1"An . . . away." (*run-on in text in* I [743.22–744.2]) (C. F. Taylor . . . 1882.) (*fn.* 22 *in* I *text*) P24
743.21 disappears.] *for continuing* P24 *text, see* Appendix I
743.22 instance] instance of the power of imagination over the sense of smell P24
744.2 away."22] ∼."˄ (*fn. follows* 'disappears.' [743.21]) P24
744.3–4 It . . . quality] Touch is a sensation; yet who has not felt the sensible quality of touch P24
744.11 someone to whom] Wollaston

when P24
744.11 showed] showed him P24
749.13 is!" . . . man] is," said Wollaston
744.16–19 In . . . everyone] As we approach the sense of Hearing, the conditions become even more like those of sight, and the deceptions which Reid's and Helmholtz's principle denies to be possible, abound. Everyone P24
744.20 they . . . their] a sensation of sound altered its P24
744.21 them] it P24
744.38 before.˄] ∼.1 | 1In . . . chase." (*run-on in text in* I [745.1–21]) (*Examen* . . . p. 61.) (*fn.* 23 *in* I *text*) P24
745.1–8 In . . . follows:] 1In an anecdote given by M. Delboeuf to prove a different point, this was probably also the case, though it is not so stated. P24
745.21 chase."23] ∼."˄ (*fn. follows* 'before.' [744.38]) P24

CHAPTER XX: THE PERCEPTION OF SPACE

Reference is made to P24, "The Perception of Space," *Mind*, 12 (January, April, July, October 1887), 1–30, 183–211, 321–353, 516–548 (McD 1887: 4), and to P21, "The Spatial Quale," *Journal of Speculative Philosophy*, 13 (January 1879), 64–87 (McD 1879:6). The variants in the parallel quotation of Fechner on p. 412 in the first printing of *Principles* are indicated by the sigil PP.

[*begin* P24 (1)]
776.0 The . . . Space] I.–THE PERCEPTION OF SPACE. (I.) | By Professor WILLIAM JAMES. P24

776.1 THE . . . EXTENSITY] 1. *The Extensive Quality.* P24
776.9 looks] *om.* P24
776.10 dizziness] vertigo, dizziness P24

776.16 extensive] extended P24
776.17 do better to] better P24
776.22 lay . . . themselves] were not wholly explained by traction on different amounts of skin and joint P24
777.21 elsewhere.1] ~.ₐ (*om. fn.*) P24
777.23 it.2] ~.ₐ (*om. fn.*) P24
777.28-29 'Extensity . . . it,3] Extensiveness,ₐ (*om. fn.*) P24
778.3 extensity] extensiveness P24
778.20 large."4] ~."ₐ (*om. fn.*) P24
779.32 sideways] sidewise PP 412.14
779.34 wherefore] and PP 412.16
779.34 speak] speak accordingly PP 412.16-17
779.36 vibrates] oscillates PP 412.18
779.36 ear. This] ear; and the PP 412.18
779.41 *Loc. cit.*] *Ibid.* P24
780.2 grasp] apprehend PP 412.24
780.6 sense-organs] several external sense-organs PP 412.28
☞780.13 which] *om.* P24 (*This variant from* I *also occurs in* P24 *at* 791.39; 806.26;820.37;825.13;827.13; 830.34 [*twice*];849.26;851.40; 852.1;855.7;870.8;883.35;889.31)
780.14 part] great part P24
780.20 attention.ₐ] ~.1 | 1Hermann's *Handb. der Physiologie*, iii, 2, p. 436. P24
780.28 hardly conscious] wholly unconscious P24
781.15 lamplighter,] lamplighter, or the end of a wooden toothpick made soft between the teeth, P24
781.22-32 The . . . -nail.] *om.* P24
781.33 ¶The] *no* ¶ P24
781.35 either . . . way] as noise P24
782.16 that] that the P24
782.19 they] *om.* P24
783.6 below] about P24
783.8-9 The . . . path.] *om.* P24 (*including figures*)
783.14 points.11] ~.ₐ (*fn. run-on as new* ¶ *in text*) P24
784.12 A.] *om.* P24
785.11-13 *Can . . . imperfectly.*] [*space*] In the facts we have thus passed in review hardly anything has been said about position, direction, or anything that could fall under the concept of

localisation. We have spoken of the mere bigness considered as a unit of each of the several feelings. What the reasons for the particular amount of this extensive muchness may be in each particular case is an interesting and important problem. P24
785.13 in the result] *om.* P24
786.11 THE . . . ORDER] *om.* P24
786.14 peculiarities] qualitative peculiarities P24
787.6 has . . . be] seemed P24
787.7 sort] character P24
787.10 or of] or P24
787.15-16 distinctly apprehended] realised P24
787.17 acts.] acts—first the whole, then the parts. P24
787.17 largenesses] sensations of largeness P24
787.18 sensations] spaces P24
787.19 and] and the various original totals of extension P24
787.19 before they can] so as to P24
787.29-788.1 As . . . with,] To make clear what the problem of finding order, the problem of subdivision and synthesis, is, let us begin by supposing a creature with several sense-organs, each of which yields its own vaguely extensive feeling. (This would probably represent an advanced stage of evolution, for it is likely that in the very earliest dawn of sensibility every impression made awakened the same vague but extensive feeling.) Now, in the creature we have assumed, so long as things do not evolve still farther, P24
788.2 a . . . creature] it P24
788.3 content] content of feeling P24
788.3-4 tend . . . to] *om.* P24
788.23 a multitude of] the several P24
788.26 *a . . . extents*] spatial feelings P24
788.28 *sensible extent*] spatial feeling P24
789.16+ *space*] 2. Space-relations. P24
790.4 *Space-relations*] *om.* P24
790.10 is] *om.* P24
790.24 of the] of the feeling of the P24
790.26 1Thought] *l.c.* P24
790.29 Let us, however,] But let *us* P24
791.16 imagined] imagined or pointed

out P24

791.16   2you] you, or your interlocutor, P24

791.33–34   Like . . . described.] *om.* P24 [*begin* P21]

792.2   blue] blue, without being able to give an idea of them in words P21,24 [*end* P21]

792.6–7   objects] elements P24

792.29   last] *om.* P24

792.29–43 After . . . enough.] facts. Cp. *Prolegomena*, §12. P24

793.4   indispensable condition] condition *sine quâ non* P24

793.23   lines,] lines &c. P24

794.5   *The . . . Localization*] *om.* P24

794.6–7   *Confining . . . us*] Let us take the problem of Locality first, and P24

794.8   receive] happen to be recipients of P24

794.30   therefore] *om.* P24

794.30   one] *om.* P24

795.12   *von vornherein*] *vonvornherein* P24

795.20   point] one of the points P24

795.22   *second*] second sentient P24

795.22   *is . . . arise*] arises P24

795.23   *one*] *om.* P24

795.24   *all relative*] with respect P24

795.25   is] is a P24

795.25–26   by virtue of] *om.* P24

795.27   absolute] *om.* P24

795.29   *isolated*] separate P24

796.3   'Local Signs'] *om.* P24

796.29–31   Whether . . . that] *in quote* P24

796.35–39   See . . . surface.] *om.* P24

797.11   felt] felt by us P24

797.30   discussed.] discussed. Some differences there must be, either in the composition of the nerve-tissue or in the manner in which, in different places, it is affected by the tissues in contact with it when they themselves are touched. These latter mechanical conditions cannot however obtain in the case of the retina, the different points of which exhibit nevertheless a wonderfully delicately graded system of sensations dependent on locality alone. P24

798.9   of where] where P24

798.15   designating] designated P24

799.1   existence] presence P24

799.1   other] other external P24

799.13   that] that the local-sign, P24

799.13   *point*ₐ SUGGESTS] ∼, when aroused, will *suggest* P24

799.28   'reminds'] will 'remind' P24

799.30   suggests] will suggest P24

800.5   point, . . . thus] point has thus its own local-sign P24

800.6   with] with those of P24

800.13   with] *om.* P24

800.14   of the] of P24

800.14   points . . . line] points, joined by an ideal line P24

800.16   comes] *om.* P24

800.20   object felt] feeling P24

800.32–33   interval or] *om.* P24

802.14   thus . . . image] by this motion P24

803.14   awakening.27] awakening.1 | *for fn. in* P24 *see* Appendix I

803.15–805.21   So . . . between.] *text in* P24

803.15–17   our . . . note] now our course begins to be tortuous P24

803.25   1is] are P24

803.29   is it] should it be P24

803.30   the . . . appear] each local-sign (or whatever other feeling now in the aggregate excitement corresponds to the local-sign) should appear out- and along-side of its neighbour in a strictly determinate position which it never abandons? Why should the sign *a* be P24

803.39–40   and . . . chorus.] within whose bulk each should be discriminated just as we discriminate a single voice in a chorus, not by its position but rather by its quality.1 | 1Remember the definition of local-sign (p. 21) [i.e., 798.32–33] as a mere "intensive" quality of feeling, which, *only in combination with other feelings, produces* a feeling of space-relation. P24

803.40   how] why P24

803.41   'sirene'] ₐsirenₐ P24

803.43–44   , by . . . eye,] *om.* P24

803.44   affected,] ∼ₐ by opening the other eye, P24

804.8 *se?*$_\wedge$] *se?*[1] | *for fn. in* P[24] *see*
Appendix I
804.14 every one] everyone P[24]
804.17 a mere] the P[24]
804.17 -process,] -process that underlies
the production of the feeling, P[24]
804.18 a] the separate feeling of P[24]
804.18 appear] result P[24]
804.20 a] the feeling of P[24]
804.25 everlasting] confessed P[24]
804.25 nexus] nexus in all cases P[24]
804.32 occurs.$_\wedge$] occurs.[1] | *for fn. in*
P[24] *see* Appendix I
805.14 points . . . line] feelings from
the mass P[24]
805.14 rank] rank in the scale P[24]
805.22–49 But . . . space.] *fn. in* P[24]
attached to 'between.' [805.21]
805.38 -order, . . . by] -~$_\wedge$ out of P[24]
805.42–43 merely . . . rank] an altogether different sort P[24]
806.1 (in a foot-note)] *om.* P[24]
806.3 and] and (in a footnote) P[24]
806.4–5 in . . . them] which voluntary
attention must follow in its movements
when it passes from one to another of
them P[24]
[*end* P[24] (1); *begin* P[24] (2)]
806.11 THE . . . SPACE] 3. *The Synthesis*
of the original sensible Bignesses. ; *for*
the introduction to pt. 2 of P[24] *see*
Appendix I
806.12 The problem] It P[24]
806.13 ¶(1)] *no* ¶ P[24]
806.15 ¶ (2)] *no* ¶ P[24]
806.17 ¶ I] *no* ¶ P[24]
806.27 1. . . . -spaces] *(a) Their Subdivi-*
sion. P[24]
806.28 How] Let us take subdivision
first. How P[24]
806.29–30 The . . . chapter.] I must
reserve a general treatment of the
subject of discrimination for another
place. P[24]
807.3 point.$_\wedge$] ~.[1] | *fn.* P[24] *(same fn. as*
attached to 'different.' *in* I *at* 807.5)
[*begin* P[21]]
807.15 there] their P[24]
807.21 2the] a P[21]
807.22 of a] *om.* P[21]
807.22,25 one] I P[21,24]

807.24 one's] my P[21,24]
807.25 region] *om.* P[21]
807.25 is] am P[21,24]
[*end* P[21]]
807.36 M.] A. P[24]
808.16 $_\wedge$ *thus*$_\wedge$] , then, P[24]
808.18 once] once by every kind of
stimulus that can be applied to it P[24]
809.8 Donaldson,] Donaldson and Hall,[1] |
[1]See MIND x. 399 and 577. P[24]
809.8 Goldscheider,[30]] ~,$_\wedge$ (*om. fn.*) P[24]
809.10 by . . . Ludwig's] in Wundt's P[24]
809.24 meeting] last meeting P[24]
809.25 for 1886] *om.* P[24]
809.29–31 Stepanoff . . . require.] *om.*
P[24]
809.43 became] was P[24]
809.43 than before] *om.* P[24]
809.44 pair of compasses] compass P[24]
810.6 *The . . . Surfaces*] *om.* P[24]
[*begin* P[21]]
810.7–8 *The . . . physiologists*] Just as
the current psychologies assume that
there can be no space before separate
positions have been accurately distinguished, so they assume the perception of motion P[21]; Psychologists generally have assumed the perception of
motion P[24]
810.8 a] ad P[21]
810.9 the] their P[21,24]
810.10 of these positions] *om.* P[21,24]
810.11 time.[32]] ~.$_\wedge$ (*om. fn.*) P[21]
810.13 we] I P[21]
810.37 another] one P[24]
810.37 call] have called P[24]
811.10 physiologist] young physiologist
P[21]
811.21 2from the] *om.* P[21,24]
811.38–39 *Sitzungsberichte . . .* 3] Wiener
Sitzungs Berichte, LXXII., Bd. III.,
Abth., §156. P[21]
811.38 *der . . . Wien*] zu Wien P[24]
[*end* P[21]]
811.24 amongst . . . these:] which seemed
to him survivals from a stage of development when motion was felt as such, but
not yet discriminated as belonging to
subject or object. Such feeling, he concluded, must be the primitive and undif-
ferentiated form of all spatial perception.

The illusions in question are, among others, these: P24

811.35–812.23　These . . . eye.] Vierordt's inferences may be rash, but his experiments certainly show to one who will repeat them how much more like an indecomposable *sensation* our perception of motion is, than like a constructive act of the mind. P24

813.18　radiates.37] ∼.ᴧ (*om. fn.*) P24

814.5　main] principal P24

814.14–15　which most of them] they P24

814.17　conformation . . . same] conformity of the latter P24

814.20–33　In . . . fall.39] And the exquisite mobility of the eyeball is thus shown, apart from those measuring uses we have noticed already and shall notice again, to be of immense service in promoting discrimination pure and simple. P24

815.1　2. . . . *Other*] *(b) Their Comparison and Measurement.* P24

815.7–816.1　The . . . operative,] If we were immovable and could only passively receive the pressure and motion of objects on our skin, without ever feeling one part of our skin with another, it is certain that we should have far vaguer perceptions of their extension and of our own form than we now possess. The differences of vastness in the feelings of different parts would have uncorrected play. Objects gliding from one part of our surface to another would appear to change their size, as in the observations mentioned at the beginning of the paper; P24

816.5　bigness] vastness P24

816.7　motion] certain motion P24

816.26–817.14　In . . . fluctuating] [¶] The readjustment of the various retinal space-feelings to a common scale is more complex still. So constantly is the same qualitative impression of colour and form changing its magnitude upon the retina (whilst from incessant reversals of the change and tactile verifications we believe the real size of the object to be unaltered), P24

817.17　magnitudes of] magnitude sub-

tended by different P24

817.24–25　retinal . . . in] relative angular or retinal magnitudes which different parts of P24

817.27　stains] flat stains P24

817.28　mean] signify P24

818.1　of them] *om.* P24

818.5　probably] *om.* P24

818.7　reduction] relation P24

818.11　1is] is, in Mr. Spencer's phrase, P24

818.11–12　, in . . . phrase,] *om.* P24

818.14　clearly] *om.* P24

818.14　mind.41] ∼.ᴧ (*om. fn.*) P24

818.16–17　extremity.] extremity. We seem to have in these joint-feelings instances of space-feelings, small *in se*, but geometrically similar to larger ones, preserving their form but suggesting the magnified scale of other sensations with which they are identified. P24

819.1　3. . . . *-spaces*] *(c) Their Identification and Summation.* P24

819.6–21　Here . . . excavates] When a dentist is excavating P24

819.22　in] in various P24

819.23　vaguely] immensely P24

819.27　is thus really] forms thus P24

819.29　outer] real P24

819.29　farther] further P24

819.31　And even] Even P24

820.1　the . . . one] them all to subdivide a common and single objective P24

820.10　perceived . . . ways] of our ordinary space-world. The two worlds P24

820.37　touch.ᴧ] touch.1 | *for fn. in* P24 *see* Appendix I

820.38–824.13　The . . . these.] *om.* P24 (*see* Appendix I *for* P24 *text*)

824.13–14　Suppose . . . toe,] [¶] Suppose the baby learning to locate the pain of a blister in his toe by P24

824.15　a] the P24

824.20　attended . . . as] as concomitantly experienced, are identified in their totalities as appearances of P24

824.21　moves] is judged to move P24

824.22　of objects] *om.* P24

824.23　Their] Both these can be reproduced at will by repeating the movement—their P24

824.29 point.[47]] ~.$_\wedge$ (*om. fn.*) P[24]

824.35–825.42 [47]The . . . whole.] *text in* P[24] *following* 820.37

824.38 he] it P[24]

824.38–825.25 [2]toe . . . really] toe". But this is all wrong. The ache *is* a space; and it will be located within whatever movement-space may call it forth, or whatever pressure-space, heat-space or what not, may envelop it. What P[24]

825.1–6 ¶ Just . . . grow. If] [*no* ¶] And the emphatic sensations that may momentarily occur imbedded in larger space-feelings not only play a part in conferring the maximum of reality upon those spaces that contain them, but they are the means of adding together spaces which can only be experienced in succession. [¶] If P[24]

825.12 common] one P[24]

825.14 The] Now the P[24]

825.16 the blind] a blind P[24]

825.20 From (*no* ¶)] ¶ P[24]

825.24 larger . . . blind.] larger. [¶] But the emphatic sensations that may interrupt a feeling of movement perform another function still. They lend their own scale of absolute magnitude to the movement. That part of the movement-feeling with which they coincide is equated in extent with them, they being more interesting than it. But as the magnitude of this part of the movement-feeling is *immediately* comparable in a more or less exact way with that of its remaining parts, the whole of the movement-space becomes measured in terms of the adventitious feeling in question. P[24]

825.26 'toe'] $_\wedge$~$_\wedge$ P[24]

825.27 'toe'] $_\wedge$~$_\wedge$ P[24]

825.31 an . . . member] *om.* P[24]

825.32 yet save] but P[24]

825.33 itself?$_\wedge$] ~?[1] | [1]Surgical operations on babies sometimes reveal an almost incredible incoherence among their earliest bodily feelings. There is lacking in them that system of pre-organised reflex "movements of defence" which in lower creatures carry the mouth or the foot straight

to the part attacked. A baby may be vaccinated without being held. P[24]

825.34 But (*no* ¶)] ¶ P[24]

825.38–39 fingers . . . let] grasp; let heating the whole foot or P[24]

825.40 gets] is being P[24]

825.42 and] and their totals P[24]

825.42 as . . . whole] *om.* P[24]

826.1 FEELINGS . . . MUSCLES] (*d*) *Muscle-feelings* versus *Joint-feelings.* P[24]

826.2 1. . . . *Joints*] *om.* P[24]

826.3–5 I . . . hitherto,] The applications of this last principle are best seen in the Feelings of Movement which arise in *joints.* These feelings have been too much neglected hitherto, and P[24]

826.19 Psychologist] *l.c.* P[24]

826.19 Delbœuf,[48]] ~$_\wedge$ of Liège, (*om. fn.*) P[24]

827.11–12 impression] sensation P[24]

828.7 way in] position into P[24]

828.9 this . . . movement] the . . . attitude P[24]

828.10 well preserved] intact P[24]

828.15 consequently] *om.* P[24]

828.34 first] nearest P[24]

829.18–830.4 Since . . . *perceived.*] *om.* P[24]

830.5 this . . . invulnerable,] these results (which, though supported by circumstantial evidence only, seem nevertheless invulnerable) P[24]

830.6 our . . . of] *om.* P[24]

830.7 of the] of localisation by P[24]

830.7–9 We . . . joints.] *for text in* P[24] *see* Appendix I

830.9 But (*no* ¶)] ¶ P[24]

830.10 is] is all P[24]

830.10 may] may well P[24]

830.16 feelings] feelings (if we abstract from eye and ear) P[24]

830.17 2, or . . . eye] *om.* P[24]

830.21 *is*] *is,* or coincides in place with, P[24]

830.21–23 skin, . . . extents] skin. The skin-spaces P[24]

830.23 things] ones P[24]

830.25 we . . . cutaneously] no skin-sensation occurs P[24]

830.25–26 -events and sights] -sensations P[24]

830.29 as] and as P24
831.8 *direction?*54] ∼?ᴧ (*om. fn.*) P24
831.24 *can identify*] may project P24
831.24-25 *with . . . way*] into this or that part of objective space P24
831.29 intrinsic] proper P24
831.29 magnitude.55] ∼.ᴧ (*fn. run-on as new ¶ in text*) P24
831.34-35 blind . . . man] blind man and the seeing P24
831.36 when . . . moves,] *om.* P24
831.37 any] any such P24
831.37-38 -tract . . . blind man] -tract as that of cheek or palm, by means of which the 'meaning' of the joint-rotation may originally have been learned. What the mind P24
831.39 other] other by blending P24
832.1-838.7 The . . . be.] *for variant* P24 *text see* Appendix I, *except for* 833.32-40 *drawn from pp.* 207-208 *of* P24
833.32 The ideal] This ideal and uniform P24
833.32 by the mind] *om.* P24
833.39 by] in advance by P24
838.8-10 Before . . . glance] We have now to pass to the great subject of Visual Space, and in view of what is to follow may best at this stage append (in a Supplementary Note) some remarks on the peculiarities of the blind man's perception. But before closing the present section, let us look back for a moment P24
838.11 once more] again P24
838.12 orderly] the more systematic and orderly P24
838.12 primitive incoherency] the more chaotic primitive ones P24
838.13 any] any other P24
838.13 beyond] than P24
838.25 suggested,ᴧ] ∼1 | 1A generic image of several space-feelings of the same sphere of sensibility may take the place of an individual image in the case of ideal suggestion, where the latter is not of a definitely measured extension. P24
838.32 HOW . . . SPACE] NOTE.—*The Space of the Blind.* P24 (*a supplementary note*)

839.6 instantly, in . . . view,] ∼ᴧ . . . view of P24
839.12 days'] day's P24
839.31 , *supra*,] *om.* P24
839.34 his] his own P24
841.17 ᴧstarts.ᴧ65] '∼'.ᴧ (*om. fn.*) P24
842.2 symbolicallyᴧ] to an intuitively manageable one, P24
842.6-7 less . . . than] not as . . . as P24
843.9 once] ∼—like Mr. Galton's correspondents quoted in MIND v. 315 P24
843.11 (cf. . . . above)] *om.* P24
843.12-14 Sir . . . blind.] Sir Wm. Hamilton (*Lects. on Metaphysics,* ii. 174) has, by resuscitating it, given to the foolish opinion of a German philosopher of the last century, Platner, greater currency among us than it deserves. P24
843.20 other."] ∼." It is needless to remark on the utterly arbitrary and fanciful character of such an interpretation. No opinion is so silly but it will find some "learned Theban" to defend it. Platner's doctrine may well pair off with that of Brown, the Mills and other English psychologists, who hold colours to be primitively seen without extension. P24
843.21-845.33 After . . . sight.69] *om.* P24
[*end* P24 (2); *begin* P24 (3)]
846.1 VISUAL] 4. *Visual* P24
847.14 *The*] (*a*) *The* P24
847.16 of volume] voluminous P24
847.16 of extension] extended P24
847.17-18 only . . . we] extended only in the first two dimensions, not in the third. At starting we have P24
847.19 objects of sensation] sensations P24
847.20 (cf. . . . ff.)] *om.* P24
847.38 Leipzig] *Sächs.* P24
848.16 which are] *om.* P24
848.37 Froriep's] *ital.* P24
849.19 separated laterally] widely separated P24
849.19 its] the P24
849.20 the latter] it P24
849.25 consider] prefer to consider P24
849.27 during the experience] *om.* P24
849.33 we . . . given] *om.* P24

849.40–850.4 ¹line . . . men?] line; the
line will visibly shrink as he advances,
and at the same time the colonel will
perceive his distance from the extreme
man at each end of the line to increase
relatively to his distance from the
midmost man whom he approaches.
When he finally touches this midmost
man, his distance from the ends is felt
by him to be at its maximum, although
the line as a whole subtends hardly any
retinal angle. *What* distance shall he
judge it to be? P²⁴

850.7 now] *om.* P²⁴

850.15 visual] *om.* P²⁴

850.24 *Helmholtz . . . Sensations*] *om.*
P²⁴

850.25 is, . . . XVII,] is∧ presumably∧
P²⁴

850.36 *the system of*] *other parts of the
nervous system than the sense-organ in
question, probably* P²⁴

851.12 *unable*] quite unable P²⁴

851.33–34 is *improbable*] contradicts
their verdict P²⁴

851.34 they] they, if left to themselves,
P²⁴

851.37 *since*] if P²⁴

852.14 ¶ More] *no* ¶ P²⁴

853.4–13 But . . . thing.] *for variant text
in* P²⁴ *see* Appendix I

853.13 So . . . Stumpf,⁷⁴] These examples,
to which I could easily add others if I
had room, are perhaps sufficient to
break down in the reader's mind the
authority of a dictum which has been
left so strangely unquestioned. So far
from its being true, as Helmholtz says,
that a genuine present sensation cannot
have its character transformed by suggestions from past experience, it would
seem as if the exact contrary were the
rule, and as if, with Stumpf,¹ we might
P²⁴

853.16 Stumpf adds:] Adding, P²⁴

853.32 *objects*] sensations P²⁴

853.33–34 sensation] one P²⁴

853.34–35 and . . . strength] *om.* P²⁴

854.2 section.⁷⁵] ∼.∧ P²⁴ (*fn. in* P²⁴
attached to a portion omitted in [I])

854.5 inferior . . . only in] only inferior

. . . in P²⁴

854.9–10 reason∧ . . . accommodation]
∼, the feeling of accommodation cannot be identical with the feeling of
distance P²⁴

855.1 Let] *(c) The Two Theories of
Retinal Perception.* [¶] Let P²⁴

855.5 ¹of] on P²⁴

855.37 concluded] found P²⁴

855.37 sensible qualities] sensations P²⁴

855.42 may . . . be] is doubtless much P²⁴

856.3–4 *The* . . . starts] *The theory of
identical points* starts P²⁴

857.37 which] that P²⁴

858.12 LOOK] *om.* P²⁴

859.13 will] should P²⁴

860.20–21 right;⁸⁰ finally] ∼.² Finally
P²⁴

861.6 *The . . . -Theory*] *om.* P²⁴ (*space*)

861.7 theory of projection] *projection-
theory* P²⁴

861.32 *et seq. this chap.* (*except* 911.23–
24) Le Conte] Leconte P²⁴

861.37 ²in] of P²⁴

862.11 Let O be . . . M] O being the point
looked at, M being P²⁴

862.12 nearer, . . . N] ∼∧ than it, P²⁴

863.8 an . . . two] a few inches P²⁴

863.32 plane] place P²⁴

863.36 can] *om.* P²⁴

864.4 *Ambiguity . . . Impressions*] *om.*
P²⁴ (*space*)

864.14 figures . . . 57] following figures
P²⁴

866.5 *Ambiguous*] *(d) Ambiguous* P²⁴

867.23 -measurer.⁸⁶] -∼.∧ (*om. fn.*) P²⁴

868.31 The (*no* ¶)] ¶ P²⁴

868.33–869.1 shall . . . try] have . . . tried
P²⁴

869.21 *The*] *(e) The* P²⁴

869.38 ⁹⁰See Chapter XXVI.] ¹Cp. "The
Feeling of Effort" in the *Anniversary
Memoirs of the Boston Society of Natu-
ral History*, Boston, 1880. The only fact
I am acquainted with which still seems
to make for a feeling of innervation is
the illusion of movement described by
Mach on pp. 65–6 of his *Beiträge zur
Analyse der Empfindungen* (1886).
Not having yet experimentally verified
Mach's observation, I am unable to criti-

cise his explanation of it. The consequence is that the theory of the *Innervations gefühl* has the last word in the discussion. But its existence or non-existence is quite immaterial, as far as my own space-theory is concerned. P24

870.8 that] all that P24

870.29 *the*] their P24

870.30 upon, so that] upon (p. 192), and P24

870.32;873.21;896.27 (*second*) that] *om.* P24

872.1 probable real thing] reality P24

872.2 thing itself] 'reality' P24

872.2 fixed] constant P24

872.4 mental . . . their] a mental image . . . its P24

872.5 definite] perfectly definite P24

872.5 *names* . . . suggest] *name* it suggests P24

872.11 *Sensations . . . Ignore*] 5. *The Intellectualist Theory of Space.* P24

874.23-24 firmness] **fineness** P24

875.11 *Sensations . . . Suppressed*] *om.* P24

876.17-18 But . . . *groups.*] *for variant text of* P24 *see* Appendix I

[*end* P24 (3); *begin* P24 (4)]

876.22-25 In . . . problem.] This chapter on space is not for the discussion of the colour-contrast problem; but I mention it here, because maybe the principles which apply to its solution will prove also applicable to part of our own problem. Hering's treatment of colour-contrast seems, in fact, to have conclusively convicted Helmholtz of error. P24

877.10+ FIG. 64] *om. fig.* P24

878.10+ FIG. 65] *om. fig.* P24

880.6-7 , that . . . facts] *om.* P24

881.18 ¶As] no ¶ P24

881.34-35 Compare . . . 174.] *om.* P24

882.25 *feel*] feel entirely P24

883.16 should] would P24

883.23 motive.99] ~., (*om. fn.*) P24

883.35 shown] *om.* P24

884.3 line] *om.* P24

884.12 excitement] *om.* P24

884.13 farther] further P24

885.24 A] An P24

886.10 is,—] ~1— (*fn. in* I *moved to*

886.10 'b.104')

888.5 gaze.106] ~., (*om. fn.*) P24

889.37-38 , and . . . 731 ff.] *om.* P24

890.5 'perceptions'] 'apperceptions' P24

891.13 whose . . . the] with facets, P24

891.16 another.110] ~., (*om. fn.*) P24

895.12-14 : right . . . everywhere] *om.* P24

895.15 liable always] equally liable P24

895.20 *Bulletin*] *Bulletins* P24

895.29 Wundt] W. Wundt P24

897.12-13 in which] *om.* P24

898.9-10 , by . . . example,] *om.* P24

898.16-18 Those . . . occurred.] *om.* P24

898.19 GENERAL] 6. *General* P24

898.32 the . . . 1of] *om.* P24

898.32 form,] form, length, P24

899.10 , primitively,] , by feeling alone, P24

899.11 are] are often P24

899.20-21 conception in all] notion in most P24

900.9 HISTORICAL] 7. *Historical* P24

900.17 touch] felt touch P24

900.19 , that] , the P24

900.20 which . . . demonstrated,] *om.* P24

901.5 nature] content P24

901.5 it] the latter P24

901.6 they] *om.* P24

902.4 an *extensive*] a P24

902.21 what I must call] *om.* P24

903.7 anyone] any one P24

903.12 , I say,] , and ~., P24

903.28;904.26 a] à P24

905.19-20 add . . . compare] aggregate and summate, they equate P24

906.17 von Volkmar] *om.* P24

906.25 sensations . . . not] may not sensations themselves P24

906.26 acts, . . . explain.] acts, upon which, of course, other acts of further reconstruction may ensue? P24

908.40 Cf. . . . 301-3.] *om.* P24

909.23 given.'] ~., P24 (*error*)

909.25 for help] to help him P24

909.25 doesn't this mean] this means P24

909.37 E.] S. P24

910.9 physiological] sensationalistic P24

910.37-38 *Psychologische* . . . 14.] *om.* P24

911.12 have] have elsewhere (MIND ix. 20) P24

911.28–912.5 writers; . . . way.146] writers. That Hering should have occassionally been fanciful in his assumptions concerning sensations of the third dimension, does not seem to me fatal to the supposition that we have such sensations. In English there is a certain amount of good anti-associationist criticism. The ablest special works are those of Bailey and of Abbott. To the latter author belongs the honour of first in England discussing the question on the basis of the *facts* of vision, of which, having been mainly discovered in Germany, the English associationist authorities were almost uninformed. Dr. E. Montgomery's papers in Vol. X. of MIND contain many valuable introspective remarks and critical observations; but with his notion of an unitary objective space known by the specific energy of a specific central organ, and at definite positions within which we locate each particular sensation, I cannot agree.︵ (*om. fn.*) P24

[*end* P24(4)]

CHAPTER XXI: THE PERCEPTION OF REALITY

Reference is made to P24, "The Psychology of Belief," *Mind*, 14 (July 1889), 321–352 (McD 1889:4), and to P30, "Rationality, Activity and Faith," *Princeton Review*, 2 (July 1882), 58–86 (McD 1882:2).

[*begin* P24]

913.0 The . . . Reality] I.–THE PSYCHOLOGY OF BELIEF. | By Professor WILLIAM JAMES. P24

913.1 BELIEF] "Mein Jetzt und Hier ist der letzte Angelpunkt für alle Wirklichkeit, also alle Erkenntniss."– THEODOR LIPPS. P24

913.7 reality.] ∼–I might, indeed, have called this paper 'The Perception of Reality'. P24

914.7 But we] We P24

916.6 have . . . 265)] in a former article, MIND ix. 22, called P24

916.39 object?] ∼, and P24

916.39 proposition] proposition about it P24

917.5–6 –these . . . belief–] *om.* P24

917.7–8 whole . . . itself.5] whole.1 P24

917.12–13 *do . . . real?*] *does this peculiar attitude of mind arise?* P24

917.14 THE . . . REALITY] *om.* P24 (*space*)

918.8–9 unintelligible.6] ∼.︵ (*om. fn.*) P24

918.26 think.] think. The contradicting thing may then itself be held for real, till it in turn is contradicted by some farther object of our thought. P24

918.29 cannot] can't P24

918.32 *the outer world*] real extra-mental space P24

918.33 'the outer world'] ︵real extra-mental space︵ P24

918.34 world] space P24

918.36 the world] space P24

919.1 contradicted] annulled P24

919.2 *world*] extra-mental space P24

919.7 the space] space P24

919.7 the realities . . . world'] outer realities P24

919.17 altered; for now] ∼. Now P24

920.21–23 The . . . WORLDS] *om.* P24

920.25–26 all . . . philosophy] all, neither the times and spaces represented in our fancy, nor the subjects and attributes appearing located therein. The only times, places, subjects, relations, which popular thought *recognises* are those which we 'adhere to' in the way described. For the erroneous things *Vae victis* is the law P24

920.26 appearances] appearances in the popular philosophy P24

920.29   though . . . . *As*] They are not the same, nor have they the same existence, as the real things. But *as* P24

921.35-36   Swedenborg's . . . *audita*] things seen and heard by Swedenborg P24

922.20-21   , they . . . them] *om.* P24

923.1-5   Each . . . *elect*] Every thinker, however, practically elects P24

923.7   he does not] there is no P24

923.7   positively contradicts] contradicts what is believed of P24

923.10   horse—*that* horse] horse. The real world's horse is the horse which P24

923.18   senses.'10] ~'.ᴧ (*om. fn.*) P24

926.8   fails] fades P24

926.22-24   Mein . . . Erkenntniss."] *om.* P24 (*but used as epigraph*)

926.28   support] ποῦ στῶ P24

927.33   THE . . . SENSATIONS] *om.* P24

930.6-7   Compare . . . above.] *om.* P24

933.36   tale.'ᴧ] ~".1 | 1The reader will be reminded of the part which real sensations play in a very large number of hallucinations or even, according to M. Binet, in all. Some sensorial process seems requisite in order that the illusory object shall appear *outwardly there*, though the *nature* of the object thus appearing may be determined by inward cerebral processes with which under normal conditions the outer *point de repère* had nothing to do. P24

934.5   former chapters.20] a former essay in MIND (vol. xii.).ᴧ (*om. fn.*) P24

935.7   THE . . . BELIEF] *om.* P24

935.10-11   Chapter . . . seek] MIND ix. 188, I have sought P24

935.14   is] more than in indifferent ones is P24

935.15   generally,] generally, and other things being equal, P24

936.10-11   in . . . man] *om.* P24

937.24   *explode*] explode convulsively P24

939.3   a woman] woman P24

939.20   BELIEF . . . THEORY] *om.* P24

939.34   forever] for ever P24

940.1   *theory*] *om.* P24

940.6   conceptions] conception P24 [*begin* P30]

940.15   -at-] -of- P30

940.32   But] Now P30

940.37   would] would all P30

940.39   is life] life is P30

941.13   Cosmos] *l.c.* P30

941.18   reaction] reacting P30

941.21   legitimate only] only legitimate P30

941.32   Horwiczᴧ] ~1 | 1Psychologische Analysen, 2. Theil, I. Hälfte, p. 82. P30

941.35   although] altho P30

942.6   though] tho P30

942.10   is] can be P30

942.10-11   agnostics] a disciple of Spencer P30

942.29   Middle Ages] *l.c.* P30

942.32   Renaissance] Platonizing renaissance P30

942.43   which] *om.* P30

943.4   enveloping] developing P24

943.11   universal essence] *init. caps.* P30

943.12   formulæ] formulas P30 [*end* P30]

943.32   also] *om.* P24

944.24   will] would P24

944.25   chapter] article P24

944.25   show.28] ~.ᴧ (*om. fn.*) P24

944.33   mere] more P24

945.19   1are.] are. Hume declared that its source was the idea's liveliness; Hartley and James Mill maintained that it was its association with other ideas; Prof. Bain has said that it was its connexion with our motor nature. Each is right in part; so that my completer account is less simple than any of its classic predecessors. I have not aspired in it to the slightest originality; I only hope to have woven the traditional doctrines into a less vulnerable whole than I have yet met in print. The absolute, uncriticised reality of the Self is the root of the whole matter, concerning which there is much more to be said, but not at this time and place. There is also much to be said about the connexion of the sense of reality with the Will. The will can change the relative power which objects have of compelling our attention. The will can increase or diminish our emotional and impulsive reactions upon them. The will can end by making us believe things through making us *act* as if they were real, although at first without belief. Belief and will are thus inseparable functions. But space is lacking to treat of their connexion, which I leave willingly untouched, since the masterly treatment of the subject by Renouvier is so readily accessible to every reader.[1] |

[1]*Psychologie Rationelle* (1875), ii. P[24]

[*end* P[24]]

CHAPTER XXII: REASONING

Reference is made to P[21], "Brute and Human Intellect," *Journal of Speculative Philosophy*, 12 (July 1878), 236-276 (McD 1878:4), and to P[31], "Report of the Committee on Hypnotism," *Proceedings of the American Society for Psychical Research*, 1 (July 1886), 95-102 (McD 1886:1).

[*begin* P[21]]

966.15   1. Suppose] Suppose P[21]
966.18   correct] quite correct P[21]
966.18   not . . . [1]but] *om.* P[21]
966.19   there] *om.* P[21]
966.20   fade] not last P[21]
966.22   parts] ingredients P[21]
966.26-29   In . . . . But] A child may open a refractory door by lifting it bodily on its hinges; or he may know enough to tip sideways a stopped mantel-clock, to make it tick again after winding it up— in each case, because the process "always" has the desired effect—and in none of these cases could the result be anticipated without full previous acquaintance with the entire phenomenon. [¶] *It is not reasoned*; but P[21]
966.33-34   eye,— . . . objects,] eye; who should perceive that this particular door sags on its *sill*, or should reflect that no clock can tick until its pendulum swing, and that tipping may start the oscillations of a hidden pendulum—such a man would handle all these objects intelligently, P[21]
966.37   would] *om.* P[21]
967.5   I . . . above] *om.* P[21]
967.6   a] the P[21]
967.6   in . . . be] is hardly P[21]
967.7   agree . . . they] *om.* P[21]
967.8   conclusion . . . their] consequent idea than did the antecedent in its P[21]
967.10-11   immediate data] antecedent phenomenon P[21]

967.12   conclusion] consequent P[21]
967.13-15   properties, . . . now.] properties. P[21]
967.15-16   The . . . possible] [¶] These simple examples show sufficiently that our first point is true. Each P[21]
967.17-18   about, . . . whilst] about. Whilst P[21]
967.18   phenomena] the phenomena P[21]
967.21   2.] *om.* P[21]
967.21-22   , consequences, and implications] *om.* P[21]
967.23-24   reasons. [¶] First] ~: (*no* ¶) First P[21]
967.26   having] as having P[21]
967.31   comparatively] *om.* P[21]
967.34   ¶ The] *no* ¶ P[21]
968.2   all] all of P[21]
968.28   phenomena] concrete phenomena P[21]
968.35   these notions] such a mathematical notion P[21]
968.36   those which concern] the one which concerns P[21]
968.37 *et seq. this chap. Sagacity* . . . *Essence*] *om. headings* P[21]
968.38   characters,—] ~,ᴧ and P[21]
969.4-5   Why . . . else?] *om.* P[21]
969.13   whole.[14]] ~.ᴧ (*om. fn.*) P[21]
969.25   Charles] Mr. P[21]
969.33   corner] point P[21]
969.34   they] *om.* P[21]
969.34-37   It . . . idea.] Knowledge, then, if it begins thus with vague confusion, is not, as some philosophers say, purely

and simply the result of association. To quote Mr. Martineau, in an admirable passage, "It is an utter falsification of the order of nature to speak of sensations grouping themselves into aggregates, and so composing for us the objects of which we think; and the whole language of the theory [of association], in regard to the field of synchronous existences, is a direct inversion of the truth. Experience proceeds and intellect is trained, not by association, but by *Dissociation*; not by reduction of pluralities of impression into one, but by the opening out of one into many; and a true psychological history must expound itself in analytic, rather than in synthetic, terms.4 | 4James Martineau: Essays Philos. and Theolog., p. 273. Boston, 1866. | [¶] According to this, any original Whole of experience is an eternal well of ever new and more delicately differenced ingredients, which little by little come to light. A man's reasoning powers may, then, if our previous account of reasoning is correct, be said to be in direct proportion to his ability to break up these wholes and dissociate their ingredients. P21

969.38–970.2 How . . . alternately] How, then, do we come to dissociate the elements of the originally vague syncretism of consciousness? By noticing or attending to them P21

970.4 or instinctive] *om.* P21
970.7 , and . . . creatures] *om.* P21
970.8 infant] child P21
970.9 those] these P21
970.21 instinctive impulses, or] *om.* P21
970.25 instincts,] *om.* P21
970.25 and] and his P21
970.29–38 The . . . here.] *om.* P21
971.1 when he] who P21
971.8–9;974.18 embedded] imbedded P21
971.22 stand] stand revealed P21
971.22–27 This . . . mind.] Spencer's account omits this last condition, which will immediately be recognized by the reader as the ground of utility in Mill's famous methods of induction, the

"method of Agreement," that of "Difference," of "concomitant variations," etc. P21
971.28–32 Now . . . F,–] But, now, is it not immediately obvious that this condition is supplied in the organization of every mind in which similar association is largely developed? If the character *m* in the midst of A will call up C, D, E, and F immediately— P21
971.35 reader's] *om.* P21
971.37 consideration] simultaneous consideration P21
971.37–38 , and . . . way] *om.* P21
971.40–972.1 chief . . . noticing] only instrument for dissecting out P21
972.2–3 class . . . terms,] *om.* P21
972.13 Figure] Diagram P21
972.20 the] *om.* P21
972.24–973.11 Geniuses . . . MAN] *om.* P21
973.12 first try] try now P21
973.16 who scatter] as scattering P21
973.32–34 It . . . 954.] *om.* P21
974.6 he trotted] trotted the latter P21
974.13 his] *om.* P21
974.29 always] *om.* P21
974.29 peculiar . . . interests] mere . . . interest P21
974.35–38 however . . . idea–] whether represented in his mind by images of further hostile or friendly acts, or in whatever other way, P21
974.40 playing with you] the reverse P21
975.2 which] *om.* P21
975.4 I] We P21
975.7 over, . . . dived] overboard from a boat, . . . dove P21
975.10 things.16] ∼., (*om. fn.*) P21 [*begin* P31]
975.28–31 Just . . . surrender] This puts us on the track of a distinction between the normal and the trance mode of perception, which partly explains the latter. The evolution of man's mind is altogether in the analytic direction. He deals with objects by picking out their "essential" character, tracing its consequences, and ignoring other features. He remembers a house in a street by the one little inconspicuous detail of its number, very

likely observing nothing else about it; and similarly he retains the line on the foolscap paper by not dispersing his attention over the sheet, but counting the number of lines between the one selected and the nearest edge. The number thus obtained is a permanent part of the mind's possession, and is obviously for practical purposes more exact than any reminiscence of the "general look" of the line in its place would be. [¶] The trance-subject, however, surrenders P31

975.32,34 total] general P31
975.45 'it looks so.'] it "looks so." P31 [*end* P31]
976.2 was probably] may have been P21
976.5 is] is probably P21
976.16 me far to] us to far P21
976.18 belonging] mere belonging P21
976.20 been no] hardly been P21 [*begin* P31]
976.35-36 off altogether ... 1the] out altogether. The P31
976.36 may] may then P31 [*end* P31]
977.11 mind] sensorium P21
977.12 there.18] ∼.ᴧ (*om. fn.*) P21
977.13 be found to] *om.* P21
977.14 but] but only P21
977.21-979.20 Professor ... think."19] *om.* P21
977.31 are] were P21
977.31-37 I ...-headed.] There are, however, other and more subtle considerations which intervene and prevent us from treating the matter further in this place. P21
979.21-24 Other ... animal.'] Another well-known *differentia* of man is that he is the only laughing animal. P21
979.24 often] *om.* P21
979.24-25 identities] certain identities P21
980.1-2 Man ... assuredly] *Language* is certainly P21
980.31 1thing] *om.* P21
980.37 It arises as] As P21
980.38 a *sign*] the sign P21
980.39 this notion] it P21
981.1 several ... natures] import—and as to their own physical constitution P21

981.5 probably thereupon] have P21
981.5-6 general ... or] *om.* P21
981.8 laid down (p. 478)] so often repeated P21
981.20-21 idea of the] *om.* P21
981.21 2of] *om.* P21
981.22 these] they P21
981.22 idea] *om.* P21
982.20 for] *om.* P21
982.38 See] See an interesting article on P21
982.39-983.38 Dr. ... also.] *om.* P21
983.9 (*twice*) his] *om.* P21
983.21-22 *elementary*] characteristic P21
983.27-32 If ... out.] But *other* characters (few and far between) may be singled out by practical interests. P21
984.4 men. And] ∼, and P21
984.9 question] question we asked sometime back, P21
984.12 selection] approbation P21
984.13 as ... said,] *om.* P21
984.14 *similar association*] init. caps. P21
984.15 Bain] Bain, in his admirable work on the "Study of Character," P21
984.18 Alike] He proceeds to show how alike P21
984.20 ¶ But] *no* ¶ P21
984.22 farther] further P21
984.25-26 properly so called,] *om.* P21
984.35 similarity] association P21
985.2 suggestion] suggestions P21
985.16 ¶ Or] *no* ¶ P21
985.26-27 is ... to] should not P21
985.39 *Study*] Bain: "Study P21
986.21-22 Association] We saw sometime back how association P21
986.22 may have identical] were identical in their P21
986.34 does not] doesn't P21
987.17 2of] *om.* P21
987.23 can work] *om.* P21
987.23 adjectives] words are probably names of entire things and entire actions—extensive, coherent groups. Similarity working before abstraction, which as a rule we have seen to be based upon it, the first adjectives P21
987.24 therefore probably] *om.* P21

987.28 concrete;just] ∼. Just P21
987.37 one and] *om.* P21
988.7 basis] bases P21
988.8 immense departments] an immense department P21
988.22–23 bare . . . joints] mere reclining figure P21
988.23 so suggest] suggest all P21
988.24 cannot] can't P21
989.1 *physiological*] final P21
989.1–2 If . . . true,] If the theory be true which assigns to the cerebral hemispheres definite localities in which the various images, motor and sensible, which constitute our thoughts are stored up, P21
989.3–4 must be] is P21
989.10 This] But this P21
989.12–14 we . . . be] which is the basis of similar association, seems P21
989.15 localized‸] localize- P21
989.22 figure] Diagram P21
989.22 p. 972] *om.* P21
989.24 possible] at least possible P21
989.30–31 little . . . own.] little. We have ourselves tried our best to form some hypothesis, but wholly without success.

We bequeath, therefore, the problem to abler hands. P21
989.33 inferences] inferences, with which we may conclude P21
989.35 makes] make P21
990.10 the] Spencer's P21
990.12 principle‸] ∼, both by Mr. Spencer and by others, P21
990.14–15 In . . . call] The pointer pup, the birds on desert islands, the young of the tame rabbit, and Brown-Séquard's epileptic guinea-pigs constitute P21
990.18 possibly] *om.* P21
990.18 law] probable law P21
990.20 children.] ∼, and that is not a *mental* law. P21
990.20 certainly] *om.* P21
990.25 law] law of Spencer's P21
990.34 of intellect] *om.* P21
990.39–991.1 ²the . . . inherited] Spencer's law P21
991.13 may probably] probably could P21
991.17 placed.25] ∼.‸ (*om. fn.*) P21
991.28 ground on] condition by P21
991.29 grow up] are formed P21
[*end* P21]

CHAPTER XXIV: INSTINCT

Reference is made to P37, "What Is an Instinct?" *Scribner's Magazine*, 1 (March 1887), 355–365 (McD 1887:6), and to P29, "Some Human Instincts," *Popular Science Monthly*, 31 (June, September 1887), 160–170, 666–681 (McD 1887:8).

[*begin* P37]
1004.0 Instinct] WHAT IS AN INSTINCT? | *By William James.* P37
1006.39 in] it P37 (*error*)
1007.3 ¶ In] *no* ¶ P37
☛1007.17 towards] toward P37 (*This variation from I also occurs in P37 or P29 at* 1032.30;1046.13;1052.14; 1055.2)
1008.35 G. H.] *om.* P37
1008.36 *Der*] *om.* P37
1009.29 a bird] the bird P37
1010.10 *et seq. this chap.* INSTINCTS . . .

INVARIABLE] *om. headings* P37
1010.19 been] been used P37
1011.32 will be] are P37
1011.36 associative] mental P37
1012.39 W. L.] *om.* P37
1012.40 K.] *om.* P37
1013.25 lacks. On . . . possesses] ∼, but to his possessing P37
1013.30 *excite . . . to*] *om.* P37
1014.23–24 1. . . . 2.] *om. numbers and text run-on* P37
1014.25 ¶ Taken] *no* ¶ P37
1014.25–26 the same] an P37

1014.31 1. The . . . habits] Take first the inhibition of instincts by habits. The law P37

1015.23 object] objects P37

1015.33 it] if P37 (*error*)

1016.23 ¶ But] *no* ¶ P37

1016.39 *Macmillan's* . . . 1873] *op. cit.* P37

1016.40 *Ibid.*] *op. cit.* P37

1017.5 the earliest] some P37

1017.15 which] *om.* P37

1017.33 2.] *om.* P37

1017.33 *Many*] That *many* P37

1019.9-10 with which . . . played] which . . . played with P37

1019.16 should] could P37

1020.10 writes] tells P37

1020.16-17;1052.13 afterwards] afterward P37 (*or* P29)

1020.39 Stebbing] Spedding P37 (*error*)

1022.7 *instincts*] of them P37

1022.16 risk.] rule. [¶] The most interesting thing possible now would be to test our principles by going through the human instincts in detail. But as I have already exceeded my allotted space, that must be reserved for another opportunity. P37

[*end* P37; *begin* P29 (1)]

1022.17 SPECIAL . . . INSTINCTS] SOME HUMAN INSTINCTS. | BY WILLIAM JAMES, | PROFESSOR OF PHILOSOPHY IN HARVARD COLLEGE. P29

1022.18-1028.18 Let . . . consider.] *for variant* P29 *text see* Appendix I

1028.19 *Pugnacity* . . . *resentment.*] Pugnacity and' anger. P29

1028.23 *et seq. this chap.* cannot] can not P29

1029.13 board . . . other] *om.* P29

1029.16 adult‸ . . . friend‸] adult, beloved, and friend, P29

1029.18 the . . . of] *om.* P29

1029.19 Cattle] Sheep and cattle P29

1029.30 as] as, in Spencer's opinion, P29

1029.30-31 , even . . . opinion,] *om.* P29

1029.38 reinforce one's sympathy] re-enforce P29

1030.4 gone.13] ~.‸ (*om. fn.*) P29

1030.6 race.14] ~.‸ (*om. fn.*) P29

1030.18 rather] either a semblance or P29

1031.1 both] both of P29

1032.13-14 downwards] downward P29

1032.21 is.16] ~.‸ (*om. fn.*) P29

1033.22 it] him P29

1035.30-1036.6 One . . . child.] *om.* P29

1036.7 ¶ Preyer] *no* ¶ P29

1036.8-9 The . . . solitude. (*no* ¶)] ¶ *Solitude* is a source of terror to infancy. P29

1037.2 they are] this is P29

1037.5-6 The . . . another] The impulse is so much of an individual idiosyncrasy P29

1037.13 has] has recently P29

1038.22 work] work on P29

1038.32 in . . . language] *om.* P29

1039.35 play?] ~? [¶] In a subsequent paper I shall try to consider man's remaining instincts in a similar way. P29

[*end* P29 (1); *begin* P29 (2)]

1039.36 *Appropriation* or *Acquisitiveness.*] In a previous article I passed in review a certain number of those instincts which may be considered fundamental in man. In the pages which follow I propose to complete the list. The reader will perhaps remember my main thesis, which is that man, so far from having an unusually small number of instincts, is more richly endowed in this respect than any other mammal; so richly, indeed, that his instincts often block one another's path. This phenomenon, combined with the transitoriness of many of them, and with what I have called the law of inhibition of instincts by habits, sufficiently account for the indeterminateness of man's conduct in presence of the same objective stimuli—an indeterminateness which has usually been supposed incompatible with his possession of any instincts at all. [¶] The last instinct I touched upon was fear. Let me next say a few words about *appropriation* or *acquisitiveness.* Once more the reader will remember that an instinct is nothing more than an inborn path of reflex discharge in the nervous centers, such that a certain sort of object falling on the senses awakens an impulse to act in a determinate way. P29

1040.5   Everyone] Every one P29
1040.39   President] Professor P29
1040.39   has given] gives P29
1041.24   they . . . se] om. P29
1042.11   'the Miser'] the "miser" P29
1043.5   things] om. P29
1043.6   his] the P29
1045.13–14   civic . . . their] civic power symbolizes its P29
1045.24   our] the P29
1047.2   scientific] om. P29
1047.10   Chapter XXVIII] another place

P29
1048.39   a . . . woman] some lady P29
1048.40   compared] om. P29
1054.25   whom] with whom P29 (error)
1054.33   instinct . . . aversion] anti-sexual impulse P29
1055.38   But (no ¶)] ¶ P29
1055.38   only . . . bare] merely . . . mere P29
1056.22   fading] fading off P29
1056.22   and into] and P29
[end P29(2)]

CHAPTER XXV: THE EMOTIONS

Reference is made to P24, "What Is an Emotion?" *Mind*, 9 (April 1884), 188–205 (McD 1884:2).

1065.27   coarser] standard P24
1065.30   theory] thesis P24
1066.7   should] could P24
1066.18   The] And the P24
1066.22   The (no ¶)] ¶ P24
1067.12   on.ₐ] ∼.1 | 1Of course the physiological question arises, *how* are the changes felt?—*after* they are produced, by the sensory nerves of the organs bringing back to the brain a report of the modifications that have occurred? or *before* they are produced, by our being conscious of the outgoing nerve-currents starting on their way downward towards the parts they are to excite? I believe all the evidence we have to be in favour of the former alternative. The question is too minute for discussion here, but I have said something about it in a paper entitled "The Feeling of Effort," in the *Anniversary Memoirs of the Boston Natural History Society*, 1880 (translated in *La Critique Philosophique* for that year, and summarised in MIND XX, 582). See also G. E. Müller's *Grundlegung der Psychophysik*, § 110. P24
1067.15   *its*] its characteristic P24
1067.35   feeling] feelings P24
1067.38   for me] om. P24

1067.39   ebullition] ebullition of it P24
1068.19;1073.8;1077.37   which] om. P24
1072.2–4   Let . . . said,] But now, this objection disposed of, there arises a more general doubt. Is there any evidence, it may be asked, P24
1072.8   *Reply.* There] The only possible reply is, that there P24
1072.31–1073.2   Professor . . . them."10] om. P24
1073.11   an anticipation] a representation P24
1073.15–16   In . . . seems] I am told of a case of morbid terror, of which the subject confessed that what possessed her seemed P24
1073.16–17   fear of the] the fear of P24
1073.27–28   vivid . . . and the] presented feeling, or the idea, of the manifestations; which P24
1073.29   and . . . substance] its sum and substance, and its stock-in-trade P24
1073.33–36   The . . . easily] The last great argument in favour of the priority of the bodily symptoms to the felt emotion, is the ease with which we P24
1074.6   causes] will cause P24
1074.7   and] and as a consequence P24
1074.41   and . . . believe,] om. P24
1074.42   repose.] repose. Whether the

subjective strength of the feeling be
due in these cases to the actual energy
of the central disturbance, or merely
to the narrowing of the field of consciousness, need not concern us. In the
asylum cases of melancholy, there is
usually a narrowing of the field. P[24]

1077.10   this:] *om.* P[24]

1077.10   and cold-blooded] *om.* P[24]

1077.12-16   Now . . . . In] Of course in
p[24]

1077.18   voluntary] volitional P[24]

1077.18-19   Few . . . . But,] Still, P[24]

1077.20-21   corroborates . . . rests] fully
corroborates this test P[24]

1077.37   *movements*] *motions* P[24]

1080.26-34   *Reply . . . on.*] I feel per-
suaded there is no real exception to
the law. The formidable effects of
suppressed tears might be mentioned,
and the calming results of speaking out
your mind when angry and having done
with it. But these are also but specious
wanderings from the rule. Every perception must lead to *some* nervous result.
If this be the normal emotional expression, it soon expends itself, and in the
natural course of things a calm succeeds.
But if the normal issue be blocked from
any cause, the currents may under certain circumstances invade other tracts,
and there work different and worse
effects. P[24]

1081.2-11   This . . . strong."] *om.* P[24]

1081.12   ¶When] *no* ¶ P[24]

1081.12-13   emotional . . . display]
emotions P[24]

1081.14   currents] nerve-currents P[24]

1081.16-24   brain.ʌ In . . . child.] brain.[1] |
[1]This is the opposite of what happens in
injuries to the brain, whether from outward violence, inward rupture or tumor,
or mere starvation from disease. The
cortical permeability seems reduced, so
that excitement, instead of propagating
itself laterally through the ideational
channels as before, tends to take the
downward track into the organs of the
body. The consequence is that we have
tears, laughter, and temper-fits, on the
most insignificant provocation, accom-

panying a proportional feebleness in
logical thought and the power of
volitional attention and decision. P[24]

1081.24-25   It . . . expressed] The only
exceptions to this are apparent, not real.
The great emotional expressiveness and
mobility of certain persons often lead
us to say "They would feel more if
they talked P[24]

1082.1   is] be P[24]

1082.5-6   But . . . this] But it was said at
the outset that this would be affirmed
p[24]

1082.7   called the 'coarser'] agreed to call
the "standard" P[24]

1082.8   states . . . which] sensibilities that
p[24]

1082.9-13   We . . . are] We had better,
before closing, say a word or two about
these latter feelings. [¶] They are, the
reader will remember, P[24]

1082.18   distinguished] tried to distinguish
p[24]

1082.19   mathematical] geometrical P[24]

1082.21   seem] seem here to be a pure
matter of sensation, and there P[24]

1082.24   'coarser'] so-called "standard"
P[24]

1082.30;1085.14   'coarser'] "standard"
P[24]

1082.31   other . . . objects] the presence
of objects or the experience of events
p[24]

1082.34-1085.3   In . . . like.] But a sober
scrutiny of the cases of pure cerebral
emotion gives little force to this assimilation. Unless in them there actually be
coupled with the intellectual feeling a
bodily reverberation of some kind, unless we actually laugh at the neatness
of the mechanical device, thrill at the
justice of the act, or tingle at the perfection of the musical form, our mental condition is more allied to a judgment of *right* than to anything else. P[24]

1085.3   Such . . . is] And such a judgment
is rather P[24]

1085.4   As] But as P[24]

1085.4-5   , however,] *om.* P[24]

1085.5   moral . . . do] intellectual feeling
hardly ever does P[24]

1085.8-9 , even ... ones,] *om.* P24

1085.9 mere ... excitability] emotional sensibility thereto P24

1085.10 taste] the taste P24

1086.11-1087.18 And ... by] Cognition and emotion are parted even in this last retreat,—who shall say that their antagonism may not just be one phase of the world-old struggle known as that between the spirit and the flesh?—a struggle in which it seems pretty certain that neither party will definitively drive the other off the field. [¶] To return now to our starting-point, the physi-

ology of the brain. If we suppose its cortex to contain centres for the perception of P24

1087.21 capable] perfectly capable P24

1087.22-23 affects ... perceived] and is apperceived by the appropriate cortical centre P24

1087.23 inwardly] in some other way P24

1087.26 perceived,] apperceived‿ P24

1087.27 portions] specific portions P24

1087.30 nothing] nothing is P24

1087.30 circuits] circuit P24

1087.31 local] topical P24

CHAPTER XXVI: WILL

Reference is made to P37, "What the Will Effects," *Scribner's Magazine*, 3 (February 1888), 240–250 (McD 1888:1), and to P42, "The Feeling of Effort," *Anniversary Memoirs of the Boston Society of Natural History* (1880), pp. 3–32 (McD 1880:3).

[*begin* P37]

1099.17-18 this youngster] that child P37

1099.18 much] *om.* P37

1099.20 has] has already P37

1099.22 But if (*no* ¶)] ¶ But P37

1099.23 must be] is P37

[*end* P37; *begin* P42]

1101.36 ¶ Or we] (*no* ¶) We P42

1102.8 ¶ Or] *no* ¶ P42

1102.32 *Gazette*] in Gazette P42

1102.35-36 Concerning ... -841.] *om.* p42

1107.7 It ... Psychology] Plausibility accrues to this presumption when we call to mind this general law: P42

1107.7 deserts] seems to desert P42

1107.8 use] any use P42

1107.10 1law] law in Psychology P42

1107.10 2law] logical law P42

1107.10 in logic] *om.* P42

1108.1 work] function P42

1108.8 That] The P42

1108.10 ends by thinking] thinks P42

1108.12 of the pole] in space P42

1108.13 counteract] counteract by movement P42

1108.36 remote,9] *fn. keyed to* 1110.30 'intensity.' P42

1109.13 For] Now P42

1109.14 relay] second relay P42

1109.14 of the movement] *om.* P42

1109.16 of movement] *om.* P42

1109.17 centres,‿] feelings,1 | 1The association between the two orders of feeling being of course brought about by a separate neural connexion between the tracts supporting each. P42

1109.17-18 with ... discharge] specific P42

1109.20-21 2the ... innervation] they p42

1109.22 idea ... movement] notion of the end P42

1109.24-25 our ... ideas] "ends" P42

1109.27,30 (*twice*) idea] end P42

1109.36-37 , and ... cues] *om.* P42

1110.24 expressively] expressly P42

1110.30 intensity.‿] ~.2 | 2Harless, in an article which in many respects forestalls what I have to say, (Der Apparat des Willens, in Fichte's Zeitschrift f. Philos., Bd. 38, 1861) uses the con-

venient word *Effectsbild* to designate
our idea of this sensory result of a
movement. P42 [*see* 1108.38-40]

1110.31 which] *what* P42

1110.33 altogether?12] ~?₍ (*om. fn.*)
p42

1110.37 1st ed.,] *om.* P42

1111.19 result,₍] result,3 | 3We speak here
only of the *muscular* exertion, properly
so called. The difficulty often involved
in making the *fiat* still remains a reserved
question. P42

1111.28 are . . . feelings] feelings are
afferent P42

1111.32 There is indeed] Except, indeed,
what I have called P42

1111.38-39 arm . . . left] or the left arm,
for example, P42

1111.40-1112.7 *An . . . on.*] So far then,
we seem free to conclude that an anticipatory image of the sensorial consequences of a movement, hard or easy,
plus the fiat that these consequences
shall become actual, ought to be able
to discharge *directly* the special movement with which in our past experiences
the particular consequences were combined as effects. Furthermore, there is
no introspective evidence whatever of
the existence of any intermediate feelings, possessing either qualitative or
quantitative differences, and accompanying the efferent discharge.1 [*space*]
| 1The various degrees of difficulty with
which the fiat is given form a complication of the utmost importance, reserved
for discussion further on. P42

1112.34 air.13] ~.₍ (*om. fn.*) P42

1113.9-12 Since . . . is.] Is there, not-
withstanding, any circumstantial evidence? At first sight, it appears as if
the circumstantial evidence in favor
of efferent feelings were very strong.
p42

1113.12 says₍ ₍] says,2 | 2Vorlesungen
über Menschen und Thierseele, Bd. i,
p. 222. P42

1113.26 formerly."16] ~."₍ (*om. fn.*)
p42

1113.38-39 evidence . . . being] evidence
is P42

1113.40-41 , is . . . Bd. XX] *om.* P42

1114.3 But] *om.* P42

1115.31 add.18] ~.₍ (*om. fn.*) P42

1116.7 next] *om.* P42

1116.9 small] last small P42

1116.10 inexpugnable.] ~. And, to say
the truth, it may well be excused for
its confidence; for Ferrier alone, so far
as I know, has ventured to attack it
there, and his attack must be deemed
a very weak failure. P42

1116.12 recall our] examine the position
with a little care, laying down first a
few general P42

1116.23 get] shall get P42

1116.23 judge] shall judge P42

1116.35-36 (See . . . -736.)] *om.* P42

1117.33 recent] very recent P42

1117.41 pp. 18-21] S. 18 P42

1118.16 vision."₍] ~."1 | 1*Ibid*, p. 21.
P42

1118.40 show.22] ~.₍ (*om. fn.*) P42

1119.19-20 left . . . right] right . . . left
P42 (*corr. in errata*)

1120.11 alone.23] ~.₍ (*om. fn.*) P42

1120.12-13 It . . . not] ¶ Not P42

1120.17 The] Now the P42

1120.18-19 naturally . . . respects] also
to a great extent absolutely indistinguishable, namely, where they fall in
corresponding points. But even where
they are *numerically* distinguishable,
they are indistinguishable with respect
to P42

1121.2 severally] respectively P42

1121.2 Similarly (*no* ¶)] ¶ Now P42

1121.3 are] are also P42

1131.28;1167.44 one's self] oneself P42

1131.32 thought."34] ~."₍ P42 (*fn.*
follows 'says:' [1131.23])

1131.33 p. 293] 1852, p. 293 P42

1131.33 Will] will P42

1131.40 such] so P42

[*end* P42; *begin* P37]

1132.23 We] We all P37

1132.25 persons] of us P37

1132.26 themselves] ourselves P37

1135.12-14 It . . . does.] Not that the
refusing of consent need imply energe-
tic volition either. Quite as little as the
execution of a movement does its

inhibition always require an express effort or command. P37

1135.14   it] it, as we shall presently see P37

1135.15   prompts] will prompt P37

1135.22   all.ˏ] ~.* | *It always takes place insensibly even when the brakes are on. The skill of such muscle-readers as Mr. Irving Bishop depends on the fact that hardly anyone in thinking of a movement is able entirely to suppress the tendency to carry it out. The muscle-reader feels this tendency in the "Agent's" hand which is laid upon his person. P37

[end P37; begin MS]

1150.17   would,] ~ˏ MS

1150.17   death.] ~ˏ MS

1150.18-19   , 1775,] ˏ~ˏ MS

1150.20   bounds,] ~ˏ MS

[end MS; begin P42]

1154.29   the] its P42

1154.30   is in] follows P42

1154.31   traction.] traction. When we deliberately symbolize the mental drama in mechanical language, we also say that belief and will follow the lines of least resistance, or of most attractive motivation. P42

1154.32   never ... way] is by no means compatible with the law that mental action always follows lines of least resistance P42

1154.34-39   physical .... He] law must hold good. But in all hard cases either of belief or will, it seems to the agent as if one line were easier than another, and offered least resistance, even at the moment when the other line is taken. The sailor at the pumps, he P42

1155.1   social obloquy] ostracism P42

1155.8   springs ... propensities] motives as sensual P42

1155.8   ideals] moral P42

1155.10   ideals] conscience P42

1155.11   propensities] appetite P42

1155.12   ideals] ideal P42

1155.13   ideal] moral P42

1155.15   propensities] sensual impulse P42

1155.15   ideal impulse] moral one P42

1155.18   force of propensity] sensual force P42

1155.19   ideal force] moral P42

1155.20-21   an ideal motive] moral force P42

1155.22-23   propensity is] impulses are P42

1155.23   effort] moral effort P42

1155.24-25   ideal or] om. P42

1155.28-29   P ... impulse,] S standing for the sensual motive, M for the moralˏ P42

1155.30-31   I ... P.] M per se < S. | M + E > S. P42

1155.32   I, P] M, S   P42

1155.34   I] M   P42

1165.6-7   then ... not] do follow or not upon the representation P42

1165.7   itself] of the act represented P42

1165.13   write.[60]] ~.ˏ (om. fn.) P42

1165.14   stable ... idea] intention or consent P42

1165.15   motion] motion upon its completion P42

1165.16-17   depending ... mind] belonging to the department of physiology exclusively, and depending on the organic structure and condition of executive ganglia, whose functioning is quite unconscious P42

1165.22   anticipated] which they prefigure P42

1165.26   remains.] remains.[1] | [1]In ataxy it is true that the sensations resultant from movement are usually disguised by anasthesia. This has led to false explanations of the symptom (Leyden, Die graue Degeneration des Rückenmarks, 1863). But the undeniable existence of atactics without a trace of insensibility proves the trouble to be due to disorder of the associating machinery between the centres of ideation and those of discharge. These latter cases have been used by some authors in support of the Innervationsgefühl theory: (Classen: das Schlussverfahren des Sehactes, 1863, p. 50); the spasmodic irregular movements being interpreted as the result of an imperfect *sense* of the amount of innervation we are exerting. There is no subjective evidence whatever of such a state. The undoubtedly true theory is best expounded by Jaccoud: Des Paraplegies et de l'Ataxie Motrice, 1864, part iii, chapter ii. P42

1165.26 Paralysis (*no* ¶)] ¶ P42

1165.26-27 associated] associative P42

1166.3 as before] *om.* P42 (*fn.* 61 *follows* 'passive.' [1166.3])

1166.35 make a muscular] will the P42 [*end* P42; *begin* P37]

1167.6 ¹to . . . one,] *om.* P37

1167.7 squander . . . cupidities,] pay it out, and as easy P37

1167.8 towards] in the direction of P37

1167.14-15 those . . . if] that tomb which certainly awaits us—try it now, sanguine reader! If P37

1167.15-16 travels . . . joys] flowers and spring P37

1167.21 objects] ideas P37 [*end* P37; *begin* P42]

1167.24 These] Muscular P42

1167.27-29 must . . . about] has difficulty in consenting to their reality P42

1167.29 muscular] our bodily P42

1167.31 from his muscular] engendered by his bodily P42

1167.31 sustaining] *consenting to* P42

1167.32 required . . . effort] of the sailor rising to go to the pumps P42

1167.42 Again (*no* ¶)] ¶ P42

1167.42 fiat] volitional fiat P42

1167.43 volitional] *om.* P42 [*end* P42; *begin* P37]

1168.13 a] like a P37

1168.20 difficult object] moral idea P37

1168.20 begins to call] succeeds in calling P37

1168.21 the . . . of] *om.* P37

1168.22-23 action . . . once] actions change. The new ideas, as soon as they are P37

1168.23-24 field . . . own] mental field, infallibly produce their P37

1168.24-31 The . . . . For the] The struggle, the difficulty is all in their getting possession of the field. The strain of the will lies in keeping the attention firmly fixed upon them, in

spite of the fact that the spontaneous drift of thought is all the other way. That is what takes the moral effort. And when the moral effort has victoriously maintained the presence of the moral ideas, its work is over. The P37

1168.32 thought . . . centres] ideas and the cerebral motor-centres P37

1168.35 how] that P37

1168.36 volitional] voluntary P37

1168.36 lies exclusively] does not lie in the physical world at all, but P37

1168.36-1169.1 The whole . . . that] *om.* P37

1169.9-10 If . . . a] There is no other possible sort of consent than this. If the idea be that of the beginning or stopping of some P37

1169.10 then] *om.* P37

1169.11 motor] *om.* P37

1169.11 For] The movement in this case becomes real as soon as we agree to the notion that it shall be real. P37

1169.13 on . . . . She] of her own. Nature P37

1169.14-16 instance . . . will!] instance than this one of our own bodily movements. P37

1175.13-14 It . . . choose.] The effort which such attention implies seems to be indeterminate in quantity, as if we might make more or less as we chose. P37

1175.18 objects] ideas P37

1175.18 object] idea P37

1175.20 effort] effort of attention P37

1175.24 or consent] *om.* P37

1175.26 object . . . they] idea attended to or P37

1175.26 effort] attention P37 [*end* P37; *begin* P42]

1176.20 doubts‸] doubts and probabilities, P42

1176.21 the point] *om.* P42

1176.23 reasons . . . on] evidence for P42

1176.24 discussion more] question more exquisitely P42

1176.24-25 our . . . be] his . . . is P42

1176.26 genius‸] ∼¹ | ¹J. Lequier: La Recherche d'une Première Vérité, 1865.

p. 90. P42

1176.28   us] him P42

1176.29   our] his P42

1176.29   we] he P42

1176.29-30   alternative views₋] alternatives in his mind, P42

1176.30-31   us . . . creed] *him* P42

[*end* P42; *begin* P37]

1181.33-38   He . . . ²in] They find a zest in this difficult clinging to truth, or a lonely sort of joy in pressing on the thorns and going without it, which no passively warranted possession of it can ever confer. And thereby they become

the masters and the lords of life. They must be counted with henceforth; they form a part of human destiny. No more in the theoretic than in P37

1182.5-8   The . . . own.] Ever there rises up the prophet, the hero of belief, who drinks more deeply than any of the cup of bitterness; but his countenance is so unshaken and he speaks such mighty words of cheer, that his thought becomes our thought, and to later generations he seems a being half divine. P37

[*end* P37]

CHAPTER XXVII: HYPNOTISM

Reference is made to P31, "Report of the Committee on Hypnotism," *Proceedings of the American Society for Psychical Research*, 1 (July 1886), 95-102 (McD 1886:1). Reference is made to R-P, the reprint entitled "Hypnotism: Modes of Operating and Susceptibility" in the *Religio-Philosophical Journal*, 1 (1890), August 23, p. 196; August 30, p. 212; September 6, pp. 228-229; September 13, pp. 245-246; September 20, p. 260.

[*begin* R-P]

1194.5   relax] relaxes R-P

1194.20   methods] method R-P

1194.20   and] or R-P

1194.23   his] the R-P

1195.39   *must not* have] must stop having R-P

1197.6   *animal-magnetism theory*] first of these theories R-P

1197.11   with.₋] ∼.† | †Gurney, Liébault, etc. R-P

1197.17   admit] admits R-P

1198.8   expectation] expectations R-P

1198.14   hemisomnambulic] hemisomnambulistic R-P

1198.31   what] that R-P

1202.10   earlier] early R-P

1202.35   alterations] alternations R-P

1203.12   for] for an R-P

1203.13   subject's] patient's R-P

1203.33   by] of R-P

1204.14   or a] or R-P

1204.39   ¹by] be R-P (*error*)

1205.29   of] to R-P

1206.17;1208.10   subjects'] subject's R-P

[*begin* P31]

1207.19   all!₋] ∼!¹ | ¹M. Ch. Féré was, so far as I know, the first to make this remark. P31

1207.37   state.₋] ∼.² | ²The phenomenon is described as it most frequently happens. There have been some exceptions, and there are some curious variations in the visibility of the finger with which the subject points out the line he sees when he looks at it with both eyes open and the prism before one; but these we reserve for further study. P31

[*end* P31]

1208.20   I] *om. with space* R-P (*error*)

1210.14   not] no *with space* R-P (*error*)

1210.27   or] *om.* R-P

1211.11   assures] assured R-P

1211.23   forehead] foreheads R-P

1211.30   remain] remains R-P

1211.33   patients] patient R-P

1212.27   really] *om.* R-P

1213.31   the] *om.* R-P

1214.5   ²the] this R–P
1214.15 (*twice*)   1889] 1890 R–P
1214.20-24   —In . . . -274.] To which
may be added J. Cadwell, "How to
Mesmerize." C. Lloyd Tackey [*i.e.*,
Tuckey] , "Psycho-Therapeutics,"
Second Edition 1890. Bjornström,
"Hypnotism: its History and Present
Development," 1890. J. G. McKendrick,
article Animal Magnetism in Encyclopedia Britannica, 9th Edition, (Reprinted). R–P
[*end* R–P]

Word-Division

The following is a list of actual or possible hyphenated compounds divided at the end of the line in the copy-text but which were not confirmed in their forms as printed in the present edition either because the copy-text did not derive from a learned journal at that point, the journal printed the hyphenated form as two words which was not adopted as an emendation, the journal was variant at that point, or it also broke the compounds at the end of the line and so was not evidential. The last group are distinguished by prefixed asterisks. When the form of a hyphenated compound could be confirmed in an English quotation, it was also not printed here. In a sense, then, the hyphenation or non-hyphenation of possible compounds in the present list is in the nature of editorial emendation.

22.17 shotgun	452.16;553.11 sub-excitements
50.7 right-handedness	528.24 subdivide
60.42 brokendown	528.38 sixfold
76.1 re-established	618.25 substratum
93.27 stop-watch	625.18 school-boys
147.15;314.16 common-sense	628.8 fourfold
169.19 co-operation	655.25 by-gone
181.5 anti-spiritualistic	675.20 earth-born
191.4 offhand	731.33 penholder
215.3 to-day	740.29 churchyard
229.28 footprints	*782.35;1026.11 well-marked
230.34;447.17 self-identical	*864.18 left-hand
256.15 butter-dish	*870.34 wall-papers
268.3 non-existence	873.1 non-attention
274.1 ultra-violet	*899.32 self-mobility
283.18 self-satisfaction	923.29 sub-universe
311.30 *self-regarding*	1061.29 goose-flesh
312.14 self-measuring	1133.30 mind-reading
313.41 self-gratulation	1181.17 heart-strings
426.4 pre-existing	1202.36 heart-beat
432.34 well-known	

The following is a list of words divided at the ends of lines in the present edition but which represents authentic hyphenated compounds as found within the lines of the copy-text. Except for this list, all other hyphenations at the ends of lines in the present edition are the modern printer's and are not hyphenated forms in the copy-text.

12.38 non-|uniformity	18.29 heart-|beats
13.33 front-|door	19.30;313.35 old-|fashioned
18.14 brain-|experiences	21.33;426.7;1080.29 nerve-|centres
18.21 brain-|physiology	23.2 main-|spring

552.13   co-|operative
565.36   previously-|experienced
570.21   bead-|like
573.29;586.30   time-|perception
576.19   time-|sense
577.16   sub-|groups
594.37   space-|intuition
597.14   time-|feeling
597.16   association-|time
598.18   foot-|note
616.18;647.26   brain-|paths
621.17   brain-|substance
621.36   law-|dissertation
627.17   self-|discipline
634.34   just-|excited
636.28   nonsense-|verses
653.33   training-|institutions
655.12   well-|worn
659.1   neo-|hegelian
661.8   non-|presence
668.28;729.24;730.13;773.24;890.35
   after-|image
680.24   arm-|chair
684.31   elbow-|joint
698.4   bread-|crust
706.40   dearly-|beloved
710.35;868.6   eye-|movements
713.32   full-|face
716.40;760.11;764.5   pseudo-|hallucina-
   tions
717.23   bluish-|green
718.28;719.5   *sensation-|process*
735.22   eye-|muscles
741.29   gauze-|robed
768.22   dream-|fantasms
771.26   supra-|ideational
773.31   perception-|time
780.25   semi-|circular
781.31   -finger-|nail
783.28;889.21   visiting-|card
787.34   space-|or
787.35   quality-|order
790.5   space-|*relations*
801.32   semi-|conscious
807.38   Skin-|sensations
818.5   touch-|feeling
820.1   space-|world
826.28   skin-|patches
827.9   finger-|*tip*
829.8   knock-|kneed
829.29   hip-|joint
829.32   induction-|currents

830.25   skin-|events
831.21   joint-|difference
835.24   space-| significance
836.24   eyeball-|muscles
841.13   -circular-|canal
846.19   differently-|shaped
848.8   wash-|basin
849.33;850.7   *depth-|feeling*
857.20   finger-|tip
861.24   *projection-|theory*
862.2   *identity-|theory*
868.32   space-|theories
869.8   *eye-|feelings*
870.12   slant-|legged
876.20   color-|contrast
888.18   space-|yielding
899.27   space-|giving
900.4;911.8   space-|sensations
905.22   space-|system
916.7   It-|thunders
916.8   -discovered-|America-
916.9   -the-|world
920.36   sub-|universes
923.37   dream-|objects
934.29   *pleasure-|or*
938.1   child-|bearing
938.33   note-|book
958.32   self-|education
962.14   soap-|boiler
975.21   non-|analytic
975.38   trance-|method
976.6   lumber-|camp
980.18   rat-|hunt
989.24   molecular-|mechanical
989.33   brain-|activity
990.4   by-|considerations
1006.15   perception-|impulses
1006.16   sensation-|impulse
1011.39   excito-|motor
1020.23   boon-|fellowship
1037.18   *fear-|paroxysm*
1040.34   would-|be
1042.30   store-|room
1043.16   dining-|room
1049.9   stage-|fright
1072.16   all-|overishness
1080.24   *pent-|up*
1081.20   temper-|fits
1109.3   memory-|image
1123.11   oil-|cloth's
1124.17   India-|rubber
1126.3   nerve-|trunks

1146.5,32 self-|control
1160.21 never-|dying
1162.28 pleasure-|theory
1163.12 pleasure-|philosophers
1164.6 what-|we-
1166.34 non-|performance
1169.19 anti-|impulsive
1173.28 -and-|their-
1173.29 -true-|or-
1173.30 -desirability-|of-
1179.20 free-|will
1191.19 drainage-|channel

1193.11 hearing-|centre
1198.19 speech-|centre
1203.40 hyper-|excitability
1205.28 background-|thoughts
1208.32 non-|reflecting
1212.32 post-|hypnotic
1224.6 brain-|pathology
1226.2 *-door-|way*
1229.35 time-|and
1249.11 number-|sensations
1274.7 orphan-|child

Special Cases:

(a) The following are actual or possible hyphenated compounds broken at the end of the line in both the copy-text and the present edition.

19.11 self-|preservation (*i.e.*, self-preservation)
71.33 brain-|surface (*i.e.*, brain-surface)
123.25 long-|familiar (*i.e.*, long-familiar)
152.41 chromo-|philosophy (*i.e.*, chromo-philosophy)
182.21 mind-|dust (*i.e.*, mind-dust)
226.17 moon-|light (*i.e.*, moonlight)
235.25 brain-|tract (*i.e.*, brain-tract)
249.17 brain-|processes (*i.e.*, brain-processes)
407.10 reaction-|times (*i.e.*, reaction-times)
419.11 looked-|for (*i.e.*, looked-for)
490.8;1219.6 so-|called (*i.e.*, so-called)
492.18 nerve-|fibres (*i.e.*, nerve-fibres)
505.39 pound-|weight (*i.e.*, pound-weight)
589.4 long-|drawn- (*i.e.*, long-drawn-)
592.10 non-|existent (*i.e.*, non-existent)
704.5 breakfast-|table (*i.e.*, breakfast-table)
704.11 table-|cloth (*i.e.*, tablecloth)
753.5 apperception-|product (*i.e.*, apperception-product)

753.18 four-|cornered (*i.e.*, four-cornered)
759.13 pseudo-|hallucinatory (*i.e.*, pseudo-hallucinatory)
806.7 space-|experiences (*i.e.*, space-experiences)
832.9 joint-|feeling (*i.e.*, joint-feeling)
873.36 ground-|tone (*i.e.*, ground-tone)
876.19 space-|perception (*i.e.*, space-perception)
936.35 anti-|Catholicism (*i.e.*, anti-Catholicism)
940.35 dreary-|feeling (*i.e.*, dreary-feeling)
942.13 co-|operative (*i.e.*, co-operative)
975.5 fish-|basket (*i.e.*, fish-basket)
1039.21 self-|command (*i.e.*, self-command)
1177.27 pre-|exists (*i.e.*, pre-exists)
1180.24 long-|treasured (*i.e.*, long-treasured)
1218.16 experience-|hypothesis (*i.e.*, experience-hypothesis)
1219.37 *non-|ego* (*i.e.*, *non-ego*)
1220.29 pre-|existence (*i.e.*, pre-existence)
1257.8 self-|evident (*i.e.*, self-evident)

(b) The following compounds hyphenated at the ends of lines in the present edition are silent emendations except for 1057.16 which can be found in the list of Emendations.

115.7 newly-|forming
116.31 consciously-|formed
139.7 beef-|steak

1057.16 bringing-|up
1248.39 *Doctor-|Jubiläum*

Index
Key to the Pagination of Editions

This index is a name and subject index for the text of *The Principles of Psychology* and Appendixes I, II, and III. It is an index of names only for the "Notes," "A Note on the Editorial Method," "The Text of *The Principles of Psychology*," and Appendix IV.

Names of persons, localities, and institutions, and titles of books are indexed. However, such items are not indexed if no information about them is provided—if they are only a part of the identification of a discussed item or are merely used to indicate its location. This excludes, most of the time, names of editors, translators, and libraries, and titles of reference books consulted by the editors of the present text. In contrast to the practice of earlier volumes, titles of articles in periodicals, except those by James, are not indexed.

Generally, references to books are not indexed when the title of the book does not appear in the citation. The index therefore provides an extensive but incomplete list of James's references to individual works.

The index in most cases does not include the technical names for the various parts of the brain and nervous system.

Throughout his text James frequently offers introspective evidence, makes observations about the behavior of his own children, or refers to informal studies conducted on students and friends. Since such observations bear on the question of James as an experimental psychologist, they are listed in the index under James's name. Otherwise, references to James are not indexed.

The two introductions to the present edition also are not indexed.

Index

Index

Anesthesia: and motor zone, 67–70; hysterical, 200, 201, 202, 204, 205, 222, 223–224; and hypnotism, 208–209, 1205–08; and sleep, 210; total, 355n; and amnesia, 369n; false, 377; and volition, 749, 1100–04, 1129n; cutaneous, 828, 829; and emotion, 1070–71; and innervation, 1123–24

Anesthésies hystériques, Des (A. Pitres), 1338

Anger, 293, 294, 1028, 1076n

Angular gyrus, 51–52, 56, 64

Animal Life and Intelligence (C. L. Morgan), 1404

Animal Magnetism (Binet and Féré), 771n, 1214n, 1387, 1421

Animal Magnetism (R. P. H. Heidenhain), 1421

Animals: and purpose, 21–22, 28, 33–34, 38, 132; motor zone, 42–43; blindness, 51–57; deafness, 62; and localization, 69, 82; vivisection, 71; and consciousness, 74, 141–142; lower centers, 84–85; and habits, 109; automatism, 118, 125, 134; and psychology, 193; and conception, 437–438; and movement, 812–813, 1002–03, 1025; and reason, 952, 970, 1245; intelligence, 973–983; and signs, 980–981; and instincts, 1005, 1010–14, 1017–20, 1056; and impulses, 1006–10; and inhibition, 1014–17; and imitation, 1027–28; ferocity, 1028; and sympathy, 1029–30; and fear, 1033, 1037–38; and acquisitiveness, 1041–42; and shelter, 1044; and sociability, 1047; and cleanliness, 1051; and men, 1443; and abstraction, 1470

Anthropoid Apes (R. Hartmann), 1035n, 1407

Anthropologie (I. H. Fichte), 1339

Anthropologie der Naturvölker (T. Waitz), 1052n, 1408

Anthropologische Vorträge (J. Henle), 1061n, 1409, 1410, 1412

Anticipation, 411, 415–420

Aphasia: and motor zone, 49–51, 53, 63; and alexia, 59; study of, 60n–61n, 63, 65; sensory, 63–64, 69, 70, 177; and summation, 92; and apperception, 557; and time, 602; and memory, 644; and imagination, 704–707; and consciousness, 728; and volition, 1165; and hypnotism, 1198

Aphasische Symptomencomplex, Der (C. Wernicke), 63n, 1308

Apoplexy, 58

Apperception: Wundt on, 73n, 95, 96n, 289n–290n, 416, 675, 1456–57; and

reaction time, 98n, 1453; Leibniz on, 166; Kant on, 315n, 341–342; Herbart on, 423, 426; and similarity, 557; and perception, 750–755

Appetite, 15

Applied Psychology (J. A. McLellan), 1467

Appropriateness, 26, 28

Appropriation, 323, 326, 340

Apraxia, 61

Arch-cell, 179–180, 181

Arch-ego, 322, 325

Archer, William, 1079–80, 1410

Archimedes, 396

"Are We Automata?" (W. James), 1509, 1541n, 1542, 1592, 1593

Aristotle: on the soul, 211, 326; and knowledge, 453; and association, 559, 562; on illusions, 731; on touch, 934; on emotions, 1065, 1473; on moral effort, 1170n; note on, 1419; mentioned, 138, 658n, 916, 1339, 1365, 1376, 1383, 1400, 1469, 1472

Arithmetic, 1248–50, 1256, 1268

Arnold, Matthew, 1420

Art, 420, 874–875, 1083–84

Asceticism, 130

Assimilation, 751

Association: laws, 36, 64, 88, 533–538, 1432–33; and mental blindness, 59; disturbances, 60; and reflexes, 83, 86; and summation, 92; and time, 100, 597n; and space, 170–171, 823, 825n, 831n, 853, 899–900; and tendency, 246; and fatigue, 247; and ideas, 267–268, 451, 1184; and attention, 384–385, 426, 427, 559; and suggestion, 439–440; history, 458–461, 559–563, 565–569; and abstraction, 478–480; and discrimination, 482, 486; and thought, 500, 519–523, 1090; and habit, 522–525, 541, 543, 1432, 1435; rapidity, 525–529; and contiguity, 529–533; and interest, 538–541; and vividness, 542–543; and emotion, 543; and similarity, 544–549, 555–559; and problem solving, 553–555; as explanation, 563–565; and memory, 615–617, 622–623, 625, 633–636, 637; and perception, 723, 727, 729; and illusion, 737; and apperception, 751; and hallucination, 769–770; and local signs, 798–800; and novelty, 901, 902, 908–909; and belief, 931–932; and reason, 952–953, 967, 970–973, 984–987; and animals, 974, 976, 977n, 982–983; and laughter, 979; and language, 980–982, 987–988; and brain, 989, 1191, 1235; and aesthetics, 1084; and effort, 1166; and inhibition,

Index

Index

Index

Correspondence, 183

Cortex, cerebral: irritation, 42–43, 83n; ablations, 43–46; degeneration, 46–47; motor zone, 49–51, 57, 67; and sight, 52–54, 58–60; functions, 73, 86; and restitution, 75–79; injuries, 82–83; and summation, 90–91; and purposes, 133; compounding, 158–159, 177; and reaction time, 496. *See also* Brain; Hemispheres, cerebral

Cosmic Consciousness (R. M. Bucke), 1410

Counterparts, incongruent, 792n

Counting, 577n

Countway Library of Medicine, 1303

Cours de philosophie positive (A. Comte), 187n, 1335

Course of Elementary Practical Physiology, A (Foster and Langley), 24n, 1305

Couty, Louis C., 996, 1405

Cowles, Edward, 1152n, 1417–18

Cramming, 623–624

Creation, 165

Critical Account of the Philosophy of Kant, A (E. Caird), 445n, 660n, 1357, 1377, 1454

Critical Philosophy of Immanuel Kant, The (E. Caird), 1357

Critique of Practical Reason (I. Kant), 1477

Critique of Pure Reason (I. Kant), 925n, 1346, 1400, 1425, 1446, 1487

Crothers, Thomas Davison, 1275n, 1427

Cudworth, Ralph, 658n–659n, 1376, 1377

Cumberland, Stuart C., 1133n, 1417

Curiosity, 754, 1046–47

Curtis, Thomas B., 1062n, 1409

Cutler, John, 352n

Cuvier, Georges, 400n, 1354

Cyclopean eye, 857, 858, 860, 1120

Czermak, Johann Nepomuk, 485, 809, 810, 814; notes on, 1359, 1389, 1390

Danilewsky, B., 998n, 1405

Dante Alighieri, 470, 1081, 1156, 1411, 1418

Darwin, Charles: and selection, 34; his method, 193; his memory, 623; on animal intelligence, 955, 973; on instincts, 1012n, 1270, 1273, 1274, 1275; on fear, 1038, 1062–63; on shyness, 1048, 1049; on coyness, 1054; on expression, 1091n, 1092, 1093, 1094, 1096–97; on variation, 1216n, 1224; notes on, 1306, 1336, 1402, 1406, 1408, 1426; mentioned, 144, 754, 984, 1263n, 1403, 1409, 1411, 1412

Darwin, Erasmus, 713

Darwin, and after Darwin (G. J. Romanes), 1480

Darwinism in Morals (F. P. Cobbe), 166n, 1333

Data of Ethics, The (H. Spencer), 1164n, 1418

Dauriac, Lionel Alexandre, 1446

Davey, S. J., 1349

Davidson, Thomas, 448n, 1357, 1519, 1536, 1542–43

Davy, Humphry, 744, 1384

Deaf-mutes, 256–259, 734n, 982, 1104

Deafness, 60, 62, 63–64, 177

Dean, Sidney, 373–374, 1351

De Anima (Aristotle), 1065, 1376, 1400, 1473

Decision: and psychology, 15; and doubt, 1137; kinds, 1138–42; object, 1173–74; and effort, 1178–79

Delabarre, Edmund Burke, 662–674, 717n, 1594; notes on, 1377, 1378, 1383

De la certitude morale (L. Ollé-Laprune), 949n, 1402

De la névropathie (M. Krishaber), 357n, 1350

De l'aphasie (D. A. F. Bernard), 61n, 65n, 70n, 1311, 1381

De la physionomie (P. Gratiolet), 1412

De la recherche de la vérité (Malebranche), 199n, 1337

De la suggestion (J. Liégeois), 1214n, 1420, 1422, 1423

Delboeuf, Joseph Remi Léopold: on comparison, 501; on psychophysics, 509n, 510, 511, 512, 517; on illusions, 745, 880–881, 894–895; on muscular feelings, 826; on hypnotism, 1202, 1205, 1210, 1211; on sensitivity, 1208; on the self, 1486; notes on, 1321–22, 1342, 1360, 1361, 1374–75, 1384, 1391, 1396, 1421, 1422; mentioned, 98n, 254n, 431n, 516n, 643n, 1362, 1423

De l'électrisation localisée (G. B. A. Duchenne), 828n, 1391

De l'erreur (V. Brochard), 949n, 1401

Deliberation, 126–127, 1136–42, 1173

De l'intelligence (H. Taine), 355n, 357n, 1331, 1348, 1349, 1350, 1404

Delusion, 758n

De Memoria et Reminiscentia (Aristotle), 1365

De Morgan, Augustus, 481, 1254n, 1359, 1425

Denken und Gedächtnis (F. W. Dörpfeld), 1462

Denken und Wirklichkeit (A. Spir), 1255n, 1258n, 1270n, 1425

Index

Index

Essays Moral, Political, and Literary (D. Hume), 1328
Essays on Darwinism (T. R. R. Stebbing), 1020n, 1406
Essays on the Anatomy of Expression (C. Bell), 1411
Essays on the Intellectual Powers of Man (T. Reid), 162n, 447n, 574n, 731n, 1330, 1376, 1487
Essays upon Heredity (A. Weismann), 1278n, 1427
Essay towards a New Theory of Vision, An (G. Berkeley), 689n, 723, 724n, 737n, 846, 912n, 934n, 1380, 1388, 1393
Essence, 959-963, 968-970, 1231
Estel, Volkmar, 577, 580n, 581, 582, 585n, 1512; note on, 1367
État mental des hystériques (Pierre Janet), 1451, 1457, 1474, 1476
Ethics: and physiology, 130-131, 276-277, 299-302, 429-430, 1235; and belief, 940; education in, 948-949; and character, 1153-54; and effort, 1155; motives in, 1158-59; and free will, 1176-77, 1182; and reality, 1264-68, 1269
Ethics (Spinoza), 692n, 918, 1399, 1446, 1458, 1460, 1463, 1469, 1471
Ethics of Aristotle, The (A. Grant), 1419
Étude critique et clinique de la doctrine des localisations motrices (Charcot and Pitres), 1311
Étude psychophysique (J. R. L. Delbœuf), 1361
Étude scientifique sur le somnambulisme (P. Despine), 1196n, 1420
Études de pathogénie et de sémiotique (S. Jaccoud), 1414
Études de physiologie (J. Luys), 1314, 1373
Études élémentaires de philosophie (J. J. de Cardaillac), 240n, 1341
Études médicales (E. C. Lasègue), 1474
Études sur les facultés mentales des animaux (J. C. Houzeau), 1402
Étude sur quelques paralysies (Alfred Grafé), 1476
Eulenburg, Albert, 828n, 1310, 1391
Evans, William Lemuel, 1373
Everett, Charles Caroll, 1141n, 1417, 1487, 1504
Evolution: of brain, 85-87; and mind-stuff, 149-152; and consciousness, 157n; and self-love, 307-309; and attention, 424-425; and diffusion, 1003; and hunting, 1030; and fear, 1038; and instinct, 1106, 1270-80;

and the a priori, 1215-16; and experience, 1218-22; zoological, 1224; scholasticism on, 1263n; and psychology, 1482-83
Evolution and Disease (J. B. Sutton), 1479, 1480
Evolutionism, 164, 309, 313n, 1226-30, 1232n
Examen critique de la loi psychophysique (J. R. L. Delbœuf), 745n, 1384
Examination of Sir William Hamilton's Philosophy, An (J. S. Mill), 166n, 167n, 338n, 339n, 445n, 660n, 901n, 912n, 1332, 1333, 1348, 1377, 1390, 1391, 1392, 1486, 1487
Existence, 917-918, 919n, 925
Exner, Sigmund: on cortical injuries, 46-47; on hemiopia, 54, 1502; on decussation, 57n-58n; on aphasias, 69n; on motor center, 73; on summation, 89n, 91n; on psychodometer, 94; on reaction time, 96n, 97, 98n, 100, 101, 406n, 1496, 1498; on attention, 387-388, 415-416; on time, 578, 579; on memory, 600, 607-608; on contrast, 673; on movement, 749-750, 811, 813n; on innervation, 1125n; notes on, 1307-08, 1314, 1315, 1318, 1320, 1321, 1322, 1324, 1378; mentioned, 102, 382, 580n, 1323, 1355, 1371, 1390, 1416, 1508
Expectation, 563-564
Experience: and memory, 17; development, 227-228, 1223-25; and selection, 273-277; and attention, 380-381; and thought, 455, 1253-58, 1280; objects, 461; law of, 472; analysis, 474-475; novelty in, 753-755; and space, 805, 849, 869, 908, 911; and sensation, 875-876, 879-880; and instincts, 1011-14; and volition, 1099; and the a priori, 1215-17; meaning, 1217, 1226; and evolution, 1218-22; and supernatural, 1222-23; and reality, 1229-30; and science, 1232-33, 1237-40; and ideals, 1235-36; rationality, 1242; and classification, 1244, 1246; and mathematics, 1247-53
"Experience of Activity, The" (W. James), 1345
Expériences sur les centres modérateurs (A. Herzen), 1313
"Experimental and Critical Contribution to the Physiology of the Semicircular Canals" (W. James), 1305
Experimentalphysiologie des Nervensystems (C. Eckhard), 1319

Index

Index

Index

Index

Index

"Original Datum of Space-Consciousness,
The" (W. James), 1389, 1466
Orschansky, Isaak G., 101n, 103, 1323
Osborn, Henry Fairfield, 702n, 1380,
1479, 1480
Othello, 986, 1079
Othello (W. Shakespeare), 1344
Ottolenghi, Salvatore, 717n, 1383
Oughton, D., 1493
Outlines of Cosmic Philosophy (J. Fiske),
114n, 1180n, 1326
Outlines of Metaphysic (H. Lotze), 1302,
1330
Outlines of Psychology (H. Höffding),
1373, 1458
Outlines of Psychology (H. Lotze), 212n,
1330
Outlines of Psychology (J. Sully), 7, 470n,
725n, 798n, 912n, 1183n, 1301, 1358,
1388, 1390, 1397
Outlines of the History of Ethics (H. Sidg-
wick), 1418
Ovid, 1418

P., Mr., quoted, 950n–951n
Pain: study of, 5; and harm, 146–147; and
self, 285; idea of, 470; perception of,
677, 757; and space, 679, 682; and
belief, 934; and action, 1156–64; and
will, 1185; and pleasure, 1477
Palmer, George Herbert, 985, 1404
Palsy, 46, 69, 71, 77
Paneth, Josef: on cortical irritations, 43n;
on motor centers, 71, 72, 73; on hemi-
spheres, 83n; notes on, 1307, 1314,
1317; mentioned, 1315, 1504
Pangloss Bookshop, 1330
Panum, Peter Ludwig, 785, 855n, 1388,
1393
Papillon, Fernand, 1275n, 1427
Paradise Lost (J. Milton), 627n
Parallelism, 182
Paralysis: and motor zone, 44, 45, 68, 69,
82; and innervation, 1113–15, 1117–
18; and volition, 1165
Paraplegics, 29
Paraplégies, Les (S. Jaccoud), 1110n, 1414
Parinaud, Henri, 717n, 1382–83
Paris, 119, 549, 1174
Paris, John Ayrton, 1384
Parker, George, 1464
Parole intérieure, La (V. Egger), 261n,
270n, 1343, 1344
Parts and wholes, 268n–269n
Pascal, Blaise, 396
Passion, 111
Passions de l'âme, Les (R. Descartes),
1065, 1327, 1339, 1363, 1473

Pastness, 570, 591–594, 611–612
Pathologie, Die (W. Griesinger), 356n,
927n, 1349, 1400, 1469
Pathology, 57, 71
Pathology of Mind, The (H. Maudsley),
1315
Paths, cortical, 112–114
Paulhan, Frédéric: on relations, 242n; on
attention, 385, 386; on similarity,
556n; on delusions, 630–631; on
Stricker, 711n; on emotions, 1090n;
notes on, 1341–42, 1353, 1365, 1373,
1382; mentioned, 1083n, 1465, 1487,
1583
Paura, La (A. Mosso), 104n, 996n, 1037,
1091n, 1096, 1324
Pearson, George, 1384
Peasants, 92n
Pease, Edward Allen, 628n, 1107n, 1372,
1414
Peirce, Charles Sanders, 7, 1303, 1459
Pellacani, P., 1000, 1405
Perception: and sensation, 32, 651–653,
722–724, 747, 757; and movement,
83, 733–734; Wundt on, 95; and unconscious, 167, 170–171; and psychology, 195; and selection, 273–277; and
self, 285; and attention, 406; and feelings, 431; described, 488, 725–727;
and reaction time, 496, 497, 498; of
likeness, 499–500; object of, 727–730;
and illusion, 731–747, 888; physiology,
747–750; and apperception, 750–755;
and inference, 755–756, 953–954; and
hallucination, 757–766; time, 773–775;
of points, 800; and motion, 810–814;
of distance, 846–855; and habit, 889,
891; of things, 890; and hypnotism,
1205–10; and thought, 1439–40
"Perception of Space, The" (W. James):
variant readings, 1433–40; James's
notes, 1488–96; writing of, 1537,
1538, 1541, 1547, 1548, 1550–52,
1553; use in Principles, 1594; mentioned, 1384, 1389, 1393, 1545, 1546,
1558
Perception of Space, The (J. E. Walter),
211n, 912n, 1339, 1438n
"Perception of Time, The" (W. James),
1508, 1543–44, 1594
Perez, Bernard, 422–423, 1034–35, 1355,
1407, 1454
Perkins Institution for the Blind, 840,
1388
Perry (unidentified person), 1467
Perry, Ralph Barton, 1299, 1301, 1403,
1485, 1501, 1511, 1535, 1582n
Persia, 1267n

Index

Piderit, Theodor, 1091n, 1094, 1411, 1412
Pigeons: experiments on, 32, 42, 76, 81, 84, 86; sexual functions, 34; and blindness, 52-53; spinal cord, 80
Pikler, Julius, 949n, 1402
Pillon, François, 556n, 1365, 1509
Pilzecker, Alfons, 1451, 1452
Pinel, Philippe, 1170
Piper, Leonore, 1351-52
Pitres, Albert, 203, 1195, 1311, 1474; notes on, 1338, 1420
Planchette, 205-206, 1213
Plan des menschlichen Gehirns (P. E. Flechsig), 1308
Plants, 22
Plasticity, 109-110, 112
Plateau, Joseph Antoine Ferdinand, 501, 1360, 1395
Plateau's spiral, 878
Platner, Ernst, 843, 1392, 1490
Plato: on the soul, 211, 326; on knowledge, 453; his intellect, 985; note on, 1339; mentioned, 437, 658
Platonism, 452n
Play, 1044-46
"Plea for Psychology as a 'Natural Science', A" (W. James), 1303
Pleasure: study of, 5; and benefit, 146-147; and self, 285; idea of, 470; and recalling, 550-551; intellectual, 754; awareness, 757; and belief, 934; aesthetic, 1082-86; and action, 1156-64, 1477; and will, 1185-86
Plethysmograph, 103-104, 996
Plotinus, 658n, 659n, 1377
Plumer, William Swan, 359n, 1350, 1352
Pluralism, 221, 424
"Pluralistic Mystic, A" (W. James), 1360
Pluralistic Universe, A (W. James), 1328, 1330, 1341, 1343, 1421
Podmore, Frank, 1349
Poems (R. W. Emerson), 1346
Polyzoism, 179
Pomeroy, Jesse Harding, 1032n, 1407
Pope, Alexander, 352n, 1349
Populäre wissenschaftliche Vorträge (H. Helmholtz), 226n, 1341
Popular Lectures (H. Helmholtz), 217n, 418n, 908n, 1340
Porter, Noah, 1339, 1438n, 1487
Porter, Samuel, 259n, 1343
Position: perception of, 733, 795; sensation of, 790, 791, 811; and local signs, 798-803, 803n-805n
Positivism, 6, 182
Possession, 371-377
Pratt, W. H., 1496

Prayer, 301
Predication, 1242-47
Prediction, 544-545, 956
Predisposition, 170
Preisschrift über die Freiheit des Willens (A. Schopenhauer), 1344
Preliminary Discourse, A (J. F. W. Herschel), 1416
Preludi della vita, I (L. Luciani), 1310
Preperception, 416, 419, 420, 421, 427
Preyer, Wilhelm Thierry: on time, 579n; on contrast, 663n; on instincts, 1022-24, 1441; on imitation, 1027; on fear, 1036; notes on, 1368, 1377, 1407; mentioned, 1408
Pride, 305-306
Priestley, Joseph, 562, 564n, 1366, 1432
Prince, Morton, 162n, 1332, 1510
Principles of Biology, The (H. Spencer), 114n, 1225n, 1274n, 1275n, 1326, 1478, 1479
Principles of Logic, The (F. H. Bradley), 448n, 556n, 569n, 658n, 914n, 1241n, 1243n, 1357, 1367, 1376
Principles of Mental Physiology (W. B. Carpenter), 114-117, 122n, 123n, 124, 166n, 249, 397n, 422n, 642n, 1133n, 1163n, 1326, 1333, 1349, 1354, 1374, 1416, 1417, 1445
Principles of Morals, The (T. Fowler), 1030n, 1407
Principles of Psychology, The (W. James): origin, 5; reading of, 5-6; viewpoint, 6-7, 1483-84; bibliography, 7; references, 1299-1300, 1602-04; Ladd's review, 1303; Marty's review, 1321; James's copy, 1443, 1590-91; Italian translation, 1482, 1484, 1577-79; James's notes, 1485; plate-changes, 1524, 1601; history of text, 1532-75; English printings, 1575-76, 1590; manuscript, 1580-82; bibliographic description, 1585-86; printings, 1586-90; copy-text, 1598; and *Briefer Course,* 1598-1601; mentioned, 1315, 1384
Principles of Psychology, The (H. Spencer), 114n, 118n, 149n, 150n, 151n, 152n, 154-156, 241n, 438n, 479n, 565n, 586n, 601n, 610n, 634n, 722n, 727n, 755n, 757n, 902, 910n, 912n, 1092n, 1093n, 1095n, 1179n, 1218-22, 1270n, 1277n, 1301, 1304, 1326, 1328, 1329, 1357, 1359, 1366, 1385, 1390, 1398, 1399, 1407, 1412, 1419, 1423, 1471
Problèmes de l'esthétique, Les (M. J. Guyau), 1083n, 1411

Index

Problems of Life and Mind (G. H. Lewes), 166n, 261n, 422n, 751n, 835n, 1020n, 1304, 1333, 1355, 1385, 1426, 1436, 1478

Problems of Philosophy (H. Höffding), 1364

Proctor, Richard Anthony, 636n, 1373-74

"Professor Wundt and Feelings of Innervation" (W. James), 1413

Projection: and sensation, 678-689; and hallucination, 759, 760; of images, 768; of feeling, 832; and space, 841, 856, 885, 1437-39; theory, 861-864; and after-images, 884-885, 889

Prolegomena (I. Kant), 345n, 792n, 1348, 1388

Prolegomena Logica (H. L. Mansel), 1487

Prolegomena to Ethics (T. H. Green), 347n, 348n, 654n, 659n, 660n, 1163n, 1349, 1376, 1377, 1487

Property, 281

Propositions: and belief, 916-917, 919-920; general, 958, 963-966; and necessity, 1215-16; kinds, 1239-40; empirical, 1247; a priori, 1255n, 1257-58, 1269

Proverbs, 987

Prudence, 32, 33-34

Pseudoscope, 732-733

Psychiatrie (E. Kraepelin), 1387

Psychiatrie (T. Meynert), 1090n, 1305, 1473

Psychiatry (T. Meynert), 38n, 1305, 1306

Psychical research, 213-214

Psychic synthesis, 163

Psychodometer, 94

Psychogenesis, 84n, 1280

Psychologia Empirica (C. Wolff), 386n, 613n, 1353, 1372

Psychologia Rationalis (C. Wolff), 199n, 1337

Psychological Inquiries (B. C. Brodie), 199n, 1337

Psychologie (F. Brentano), 163n, 187n, 234n, 516n, 916, 1332, 1335, 1341, 1362, 1487

Psychologie (H. Cornelius), 1458

Psychologie (I. H. Fichte), 1339

Psychologie (J. K. F. Rosenkranz), 1348, 1487

Psychologie allemande, La (T. Ribot), 1322

Psychologie als Wissenschaft (J. F. Herbart), 395n, 568n, 573n, 589n, 595n, 750n, 906n, 1348, 1366, 1370, 1385, 1486

Psychologie anglaise, La (T. Ribot), 563n, 1366

Psychologie comme science naturelle, La (J. R. L. Delboeuf), 1322, 1486

Psychologie de l'association, La (L. Ferri), 559n, 1365

Psychologie de l'attention (T. Ribot), 420n, 423n, 1355

Psychologie de l'effort, La (A. Bertrand), 1127n, 1416

Psychologie de l'enfant, La (B. Perez), 1035n, 1407

Psychologie der suggestion (H. Schmidkunz), 1477

Psychologie du raisonnement, La (A. Binet), 707-709, 717n, 755n, 954n, 1381, 1382, 1383

Psychologie in Umrissen (H. Höffding), 634n, 1070n, 1089n, 1373, 1410, 1411

Psychologie naturelle (P. Despine), 1420

Psychologie physiologique, La (G. Sergi), 681n, 717n, 1379

Psychologische Analysen (A. Horwicz), 309-311, 1346, 1460, 1487

Psychologische Studien (T. Lipps), 836n, 855n, 1392, 1393, 1398, 1436

Psychologist's fallacy: and psychology, 96, 195-196, 268, 463, 810n, 911; and associationism, 335; and idealism, 346n-347n, 660n; in Helmholtz, 493n

Psychology: and metaphysics, 5, 180, 182, 328, 1450; as science, 6-7, 141, 183-184, 655; described, 15, 17, 19, 189, 379, 461, 909; on the soul, 15-17, 181-182; and physiology, 18-19; and consciousness, 21-22; and phrenology, 39; and medicine, 51; and volition, 67, 1110; and summation, 92; and reaction time, 92; and habit, 110, 558; and interaction, 140; concepts of, 148, 185-186; and mind, 149, 172, 197; and unconscious, 166; error in, 173, 193-196, 243, 498, 725; and identity, 175-176, 435, 454-455; data of, 184-185, 196, 219-220, 246, 350n; and introspection, 185, 186-191; methods, 191-193, 196; and knowledge, 212-216, 262-263; and personal form, 221-222; and ideas, 225, 447, 691-692; and objects, 265, 266; and personal identity, 314, 315-316; idealistic, 345-350; and attention, 380-381; and education, 423; and ethics, 429-430, 1158; and categories, 520; and association, 521-522, 566, 568-569; and measurement, 525-526; and memory, 649; and mediums, 742; and logic, 753; explanation in, 806, 1166; on emotions, 1064-65; and free will, 1176, 1179; condition, 1482-84

Index

Psychology, congresses of, 760n, 773, 1174
Psychology (J. Dewey), 7, 447n, 654n, 1302, 1376
Psychology (J. McCosh), 556n, 1365
Psychology (M. Maher), 1454
Psychology (A. Rosmini-Serbati), 1357, 1487
Psychology: Briefer Course (W. James), 1305, 1419, 1470, 1541, 1591, 1598–1601
Psychology: Descriptive and Explanatory (G. T. Ladd), 1304
Psychology and Life (H. Münsterberg), 1317
Psychology for Teachers (C. L. Morgan), 1404
"Psychology of Belief, The" (W. James), 1400, 1553, 1595
Psychology of the Belief in Objective Existence (J. Pikler), 949n, 1402
Psychophysics: processes, 95–96; law of, 182, 503–509, 514, 518, 1456–57; meaning, 192; methods, 510–512; results, 512–514; theory in, 515–517; and physiology, 517–518; and time, 580
Psychosis, 133, 185, 236
Psycho-Therapeutics (C. L. Tuckey), 1423
Psychotherapy (H. Münsterberg), 1317
Pugnacity, 1028–29, 1030, 1033
Punishment, 352
Purkinje, Johannes Evangelista, 489, 734n, 873, 1383
Purpose: and animal actions, 20–21, 22–23, 28, 132; and mind, 21; in nature, 144; and restitution, 146; and selfishness, 305; and conception, 456; and association, 549; and classification, 961; and instincts, 1004–05; and fear, 1037; and sameness, 1245n
Putnam, James Jackson, 7, 69, 1062n; notes on, 1303, 1313–14, 1409
Pyramids, 47, 48–49, 57, 78

Quintilian, 404

Rabbits, 53–54, 82, 86
Rabier, Élie: on conceptualism, 444n; on similarity, 556n; on association, 569, 1458; on voluntary belief, 949n; notes on, 1357, 1401; mentioned, 1365, 1491
Radestock, Paul, 1445
Raehlmann, Eduard, 1466, 1467, 1469
Rahn, Marie Johanne, 1400
Rapport in der Hypnose, Der (A. Moll), 1420

Rapports du physique et du moral (P. J. G. Cabanis), 1325
Rationalism, 1215–17
Rationality: feeling of, 253, 254–255; and series, 1253–58; and metaphysics, 1262–64; ideal, 1269–70
"Rationality, Activity and Faith" (W. James), 940n, 1595
Reaction time: meaning, 92–93; instruments for study, 93–94; simple, 94–95; Wundt on, 95–96, 98–99; and consciousness, 95–97; and summation, 97; and reflex action, 98n; kinds, 99–100; variations, 100–103; and attention, 388–392, 397n, 404–410, 1453; and discrimination, 494–498, 773–775; and association, 526; and anticipation, 1191n
"Reaction-Time in the Hypnotic Trance" (W. James), 1324
Read, Carveth, 478n, 1097, 1455; notes on, 1359, 1413
Read, Louis H., 370, 371n, 1351
Reading, 525
Reality: recognition, 262–263; and belief, 343, 913–920, 946; and thought, 455, 1268; sense of, 613–614; and sensations, 687–688, 927–935; and appearance, 724; and selection, 869–872; kinds, 920–923; and activity, 923–927; and emotion, 935–939; and concepts, 939–945; and relation, 959; and will, 1153; and experience, 1216, 1229–30; and knowledge, 1226–30; and science, 1230–35, 1237–40, 1250, 1258–62; and ideals, 1235, 1236; and logic, 1242–47; and metaphysics, 1262–64; and morality, 1264–68; perception of, 1436
Reason: and comparison, 464; and thought, 520–522, 952–954; and recepts, 954–956; described, 956–958, 966–968; and essence, 959–963; and general propositions, 963–966; and sagacity, 968–970; and similarity, 970–973; and animals, 973–983; and association, 984–987; and brain, 989–990; and habit, 990–991; and selection, 992–993; and instinct, 1010, 1013; and decision, 1138–1139; and passion, 1168; and classification, 1242; and predication, 1242–47; and experience, 1253–58; and psychology, 1431–32
Reasoning, 15, 276, 287–288, 564
Rebecca and Rowena (W. M. Thackeray), 922n, 1399
Recalling, 243, 550–552
Recepts, 954–956, 975n–976n

Index

Index

Index

Index

Index

Index

and effort, 1142-44, 1169-70; and free will, 1173-76; and hypnotism, 1203. *See also* Will

Volkmann, Alfred Wilhelm: on discrimination, 485-486; on Weber's law, 512; on sensation, 745n-746n; on muscular feelings, 834, 836n, 1436; on Wheatstone, 860n; on illusions, 866, 885; on double images, 883-884, 1490; on projection, 894; on space, 911; notes on, 1359, 1384-85, 1394, 1396; mentioned, 1361, 1397, 1488

Volkmann, Wilhelm Fridolin, Ritter von Volkmar: on the soul, 211; on tedium, 590; on time, 592, 594n, 595n; on space, 906; and association, 1431; notes on, 1301, 1339; mentioned, 7, 1370, 1371, 1472, 1473

Voltaire, 658

Voluminousness, 776-787, 847, 1434, 1435, 1437

Vom Fühlen, Wollen, und Denken (T. Lipps), 1322

Von Magdeburg bis Königsberg (J. K. F. Rosenkranz), 1348

Vorlesungen über allgemeine und experimentelle Pathologie (S. Stricker), 249n, 1342

Vorlesungen über die Menschen- und Thierseele (W. Wundt), 393n, 504-508, 675n, 714n, 755n, 796n, 797n, 1113n, 1353, 1378, 1456, 1462-63, 1486

Vorlesungen über Physiologie (E. W. von Brücke), 1319

Vorschule der Aesthetik (G. T. Fechner), 1079n, 1410

Vulpian, Edme Félix Alfred, 75n, 80-81, 1114, 1501; notes on, 1315, 1317

Wadsworth, Oliver Fairfield, 491n, 1359

Wahle, Richard, 467n, 543n, 556n, 1358

Wahrnehmung und Empfindung (G. K. Uphues), 689n, 1380

Waitz, Theodor, 382n-383n, 595n, 1052n, 1352, 1408

Walitzky, Marie, 528n, 1363

Walter, Johnston Estep, 211, 912n, 1339, 1438n

Ward, Artemus, 1233

Ward, James: on summation, 89n; on series, 164n; on activity, 430n; on sensations, 516n; on psychophysics, 517; on association, 529, 530n, 1458; on similarity, 556n; on time, 592-593, 595n-596n, 597n, 1460; on space, 777, 911, 912n, 1435n; on recognition, 1461; on images, 1464; notes on, 1318, 1332, 1335, 1356, 1358, 1363, 1371,

1399; mentioned, 184n, 468n, 598, 1362, 1389

Warner, Charles Dudley, 960, 1402

Warren, Joseph Weatherhead, 102-103, 1320-21

Washburn, Margaret Floy, 1468

Washburn (unidentified person), 1464

Waterfall illusion, 877

Watseka Wonder, The (E. W. Stevens), 375-377, 1352

Watson, John, 1487

Watt, James, 567

Watteville, Armand de, 90n, 1319

Wayland, Francis, 329, 1346

Weber, Eduard Friedrich Wilhelm, 528n, 597n, 1336, 1363

Weber, Ernst Heinrich: his method, 192; his law, 507-509, 510, 511, 512, 513, 514, 516, 517, 518, 581n, 675n, 1456, 1457; on sensations, 676; on sense of direction, 683n; on space, 783, 784, 800; on muscular feelings, 834, 1436; notes on, 1361, 1379, 1388; mentioned, 1336, 1362, 1378, 1389

Weber, Wilhelm Eduard, 528n, 597n, 1336, 1363

Weber (unidentified person), 1489

Weed, Thurlow, 626-627, 1372

Weismann, August, 1278-79, 1479, 1480, 1481; note on, 1427

Wellington, Arthur Wellesley, Duke of, 124

Welt als Wille und Vorstellung, Die (A. Schopenhauer), 848n, 1344, 1393

Wernicke, Carl, 49, 61n, 63, 64, 1502; notes on, 1308, 1312

Wesley, John, 396, 1353

Wetterstrand, Otto G., 1195, 1420

Whately, Richard, 991n, 1404

"What Is an Emotion?" (W. James), 1409, 1410, 1543, 1596-97

"What Is an Instinct?" (W. James), 1545n, 1548, 1596

"What Psychical Research Has Accomplished" (W. James), 1330

"What the Will Effects" (W. James), 1597

Wheatstone, Charles: on pseudoscope, 732, 889; on binocular vision, 859-860; on convergence, 867; notes on, 1320, 1383, 1394, 1395

Whewell, William, 961n, 1403

Whitman, Sarah, 1565

Whittaker, Thomas, 162n, 1331

Whitton, Frederick, 1387

Widener Library, 1299

Wigan, Arthur Ladbroke, 369, 635-636, 1170-71, 1351

Wilbrand, Hermann, 59, 60n-61n, 704n, 1311, 1381

Index

Key to the Pagination of Editions

The plates of the Henry Holt first edition of *The Principles of Psychology* have been reprinted a number of times, but always with the same numbering regardless of the date. Since the original edition has been widely used in scholarly reference, a key is here provided by which the pagination of the original Holt printing can be readily equated with the text in the present ACLS edition. In the list that follows, the first number refers to the page of the September 1890 original edition and its printings of different date. The number to the right after the colon represents the page(s) of the present edition on which the corresponding text will be found.

Volume I	34:45	75:82–83	116:120–121
v:5–6	35:45–46	76:83	117:121–122
vi:6	36:46–47	77:83–84	118:122–123
vii:6–7	37:46–49	78:84–85	119:123–124
ix:9	38:48–49	79:85–86	120:124–125
x:9–10	39:49–50	80:86–87	121:125–126
xi:10–11	40:50–51	81:88–89	122:126–127
xii:11	41:51–52	82:89–90	123:127–128
[1]:15	42:52–53	83:90	124:128
2:15–16	43:53	84:90–91	125:129
3:16–17	44:53–54	85:91–92	126:129–130
4:17–18	45:54–55	86:92–93	127:130–131
5:18–19	46:55–56	87:93–94	128:132–133
6:19–20	47:56–57	88:94–95	129:133
7:20–21	48:57–59	89:95–96	130:133–134
8:21	49:58–59	90:96–97	131:134–135
9:21–22	50:59–60	91:97–98	132:135–136
10:22–23	51:60–61	92:98–99	133:136–137
11:23–24	52:61–62	93:99	134:137–138
12:25–26	53:62–63	94:99–100	135:138–139
13:26–27	54:63	95:100–101	136:139–140
14:27–28	55:63–64	96:101–102	137:140–141
15:28–29	56:64–65	97:102–103	138:141–142
16:29	57:65–66	98:103–104	139:142–143
17:29–30	58:66–67	99:104–105	140:143
18:30–31	59:67–68	100:105–106	141:143–144
19:31–32	60:68–69	101:106–107	142:144–145
20:32–33	61:69–70	102:107–108	143:145–146
21:33–34	62:70	103:108	144:146–147
22:34–35	63:70–71	104:109–110	145:148
23:35	64:71–73	105:110	146:149
24:36	65:73–74	106:110–111	147:149–150
25:36–37	66:74–75	107:111–112	148:150–152
26:37–38	67:75–76	108:112–113	149:151–152
27:38–39	68:76	109:113–114	150:152–153
28:39–40	69:76–77	110:114–115	151:153–154
29:40–41	70:77–78	111:115–116	152:154–155
30:41–42	71:78–79	112:116–117	153:155–156
31:42–43	72:79–80	113:117–118	154:156–157
32:43–44	73:80–81	114:118–119	155:157–158
33:44	74:81–82	115:119–120	156:158–159

Key to the Pagination of Editions

157:159-160
158:160-161
159:161-162
160:162-163
161:163-164
162:164-165
163:165-166
164:166-167
165:167
166:167-168
167:168-169
168:169-170
169:170-171
170:171-172
171:172-173
172:173-174
173:174-175
174:175-176
175:176
176:176-177
177:177-178
178:178-179
179:179-180
180:180-181
181:181-182
182:182
183:183-184
184:184
185:184-185
186:185-186
187:186-187
188:187-188
189:188-189
190:189-190
191:190-191
192:191-192
193:192-193
194:193-194
195:194
196:194-195
197:195-196
198:196
199:197-198
200:198
201:198-199
202:199-200
203:200-201
204:201-202
205:202-203
206:203-204
207:204-205
208:205-206
209:206
210:206-207
211:207-208
212:208-209

213:209-210
214:210-211
215:211-212
216:212-213
217:213
218:213-214
219:214-215
220:215-216
221:216-217
222:217-218
223:218
224:219-220
225:220
226:220-221
227:221-222
228:222-223
229:223-224
230:224-225
231:225-226
232:226-227
233:227-228
234:228
235:228-229
236:229-230
237:230-231
238:231-232
239:232-233
240:233-234
241:234-235
242:235-236
243:236
244:236-237
245:237-238
246:238-239
247:239-240
248:239-241
249:240-242
250:240-243
251:243
252:243-244
253:244-245
254:245-246
255:246-247
256:247-248
257:248-249
258:249
259:249-250
260:250-251
261:251-252
262:252-253
263:253-254
264:254-255
265:255-256
266:256-257
267:257-258
268:258-259

269:259-260
270:260-261
271:261-262
272:262-263
273:263-264
274:264-265
275:265-266
276:266
277:267
278:267-268
279:268-269
280:269-270
281:270-271
282:271-272
283:272-273
284:273-274
285:274-275
286:275
287:275-276
288:276-277
289:277-278
290:278
291:279-280
292:280
293:280-281
294:281-282
295:282-283
296:283-284
297:284-285
298:285-286
299:286-287
300:287-288
301:288
302:288-289
303:289-290
304:290-291
305:291-292
306:292-293
307:293-294
308:294
309:294-295
310:295-296
311:296-297
312:297-298
313:298-299
314:299-300
315:300-301
316:301
317:301-302
318:302-303
319:303-304
320:304-305
321:305-306
322:306-307
323:307-308
324:308

325:309
326:309-310
327:310-312
328:312
329:312-314
330:313-314
331:314-315
332:315-316
333:316-317
334:317-318
335:318-319
336:319
337:319-320
338:320-321
339:321-322
340:322-323
341:323-324
342:323-325
343:325-326
344:326-327
345:327
346:327-328
347:328-329
348:329-330
349:330-331
350:331-332
351:332-333
352:333-334
353:334-335
354:335-336
355:336-337
356:337-338
357:338-339
358:339-340
359:339-340
360:340-341
361:341-342
362:342-343
363:343-344
364:344-345
365:345-346
366:346
367:346-347
368:347-348
369:348-349
370:349-350
371:350-351
372:351-352
373:352-353
374:353-354
375:354-355
376:355-356
377:356-357
378:357-358
379:358
380:358-359

381:359-360	437:413-414	493:466-467	549:518
382:360-361	438:414-415	494:467-468	550:519-520
383:361-362	439:415-416	495:468-469	551:520
384:362-363	440:416-417	496:469-470	552:520-521
385:363-364	441:417-418	497:470-471	553:521-522
386:364-365	442:418-419	498:471-472	554:522-523
387:365-366	443:419-420	499:472	555:523-524
388:366-367	444:420-421	500:472-473	556:524-525
389:367-368	445:421-422	501:473-474	557:525-526
390:368-369	446:422-423	502:474-475	558:526-527
391:369-370	447:423-424	503:475-476	559:527-528
392:370-371	448:424-425	504:476-477	560:528-529
393:371-372	449:424-425	505:477-478	561:529
394:372-373	450:425-426	506:478-479	562:529-530
395:373-374	451:426-427	507:479-480	563:530-531
396:374-375	452:427-428	508:480-481	564:531-532
397:375-376	453:428-429	509:481-482	565:532-533
398:376-377	454:429-430	510:482-483	566:533-534
399:377-378	455:430-431	511:483	567:534-535
400:378-379	456:431-432	512:483-484	568:535-536
401:379	457:432-433	513:484-485	569:536-537
402:380-381	458:433	514:485-486	570:537
403:381	459:434-435	515:486-487	571:537-538
404:381-382	460:435-436	516:487-488	572:538-539
405:382-383	461:436	517:488-489	573:539-540
406:383-384	462:436-437	518:489-490	574:540-541
407:384-385	463:437-438	519:490-491	575:541-542
408:385-386	464:438-439	520:491-492	576:542-543
409:386-387	465:439-440	521:492-493	577:543-544
410:387-388	466:440-441	522:493-494	578:544-545
411:388-389	467:441-442	523:494-495	579:545-546
412:389-390	468:442-443	524:495-496	580:546-547
413:390-391	469:443-444	525:496	581:547-548
414:391-392	470:444-445	526:497	582:548-549
415:392-393	471:445-446	527:497-498	583:549
416:392-394	472:446-447	528:498-499	584:549-550
417:394-395	473:447-448	529:499-500	585:550-551
418:395-396	474:448	530:500-501	586:551-552
419:396-397	475:448-449	531:501-502	587:552-553
420:397-398	476:449-451	532:501-503	588:553-554
421:398	477:451	533:503-504	589:554-555
422:398-399	478:451-453	534:501	590:555-556
423:399-400	479:452-453	535:504-506	591:556-557
424:400-401	480:453-454	536:506-507	592:557
425:401-402	481:454-455	537:507-508	593:557-558
426:402-403	482:455-456	538:508-509	594:558-559
427:403-404	483:457-458	539:509	595:559-560
428:404-405	484:458-459	540:509-510	596:560-561
429:405-406	485:459-460	541:510-511	597:561-563
430:406-407	486:460-461	542:511-512	598:563-564
431:407-408	487:461-462	543:512-513	599:564
432:408-409	488:462-463	544:513-514	600:564-566
433:409-410	489:463-464	545:514-515	601:565-566
434:410-411	490:464	546:515-516	602:566-567
435:411-412	491:464-465	547:516-517	603:568
436:412-413	492:465-466	548:517-518	604:568-569

134:776–777	190:826–827	246:877–878	302:930–931
135:777	191:827–828	247:878–879	303:931–932
136:777–778	192:828–829	248:879–880	304:932–933
137:778–779	193:829–830	249:880–881	305:933–934
138:779–780	194:830–831	250:881–882	306:934–935
139:780–781	195:831–832	251:882–883	307:935–936
140:781–782	196:832–833	252:883–884	308:936–937
141:782–783	197:833	253:883–885	309:937
142:783–785	198:833–834	254:885–886	310:937–939
143:785	199:834–835	255:886	311:938–939
144:785–786	200:835–836	256:886–887	312:939–940
145:786–787	201:836–837	257:887–888	313:940–941
146:787–788	202:837–838	258:888–889	314:941–942
147:788–789	203:838–839	259:889–890	315:942–943
148:789–790	204:839–840	260:890–891	316:943–944
149:790–791	205:840–841	261:891–892	317:944–945
150:791–792	206:841–842	262:892–893	318:945–946
151:792–793	207:842–843	263:893–894	319:946–947
152:793–794	208:843–844	264:894–895	320:947–948
153:794	209:844	265:895–896	321:948–949
154:794–795	210:844–845	266:896–897	322:949–950
155:795–796	211:845–846	267:897–898	323:950
156:796–797	212:846–847	268:898–899	324:950–951
157:797–798	213:847–848	269:899–900	325:952–953
158:798–799	214:848–849	270:900–901	326:953–954
159:799–800	215:849–850	271:901–902	327:954
160:800–801	216:850–851	272:902	328:954–955
161:801–802	217:851–852	273:903–904	329:955–956
162:802–803	218:852	274:904–905	330:956–957
163:803	219:852–853	275:905–906	331:957–958
164:803–805	220:853–854	276:906	332:958–959
165:804–805	221:854–855	277:906–907	333:959–960
166:805–806	222:855–856	278:907–908	334:960–961
167:806–807	223:856–857	279:908–909	335:961–962
168:807–808	224:857–858	280:909–910	336:961–963
169:808–809	225:858–859	281:910–911	337:963
170:809–810	226:859–860	282:911–912	338:963–964
171:810	227:859–860	283:913–914	339:964–965
172:810–811	228:860–861	284:914	340:965–966
173:811–812	229:861–862	285:914–915	341:966–967
174:812–813	230:862–863	286:915–916	342:967–968
175:813–814	231:863–864	287:916–917	343:968–969
176:814–815	232:864–865	288:917–918	344:969–970
177:815–816	233:865–866	289:918–919	345:970–971
178:816–817	234:865–867	290:919–920	346:971
179:817	235:867–868	291:920–921	347:971–972
180:817–818	236:868–869	292:921–922	348:972–973
181:818–819	237:869	293:922–923	349:973–974
182:819–820	238:870	294:923–924	350:974–975
183:820–821	239:870–871	295:924	351:975–976
184:821–822	240:871–872	296:925	352:976–977
185:822–823	241:872–873	297:925–926	353:977
186:823–824	242:873–874	298:926–927	354:977–979
187:824–825	243:874–875	299:927–928	355:979–980
188:825	244:875–876	300:928–929	356:980
189:826	245:876–877	301:929–930	357:980–981

358:981-982
359:982-983
360:983-984
361:984-985
362:985-986
363:986-987
364:987-988
365:988
366:988-989
367:989-990
368:990-991
369:991-992
370:992-993
371:993
372:994-995
373:995-996
374:996
375:997
376:996,998
377:998-999
378:998-1000
379:1000-1001
380:1001-1002
381:1002-1003
382:1003
383:1004-1005
384:1005-1006
385:1006
386:1006-1007
387:1007-1008
388:1008-1009
389:1009-1010
390:1010-1011
391:1011-1012
392:1012-1013
393:1013-1014
394:1014-1015
395:1015-1016
396:1016
397:1017
398:1017-1018
399:1018-1019
400:1019-1020
401:1020-1021
402:1021-1022
403:1022-1023
404:1023-1024
405:1024-1025
406:1025-1026
407:1026
408:1026-1027
409:1027-1028
410:1028-1029
411:1029-1030
412:1030-1031
413:1031-1032

414:1032-1033
415:1033-1034
416:1034-1035
417:1035
418:1035-1037
419:1037
420:1037-1038
421:1038-1039
422:1039-1040
423:1040-1041
424:1041-1042
425:1042-1043
426:1043-1044
427:1044-1045
428:1045
429:1045-1046
430:1046-1047
431:1047-1048
432:1048-1049
433:1049-1050
434:1050-1051
435:1051-1052
436:1052-1053
437:1053-1054
438:1054
439:1054-1055
440:1055-1056
441:1056-1057
442:1058-1059
443:1059-1060
444:1060-1061
445:1061-1062
446:1062-1063
447:1063-1064
448:1064
449:1064-1065
450:1065-1066
451:1066-1067
452:1067-1068
453:1068-1069
454:1069-1070
455:1070-1071
456:1071-1072
457:1072-1073
458:1073
459:1073-1074
460:1074-1075
461:1075-1076
462:1076-1077
463:1077-1078
464:1078-1079
465:1079-1080
466:1080-1081
467:1081-1082
468:1082-1083
469:1083-1084

470:1084
471:1084-1085
472:1085-1086
473:1086-1087
474:1087-1088
475:1088-1089
476:1089-1090
477:1090-1091
478:1091-1092
479:1092
480:1092-1093
481:1093-1094
482:1094-1095
483:1095-1096
484:1096-1097
485:1097
486:1098-1099
487:1099
488:1099-1100
489:1100-1101
490:1101-1102
491:1102-1103
492:1103-1104
493:1104-1105
494:1105-1106
495:1106-1107
496:1107-1108
497:1108-1109
498:1109
499:1109-1110
500:1110-1111
501:1111-1112
502:1112-1113
503:1113-1114
504:1114-1115
505:1115-1116
506:1116-1117
507:1117-1118
508:1118-1119
509:1119
510:1119-1120
511:1120-1121
512:1121-1122
513:1122-1123
514:1123-1124
515:1124-1125
516:1125-1126
517:1126
518:1126-1127
519:1127-1128
520:1128-1129
521:1129-1130
522:1130-1131
523:1131-1132
524:1132-1133
525:1133-1134

526:1134
527:1134-1135
528:1135-1136
529:1136-1137
530:1137-1138
531:1138-1139
532:1139-1140
533:1140-1141
534:1141
535:1141-1142
536:1142-1143
537:1143-1144
538:1144-1145
539:1145-1146
540:1146-1147
541:1147-1148
542:1148-1149
543:1149-1150
544:1150-1151
545:1151-1152
546:1152-1153
547:1153-1154
548:1154-1155
549:1155-1156
550:1156-1157
551:1157
552:1157-1158
553:1158-1159
554:1159-1160
555:1160-1161
556:1161-1162
557:1162-1163
558:1163-1164
559:1164-1165
560:1165
561:1165-1166
562:1166-1167
563:1167-1168
564:1168-1169
565:1169-1170
566:1170-1171
567:1171-1172
568:1172-1173
569:1173
570:1173-1174
571:1174-1175
572:1175-1176
573:1176-1177
574:1177-1178
575:1178-1179
576:1179-1180
577:1180
578:1180-1181
579:1181-1182
580:1182-1183
581:1183-1184

582:1184–1185	609:1208–1209	636:1232–1233	663:1256–1257
583:1185–1186	610:1209	637:1233–1234	664:1257–1258
584:1186–1187	611:1209–1210	638:1233–1235	665:1258–1259
585:1187–1188	612:1210–1211	639:1235–1236	666:1259–1260
586:1188	613:1211–1212	640:1236	667:1260–1261
587:1188–1189	614:1212–1213	641:1236–1237	668:1261–1262
588:1189–1190	615:1213–1214	642:1237–1238	669:1262–1263
589:1190–1191	616:1214	643:1238–1239	670:1263–1264
590:1191–1192	617:1215–1216	644:1239–1240	671:1263–1264
591:1192–1193	618:1216	645:1240–1241	672:1264–1265
592:1193	619:1216–1217	646:1241–1242	673:1265–1266
593:1194–1195	620:1217–1218	647:1242–1243	674:1266–1267
594:1195	621:1218–1219	648:1243–1244	675:1267–1268
595:1195–1196	622:1219–1220	649:1244	676:1268–1269
596:1196–1197	623:1220–1221	650:1244–1245	677:1269–1270
597:1197–1198	624:1222	651:1245–1246	678:1270–1271
598:1198–1199	625:1222–1223	652:1246–1247	679:1271–1272
599:1199–1200	626:1223–1224	653:1247–1248	680:1272–1273
600:1200–1201	627:1224–1225	654:1248–1249	681:1273–1274
601:1201–1202	628:1225–1226	655:1249–1250	682:1274–1275
602:1202	629:1226–1227	656:1250–1251	683:1275
603:1202–1203	630:1227–1228	657:1251–1252	684:1275–1276
604:1203–1204	631:1228	658:1252	685:1276–1277
605:1204–1205	632:1229	659:1252–1253	686:1277–1278
606:1205–1206	633:1229–1230	660:1253–1254	687:1278–1279
607:1206–1207	634:1230–1231	661:1254–1255	688:1279–1280
608:1207–1208	635:1231–1232	662:1255–1256	689:1280